While You Were Gone

A Report on Wartime Life
in the United States

ALLAN NEVINS — PAUL GALLICO — ANNA W. M. WOLF
IRMA SIMONTON BLACK — CAREY MCWILLIAMS — JONA-
THAN DANIELS — THOMAS L. STOKES — HENRY F. PRINGLE
R. J. THOMAS — DONALD M. NELSON — RUSSELL LORD
GERALD WENDT — MARGARET MEAD — DAN PARKER — JAMES
THURBER — LESTER MARKEL — NORMAN CORWIN — ERIC
HODGINS — RAYMOND RUBICAM — LEWIS GANNETT — WOL-
COTT GIBBS — MILTON CANIFF — BOSLEY CROWTHER
CHARLES HURD — CHARLES BOLTÉ — JOSEPH H. BALL

Edited by Jack Goodman

SIMON AND SCHUSTER, NEW YORK, 1946

E 806 .G65 1946

Goodman, Jack.

While you were gone

Table of Contents

Editor's Introduction

THE ORIGINAL IDEA *for this book was suggested in December, 1944, by Captain Joe Thompson, U.S. Signal Corps. He conceived it while stationed on a lonely assignment somewhere in the Pacific, and wrote suggesting that I take on the job of getting it together. Because it seemed to me to be a superb idea, I promptly started to do so.*

Captain Thompson's outline has been changed a good deal and expanded a good deal more, but I believe the resulting book is pretty much the one both of us wanted.

Its purpose is to give, so far as is possible in a volume in which each chapter is a potential book, a capsule over-all survey of the way life was lived, of the way we thought and behaved, of the way we did our jobs or failed to do them in the United States during the war against Axis aggression.

In its pages, twenty-four phases of the American home front at war are seen through the eyes of twenty-six people (two of the chapters are collaborative). Each contributor is, in the opinion of the editor, well equipped to write, authoritatively and fairly, the chapter for which he or she has been asked.

A different set of twenty-six people would unquestionably have produced a thoroughly different book. Obviously, a total impression different to that conveyed by While You Were Gone *would be gleaned from a symposium in which, say, the chapter on race relations was written by Senator Bilbo and that on labor by Westbrook Pegler. Equally, still another effect would be created by a book to which William Z. Foster had contributed the chapter on industry and Earl Browder that on the Congress.*

In While You Were Gone, *the editor attempted to steer some-*

thing of a middle course. The resulting book is not, however, an impartial study. It contains a good deal of opinion. Sometimes, indeed, those opinions will be found very much at variance with each other. The editor has made no attempt to smooth out certain controversial presentations, in the belief that the reader may better arrive at his own conclusions through the stereopticon of varied points of view.

Miss Amy Loveman helped immeasurably in the preparation of the book, from idea stage through final galleys. Miss Beverly Harmon was indispensable to its assembly. I am also indebted, for their generous help, to Miss Ann Honeycutt, to Joseph Barnes, to James Thurber, to Albert Rice Leventhal, to Albert Z. Carr, and, above all, of course, to Captain Joe Thompson.

J. G.

Part One

How We Thought and Behaved

I. HOW WE FELT ABOUT THE WAR

by ALLAN NEVINS

ALLAN NEVINS (age 55) is Professor of American History at Columbia University. He is twice winner of the Pulitzer Prize for the best biography of the year. He was in England as Harmsworth Professor of American History at Oxford during the blitz winter of 1940–41. In 1942 he returned to England to work for the English Board of Education, and was in Australia and New Zealand for OWI in 1943–44.

EVERY great war begins with a sharp crystallization of opinion —or generally it would not begin at all. Confusions, doubts, a maelstrom of conflicting interests and opinions, spread a curtain of fog across the future; and then the nation suddenly breaks through it to light, conviction, and a clear path. The shots at Concord and Lexington rent away a murk of hesitations. The news of Fort Sumter brought the North and South to their feet in fighting trim. The sinking of the *Maine* meant war almost as clearly as if the decree had been written in the heavens, for it made American opinion fixed and definite. The declaration of unrestricted submarine warfare in 1917 and the Zimmermann note inviting Mexico to reannex our Southwest ended all doubt. And yet, looking back of these seemingly rapid crystallizations, we can see that they had usually been long in preparation; that all the needful forces were present in solution, and if one dramatic event had not acted as precipitant, another would have done so. Thus it was with Pearl Harbor. We can now perceive that the Japa-

nese onslaught did not really cause our participation in the war;
rather, the Japanese struck at us because we were so inexorably
moving to resist Axis aggression.

It requires a good deal of effort to recall the nation's fluctuat-
ing, uncertain, anomalous state of mind at the beginning of 1940.
During the previous fateful year the Spanish Republic had ended
its long death agony; Czechoslovakia and Poland had perished;
Finland had been attacked; and Germany (with, as a number of
people felt, some assistance from a Russian pact) had opened
the second World War. All this constituted a titanic disaster for
the globe. Yet because the Anglo-French forces still held the
Maginot Line, the world at the opening of 1940 was full of
illusions. Many Britons shared Chamberlain's belief that Hitler
had somehow missed the bus. Genevieve Tabouis was recording
the conviction of numerous French intellectuals that by spring
Bolshevism would have fatally sapped Germany's strength. The
general feeling in France, she declared, was that while 1939 had
been the worst year that men could remember, 1940 would prove
"the happy year of peace."

And in the United States? Many Americans hoped that the in-
active war would yet be stopped by President Roosevelt or Pope
Pius. The Gallup polls, the newspapers, and the utterances of ordinary men were all overwhelmingly against any embroilment in
the conflict. So optimistic was the country that millions of citizens
grew indignant over the "staggering" Administration proposals for
new naval expenditures. Only a year earlier, Congress had authorized an outlay of one and a quarter billion dollars for new
warships; and now in the early weeks of 1940 legislation was
being shaped for a flat addition of one and a third billions more.
Could the country stand such enormous expenditures?

Then came the thunderclaps which shook men awake from
their illusions. The tremendous Battle of Belgium and Flanders;
the break-through at Sedan; the crumpling of three French armies; the race of the Germans to the Somme and the Channel; the
British evacuation of 335,000 men through Dunkirk; the fall of

France. The tempest swept Churchill into Downing Street. It erased all party lines in Britain as the nation prepared to fight on the beaches and in the fields and streets. It sent a wave of apprehension around the world. The emotional temperature of the United States rose. As Italy delivered her stab in the back of France, and as Germany got ready her bombers and invasion barges for the Battle of Britain, multitudes of Americans felt that in a war between civilization and tyranny they should be in the battle line. It was with a majority of the country behind him that Roosevelt at once promised to put "the full material resources" of the United States behind Britain, and with the approval of the Republican leader Wendell Willkie that he shortly transferred fifty destroyers to the British Navy. It was with universal approbation that Congress appropriated fourteen billions (this time nobody asking whether we could afford it) for battleships, tanks, and airplanes. The country had begun its march to war because forces so evil and powerful were loose in the world, ravening for blood and spoils, that it was clearly safer to begin fighting while allies remained than to wait until after the last had been struck down.

With the events of May and June, 1940, all but one of the ingredients which were to bring an eventual crystallization of opinion were ready. Men waited to see whether Britain could survive. As she did, the Dominions rallying to her side, the last ingredient was added. On the emotional plane, Americans were equally harrowed by the threatened destruction of democracy in the two lands, Britain and France, which had done most for its modern development, and by the Nazi brutalities against helpless little nations and inoffensive minorities. On the plane of cold hard calculation, men could see that waiting offered much risk and little gain. We might, by letting other nations go down and shrinking into our shell, postpone war for years or even decades. But at what price? At the cost of arming to the teeth, keeping our children and our grandchildren ready for momentary conflict, remodeling our economy to make it self-sufficing, and maintaining the strictest government controls over that economy—at the cost, that is, of ourselves' becoming a militarized totalitarian state; of surrendering our finest traditions and most fundamental principles. Heart and mind alike urged us to meet the enemy in the gate, not on our hearthstones; to harden our morale by fighting betimes, not sap it by shivering over the plunge. We were moving fast toward open conflict when Japan rushed to meet us; and the instant declaration of war by Germany and Italy showed that they had encouraged Tokyo's attack.

What did the American people think of the war once it was in progress? The question is too comprehensive to answer in a chapter, or a volume. Their thought covered the whole complex panorama of battles, politics, economic reorganization, and social change; their emotions ran the gamut from the most idealistic impulses to the basest, most selfish instincts. When we look at our previous wars, we can see that the contemporaneous observer was always likely to estimate the nation's purposes somewhat too highly. So much rhetoric is poured out by politicians and publicists upon the noble objects and sublime effort of any war that the hasty student is in danger of being misled. While the Civil War lasted most men wrote of it in James Russell Lowell's terms —"Oh beautiful! My country!" When it was over they saw that it had also to be described in terms of skulkers, thieves, shoddy speculators, and cheap-Jack demagogues. Lincoln stated one side of what the North thought of the Civil War in his Gettysburg Address; Artemus Ward stated another side when he said that he would gladly sacrifice on the battlefield all his wife's relatives. As E. L. Godkin wrote, the men who bled in the crusade to save the Union found in 1865 that they were in the predicament of Cromwell's troops at Marston Moor; they drove the enemy from the field only to learn that a foul crew of camp followers was meanwhile looting their own base. Wartime attitudes cannot all be taken at face value. But happily they cannot all be taken cynically, either.

The returning warrior will take one step toward a comprehension of our wartime attitudes if he realizes that the distinction between the home front and fighting front is partly unreal; unreal, that is, in terms of basic psychology. The fighters of course suffer far greater perils, pains, and hardships. All honor to them! But this does not mean that soldier and civilian attitudes are fundamentally different. The fighter justly resents the slack complacency of some stay-at-homes, the cowardice of others, and the profiteering of still more. They should be put into the foxholes for five minutes! But if left at home, the fighters as a body would doubtless behave much as did the civilians as a body. And if compelled to go into the front lines, the civilians would have behaved much as the fighters did. The people of England proved that. There were times in the war when London streets and Sussex villages were more dangerous than camps and battleships. "The bombs came down and the people stood up," as J. B. Priestley remarked. There was no lack of bravery and self-sacrifice on the part of men and women who, if the war had been a trench conflict like that of 1915–18, would have been abused by many soldiers as shirkers. Nor should it be forgotten that mothers find it about as nerve-racking to wait at home as their sons find it to serve in the lines.

Another long step toward the comprehension of war attitudes will be taken when it is realized that every great conflict constitutes a social and economic revolution. It produces violent torsions and sweeping changes. The War of Independence was accompanied by a revolution in political ideas, social customs, and habits of thought. The Civil War was an economic revolution for the whole country and a social revolution for the South. The first World War created vast new industries, changed race relations, made us a true world power, and altered our psychology. The second World War has had its deep revolutionary effects, the brunt of which has fallen on the civil population.

It has been a war in which big business has gotten bigger, while tens of thousands of small industrial plants have suffered acutely (with their managers and employees) from the high-speed mobilization. It has been a war in which the country has

had to increase its forty-five millions of gainfully employed to
sixty-five or seventy millions, which has meant working millions
of semi-fit people long hours. Literally millions of workers have
been moved by irresistible economic forces from one section of
the country to another; millions have been shifted, or have rest-
lessly shifted themselves, from one industry to another—the labor
turnover at certain places and times has reached 30 per cent a
month. Multitudes of families have been uprooted, and multitudes of children hurried into jobs. The result has been a painful
strain on family ties, and a spectacular increase in juvenile delinquency. Crimes against the person—murder, rape, assault—
have sharply risen. The population has had to adjust itself to the
jamming of cities, the dislocation of transport, the pinch of a
thousand shortages, the unpredictable shift of prices, the intrusion of government into new spheres. It has seen some groups enriched and others impoverished. The violence and confusion of
these changes test many people severely even if they never see a
gun. It is true that the revolutionary churn of war brings many
crude, selfish, hard-hitting scoundrels to the top. But it is also true
that it gives other men an opportunity to display selfless heroism,
and to prove that not all the wartime casualties die in uniform.
A distinguished American poet, Stephen Vincent Benét, succumbed to his devotion to war work, for which he had put everything else aside; the most useful of the younger college presidents
of the country, Dixon Ryan Fox, died laboring tirelessly to
mobilize his institution for war.

The important questions which we must ask are three or four.
The mood of the United States in this war differed perceptibly
from that in previous conflicts. There was less of parades, brass
bands, and fireworks; there was more of grim, determined, businesslike attention to the job. Why? Unquestionably, too, we
showed a closer national unity than in the first World War. Despite Gerald Nye, Hamilton Fish, and the Chicago *Tribune*;
despite Gerald Smith, Father Coughlin, and the forces exposed
in John Roy Carlson's *Under Cover*; despite grumbling, sniping,

and dishonest criticism, the country was better integrated than under Wilson. Why? What contributed to disunity and to unity?

In all our wars we may differentiate between two objects: the immediate purpose of defeating the enemy, and a larger purpose which gives moral meaning to the war. What did men think was the moral purpose in this conflict? How far would they pursue it beyond the last shot? Another set of questions pertains to our enemies and our allies. Was a brisk hatred of Germany and Japan fanned up? What did the country think of Britain, of China, and of Russia? Still another set pertains to morale. Was America unduly depressed in the first bad months, or unduly self-confident when the tide turned to victory?

The first of these questions—the question why the national mood was grimly sober—has some obvious answers, and one that lies beneath the surface. In previous conflicts Americans filled the streets with flags, staged wild recruiting rallies, cheered departing fighters madly, and roared patriotic songs—"We'll Rally Round the Flag, Boys," "A Hot Time in the Old Town," "Over There." In this war there was happily no such straw fire of frothy enthusiasm. For one reason, the sight of what Europe and Eastern Asia, both trodden into bloody mire, had endured, exercised a sobering effect. Americans in 1861, 1898, and 1917 had thought that the war would be easy. They knew full well in 1941 that it wouldn't. They knew that it was a war they might even lose—that it would cost, in treasure, effort, and possibly lives, far more than any previous struggle. They were too anxious, busy, and determined to waste time cheering. The example of Britain, which had been stimulated not by cheap rhetoric but by a stern promise of strain and agony, had its effect. There were no troop movements to cheer, anyway, for the troops moved secretly.

The grimness of temper was aided by another fact: that the memories of the first World War, and above all of its sickening aftermath, were still fresh. For the first time in their history Americans had fought two great wars in rapid succession. Eighty years had intervened between Yorktown and Bull Run; fifty years be-

tween Appomattox and Château-Thierry. The men of 1861 had
never known what a really bloody and devastating conflict meant,
nor had the men of 1914. It was easy then to march to battle with
pomp and fanfare—but not easy for a generation which vividly
remembered the ten million young men slain in Woodrow Wilson's day. We were in for it all again; we knew that it would be
a nasty ordeal; and we knew, too, that Norman Angell was right
when he declared that while defeat was the worst of disasters,
victory was a disaster too. This Spartan temper did not represent
apathy, nor distaste for our allies. It did not in the least stem from
pessimism; a people which had won all its wars, and had licked
the great rough North American continent into shape, never really
doubted that it could win one more encounter and help lick the
world into shape. It was just the acceptance at face value of a
tough, mean contract which had to be carried through, and
would be carried through.

But there was a deeper element which went into American
thinking and gave it a graver tinge. Many millions of reflective
people were troubled by a feeling for which no counterpart had
existed in the first World War; a feeling that the nation was
partly to blame for the catastrophe. The origins of the first war
were not our affair. It had flared up in the Old World as a result
of purely Old World forces. We were dragged into it—or so we
believed. But not so with this far greater collision. It was our affair, because we had been given a chance in 1918–20 to help stop
all future conflicts, and had turned our back on the opportunity.
When we might have furnished mankind continued leadership,
we had failed it. We were paying the penalty. Beyond question
this sense of a partial responsibility, this troubled conscience, im-
parted to tens of millions of Americans a feeling of moral obligation. Never had we been more acutely conscious of both past
failure and future opportunity. We had been given a second
chance, in which we could rectify our errors, atone for our failure,
and write a better page. The feeling that the war was to some
extent an atonement could not be translated into Sousa marches

and hip-hooray oratory; but it lent an underlying moral power to the national effort that could not be mistaken. Self-blame is not the most delightful spur to effort, but it can be a very healthy incentive.

Unity of sentiment is all-important in war, and historically the United States has found unity harder to attain than some other powers. The sectional diversities of a large country; the mixture of many national stocks in our population; our strong pacifist tradition running down from William Penn; our principle of free speech, which encourages dissent; the sharp difference of outlook between seaboard and interior on most issues of foreign policy— all these factors have militated against unity. Our discontented elements were so large in the War of 1812, the Civil War, and the first World War as to be positively dangerous. It is universally agreed that the second World War found us much more fortunate. Had we drifted into conflict on the Atlantic, some divisions might have remained acute. But the foully treacherous attack at Pearl Harbor gave every citizen, East and West, a sense of the deepest outrage. In 1917 there had been many pro-Germans; in 1941 nobody was blind enough to be pro-Japanese. For that matter, few people, whatever their blood, were even secretly pro-Nazi. The oppressions and cruelties of the Nazi and fascist systems, described for ten years by a host of keen-eyed American journalists and driven home to our consciousness by the arrival of throngs of refugees, had deeply offended all lovers of democracy and justice. Everybody had read newspaper articles of the sort later gathered into *I Saw It Happen.* Most literate people had read some of the books—*Germany Turns the Clock Back, Sawdust Caesar, The Voice of Destruction, You Can't Do Business With Hitler,* and so on into scores of titles. When we add the clear perception of national peril, and the emotional pull furnished by the sight of nations of kindred ideals struggling for life, the integration of America after Pearl Harbor seems entirely natural.

But here, too, a more fundamental element came into play. Before a peace-loving democracy like the United States can be even passably united in war, it must feel an intense moral conviction. We have always fought in part for ideals. In the Revolution we struggled for freedom; in the Civil War, the North fought for union and emancipation, the South for state rights. During the first World War a dozen great leaders—Wilson, Smuts, Borden, Lloyd George, and so on—tried to convince the English-speaking lands that they were fighting for the regeneration of the world. So far as the United States was concerned, they never completely succeeded. Such a goodhearted democrat as William Jennings Bryan and such a clearheaded lover of peace as Elihu Root refused to believe unreservedly in the higher aims of the war. The country never shook off all its doubts, as the events of 1919–20 proved.

But this war had been preceded by a thorough process of education—the education offered by the Great Depression, the failure of isolation, and the decade of open aggression and international anarchy. Between 1930 and 1940 events taught us that we *do* have a major part to play in shaping the destinies of mankind, and that we cannot escape our responsibility even if we wish to do so. We can evade it for twenty years; we can hide our heads in the sand of Neutrality Acts; but then it confronts us more starkly than ever. Few educated and thinking Americans did not know by 1941 that for better or worse they must henceforth share the general future of mankind. They could play a cheap, mean, shrinking part to their own injury, or a firm, generous, well-planned part to their own benefit. But the world has shrunk too far and fast to make it possible to play no part at all. Epidemics of disease in backward nations can menace our health. Economic depressions in other lands will injure our economy. Sequences of boom and depression, such as we gaily staged in the 1920's, will hurt everybody on the planet. Disruptive social and moral ideas, spreading from one stricken country to another, can lay a blight on far corners of the globe. "Any war, anywhere, is the concern of every nation, everywhere." In short, the country had been educated to a conviction that in essentials Woodrow Wilson had been right about the high moral purpose of the first World War, and his critics had been wrong. The two wars were simply successive phases of a grand continuing struggle to save democracy, peace, and the future of mankind. Agreement on this truth was so general as to make a mighty contribution to national unity—and national fervor.

One indication of this fact lay in the readiness with which the United States accepted the idea that the United Nations must be a continuing body. Another indication was furnished by the general initial approval of the United Nations Relief and Rehabilitation Administration program; of the two billion dollars to be initially spent, America was to furnish $1,350,000,000—and nobody complained. We were ready to spend for the peace as well as the war. When the Connally resolution committing the United States to a full role in a new world organization came to its final vote in the Senate, only six men opposed it. Six out of ninety-six —this perhaps represented the ratio of the population which had not been converted to a unifying moral conviction of the mission of the United States during and after the war.

Hatred of the enemy was not needed to harden the determination of the country, but more than in the first World War hatred existed. Probably in all our history no foe has been so detested as were the Japanese. The infamy of Pearl Harbor was enough; but to it were soon added circumstantial accounts of Japanese atrocities at Hong Kong, Singapore, and finally and most appallingly, upon American prisoners in the Philippines. Casualty lists made it plain that less quarter was being given on both sides in the Pacific war than in any previous conflict. Emotions forgotten since our most savage Indian wars were reawakened by the ferocities of Japanese commanders. Italy was viewed very differently; Winston Churchill expressed our contempt for the "jackal" Mussolini, and that was enough. Germany, too, was at first regarded mildly. But in 1942–44 came increasingly detailed accounts of what the Moscow Declaration, signed by Roosevelt, Churchill, and Stalin, termed "atrocities, massacres, and cold-blooded mass executions." Men's blood ran cold over descriptions of the Nazi murder camps; the slaughter of French, Dutch, Belgian, and Norwegian hostages; the wanton killing of hundreds of thousands of Russian civilians; and the deliberate starvation forced upon Greece. Estimates of the number of Jews done to death in one fashion or another ran as high as four millions. Anger mingled with horror over these histories. If it could not be said that the German people as a whole came to be hated, certainly the German *system* was detested as Americans had seldom detested anything. That satanic cancer they were determined to excise from the world at any cost.

The esteem of Americans for their allies, naturally enough, tended to rise and fall with the fortunes of war. They were most criticized in defeat and most popular in victory. This fact, clearly exhibited by newspaper comment and popular talk, was scientifically verified by OWI and other polls. British repute, for example, fell low just after the loss of Malaya and Singapore, and the sinking of the *Prince of Wales* and the *Repulse*; it rose again after the first thousand-plane raid on Cologne, and the decisive victory over Rommel at El Alamein. China's heroic resistance was almost universally extolled during 1941–43. When that gallant nation lost ground in 1944 it became less popular, and the revelation late that year that civil divisions had largely put it out of the war gave the signal for a storm of criticism. This reached its height when General Joseph Stilwell was recalled following a quarrel with Chiang Kai-shek. As for Russia, general opinion ran through violent oscillations. Indignation over the Russo-German pact and the invasion of Finland made even the *New Republic* call Stalin in 1940 "a bloody tyrant." The German invasion in June, 1941, produced a suspension of judgment as hopes alternated with fears. Finally, admiration for Soviet fighting prowess rose to wild enthusiasm, which reached its apex after the liberation of Stalingrad and again with the invasion of Germany.

But it must be said that a clear difference always existed between sentiment for Britain and the Dominions and sentiment for

Russia. More of family feeling, with all its superficial irritations and fundamental loyalties, entered into the former; more of ideological likes and dislikes into the latter. At all times Winston Churchill was one of the most admired figures of the conflict. Even before Pearl Harbor the boundary line between the United States and Canada had become thin and insubstantial. Hundreds of thousands of American soldiers and sailors found Australia and New Zealand another home. Well-informed people knew that the Anglo-American effort in North Africa, Italy, and on the Western Front was admirably co-ordinated. Eisenhower and Montgomery were ruthless in weeding out officers who betrayed any national prejudice. The joint chiefs of staffs labored without visible friction. The Anglo-American Combined Production and Resources Board, and the Anglo-American Food Board, both did admirable work from 1942 onward. An Anglo-American Commission on Social and Economic Co-operation in the Caribbean offered an interesting experiment in the colonial sphere. We generally admired Great Britain and her Dominions—and trusted them; we generally admired Russia—and were not quite so trustful. The Russian war was to a considerable extent a secret war, American observers long being kept back from the fighting fronts. British diplomacy seemed more open than Russian diplomacy.

While by 1945 our regard for the British had wide cordiality, the American attitude toward Russia represented some violently conflicting opinions. C.I.O. circles and radicals generally declared that the Soviet system stood completely vindicated and was the hope of the world. Conservative labor groups and the Socialist school supporting the *New Leader* were fiercely critical of some phases of the Russian system. Businessmen, most churchmen (especially Catholics), and many politicians viewed Russia, for all her magnificent war effort, with reservations. When in 1944–45 feeling between Russia and the London Government of Poland became strained to the point of total rupture, great numbers of Americans heatedly took sides. The Polish National Council maintained an unchangeable demand for the eastern boundary of September 1, 1939; the Russian Government insisted upon "the historic right of the Ukrainian and White Russian peoples to be united within their national states." To American Catholics in particular, the Soviet demand for what was roughly the Curzon Line seemed arbitrary and unfair. Yet the majority esteem for Russia remained high, and belief that a fair solution would be reached was still general. The average American felt that the United States was fortunate in its allies; fortunate in the brotherhood of Britons, Russians, Chinese, and Free French.

What then of the factors which made for national disunity? Did any obtrude themselves? Of course they did; but it could be said that they were less troublesome than in 1917–19.

In the second World War Americans never faced the most dangerous of disruptive forces, a feeling that the leaders of the armed forces were not measuring up to their tremendous responsibilities. The Civil War distrust of McClellan, Pope, and Halleck, of Bragg and Longstreet, found no duplication in 1941–45. Nothing took place to recall the outcries of admirers of T. R. and Leonard Wood in the first World War. Instead, the American people felt and expressed the heartiest admiration for Eisenhower, Bradley, and Patton, for MacArthur and Kruger, for Nimitz and Halsey. In due time the work of these men would demand a critical appraisal. But this could wait till full data were available, for the results showed a high competence. Nor was there much real dispute over war policy. The great decision to win the war in Europe first, though criticized by MacArthur's friends and (for purposes strictly their own) by the McCormick-Patterson newspapers, was approved by the country and justified by events. Such men as Major Alexander de Seversky (his *Victory Through Air Power* was widely read) declared that battleships were outmoded and that long-range planes might displace even carriers; but the people were content to accept the judgments of the staffs. Never has the American high command, in a long, arduous, and costly war, been less criticized. General George Marshall and Admiral King had a hundred words of commendation for one of doubt.

The civil administration enjoyed less confidence and got at least a wholesome amount of criticism. Much of it was concentrated upon President Roosevelt; more upon Vice-President Wallace, who in 1944 was temporarily shelved at the behest of Southern and Western reactionaries; and most of all upon the "bureaucrats," target of politicians and businessmen alike. The assault upon vestiges of the New Deal and upon wartime restrictions became acutest in 1942–43, midway in the third term. Republicans attacked "mismanagement, bungling, and confusion" in Washington. Promising a housecleaning, they won a gain of forty-seven seats in the House and ten in the Senate. A grand old Progressive, G. W. Norris of Nebraska, disappeared. Congress was still nominally controlled by the Democrats, but it numbered plenty of men who, in Mark Twain's phrase, had "one eye on the constituency and one on the swag," and plenty in both parties who wanted to slap the Administration. The sequel was the unhappy record of the first half of 1943. Congress passed over the President's veto the Smith-Connally Strike Limitation Bill; struck down the domestic branch of the OWI; destroyed the National Resources Planning Board by denying it any funds; abolished the National Youth Administration; lifted the $25,000 net ceiling on salaries favored by the President; cut the appropriation of the enforcement division of the Office of Price Administration, and tried to stop the use of federal money in price roll-backs.

This congressional foray, though proof that the legislative branch was in due working order, was a poor contribution to national unity. Meanwhile, the State Department was becoming a storm center. Its policy upon the Franco government in Spain and the Vichy regime in France was hotly attacked and defended. Critics of Secretary Hull's policy declared that in both countries he was betraying democracy and aiding fascism. Friends of the State Department asserted that it was doing nothing of the kind; that it disliked Franco and Pétain as much as anybody, and handled both firmly; and that its touches of appeasement were indispensable to prevent Vichy from handing the French fleet over to Hitler, and to preclude all risk of a sudden Spanish attack on the Anglo-American flank in the North African invasion. The authorized publication in *Harper's Magazine* of a documented article on Ambassador Hayes's work in Madrid offered evidence of efficient activity there. But criticism of State Department policy toward Vichy, De Gaulle, and the provisional Italian Government in 1944–45 remained high. More than any other home-front battle (the feud of Henry Wallace and Jesse Jones, for example, or the storm that forced Leon Henderson out of OPA), the warfare against and within the State Department definitely threatened to impair American earnestness in the war effort.

The struggles of rival economic groups, too, inevitably shook the country. National income rose to a hundred billions, a hundred and twenty-five billions, a hundred and fifty billions. What element should get most of the increase? The antagonism of little business toward big business remained keen. Farmers (though their income increased 90 per cent in the three years 1941–43) felt abused because government controls kept prices from reaching the high levels of the first World War, while manpower and machinery shortages troubled them. The vociferations of Western stockmen over OPA meat ceilings were loud and constant. As for the millions of white-collar wage earners and salaried workers, few received anything like the 15 per cent increase which the Little Steel formula gave most union workers (as a minimum) to meet the heightened cost of living.

Unquestionably there was a general feeling by 1944–45 that big business and union labor were taking more than their proper share from the common pot. Profits of all corporations after taxes had been $8,100,000,000 in the peak year 1929; in 1943 they were estimated at $8,500,000,000. Dividends had risen to striking figures, and the stock market followed them up. The President's efforts to have greatly increased amounts of money collected in 1944 and 1945 by taxes, loans, or both had been foiled by Con-

gress. The strength of the labor unions, which by the beginning
of 1943 counted more than twelve million members, was exciting
some apprehension. Those familiar with the history of older democracies, especially Great Britain, knew that this strength constituted a great national gain. But many rural groups of low income, and many ill-paid clerical workers in stores and offices,
resentfully felt that they had been forgotten. An OWI press release in 1943 declared that twenty million Americans were receiving inadequate incomes. More specific were the figures of FDA
economists, who that year declared that more than ten million
families were still making less than the $1,675 required to main-
tain a sound minimum standard of living. It was clear that if an
impassioned upflare of resentment against business (especially
the big corporations) and an irrational assault upon labor unions
were to be avoided, legislation would have to be undertaken to
diffuse the national income more equitably.

To the ups and downs of the war Americans responded with an
equanimity born of their general grimness of temper. They indulged neither in sackcloth-rending over defeat nor in hat-
tossing over victory. The first year was the most discouraging in
American memory—as dark as the first year of the Civil War in
the North. The terrible losses of Pearl Harbor—five battleships
sunk or beached, three more heavily damaged, ten smaller warships destroyed or badly hurt—and the smashing at Clark Field of
the whole bomber command in the Philippines, were the harder
to bear because they showed gross negligence. Few nations have
been so stupid as to sink 80,000 tons of vitally needed merchant
shipping at the pier in one afternoon; the United States did it
when it let the *Normandie* burn and capsize. For a full year after
Pearl Harbor the skies grew blacker and blacker. The Japanese
drove to the borders of Australia; Rommel planted himself at the
gates of Cairo and Suez; Hawaii was threatened; the Germans
seemed about to seize Stalingrad and the oilfields of the Cau-
casus. But Americans showed that, like the British and the Rus-

sians, they are good at endurance of defeat. Perhaps, despite differences of temperament, they are good for fundamentally the same reason, because they are so sure of ultimate success.

But then the tide swiftly turned in every quarter of the globe. At El Alamein the Imperial Army under Alexander defeated Rommel's arrogant forces and began to drive them back across the deserts; at Stalingrad the Russians first stopped the enemy in his tracks, and then by brilliant strategy crushed the flower of his army; in the magnificent victories of the Coral Sea and Midway the American Navy passed from defensive to offensive; and in North Africa the Anglo-American forces landed to take Algeria and Tunis. It was "the end of the beginning." Depression gave way to restrained optimism.

Two traditions merged in the quiet exhilaration which appeared among Americans in 1943 and which grew steadily in 1944 and 1945. One, we need not say, was our tradition of pride in the sheer fighting capacity of Americans. Officers who knew both armies reported that the generation of 1941 was in some ways distinctly superior to that of 1917. At any rate, it fought fully as well. In part, we took pride in dashing individual exploits: to name but one in thousands, the valor of John J. Powers at the Battle of the Coral Sea in planting a half-ton bomb in the carrier *Ryukaku* at five hundred feet, when he knew that he could not come out of the resulting explosion. In part, we were proud of battles desperately fought to victory: the marines carrying Tarawa and Iwo as their forefathers had carried the Yorktown redoubts, the amphibious forces storming the Normandy beaches as an older army had stormed the Bloody Angle at Spotsylvania. Americans were not least pleased at the ability of their navy to outthink the Japanese admirals and of their army to outmaneuver the German generals. In the Pacific, the onset usually seemed to fall just where the enemy did not expect it. In Northern France, Bradley and Patton seized a dexterous opportunity to place themselves in the German rear. And on the Rhine, young officers and privates took the Remagen Bridge in the ten minutes that the foe's confusion allowed them.

But American exhilaration was equally a pride in the careful planning, the systematic production of overpowering armaments, and the skillful massing of strength which made large operations so swiftly successful. A British observer, D. W. Brogan, remarked during the conflict that "to the Americans war is a business, not an art." He meant that the Americans approached it with business resourcefulness and efficiency, as they had approached the harnessing of the Tennessee Valley or the exploitation of the Mesabi iron ranges. To the French, war might be a matter of dash and parade; to the Germans, of professional military skill. But to the Americans it meant a relentless massing of resources in the right place at the right time. It meant large-scale manufacture, logistics, and final deployment. It meant, in short, enough strength to win successively in North Africa, Sicily, France, and Germany; enough strength to drive a path across the tremendous distances of the Central Pacific, to take the Philippines, and to convert them in a few weeks into a base for further operations.

Never before had war demanded such technological expertness and business organization. Americans first comprehended the fact when they studied that Battle of the Coral Sea in which the Japanese and American warships never saw each other, but simply maneuvered to send death-dealing squadrons of airplanes to their targets. The subsequent actions in the Battle of Midway, where the Japanese lost four of their largest carriers, in the waters off Guadalcanal, and above all in the battles of the Philippine Sea, would have been equally difficult for Perry or Farragut to understand. They involved more comprehensive preparations and intricate calculations than were dreamed of in previous wars. The modern American genius, the genius of the country of Whitney, Morse, and Edison, precisely fitted such a war. After our invasion of France, we were told that our armies lurched forward to the Siegfried Line like a vast armed workshop; a congeries of factories on wheels with a bristling screen of troops and a cover of airplanes; the most highly mechanized advance in history. We were proud of our forces because they were brave; we were proud of them also because they were efficient in the hard temper of the American planner and engineer.

People found a growing exhilaration, moreover, in the vast productive feats of America's rapidly mobilized war industries. Many observers had refused to take seriously Mr. Roosevelt's initial challenge to the country to produce within two years 125,000 airplanes, 85,000 tanks, and 25,000,000 dead-weight tons of shipping. They saw the importance of the principle involved: to spare life and limb as much as possible, the government intended to amass the greatest panoply of war machines ever seen. But they doubted the possibility of attaining such totals. The first months, with an overproduction of bickering and excuses and an underproduction of implements, seemed to justify this skepticism. Factories had to be built or converted; machine tools devised; the new machinery produced in quantity; hands and foremen trained. But early in 1943 industry began to report its first spotty successes. The greatest airplane factories the world had ever seen were being equipped and set running. The largest shipyards ever built were being put in operation. Mass-production methods were being applied to planes, ships, guns, tanks, and nearly every other weapon demanded. New captains of industry—Higgins, Kaiser, Douglas— were emerging. In some respects the showing of industry was open to criticism. American tanks somehow never equaled the best German tanks. But in general the production far exceeded most expectations, and justified Mr. Roosevelt's boast early in 1943: "The arsenal of democracy is making good."

There were special reasons why Americans found elation in the results soon observable—in the output of 10,000 planes a month; in the building of 14,000-ton Liberty ships in a few weeks or even days rather than months; in a production of medium tanks so rapid that it had to be cut back; in the flood of ordnance, shells, bombs, and small arms; in warship-building that ran far ahead of schedule. This, too, was in an old American tradition. But we had been told in the 1930's that the tradition of individual initiative and large-scale feats of production was ended. The depression, continuing down to 1939, had numbed multitudes of people. They had accepted those voices of discouragement which declared that the great days of free enterprise were dead; that the nation had entered upon a tamer, more restricted phase of economic development; that commanding captains of industry and tremendous corporate undertakings were gone forever. Millions had feared that these prophecies of a weaker, more pedestrian, and less adventurous America were true. The home-front effort proved that they were false. With pleased wonder, men heard that American and Canadian production of synthetic rubber had risen above the prewar importation figures. They learned that aluminum production was reaching up toward a million tons a year, and magnesium production surpassing the wildest dreams of its users. They read of heavy ships built in sections all over a wide yard, and welded together on a central way in a matter of hours. They heard that clouds of bombers were being ferried across the Atlantic in six to eight hours. They knew that steel production, running close to capacity, exceeded the whole output of the world a few years earlier. The old self-confident America was coming into its stride again.

But the greatest reason for elation in the production totals was clear enough to all. They meant not only speedier victory, but victory purchased with fewer lives. An officer who was smothering a hill in Tunis with artillery fire spoke to a war correspondent. "I'm letting the American taxpayer take this hill," he said. That was obviously the way an American war should be fought; industry and the taxpayer doing as much of it as they could.

Some circles naturally translated their pride in the feats of American fighters and the achievements of industry into a blatant nationalism; a swaggering assertion that after the war we would do better than co-operate with other nations—we would tell them! Demands for bases all over the globe sprung up. This nationalism

failed to seduce most thinking Americans, who were too conscious of unsolved problems at home to forget a due humility,
and too well aware of the staggering size of world problems to
ignore the need for united world effort. They knew that they had
not controlled prices so efficiently as Australia and New Zealand;
that they had not taxed away the threat of inflation as courageously as Britain; that they had hardly begun to deal with the
Negro problem as it required; that their handling of the west
coast Japanese was a blot on the war record; that they could take
lessons from Sir William Beveridge on social security, and from
little Sweden on the relations of government and industry. They
knew that the program of Dumbarton Oaks and the San Francisco Conference was indispensable to the welfare of all mankind, including themselves, and that it could be carried out only
by the united effort of all peace-loving nations.

As other wars drew to a close, Americans had looked forward
to a relaxation of effort and a return to the comforts of normal
life. No dream of a folding of hands beneath their own vine and
fig tree could beguile thoughtful citizens of the republic as victory approached in 1945. They had seen their fighters add proud
new pages to the history of the nation. Successive generations
would never forget Bataan and Guadalcanal, Casablanca and
Bizerte, the Coral Sea and the Philippine Sea, the Battle of the
Rhineland and the sweep toward Berlin. They would never forget the returning veterans that men applauded in 1945–46, or
still more, the heroes who, like the gallant Pelham of whom John
Esten Cooke sang, never returned from the battlefield:

> *Oh, band in the pine-wood, cease!*
> *Cease from your mournful call!*
> *The living are brave and noble,*
> *But the dead were the bravest of all!*

Early in 1945, with the winning of the Battle of the Bulge, it
became clear that the end of the war was in sight, and that, as
most Americans had always believed, it would terminate in

Europe before it did in the Pacific. Americans tightened their belts for the last heavy pull—a pull that might go into 1946, but which would bring complete victory.

It can be said that the final curtain dropped in Europe more slowly than most people had anticipated, for the last-ditch battle of the Germans at Breslau and Berlin, Frankfurt and Nuremberg, was irrational to the point of insanity. The Nazis fought that battle so they might leave the victors a heap of ruins. On the other hand, the Japanese war then ended far more quickly than most people had expected, and with far less cost in life. Most Americans saw the victory in Europe as primarily an achievement of the Army. Co-ordinated with air power, the land forces under Eisenhower, Bradley, Hodges, and Patton first cracked the coastal defenses and then smashed the Wehrmacht—the British and Russians doing their full part. On the other hand, Americans credited the Navy with the major share of the victory in the Pacific. It defeated the Japanese fleets wherever they met in large-scale action, and finally all but wiped out the last enemy forces in the Battle of the Philippine Sea. It drove the Japanese from outpost to outpost, cleared the sea lanes, sank most of the Japanese merchant shipping (submarines co-operating with air forces), and established bases from which air power was able to smash Japanese cities and industries. The Army was ready in the Pacific, but happily it never had to meet its most fearful test— a death grapple with the still unbeaten two million Japanese warriors mustered in the home islands, and the million on the Asiatic continent. Navy, air power, and the atomic bomb saved us from that bloody ordeal.

A fiercer exultation naturally went into V-J Day than into V-E Day. After all, from the moment the Rhine was crossed Americans had discounted their European triumph. They not only knew that it was coming, but they knew that it would bring tasks of relief, reconstruction, and reshaping that would be as difficult as any of the war. They knew that ruined Germany would cast down its arms only to ask us for crutches. But V-J Day

came as a sudden relief from dark forebodings of slaughter on
the beaches and suicidal mass attacks along every mile of our
inland thrust. It meant that hundreds of thousands of our young
men had been reprieved from death. It meant, too, that war was
over, everywhere, and perhaps for all time. It meant that the
enemy which had dealt us the foulest blow in our history had
been compelled to the most abject capitulation. Long before
V-E Day and V-J Day people had been exhorted to flock to
churches, not bars, and think of the doxology, not the dram. That
admonition was widely heeded on V-E Day, but a wild passion
of relief, pride, and joy shook a hundred and forty millions the
night that news came of Japan's surrender.

The atomic bomb might or might not be credited with a major
share in the Pacific victory; on that point men would long differ.
It was clear that Japanese fighting power had been largely
crushed before the first bomb fell, and that Hirohito as early as
June 22 had been trying to initiate peace negotiations. It was
also true that the cataclysms in Hiroshima and Nagasaki made
continued resistance absurd, and that the new weapon gave
Japan an excuse for quitting. But reflective men saw that the
chief significance of the bomb lay elsewhere. It lay in its implications for world peace. A Gallup poll showed that most Americans approved of spending two billions to develop it; that most
of them wished to keep it in Anglo-American rather than United
Nations hands; and that a majority of those who expressed any
opinion were optimistic that industrial use of atomic energy
would begin within ten years.

It was only the second of these three views, that favoring
Anglo-American secrecy on the bomb formula, which had any
significance, and it rested upon a misconception that scientists
were quick to dispel. Prolonged secrecy would be impossible.
The bomb was actually an international achievement. American,
British, and Canadian scientists had done most of the work, but
a Danish professor, a German woman scientist, an Italian physicist,
and a number of German-Austrian refugees had aided them. No

such discovery could long be the secret of two Powers any more than Faraday's discovery of electromagnetic energy or Watt's steam engine could be a secret. There was but one way to control the destructive use of atomic energy: to control legalized destruction. There was but one way to prevent a holocaust of life and property beyond any historical precedent; that was to prevent war. The new atomic age, when it fully dawned, would open revolutionary vistas in industry and in all social relationships. It would also open a vista of compulsory world unity and world organization for peace—for the alternative would be the destruction of world civilization.

Americans suddenly seemed to stand, as the war closed, beholding a new heaven and a new earth, to which they somewhat dazedly tried to adjust themselves. This adjustment was not made easier by the fact that a new leadership had suddenly been imposed. Roosevelt was gone, his greatness looming up more unmistakably than ever for his swift removal in the hour of victory. Churchill was gone, swept under in a dramatic election overturn—though his organ voice pealed out as loudly as ever in Opposition ranks. These changes simply emphasized the fact that the democratic peoples of the world must, as always, find their chief strength in their rank and file; in the resources of the common people who had made democracy what it was. They had always risen to meet their greatest crises, and in this time of unexampled want, woe, and confusion the world over, they would answer the challenge again.

II. WHAT WE TALKED ABOUT

by *PAUL GALLICO*

*PAUL GALLICO (age 48), ex-sports columnist,
feature writer, and war correspondent, describes
himself as an inveterate newspaper reader, gos-
sip-column addict, and comic-strip fan. He is
perhaps best known for his short stories. In the
summer of 1944, as a war correspondent for*
Cosmopolitan Magazine, *he entered Paris with
the French 2nd Armored Division to witness
the fall, or rather the rise, of that city.*

THERE was the war. And then after that there were the hundreds and the thousands of little things and big things, tragic,
funny, profound, silly, vital, unimportant, American things that
went to make up the rest of life at home during the war years,
the things that you would have laughed, or gossiped, or shed a
tear about had you been a civilian in these United States, those
years from the spring of '42 to the summer of '45, while you were
gone.

Nothing much happened here at home while you were gone,
and a million things happened, day in, day out, things you would
have talked about, shuddered or marveled at, laughed about, repeated, or discussed with your friends; births, deaths, engage-
ments, marriages and divorces, fire and flood and train wreck,
romance and scandal, new customs, fads and fashions, popular
songs, books, plays, movies, radio shows and the people who
made them, juicy murders that in peace times would have filled
the tabloids and the big papers too, for weeks, new stars of stage,
sports, and screen arising, plus all the turmoil of wartime living
here at home, blackout and scarcities and rationing, conniving

and finagling and black marketing, the struggle for gasoline and sugar and meat AND cigarettes, in all of which you would have played your normal civilian part for better or for worse had you been one of us instead of a soldier.

While you were gone, many an old friend and famous national name vanished from the scene through death, and the passing of all of them gave us pause here at home for comment, for regret, or memories of their contributions.

Nineteen forty-two saw the exit from the national scene, among others, of General Hugh Johnson of NRA and Blue Eagle fame, a damned competent, crotchety newspaper columnist in his final years; Jack Blackburn, who trained Joe Louis and taught him all the boxing Louis knows; and Graham McNamee, famous old-time radio announcer who grew up with the infant industry.

Gone too by the year's end were four great figures of the stage, John Barrymore, George M. Cohan, Joe Weber, the little fat one of the old-time comedy team of Weber and Fields, relic of the era of Shanleys and Reisenwebers, and onwards too passed at the age of sixty-nine a little man named Joseph Francis Jiranek, but better known to America and the world as Joe Jackson, the tramp bicyclist of the vaudeville stage and one of the great clowns and pantomime artists of all time.

In that year, too, died Arthur Pryor, the band leader; Maury Paul, who as Cholly Knickerbocker, social arbiter and blue-blood gossip columnist, ended an era with his passing; Condé Nast, founder of *Vanity Fair* magazine; Tony, nationally known horse of the late Tom Mix; and Philadelphia Jack O'Brien, old-time fighter who once won a decision while lying with his head in the resin box, knocked cold in the last seconds of a fight he had won up to then.

Billy Beck died. He invented and drew Barney Google and his famous blanketed horse, "Sparkplug," Snuffy Smith and Bunky, who used to say, "Youse is a viper." With him vanished from the scene Bob Davis, editor, newspaperman, and storyteller, and the sporting man Jack Doyle, proprietor of Jack Doyle's billiard parlor on Broadway, whence stemmed the odds on every important prize fight, World Series, horse race, or football game, the country over.

A lot of other things happened in that beginning year of '42, to get themselves talked about. There was a flash fad for high school girls, who wore guard rings of black jet denoting absent soldier friends; Joe Louis flattened Abe Simon in six rounds in his last fight before enlisting in the Army; and a girl named Oona O'Neill was named Stork Club debutante of the year, much to the disgust of her father, the great playwright, Eugene O'Neill. Remember that name, Oona O'Neill, for you will meet her again in connection with another great personality.

That was the spring when women took to wearing slacks in the streets (a great blow to the human race), old toothpaste tubes had to be turned in for new ones, men's trousers were commanded to be cuffless, and a radio comedian named Bob Hope began to play soldiers' camps around the country. Lili Damita divorced Errol Flynn, turning her superwolf back into circulation, with consequences yet to develop. Superman took his army physical and was rejected as a 4F when his X-ray eyes unfortunately read the chart in the next room instead of the one he was supposed to read, and Hitler, Mussolini, and Hirohito all breathed easier.

Shipwreck Kelly the flagpole sitter fell off a ten-foot pole at Palisades Park, New Jersey, and went to the hospital; the New York *Post* turned tabloid; a national drive was begun to salvage tin cans and we first began to hear of a new bug-eyed gravel-voiced comic named Zero Mostel on a new radio program called the "Chamber Music Society of Lower Basin Street." An itinerant newspaper columnist named Ernie Pyle, who used to wander up and down the U.S.A. in an old Ford writing pieces about people, divorced his wife Geraldine, known as "that girl . . ." to his column readers, in Albuquerque after sixteen years of marriage.

That was the spring we first heard about sugar rationing, with gasoline rationing to come. Ice cream was reduced to ten flavors, and civilian suffering really hit its stride when the War Production Board banned the use of metals for asparagus tongs, beer mugs, spittoons, bird cages, cocktail shakers, hair curlers, corn poppers, and lobster forks. New York blacked out, and for days we talked about how beautiful the great city looked stark and naked, silhouetted against the moon and the stars. The draft made a pass at the body of Vic Mature, the beautiful hunk of man, just about the time that Pat Di Cicco, Gloria Vanderbilt's husband, enlisted. You'll hear more about Pat and Gloria later.

Gas rationing came in with a nasty shock—three gallons a week for A Card holders. Within a fortnight practically the entire nation had perjured itself to get B2 and B3 and X cards. Don't gripe, soldier. If you were a civilian in those days, you did it too. Or you would have. Undisciplined to wartime sacrifices, we all made sweet pigs out of ourselves and in no time at all were in the throes of a national scandal, so all-encompassing in scope that public opinion forced most of the hogs to cough up their B and X cards and put up with their three gallons. In the meantime, we were singing "Don't sit under the apple tree with anyone else but me," and Billy Conn paid a social call to his father-in-law, Jimmy Smith, in Pittsburgh to bury the hatchet for running off with his daughter. Smith asked: "Are you afraid of me?" Conn replied, "I'm not afraid of anyone," and let go with the right—BLAM! When the dust of battle settled, Conn had a broken hand and the projected return match with Joe Louis was off.

Things were building up. The wedding of seventeen-year-old Nancy Oakes, daughter of Sir Harry Oakes of Nassau in the Bahamas, to Count Alfred de Marigny, was announced, and none foresaw the tragedy that was to ensue. We were too busy following the trial of a girl named Madeleine Webb who with her sweetheart Eli Schonbrun was accused of luring a rich old woman to a Manhattan hotel and strangling her. Ted Williams, Boston's batting star, enlisted, and the *Saturday Evening Post* changed its cover and interior format, dropped Benjamin Franklin and *Saturday Evening,* and became just plain *Post.*

That spring of '42 was hellish, the worst in sixty years. There

were floods, tornadoes, ice jams, cloudbursts, forest fires, hail-
storms, but weather had become a military secret instead of a
favorite topic of conversation. We could talk about it locally but
not nationally.

But we had other matters to discuss. The vacation problem
popped up for the first time on the national consciousness. Where
to go, and how to get there? Both coasts were shut off to visitors;
transportation difficulties were beginning to arise, automobiles
were out. To keep our minds off our troubles we contemplated
the annual salary of Louis B. Mayer, head of MGM Pictures,
which was reported at $704,425.60.

A dark-haired, throaty beauty named Dinah Shore was singing
a song about "One Dozen Roses," movie-goers thrilled over a new
screen tough guy, a 4F named Alan Ladd who turned up in a
picture called *This Gun for Hire*, and the Hollywood divorce and
marriage mills ground merrily. Myrna Loy divorced producer
Arthur Hornblow and immediately married John D. Hertz, Jr.,
Chicago taxicab heir, while Charlie Chaplin divorced Paulette
Goddard. Are you keeping track?

That spring came to an end with the conviction of the Webb-
Schonbrun pair. Madeleine got life, Eli the chair. The Dionne
Quintuplets had their hair cut short, their five shorn heads appearing in every newspaper, and feminine hearts the land over
shuddered at the news that Clark Gable had passed his physical
examination for admission into the Air Forces.

Summer was icumen in not with lhude sing cuccu, but with
street urchins, radios, and juke boxes intoning something called
"I've got spurs that jingle, jangle, jingle," and the home front began to shift into high with the realization of the steel and rubber
shortage, the latter a national scandal, and the organization of the
great scrap drives.

It was in the heat of July that we learned that the FBI had
captured eight Nazi spies and saboteurs landed at Ammagansett,
L. I., and Jacksonville, Florida. All were tried and electrocuted.
The story was a three-day wonder. So was the acute gasoline

shortage, and had you been around the big cities of the East you would have seen the fantastic spectacle of processions of cars burning up gasoline following tank trucks through the streets to filling stations so that when the trucks pumped their loads into the service station tanks, the citizens could buy more gasoline to follow more trucks to more gas tanks. The arrival of the A, B, and C stickers finally put an end to that screwball merry-go-round.

Victor Mature turned his torso over to his country via the Coast Guard, and Babs Hutton took another palpitating male out of public and dream circulation by marrying Cary Grant. The libidos of the male population suffered two blows when Lana Turner married one Stephen Crane, a businessman, and Joan Crawford took unto herself Philip Terry, a movie actor, but recovered somewhat at the news that Mae West won a divorce from her husband, Frank Wallace. Harry Hopkins married Louise Macy in a tender if slightly public White House romance. Detroit's home run slugger, Hank Greenberg, was commissioned a Second Lieutenant, and Jimmy Stewart was promoted to First Lieutenant in the Air Corps.

Life in these United States rolled on. A kid in the Army published a book called *See Here, Private Hargrove*. Local officials squabbled publicly and in the newspapers over the best way to deal with an incendiary bomb—spray, solid stream, or pick it up with the sugar tongs and dump it into a pail of water—and people were made very happy by the story of the lady hoarder who filled her cellar from top to bottom with canned goods. A flash rainstorm flooded the cellar and washed all the paper labels off the cans. The lady now had not only a fine, hoarded food supply, but a delightful lottery to keep her entertained, since there was no longer the slightest clue as to what was inside any can.

Bertie McCormick, proprietor of the Chicago *Tribune*, made the mistake of attacking Marshall Field, publisher of the rival *Sun*, as a slacker, and grew long, furry ears when it developed that Field had a hot combat record in the last war. And the East had a corking three-day spy scare when the Army released air pictures of fields apparently plowed to arrow design with arrows pointing towards airplane factories. Then the pictures proved to be a hoax and an army publicity officer was fired. People wondered whether Attorney General Francis Biddle could convict Liz Dilling and the twenty-seven other crackpots, hate-spreaders, home-grown fascists, and Hitler-lovers he had at last succeeded in indicting.

By summer's end a dreadful phrase had come into being out of the mouths of clerks in stores, hotels, service companies—"Hey, don'tcha know there's a war on?"

We should have been aware irrespective of the war news, which was all bad, so bad that General Brehon Somervell warned us, "We are losing the war." Rommel was nearing Suez, the Japanese dominated Asia and the Western Pacific. Mr. Roosevelt suggested a meatless day, and ration books were promised after election with fuel oil rationing likewise in prospect. One began to hear of the servant question as domestic help vanished from homes into factories. Cosmetics, hairpins, tinfoil, and alcohol were disappearing.

But the home front shenanigans went on just the same, with night spots, bars, theatres, and places of entertainment jammed, silk shirts, fur coats, and diamonds moving off counters at a fantastic rate, and names continued to make news.

Paul Robeson made a minor sensation by overplaying Othello; Jackie Coogan, "The Kid" of the Golden Era when Charlie Chaplin was a comedian instead of a somewhat ridiculous public Lothario, became a glider pilot. Norma Shearer married her ski instructor, Martin Arronge, aged twenty-eight, Gypsy Rose Lee, the literary strip teaser, wed actor Alexander Kirkland, and Ava Gardner married Mickey Rooney.

Glenn Miller went into the Army, and Harry James the sweet swing trumpeter took his place in the affections of the disk devotees. Russia sent us a pretty girl sniper named Ludmilla Pavlichenko, with a record of 311 bull's-eyes scored on Nazis, and Sex reared its pretty head in factories as an occupational hazard. Girls were requested to quit wearing sweaters, peekaboo waists, halters, and other revealing garments. The boys were rubber-necking themselves into too many accidents.

The fall of '42 began with a wreck on the B. & O. that cost twenty lives, the cry for scrap and more scrap to feed the mills, OPA tire inspection, the thirty-five-mile-an-hour speed limit, and the total disappearance of alarm clocks, cameras, and field glasses from store shelves.

Mayor La Guardia and the New York press fell out and called each other names, and a wonderful Negro jazz pianist named Hazel Scott was discovered, but more and bigger news was yet to come. This was the season in which we sang Frank Loesser's great song, "Praise the Lord and Pass the Ammunition," and sang it and sang it until it was no longer bearable and radio stations rationed themselves on performances of it. Not coming out of the radio was another song, a lil, called "In Der Fuehrer's Face," because it was not considered a nice song, for what you did in the Fuehrer's face was "Bra-a-a-a-a-a-ack," which is the nearest one can come to spelling out the mouth sound made to imitate breaking wind. People loved it.

Wendell Willkie came home from his world tour just in time to have all available newspaper space grabbed by the juiciest Hollywood scandal in years. Errol Flynn, restored to circulation by Lili Damita, as we have seen, was charged with statutory rape after a party at the Bel Air home of one Fred McEvoy, listed as a British sportsman, by a toothsome bit of jail-bait named Betty Hansen. "He took me upstairs to a room," testified Miss Hansen, and then went into considerable meaty detail as to what had happened there. The charge of statutory rape has to do with the age of consent, not the amount of struggle put up, for there wasn't any.

That was what we talked about at a time when you were compressed in the bowels of great transport ships setting out upon the greatest adventure of your lives, but can you blame us?

Wendell Willkie made his famous radio speech about the "reservoir of good will," and Eddie Rickenbacker disappeared into the void of the Pacific when his special mission plane vanished and never made a landfall. Rick was dear to us all as a former war hero, a national character in aviation, and a friend, and for days the nation discussed his disappearance and the great search that was on for him until the newest monkeyshines from Hollywood gave us a new topic for gossip. It was only an addition to the woes of actor Errol Flynn. A darling little night club dancer likewise in the jail-bait bracket bethought herself back to events that had occurred two years ago on a little yachting trip in the company of some Hollywood greats, and darned, now that she thought of it in the light of Miss Hansen's testimony, if she too hadn't been raped a little by Mr. Flynn. Help! Police!

Then coffee disappeared from grocery shelves just like that, with the OPA still unprepared for rationing. The howl that went up from the coffee drinkers smothered the news that the Big Inch Pipe Line was at last under way and that Clark Gable had graduated as a second looey in the Air Forces. It drowned out Ella Mae Morse shouting "Cow Cow Boogie," and Gracie Fields singing "The Biggest Aspidistra in the World," over a national hookup from 9:55 to 10 P.M.

Election Day came and went, and to the Congress went Will Rogers, Jr., and Clare Booth Luce. Gloria Vanderbilt professed herself ecstatically happy with Pat Di Cicco at an army camp in Red Bank, N. J. Eddie Rickenbacker was found alive after drifting twenty-four days in an open raft. Africa was invaded.

The war was getting on, but culture at home was far from neglected. Toscanini had performed the Shostakovitch Seventh Symphony. In St. Louis, Vladimir Golschmann, conducting the "1812 Overture," had two shotguns fired offstage in the finale, scaring the pants off the audience and bringing out the gendarmes. There was considerable to-do over Joe Palooka, the comic strip character, shooting a Nazi and a public debate as to whether Joe should go to Officer's Candidate School, which was settled by a pronouncement by Major General Surles that as an officer Joe would cease to represent the average soldier. Joe remained a private. Jimmy Fiddler accused Gene Tierney of smoking a cigar, and there were some comic cracks about the diaper shortage which weren't funny to the parties who were short of them.

Folks discovered the intimate and obscene meaning of the army words "snafu" and "tarfu," and immediately adopted them into civilian drawing room language.

The anniversary of Pearl Harbor, December 7, was met with ceremony, prayer, and a yell from the isolationist press, still trying to pin it on Mr. Roosevelt, that blame for the disgrace had not yet been fixed. It was also announced that the sale of heavy cream was stopped, ending the whipped cream era. Society saw its duty and did it at the opening of the Metropolitan Opera season. It came in black tie.

In that week, the nation mourned another tragedy. Boston's Coconut Grove night club was jammed with eight hundred people after the Holy Cross–Boston football game. A bus boy lit a match. The unfireproofed artificial palm trees caught. There was a flash blaze that swept through the cabaret. Panic did the rest. Four hundred and eighty-four dead were taken from the holocaust. Fire marshals all over the country became vigilant as hell over night club furnishings—after the disaster. . . .

The old year was drawing to a close. We celebrated Christmas and New Year's with considerable heartlessness and a stubborn refusal to face the horrors of the wars in which we were engaged. Guadalcanal had just been won, and in Des Moines, Iowa, a lassie yclept Amber D'Georg, a strip teaser in a bush league burlesque show, suddenly turned out to be Auxiliary Kathryn Doris Gregory, 15th Co., 3rd Regiment WAAC, who was AWOL from her camp at Ft. Worth, Texas, and picking up pin money. The nation paused to savor that scandal while Miss D'Georg, née Gregory, was snatched back to Ft. Worth and confined to quarters.

The nasty zoot-suiters with the reet pleats had appeared on the national scene before you went away, but in New York, at the year's end, two particularly vicious ones, Joe Annunziata and Neil Simonelli, shot their mathematics teacher in the back and killed him. We began to hear talk of juvenile delinquency.

Hedy Lamarr played Tondelayo, the warm-blooded native girl, in the movie version of *White Cargo*. And how!

Good-by, '42. The Pat Di Ciccos were on the move, leaving bills behind them. Noel Toy, Chinese fan dancer, and Margie Hart, strip teaseuse, appeared in court in defense of a smut musical entitled *Wine, Woman, and Song,* which was given the heave-ho from the New York boards. Joe DiMaggio's wife Dorothy Arnold went to Reno. Walter Winchell turned up in a lieutenant commander's uniform on a secret mission to Brazil, and the pro-Nazi gang in Congress sputtered. Jackie Coogan the glider pilot, whose first wife had been Betty Grable, was sued for divorce by Flower Parry, his second. Rick told the nation his tale of privation and prayer and the sea gull that saved them in their hour of need. The nation listened to him and to the rumblings of the black market in tires, sugar, gasoline, and coffee. . . .

New Year's Eve was celebrated in hotel, bar, cabaret, and night club the country over by fools in paper hats tooting horns and slopping over with liquor.

The clock struck twelve. Happy New Year!

Nineteen forty-three was the year in which the people at home began to grow more conscious of the nature of the struggle in which we were engaged. Not that there was cessation of national flapdoodle and monkeyshines, but there seemed to be less of it. There were casualty lists from Africa and Italy now as well as from the Pacific, and mostly we talked about the war and the men who were fighting it. And since bitching and griping are not by any means an army monopoly, we squawked and complained and beefed about our growing shortages but, in the main, behaved better about them. And in the meantime, news in civilian life continued to unfold and provide us with the fun, fuss, thrill, life, and color that make these United States like no other spot on earth, thank God.

A dozen or so of great names familiar to you passed into history during the year. Alex Woollcott, literary figure and famous over the radio as the "Town Crier," died, as did the American poet, Stephen Vincent Benét, Sergei Rachmaninoff, great Russian composer whose second piano concerto once rang from every juke box in the country, and J. P. Morgan the financier.

Leslie Howard, the actor, was shot down in a flight between Lisbon and London; the famous Dr. Allan Roy Dafoe, who brought the Dionne Quintuplets into this world, himself journeyed on into the next. Frank Crumit, musical comedy star and partner of Julia Sanderson, died, as did Fats Waller, genius of jazz, and Max Reinhardt, genius of the theatre. It was the last year for Elinor Glyn, who more than forty years ago startled the world with her novel *Three Weeks*, for little Lorenz Hart, who wrote the words for more than a thousand songs sung by America during his lifetime, and, finally, for another well-known and well-loved figure of the entertainment world, Ben Bernie, the Old Maestro.

The year began mildly. We were singing a song by Don (Beat Me Daddy) Raye called "Mister Five by Five," listening to a sultry, sexy new singing star, colored Lena Horne, and discussing the recapture of Roger "Terrible" Touhy, Basil "Owl" Banghart, arch gangster, and five others who escaped from Illinois State prison and were taken, after a terrific man hunt, in a rooming house in Chicago.

Polish conductor Artur Rodzinski was appointed to replace Barbirolli as leader of the New York Philharmonic, amidst general rejoicing, and Ursula Parrott, four-times-married novelist, got herself into the news as well as into the local pokey for helping a soldier prisoner escape from the Miami Beach Army Stockade. Ursula took him home in her car and outfitted him with civilian clothes, but explained "it was just an impulse." And—here we go again—Lana Turner sued Stephen Crane for annulment of their seven months' marriage. But don't get this one wrong. It developed that Crane's first wife's divorce was not yet final. To complicate matters La Turner was expecting. Mr. Crane issued a statement: "Miss Turner should do everything legally necessary for protection of the child soon to be born."

Jack Dempsey sued his "Cheerful Little Earful," Hannah Williams Dempsey, for divorce after ten years of marriage.

The new year was hardly a month old when Amos and Andy, after fifteen years and more than four thousand consecutive nightly broadcasts, left the air. Since March, 1928, they had had but one vacation. They returned later in a once-a-week program, but the country wasn't the same any more. Phil Wylie wrote a book called *Generation of Vipers,* in which he took the nation over his knee and spanked it hard. Not enough people read it. And War Correspondent Dick Tregaskis's *Guadalcanal Diary* made book history.

History too noted the meeting of Churchill and Roosevelt at Casablanca, and Warner Brothers continued to cash in on their picture of the same name with Ingrid Bergman, Humphrey Bogart, and Dooley Wilson. The song from the film, "As Time Goes By," became a best seller, and the most popular radio programs for 1942 were listed in the following order: Fibber McGee and Molly, Jack Benny, Charlie McCarthy, Bob Hope, Aldrich Family, Lux Radio Theatre, Maxwell House, Kraft Music Hall, Walter Winchell.

Ginger Rogers married Marine Private John Calvin Griggs, the lucky stiff, breaking the hearts of the Army, the Navy, and the Air Forces, and Tommy Manville, forty-eight, divorced his sixth wife, Billy Boze, aged twenty, four months after marriage, making everyone a little ill. Shoe rationing was announced without warning by the OPA.

In the first open revolt against the nauseating institutional advertising flooding the magazines and air waves, Dan Golenpaul took his program "Information Please" (Fadiman, Kieran, Adams, Levant, and guest) away from the sponsorship of Lucky Strike because he couldn't stomach Lucky's line—"Lucky Strike Green has gone to war," referring to the color on the package. Heinz got the show, which went merrily on.

In Hollywood, Errol Flynn was acquitted on three counts of statutory rape, which ended that particular bit of nastiness, to everyone's relief, but did not end Mr. Flynn's troubles, so don't go away. Joe DiMaggio went into the Army as a private, and Bill Saroyan got married. Also a war bond rally auction was held in Gimbel's basement with a crowd of 750 present to bid for precious items such as Jefferson's Bible and George Washington letters. Jack Benny's violin, a $75 imitation Amati nicknamed "Old Love in Bloom," was put up, and the nation fell right flat on its collective face when a gent by the name of Julius Klorfein bought it for ONE MILLION DOLLARS. Nobody had ever heard of Mr. Klorfein, who turned out to be the president of Garcia Grande cigars.

That was about the time of the fatal crash of the Yankee Clipper in Lisbon, Portugal, killing fifteen. Among the survivors, radio singer Jane Froman and night club accordionist Gypsy Markoff. Among the dead, Tamara ("Smoke Gets in Your Eyes") and Ben Robertson, fine foreign correspondent. And Louis B. Mayer's salary and bonus for 1942 was reported as 35 per cent above his 1941 earnings, namely $949,766.00. Somehow he missed out on the sixty cents of last year.

It will be some consolation to the G.I. reader to note that thus far he has not missed too much by being out of the country, except the doings in the comic strips. Dick Tracy had captured Pruneface early in '43 and almost immediately became involved with two other charm characters, "88 Keys," a villainous orchestra leader, and Mrs. Pruneface, who tried to avenge her husband. Tracy won, but it was a damned close call.

While this was going on, Skeezix Wallett, now a G.I. in Ordnance, was lost in the Libyan Desert, and Orphan Annie, abandoned by Daddy Warbucks again, got herself involved in a small-town political mess in which the characters made noises sufficiently like local politicos to bring protests from newspaper editors and outraged readers. Young Terry of "Terry and the Pirates" went into the Air Forces in China, as a flying cadet, and real life character Colonel Philip Cochrane of the Air Forces got himself into the comic strip as the character Col. Flip Corkin, Terry's flying instructor and friend. The usual bosomy and nifty bunch of dames were involved, all of whom looked more or less like Lace of "Male Call."

And in New York, Richard Knight, disbarred lawyer and town crackpot, went on another bender and made a public ass of himself at Fifty-ninth Street and Fifth Avenue until the police arrived. An odd remarriage took place in Albuquerque, New Mexico. "That girl," Geraldine Siebalds Pyle, was remarried to Ernie Pyle, veteran Scripps-Howard columnist, by proxy after eleven months of divorce. The reason it was done by proxy is because Ernie was in North Africa, getting ready to begin to become the greatest war correspondent and one of the great figures of the war with which you were engaged.

And by that time, spring had come again. We were beginning to be rationwise by then, we all had books, housewives and grocers were going crazy, and the OPA warned that shortly meats, fats, and cheeses would be added to the point system. You probably heard us gripe clear across two oceans.

Spring, baseball nervously eying Washington, the opening of *Oklahoma!*, a nation singing "Oh what a beautiful morning . . ." and reading *One World* by Wendell Willkie. Lana Turner re-wed Steve Crane six weeks after their first marriage was annulled; John Steinbeck got married; so did Tommy Dorsey, and Linda Darnell, and Margie Hart, AND, doggone it, Dorothy (Sarong) Lamour. Dotty succumbed to a soldier she met on tour, one Captain William Ross Howard, III, of the Army Air Forces.

There was also another matrimonial adventure worth mentioning to fill you in. A little stinker by the name of Merry (Madcap) Fahrney paid a Swedish waiter $1,500 to marry her, divorce her eleven days later. But it got her a Swedish passport, with which she skipped out to Buenos Aires with a half million bucks in cash to join her Nazi boy friend there.

After seventy-five years disturbed only by babies crying for it, Fletcher's Castoria suddenly went sour from a change in the formula due to sugar rationing and began to make people sick. Alarmed, the company spent hundreds of thousands of dollars warning purchasers and calling in outstanding lots. Rosalind Russell, married to Army Captain Fred Brisson, had a baby. A pair of Sally Rand's old fans were enshrined in the museum of the Chicago Historical Society, and just as you began to sample Sicilian Grappa, and other varieties of Dago red, not to mention gin and tonic and pints of mild and bitter, these United States of America began to run short of drinking liquor.

It also ran short of gasoline, but good. All pleasure driving was temporarily banned, bus schedules were cut, deliveries curtailed, every service cut to a minimum. New York looked like a dead city. You could have fired a bazooka down any Main Street in the country without hitting a vehicle. The war was really putting the squeeze on civilian life, slowly but surely. Lack of manpower was pinching laundries, hotels, railroads, shops, service agencies such as plumbers, electricians, and gadget men. Sales people had a field day insulting would-be buyers. And Lucius Beebe reported in his syndicated chitchat for the stiff and stuffed shirts: "The greatest wartime grief of the town's exquisites is not the curtailment of those essentials of living like food and transportation, but the complete disappearance from circulation of Floris' mouthwash, formerly imported from England. . . . There isn't a flagon of this choosy smell left on any chemist's shelf in town." Hold on, now, you were fighting for our right to be just that daffy if we pleased.

Well, Mickey Rooney and John Jacob Astor, III, were divorced from their helpmeets, Vera Zorina (*I Married an Angel*) became a U. S. citizen, Hedy Lamarr took herself out of circulation again by marrying John Loder, and a fine new tidbit broke out of Hollywood, where, one might say, there had been practically never a dull moment. Charles Spencer Chaplin's ex-protégée, Joan Barry, filed suit against him for $10,000 prenatal care, $5,000 court costs, and $2,500 a month for support of an expected baby she claimed was his, setting off a new powder train of toothsome scandal and public sex shenanigans.

We also became acquainted with a new crime born of the dimouts and blackouts. It was known as "mugging." Citizens were hauled into dark doorways, knocked unconscious, and robbed. We were also learning something of war's price in sex delinquencies and trouble for young girls of high school age and even younger.

June, '43, was one hell of a month in the U. S. A.; and maybe you were just as well abroad. In Los Angeles, prurient, pimply-faced young town rats in their disgusting zoot suits entertained their libidos by attacking Mexican kids and foreigners in the nasty Zoot Suit War, finally broken up by the police. And in Detroit we experienced our most shameful moment as civilians at war during the dark days of the race riots. Everything for which we were at war—decency, humanity, the dignity and rights of man—was set at naught while citizens of the United States, white and colored, fought one another with the white brother taking the initiative.

And yet withal, there was a ray of hope. The riots, most probably Nazi instigated, either foreign or home-grown, were quickly quelled.

The nation breathed easier and turned to other topics of conversation. There were plenty. Oona O'Neill, '42's Stork Club debutante of the year, daughter of brilliant, dignified playwright Eugene O'Neill, married Charlie Chaplin one week after he had agreed to pay Joan Barry $2,500 legal costs and support until the blood test which might or might not show that he was father to her yet unborn child. And in Nassau, Sir Harry Oakes had been found bludgeoned to death, and the nation took time out from the war to read the day-by-day accounts of the trial of Count Alfred de Marigny (husband of Sir Harry's daughter, eighteen-year-old Nancy), who was arrested and charged with the murder of his father-in-law.

Add celebrity marital sweepstakes, Betty Grable and Harry James, Greer Garson and Richard Ney. Add divorces, Bill Bojangles Robinson. Add celebrity in crime, Gene Krupa, jazz drummer, to San Quentin, convicted by a San Francisco jury of using a minor to transport marijuana cigarettes. Life marches on, eh?

Then there was the fantastic rage for a nice, clean, skinny, practically voiceless kid with jug-handle ears and golf ball Adam's apple, named Frank Sinatra, who mooed into a microphone and caused teen-agers, males and females generically lumped under the name of "bobby-soxers," to go into spasmodic imitations of sex convulsions in his presence. Helplessly caught in the tide of national public hysteria, young Sinatra was made "It" and catapulted into national fame with Bing Crosby his only rival.

That old satyr Tommy Manville did it again with something called Sunny Ainsworth. This beautiful marriage lasted seven hours, forty-five minutes flat. Rudy Vallee got engaged again. The War Production Board said the birthrate was about 25 per cent over prewar levels and ordered more baby carriages, doubles and singles. Betty Smith wrote *A Tree Grows in Brooklyn* and became famous and wealthy overnight. When the Army snatched Bell Township High School's football coach in Salina, Pa., Pauline Reagh, the twenty-two-year-old physical instructor, took over the job. And the pro-Roosevelt Louisville *Courier-Journal* tossed out the Little Orphan Annie comic strip on the grounds that it had been made into a vehicle of Republican propaganda. Wow, what a country!

And lest we forget. Errol Flynn and nineteen-year-old Nora Eddington, up to then an aircraft worker, discovered cruising on a yacht off Acapulco, Mexico, denied being married and just asked everybody to go away and leave them alone.

As another war year began to draw to its close at home, the

Congressional Limited piled up in a ghastly wreck, killing seventy-five persons, including many servicemen, three miles outside of Philadelphia when a wheel-bearing burned out.

Orson Welles married Rita Hayworth, and oh God, here we go again, Errol Flynn was charged by one Shirley Evans Hassau, the wife of a singer, with being the father of her three-year-old daughter. She sued for $1,750 a month support and $17,000 for hospital and legal expenses.

Postmaster Frank Walker, out to "get" *Esquire* magazine for reasons that were never made quite clear, began hearings to see whether he could get away with denying second-class mailing privileges to the G.I.'s favorite magazine and the Varga girl. Walker lined up a choice panel of bluenoses, *Esquire* countered with college professors, liberals, and assorted trained seals, and the battle was joined while the country shouted with ribald laughter.

One murder trial ended when Alfred de Marigny was acquitted of the murder of Sir Harry Oakes, with the jury recommending immediate deportation for him, and another murder sensation took its place when the handsome brewery heiress Patricia Burton Lonergan was found battered to death in her Beekman Place home in New York. Her husband, Wayne Lonergan, was arrested after some smart detective work, and suddenly the murder story took on dreadful overtones of sexual perversion. The press had a field day, and so did the citizens.

Frank Sinatra was classified 1A pending an induction physical examination, and a new crackpot radio program, "It Pays to Be Ignorant," hit the air waves. Screen and stage celebrities continued to swap and acquire mates. Deanna Durbin sued her Navy Lieutenant Vaughn Paul for divorce; Dinah Shore married Signal Corps Corporal George Montgomery. Broadway talked about Johnny Van Druten's *Voice of the Turtle*, whose soldier-meets-girl theme artfully and innocently exposed one of the most erotic plays ever seen on a New York stage.

We whipped ourselves up to meet the demands of Christmas.

Good whisky and gin were gone from the shelves, leather goods, handbags, gloves, stockings, toys were missing. Prices were up. Millions of our men were gone from the country. The words "Merry Christmas" had a hollow ring to them.

New Year's Eve was celebrated in hotel, bar, cabaret, and night club, the country over by fools in paper hats, tooting horns and slopping over with liquor. The clock chimed twelve again. Happy (hic) New Year. Would we never learn?

Nineteen forty-four was your year. We actually found out there was a war on. We thought about you, talked about you, worried about you, bought bonds and worked for you. Life at home went on apparently as usual, but there was that difference. We did sweat for you. Two weeks before D Day, national tension was at or close to the bursting point. You could see it in people's faces, feel it in their nervousness and irritability. We were civilians and our men were preparing to go into hell and there was nothing we could do but wait and go on doing the things we had grown used to doing all of our lives, the things you would have done or read or talked or laughed about had you been here instead of us.

The year began with a mild influenza epidemic which knocked people flat for three days and got itself nicknamed "cat fever." Gene Krupa was paroled from San Quentin and wept when he got an ovation at New York's Paramount, Doris Duke finally divorced Jimmy Cromwell, and Frank Sinatra and Bing Crosby met for the first time in a hallway of the NBC studios in Hollywood and shook hands without the building collapsing.

It was a dirty winter. There was a coal shortage, and it was the turn of the West Coast to run out of gasoline and start screaming. Unpleasant things were happening, such as the first hint of a soft peace for Germany, and the Ambassador Grew policy of coddling Hirohito, and a victory for the forces of suppression when Postmaster Frank Walker overruled his own court and denied *Esquire* the mailing privileges that were necessary to the life of the magazine.

Responsible elements began to lambaste us for the lack of public spirit shown the year before. Fitzpatrick in the St. Louis *Post-Dispatch* drew a cartoon showing characters labeled "Labor-bloc, Farm-bloc, Oil-bloc, Anti-higher-taxes-bloc," all singing "My country 'tis of ME." *Time, Life,* and others castigated the mid-winter vacation spending boom in Florida.

Jimmy Durante, one of our greatest clowns, made a smashing comeback to the cabaret world with his "Mr. Umbriago," who soon became a national character. And we heard for the first time of another name that was to become beloved and national in scope—a kid named Bill Mauldin, first mentioned as cartoonist of the 45th Division *News.*

The flu got worse. Everybody got it, including Rita Hayworth, Hedy Lamarr, Marlene Dietrich, and Gypsy Rose Lee, but the nation really took time out to consider the plight of a four-year-old boy in Dallas named Billy Meers, who suffered from an illness known as renal edema and necessitating the infusion of a pint of blood a day. Baylor Hospital was running short. A brief newspaper campaign brought Billy enough blood to keep him going.

Louis "Lepke" Buchalter, gangster killer, was extradited to New York State to stand trial for murder, and possibly to "sing." The USO and Y.M.C.A. lost their nerve over a pamphlet called *Races of Mankind,* which showed up the Nazi racial theories for the hooey they were, and banned its distribution to soldiers, an odd performance in a democracy. Sybarites breathed easier with the announcement of a new fur, blue mink, costing $20,000 for one benny. And grown people were going around singing "Mairzy Doats and Dozy Doats and Liddle Lamzy Divy" because that was the newest popular song by Milton Drake, Jerry Livingston, and Al Hoffman. Milton got the idea from a kid rhyme his little daughter Neila Bonni Drake recited.

Congressman Rankin distinguished himself during the soldier-vote debate in Congress by referring to Walter Winchell as a "little kike." Louis Bromfield said the nation would run out of food by April, and Preston Sturges made and released one of the funniest and most daring pictures of all time, *The Miracle of Morgan's Creek*. Mickey Walker, the ex-welterweight champion, took to painting and had an exhibition which was attended by Two-Ton Tony Galento wearing a monocle, and the gags flew thick and fast. But entertaining wounded men in a hospital, Mickey said seriously, "You guys ought to try painting. It's the most wonderful thing in the world to occupy your mind. It does something for you."

It was about this time that the nation was profoundly shocked, angered, and sobered by the release of the story of the Death March on Bataan, and talked of nothing else.

In the new spirit of self-criticism, William J. Caldwell, a veteran copywriter, wounded twice and discharged from the Army, warned of the disgust engendered in G.I. readers abroad by American advertising in which companies making engine or gun parts, tanks, radios, or so much as the smallest gadget used in combat were boasting individually of their products' winning the war, which was yet far from won.

And Charlie Chaplin was indicted by a Federal Grand Jury in Los Angeles for two violations of the Mann Act, four months after Joan Barry bore the disputed daughter, and his wife Oona announced she expected a baby herself in August. A daughter was born to Betty Grable and trumpeter husband Harry James. But the father who really rocked the nation was Staff Sergeant Bill Thompson, whose girl friend Miss Norah Carpenter presented him with quadruplets in England to the mild surprise of Thompson's wife Eleanor back home, who allowed she didn't think she'd give him a divorce.

There was vast indignation when twenty-eight U. S. clergymen and writers protested the "obliteration bombing" of German cities. Nearly every responsible newspaper in the country pointed out that these same twenty-eight had failed to protest when Warsaw, Rotterdam, Belgrade, and Coventry suffered "obliteration bombing" at the hands of the Germans.

The snow was off the ground when Louis "Lepke" Buchalter, head of "Murder, Inc.," was burned at Sing Sing for the killing of clothing trucker Joseph Rosen; Sophie Tucker made a smash comeback singing "Some of These Days," and Colonel Elliott Roosevelt was sued for divorce by his wife in Texas.

Two trials watched by the civilian nation ended. Charlie Chaplin was acquitted of the Mann Act indictment and Wayne Lonergan, one of the nastier characters crawling around Manhattan, was found guilty of the murder of his wife and was sentenced to from twenty years to life imprisonment. But it was the latter case which gave rise to two of the best New York cab driver gags of the year. Reported by patrons the following: Cab driver, commenting on the Lonergan case—"You know, it's guys like that give degeneracy a bad name." Another cab driver to patron: "Ya know, I been readin' all about this case an' I guess I'm a homosexual all right." Patron (studying the tough and definitely virile back of the driver): "You're a what?" Hackie: "I'm a homosexual. I always say sex oughta be performed in the home."

AND, Lana Turner was returned to circulation. ι just didn't work out somehow. Two years after their marriage, fourteen months after its annulment, ten months after their remarriage, nine months after the birth of their daughter, she sued Stephen Crane for divorce. Also, as long as you are following the Errol Flynn serial, Dan Topping, Sonia Henie's husband, hit Errol a belt in the nose during a party at their home and then vanished after throwing the punch. And while we're on the subject, Pat Di Cicco, Gloria Vanderbilt's husband, picked on the wrong guy in a New York night club, the best rough-and-tumble fighter in Texas, identified only as Benny, and got himself flattened twice, once inside, once again outside the club.

On May 9, the second most famous photograph of the war was published in every newspaper in the country. The first most famous was to be the flag raising on Iwo Jima, more than a year away. This one showed a crusty-looking little old man being carried "chair fashion" by two embarrassed-looking G.I.'s. It was

Sewell Avery being lugged out of the Montgomery Ward plant in Chicago after refusing to turn it over to the government, which had seized it on Roosevelt's orders as the result of a labor dispute.

The government had slapped a 30-per-cent luxury tax on cabarets, and the owners were screaming about the resultant drop in business. Fact was that the tax did not disturb the rich gluttons at whom it was aimed, but hurt the G.I. on leave in town for a night's fun.

June returned to our land and brought with it invasion jitters. Minor news items were taking place: a crackpot Czech alien threw a couple of eggs that spattered at the feet of Archbishop Spellman in St. Patrick's Cathedral, Paulette Goddard and Captain Burgess Meredith were married, Jim Farley quit his fourteen-year-old post as chairman of the N. Y. State Democratic Committee, Joan Fontaine divorced Brian Aherne, but nobody cared and nobody talked about such trivia. All nerves, all emotions, all fears and prayers were tensed and directed towards Europe. D Day was a military secret, but somehow, everybody here knew it was coming—and soon. Frazzled civilian nerves went sky-high June 5 when the false invasion was broadcast over the radio.

The nation was never more sober than on June 6 when your life and the fate of the world hung in the balance. For the next three weeks until the beachheads were secure and Normandy was falling to Eisenhower's attack, we hung about our radios, bought every edition of the newspapers. And then like the Bandar-log who could not keep their minds on any one thing for very long, we began to drift and be aware of the things going on in the country all about us.

We watched the Republican Convention, with a collective expression on its collective face as though something didn't smell good, nominate Tom Dewey for the presidency of the United States, noted that Mickey Rooney had become the smallest soldier in California's Fort MacArthur, and that Rudy Vallee's wife of six months, Betty Jane Greer, left him. The crooners, the torch-ers, the radios, and the juke boxes were giving out "Swingin' on a Star," and a couple of oldies, "I'll Get By" and "I'll Be Seeing You." Scuttlebutt had Col. Elliott Roosevelt about to marry a WAC captain named Briggs, and the worst circus fire in history took place in Hartford, Connecticut, when the Barnum and Bailey big top caught fire during a performance, and 158 died in the flames and the ensuing panic.

By midsummer it was apparent that the U. S. was running out of automobiles, there being only 30,000 new ones left, normally a three-day supply. That great emotional actress Mae West opened a *schmier* called *Catherine Was Great* in Philadelphia, and the boobs knocked one another down to get in. Joan Blondell divorced Dick Powell to keep the Hollywood marriage market fluid, and the rest of the nation laughed when Mayor La Guardia cracked down on all the hot-shot New York night clubs for back taxes, including the Stork Club. In Chicago, just for auld lang syne, irritated parties filled Lawrence "Dago" Magnano, onetime Capone lieutenant, and Big Mike Pontelli, his not too well functioning bodyguard, with two hundred shotgun pellets and six .45 slugs, thereby concluding whatever the argument was about. Hollywood had another one-punch fight. Tommy Dorsey swung on Jon Hall and reportedly busted his beezer for allegedly embracing Dorsey's wife, Pat Dane.

At Santa Monica there was born to Charles Spencer Chaplin, fifty-five, and Oona O'Neill Chaplin, nineteen, a daughter, and in New York the Gallup Poll predicted a Dewey victory over Roosevelt. This sounds funny now, but at the time it scared the pants off everybody. Babs Hutton admitted that she had separated from Cary Grant, and Westbrook Pegler ditto from Scripps-Howard. There was one hell of a big scandal over the surplus egg situation, and the day Paris fell, morons all over the country began to make preparations to celebrate V-E Day, and were promptly slapped down by outraged public opinion.

And as long as you were in on the marriage of Myrna Loy and John D. Hertz, Jr., the taxicab heir, you might like to know how it turned out. It didn't. After two years, divorce in Cuernavaca, Mexico. Harry S. Truman returned to his home town of Lamar, Mo. (Pop. 3,000), to be notified that he was the Democratic nominee for Vice President on the ticket with F.D.R. Everybody was raving about the smash box-office hit movie of the decade—Bing Crosby and Barry Fitzgerald in *Going My Way*. Oscar Levant, pianist composer who for years functioned as an irritant on "Information Please" by rubbing millions of people the wrong way, left the programs to Adams and Kieran and general relief including his own. Frank Sinatra, now known as "The Voice," had tea at the White House and decided to campaign for Roosevelt. Mickey Rooney got married; Carole Landis and Artie Shaw got divorced, and Drew Pearson was dropped from the 1945 edition of the swank Washington Social List, apparently not for the crime of writing a column but for the more serious one of being right too often.

The United States lost two of its great citizens by death in one October week, Wendell Willkie, aged fifty-two, of a broken heart, and Al Smith, aged seventy.

We were now in the fall when everyone went around singing "Clang, clang, clang, went the something . . ." the nearest they could come to "The Trolley Song," and Ernie Pyle, now at the height of his fame as a great war reporter, was vacationing at home, pursued by honors and pests.

Sex had its innings when 421 policemen, 20 policewomen, and 20 patrol cars responded to the riot call at the Paramount Theatre, where 30,000 bobby-soxers reacted to Frank Sinatra; Kathleen Winsor, herself a stunning number, published the year's bawdiest book, *Forever Amber*; and Howard Hawks catapulted a new screen siren to fame in an opus called *To Have and Have Not*, a sultry brunette with insolent, smoldering let's-get-to-doing-it eyes by name Lauren Bacall, immediately nicknamed "The Look." She played opposite Humphrey Bogart, who announced shortly after that he was separating from his wife and sparring partner, Mayo "Sluggy" Methot, but failed to add that it was preliminary to the public courtship of La Bacall—or "Baby," as he preferred to call her—which followed.

Mr. Roosevelt and Clare Booth were re-elected, Mr. Hamilton Fish was kicked out. People were sending one another rabbits, or pretending to see one where it wasn't, because of the new show *Harvey*, one of the cutest ideas and, to my mind, worst plays ever to be seen on Broadway. Brooklyn, apparently the heart of the United States, was thrown into an uproar spreading to the rest of the country by a line in Noel Coward's new book, *Middle East Diary*, speaking slightingly of Brooklyn soldiers. Congressmen made speeches, and Coward immediately supplanted Adolf Hitler as the guy most hated out loud.

We had our sentimental spell over three-year-old Forest (Nubbins) Hoffman, bedridden with what the doctors pronounced an incurable sarcoma of the bladder, and who because he could not live until Christmas had the sweet day celebrated for him on November 27, with gifts coming in from all over the country.

Store shelves were really empty for the Christmas rush, and prices were staggering. The season's ritziest gift was a carton of cigarettes. For the first time in history cigarette counters were bare. At first only the popular brands had vanished. By the close of the year there wasn't a butt to be bought except on the black market. New York had its first view of long lines of would-be-purchasers outside cigar stores at six in the evening, when a limited ration went on sale. There were the usual gags about the famine, but amazingly little griping. Colonel Elliott Roosevelt, the President's second son, did not marry the WAC captain. He married a tall, blonde movie actress by the name of Faye Emerson.

In December the news of the Battle of the Bulge hit the home front and frightened everyone into a semblance of decent and restrained behavior. The German break-through scared the daylights out of the home folks and made us good as gold. Nobody felt much like celebrating. Just before Christmas, poor, gay little Lupe Velez committed suicide over an unhappy love affair.

Other celebrated names on the roster of those who died in 1944 included Mrs. Herbert Hoover, wife of the ex-President, William Allen White, the great editor, writers Irving Cobb, George Ade, Harold Bell Wright, and Hendrik Willem van Loon, Teddy Roosevelt, Jr., and Frank Knox, Secretary of the Navy. The President lost his trusted secretary, Margaret "Missy" LeHand. Ray Clapper was killed in the Pacific, and Aimee Semple McPherson died in California.

Nobody was sorry to hear the clock strike out the old year. . . .

Nineteen forty-five—the home stretch!

You won two wars, and at home we lived a lifetime in eight months—eight months of all the usual, normal, silly, sensational things we like to read or talk about, plus the tragedy of losing the leader of our nation just as victory was in sight, plus the breaking of the greatest story next to war—peace. And through it all was laced our reaction to the shortages that pinched the nation more and more, meat, cigarettes, liquor, apartments, cabs, hotels, railroad seats, eggs, radios, coal, oil. Our standard of living was really on the verge of falling apart. The only thing that was plentiful was printed paper laughingly called money.

It was a filthy winter for weather, the worst in fifty years, with freezing, stinging cold and blizzards that tied up rail transportation and disrupted the movement of coal, food, and troops. Much of the time, town and country lay buried beneath mounds of snow. Urban and interurban traffic was paralyzed. In New York when the snow fell the hackies simply kept their ancient cruisers in the garages rather than risk them further on the streets. There had been no new parts for two years.

But we read avidly about the first meeting of Faye Emerson Roosevelt with her in-laws in Washington, and even more avidly the testimony of the Chaplin paternity trial in Hollywood which resulted in Charles' being adjudged the father of little Carol Ann Barry, appeal for new trial denied. Chaplin went for a rough ride. Testimony was introduced that he paraded quite in the all-together before his Joan and a mirror, flexed his muscles towards the glass, and said, "You know, Joan, I look something like Peter Pan, don't you think?" It was all very funny and ribald, and Charles hadn't behaved up to his responsibilities, but many of us remembered the joy the little man had brought us in the old days. . . .

Merle Oberon said "enough" to her husband, Sir Alexander Korda, the movie director, and the OPA brought screams of anguish from housewives by invalidating 34 red stamps, 34 blue stamps, and fifteen pounds of sugar. The nation's housekeepers charged "breach of faith" and moaned, "Can we ever trust the OPA again?" The OPA said nothing and got away with it, covering up a scandalous shortage of food.

New York turned up a lady Robin Hood, Madeline Dunnigan, twenty-two-year-old Brooklyn shipyard worker's wife, who, working as cashier for the Oscar H. Gropper luggage store on Fifth Avenue, embezzled $35,000 and gave it all away in salary raises, bonuses, gifts, to employees and friends, keeping nothing for herself. It would have been funny as hell except old man Gropper, proprietor of the store, ruined financially, stepped out of a ninth-story window.

Bing Crosby, Barry Fitzgerald, and Leo McCarey won all the Oscars with *Going My Way*, and *Radio Daily* listed "Information Please," Bob Hope, Bing Crosby, Lowell Thomas, the N. Y. Philharmonic concerts, and "One Man's Family" as the most popular radio shows.

John F. (Jafsie) Condon, the famous go-between of the Lindbergh kidnaping, died; Mayor La Guardia went on the radio to sell the idea of cooking Pasta Faggiol to exasperated housewives; but the real red-hot news story of the beginning of the year was the bumping of Seaman 1/C Leon Le Roy from an airplane while on emergency leave to see his ailing, widowed mother, along with a Seabee and an army technical sergeant, also on their way home to see sick wives, by a 115-pound tawny mastiff named Blaze, the property of Col. Elliott Roosevelt, that was being shipped to his wife Faye Emerson in California on a double A, double 1, gilt-edged priority.

Elliott had sent the pooch from England via Air Transport Command. The White House, apparently short on red points, bucked it on to Faye. Citizens yelled and screamed more than if their taxes had been raised. The very foundation of democracy tottered. Mrs. Eleanor Roosevelt, Stephen Early, presidential Secretary, and Major General Harold George of the ATC all made public apologies and went around with red faces. You'll find out all about it in Jim Thurber's chapter. Just in time to distract the Republic and save the Union came the news that Shirley Temple, now grown into a big girl, had at last been kissed in a picture (*Kiss and Tell*) for the first time.

Likewise to help us to forget, though Congressmen as well as private citizens were still mumbling, was the not exactly surprising information that Gloria Vanderbilt and Pat Di Cicco were separating. Dr. Ella Boole, world president of the Women's Christian Temperance Union, got her kisser in the newspapers with a squawk about natives giving our dear, innocent soldiers W I N E abroad, when they might just as well refresh them with fruit juices. . . . C. B. DeMille quit the radio in a fight over a $1.00 union assessment which he considered an infringement on his rights, Joe Pendergast, notorious Kansas City boss, died, and in the nation-wide brownout resulting from the fuel crisis, resulting from the lousy weather, people forgot about Elliott's big mutt pushing servicemen off airplanes and turned to more serious matters.

There was the beginning of the public indignation over coddling of German prisoners of war in this country when civilian and servicemen travelers stood in line waiting to get into a Pennsylvania railroad diner while inside, sixteen Nazi P.W.'s supped leisurely on stewed chicken, white bread, and ice cream. Mississippi's Rankin and Michigan's Hook had a hair-pulling match in the sacred halls of Congress, and Ernie Pyle said good-by and was off to cover the war in the Pacific and keep his rendezvous with "It." Forest (Nubbins) Hoffman, the "early Christmas" boy, didn't die but walked out of the hospital, cured by an operation. Gloria Swanson married her fifth husband, the basketball scandal broke, and Bogart and Bacall played satyr chasing nymph from coast to coast, "The Look" ending up in the picture papers, photographed sitting on a piano being played by Vice President Truman, that is to say, Mr. Truman was playing the piano. The press agents were playing Miss Bacall, *fortissimo ad nauseam.* Jimmy Byrnes slapped his midnight curfew on us in March, or, as it was called, the "Byrne-out."

The holler that arose from night spot proprietors over that one probably reached you all the way over to the Hürtgen Forest or Okinawa. The purpose of it, ostensibly, was to save power, coal, and electricity, but actually it was to illustrate that by now stale crack to civilians—"Don'tcha know there's a war on?" Oddly, the ukase backfired. It hurt not the civilian but the serviceman on leave in town. Civilians had their homes, but when the joints shut down at midnight, sailor and soldier had no place to go but into trouble. New York's Mayor La Guardia indignantly refused to play. The Army backed Byrnes and sent military police and the navy shore patrols to sweep servicemen out of the bistros. It was a grand fizzle, but both we and Jimmy were stuck with it.

The scandal over Nazi prisoner coddling went into high, as did the indignation throughout the nation over the Hood River, Oregon, Post of the American Legion banning from their honor rolls the names of sixteen Nisei soldiers who had fought and bled and died in Italy. The Legion voted to restore fifteen of the sixteen names, and the Duke of Windsor resigned as Governor of the (This is Elba) Bahamas. Babe Ruth announced his intention of becoming a wrestling referee.

Bill White's *Report on the Russians* stirred up a hornets' nest. Everyone talked about Joe Rosenthal's Flag Raising on Iwo Jima, unquestionably the great picture to come out of the Pacific. The song hit was "I'm Confessin'" (That I Love You) and the top U. S. singer of all time was still der Bingle. In two decades,

Crosby had sold seventy-five million records. When Bing signed a contract with Decca until 1950, it was revealed that his recording of "White Christmas" had sold 1,700,000, "Silent Night" 1,500,000, "Don't Fence Me In" had done 1,250,000, and "Sunday, Monday, and Always" a cool 1,000,000.

The United States of America, as pointed out by frank, vulgar Earl Wilson, syndicated saloon editor of the New York *Post*, was finally admitting breast fetishism. Whereas ladies in the courts of France frequently exposed theirs completely, American girls revealed bumps of all shapes and sizes more tantalizingly by wearing and letting themselves be photographed in tight-fitting sweaters. Al Jolson married again, a Southern-style cinema starlet named Erle Galbraithe. Joe Louis divorced Marva Trotter. And Hy Zarett rewrote an old song, "The Lone Fish Ball," and soon Jimmy Savo and the rest of the country were singing "You gets no bread with ONE meat ball. . . ."

In April, an eight-pound, ten-ounce son, "Chipper," was born to Nina and Skeezix Wallett of Gasoline Alley. A rumor spread that Frank King, the creator of the comic strip characters, was going to kill Skeezix off in the war. For three days the switchboards of the *Daily News* in New York and the Chicago *Tribune* were clogged with calls saying "Don't you dare," until the rumor proved unfounded.

Dick Tracy had worked his way through a dope peddler named Laffy and a dirty little gangster named Flattop, who nearly got the indestructible dick. Thereafter in quick succession he became involved with the Summer Sisters, the sinister Brow, Gravel Gertie, and a bad little girl called Breathless. He's still ahead.

By 1945, Milt Caniff had Terry promoted from Warrant Officer to Second Lieutenant and introduced a new character in his strip, a frog-faced kid pilot from Boston named Hot-Shot Charlie. We had a glimpse of the Dragon Lady, Hu-shee, and April Kane.

Orphan Annie was railroaded to jail on a bum murder rap. Readers of this strip raised so much hell over the death of Daddy Warbucks that Harold Gray, the cartoonist, had to resurrect him, even as Conan Doyle was forced to resurrect Sherlock Holmes. Daddy came back and got Annie out of her jam with the law. You straight on that now? Daddy Warbucks isn't dead, and neither is Punjab, nor the Asp. Pick it up from there.

Good God, none of us are getting any younger. Shirley Temple announced her engagement to a sergeant in the Air Forces. A little birdie coupled the name of Leopold Stokowski with that of Gloria Vanderbilt Di Cicco, who was in Truckee, Nevada, getting rid of the Di Cicco tag. Later the tabloids had a field day pursuing Gloria and "Stokie," all over Nevada.

On April 12 the nation was stunned by the death of Franklin D. Roosevelt. Not since Mr. Lincoln died had there been such genuine, heartfelt grief overflowing from the hearts of simple people, brimming in tears from their eyes and marked on their faces, as was felt and seen in the streets and homes throughout the land. For twenty-four hours the entire nation was in a state of shock.

But the Rhine had been crossed by the end of April, and the nation next reacted with deep disgust to the foul obscenities of the Nazi concentration camps. And again we mourned a friend and hero when little Ernie Pyle was killed on Ie in the Pacific.

Came the false surrender bulletin from San Francisco and the naming of Senator Happy Chandler to be baseball's high commissioner, replacing the late Judge Landis, amidst practically no cheers. Leopold Stokowski and Gloria Vanderbilt were joined in holy wedlock, and plans for a similar ceremony for Mr. Bogart and Miss Bacall, who had had about all the publicity that the citizens could bear, were made by Mr. Louis Bromfield, the novelist, whose continued dire predictions about food shortages eventually were caught up with by events. The national howl about Nazi POWs got results. At the Pierre Cotillion Room in New York, Margaret Scott sang "Lili Marlene," and Lady Doverdale and Mary Hoyt walked out. *Cosmopolitan* magazine ran a stunning exposé of appalling conditions in veterans' hospitals the nation over, and the sweet-smelling Rankin, chairman of the Veterans Committee in Congress, immediately laid in a couple of tanks of whitewash and proceeded to apply. Billy Mitchell was awarded the rank of Major General and the Medal of Honor posthumously by the United States Senate. A high court reversed the *Esquire* ban, and the Varga gal was free again.

We behaved like adults when V-E Day came. The celebration was moderate, and genuine gratitude replaced the desire to go out and get drunk. But we debated for days: "Was Ed Kennedy of the AP right or wrong in sending that flash and scooping the world?" When the facts were published and it developed that any of the other correspondents could have done the same thing had he wanted to break his word, the consensus was that Mr. Kennedy's scoop was not so hot.

An unconscionable amount of hooey on how to treat the returned soldier began to appear in American publications. And the entertainment world switched into high with the lifting of the curfew and the ban on horse racing. We discussed the odd case of Mrs. Helen Goad MacDowell. Married first to Lieut. Harold Goad, A.A.F., she wed Ensign Robert A. MacDowell, U.S.N.R., when Lieut. Goad was reported dead. But Goad was found alive in a Rangoon hospital. Helen had marriage no. 2 annulled, went back to no. 1.

By the end of May there was no beef in the big cities, and the miners of Kentucky and West Virginia went on strike for meat in their diet. Pete Reilly, a fight manager, fed oxygen in the corner to his fighter, Benny Goldberg, and Benny, he win. Norman Corwin wrote and produced a magnificent piece of poetry on the radio, *On a Note of Triumph*, which you should ask to hear because it concerns you and your victory. Arlene Whelan, a redhead, was named the most perfect over-all beauty of all time by a committee of sixty-five illustrators. You might ask for a gander at Arlene too.

The country sighed with relief when Humphrey Bogart finally

married Lauren Bacall, alias "Baby," alias "The Look," at Louis Bromfield's Mansfield, Ohio, farm. The Dionne Quints celebrated their eleventh birthday. Doesn't seem that long, does it?

And now we are about ready to say, "This is where you came in. . . ."

General Eisenhower came home, and every man, woman, and child in the country fell in love with him. A wealthy merchant named Langford whose wife was prominent in that demi-world known as café society was shot to death in the Hotel Marguery, Park Avenue, New York, and the cops never did find out who did it. The *Queen Mary* and the *Queen Elizabeth* shed their war incognitos and came sailing up the harbor loaded to the gunnels with returning G.I.'s, whose families back home were counting points.

New York went through a newspaper delivery strike and for three weeks went without newspapers. Citizens formed lines a half mile long at the newspaper plants to buy copies—not for the news, which we got over the radio, but for the funnies, which is what we're like, and what of it? Spring came in March. It rained all July. Cigarettes returned, but sugar fled.

The impossible happening, the accident of accidents, occurred one wet, foggy Saturday when a B-26 bomber piloted by a war veteran unfamiliar with the New York terrain flew headlong into the 77th story of the Empire State Building, killing all its crew and more than a score of office workers in the building. Burning gasoline made the tower a torch. The Fire Department conquered the world's highest blaze.

And then one morning, in August, the voice of an excited radio announcer intoned: "President Truman has just announced that an atomic bomb has been dropped on Hiroshima. . . . American and British scientists have succeeded in splitting the atom. . . ."

A bartender in a Fifty-second Street booby trap immediately compounded an atomic cocktail, and six press agents wired columnists that their clients had just got off the crack about Japan suffering from atomic ache. A comedian named Milton Berle made news by *refraining* from composing an atomic bomb joke.

But the great majority of us trod softly that day and for many days thereafter thinking of the terrible and deadly force let loose in the world. We went through the week of radio and news tension and jitters awaiting the news of the surrender of Japan and the return of peace to our sore and battered world.

When it came, the nation, from its tiniest hamlets to its largest cities, broke loose in a wild two-day celebration, one grand gargantuan bust to relieve strained nerves and emotions.

But thereafter most of us thought and talked again about that old world we had all known which was finished and done with because of what was dropped on Hiroshima and Nagasaki, and what the new world and the new era would be like, the one to which you were coming home, we hoped and prayed, for all time.

III. WHAT HAPPENED TO THE YOUNGER PEOPLE

by ANNA W. M. WOLF and IRMA SIMONTON BLACK

ANNA W. M. WOLF *is senior staff member of the Child Study Association of America. The major part of her time is involved with the Association's Family Guidance and Counseling Service—involving counseling of parents who come for help on matters of child development and family relationships. She is the author of two books,* The Parent's Manual *and* Our Children Face War.

IRMA SIMONTON BLACK *is a teacher, columnist, and author of books for children. Her primary interest lies in the field of child psychology and she has been successively a teacher in the Harriet Johnson Nursery School, Associate in Research at the Bank Street Schools, and staff member of the Co-operative School for Teachers. She contributes a column for PM's weekly Pictorial News Section and her "Life with Junior" articles are soon to appear in book form.*

THERE is a general impression among civilians that servicemen hope to find their country, and in particular their homes, very much as they left them. Probably many servicemen have tended to think of their families as being unchanged by the passing of time and the speeded up tempo of war. Certainly they look forward to returning to familiar people and familiar things.

One group of people, however, no serviceman would even want to find unchanged. That group is the children. The most obvious and yet amazing feature of childhood is its capacity to grow in all directions at once. Anyone who has not seen a child for a year or more will find that child a rather different person from the one he left—bigger and heavier, with new skills and new understandings, new ideas and new ways of expressing them.

Perhaps the serviceman comes back to his own child whom he has never known at all, or known for a few brief weeks when it was either a sleeping or a yelling bundle in a bassinet. Perhaps he comes back to younger brothers and sisters of school age. Perhaps he looks forward to meeting some of his own friends only a few years younger than he, who are still in school and still technically "children." What was it like to be a child in wartime America? What have the rest of us done for the children? What have we failed to do?

To the returning veteran, American children will at first seem altogether untouched by war. Compared to Europe's children they have been well fed, well dressed, well housed. They will seem busy with their own affairs, which are not world affairs. They have had no first-hand experience of the grim business of war—of killing, of being bombed, of going hungry—as have the children of many other nations.

Yet the war has not altogether passed our children by. Some of them have lost a father or a brother. Many more have suffered through family dislocation or through living around in strange places with strange people, while mothers worked. In their own way, American children have been part of the war, and the lives of this generation will be different from those of any other, because of the war.

THE YOUNGEST CHILDREN

WORKING MOTHERS AND ABSENT FATHERS

The youngest children, up to about six years old, knew the least about the war, yet they were the group most deeply affected by it. Take Billy, aged two, who has lived with his mother, his mother's parents, and her younger brother and sister. Billy's mother has been working in a war plant while Billy's grandmother took care of him in the daytime. Billy's mother isn't unhappy about this, yet she wishes she could be with him more of the time. She wishes, too, that his grandma wouldn't coax him to eat the way she does, and wouldn't worry so much when Billy takes a notion to do some daring trick. She knows that there are too many grownups around Billy, and that he has at the same time too much attention and too much supervision.

When his father comes back, things will be different—and right. Just now Billy's father is only a shape in a picture, or something that Mommy reads out loud to him from a letter. Those things, slight as they are, are important to Billy. They give him a feeling that he has a father like other children, even if he isn't at home. Billy hasn't even a memory of his father, for he went overseas just before Billy was born. Billy's early childhood has been healthy and happy enough, but it has not been the normal babyhood that he would have had in a stable home with his own parents. Billy and his mother have both had to make adjustments to live comfortably in this situation. There are thousands of children like Billy.

Other small children have spent a fair proportion of their short lives shifting from place to place in this country until their fathers went overseas. Or perhaps their parents have had to move to get work in the factories. This kind of thing is trying for adults; it is even harder for small youngsters. Yet here too they adjusted with astonishing speed to difficult conditions. It was a common sight to see a healthy baby sleeping peacefully in a crowded, brightly lighted day coach, or waiting while his mother unearthed a bag of food from her traveling bag. The crowded camp and factory cities were hard on little children too—with their small furnished quarters where children were usually not wanted in the first place. And when the children's parents did find a place, they felt anxious every time the children slammed the door or woke up at 5 A.M. to sing cheerfully but noisily.

Even the play of young children was affected by the war. One

of the minor inconveniences of wartime was the virtual disappearance of sturdy inexpensive toys. Many a two-year-old has
never had a rubber ball. One child was utterly astonished when
an old prewar ball bounced feebly! He had known only stuffed
oilcloth things that rolled on the floor and hit the wall with a
dull thud. The standard equipment of childhood—tricycles and
doll carriages—vanished from the market early in the war. Some
of them reappeared in clumsy wooden versions that cost about
three times as much as the streamlined originals. Of course there
was a brisk trade in secondhand articles. That helped some, but
there weren't enough to go around.

There was a silver lining to this cloud, though. The complicated mechanical toys that used to clutter up many a child's play
space were an unregretted casualty. Parents were forced to buy
simple playthings like blocks or paints, dolls or stuffed animals.
These were scarce too, but they could usually be found somewhere.

Children's books took on new importance and new charm.
Moderate-priced, brightly illustrated books for the nursery ages
appeared on the shelves. Whole editions were sold out in a few
days.

These, of course, are not of major importance. The little children were most deeply affected by the absence of their fathers.
They did not worry about their fathers in any grown-up sense of
the word. But they felt their mothers' worry about their fathers
during the major campaigns, during long intervals between letters. They felt it the way young children feel things—not in any
mysterious telepathic way, but quite specifically in her expression, her tone of voice, in the tension of her muscles as she bathed
and dressed them.

Yet in spite of these upsets, many a mother has managed to
give her child a sense of stability and safety. Many mothers have
shown that they have the gift of carrying on in the same reassuring way with their children in spite of jobs, in spite of hardships,
and in spite of changes. Young children can take a lot so long as

their mother speaks to them in the same voice and with the same smile—so long as a loved toy like the old teddy bear or the moth-eaten panda or even the crib blanket can still be a part of their lives—so long as the same stories and jokes and games can go on as accompaniments to dressing, eating, bathing, and going to sleep.

Because young children have so great a need for a close relation with their mothers, they have been on the whole better off if their mothers did not leave them with relatives or neighbors or foster homes to go to work. Neither the U. S. Government nor even Great Britain in the darkest days wanted the mothers of young children on the assembly lines. Yet in many cases these mothers had little choice. They needed money to supplement their army allotments. They wanted to feel that they were actively helping the war effort and helping to speed their husbands' return.

There is, of course, no absolute rule about working mothers. We can't say, for instance, that all working mothers have problem children, that all stay-at-home mothers have well-adjusted ones. Some jobs for mothers were flexible enough so that they could be with their children in those unpredictable emergencies which are forever arising. Part-time jobs have been increasingly available to mothers. Both working women and employers have come to realize that for mothers, their children's needs must come first. There are not one but dozens of facets to the argument about jobs for mothers. We will hear all of them in the next few years, too. It is futile merely to thank them (or spank them either, as some might want to) and send these women back home now that the war is over. Thousands of children have known economic security because their mothers worked. Thousands of mothers will be willing to keep on working after the war if their families need the income. Many—perhaps most—of them will want nothing more than to go back to their homes. Yet will they want this if it means a measurable lowering of the standards they have learned to expect for their children?

CHILD CARE CENTERS

Child care centers have been the most fruitful of the attempts to meet the needs of children of working mothers. At first many mothers resisted them, and felt guilty about placing their children in the hands of strangers. But it usually turned out that the children were far happier in groups with trained people than spending the day with Aunt Ella or the next-door neighbor. Far from being unpopular, there were soon not enough child care centers to go around!

The teachers at the centers, instead of being strangers, became practically adjuncts of the families. Mothers who could not talk over the daily problems of child-rearing with fathers found a sympathetic ear at hand at the nursery school. They found too that they often got some very concrete help from the teachers—suggestions about Tommy's tantrums, and what to do about Sue's thumb-sucking. Often the group life itself had a good effect upon the children. Children who dawdled over their food at home could be seen stowing away man-sized dinners in groups. Children who had shied away from all strangers and clung to their mothers could be found at the end of a week in the thick of a three-year-old gang. There was nothing formal or intimidating about these schools, either for children or for mothers. There were no folded hands, no straight solemn lines. The schools were not mere parking places, either. They were genuine "schools," not for book learning, to be sure, but for social play, for manual and bodily skills, for creative activity. They were, above all, places where the important lessons of give-and-take among children could go forward under the guidance of understanding and trained adults.

Nursery schools were not inventions of this war, but they were tremendously extended during the war. And it is quite possible that in education, as in so many other fields of activity, the wartime necessity will prove to be a permanent and important gain. Such schools may ultimately be available to all children, whether their mothers work or not, for a few hours a day. They would promote sound social and emotional development in children during their most formative years. They would help parents to guide their own children wisely and make available to them the close detailed assistance of trained professionals.

At present, when government funds have been supplied for these centers, they are restricted to children of mothers engaged specifically in war industries. In other communities such centers have been open, so long as space permitted, to any child whose mother applied. Tuition has varied anywhere from a nominal rate of a few cents a day in those with public funds, to a sizable amount in those operated under private enterprise. Still a different type of child care center was operated by certain of the great industrial plants for the benefit of the children of their own work-ers, with mother and child turning up at the factory in the morning and leaving together at night.

Ideally, children should not be at nursery schools for such long hours as many of them have been during the war years. But even so, day care has proved immeasurably better than twenty-four-hour care. If there is one thing that nations at war have learned it is that continuous separation from their mothers is one of the most destructive experiences a young child can have. He needs someone on whom he can count when he is tired or frightened or bewildered, to whom he is sure he belongs, and who will not disappoint him no matter what happens, no matter whether he is "good" or "bad." Enforced separation over a long period can cause a child to become actually ill. He develops digestive ailments and colds, he reverts to babyish behavior, he is less alert.

WHEN FATHER COMES HOME

But the problem of young children in wartime does not stop even with the fundamental matter of keeping intact their relation to their mothers. Children have fathers as well as mothers. They need fathers not only to provide for them and to teach them; they need them also for sound emotional maturing. One of the tragedies of war is the loss of fathers through long absence as well as by death. One of the big jobs that "comes after" is the putting together again, into a fine and meaningful pattern, a home that has been torn apart, its members often growing diversely because of separation. Despite the joy of reunion, the time comes when husband and wife are likely to find that in some ways they must learn to know and love each other all over again. The child is not always the merry, confiding baby we thought we left behind us, but a shy, cautious child, a bit distrustful, perhaps even resentful of a father who in spite of letters and gifts and photographs and stories may seem, after the first excitement, a stranger and even a dangerous rival. The infant we have never seen but who was so cherubic in the pictures may seem to the disappointed veteran an irritable, disobedient, and demanding "brat," until he knows him better. Domestic life, so longed for in foxholes, may seem in the first difficult days to be a woman-dominated, intricate array of trivialities in which a man has neither the wish nor the power to find a real place. The pattern of life for his wife and children *seems* to be complete without him, and time and patience are often necessary before he can feel part of it again.

For young children the problem of the returning father may be especially acute. Older children understand why their father left them to go to war. The baby, however, who has been in sole possession of his mother, is unlikely to give her up or even share her without a struggle. Sometimes there is open jealousy and resentment. Sometimes there are such signs of emotional disturbance as bed-wetting, stuttering, sleep disturbances, unusual disobedience. In any event, the child may have to be won step by step and with patient understanding to the discovery that it is possible and necessary to share love, that two parents are better than one, and that a father is nonetheless delightful because he is different from the women he has had about him. There is no end to the variety of feelings which young children may entertain toward this new parent. Young children cannot really understand about war no matter how patiently we may have tried to explain.

They cannot understand why a loved father who once came home to them every evening with gifts and tenderness should have gone away and left them. A child may feel his father's going not as a response to a duty but as an act of desertion; the "good" father he knew and loved has become the "bad" father who went away. While he was away, the joyous love that was may have become tinged with anxiety and distrust.

Fortunately, these things do eventually get ironed out and usually the damage is not irreparable, but it is well to understand the problems beforehand, so that the returning serviceman will not hold either his wife or children to blame if the first months are not all his fancy painted them. It is natural enough for a man to expect that home and family are going to be all that in dreams they have seemed—natural too that he should expect to be, at least for a time, the central point of the household. Certainly it should be so. But sometimes, try as she may, his wife cannot make things work out according to the rules of what is fair and just. Children cannot really comprehend what their father's experiences have been, nor have they any comprehension of his hopes and dreams. They cannot be disciplined into understanding, or into loving, even into "behaving well" when they are torn with conflicting emotions. If their mother gives her attention entirely to her new-found husband they may take it hard and vent their resentment on him. If he thereupon jumps to the conclusion that they have lacked a firm hand and the benefits of fatherly discipline while he was away and then starts top-sergeant methods with them, they are likely to respond with all the anger habitually felt toward an intruder in their customary groove. Yet it is all-important that a father should persist and continue to be patient and friendly. Home is *not* complete without him, and if he gets discouraged there is a real and irreparable loss for everyone —most of all perhaps for the children. Despite difficulties, fathers *do* become reinstated, homes *are* repaired, and a soldier's final service to his country is not finished until this has been achieved.

THE SCHOOL CHILDREN

THEIR INTEREST IN THE WAR

Children in their middle years—say from seven to eleven—were more aware of the war than were their younger brothers and sisters. Paradoxically enough, it usually had less effect upon them. While they consciously missed their fathers or brothers who were away from home, their separation was in a way easier just because they could remember them, because father and brother were real people in their minds, not mere abstractions. Children of these ages often did miss their dad or older brother acutely. But they had something to compensate for that. Were they proud! They were all convinced that their particular soldier or sailor was winning the war singlehanded, and they had a distinct tendency to lord it over children who had no older brothers or whose brothers were 4F or over draft age.

Children of grammar school age are just beginning to identify themselves with groups, to take on the loyalties and ideals of their nations, their schools, their churches. They are outgrowing the normal and healthy egoism of early childhood. At playtime they are likely to divide up in "gangs." They are hero-worshipers, and their heroes are all good, their villains one hundred per cent bad. It was only natural that these children should feel a lively pride in having a father or brother who was doing his part in the war. And they were insulted if you accused their father or brother of being a sailor when he was actually a soldier —or vice versa.

Another advantage these older children had was the ability to communicate directly with the serviceman of their family. A nine-year-old can read the letters his dad wrote to him, and he can treasure the funny little cartoons in the margin. He can answer his dad directly, and tell him what happened at home or at school. He can remember little things about him, like the way he laughed, or the way he used to sit absorbed by the radio listening to a prize fight.

Many of these children keep in touch with the news. They usually do not read the papers or listen to the radio systematically, and they are likely to be hazy about geography, but they pay attention when they hear a familiar name or when something unusually exciting happens. They are just beginning to take a real interest in far-off events.

And on their home ground, they are unbeatable. The normal ten-year-old can identify twenty times as many airplanes as his mother can. He can tell you the meaning of service stripes and insignia. His alert and eager mind is taking in everything around him, and he is particularly fascinated by the evidences of war that he can see for himself.

Many of these "middle-aged" children reflected their interest in the war in their play. The old game of cops and robbers turned into Marines and Japs. Little boys' throats were remarkably adapted to imitating machine guns. They swooped down the stairs making airplane noises. Little girls played Red Cross or army nurse instead of house. And the girls, incidentally, got a great pride from having the women's branches of the services to imitate and to admire. It put them on a more equal footing with their brothers. It gave them a feeling that women as well as men had a contribution to make to the war.

They were ardent radio fans. They faithfully clustered around the radio every afternoon to follow the adventures of Hop Harrigan and Dick Tracy and Superman. All of their heroes have been engaged in fighting sabotage and espionage in a series of glamorous and exciting episodes. Secretly, they imagined that was the way their father or brother cleaned up the enemy.

The active and energetic children of school age did what they could for the war effort, and it was a very creditable amount. They pulled wagons from house to house and exhorted housewives to save their paper and tin cans so that their particular class or scout troop could have the best record in town. They took their nickels and dimes to school for War Stamps and Bonds. In the War Finance Program, schools accounted for over

$1,000,000,000 of stamps and bonds, an average of $21 for every school child per year. They bought war equipment. During 1944, schools financed 2,900 planes, 33,000 jeeps, 11,600 amphibious jeeps, 11,690 parachutes. Some school workshops made toys for the child care centers that needed them badly. They turned out rough but sturdy boats and carts and dollhouses. Little girls in grammar schools and clubs made hospital bags and knitted small squares that later were put together to make warm afghans. They made simple clothing for children in devastated areas.

The Boy Scouts of America deserve special mention for their service during the war. They aided in collections of many kinds. They took in more than 3,000,000 books, over 109,000,000 pounds of rubber, more than 23,000,000 pounds of tin, and over 370,000,-000 pounds of scrap metal, to mention only a few. In the paper salvage drive, more than 2,000 troops collected more than 1,000 pounds per registered member.

Scouts distributed more than a million posters a month for the OWI, as well as distributing millions of Price Control Pamphlets and Consumer Pledges. They planted more than a million and a half trees.

It is estimated that Scouts were responsible for the sale of approximately $8,000,000,000 worth of stamps and bonds.

AFTER-SCHOOL PLAY GROUPS

Children of these ages also suffered in the family upsets and dislocations caused by war conditions. Often their mothers, after years at home, were tempted to go back to work and earn some very usable cash. The children seemed big and capable. They didn't need her in the same way they used to—perhaps they could be left on their own in the afternoons. Many a working mother tied a key on a string around her school child's neck and sent him off in the morning with instructions to come home after school and let himself in. Sometimes he did, sometimes not. Sometimes he was simply locked out of the house to wander the streets until his mother came home from work.

While these children are obviously not so dependent upon their mothers as the younger ones, they are usually better off with a little less cash and a little more care. But here again there was not always a choice. The problem of children who wandered about completely unsupervised and unprotected became acute in some places. Some communities solved this problem of neglected older children in ways that are sound and healthy, and that may well prove to be of permanent value.

Some of the child care centers for the younger children opened their doors to the older brothers and sisters after school, and offered them a free-play period with such creative materials as paints and clay and workbench and tools. This was not entirely satisfactory, as the big children tended to take the place over completely from the little ones. Some schools kept their doors open until late in the afternoon. In New York City, for instance, the Board of Education, co-operating with the Public Education Association, set up two All-Day Neighborhood Schools in crowded, low-income areas. These schools, instead of being buildings set aside for learning the three R's, became community centers that offered children a variety of play activities as well as formal study. They became the site of clubs, dramatic groups, discussion groups. Here children could dance, paint, model, instead of drifting around the streets in the afternoons. Many educators believe that in the postwar world the school and its plant should have an enlarged function that will offer social and creative activity as well as book learning.

GETTING BACK HOME

The serviceman who comes home to children of these years does not have so delicate an adjustment to make as the one who comes to little children. These older children, provided they had a good relationship to father or brother before the war, will have no deep-seated problem centering around his return. They have been eagerly awaiting his home-coming. They have made their father's or brother's status as a serviceman one of their own chief points of pride. They have basked in his reflected glory—and we mean glory!

It may not all be completely smooth sailing. The older child who admiringly accepted a father's leadership in the days before the war may have become an independent youngster with a mind all his own in which his father seems at first to have no place. He may seem reluctant to take suggestions, and he will almost certainly resist any early attempts at discipline. But even though the older child has learned to get along without father or brother, and seems well established with his own affairs, he is more likely to take his father or brother back without serious inner conflict than are the younger children.

The returning serviceman, however, should be warned that the average high-spirited American youngster, full of beans and ideas, will not take such an exciting event as his favorite veteran's return calmly. At times his enthusiasm may be hard to take. He will speed up his play—and his noise. He'll be rather hard to live with for a few days. He'll interrupt anyone to tell his dad or brother a story—at the top of his lungs. He'll shout, "Hey, Dad— watch—you're not looking—watch!" until a Normandy beachhead will seem quiet by comparison.

Unless he has cast-iron nerves the veteran may be somewhat frayed by the antics of even the most beloved hoodlums. But if he remembers how eagerly they have anticipated his return, how much it means to them, how proud they are of him, he'll let them wear themselves down without interference. He'll tell them a story about his trip home, or get out in the yard and have a rousing game of ball.

The older child who is normally quiet and shy may go to the other extreme and be reserved and diffident with someone who seems half a stranger to him. No father or brother should feel hurt by such behavior. It does not mean that the child's affection or pride is less, but merely that he has no means of expression for them. Such a child should not be pressed to talk. Give him time, and he will relax into his old easy relationship.

ADOLESCENT BOYS AND GIRLS

WORK FOR CHILDREN?

If little children change quickly and school-age children change less, we might logically expect to find the teen-age boys and girls most like themselves when the servicemen of their families get back. But any serviceman who remembers his own adolescence, with its ups and downs, the sudden shift from childhood to adulthood and back again, will not expect any such thing. The adolescent may seem unchanged or he may have become a quite different person. You can't tell with him. He can't tell himself.

Not many servicemen have adolescent children of their own to come home to. But plenty of them have adolescent brothers and sisters and friends. The veteran will find that the war matured these young people in many respects. Boys saw their brothers and friends not much older than they were going off to war. Girls saw their older and most interesting boy friends leaving, while girls only a little older were hurrying to marry before their sweethearts had to go overseas. Many of these young wives are now mothers with a full share of adult responsibility. High school youngsters, instead of seeing jobs and parenthood as remote contingencies, saw them just ahead. They were frankly envious, too, of their friends who were just old enough to get in the war. They wished they could go too. Actually many of them did a good job on the home front.

Anything with an authentic military flavor was particularly popular with the teen-age boys and girls. The boys went in for pre-flight aeronautics wherever courses were offered. High school youngsters made model planes that were good enough to be used by the Army and Navy in teaching programs. Girls emulated their older sisters in the service by taking courses in home nursing and first aid.

Teen-age children, like the grammar school children, contributed largely to community bond and salvage drives through their schools and clubs. Many of them did real jobs, too. In the summer of 1944 about 700,000 young people helped on the farms of the United States. Aside from the minor perils of sore muscles and sunburn they had a healthy vacation that they loved. They went haying, they learned how to milk, they picked bushel after bushel of fruit that would otherwise have spoiled on the trees. In certain sections they collected milkweed pods to yield floss for over one million life jackets.

One of the troubles with jobs for high school boys and girls was that many of them liked the jobs too well. They found that they could get good paying permanent jobs as well as summer or volunteer work. Children who grew up during the depression were not likely to be blind to the advantages of having folding money in their pockets. Many of them could earn almost as much as their fathers. In 1940, before we entered the war, less than 900,000 boys and girls between fourteen and eighteen were employed. In 1941 this number doubled. By the spring of 1944 nearly 3,000,000 young people of these ages were at work full or part time—one out of three of the total population of this age group. The number was actually much greater, for these figures reflect only the employment of children who operated legally with working certificates. Child labor law violations increased by leaps and bounds. High school enrollment hit a new low. It looked as though America's much prized public education might be threatened by an attack of deep apathy. In the summer of 1944 a back-to-school drive was launched, and in the fall of that year there were signs of a reversal of the trend away from school.

Incidentally, not only children left the schools. Teachers went in droves. Even in the fall of 1944 when the shortage was less acute than in the two years preceding, there were upwards of 5,000 teaching positions unfilled. The exact number is hard to estimate because there is evidence that the "improvement" of that year was gained at the expense of the pupils. Positions were filled by hiring teachers with emergency certificates or by making classes bigger than they should be. Teacher turnover has doubled in the last five years, thus adding to the confusion and inefficiency.

Before we blame the teachers, we must remember that teachers' salaries lagged far behind the rising costs of living. Many a teacher with ten or fifteen years of experience behind her, with summer courses to her credit, has met a former student who languished in the fifth or sixth grade for years and who was making a lot better money than she was. After a few episodes of this kind, many a teacher went into the factory herself.

It could be that to the veteran returning from the battle front, the danger of work looks vastly overrated. He is right. It is. Even educators are getting around to admitting it. Up to date, most schools have operated on the theory that until the moment they leave school, children should be occupied with study or play. But contrary to many popular notions about childhood, children love to work. They like to earn money, of course, but it isn't merely the cash that appeals to them. Children like to feel, just as their parents do, that their world needs them and has a place for them. If they can measure their value in hard cash, so much the better. But money alone cannot explain the added self-respect and sense of responsibility that real work brings. Children of high school age, especially, need a solid basis for feelings of self-respect and independence. It isn't work that is wrong for children—it's the premature stopping of their education that is bad.

The war-torn countries of Europe found that children could be real assets in the actual business of war. Occupied countries found that they could be trusted in underground movements. While young Americans, snugly tucked between their two oceans, did not furnish examples of the kind of heroic endeavor that the children of Russia or England or France did, they met the needs of their particular situation for the most part well. They displayed hardihood and courage.

The trend of high school children away from the schools forced grownups to think about the place of children in the community life. Here again the sudden and drastic needs of war forced new ways of tackling the problems that arose. In some cases the working children were not merely lectured. Some schools, instead of fighting the trend, actually acted as hiring agents for the war plants in their neighborhood. This was done only when the plants co-operated and established a work and study plan whereby the children could work half a day and go to school the other half. The school kept the final say-so about which children could stand this rather demanding schedule. The fact emerged that plenty could stand it and did. Educators, while certainly not advocating a back-to-the-factory movement for the children, began to wonder if the high school shouldn't be more closely related to the life around it. Perhaps many youngsters would profit by an actual experience of work that was related to their education. Perhaps the prolonged childhood of our American boys and girls could be turned into a more gradual maturing if our schools were more flexible, if the children could have a sense of doing real jobs in school or out, along with their education. Perhaps our boys and girls could leave school better fitted to take their places in adult jobs and responsibilities.

The need for workers of all ages was also a need for workers of all classes. Children whose families felt the depression only in their bank statements responded to their country's need for them if not to their own need for money. Youngsters who had scarcely had a nodding acquaintance with one another before the war commuted back and forth to work in the same bus or car pool. The war in this country, as in others, became a leveler of distinctions of many kinds. Barriers of wealth, social position, and sex, though they still exist, have become much more fluid. High school boys and girls and college girls of all classes work at summer or part-time jobs in shipyards, airplane factories, offices, department stores, and anything else they can find. The girl from the big house on the hill and the boy whose father owns the drugstore find themselves working side by side.

Many youngsters who did not get jobs in war plants helped by taking more responsibility in their own homes. It turned out that many a girl who had seemed all thumbs in the kitchen under her mother's scrutiny could whip up a good dinner before her mother got home from the afternoon shift. And as for rationing—it might be a nuisance, but it was obvious from the results that children as well as grownups could thrive on other diets besides roast meat and mashed potatoes.

RECREATION

Since young people shared their work, it was natural that they should share their play to a greater extent than they had before. Teen Age Canteens, or Teen Towns, as they are sometimes called, sprang up spontaneously. These youth centers put on shows, ran newspapers, went in for arts and crafts or anything else that interested them. They were organized and operated largely by young people themselves with some help from adults. There are now about 3,000 such canteens which have a real chance to continue into the future.

A few of the wartime deprivations turned out to be blessings in disguise for the youngsters—or at least for their parents. They and their parents no longer had to quarrel about the family car, if they had one. The gasoline shortage took care of that. High-speed junkets and trips to roadhouses were out for the duration, and parents were unqualifiedly relieved. The young people didn't fare so badly, either. Parties at home could be good fun after all. It turned out that the young people of the nation had not lost the use of their legs as some alarmists had feared. They took up bicycling and pedaled themselves around vigorously (when Mother hadn't borrowed the bike to get the family groceries from downtown).

Although American teen-agers matured speedily with all their new experience and responsibility and hard work, these young people never looked so healthy, so tall and strong, or so alive as they do today. Perhaps, paradoxically, never so young either. With their long hair-do's or crisp short feather-cuts, their flat-soled loafers, sloppy Joe sweaters and bobby socks, it is hard to tell a girl of nineteen from one of fourteen until she speaks and you get to know her. The adolescent boy in dark wool shirt or sweater seems less self-consciously collegiate than he used to. These boys and girls are likely to be more appreciative of each other as human beings, and less artificially sexy than formerly, despite their rather complete knowledge about sex matters and the marked trend toward earlier marriages.

DELINQUENCY IN WARTIME

There were some serious troubles too. Many of them, to be sure, were only brought to the surface by the special pressures of wartime. Families on the march with war industries, children uprooted from the familiar ties and associations of their home towns, were turned loose in mushroom cities with no facilities for their expanded populations. Many of these towns had grown suddenly to five or six times their original size. Anyone who has ever tried to spend a leave in a town of this kind knows what it is like on the recreation end. Housing, schools, hospitals, as well as recreation are hopelessly inadequate. Government housing projects helped to alleviate the housing shortage and to provide people with real homes for their children, but they could not accommodate nearly all the people who needed a place to live. Newcomers in these rapidly growing towns are not always exactly welcomed either. Older children in these towns, often with mothers as well as fathers off at work all day, are in many cases lonely and friendless. Sometimes, under the influence of older unscrupulous people, they find themselves in serious difficulties.

Juvenile delinquency is a very small fragment of the total picture of American childhood. During the four or five years preceding the war delinquency was on the wane. But around 1939, the figures leaped upward. Experts argue about the causes; they blame, depending upon their prejudices, modern education, failure of community services, too much money in children's pockets, and many other more subtle psychological forces. The veteran, who has the advantage of not being an expert, will not fail to notice the correspondence of dates between the start of the war and the rise of juvenile delinquency. It is obvious that the pressures and tensions of war are closely involved. Figures for 1944 showed a rise of court cases of 56 per cent over 1939. In some places where overcrowding and family dislocation were acute it was even higher.

Figures also show a greater rise in the rate of delinquency for girls than for boys, though the actual number of boy delinquents still remains greater than the number of girls. Girls just under eighteen have experienced an even greater upheaval in their daily lives than the boys just under draft age. Many of the boys they would normally date with have gone off to war. Servicemen on leave are eager for a good time, and they have little trouble in finding these youngsters roaming the streets in twos and threes. Many a high school girl has succumbed to the lure of a good time and has found herself in serious trouble.

Delinquency is by no means, of course, a purely American problem. England has had a similar experience and has excelled us in learning some of the lessons of community responsibility for this and other social ills.

"Before any boy or girl has broken the law," said Arthur H. Crowl, of the Federal Bureau of Investigation, "some adult has committed a more serious fault, some parent has been negligent in his responsibility or some social agency has failed to fulfill completely its purpose. Before any child strays from the path of the right, the adult generation has forgotten that the most solemn obligation anyone can assume in the eyes of God and man is to guide and direct a child along the proper paths of life. And when an adult places anything ahead of that responsibility, it is akin to criminal negligence. . . . The American home today may be excused to some extent for failure to carry out its responsibilities. But the community cannot be excused and it must accept its added responsibilities."

Certain communities have met the challenge. Both the Chicago and Detroit Area Project Plans, the Sunbury (Pennsylvania) Council for Youth Welfare, and especially the Back of the Yard Plan of Saul J. Alinsky in Chicago are the best examples of what can be done to safeguard young people when the public wakes up and decides that healthy community life goes far toward keeping youth sound. Yet all students of delinquency know that such efforts, important as they are, constitute a part, not the whole, of an effective attack upon the problem. While many so-called delinquents can be helped through better social conditions, there is also a significant number with deep-seated personality disturbances who require an altogether different approach. These are the children who are as undeterred by prison sentences on the one hand as they are by the "kind approach" or by bettered social conditions on the other. These hard-to-reach youngsters are directly or indirectly of concern to every serviceman, since they affect the community in which his own children will live. The one way to help them is through increased psychiatric research and through special agencies for their guidance.

INFLUENCE OF THE VETERAN AT HOME AND IN THE NATION

How will these almost grown-up children greet their brothers and friends who come home from the front? They may be a little on the defensive at first, in fear that the serviceman, with his greater experience, will challenge their own maturity. They may put on a cocky and smart-alecky front. This will be especially true of the boys who have had in many cases to take the jobs and responsibilities that would normally have been filled by their older brothers. The returning serviceman need not be fooled by this manner for long, if he realizes that it covers up a feeling of inadequacy. The adolescent is likely to be touchy, and unstable in his maturity. In many instances he will be afraid that he will have to get back to his secondary role as younger brother or friend. He is afraid that there will be no place for him in the serviceman's world.

The girls will, most of them, have no such defenses. They will be unqualifiedly glad that the men are back. They have worked hard and done a good job, but after the job was over there has always been the sense of restlessness and loneliness that comes from having their social lives disrupted and distorted by the disappearance of most of the young men. They would much prefer to go out with their own men than to go in a female phalanx to scream at Frankie Sinatra.

At the same time, both boys and girls will be terribly eager to have the approval and the friendship of their relatives and friends who were in the service. They will have tremendous respect for their opinions. Many of them will be curious about the serviceman's experience, but it will be a warm and admiring curiosity, not a prying one. All they want, fundamentally, is to be treated like real people instead of being dismissed as "just kids."

The serviceman is in a position to be very influential with this younger crowd. Take the problem of leaving school. Any soldier or sailor who has been plucked from the midst of his own education or from the beginning of his professional life will not hesitate to urge the younger people to keep on with their own training, even if it is only part-time, while they have the chance.

The serviceman will be in a position to steer his young friends and his brothers and sisters to serious thought about some of the important issues this nation will face in the years to come—cooperation with the other nations of the world, continuing alertness toward the prevention of war. The serviceman, who has seen the enormous contribution of many people and many nations to victory, can help to give his younger brothers and sisters an attitude of respect and friendliness toward other racial and cultural groups, both in his own country and abroad.

It is to be hoped that the returning serviceman will take such a serious interest in the lives of his own children, of his younger brothers and sisters. He can be a powerful factor for healthy growth in his own family. And it is to be hoped that the terrible experience of war will open his eyes to the needs of all children— not only his own. He can be a powerful factor for good in the nation.

It becomes increasingly clear that to protect our own children we must protect all children everywhere. We cannot hope for another war to spare the American home front so miraculously. To give our children a real chance we must give all the nation's children a real chance. It is true that disease and delinquency tend to follow poverty, inadequate housing, lack of education. But we cannot keep them behind fences. Like flying bombs, they are likely to hit suddenly when we are defenseless.

When men have seen children in devastated and war-torn countries, let them not conclude, by contrast, that all is well with children here at home where they have now returned, and so gladly. If their own families are comfortable and nourished, well educated, sound in mind and body, let them not shut their eyes to the lives of children elsewhere. There are thousands of children here in the United States, undernourished, disease-ridden, miserably housed, unschooled. Much as these children need community services, medical care, proper recreation, improved schools, they need, even more, decent financial resources *within their families*. Such children will never have a chance until we find ways of keeping the incomes of American families above the level of subsistence. In the year 1940, 55 per cent of the nation's children were to be found in families with incomes of less than $1,500 per year. Families headed by women alone, about one-eighth of the total, were even more destitute. These figures are taken from the families of the urban and small-town groups. If farmers' families were included the annual income would be even smaller. Sixty million jobs by all means! But ways, too, for mothers of children to be assured adequate means even if their husbands are unemployed, or ill, or shiftless, or dead.

Today the Federal Government spends six times the amount of money on services for the aged that it does on services for children. The aged need it; they are voters; they get it. Children need it too, but they have no votes. Are there no spokesmen for them?

Unless decent living conditions prevail for American children—which means for the American family—the nation will be restless, torn by racial and industrial strife; there will be no basis for peace at home or between nations.

There are good signs in the world today, signs of a quickened conscience, of a determination to build a brave new world. Thought and planning, practical common sense and technical skill are in process of mobilization. In spite of the defeatists and the difficulties ahead, there is a spirit of working together which should give us heart. A conscience about children—not yours and ours only—but all the children, is the surest sign that the best in mankind is on the job.

IV. WHAT WE DID ABOUT
RACIAL MINORITIES

by CAREY MCWILLIAMS

CAREY McWILLIAMS (age 40) is one of the
country's leading authorities on the history of
racial minorities in the United States, on the
causes of and possible cures for racial conflict.
He was head of the California Division of
Immigration and Housing from 1939 to 1943.
He is the author of Brothers under the Skin
(April, 1943), a basic study of the various colored minority groups in the United States. He
is at present preparing a study of the Japanese
relocation program for the Institute of Pacific
Relations. Mr. McWilliams' courageous and
hard-hitting articles on the zoot-suit demonstrations in California did much to explain the
basic causes of those riots.

GREAT changes have taken place in race relations in America
since the beginning of the war. By accelerating processes long at
work in our democracy, the war has quickened the pace of cultural change. It has telescoped pre-existing tendencies, brought
to light long-dormant issues, and sharpened numerous contradic-
tions. By focusing public attention upon "the race problem," in
all its ramifications, it has aroused a new national interest in
racial minorities and stirred to life a new national conscience
toward these groups.

Outwardly "the race question" has passed through three clearly
defined phases since the war began: a period of mounting tension and friction (from the outset of the defense program to Jan-

uary 1, 1943); a period of overt hostility and aggression (through 1943); and a period in which the democratic forces of the nation mobilized to meet the menace so clearly apparent in the shocking events of 1943 (from midsummer, 1943, to date).

To fight a total war successfully on a global scale, America quickly realized that all available sources of manpower, including the racial minorities, must be utilized—in the services, in the defense industries, in all phases of the war effort. The attempt to make full utilization of the racial minorities, however, ran counter to long-established usages and customs. Since it involved the grafting of emergency wartime requirements upon a peacetime structure of race relations, the effort was naturally productive of considerable friction, particularly in the crowded defense areas, where sharp issues arose over housing, employment, and transportation. By rapidly shifting populations from rural to urban areas, the war heightened existing tensions and created new tension areas. The steady accumulation of racial "incidents" throughout 1941 and 1942 was primarily the result of the efforts of various groups to adjust to a wide variety of new situations and relationships.

To some extent these incidents were stimulated, directly and indirectly, by our enemies at home and abroad. On February 28, 1942, a savage riot occurred at the Sojourner Truth Housing project in Detroit, in which prospective Negro tenants were attacked with clubs, knives, rifles, and shotguns, resulting in many injuries and over 104 arrests. When 14 Negro families were finally moved into the project in May, 2,000 National Guardsmen were on duty to give them protection. Two of the men arrested for fomenting this riot—which was a dress rehearsal for the Detroit riots of 1943 —were members of an organization which had been disseminating pro-Axis propaganda. Spokesmen for America First, such as Father Coughlin, Gerald L. K. Smith, and Charles Lindbergh, consistently raised "the Jewish question" in their propaganda. Throughout 1941 and 1942 a legion of rabble-rousers was active in the Detroit area. Included among these troublemakers were some 2,500 self-appointed "lay ministers," many of whom preached a violent form of racial hatred. It is significant that so much of this activity was concentrated in Detroit—"the arsenal of democracy"—where open racial violence could be expected to have a crippling effect on the war program.

Also during this period enemy agents sought to foment racial discord by direct instigation. On September 14, 1942, for example, Robert Jordan, a West Indian Negro, and four leaders of "an Ethiopian-Pacific movement envisaging a coalition of Africa and Japan in an Axis-dominated world," were indicted in New York. One of the presentments in the indictment of twenty-eight Nazi agents in 1942 was that they had organized a conspiracy to set afoot preposterous rumors of a "campaign to pollute Aryan Christian soldiers" by injecting into their veins the blood of "Negroes, Jews, and Japs." Throughout 1941 and 1942 small units of the Sinarquista movement, launched in Mexico in 1937 with Nazi funds, were seeking to spread unrest and disaffection among the Mexican minority in the Southwest. The evidence would indicate, however, that these activities were not particularly successful. Even the limited effectiveness of such enemy-inspired activity was largely due to the fact that the war had momentarily created a situation which could be exploited to advantage.

Where the enemy did make effective use of racial discord in America was in their world-wide propaganda. Every racial "incident" was immediately seized upon for propaganda purposes. Not only did such incidents serve to discredit America, but they tended to support the Japanese propaganda thesis that this was a racial war. On January 25, 1942, the Japanese broadcast throughout the Far East the story of how, a few hours previously, Cleo Wright, a Negro, had been seized by a mob and burned to death in Sikeston, Missouri. A consistent theme of Japanese propaganda was indicated in a broadcast of March 15, 1942: "Democracy, as preached by Anglo-Americans, may be an ideal and a noble system of life, but democracy as practiced by Anglo-Americans is stained with the bloody guilt of racial persecution and exploitation." The Sojourner Truth riot of February 28, 1942, occasioned a great outburst of enemy propaganda. Such Nazi publications as

Die Wehrmacht carried full pictures of the rioting in Detroit. Pursuing a line of propaganda developed long before the war, the Nazis sought to make an issue, throughout Central and South America, of our mistreatment of the Indian minority.

In the United States important changes began to take place, as the war progressed, in the attitude of the minorities toward each other and toward the majority; in the attitude of the majority toward the minorities; and in the conception which the minorities entertained of their own predicament. A noticeable ferment began to develop in the minority groups, in particular the Negro minority. While this ferment was unquestionably quickened by the slogans and dynamics of the war, it really represented the expression of sentiments and aspirations which had been maturing over a long period of time. No agitators were needed, as Roy Wilkins wrote, to point out to the Negro the discrepancy between "what we said we were fighting for, and what we did to him." This was an old and bitter reality to the Negro, made particularly galling by the circumstance that we were at war. The segregation of Negro personnel in the services and the continued mistreatment of Negro soldiers in civilian communities aroused the Negro communities throughout the nation to a high pitch of excitement and indignation.

While resentment mounted, however, the minorities were quick to realize that they must wholeheartedly support the war. For they saw that the war could become a war of liberation for oppressed peoples throughout the world. As one Negro newspaper put it: "As we storm the Nazis' fortress to deliver the European people from oppression we are setting in motion forces which must not stop until every vestige of totalitarianism is abolished." Not only did the minorities want to join in the fight against the Nazi aggressors, whose ideology was premised upon racist theories, but they were well aware of the fact that, as a world phenomenon, fascism had its domestic manifestations. Early in the defense program militant Negro leadership secured the issuance of President Roosevelt's famous Executive Order No. 8802 creating the Fair Employment Practice Committee; and the same leadership continued to press the fight against discrimination. Owing largely to the intelligent character of this leadership, the mounting toll of racial incidents served, not to create disaffection among Negroes, but to encourage their determination to win full equality as citizens. At the same time the limited gains which they began to record on the domestic front tended to solidify their ranks and to strengthen their organizational efforts. By 1944 the membership of the National Association for the Advancement of the Colored People had increased from 100,000 on December 7, 1941, to around 500,000, with a substantial portion of the gain being achieved in the Deep South.

As Negroes, north and south, began to close ranks in response to the pressures of war, they also began to break away from a narrow Negro nationalism. A similar tendency was also noticeable among the other racial minorities. More important, perhaps, than any of these developments was the fact that a profound change had come over the thinking of these racial minority groups (and what they *think* about their problems is, obviously, one of the most important factors in what we call "the race question"). Throughout 1941 and 1942 the majority remained blindly unaware of the fact that these groups could no longer be cajoled, as Wendell Willkie phrased it, "by the counsels of patience and the assurances of kindly men."

Strangely enough, the wartime prejudices of the majority tended to be directed at our own racial minorities rather than, as in World War I, against enemy aliens and naturalized citizens of German descent. In fact, German-Americans and Italian-Americans have gone through this war virtually unscathed by prejudice or discrimination.

Realizing that the dynamics of the war were releasing new forces which were profoundly disturbing the racial *status quo* in America, the traditionally biased section of the white majority became increasingly provocative. Demagogues, in and out of Congress, began to indulge in rabid anti-Negro speeches which not only infuriated the Negro minority but shocked large sections of the white majority. Writing in the *Virginia Quarterly* in the summer of 1942, John Temple Graves charged that the Negroes "have chosen to go crazy with their championings, scouring the land for trouble . . . making plain beyond question an intent to use the war for settling overnight the whole, long, complicated, infinitely delicate racial problem." Other Southern liberals, such as Virginius Dabney and David L. Cohn, began "to warn the nation" about "the delicate racial problem," which the South had always treated so indelicately. Hundreds of crazy rumors began to circulate throughout the nation (documented in *Race and Rumors of Race,* by Dr. Howard W. Odum—a volume of 250 pages devoted to an analysis of these poisonous, insidiously contrived stories). Perhaps the most fantastic of these widely circulated rumors was one that had to do with the so-called "Eleanor Clubs," that is, clubs of Negro domestics supposedly organized by Mrs. Eleanor Roosevelt as part of an alleged campaign "to get a white woman in every kitchen by 1943." Careful investigation failed to reveal the existence of these fabled clubs. Throughout 1942 there was a marked stiffening of attitudes, which, in itself, was the best proof that the racial *status quo* was being seriously challenged.

Also during 1941 and 1942 a noticeable ferment began to develop among middle-class white elements on the racial question. In large part, this new interest in racial minorities was related to the emphasis which the Nazis placed on "blood" and "race." As Roy Wilkins observed, "Hitler jammed our white people into their logically untenable position. Forced to oppose him for the sake of the life of the nation, they were jockeyed into declaring against his racial theories—publicly." As the American people became more deeply involved in the war, the inconsistency between our traditional ideals and our racial practices became increasingly embarrassing and progressively indefensible. While this embarrassment was not shared equally by all the people, it began to be reflected in an ever-widening circle of opinion. Historians will recognize, during this period, the growing influence of Wendell Willkie. In numerous speeches and articles he began to outline the implications of the race question, in terms of America's new world position, with admirable candor and vigor. In this respect his interest in racial minorities has symbolic importance. For he was reflecting as much, perhaps, as he was inspiring, a growing interest and deepening concern with racial minorities on the part of a large section of the majority. It would be a mistake to write off this ferment as "crisis patriotism." For it has not abated with the end of the war; on the contrary, it has steadily expanded.

Thus, as the war developed, a triangle of forces began to form in America: better organized than ever before, the racial minorities were struggling to fight free from all restrictions of caste and color; one section of the majority, responding to the challenging issues of the war, began to rally to the defense of the minorities; while a minority of the majority redoubled its efforts in defense of the prewar racial *status quo*.

The dangers implicit in these mounting tensions were clearly apparent. For more than a year prior to the Detroit riots a score of journalists, government investigators, and labor union officials had pointed to the likelihood of serious disturbances in the area. Mounting tensions in Los Angeles were so clearly discernible in 1941 that experienced observers warned of a rapidly approaching disaster. Up to the time that the explosions occurred, however, virtually nothing was done to prevent an outbreak of racial vio-nce. To be sure, as mentioned above, President Roosevelt on June 25, 1941, had issued his Executive Order No. 8802, creating the Fair Employment Practice Committee to prevent discrimination in the defense industries on the score of race, creed, color, or country of national origin (strengthened and supplemented, at a later date, by Executive Order No. 9346). While the establishment of the Fair Employment Practice Committee was an excellent beginning, its effects were in part nullified by other actions of the Federal Government inconsistent with the spirit and intention of the order.

The commendable efforts of OWI to publicize the contributions the minorities were making to the war effort were, likewise, largely nullified by demagogic speeches on the floor of Congress and by the continued assaults upon Negro servicemen in American civilian communities throughout 1941 and 1942.

The efforts of the Coordinator of Inter-American Affairs to create a better understanding between Anglos and Hispanos, admittedly feeble in character, were more than offset by an increasingly violent "anti-Mexican" campaign that began to gather dangerous momentum in Southern California in 1942.

The explosions came in 1943. They began with the so-called "zoot-suit" riot in Los Angeles early in June (although there had been some violence in connection with a "hate" strike in the shipyards at Mobile, Alabama, on May 29). Then came the Detroit race riot of June 20–21, the worst race riot which America had experienced in twenty-five years, followed by subsequent disturbances in Beaumont and Harlem. In Los Angeles 3,000 screaming rioters severely beat and mistreated nearly a hundred victims, most of whom were Mexican youngsters. The press carried photographs of these youngsters (98 per cent of whom were American citizens of Mexican descent), stripped of their clothing, being beaten and kicked around on the sidewalks and in the streets with a large crowd watching the show. In the Detroit riots, 25 Negroes and 9 whites were killed; property damage ran into the hundreds of thousands of dollars; and the war effort was materially, if momentarily, disrupted. The swift, crazy violence of the Harlem riot resulted, in a few hours' time, in nearly a million-dollar property damage. The rapid succession of these violent and destructive riots, coming as they did in the midst of the greatest war in which America has participated, profoundly shocked the American people.

Without waiting for leadership or guidance, public opinion began to mobilize at the local level. Within a short space of time, 102 formally organized groups were formed (17 were appointed by governors, 16 by mayors, and 69 were spontaneously organized). The national press and the radio networks began to swing in behind this rapidly developing public opinion. Police training programs were instituted; adult education campaigns were launched; special programs were established in the schools; and thousands of civic organizations began to show, for the first time, an active interest in race relations. The American Council on Race Relations was established in Chicago. The churches and labor unions launched many new programs and projects.

Out of this emergency activity came a host of conferences, institutes, programs, and studies, constituting in the aggregate an enormous amount of energy and effort. Much of this activity was sporadic and unintegrated and will doubtless lapse now that the war is over. But it was this activity which accounts for the fact that few racial disturbances were recorded in 1944 (the Philadelphia transit strike and the disturbances in New Iberia, Louisiana, were about the only major outbreaks during the year) or 1945. Interest in racial minorities, moreover, has continued to increase.

Part of the changing aspect of race relations since the war consists in the growth of a new conception of the nature of the race problem. Forced to deal with the realities of the problem, if only on an emergency wartime basis, the American people have begun to see through some of the myths and fallacies which have long enshrouded their thinking about racial issues. Increasingly they have come to realize that it is not the fact of racial difference that constitutes "the race problem," but rather what people think about this difference. Coming to know the racial minorities under the stress of wartime compulsions, they have discovered for themselves the truth that racial prejudice is not based on biological antipathy but rather upon socially sanctioned or learned behavior.

While the rapidly accumulating findings of science about race have not been thoroughly popularized, sufficient progress has been made since the war to undermine, if not to demolish, the false ideology upon which the doctrine of White Supremacy has always rested. Using such popular media as pamphlets, cartoons, comic strips, motion pictures, and radio, the scientific view has been widely disseminated to mass organizations and groups throughout the nation. Merely to indicate the growth in understanding that has taken place since the war, the following, among other works of equal excellence, have been published during this period: *An American Dilemma,* by Gunnar Myrdal (the publication of this two-volume work can be said to constitute a major event in the history of race relations in America); *Patterns of Negro Segregation,* by Charles S. Johnson; *Characteristics of the American Negro,* by Otto Klineberg; *The Negro's Share,* by Richard Sterner; *When People Meet,* by Bernhard J. Stern and Alain Locke; and, at a different level, Richard Wright's *Black Boy,* J. Saunders Redding's *No Day of Triumph,* and Lillian Smith's *Strange Fruit.* In fact, more progress has been made, in this five-year period, toward a realistic understanding of the issues involved in what we still call "the race problem" than in the entire period from the Civil War to 1940.

Paralleling this growth in understanding, "the race problem," as such, has undergone some important mutations. Increasingly the emphasis has shifted from biological to sociological factors; from "prejudice" to "discrimination"; from "race relations" to "ethnic democracy." As the myth of race has begun to dissolve, public attention has been focused, with increasing sharpness and directness, upon such specific issues as the white primary laws, the poll tax, and the practice of segregation. The philanthropic and paternalistic approach has steadily given way to widely supported programs of social action based upon a scientific analysis of the facts. In much the same manner, as Alain Locke has pointed out, "minority self-assertion" has tended "to broaden out into an integrated mass movement of general social re-construction and reform." Similarly, the sharp demarcation between "northern" and "southern" schools of racial thought has tended to merge in a general concern over the race issue as "a national problem." The wide gap which formerly separated the thinking of Northern and Southern Negroes has largely disappeared. Since the war the various aspects of the race problem, seldom correlated in the past, have been drawn together so that all phases of the matter, involving Negroes, Mexicans, Orientals, Indians, Filipinos, etc., have come to be regarded as a single national problem. These changes have considerably altered the dimensions of the race problem and have brought about a growing confidence in its solubility. No longer intimidated by the formidable dimensions which the problem once possessed, a new realism has come to characterize the thinking of both majority and minority.

Some of the basic factors involved in the race problem have also undergone important changes since the war. Prior to the war virtually all the Japanese in the United States were concentrated on the west coast, most of them in California. As a result of the mass evacuation of all persons of Japanese descent from the three west coast states, some 35,000 Japanese-Americans have been relocated in other parts of the nation, primarily in the Middle West. At the same time, Negroes have moved from the Deep South to the North: 100,000 to Chicago; 60,000 to Detroit; 25,000 to Harlem; and 250,000 to the west coast. It is also estimated that 300,000 Negroes, in the South, have moved from rural to urban areas since the war (a factor of great importance). This geographical redistribution of minorities has tended to underline the national aspects of the problem and to level off sectional differences.

The outward movement of Negroes from the South has had important economic, social, and political implications. It has, for example, emphasized the significance of the Negro vote in national elections. In an analysis of the vote in the November, 1944, election, Henry Lee Moon has pointed out that the 168 electoral votes of the seven states in which Negroes contributed substantially to the margin of victory for the Democratic candidate outweigh the 127 votes of the eleven states comprising the Solid South. The history of the last twelve years shows that the Negro vote is a more intelligent, a more independent, vote than ever before. With the remarkable decline in Negro illiteracy (from 95 per cent in 1865 to less than 8 per cent in 1940), the traditional arguments used in the South to justify the exclusion of Negroes from the polls have lost whatever merit they formerly possessed. It is not surprising to note, therefore, a growing trend of opinion in the South in favor of the political re-enfranchisement of the Negro.

Nearly 5,300,000 Negroes were employed in civilian jobs in April, 1944—a million more than were employed at the time of the 1940 census. The number of Negroes employed in manufacturing and processing increased from 500,000 to around 1,200,000 between 1940 and 1944; in transportation, communications, and public utilities from less than 200,000 in 1940 to 250,000 in 1944; in government service from 60,000 to 200,000. Despite continuing resistance to the upgrading of Negroes, the number employed as skilled craftsmen and foremen doubled from 1940 to 1944; the number of those in semiskilled jobs also doubled. The number of Negro women employed in industry has quadrupled since the war. This important occupational reshifting of Negroes also has its significant economic, social, and political implications. More than 500,000 Negroes, for example, have joined trade unions since 1940. The integration of Negroes in the trade union movement, by no means thoroughly effected, implies that the solution of the Negro problem cannot be reached separate and apart from other issues but only as incidental to more general problems of human rights and liberties. With more Negroes voting in trade union elections and proceedings, the argument against their voting in general elections becomes absurdly anachronistic. It should be noted, however, that 13 national labor unions, with a membership of more than a million, still exclude Negroes from membership.

Not only have sectional differences of opinion on racial issues tended to level off since the war, but a wedge has been driven in

Southern opinion. It is no longer accurate, for example, to refer to the Deep South or the Solid South. Already two Souths have begun to emerge: the *Upper* South and the *Deeper* South. On such important issues as the white primary, the FEPC, and the poll tax, influential newspapers throughout the Upper South have tended to diverge from the traditional Southern position. Within the Deeper South, important rifts have developed. In 1945 Georgia repealed the poll tax. Recently the Atlanta *Journal* launched a campaign to win support for its four-point racial program: improved economic opportunities for Negroes; better educational facilities; a greater emphasis upon health and housing; and support for the idea that the Negro should be permitted to share in the rights and safeguards of democratic government, *including the right to vote in general and primary elections.* Similarly the Anniston *Star,* published in Alabama, has come forth in support of a general program for the improvement of living and working conditions for Negroes. Of equal importance is the fact that the one-party system has shown signs of early disintegration in the South. In the November, 1944, election, the Republican party polled, in one Southern state, the largest vote which it has received since 1876. The tendency of Southern Bourbon Democrats in Congress to align themselves with, and in fact to assume the leadership of, the more reactionary Republicans, is related to this same general trend. The defeat of Senator "Cotton" Ed Smith in South Carolina and Representative Joe Starnes in Alabama, the emergence of a leader like Governor Ellis Arnall in Georgia, and the re-election of Senator Claude Pepper and Senator Lister Hill, all point to the conclusion that a wind is rising in the South.

Of still greater significance is the appearance of a New Negro in the Southland. To quote from a recent editorial in the Michigan *Chronicle* (one of the most consistently progressive Negro newspapers published in America):

In Texas, Georgia, and South Carolina, a new Negro leadership is developing which equals in intelligence and militancy the most advanced leadership of the Northern Negro. Considering the traditions against which he must struggle, this Southern leadership is doing the job in the only way it can be done successfully. The old Southern Uncle Toms who won petty concessions from a temperamental white boss have had to concede ground to these new Southern Negroes who are allying themselves with liberal whites in the labor movement and in the intellectual fields. These new Negro leaders in Dixie have welcomed the aid and contributed their support to the NAACP and similar groups. They are taking advantage of every educational opportunity and pressing for new educational opportunities for the oppressed masses. Carter Wesley in Texas and C. A. Scott in Atlanta are developing newspapers which can intelligently present their case before the world. Taking full advantage of new industrial opportunities in this war period and living up to all the responsibilities of the war effort, they are moving toward new frontiers.

Returning from a recent visit to South Carolina, Roy Wilkins reported that "Negroes are organizing all over the state to secure their rights. They are not frightened. They are being joined, sometimes openly and sometimes quietly, by whites who believe in justice."

Throughout the war period, Negroes continued to win important victories before the United States Supreme Court, a trend that began with *Moore vs. Dempsey,* decided in 1923. Surveying the recent decisions of the court on racial questions, it is apparent that the court has begun to throw a noose around Jim Crow. In *Gaines vs. Missouri,* decided in 1938, the court in effect sounded the death knell of segregated schools. In *Smith vs. Allright,* decided in April, 1944, the court, in outlawing the Texas white primary, doomed the dominance of one-party rule in the South. In a still more recent decision, *Steele vs. The Louisville and Nashville Railroad,* the court indicated that it does not propose to sanction discrimination in the trade union movement. The most striking victories that Negroes have won since the war are represented, perhaps, in their victories before the court.

Important gains have also been registered by the other racial minorities. Early in the war Congress repealed the Chinese Exclusion Act of 1882 by giving Chinese people an immigration quota and making Chinese resident in the United States eligible to American citizenship. Similar bills are now pending in Congress to make resident Filipinos and Hindus eligible to citizenship. Since so many resident Filipinos enlisted in, or were drafted into, the armed services, most of them will acquire American citizenship under an act which makes them eligible for citizenship after serving three months in the services. At the outset of the war the resident Chinese and Filipinos, living symbols of our allies in China and the Philippines, enjoyed momentarily a new status in many communities. But, as the war dragged on, one could detect a noticeable cooling-off of attitude toward these groups, as also toward the resident Mexican minority.

As the people have come to realize that "the race problem" is amenable to social action, the movement to outlaw racial discrimination by direct legislation has steadily gained momentum. When President Roosevelt created the Fair Employment Practice Committee there were many individuals, including some unprejudiced persons, who viewed this innovation with great skepticism. But the committee, lacking legislative sanction and operating with an inadequate staff and a sorely restricted budget, made remarkable headway. In the first eighty weeks of its existence the FEPC, in the words of Dr. Malcolm S. MacLean, did more to bring the Bill of Rights closer to reality than anything accomplished in the past eighty years. Negro employment in commercial shipyards increased from 6,592 to 12,820; in navy shipyards from 6,000 to 14,000; in aircraft from 0 to 5,000. And it has continued to score equally impressive gains. With a strong national opinion being mobilized behind the proposal to create a permanent FEPC, it is interesting to note that similar proposals have been made in many states. Forty-nine different bills were introduced in twenty state legislatures in 1945. New York passed an excellent antidiscrimination measure, and, as I write, the prospects for the enactment of similar measures are reported to be excellent in a dozen Northern states.

The importance of the drive for antidiscrimination legislation consists in the fact that it provides a point around which public opinion can rally. The lobbies formed in support of such legislation have been impressive. In almost every state where antidiscrimination measures have been introduced, they have been endorsed by Catholic, Protestant, and Jewish organizations; by the Negro organizations; by State A. F. of L. and C.I.O. unions; and by influential civic organizations. In the effort to enact such legislation, the people are discovering that it is not the majority as such that endorses discrimination, but a minority of the majority. They are also discovering the folly of continuing to appease this minority. It is important to note that other groups have begun to appreciate the effectiveness of the FEPC approach, namely, of establishing uniform national fair racial practices. Early in 1945, for example, a group of American educators sent President Roosevelt a wire asking him to appoint a National Fair Educational Practice Committee for the purpose of eliminating quotas and other forms of racial and religious discrimination in the nation's colleges and universities.

Throughout May and June, 1945, the fight for the continuance of FEPC was a major, if not the dominant, issue in Congress. In the Senate, Bilbo of Mississippi staged a minor filibuster and renewed his proposal to colonize American Negroes in Africa; in the House, Rankin and his crew of merry wreckers fought the FEPC with a vengefulness and bitterness remarkable even for such diehard racists. In mid-July, Congress finally granted a niggardly appropriation of $250,000—half of the requested budget —to the FEPC. Even this appropriation had to be secured by one of the most shameful compromises in recent congressional history. One section of the bill provides that FEPC is to liquidate its affairs; but still another section, subsequently added, provides that the agency does not need to expend any portion of the appropriation on liquidation. Under the circumstances, of course, it is impossible to determine the intent of Congress. Furthermore, both in the Senate and in the House, final vote on the compromise bill was taken by a voice-vote, neither house and neither party being willing to take a roll-call vote. In the Senate, Wayne Morse of Oregon, in an hour-long speech, denounced both parties for their reluctance to take a position on the measure. Thus FEPC will be continued as a skeleton agency virtually powerless to discharge the important functions assigned to it by executive order. The reluctance of Congress to take a clear-cut position on the FEPC has, however, only strengthened the determination of the groups now fighting for a permanent Fair Employment Practice Committee. While Congress was busily engaged trying to cover up its cowardly compromise, the territorial legislature of Alaska passed an antidiscrimination measure. Of a civilian population of 72,170, some 32,458 are native Indians, Eskimos, and Aleuts. "We do not cater to native trade" has been a familiar sign in many Alaska restaurants, hotels, inns, theatres, and taverns; but the signs are coming down, just as they will come down eventually wherever the American flag is flown.

Within the last year the legislative drive against racial discrimination has broadened. Pending in Congress at the present time are a number of important measures in addition to the FEPC proposal. On January 16, 1945, the G.I. "assault bill" (H.R. 1528) was introduced. The object of this bill is to make civilian violence against members of the armed forces a federal offense. Still another bill (H.R. 1925) would amend the Interstate Commerce Act to prohibit segregation of persons in interstate travel because of their race or color. Also pending is the Hill-Thomas bill to appropriate $300,000,000 for federal aid to education, specifically aimed at bringing about an improvement in educational opportunities in the South for both Negroes and whites. Thus the legislative front has two major aspects: (1) a fight against discrimination and (2) a fight for the enactment of ameliorative measures designed to bring educational, housing, and public health facilities to disadvantaged minorities. Implicit in this tendency is a gradual abandonment of segregation as a philosophy and a racial practice. The welfare of majority and that of minority have come to

be so interwoven in the fabric of our national life that it is becoming extremely difficult to expand the economic or social frontier of the one without expanding similar frontiers for the other.
This was particularly apparent during the debate in Congress on
the G.I. Bill of Rights (a measure of profound significance to some
700,000 Negroes and some 300,000 persons of Mexican descent
now serving in the armed forces). The Bilbos and the Rankins in
our Congress quickly discovered that they would be put in the
position of opposing veteran welfare legislation for white veterans if they insisted upon the exclusion, for example, of Negro
veterans.

Most of the gains made by minorities since the war, however,
are highly precarious in nature. In employment, for example, Negroes have made their greatest gains in those occupations that
will suffer the greatest cutbacks during the present postwar period; they have made their greatest gains in those industries—
metals, chemicals, rubber, and shipbuilding—which will now experience the sharpest decline; and the most impressive Negro
gains have been won in congested production areas where the
most extensive adjustments of the labor force will occur. It should
be a sufficient warning to point out that the regions which now
face the most severe postwar economic adjustment are also the
regions in which racial tensions are already most pronounced. In
all industries in which the Negro has registered important gains,
he has been among the last hired and faces the likelihood of early
layoff.

It should also be emphasized that the Negro minority and the
other racial minorities have no intention of voluntarily relinquish-
ing the gains which they have won during the war. As Wendell
Willkie pointed out shortly before his death, "No one who has
not stopped seeing and thinking could have missed the events of
the last few years that have drawn together 13 million Americans—one tenth of the nation—into a determined, purposeful
unit." It is vitally important, therefore, that these precarious wartime gains be consolidated as rapidly as possible. For the real

test of the permanency of these gains will come in the postwar period. "The furnace is being prepared," writes Stuart Chase, "and the temperature will be high. We cannot hire smart publicity men to fake our way through it. We shall have to march through it."

What the war has done, although we have not fully realized the fact, is to make race relations an international rather than a local and national problem. In the past, the isolationism which we practiced toward racial minorities was related to the isolationism which we followed as a foreign policy.

Today we face a crisis on the race question for the simple reason that, through a process of cultural change, the racial minorities have outgrown the set of relationships that formerly prevailed between majority and minority. While the war has precipitated this crisis, it would have developed sooner or later in any case. The dominant characteristic of our prewar policy toward racial minorities was the practice of segregation. While this practice varied regionally, it prevailed throughout the nation. It was imposed, furthermore, not merely against Negroes but, with variations, against Mexicans in the Southwest, Indians throughout the West, and Orientals on the west coast. Segregation, like isolationism, has become obsolete both as policy and as practice. It is largely responsible for the increased racial tensions of the last few years. Just as we have begun to abandon isolationism, so we have tended to abandon segregation.

How rapidly we can proceed with the liquidation of all aspects of segregation, however, raises another question. The minorities issue has now become inextricably interwoven with the larger issues of securing a lasting peace and an expanding economy. "To wipe out race hatred and racial discrimination," to quote from a recent editorial in *PM*, "we must unite the races in producing food enough for all, housing for all, clothing for all, education for all, comfort for all, instead of forcing them to compete with one another for less than enough."

Needless to say, such an expansion can take place only within a world at peace. The outcome of these larger issues will, therefore, largely determine the rapidity and ease with which America can proceed toward complete racial equality. But the achievement of full employment and a stable peace will not automatically result in a solution of the minorities problem in America. To attain this goal, specific remedies of a twofold character must be applied: measures designed to secure, through the removal of all formal or legally sanctioned discriminations, a state of universal civic freedom in the United States; and special ameliorative measures, particularly in the field of housing, public health, education, and employment, designed to lift the living standards of minorities.

Just because of the magnitude of the task still before us, it is distressing to note new manifestations of racial unrest now that the war is over. While the number of organized anti-Semitic groups has hit an all-time low, owing to the fear of indictment under wartime sedition statutes, the nation as a whole has shown an increase in the latent variety of anti-Semitism. Elmer Roper, one of our leading public opinion analysts, has recently said that, in his opinion, America is faced with a revival of Ku Klux Klannism in the postwar period. His findings indicate an increase of "antiminority" feeling throughout the nation.

Other observers have sounded the same warning. In the past hundred years, as Dr. Scudder Mekeel has pointed out, America has witnessed the rise of three major "anti" movements: the Know-Nothing movement in the decade preceding the Civil War; the American Protective Association movement on the eve of the Spanish-American War; and the KKK movement after the first World War. Each of these movements was more dangerous than the one which preceded it. "So far," writes Dr. Mekeel, "we have not had a hate and super-nationalist organization that combined with prejudice a definite ideology to apply to government." The Roper polls would clearly indicate that such a combination could quickly assume dangerous proportions in the postwar period. With the death of President Roosevelt and the end of the war, the America First elements have already begun to form a united front of the various "fringe" movements in this country. Formerly isolationist, they are today nationalist. L. M. Birkhead, national director of the Friends of Democracy, conservatively estimates the potential mass base for a nationalist crusade now getting under way in America at 15,000,000 people. Disguising their antidemocratic orientation in a maze of nationalistic, pseudo-patriotic, demagogic rhetoric, these groups can always be identified by their emphasis on racial differences. In one of its orientation manuals, *Three Ways to Spot U.S. Fascists*, the Army has correctly stated that "interwoven with the master race theory of fascism is a well-planned 'hate' campaign against minority groups.

. . . In the U. S. native fascists have often been anti-Catholic, anti-Jew, anti-Negro, anti-labor and anti-foreign born." These are the telltale tags to watch for. Not all fascists are Jew-baiters, but every Jew-baiter is a fascist.

One phase of the minorities problem will serve to indicate the menace of organized racist agitation. Early in 1942 the government removed all persons of Japanese descent (around 110,000) from the three west coast states and lodged them in relocation centers. Two-thirds of these evacuees are citizens of the United States. In December, 1944, the Supreme Court upheld the constitutionality of the procedure by which this mass evacuation was effected as a proper exercise of the power to wage war. At the same time the court ruled that there was nothing in the executive orders of the President, or the orders of the War Department, or the acts of Congress that justified the detention of American citizens, against whom no charge had been filed and whose loyalty was not questioned, after removal from the area. Previously, on December 17, 1944, the War Department had lifted the ban against the return of loyal evacuees to the three west coast states. To date some 58,000 evacuees have been relocated; approximately 39,000 still remain in the relocation centers; and about 10,000 have returned to the Coast.

While a majority west coast opinion has supported the Army's decision lifting the ban against return to the west coast, an organized opposition, premised explicitly upon racial considerations, has sought by terroristic tactics and boycott campaigns to prevent these citizens from returning to their former homes. As a direct result of the provocative activities of the organized groups constituting this opposition, 59 acts of violence against returning evacuees have been reported on the west coast since December 17, 1944. Seeking to breed violence by violence, these groups have flouted a decision of the United States Supreme Court and an order of the War Department. Their activities are all the more discreditable by reason of the fact that some 17,600 Japanese-Americans are now serving with our armed forces. Such units as the 100th Infantry Battalion, made up entirely of enlisted Japanese-Americans, and the 442nd Infantry Battalion, have outstanding records of gallantry in action. It should be emphasized, also, that, contrary to widespread rumors, no acts of sabotage occurred in Hawaii on December 7, 1941, and no Japanese-American has been convicted of either sabotage or espionage on the mainland or in Hawaii since the war. That continued attacks should be made on the rights of this minority, despite their record of loyalty and good conduct, merely indicates the danger of a general nation-wide antiminority campaign in the postwar period.

What America must realize, to quote from a recent statement by John Collier, is that

wherever race persecution is tolerated, it fattens by what it feeds on. Either it must be suppressed or it will go on breeding violence by violence, undermining the foundations of free society. The suppression of inter-racial persecution, therefore, goes far beyond mere humanitarian sentiment. It is a condition to the stability and the very existence of free societies within a free world order. Freedom and peace cannot be built on oppression. "By freeing the slave," said Lincoln, with profound insight, "we assure freedom to the free." Democracy cannot exist "half slave and half free." In order to survive, it must advance until it is universal within and between nations. Democracy in race relations; democracy in the relations between nations now dominant and races now subject and dependent; democracy toward and within racial minorities in the United States and in all nations—such democracy is an imperative condition to lasting peace after this Second World War. Unless it is achieved, the Third World War is inevitable.

Part Two

How We Were Governed

I. THE PRESIDENCY

by JONATHAN DANIELS

JONATHAN DANIELS (*age 43*) *went to Washington in February, 1942, as Assistant Director of
the Office of Civilian Defense. In March, 1943,
he was appointed Administrative Assistant to
the President. In 1945 he was named secretary
to the President in charge of press relations.
In this capacity he released such stories as the
death of President Roosevelt, the accession
of President Truman, and the announcement
of victory in Europe. He has now returned to
Raleigh, North Carolina, and to his former
work of writing articles and books.*

HISTORY, being written generally by men with neat minds, will
undoubtedly divide the twelve years of Franklin D. Roosevelt
into the two periods of war and peace—war and reform. In a
sens. he himself once so divided it ih one of the lighthearted
para' les in which he liked to dress serious concerns.

He spoke of two entirely different gentlemen: Old Doc New
Deal and Dr. Win-the-War. And somehow, as he described them,
Doc New Deal seemed an old-time practitioner who came with
his bags and his goodness to the bedside. Dr. Win-the-War
seemed a precise scientific gentleman to be seen by appointment
only in the midst of the finest scientific apparatus, efficient undoubtedly but a colder individual expecting a much bigger fee—
and getting it.

I doubt that there were any such different doctors. Indeed, I
believe that there was only one doctor, only one disease, and that
in the whole twelve years the one remedy steadily applied was a

determination to make democracy effective for the security and in
the defense of free men. It worked—it worked, indeed, to an almost scientific demonstration that there are no limits to the
powers and the possibilities of democracy gallantly led and
confidently following.

Certainly only a person precise to the point of insanity would
date the war service of President Roosevelt from 1:47 P.M. EWT,
December 7, 1941. Then he received the first news almost accidentally, in a picked up message of first alarm to naval personnel
in Hawaiian waters, that the Japs were bombing Pearl Harbor.
No sensible person had talked with a true sense of security in
peace since Hitler marched into Poland in late August, 1939. A
better birthdate for war in the world might be the time in 1931
when the Japs moved into Manchuria. It was a strange item in
history that Hitler, who believed in stars, came into power just
five weeks before Franklin Roosevelt and on Franklin Roosevelt's
birthday. The stars may not have been fixed, but tragedy and
destiny already had fallen into shape for mankind.

Twelve years later it somehow seems more than a coincidence
that Roosevelt died in April as Lincoln died. The lilacs of the
Lincoln legend were in bloom again. When Lincoln fell, Lee had
surrendered, but a mourning nation had to wait eleven days beyond his death before Johnston ended his fighting with Sherman.
Roosevelt saw the Americans across the Rhine. All that remained
for victory in Europe were the signed and dated documents of
the "unconditional surrender" he had demanded. The proclama-
tion of victory which his successor read on May 8, 1945, had already been written before Roosevelt died.

American carriers, built under Roosevelt's devoted direction of
the Navy, had stood in the roadsteads less than fifty miles off
Tokyo and sent their planes with implacably increasing destruction upon the Japs. Beyond the recaptured Philippines, Iwo Jima
had fallen. Okinawa had been invaded. The atomic bombs, on
which he risked billions, were already growing from theory to
deadly reality for Hiroshima and Nagasaki. He held, long before

he died, the dependable assurance that the Russians would swing their great land forces against the Japs when the time came for final irresistible pressure upon them. In the rubble of Berlin, Adolf Hitler survived. But he survived only as the malefactor condemned by the American who paralleled his period and prevented by effective democratic leadership his purposes against human freedom.

It was a triumphant time for a great man to die. And his death gave a day upon which Americans could not only measure the growing dimensions and meaning of their victory, but also the world's debt and devotion to the man. It was clear, before the bugles sounded last inside the hemlock hedges at Hyde Park, that he was not merely a great man dead but that he stood already as the symbol of the American destiny in his time.

Better than any other man he understood that destiny. He was no solemn statesman in a plug hat. He had been wearing a pullover sweater when he began his confident direction of the war as Commander-in-Chief on Pearl Harbor Sunday. Afterwards, war workers and soldiers, sailors and statesmen saw him in a flannel shirt, old hat, and casually knotted bow tie. He was a shirt-sleeves man in an informal America and he spoke its language to its understanding in great matters and small. As no other man in his time, he could speak to the American confidence always underlying American fears. And because he believed in the dignity of the American, he was never afraid to ask or expect America's courage.

He was speaking of war in the world and democracy at home, as two inseparable parts of his work and his time, in 1936, at Philadelphia when he declared that this generation of Americans had a rendezvous with destiny. It was no casual utterance. Made in an already darkening peace then when the validity of democracy was questioned at home and abroad, he repeated it in January, 1939, when the imminence of war was obvious to all but the most blind of those Americans who sought to exorcise war by denying its danger.

"Once I prophesied," he told the Congress, "that this generation of Americans had a rendezvous with destiny. That prophecy
comes true. To us much is given; more is expected.

"This generation will 'nobly save or meanly lose the last best
hope of earth.'"

When he died the chance of salvation was certain, but certain
only because of the great burdens he had seemed almost gaily to
bear until the day he died under the long weariness of his load.

It is difficult to remember any great American who was so be-
labored in his lifetime and so beloved by so many at the same
time. He did not come to the storm of war from a cloudless
America. The fighting at home continued straight up to the war—
and beyond. But it was the same fighting for Roosevelt. He believed that democracy must be effective to survive. It was a consistency which seemed incomprehensible to Western Senators
who had supported his reforms in the domestic democracy but
turned from him in anger to isolation. It seemed equally inconsistent to Southern Senators who had fought his reforms at home
but stood with him for the collective security of the democracies
in the world. But the people understood the prudent and auda-
cious consistency of the man whom the same enemies would have
made a headlong warmonger in 1940 and a man who had failed
to move fast enough early enough when as new heroes of hindsight they tried to attack him in 1944.

It was no accident that he chose the occasion of the dedication
of a bridge, one of the public works built by his administration
for the peaceful convenience of a creative people, for his first
clear, vigorous warning to both Americans and the dictators. In
that famous Quarantine Speech in Chicago on October 5, 1937,
he did not mention Old Doc New Deal or Dr. Win-the-War but
he did use the metaphor of medicine when he spoke of the plague
of international lawlessness already apparent in the world. It did
not please the dictators. Some Americans did not like it. But he
made clear his warning that if the disease were permitted to
spread, "let no one imagine that America would escape."

He understood that warning as the man first responsible for its meaning in America. He was grim as he spoke it—grim as he could be with his great shoulders forward, his eyes hard blue. He looked young still. He was fifty-five in vigorous middle life, son of a mother still living at eighty-two and a father who had lived to be seventy-one. The paralysis which had steeled his mind seemed to have strengthened his body also. He seemed even a bigger man above his useless legs.

He had reason to be confident. The year before he had received the greatest vote any President had ever received in a contested election. Washington and Monroe had been elected without opposition, but in a bitter contest he had received the electoral votes of all the states save two. No President had ever come to the White House in the midst of such domestic crisis as he did, save only Lincoln. In four years he had given America long pent-up and long blindly resisted social and economic safeguards essential to the vitality of its democracy. True enough, he had been halted in some of his plans; not every reform had worked perfectly, but he had won the overwhelming confidence of people who wanted democracy to work. There were more fights to make for them. Then, at fifty-five, in the fullness of his powers and the powers of America for its people, he knew that forces grew in ruthlessness—and determined ruthlessness—whose patent purpose was to see democracy destroyed.

It is a very easy thing to note now that the war began less than two years later. It is less easy to remember those ghostly symbols of world security, the Maginot Line, the French Army, the strange powers attributed to and expected from the British Fleet. In terms of the crackpots who have persisted, it is not easy to recall the respectability of rigid isolationism in the years before the war—and after it before Pearl Harbor. Not many people remember that in the summer before Hitler marched into Poland the Congress declined to modify the Neutrality Act of 1935 which bound the President's hands and made it impossible for American industrial power to stand with the French Army and the British

Fleet as potentials against German aggression. The late Senator Borah, who did not live to see the full content of his magnificent misinformation, told the President and Secretary Hull directly that he had more confidence in his information than theirs about the possibility of war. His information, at the time when Hitler must have been making the last arrangements for the movement into Poland, was that there wasn't going to be any war.

The purpose of the man in the White House is clear in the record. He hoped for peace for America but he did not mean that America should idly allow the dictatorships to destroy the democracies. When war came he made a point of describing the peculiar quality of our neutrality by his pointed statement that "even a neutral has a right to take account of facts. Even a neutral cannot be asked to close his mind or his conscience." He moved immediately—and successfully this time—to secure such change in the Neutrality Act as would make it possible for American industry to supply French and British fighting forces. It was "cash and carry" then but only the Allies could come and get it.

There was not a moment after Hitler moved when American antagonism to his armies was not clear. Some historians given to labels have called America's part before Pearl Harbor America's "soft" war. After the fall of France it became quickly tougher in presidential utterance as well as presidential act. The whole surplus store of American arms went by fast freighters to a Britain left unarmed after Dunkirk. By September the President had found a way to let Britain have fifty destroyers in a deal for bases in this hemisphere. Even then, war production in the United States was growing to the possibility of the President's invention of the great American war weapon of Lend-Lease.

In September also—and in the midst of a national election—he secured the Selective Training and Service Act providing the first draft of men in peacetime in American history. In peacetime, too, he secured the right to seize industrial plants not co-operating on defense orders. Camps grew, ships rose on the ways, new American fleets took the seas. Production began to answer the incredulity that had greeted the President's goal of 50,000 planes. In the archives in Washington there are memoranda bearing the big scrawl of approval and injunction, "Work Fast—FDR."

During those months, when despite the change in the world many isolationists were still loud in the land, the President heard a story which he liked. Down near Warm Springs a very old man had told it to him. In the Civil War he had had strong convictions against fighting. He stood bravely by them while the war surged in Virginia. Then Sherman came toward Georgia. He came closer and closer, and the nearer he came the less certain the man was in his mind. Finally there came a time when he flung down his old convictions and picked up his gun. It was too late then, of course. And for sixty years or more the old man had been puzzled.

"I haven't figured it out exactly right yet whether I went to fighting too late or too soon."

Fortunately, the Japanese solved that problem for America. And solved it on a Sunday afternoon while the President, relaxing for a little in the oval study at the White House and nursing the sinuses that plagued him all his life, was working at his stamp book. Harry Hopkins was with him. Before he went late to bed almost every major participant in the "defense" effort had been with him on the first day of war. The attack, which had come under the mask of negotiations still under way in Washington when the bombs dropped, was surprise and naval disaster but it found Washington in full stride of preparation for the greatest war ever undertaken.

That day the Commander-in-Chief commanded in person. In his oval study he gave orders like a commander on the bridge of a ship. One who watched him work has spoken of his "genius in disorder" and said that his command on that crowded seventh of December was to be compared only with his confident leadership on his first days in the White House when the national economy seemed tottering. The crowds which had heard the news gathered outside the White House fence. The cabinet members, the generals, and the admirals came in. They found a leadership which did not relax while he lived.

Nobody knows yet how to count or measure such a war. The greatest war we had ever fought before was concerned with only a single European land front and the Atlantic Ocean. Roosevelt's leadership in this war concerned men on every continent and every sea. In what we had called the World War before we were engaged for only nineteen months, and only for a part of that time were large American forces engaged. This war began with men dying, and the fighting had gone on for three years and five months when Roosevelt died.

In this war Lend-Lease to our allies alone cost more in dollars than our total spending before. That whole first World War cost thirty-six billion dollars. Since June 1, 1940, we have spent eight times that much. For this war American industrial production is more than three times as great as in 1918, and nearly half of the total national production has been for war purposes, a proportion twice as great as that in the peak year of the last war. We added this time twenty billion dollars in new manufacturing facilities—seven times as much as in the first World War. The arsenal of democracy was working as the arsenal of destruction.

Twelve million men and women were in the armed forces— three times the total before.

All this production and power and treasure was to be under the direction of the one man who received the news of war in his study that Sunday afternoon. He took the direction and held it. A President of the United States can delegate jobs but not responsibility. When war came the military and naval leadership that was to fight the war was, in effect, already fighting it. The President seemed to have less luck with his choices in production administration but no lack of luck in production itself.

He called tough old Admiral William D. Leahy to the White House as his personal chief of staff and through him kept in close touch with both the Joint (U. S.) Chiefs of Staff and the Combined (Anglo-American) Chiefs of Staff. On the ground floor of the White House a specially guarded and staffed Map Room was set up where messages were received about the progress of our forces everywhere. On the maps he watched the war of men and supplies, of strategy and logistics, of heroism and death and victory.

It was a dark story at first—Guam and Wake and Midway and Bataan. Then slowly the men and production and ships and planes which were his concern became his concern also in Coral Sea, Midway again, Komondorski Straits, Guadalcanal, Attu, Kiska, Bougainville, Tarawa, Kwajalein, Eniwetok, Hollandia, Saipan, Guam again, the Palaus and Leyte, on toward Japan. The first great secret enterprise came at last to other maps: Casablanca, Oran, Algiers, Tunis, Kasserine Pass, and on to Gela, Salerno, Messina, bloody Anzio, tough Cassino, to Rome. Rome somehow seemed the signal for the greatest secret and toughest job of all, Normandy. The President had been sick, but he was gay that June day.

"What are you fellows grinning about?" he wanted to know, grinning wide and happy himself.

Within five months the Americans alone sent more fighting men to France—men fully equipped—than the entire expeditionary force of the last war. And yet within the same period at the other side of the world we landed a force sufficient to ensure the liberation of the Philippines. We were clearly already on the victory road.

We can be as impressed as our enemies should be by the Navy built under Roosevelt's direction, a Navy greater than the combined navies of all our allies and enemies. No greater Army ever marched under the American flag—or in equipment and quality under any other. The air power we built broke Germany and shattered Japan. These are the parts of victory certainly but only a part of the evidence of leadership which Roosevelt provided in this war. In the faith he created among the three great Allies and all the United Nations, he was a force for victory in himself.

A whole decade before he met the monolithic Stalin in Teheran, he had extended the first hand of recognition to the almost pariah Russians in 1933. Our full safety and solidarity in the Western Hemisphere grew straight from the Good Neighbor policy and its observance which proved not merely to the Americas but also to the world our international good intentions. Roosevelt's ardent and early aid to Britain made the simplest Briton as well as its first war statesman regard him as friend. In a whole world in trouble he seemed the man men everywhere believed they could trust.

Such faith is not to be counted in terms of divisions or battleships. It meant much at home in terms of production. He was a man as well as a commander to our fighting men. In America his train moved to war plants and military camps. His friendship for Churchill, formally begun on the foggy seas of the Newfoundland bight where they bound their purpose to freedom in the Atlantic Charter, was a good affection, warmed by many meetings. The President was not bothered by Churchill's occasional intellectual arrogance. He was not unduly impressed on a visit to his Maryland hideaway when Churchill recited the whole of *Barbara Frietchie* and then turned in casual erudition to the *Nonsense* verse of Edward Lear. He was sometimes amused by Churchill's Tory fears. I had a feeling as he talked of him that he liked to bait him a little, even to tease him in the deadpan presence of Stalin, who, he discovered, could laugh. The President had, I am sure, a deep respect for Stalin. I remember once his speaking of a plan for the solution of some problem he had outlined to the Marshal. He mimicked Stalin's brief, decisive thoughtfulness.

"I had not thought of it," he quoted the Marshal as saying. "It is a good idea. I will sign."

And that was that. It was very different with Churchill at that time. Describing him and imitating him, the President put his hands up defensively.

"Churchill is acting now as if he is always afraid of getting hit."

The nature of the differences of the Marshal and the Prime Minister placed Roosevelt between them. In the deepest sense he had the trust of both. It was not accident that at Yalta by general consent he served as the chairman of the last great conference of his life.

There can have been few greater moments in history than that time at Yalta. Victory in Europe was clearly before them. They reached decisions which the happiness of the world cannot allow to disintegrate. There was no indication of any coming disagreements then. It was a great time—and a happy one as well.

But it was not a happy voyage home. Before the Cruiser *Quincy* turned toward home, they knew that "Pa" Watson was dying. General Edwin Watson was a good deal more than the President's Secretary and Military Aide. He was an arm upon whom the President literally leaned when he undertook to walk in his steel braces. More than anybody else, perhaps, he was the President's "tonic." It was his job to protect the President from overlong and overtalkative appointments. It was his gift and grace that he had warmth and charm and great good laughter. Also, he loved the President very much. And somewhere between Gibraltar and the Azores he died—of a cerebral hemorrhage.

The President came home to the piled mass of the details of his leadership, which included more work and worry than exaltation. There was nothing dramatically new about any of it. His report on Yalta was received with acclaim. But there were—when were there not?—complaints on the home front. It was true, as it had been from the beginning of the war, that bickering continued about food (though the average American was better fed than at any time before in peace or war), about OPA (though price controls had protected Americans in this war as they had never been protected in any war before), about an endless variety of men and measures and details.

There was politics still. Politics had never abated for one moment. When it was worst it pretended to a greater patriotism than the President's. Fortunately, sometimes it amused him. His favorite story in the second tough winter of the war was about the soldier crying as he was about to leave Guadalcanal because he hadn't killed a Jap. A sympathetic colonel told him that if he would go out and shout, "To hell with the Emperor," a Jap would jump out and he could shoot him. Later, however, the colonel found the soldier crying still.

"What happened?" the colonel wanted to know.

"I did what you said," the soldier reported, "but the Jap jumped up hollering, 'Ruzvelt a son-a-beetz!' I couldn't shoot him, I'm a Republican, too."

It was the sort of story that made him throw his head back in laughter. Indeed, nothing seemed as eternal about him as his full-bodied laughter. It was one of the qualities which made him seem almost a man designed by nature to survive the strain of the American Presidency in such a war as this. His gaiety was like Lincoln's humor—the releasing levity of a deeply serious man. Certainly as he grew older and more weary, he was not the debonair Roosevelt of the first crowded days in the White House. But he seemed in conversation still the self-confident, laughing, sometimes outrageous Roosevelt who used humor as a tool and a weapon and a release. It was not the humor of an easygoing man. It could arm indignation, as he showed a year before he died in his famous speech to the teamsters. Humor was a part of his famous characteristic of reducing the most serious things to simplicity: Lend-Lease was a garden hose lent to a neighbor whose house was on fire. Such an enterprise as the United Nations could at the same time be not only close to his heart but close also to his risibilities.

He loved to tell the story of the origin of its name during Churchill's first swift visit to Washington after Pearl Harbor. They had struggled over combinations of fine words for a name for their league of belligerents. None of them seemed satisfactory. "United Nations" came to F. D. R. at night. Next morning he rolled into Churchill's bedroom. The Prime Minister was bathing. The President waited and Churchill came out of the bathroom without a stitch of clothing on.

"He looked like a fat cherub," the President recalled.

But that morning he said, "Winston, I have found the name, 'United Nations.'"

The naked Churchill considered it solemnly, and gave it his approval. Only after he had indicated his agreement did he seem to become aware of his nakedness.

"Later," said the President, "he told the King about it: 'Your Majesty, you are the only King of England whose Prime Minister has been received by the Chief of a State while completely nude.'"

Some people with neat little minds sometimes found the easy-ranging mind of Roosevelt disorderly. They were shocked by his humorous memories of solemn occasions. It could, of course, be disconcerting to call about a job and spend your time talking stamps, or the venereal disease rate in Liberia, or a plan for the reforestation of the shores of the Persian Gulf. Conversation could be a defense with him as laughter was. But he could in the first years of the war turn easily to diversion for its own sake.

Much will be written about his collections of books, stamps, prints. His greatest collecting was not tangible: Everywhere he went—Casablanca, Teheran, Yalta even—he collected an amazing amount of unessential but lively details about life and people. His interest in geography was never limited to maps. He even collected such evanescent things as birdcalls. I know that during the earliest and most jittery days of the war he disturbed the Secret Service detail by a strange postmidnight sortie. His companions were some learned ornithologists who had come to join him in a contest as to which of them could identify the greatest number of night sounds made by Dutchess County birds. He was proud of his long-standing membership in the American Ornithologists Union but enjoyed claiming that that membership had greatly befuddled investigators of the Dies Committee when they were looking for left-wing organizations. "They couldn't tell," he said, "whether it was A. F. of L. or C.I.O."

He collected also, or invented—for private conversation and for his speaking to millions—parables to show his problems and make his points. And there was the proverb he brought back from Casablanca for those New Dealers, old friends and supporters, who had grown more worried as the war went on. They became particularly worried about American dealings in the conquest of North Africa with the Vichy French. Many of them had felt that the war had pulled him away from his progressive policies. They made wry jokes about the reactionaries he permitted in his departments. I think he had been waiting a long time to give them his precise answer.

The President had faith in people as well as affection for them, but he was a realist about people, also. Sometimes he was too kind to people upon whose affection and loyalty he knew he could depend even though their abilities were limited. Also, he used some people who were simple enough to think they were using him. He did not feel called upon to explain himself to his friends. He himself was confident of his goals. In peace and in war he used some strange people for their accomplishment. He understood that he could not always attain his ends by plunging straight ahead. His genius for timing rarely failed him. But he also knew that he never lost sight of his destination. He attributed the proverb which he brought back from Casablanca to one of the Balkan countries, but it always sounded pure Roosevelt to me. I remember his telling it first to a group of newspapermen:

"In time of trouble, my children, it is given to you that you may go with the devil as far as the bridge."

He never would have asked for patience directly, but the request was there. He had a war to fight. His whole life was bound up in determination to end it victoriously and as swiftly as possible. Nothing seemed to him so important as winning it with the least loss of American lives and in such a way as to assure the continuance of democracy in security for all Americans. Somehow nobody ever seemed to remember that he had four boys in that war—none of them hidden in safety zones. For them, for other Americans, for himself victory meant making democracy work for men, women, and children.

It is important to remember that the steps he took in building power for war were accompanied all the way by the clearest insistence upon the purpose of the war as the protection and fulfillment of the possibilities of democracy. That insistence was the essence of the Four Freedoms attached to the Lend-Lease proposal of 1941. The same essential freedoms were fixed in the fighting purposes of Britain and America in the Atlantic Charter in 1941. In 1944 he advanced from freedoms to rights in the economic bill of rights which he embodied in his January message to Congress on the state of the union. He repeated that bill of rights in his speech at Soldier's Field at Chicago in October as pledge with regard to his plans and his purpose for the future. It is worth remembering now:

The right to a useful and remunerative job in the industries, or shops, or raims, or mines of the Nation;

The right to earn enough to provide adequate food and clothing and recreation;

The right of every farmer to raise and sell his products at a return which will give him and his family a decent living;

The right of every businessman, large and small, to trade in an atmosphere of freedom from unfair competition and domination by monopolies at home and abroad;

The right of every family to a decent home;

The right to adequate medical care and the opportunity to achieve and enjoy good health;

The right to adequate protection from the economic fears of old age, sickness, accident, and unemployment;

The right to a good education.

"All these rights," the President said, "spell security. And after this war is won we must be prepared to move forward, in the implementation of these rights, to new goals of human happiness and well-being."

He understood the opposition to such ideals as well as to the ideals of the Atlantic Charter. He knew better than most Americans that there were men who regarded the war as a new phase, a new turning, to the right away from the program he and the great mass of Americans, who had four times elected him, had worked out together.

Just a week before he died he wrote again his determination and his faith to an old political friend who was serving in an advisory capacity on plans for the reconversion of a war-making America to a victorious America moving again toward "new goals of happiness and well-being."

He wrote:

... I am sure that Americans who have done so much in the winning of the war have no doubt that we can give victory the rich meaning of full employment in the United States and of assistance to other nations in their reconstruction. Victory, without the use for abundance of the powers we have developed in production for war, would be, indeed, a hollow victory. We must plan security and abundance together. Such a stronger American economy will be essential to carry out the responsibilities that lie in plans made at Bretton Woods, Hot Springs, and Dumbarton Oaks. Similarly, abundance at home depends upon organization for order and security in the world.

He was tired then, but not changed. He understood the American destiny of which he had been both the prophet and the leader. It had not altered. Treasure had been spent for it; power had been made for it; men had died for it. All that had not been done to open a back door into the past for an American retreat beyond victory.

Better than anybody else he knew how weary he was, how suddenly, quickly the war had made him old. He could see the wavering signature where so recently the bold scrawl had been. He was not fooled. But others were—some who loved him most. The spark of humor and liveliness never left his face, and somehow, I think, that misled his friends, as people who saw only the photographed image were not misled.

Well, perhaps he died right for history. We can say that easily remembering the abortive tragedy of Wilson, who had no historic right to live after he was stricken at Wichita. He not only failed to get peace; he lingered in its dissolution. Somehow there seems no tragedy now about Lincoln's dying. He departed in fitness with victory. But we forget much about Lincoln: we remember the funeral train and Walt Whitman's lilacs and forget that death interrupted his devotion to freedom for people. And peace and people made the joint heritage Roosevelt left us. He knew that peace and freedom are inseparable and that there can be no enduring peace except upon a decent earth.

We shall have to wait to know his full greatness—and our own.

Harry S. Truman, who came down from the Capitol late that April afternoon to succeed Franklin Roosevelt as President, seemed almost miraculously fitted to hold the unity of all Americans in that hour of difficult transition. Somehow he seemed, in no weak way, all things to all men. Liberals counted on his voting record; conservatives expected from him a new sympathy. Both respected his excellent work as chairman of the vigilant Truman Committee of the Senate. All Americans knew they could count on the vigor of his war leadership to the victory Roosevelt had already assured and toward the enduring peace Roosevelt had steadily sought.

Truman himself accepted his task with a demonstration of humility and devotion which brought him response and support from the people. He gave to his colleagues in the Congress a reassuring sense of their importance, which sometimes they had lacked under Roosevelt's dominating executive leadership. The war was won without misstep. The beginnings of world security were made with almost complete unanimity in the Senate's ratification of the United Nations Charter.

Some Americans expressed a sense of relief from the national strain of greatness in the White House. Truman seemed an ordinary American when Americans hoped again for normal times. But great problems remained. No man had come to a harder job in the American Presidency, shadowed by greatness and given tasks under which even greatness might have faltered, since Andrew Johnson. There were other parallels in the fortunes of the tailor who followed Lincoln and the haberdasher who came after Roosevelt.

One of the most forgotten of them is the national popularity which Johnson enjoyed for months after Lincoln's death. Truman has characteristics of graciousness and tact which Johnson lacked. But Truman has tasks, too, hardly less difficult and certainly not less emotional than those which almost harried Johnson from the White House.

Truman came to the White House free of all the antagonisms Roosevelt had acquired in twelve years in the Presidency. Those antagonisms would undoubtedly have attended efforts Roosevelt might have made in dealing with the problems Truman must face. But most of them are implicit in the Presidency itself. Truman can count upon the proper and vigorous opposition of the Republicans in the American two-party system in the years ahead. The Democratic party, which he leads, is no more homogeneous now than it was while Roosevelt lived. It is still composed of Negroes and Bilbos, labor baiters and labor leaders, Northern liberals and Southern reactionaries, Henry Wallace and Harry Byrd.

The country, emerging from its greatest war, is not less complex than its politics.

The one certain thing, as the war ended and the peace began, was that Harry Truman, of Missouri, had succeeded not only to the Presidency but to the toughest job on earth.

II. THE CONGRESS

by *THOMAS L. STOKES*

THOMAS L. STOKES (*age 47*) *has been a Washington correspondent for twenty-four years. His column, syndicated by United Features, appears in one hundred twenty-seven papers. In 1938 he won the Pulitzer Prize for reporting for a series of articles exposing political exploitation of the WPA in the 1938 Kentucky primary election.*

VERY likely you did not pay a great deal of attention to Congress before you went away, that is, most of you. Most people don't, normally. Certainly you had little time, even if so inclined, to think much about Congress where you have been in these months and years immediately back of you.

Yet Congress is very much a part of the life to which you return. While you were gone Congress worked steadily with little surcease. It has had its influence in shaping the world in which you are now beginning to live again, for it has concerned itself with that, too, while it was doing all the many necessary things to adjust the national economy to war and to carry on that war. War and peace policies are intermingled because of the very nature of the gigantic conflict which finally drew every citizen into its whirling vortex, either at home or abroad. They react on one another. The pattern designed for war undoubtedly will carry over, in some of its aspects, to the pattern of our national economy for peace.

Certainly the far-reaching effects of an over-all war will be manifest in all our lives for a long time to come, as will the modes of thinking we have followed during the hard and bitter days, and some of the regulations imposed to help us carry on war will continue for a time in the transition back to peaceful living until we can readjust ourselves.

Congress has had an important part in all of this and will continue to do so through its influence on policy, in either a positive or a negative way. It may be helpful, then, to run over again the reel with which we who stayed at home are fairly familiar, but which you missed, in order to get some idea of the influences at work among those men and women drawn from all sections of the country, representing all sorts of diverse interests, and, all together, in Congress assembled, supposed to represent all of us.

It would be well for all of us, too, to discard the general conception of Congress as a body of men away off in Washington going through motions, sometimes strange, that seem to have little interest for us or little to do with our lives, a body that is depicted too often in flashy headlines detailing the idiosyncrasies of some individual or other there, or some unimportant quarrel over trivialities or clash of personalities, and too infrequently about the real meaning of what goes on.

It would be wise, too, to lay aside our conception of the stock Congressman, a freakish caricature of a man with bushy locks and a big belly wrapped in a fancy vest, a man of many words and gestures and a terribly inflated ego—though there are still some of those—and think of him as a human being a good deal like the rest of us, a person there to serve us. He may serve us better if we will only insist that he do that.

For there are critical days ahead in a strange and confused world.

Congress was a much sobered body for a time after Pearl Harbor. It finally had been stirred, in the months before, to begin to prepare for our probable entry into the war, but it did not go about this too wholeheartedly in spite of the constant prodding of President Roosevelt and other intuitive people in government and outside of government. It provided for Lend-Lease to those nations which later became our allies only after some wrangling and after pressure by President Roosevelt and Secretary of State

Hull and Wendell L. Willkie. It almost made a costly and tragic mistake in military preparedness. Only by a single vote was extension of the draft act beyond its first year saved in the House, with the bulk of Republicans in opposition.

But that was all before that sudden Jap attack from the Sunday morning skies. Congress settled down then and went speedily about the necessary business of getting ready for what it woke up gradually to discover probably would be our most trying ordeal as a nation. Without stint and without partisanship it began to vote the essential billions for this greatest of all wars, and it continued to vote them, without stint and without partisanship.

There were many things necessary to prepare the civilian for the strains and sacrifices of total war and to protect him, as far as possible, from those who would seize a war emergency to exploit him. It was necessary, too, to protect him from himself in some ways. So Congress set up the Office of Price Administration, the OPA, to fix prices as a guard against inflation and to ration food and other things so that everybody would have an equal opportunity to share in the restricted supply. It authorized the President to fix wages and salaries as another hedge against inflation. It passed a ten-billion-dollar tax bill as a starter to pay the exorbitant costs of war, as well as to sop up some of the excess cash as another inflation preventive, the first of three tax measures during the war. It voted the President still more extraordinary powers to act in prosecution of the war without recourse to Congress for specific authority. It did a multitude of other things in those early, hectic, fearful days, such as creation of the Office of Civilian Defense to train citizens in precautionary measures for possible air raids, and even provided bombing insurance against possible damage by air raids.

The American people were regimented as never before, and all their gripes and resistances reacted in Congress to provoke constant controversy and ferment, with a clash of interests among businessmen and farmers and labor and plain citizens belonging to no particular group, and with clashes among groups within these groups. Through all this ran a basic conflict, the continual conflict in our country between conservatism and progressivism, to define it very broadly, but now more sharp and clear because of its intensification by President Roosevelt's New Deal.

This is most important in any consideration of Congress while you were gone, and especially for your consideration, as it is important from now on. It is worth while to see in what ways it worked itself out, and with what result, while you were gone.

In the first place, it can be pointed out that Congress, as a body, continually kept its composite mind separated into two fairly distinct compartments.

As to the war, it did everything asked for its promotion in the way of voting money and setting up and supplying the various special agencies needed and providing you as soldiers, sailors, and marines with what you required to fight and live as comfortably as is possible in modern combat. In connection with the war Congress performed a valuable service, too, in spying out weaknesses and inadequacies in the war program through numerous investigating committees, including the one once directed by then Senator Harry Truman. It ferreted out waste in time and methods and money and energy, exposed shortages and inadequate materials and equipment, and tracked down some of the profiteers and gougers on war contracts. We had our quota of the last. Senator Truman's theory was that Congress should investigate while the war was going on instead of waiting until afterward, as in the last war. This turned out to be wise. For the Truman Committee contributed much by helping to channel the war program and to check graft and corruption, as did special House Military and Naval Investigating committees.

On the other hand, and at the same time, Congress kept a close watch on the domestic economy and its direction, both of itself and as it was affected by the regimentation of war. This involved policies that had to do with our own everyday lives, then and hereafter.

Here was the irrepressible conflict. Broadly, on basic issues, it divided Congress into conservative and progressive camps. This conflict is not new, as has been said, and, as has also been said, it was intensified by the New Deal—by the fervent loyalties on the one side and the bitter antagonisms on the other aroused in the prewar years by the New Deal, its program, and its chief figure.

The conservatives continually raised the alarm that the New Deal was moving the country toward a centralized, planned economy. They sought to ease controls of various sorts—price-fixing, rationing, and the like—carrying on continued resistance to these established restrictions and vigorously opposing the imposing of others. As the war neared its end, they waged a constant campaign to shake off war controls and others prescribed earlier wherever opportunity offered. They feared that the war might be used to fasten a planned economy on the United States so tightly that it could never be shaken loose.

New Dealers are frankly for more planning in government. Only in this way, they argued and still argue, can the complex machine civilization of today be directed properly to function so that everybody will have a job. They sought more government assistance in all directions, including unemployment benefits and social security to cushion any shocks in reconversion from war to peace and to meet possible demands from future depressions, as well as public housing, expansion of public ownership and control of public utilities, federal health and medical programs, among others.

The New Dealers and milder progressives had their heyday in the early years of the New Deal, writing into fundamental law that great body of reforms which has, for the most part, withstood assault. But their foes in Congress began to increase numerically and proportionately to put more vigor into their attack well before the war. In 1938, only two years after the tumultuous 1936 election in which President Roosevelt swept to victory with all but two states, Maine and Vermont, a reaction exhibited itself in the congressional elections. Republicans picked up 80 seats in the

House and, for the first time since the New Deal came into power, began to approach the pretensions again of a major party, with 169 seats in the House compared with 262 for the Democrats. In the Senate Republicans had but 17 members, an innocuous corporal's guard. They picked up six seats in the 1938 election to present a slightly more respectable front there. In President Roosevelt's decisive defeat of Wendell Willkie in 1940 Republicans backslid a bit in the House, with a loss of seven seats. They picked up five more in the Senate.

But, in 1942, even though the country was in the midst of war, Republicans took another spurt. They ran their House membership up to 209. This was nine short of the majority of 218, but it was better than it looked, for the Democrats, who had 222, discovered before long that their majority was really only on paper on vital issues. In the same wartime, mid-term election Republicans gained ten seats in the Senate, to bring their total there to 38. A majority in the Senate is 49.

The election was interpreted to indicate some dissatisfaction with conduct of the war. Republicans had stressed that as an issue, and we were on the defensive all around the world. But there was reflected also, undoubtedly, the discontent with regimentation to which we had not become accustomed. The election served as an outlet for lots of minor grievances in those days before we had found out how minor they really were and in what a big war we were engaged. The election could not, however, be interpreted entirely as previously stated. As in all elections, there were many factors contributing to the result. There were other circumstances which certainly had a part and which must be taken into account, for one reason, because they had an interesting aftermath in bringing a new force—labor—actively into American politics.

For one thing, Democrats always had proved weaker in off-year congressional elections when President Roosevelt's name was not on the ballots, at the head of the ticket, to attract his followers to the polls. There was not the same keen interest. But beyond that there were other factors unfavorable to the Democrats in this particular 1942 election which, in so many ways, turned out to be such an important one for what followed in Congress.

Many persons who normally voted Democratic did not vote that year, beyond the customary falling-off due to Mr. Roosevelt's absence from the ticket. That was because of the migration of hundreds of thousands of workers from their homes into war industry in other states. They had to qualify anew under the laws of those states to which they had moved. This took a certain period of residence. Many did not qualify for this reason and some just didn't bother. There were, too, physical handicaps in voting in that many worked in plants far away from their homes and far away from the polling places and so did not vote.

The Democrats and their labor allies woke up too late to find themselves in an unfortunate, if not precarious, position in Congress, now the center of important battles affecting their interests, as they well knew. The C.I.O., which was loyally behind the President, decided to do something about failure to get the vote organized and out to the polls in the 1942 congressional election. They didn't want to see that happen again. The C.I.O. thereupon created its Political Action Committee (PAC), which developed by the 1944 elections into a really efficient, practical, political organization which deserved most of the credit it got for the re-election of President Roosevelt to a fourth term and the return of more comfortable majorities in the Congress which began to sit in January, 1945. C.I.O. taught its members the elementary lessons in practical politics—in organization of voters, door-to-door canvasses, as well as the value of money in politics and elections. They learned how to levy on their membership at so much a head and saw how quickly many such small contributions can roll up into a nice fat wad for political organizing expenses.

But this was after some damage had been done them in Congress.

For conservatives were in the saddle, and effectively so, during most of the war years, and this had a particular relation to domestic issues in which New Dealers, their progressive satellites, and labor were interested. Even before the 1942 congressional elections the conservative influence was more potent than might appear from a bare list of party divisions. The reaction that occurred in Congress after the 1938 elections had other than strictly Republican sources. Southern conservative Democrats, who had long been irked over invasion of the South by such New Deal reforms as TVA, wage and hour legislation, financial assistance to tenant farmers, and collective bargaining, finally began to break away and join common cause with Republicans in a coalition, first loose and occasional, but eventually fairly well organized. The Southerners, because of their peculiar legislative skill from long experience and because of their key positions through operation of the seniority rule, provided most of the leadership in this coalition. They supplied what came to be called in war agencies of the government "the know-how." They deserted the President, despite his popularity among the rank and file of their people back home, as demonstrated so conclusively in every election since he had entered the White House, and despite all that the New Deal had done for the plain people of the South. But now that they were reinforced in Congress, they did more boldly the bidding of their real masters—the industrial and planter oligarchy of the South. They were comparatively safe against the wrath of the masses in the South, first, because the people could not always find out how they were being betrayed and, second, they were protected by the restricted suffrage through poll taxes and "white primary" laws. They had a select voting constituency loaded in their favor by the so-called "respectable element."

This coalition could outvote the Administration on strictly New Deal domestic issues even before Republican gains in the 1942 elections, and after that it was able to check any really progressive legislation. At the same time it made some gains of its own in tax and postwar legislation which become clearer as the country looks ahead to the problems of transition from a war to a peacetime economy. The coalition took care of its friends.

While New Dealers and their progressive associates could make no headway on fundamental social and economic measures during the war, they were able for the most part to hold the basic structure of reform erected in the early New Deal years. This was chiefly because those reforms had become so well entrenched with the people that the conservatives dared not attack them too openly and boldly for fear of political retaliation, though they have not given up the fight and you may look for its revival if, and when, the opportunity is offered. They have capitalized the natural reaction from reform that always follows such a dazzling era of change as that of the early New Deal. Likewise, they have exploited war weariness. They will overlook no chance here. You can be sure of that. The acceptance of major New Deal reforms by so large a part of the American public was illustrated in a practical way not only by the Republican party's 1944 platform but by espousal of them, with added flourishes, by Governor Dewey of New York, the party's 1944 presidential candidate. His only criticism was that they might be administered better, and that he pledged himself to do if elected, even as Wendell Willkie had done four years before.

But even they are not safe. It does not necessarily take outright repeal to do away with reforms in our system. This is not going to happen. Nothing so crude would be tried. They can be weakened and rendered ineffective, made in fact virtually inoperative, by replacing sincere administrators with persons who are not sympathetic and will nullify them by that sin called "the sin of omission." That is what happened in the twenties to the reforms of the Woodrow Wilson Administration. They went virtually by default because of the type of administrators placed in command in postwar Republican regimes.

The enemies of the New Deal body of reform—and they are clever and resourceful—are more active than ever before. They have tested out the defenses during the war years—a thrust here, a sally there—and in some cases have come off very nicely in minor salients.

Congress has been the proving ground.

A backward look will tell the story.

An influence that was most difficult to combat because it was
somewhat intangible grew out of the very circumstances of a
global war and the vital importance of industrial production to
meet it. This was the infiltration of big business interests, the
open and avowed natural enemies of the New Deal, into the top
civilian war command, into the various special agencies created
to supervise and direct production, and into the War and Navy
Departments themselves. The Administration drafted literally
droves of businessmen, some of them top-flight managers and
operators, from paneled offices of industry all over the country.
This represented President Roosevelt's compromise with big business to get war production.

New Dealers watched this invasion with some trepidation.
Their alarm was somewhat justified. It gave a conservative complexion to government as a whole, since the war was predominant
and overshadowing, and thus affected the formulation of policies
for Congress. It encouraged conservatives in Congress to take advantage of the war situation. They could now cite, for their own
purposes, the desires and opinions of big industrial leaders whose
natural glamour to the public at large was enhanced by their sacrifice in going to Washington to take government positions to
serve their country and help win the war. It was a convenient
cover behind which to operate.

This was reflected, for instance, in the suspension of a number
of big antitrust suits for the duration of the war. It was argued by
leaders in the War Production Board and in the War and Navy
Departments that prosecution of antitrust suits was interfering
with war production because it required the time of top officials
of these companies in the courts. This was a flimsy argument, as
was demonstrated very easily by Thurman Arnold, brilliant and
energetic head of the Justice Department's antitrust division. But
it was all that conservatives in Congress needed. They brought
forward a bill permitting postponement of antitrust suits on rec-

ommendation of the head of the War Production Board. Progressives in Congress finally were able to attach a condition that such postponement must be approved by the Attorney General. It was clear, however, that "antitrust" was to become a less meaningful phrase thereafter. Thurman Arnold, who had directed such an effective attack on business and labor restraint as well as against contracts in international cartels that were impeding our war program, discovered that his hands were tied. He gave up in disgust and accepted a federal judgeship in Washington.

Insurance, one of the nation's biggest and most powerful businesses, broke through the defenses for a partial gain. Its opportunity developed from a suit the Justice Department had brought against a host of fire insurance companies in the Southeast for alleged combination to fix rates. The government lost in the lowest federal court and appealed directly to the Supreme Court. All insurance companies became anxious and very active. They claimed they had been exempted by a seventy-five-year-old Supreme Court decision from prosecution under federal laws, since the court had held in that dim, distant past that their regulation was a function of the states. Immediately they sought relief from Congress. Companion and identic bills which would exempt them by act of Congress from antitrust prosecution were introduced in the Senate by Senator Josiah W. Bailey of North Carolina, one of the Southern conservative leaders, and in the House by Representatives Clarence E. Hancock of New York, a Republican, and Francis E. Walter of Pennsylvania, a Democrat, the latter jointly sponsored. The old cry "states' rights" was raised and the battle was on. The goal was to get the bill enacted before the Supreme Court rendered its decision. The House passed the bill, but alert Senator Joseph C. O'Mahoney of Wyoming, a Democrat, a strong champion of the antitrust laws, held it up in the Senate for an investigation of fire insurance and fire insurance rates, with the assistance of the Justice Department. He delayed the measure for weeks, meanwhile laying facts about the insurance business before the public. The insurance companies organized an imposing lobby. The Supreme Court, in a four-to-three decision, upheld the right of prosecution under federal antitrust statutes. Eventually a compromise bill was passed which exempted insurance companies from the operation of the antitrust laws and the Federal Trade Commission Act until January 1, 1948, thus giving the states a chance to improve and tighten laws which in some cases were inadequate. Thereafter those federal laws will apply to the insurance business "to the extent that such business is not regulated by State law."

This was an interesting fight, as well as a revealing one, for it showed the continual pull and tug in Congress on purely domestic issues which went on during the whole war period.

Conservative interests did very nicely in protecting themselves in reconversion legislation and in tax legislation affecting reconversion from war to peacetime production, to such an extent, as a matter of fact, that President Roosevelt vetoed one of the three tax bills passed during the war with a stinging rebuke to Congress. It was the first veto of a tax bill in the nation's history. Congress was highly resentful of this executive interference in a field in which it cherishes its prerogatives, control of the purse, though it had been forewarned of a possible veto. The blow was all the harder because of the President's harsh language, describing the measure as "providing relief not for the needy, but for the greedy." He said it was "replete with provisions which not only afford special privileges to favored groups but set dangerous precedents for the future." Mr. Roosevelt was swinging a haymaker from the left, and it was highly pleasing to his ardent New Deal following. Congress foamed up into self-righteous anger that spilled over beyond all expected bounds when the loyal and faithful Senator Alben W. Barkley, of Kentucky, rose in his wrath in the Senate, denounced the President, and resigned his position as Administration leader in a gesture of congressional fury. He was, of course, immediately re-elected, and Congress completed its defiance by passing the bill promptly over the President's veto with overwhelming majorities in both House and Senate.

So strong had the conservative element in Congress become that when the time came to enact legislation to assist in reconversion of industry from war to peace, it was successful in getting priority for a measure to take care of termination of contracts for industry, with provisions for handsome cash allowances, administered by an elaborate setup with an over-all top command directly under the Office of War Mobilization. It was President Roosevelt's idea that, at the same time, Congress should take care of what he called "the human side of reconversion," that is, the workers who would be thrown out of their jobs, at least temporarily, when plants stopped war production and were retooling for normal peace production. But Congress attended first to business and industry. This caused a howl, particularly from organized labor. When Congress got around to this phase of reconversion in another bill it was very niggardly. President Roosevelt signed it with the admonition that it did not "deal adequately with the human side of reconversion." This put it mildly in the view of labor. Even conservatives were surprised, some outside of Congress, some in the Senate.

For it was the House which made such a sham out of this measure. Conservatives had won in the Senate, but when the House finished with its version of the bill it looked like the work of arrant reactionaries. "Makes us look like radicals" was a comment from Senate conservatives. A New Deal group in the Senate, led by Senators James E. Murray of Montana and Harley M. Kilgore of West Virginia, both Democrats, sought to install a complete federal system of unemployment benefits, under which benefits would be paid for the entire time of unemployment up to two years, and with a maximum of $25 a week for a family with dependents. Their measure had other features, including blanketing in some three million federal workers not covered by existing law, as well as travel expenses for workers moving from war jobs to other jobs. But conservatives insisted on retention of the unemployment benefit system in the states, in which compensation in many cases was low and was paid for only a few weeks, and succeeded in passing the bill sponsored by Senator Walter George of Georgia, Democrat, chairman of the Finance Committee, which continued the state systems. The Senate measure, as passed, also included the federal workers, authorized loans to state unemployment compensation systems, if necessary, to keep them solvent for two years after the end of the war, and provided for payment of transportation costs to workers up to $200.

The House retained the state unemployment benefit systems, beating back all attempts to install a federal system, and left none of the other features of the Senate bill except the federal loans to state unemployment systems, so that the current description of the bill as "a mere shadow" of the Senate bill was most apt. This was the way it went to the President.

The inadequacy of the law was generally recognized, and after the end of the war in Europe President Truman recommended to Congress a compromise between federal and state systems by which the Federal Government would make up the difference in state benefits to provide a maximum of $25 a week for workers with dependents for a maximum of 26 weeks. The President, when in the Senate, had been among supporters of the defeated Murray-Kilgore bill.

Congress, however, still resisted. It voted itself a recess in the summer of 1945 without acting on the President's recommendations and was caught off guard, in recess, when the war with Japan ended. This unemployment compensation measure was still among the unfinished business when Congress came back to Washington, a month ahead of its scheduled time, on the call of President Truman. Before it took its summer recess, however, Congress had put through hurriedly a bill making available to business and industry some $5,000,000,000 in refunds authorized by the reconversion act of the previous year but postponed in that statute until after the end of the war.

In other ways Congress neglected to take sufficient heed of the reconversion and postwar period. One of the earliest forays of the conservatives, when they had caught their breaths after the dizzy early pace of war legislation, was to kill off the National Resources and Planning Board, which, among other projects, had been devising postwar plans of various sorts. Conservatives hated the very word "planning." Perhaps it was not wise to include it in the title of this agency. The NRPB had been established fairly early in the New Deal. Among other tasks, it was working out a postwar program of public works, federal, state, and local, to help take up any slack in unemployment. This job was transferred to the Federal Works Agency when Congress abolished NRPB. But Congress was very sparing of funds, and FWA was unable to get planning started on anywhere near the scale necessary at the local and state level, where most of the work projects would have to be provided. Meager funds were voted for the necessary loans to states to undertake this planning. Only the bigger states consequently were able to do much planning of this sort.

Early in the war the conservatives began to test out New Deal defenses around special agencies created during the dazzling reform era. It was fairly easy to dismantle and abolish the Works Progress Administration—the WPA of haunting memory—which had fed and clothed so many millions in the lean years when bread lines wound around windy corners. It was no longer needed. No longer needed, either, was the Civilian Conservation Corps (CCC), which had taken young men out of the soup lines and slums and put them to work in the forests. These young men were absorbed into the Army. It was eliminated without any serious quarrel. But the New Dealers did fight to try to save the National Youth Administration (NYA), directed by the zealous Aubrey Williams, once a top figure in WPA under Harry L. Hopkins. NYA had led a continuously stormy and tempestuous career, being under attack constantly from conservatives as a coddling institution infiltrated with communism, though it was defended by a number of university and college heads. It had helped to keep these institutions going and open by loans to students when depression cut so deeply into college enrollment. Senator Truman tried to keep NYA as a training school for young workers for war industry, to which it had largely devoted its energies in the preparedness period. But the House refused to accept his ameliorating amendment, and it went the way of WPA and CCC. It was in this same general attack of the conservatives that the NRPB fell a victim.

Labor was not overlooked in the general conservative offensive during the war years. It had fared well at the hands of the New Deal, the beneficiary of a whole body of statutes to guarantee collective bargaining, to put a floor under wages and a ceiling on hours, to provide machinery for settling disputes. But during the war it was constantly on the defensive. Successive efforts were made by the House to revise the National Labor Relations Act, but these were blocked in the Senate, chiefly because Senator Elbert Thomas of Utah, a staunch New Deal Democrat, bottled up all bills proposing changes in the Senate Education and Labor Committee, of which he was chairman. Occasionally the bills were given a hearing—but no action.

Eventually, however, the lines cracked for passage of the so-called antistrike bill, which turned out to be a misnomer. In the meantime Senator Thomas had given up the Education and Labor chairmanship to become head of the Military Affairs Committee, but it is doubtful that he could have bottled up this bill in view of an increasingly disturbed feeling in the public mind about strikes in the midst of war. The measure was vetoed by President Roosevelt, but Congress promptly passed it over his veto.

John L. Lewis's defiance of the government in a coal strike was capitalized to push this measure through Congress. The United Mine Workers' chieftain had become very unpopular with the Administration and New Dealers, for one thing, because of his known antipathy to President Roosevelt—which was mutual—and, for another, because he who had been so powerful an influence once politically for the Administration translated his personal feud with the man in the White House to a bolt from the Democratic party in 1940 to support the late Wendell L. Willkie. Conservatives, who never cared much for Mr. Lewis either though willing to use him when he was headed their way, were able to exploit a favorable psychological situation.

The so-called antistrike law as it finally emerged from Congress, and not before considerable controversy, was a combination of provisions embodied in a bill (sponsored by Rep. Howard Smith of Virginia, a Democrat, perhaps the most consistent and persistent foe of labor in the whole of Congress) which had passed the House but never the Senate, and a measure by Senator Tom Connally of Texas, another Southern Democrat, which empowered the President to seize plants where there was interference with war production by strikes or labor disturbances. This bill had passed the Senate in 1941 but had never come before the House.

With the 1943 walkout in the coal mines Senator Connally brought his bill again before the Senate. To the original plant seizure provisions he added another to include mines to get at John L. Lewis, as well as a prohibition against any sort of activity by employer or employees to provoke lockouts, strikes, slowdowns, or other interruption with production in plants or mines while in the hands of the government. In the Senate another amendment was adopted which clothed the War Labor Board with statutory powers so that it could subpoena witnesses, books, records, and papers. By the time the bill got to the House another strike was getting under way in the coal fields. Mr. Lewis was throwing his weight around zestfully. The House committee accordingly went literally wild—the House Military Affairs Committee, it was—seizing the excuse offered in Mr. Lewis's continued defiance of the government. It added all sorts of features which would have penalized organized labor generally, restricting the right to picket, outlawing secondary boycotts, jurisdictional strikes and sympathetic strikes, and requiring federal registration of trade unions and public accounting of their finances.

Labor as a whole, not only John L. Lewis, was confronted with a real threat. Cooler heads prevailed in the House itself, and most of the severe sections striking at some of labor's long-recognized rights which the House committee had included in its frenzy were deleted on the floor. As the bill was finally enacted and sent to the President it included the presidential plant and mine seizure powers, statutory powers for the War Labor Board, prohibition against strike activity by union leaders in plants or mines seized by the government, a ban against political contributions by labor unions, and a proviso for a thirty-day "cooling-off" period after official noting of a strike threat by the President, during which a settlement would be attempted, and, if no settlement could be reached, provision for a vote by the workers as to whether they wanted to strike.

The President objected particularly to the last-mentioned provisions in his veto message, arguing that because of them the measure was an invitation to strikes, rather than a strike-preventive measure. The C.I.O. was particularly alarmed over the ban against political contributions by labor unions, which it feared would restrict its projected activity on behalf of re-election of President Roosevelt to a fourth term, for which it was busy organizing and raising money. This alarm was shared privately by Administration political generals, including the President himself, so it was said. However, despite this attempted curb on C.I.O. political fund-raising, the PAC was able to collect substantial campaign funds through so-called "voluntary contributions" from members. Republicans and conservative Democrats charged repeatedly that the C.I.O. and its PAC were not living up to either the letter or the spirit of the law, and Representative Smith, co-author of the act, demanded an investigation by the Justice Department. Attorney General Biddle exonerated the labor organization of any violation of law. The Connally-Smith Act was a wartime measure, with provision for its expiration six months after the end of the war as proclaimed by the President. Agitation for its repeal started even before the end of the war and came from both labor and industrial quarters. It was a slipshod law, though utilized quite often by both Presidents Roosevelt and Truman to seize plants.

On the positive side New Dealers and progressives, including labor, made little headway on measures they sponsored during the war years. President Roosevelt repeatedly urged expansion of the Social Security Act, and bills were introduced, but nothing at all was done on his proposals to broaden its coverage to include millions not now benefited, nor on recommendations for increased public health facilities, medical care, health insurance, and the like. This was a heritage which President Truman accepted sympathetically for attention.

New Dealers were checkmated in other directions.

All through the war, in which Negroes fought along with their white countrymen for democracy and against fascism, there continued at home and in Congress a futile battle to secure for them some of their rights as American citizens guaranteed under the Constitution.

Time after time the House passed the bill to abolish the poll tax as a prerequisite to voting for federal officials. Every time the Southerners successfully filibustered against it in the Senate. Their stock argument was that this should be done by the states themselves. But little progress was made in that domain of action during the war. At the beginning of the war there were eight Southern states which imposed a poll tax as a prerequisite to voting. At the end of the war in Europe there were still seven. Georgia repealed hers under the courageous leadership of Governor Ellis Arnall. Tennessee also had repealed hers, but the state Supreme Court nullified the act of the legislature, so that the law remained in effect.

The poll tax acted as a deterrent to voting (though its effect has been perhaps somewhat exaggerated), not only as regards Negroes but also poor whites. There is, however, another restriction on the franchise of the Negro in the South which is much more effective and is, in fact, conclusive. It is still a bar even if poll taxes are paid up. This is the so-called "white primary" prevalent in Southern states which keeps Negroes from voting in the primary elections, which are the important elections in the one-party politics of the South. They are the only elections in which there is a choice of candidates. Congress heard occasionally about these laws during the war, as it has through the years, and every so often a familiar corrective would be offered, which also has been suggested through the years, which is to prohibit the counting of Negroes in apportioning members of Congress to the Southern states, which would cut down their representation in Congress. This is never taken seriously and is seldom offered seriously, except to dramatize the disfranchisement of Negroes in the South. There was some discussion, too, in Congress of another decision by the Supreme Court ruling white primaries out of order as unconstitutional, this time as before in the case of Texas, but nothing seemed to come of this. The Southern states are quick and clever to devise other subterfuges.

To protect Negroes and members of other racial as well as religious groups from discrimination in industry President Roosevelt created by executive order the Fair Employment Practice Committee, which, though it had only persuasive powers, nevertheless was helpful in protecting minorities in their employment rights. Southerners in Congress tried repeatedly to destroy this agency by depriving it of appropriations. They resisted strenuously likewise President Truman's recommendation that a permanent Fair Employment Practice Commission be established by law.

Farmers never lacked for friends in Congress during the war, which was also true for several years before the war, and some of the most dramatic congressional episodes during the war revolved about the conflict of their interests with those of labor and the consumer. There was almost a continuous running battle. In fact, group interests were more accentuated than ever and new alliances appeared that resulted in shifts in balances of power, a constantly recurring phenomenon that gives American political economy its resilience.

Outstanding perhaps, and certainly of the most significant influence, was a drawing together of businessmen and the more substantial farmers in a tacit alliance that directed its energy to curbs on labor and curtailing of New Deal aids to the smaller and less prosperous farmers and to efforts to lift the controls on farm production and prices so that the farmers, especially the larger ones, could reap even more handsome profits out of the war.

This translated itself in Congress into renewed activity by the coalition of Southern conservative Democrats and Republicans which was strengthened, as we have seen, by Republican victories in the 1942 elections. In that election Republicans recaptured virtually the whole Midwestern farm area which they had once dominated. The only Democratic oases left were in the cities.

Under the influence of a return of prosperity, first through New Deal measures and later through war demands, the psychology of the Midwestern farmer gradually changed. Again he was a minor capitalist, and again he found it comfortable to go back to the Republican party, comfortable and reassuring to his restored confidence and well-being. Forgotten were the dark days of the late twenties and early thirties when Midwestern farmers rose up in a mighty army and swept Republicans out of Washington. Then they hailed Franklin D. Roosevelt as their deliverer. The deliverer delivered for them. But, fat and healthy again, the farmers forgot their deliverer. Their worries now were the controls they had accepted a few years before as their salvation. Now they wanted to shake them off, to get free. They were getting good prices. But they wanted better prices. The farmer had reverted to capitalism and individualism. Slogans about a free economy and free enterprise began to sound good again. These were the aims, too, of the businessman who was now back on his feet again and who was growing increasingly weary of regulations and regimentation. All this pulled the farmer and the businessman closer together, particularly the more favored of each

group, coupled as it was with a common antipathy to labor and
New Deal encouragement to labor and a common resentment of
continued New Deal spending, now that the spending was no
longer almost the sole support of their markets but was viewed
only as it showed up on their tax bills.

This feeling worked itself out in various ways through their
representatives in Congress, who were constantly prompted by
skillful representatives of big farm and big business organizations. The alliance between Republican Midwest and Democratic South was perfectly sealed and symbolized, as far as farm
interests were concerned, in the persons of two figures very influential in the American Farm Bureau Federation, the biggest and
most powerful of the farm organizations. One was Edward A.
O'Neal, president of the Federation, who comes from an Alabama planter background, and is smooth and persuasive with
members of Congress. The other was Earl C. Smith, head of the
potent Illinois Agricultural Association, a Vice President of the
Farm Bureau Federation, an extremely shrewd political operator
with Republican leanings. It was an effective team. O'Neal was
the Washington front. Smith kept always in the background.

Constant targets of the farmer-businessman alliance were what
might be called the social reform programs along the agricultural front, measures designed to improve the opportunities of
farm tenants and substandard farmers, notable among them being the Farm Security Administration. The aim was to make
these less-favored farm folks self-supporting owners of their own
farms, rather than hired labor on somebody else's farm. This was
a blow at the low wage system in the South in particular and at
its paternalistic society established before the Civil War and still
prevalent in agriculture. The FSA represented perhaps the most
fundamental of all New Deal reforms, at least as far as the South
was concerned, for its object was reform of a social and economic
system deeply rooted in the thinking and customs of the people.
The House virtually killed the FSA at one time, but the Senate

restored it. The agency's funds were frequently reduced in the effort to hamstring its operations.

It was the House, too, which led the way in abolishing the crop insurance program. Here the Senate acquiesced. But this proved only temporary. As the election approached in 1944 the politicians discovered this was a mistake. Both parties were angling, as usual, for the farm vote, and crop insurance was restored.

The big farm battle in Congress during the war—and it never let up—was over OPA price control and the related issue of food subsidies. Farmers and business joined here, with labor and consumer groups backing up OPA. The farmer-business coalition tried, again and again, to break down the OPA price structure. The philosophy was to let prices find their natural level, without restriction. The coalition would win now in the House, now in the Senate, but every time one or the other body would break through to make a decided change in the price control system, the lines would be held in the other branch, or the issue would be compromised in conference between the two houses so that no irreparable injury was done. Twice, however, Congress voted to stop the food subsidy program, only to be blocked by presidential vetoes. Some minor victories were won in the fight against OPA in the way of concessions on price for this or that commodity and in forcing revision of administrative procedure for the benefit of this or that crop or group of processors and producers. At best the price control system was highly complicated, and necessarily so, and injustices were bound to occur.

Toward the middle of 1944, after the end of the war in Europe and with the stepped-up campaign against Japan, the fight on OPA in Congress attracted more than usual public support, owing perhaps to general war weariness and to pent-up harassment over rationing and shortages, particularly acute in meat, incident to the need for food for the destitute populations of Europe added to the continuous demands from our troops and those of our allies.

The Administration and Congress were kept conscious constantly of the citizen as consumer. Perhaps in no other field did organized labor make itself felt so during the war. Especially effective were the campaigns of education sponsored by C.I.O. The food subsidy program was devised to protect the consumer. In order to hold down prices to the consumer on essential staple items of food—bread, meat, butter, and milk, among them—subsidies were paid to the processors representing the increase in cost to them of raw materials. It was a "roll-back" system, rolling back the cost from the consumer to be taken up by a subsidy to processors and hence, in the end, by the taxpayers as a whole, and few escaped taxation during the war period. This subsidy program was under continual attack from conservative interests, partly as a matter of principle, partly because of the influence of special groups which wanted to let prices move without interference and without regulation. When President Roosevelt vetoed the second bill to abolish the subsidy program he called it "an inflation measure, a high-cost-of-living measure, a food shortage measure."

The Commodity Credit Corporation which administered the food subsidy program once was voted out of existence for a brief period, only to be restored, and efforts were made constantly to impede the program by cutting down its appropriations. But it survived all vicissitudes and the program was extended, after its last test in Congress, until June 30, 1947.

As well as from labor, the Administration also received substantial help in maintaining the food subsidy program from one farm organization, the National Farmers Union, which represented mostly the smaller and marginal farmers and had associations with labor unions. This farm organization had received encouragement from the New Deal. It was active, also, on behalf of incentive subsidies to increase the output of the smaller and less prosperous farmers, itself a considerable contribution to the big over-all total required to feed us, our armies, and those of our allies.

Almost as unpopular as OPA with some in Congress, principally Republicans, was the Office of War Information. This information and propaganda agency was the subject of almost ceaseless investigation, and always had to fight for its life in Congress every year when the matter of its funds for the ensuing year came up for consideration. Republicans saw in it, as the 1944 elections approached, a propaganda agency for a fourth term for President Roosevelt. They were irritated by frequent mention of President Roosevelt in pamphlets, including those distributed among soldiers overseas. OWI took, too, for a time to issuance of pamphlets on controversial domestic problems before Congress. Though intended, as OWI represented, to be factual, they were interpreted otherwise in Congress. This was a contributing factor to a campaign in Congress to abolish the domestic branch of OWI entirely. But the legislative body finally worked off its spleen by cutting down operations of the domestic branch very sharply and writing into law a strict injunction against use of any of its funds "for the preparation of any pamphlet or other literature for distribution to the public within the United States." The foreign branch, which was engaged in propaganda in enemy and neutral countries with both printed material and elaborate radio programs, survived the hurricane, but with smaller appropriations than OWI officials had requested. The end of the war in Europe brought a renewed campaign in Congress to do away with OWI completely.

After the end of the war with Japan its foreign propaganda and information functions were transferred to the State Department, along with necessary personnel, but its staff was sharply reduced from that maintained by OWI as an independent agency during the war.

OWI was branded with "New Dealism" and also with "communism," two handy catchwords during the war, as before the war. They were used also against various domestic measures supported, with little success, by progressive forces in Congress and previously discussed. As we have seen, progressivism as represented in purely domestic matters made little headway during the war.

President Roosevelt gave such domestic projects less and less attention. The war absorbed him more and more, necessarily, as did his plans for the peace and for a postwar international security organization to check aggressors in the future and keep down wars. He was most careful to woo Congress on this last objective, seeking to avoid the mistake which he had seen Woodrow Wilson make twenty-five years before. Congress responded nobly, as it had in supporting war measures, and the change that occurred in its attitude on international co-operation is remarkable when you consider the isolationism with which it once had been so steeped. The President and Secretary of State Hull consulted congressional leaders of both parties at every step. Both branches of Congress put themselves on record for international co-operation and for adequate machinery to effectuate it, the House in the Fulbright resolution, the Senate in the Connally resolution. Both parties contributed to the majorities, overwhelming in each case.

This paved the way for the Dumbarton Oaks Conference in Washington, at which was drawn up a preliminary draft of a world security organization by representatives of the United States, Great Britain, Russia, and China, which led, in turn, to the San Francisco Conference of United Nations at which the Charter itself was formulated. Republicans, including members of both Senate and House, were represented in the American delegation at San Francisco by appointment of President Roosevelt shortly before he died. This foresight was richly rewarded in the subsequent 89 to 2 Senate vote ratifying the San Francisco Charter.

Congress likewise co-operated, though somewhat less enthusiastically, in international trade and financial programs which the Truman Administration linked up with political co-operation, most important being the extension of the reciprocal tariff program with authority for the State Department to bargain for still another 50 per cent reduction in tariffs in negotiations with other nations, and the Bretton Woods agreements providing for an international bank and an international monetary fund for financial rehabilitation of war-ravaged countries and stabilization of exchange and currencies. Republicans supplied the bulk of opposition to these measures, and they sought to make a party issue against the reciprocal tariff program in so far as the additional 50 per cent reduction was concerned. But both measures were approved by Congress.

As disappointing as Congress proved in treatment of domestic problems while you were gone, it accepted its full responsibility and acted with courage and vision in the sphere of foreign affairs, which is important for you and your families and your children. This demonstrated, among other things, that public pressure can move Congress, slowly perhaps, but inevitably. Which is something for you to consider. For great political power rests in your hands.

Congress is aware of that. It is very conscious of you. It has been generous with you, as soldiers, sailors, and marines, providing well for your training, equipment, and comfort, your food and quarters, for your hospital care if sick or wounded, for completing your education, for priority in the jobs you left when you went away, for loans to help you get started in business or farming.

Yes, Congress has thought a great deal about you. It has done that honestly and sincerely. That is certainly true. But Congress is a body of human beings, and human beings are creatures of mixed motives, handsomely unselfish in part, ingloriously selfish in part, even like the rest of us. So it has thought of itself, too. For, to tell the truth, Congress is a little bit afraid of you and your millions of votes. Congress is fearful that some of you are going to want its jobs, and it is a good thing if some of you do. Congress was worried about your votes in the last election, and it higgled and haggled for months merely writing a law permitting you to vote.

Some members weren't overanxious to make it too easy for you to vote. That's no secret to anybody who watched that performance and knew what some members were trying to do, despite their public explanations and protestations. Some Southern Democrats who lived in districts where there was a large Negro population, and which consequently had a large representation of Negroes in the service, wanted to make sure they didn't vote as members of the armed forces when they would not be permitted to vote if they still were back home. That might have ended some political careers abruptly. So they insisted that regular state election laws which barred Negroes from voting apply to those in the service. Some Republicans weren't too anxious for you to vote in too great numbers. They were afraid too many of you might be inclined toward the late President Roosevelt, and that would be unfortunate for their candidate for the presidency, who could not be as well known among you as President Roosevelt, no matter who he might turn out to be. They were afraid, too, that the partiality they suspected in you toward President Roosevelt would lead you to vote the straight Democratic ticket. That would affect their chances of re-election. Too, they had a theory that the fewer votes cast altogether the better chance their party would have to win, which was a good theory.

As the upshot of all of these inclinations, there was formed a coalition of Republicans and Southern Democrats—not all, by any means, of either group—which was successful in writing a bill that was more complicated than it might have been. It did not make voting the free and simple right that is guaranteed by the Constitution. At one point the bill was shaping up so unsatisfactorily that President Roosevelt called it by the short and ugly word "fraud." The final bill was some better. But it wouldn't have worked so well had not the Army and Navy, which were challenged, so to speak, done a very remarkable job of organization and delivered the ballots to as many of you as was physically possible, with the result that nearly three million soldiers and sailors voted in the election.

You may gather from all this, and what has been related previously, that Congress is quite a human institution, and it is. It is like a human being, now worried and harassed, confused and stumbling, now clear and farsighted, now selfish, now unselfish, now petty and stupid, now rising to heights, now full of prides and prejudices, now sincere and straightforward. It has its moments of great confidence, even arrogance, and it has its periods of depression and its spells of inferiority.

Off and on, Congress has suffered from an inferiority complex ever since the New Deal came into being, which is another part of its story while you were gone, for it had interesting developments. It was a natural and inevitable result of the growing complexity of government that Congress should find itself subordinated somewhat in the swift, early days of the New Deal, when the world was practically upside down, and it had to be turned right-side up in a hurry. It was no longer possible for Congress to cope with the many problems brought about by the depression, which became the first concern of the Roosevelt regime by force of circumstance, without calling more and more upon experts in the executive departments and special agencies familiar with the various fields affected. These came to be called the "Brain Trust" and were vilified as such during the early New Deal, though this was not exactly a new adjunct to government. There were just more of their sort now. The field of specialists had been growing gradually through the years. Herbert Hoover had lots of them around him, as a matter of fact. They were essential. The Roosevelt Administration built a great superstructure of special agencies, boards, and bureaus to handle the new social reforms it had created with the approval of Congress. In time they aroused the suspicion and jealousy of Congress. During the war a great many more necessarily had to be established to grapple with the manifold problems of an over-all war which required regulations affecting every citizen, his normal life, his habits. This aggravated the inferiority complex. The individual member of Congress felt himself a very small cog in a great whirring machine. He could not possibly find the time, even if he had the energy to work twenty hours a day, to inform himself on all the manifold problems. More and more Congress had to rely upon the experts in the downtown agencies for information, and upon its own committees to advise it on particular policies which came under their purview.

All of this created a natural rebellion, stemming partly from frustration, which broke out sporadically. New Deal haters called Congress, in its early Roosevelt period of hasty ratification of depression relief measures, a "rubber stamp Congress." Republicans picked this up and shouted it from the floors of Congress. They did not have in those days enough members to do any more than shout. Of course, in time, as has been pointed out, Congress became anything but a "rubber stamp." The Administration came to think of it as a ball and chain.

Out of this rebellion grew a movement for restoration of congressional authority. Congress must reassert itself. That was the way it was put usually. It must recover its ordained place in the tripartite scheme of government—executive, legislative, and judicial. This movement to restore the prestige of Congress drew strength from two sources. It came from students of government who were sincerely convinced that Congress had fallen down in its responsibilities. Such sympathetic critics were in Congress and government and outside of Congress and government. The reform movement was pushed, too, by those whose main purpose in strengthening Congress was to make it the dominant power in government—as it has been occasionally in the past, though usually in a negative way—so that it might overawe and check the executive branch which had become so powerful under a strong figure in the White House. These mixed motives were concentrated eventually in a stream of action with a number of aims contributed by each group.

The purpose, as it was put, was to "streamline" Congress, both to improve its efficiency and to restrict the power and influence of special executive agencies. It embodied many proposals. They included giving congressional committees more expert help through trained and specialized staffs, both so they could institute research, themselves, and so they could check on information supplied them by representatives of special agencies, the latter naturally inclined to be zealous in their own interests. It included, too, such proposed reforms as reducing the number of committees of Congress through consolidation and rearrangement of their jurisdictions, and improving the leadership of committees and thus the leadership of Congress itself by abolishing or modifying the seniority rule of selecting committee chairmen. Another proposal was to increase the salaries of members of Congress. On the side of the executive agencies, recommendations included the reduction of such special agencies and the regrouping of those which must be retained under regular government departments and a responsible cabinet officer; more exact definition of the powers of such special agencies to make sure they do not invade the legislative field; and review of their decisions by the courts.

All this composed a big legislative program which no one expected to be executed overnight or *in toto*. But, for the first time, congressional reform seemed to make a real impression because of the increasing feeling of inferiority that pervaded and permeated the legislative body.

This was a major postwar project of Congress itself.

This review, which is drawing to its conclusion, is but a brief sketch of Congress while you were gone. Volumes would be required for the whole story. The moral is that Congress probably has done a lot of things you didn't like, and it's up to you, now you are back, to do your part in seeing that your voice is heard in what it does henceforth. For it's your Congress, after all. And it's a very important part of your government. A personal chore that is suggested is that you take a little time to look up the record of your Congressman and your Senators and keep tab on it from now on. You'll find detailed records of individual members of Congress for the period while you were gone, on major pieces of legislation, in the back of this book.

You can make your country more as you would like to have it. Congress has a share in that. It is a different country in many respects to which you return, which may not be easily discernible at first. Government has become more directly involved in the lives of all of you. That has been the trend.

It is up to you to see that it serves your needs, as it can, without at the same time depriving you of the essential liberties which are the tradition of this nation, and for which you fought. That is to be the irrepressible conflict of the future. Congress, representing you, has its responsibility in all of that. It is well for you to keep your eyes on it.

III. THE WAR AGENCIES

by HENRY F. PRINGLE

HENRY F. PRINGLE (age 48) won the 1931
Pulitzer Prize for biography and was last year
awarded a Guggenheim fellowship for the popular history of the war on which he is now at
work. In December, 1941, he joined the Office
of Facts and Figures as a writer and became
chief of its Bureau of Production in March,
1942. He continued in this capacity when the
OFF was absorbed by the Office of War Information. He is at present a free-lance writer and
a Washington member of the Writers' Board,
formerly the Writers' War Board.

THE changes in our form of government really date back to the
depression, to almost a decade before Pearl Harbor. A few go
even further back than that. The Federal Government had to adjust itself to a radically different United States. Some of the new
things in America were bad. Most of them were, in the main,
good. All of them brought new problems which had to be solved.

The process of change was enormously accelerated when, in
1940, France fell and Great Britain rescued her helpless armies
from Dunkirk. For most Americans then knew in their hearts that
they would have to help in the war against dictatorship. They demanded that the Federal Government get ready for war if war
came. To do this quickly many new agencies had to be created.
Some were abolished. Others were consolidated.

The process continued until it was almost impossible to recognize the Federal Government. For good or for evil, Washington
no longer means just the silver dome of the Capitol on the banks

of a sleepy river. Washington—that is to say, the Federal Government—is now everywhere in the United States. It is interesting to note that almost ten times as many federal employees worked outside of the District of Columbia as within its crowded boundaries during the war. And, of course, the influence of Washington has spread to every nation in the world.

Washington had never been a world capital in the sense that London and Paris are. It probably never will be. New York will remain the center of the drama, music, and the other arts. Washington has no harbor and cannot become a great commercial city. Old-time Washington was the seat of the Federal Government, the home of Congress and the Supreme Court; the principal stamping ground for that curious breed of men called politicians. A handful of wealthy people lived there, in great houses on Massachusetts Avenue or in Georgetown. They enjoyed the rigid formality of social life with high government officials and members of the diplomatic corps. They fled to Newport or Narragansett Pier when the first stifling heat of May settled down. But for the most part Washington was inhabited by middle-class government workers who lived complacently, under the protection of civil service, for the day when they could enjoy their pensions.

Like the structure of the Federal Government, all this began to change with the last war, and Washington has never been the same since. "Temporary buildings"—so-called—were hastily erected in 1917 and 1918. Many of them, with scores of other "temporary buildings" thrown together in 1940 to 1942, are still in use today. Even before Pearl Harbor it was almost impossible to get a room in a hotel or a meal at a restaurant. Then the district mushroomed in all directions. Agencies not directly connected with the war were moved to St. Louis, New York, Philadelphia, and other cities. But the population soared by thousands every week. It was still rising after the German collapse.

Typical advertisements in the Washington *Post* as late as August, 1945, read:

A returned wounded infantry officer hates to believe it is easier to billet thousands of men overseas than it is to find a house for

1 small boy in Washington. If you have a 2 or 3 bedroom furnished house and yard we will give you references on everything, including our child.

Middle-aged couple, no children or pets, frantically desire one or two bedroom, furnished or unfurnished house or apartment in Silver Spring or northwest area.

Before the war was many months old legends began to circulate about the housing shortage.

A favorite concerned a man who had fallen into the Potomac. His cries for help attracted a passerby. "What is your name and where do you live?" the passerby demanded.

"John Jones, 14 North S Street. Help!" said the drowning man.

The passerby immediately left the scene and ran all the way to 14 North S Street. Breathlessly he said to the landlady: "I want to rent John Jones' room. He won't be here any more. He just drowned."

"Sorry," said the landlady, "it was just taken by the man who pushed him in."

It is not legend, but fact, that one new Washingtonian liked to boast of his own particular method of celebrating when the end of the war came. He described how he had been shunted from hotel to hotel, snubbed by managers and room clerks and bellboys. On V-J Day he proposed to make the rounds of all these hotels.

"I'll go to the desk and ask for a room," he explained. "The room clerk will be very, very courteous. 'Yes, sir!' he will say. 'And just what kind of a room would you like, sir?' And then I'll draw myself up to my full height. 'I don't want your lousy room!' I'll say—and go on to the next hotel." The story is already dated. There were no rooms available on V-J Day.

Thousands of businessmen, some of them giving their services for one dollar a year and nearly all of them making financial sacrifices, arrived in the capital to help win the war. The ones who came within the first year contrived, somehow, to find a place to live. The later arrivals were less lucky. Many, including ranking officers in the Army and Navy, concluded that it was impossible to bring their families to the Washington madhouse. They got along at hotels, in dreary bachelor quarters. Some of them, in their loneliness, drank too much. Others suffered nervous breakdowns. Psychiatrists and nerve specialists began to open offices in this new and fertile field.

The alcoholics, the men developing ulcers, and the neurotics were a microscopic minority, of course. Most of the new officials worked harder than ever before in their lives. They wrestled with the unfamiliarities of government. They did the best they could with inadequate staffs. They ate indigestible meals, served by incompetent and disgruntled waiters, or stood in long cafeteria lines. They learned that space shortages were not limited to residential housing. Office space was soon almost unobtainable, despite all the new "temporary" buildings. The armed services, demanding a priority, moved efficiently and swiftly to capture what there was. Meanwhile, in the early months, the war news was bleak. Allied forces were dropping back, particularly in the Pacific.

"If the Army and Navy could capture territory as well as they grab office space," growled the head of one civilian agency, "we might win the war."

A degree of fantasy began to color wartime Washington. Broadway roared at a farce called *The Doughgirls,* based on the hotel crisis and its effect on the lives of big business men and their mistresses in the capital. At least one motion picture used the housing shortage as its theme. Certain Hollywood patterns began to appear. At noon the dining rooms of the Mayflower, the Statler, the Willard, and other large hotels would be jammed. People would crane their necks when Secretary of the Interior Ickes, Donald Nelson of the War Production Board, General Marshall, or Admiral King came in.

"It's just like Hollywood," said a Hollywood director who had arrived to make films for the army indoctrination courses. "Out there we went to the Brown Derby or Dave Chasen's and watched Orson Welles playing the part of Orson Welles, Chaplin being Chaplin, and the like. Here we watch Leon Henderson playing the role of Leon Henderson, Tommy Corcoran being the powerful, mysterious, faintly sinister Tommy the Cork."

Washington became, in a way, an offshoot of Broadway. Such columnists as Winchell and Danton Walker published daily hints on forthcoming legislation. They made flat statements, often wrong, about Who Would Succeed Whom in What High Place. Drew Pearson, on the air for a laxative concern, electrified the nation with his own series of predictions. Government officials were cited for peculiarities of dress or manner, without relation to their abilities. Elmer Davis of the Office of War Information, for instance, had worn a black bow tie for years, and apparently saw no reason to change. One day, quite by chance, his secretary happened to wear a white shirtwaist with an identical black tie. This astonishing war news was duly chronicled in the New York press.

Such were some of the superficial changes in the nation's capital, possibly symptomatic of the deeper and far more important alterations in the structure of government itself. The heritage of America had been local government. We had had our fill of control from afar, and, when the country was new, we trusted government from any one place, whether New York or Philadelphia or Washington, about as little as we had trusted government from England. So in the Constitution we imposed a great many restrictions on the Federal Government. Our ancestors who wrote the Constitution were far more interested in freedom than in government, because they had hardly known anything except bad government.

The system of checks and balances worked fairly well, as long as the country was at peace, for over a hundred years. It probably didn't work as well as a good many people who yearn for the Good Old Days like to think. The country was frequently torn by violent depressions. Men sometimes had jobs and sometimes starved, and nobody could do much about it. Clever men made unbelievable fortunes without bothering to obey the law. But life, like government, was relatively simple. The average American came in contact with the Federal Government only through the kindly postman with the morning mail. No direct federal taxes existed. It was an age when Washington could not pry into private business by demanding answers to scores of questionnaires. No bewildering swarm of alphabetical agencies existed.

One trouble was that the checks and balances simply did not work when war came. Abraham Lincoln, whose trust in democracy was profound, quickly learned this when he had to preserve the Union. The people found out, too, that control by government was a far lesser evil than destruction of the nation. The whole thing came to a head with the last World War. Germany and Austria would not hold off while Congress debated or quarreled with the President. So Woodrow Wilson, another profound believer in democracy, acted swiftly. Congress gave him most of the powers he needed, and the United States never returned to its traditional ideal of a severely restricted Federal Government. Thomas K. Finletter has stated it accurately in his recent excellent book, *Can Representative Government Do the Job?*:

Many of these statutes remain on the books today and were the nucleus of the huge authority granted by Congress to prosecute World War II. Almost no restriction has been placed on the President's power to use the entire resources of the nation to defeat Germany and Japan. To this end Congress has not only abandoned the checks and balances but has gone to the other extreme of helping to centralize power in the Executive as long as the war is on.

". . . as long as the war is on." Few Americans objected during this war to the theory of centralizing power to defeat the Axis, although millions have criticized the exact way it was used. The problem now is to decide what to do in time of peace. Will the ancient, honored system of checks and balances permit the United States to make war on depression, to see that good jobs are open to veterans and to war workers, to play a strong and intelligent role in the world federation which must prevent another war? First, though, let us look at the Federal Government of 1940 to 1945.

One trouble with understanding it is the enormous size of today's Federal Government. Merlo J. Pusey in his book, *Big Government*, points out that it had 30,000 more employees in 1939, when war began in Europe, than at the close of the last war. The total soared to over 3,000,000, and then was cut slightly. They were paid about $7,000,000,000 a year, and this did not include men and women in the armed services. During four years of preparing for war and fighting it, the government spent almost $400,-000,000,000. Uncle Sam is now an industrialist beside whom Ford and Kaiser are mere pygmies. He has financed, and now owns, an estimated $25,000,000,000 in factories and other war facilities. These include steel, rubber, and aluminum mills, aircraft factories —even an ice plant.

Another obstacle to comprehension of the war government lies in the heated argument it has inspired. Politics has been partly responsible. But even citizens with no political prejudices at all have found themselves bewildered by the jungle of alphabetical agencies, by the shifts and reorganizations and changes. They can't tell FEA from FEPC or the ODT from the OSS, and should not be expected to do so. If they are unfortunate enough to have business in Washington or some other city where agencies are located they grow frustrated and angry as they attempt to solve the insoluble.

Out of the citizens' frustrations and irritation has grown a widespread anger toward what is called bureaucracy. This is described as a vast, sinister machine, on the one hand, which will surely seize control of the government if it does not bankrupt the nation first. On the other, it is held to be a milling job of incompetents whose lack of intelligence and industry endangered the victory over Hitler and made improbable the defeat of Japan. This is sheer nonsense. The so-called bureaucrats consist of Republicans, Democrats, and even a few Socialists who managed to slip by the Federal Bureau of Investigation's careful screenings. Among them are lawyers from New York who have never failed to vote the Republican ticket. They include industrialists, journalists, scientists, engineers, economists, bankers, college presidents, and college professors. They include hundreds of thousands of young women who answered the plea of the United States Civil Service Commission and flocked to Washington so that the war might end sooner. Without their nimble fingers, it may be flatly stated, V-E and V-J days would surely have been delayed.

The best definition of a bureaucrat I have heard was offered by the wife of one of them, Jonathan Daniels.

"A bureaucrat," she said in effect, "is a man who is living in Washington when he would rather be somewhere else. He is doing work he would rather not be doing. His salary is considerably lower than in private life. He has a wife and two children whom he can't support on that salary."

Yet the prejudice toward this bureaucracy is partly justified. Some of the agencies had too many employees and used them inefficiently. An occasional bureau or division chief did expand his organization needlessly, often because of the Civil Service Commission's idiotic tendency to raise executive salaries in proportion to the number of subordinates. Finally, no doubt whatever exists that the war agencies overlapped and conflicted. A vital war matter may have fallen under the jurisdiction of half a dozen or more branches of this new, confused, and sprawling Federal Government. Agency heads time and again disagreed on important policies and fought their battles in the newspapers.

The blame, I think, rests squarely on the shoulders of President Roosevelt. Without Roosevelt's leadership the United States might well have lost the war. All of the great war measures which first saved England and Russia and then sent Germany and Japan tumbling to their doom were either the conception of the President or received his vigorous support. He was convinced that England would stand and that Russia would in due course turn back the Nazi armies. So he threw the lot of America in with the foes of fascism. He called for a citizens' army, for the transfer of American destroyers to England in return for bases, for the repeal of the Neutrality Act which aided the Axis, for the Lend-Lease Act of 1941 whereby the United States shipped guns, tanks, aircraft, ammunition, and all the other essentials of modern war to the democracies before it could send armies. He ordered research on the atomic bomb, however great the cost.

Men of vision can plan. The President set production sights high when the heads of the Army and Navy were conservatively cautious. In due course the goals were met. But men of vision are not necessarily good managers, and no honest friend of Roosevelt can claim that he shone as an administrator. He was terrible. Among his weaknesses was a violent distaste for dismissing men who had failed him. He tried to find excuses. He nearly always compromised by permitting the official to continue on the job, and then created a new agency to do the work. As the months passed and the pressures of war increased, he virtually emasculated some of the older government departments. Notably, the Labor Department was stripped of nearly all powers relating to labor and the war. Functions which belonged in the State Department, such as economic warfare and psychological onslaughts against the enemy, were also transferred to new agencies.

The Federal Government grew so vast that nobody, including the President, could conceivably understand or operate it. Meanwhile Congress, crippled by its archaic organization, could not function with the speed which war demands. It signed blank checks for scores of billions and left the President or the armed services to decide how they should be spent. Agencies were created without the knowledge of the supposedly equal legislative branch, often under broad and sweeping powers delegated to the executive arm. Executive orders flowed in unprecedented numbers from the White House, and no one man understood these wholly, either.

It was to be total war. The Navy had suffered its most crushing defeat at Pearl Harbor, and the Japanese were pushing Great Britain and the Netherlands farther and farther from their empires in the East. The people were to be asked to make sacrifices such as no Americans, save in the South during the War between the States, had ever been asked to make. But aside from the messages and fireside talks of the President, they had little knowledge of the ebb and flow of the struggle. For almost a year it was as though this was a private war, in the sole hands of the armed services.

The United States fought, said Archibald MacLeish, who had become director of the Office of Facts and Figures, with "the strategy of truth." Handicapped by inadequate authority and subjected to unending abuse by divisionist newspapers, MacLeish struggled to tell his fellow citizens why they were at war, about the goals for which they fought. He succeeded, to a degree. In the late spring of 1942 his office published a document unique in the history of governments which was read by millions of Americans. This defined the Four Freedoms enunciated by President Roosevelt.

The Axis nations, the pamphlet said, promised "a world in which the conquered peoples will live out their lives in the service of their masters." It continued:

The United Nations, now engaged in a common cause, have also published their design, and have committed certain common aims to writing. They plan a world in which men stand straight and walk free, free not of all human trouble but free of the fear of despotic power, free to develop as individuals, free to conduct and shape their affairs. Such a world has been more dream than reality, more hope than fact; but it has been the best hope men have had and the one for which they have most consistently shown themselves willing to die.

This free-ness, this liberty, this precious thing men love and mean to save, is the good granite ledge on which the United Nations now propose to raise their new world after victory.

Other important war documents were issued by the Office of

Facts and Figures and by the Office of War Information, with which it was merged. These exposed German propaganda, gave details about the United Nations, reported on the quality of American airplanes, extolled the war activities of American Negroes. But MacLeish had been succeeded by Elmer Davis as head of the government's information agency, and soon a swarm of advertising men were happily painting the war in glowing terms.

Yet OWI played a very important part, too, in winning the war. Congress virtually abolished its domestic functions in 1943. By that time, however, OWI had encouraged the Writers' War Board, a private organization, to mobilize the writing talent of the country. Its work was highly effective. Writers accustomed to big fees donated their services freely to the Army, the Navy, and to nearly all the war agencies. Writers of magazine serials caused their heroes and heroines to hold forth on phases of the war. Nonfiction authors wrote pamphlets and books. Radio specialists prepared or took part in coast-to-coast programs. A similar committee in Hollywood used the screen to the same end and also persuaded the industry's glamour girls to stimulate attendance at bond rallies.

OWI's own most effective work was abroad. The Germans had long been waging psychological warfare. Their propaganda had contributed materially to the fall of France. The United States used similar weapons in the North African, Italian, Sicilian, and French invasions and also against Japan. Portable loud-speakers, pamphlets, and newspapers urged surrender. In captured territory radio stations were operated to tell the civilian population the aim of the democracies. OWI worked closely with the Army in its psychological warfare operations and also with the British. That it saved many American lives and shortened the war on all fronts was confirmed by commanding generals.

The first year and a half were marked by wide confusion on the home front. Gasoline, coffee, sugar, certain canned goods, and meat had been rationed by the summer of 1943. The battle against inflation had been started by fixing wages, rents, and the prices of essential commodities. The President had called for a seven-point national economic policy which specified: 1. Tax heavily and hold profits down; 2. fix ceilings on prices and rents; 3. stabilize wages; 4. stabilize farm prices; 5. save more, buy less; 6. ration all essential commodities that are scarce; 7. discourage installment buying and encourage paying off debts. The program had gradually gone into effect, but to the accompaniment of contradictory statements by members of the Cabinet and by agency heads. Meanwhile the Army and Navy, also honeycombed with advertising men called Public Relations Officers, had been issuing voluminous reports on victories gained and saying as little as possible about defeats.

Yet somehow, despite all the blundering and the contradiction, the United States changed successfully from peace to bitter war. How great this achievement was is better understood if we recall the economic thinking which preceded it. Nearly everybody had preached the gospel of plenty. The good American bought a new car before his old had even approached obsolescence. He discarded tires which had been driven a few thousand miles. He was urged to do so—to buy new houses, new clothes, new radios, new iceboxes and everything under the sun—by advertisements which shouted at him from newspapers, magazines, and billboards or, literally, from radios. Suddenly the good American was told to do without; to patch, mend, and save. For the factories of the nation were being converted, if tardily, to total war.

Typewriter factories made machine guns. Automobile plants achieved assembly line production of fighters and bombers. The part played by labor and management in winning the war has not been given proper credit. The British expert, Major General J. F. C. Fuller, described its vital importance in a recent issue of the magazine *Army Ordnance:*

. . . for the first time in the history of war, battles were as much tussles between competing factories as between contending armies. The production of weapons, more so than the conscription of men, was the deciding factor in battle. God now marched with the biggest industries rather than with the biggest battalions. . . .

The production job was done; not without prolonged bickering. A start was made in May, 1940, when Germany began to invade the Low Countries. The President called back into being the Council of National Defense and appointed a National Defense Advisory Commission, with Lieutenant General William S. Knudsen, then a civilian, as its chairman. This was the first of four agencies, finally culminating in the War Production Board, which handled production. NDAC's troubles were legion. The armed services did not know what kind of war they would have to fight, or where. The generals and the admirals consistently underestimated America's capacity. A good many manufacturers delayed things, too, by opposing conversion. The war was still three thousand miles away. Civilian goods were rising in price, and maybe something would happen to preserve peace.

The Japanese attack on December 7 changed everything. The armed services now knew all too well whom they would have to fight. It was almost everybody and it was everywhere. So they adopted what was to be their policy for the duration: astronomical quantities of everything and to hell with civilian needs. Twelve months earlier President Roosevelt had tried to smooth out the production tangle by changing NDAC into the Office of Production Management—OPM. He also created the Supply, Priorities, and Allocations Board—SPAB—which was supposed to iron out disputes in the scramble for critical materials, but which was often confused with Spam. It was not until OPM became the War Production Board—WPB—that a single civilian, Donald M. Nelson, was put in charge of war production. And even Mr. Nelson was constantly embroiled with the military.

Even so, the goods came off the line in quantities which must have made gloomy reading for the dictators. They were carried to the fighting fronts in the staggering 45,000,000 tons of shipping which would slide off the ways by June, 1945. Training camps were thrown together throughout the country. By the close of 1941 the Army numbered more than 1,500,000 men.

Months before Pearl Harbor a group of scientists had started work on the most stupendous secret, and most terrible discovery, of the war. In all the major warring nations men had been engaged in a frantic race to unleash atomic power. In this lay, beyond any doubt, victory. But that the secret would be found seemed fantastically improbable. Hardly more than a dozen men in the United States knew the whole story of the gigantic project, ultimately to cost $2,000,000,000, handled by the Office of Scientific Research and Development. Out of the researches of the most renowned American and British scientists into unexplored realms of knowledge grew vast factories in Tennessee, New Mexico, and Washington. Tens of thousands of men and women were employed making—but they did not know what they were making.

They learned, along with their fellow citizens, on the morning of August 7—possibly the most momentous day in history. An atomic bomb had been dropped on the Japanese industrial city, Hiroshima, President Truman announced. It was 12,000 times more powerful than the most modern TNT. Hardly more than 100 bombers, each with a single atomic bomb, could equal the devastation hurled against Europe in all the war's raids. A second atomic bomb was dropped on Nagasaki. Then Japan surrendered. Men celebrated throughout the world, of course. But they also pondered the awesome significance of the discovery of atomic energy. Wisely used, it meant a new age of power and of untold wealth. Unwisely used, it probably meant the end of mankind.

Part of the mystery which had surrounded OSRD and Dr. Vannevar Bush, its director, was lifted. It became known that the agency had also supervised the perfection of radar. It had worked on DDT, the powerful insecticide which had made life more tolerable in Pacific jungles. In co-operation with Army and Navy experts it had improved innumerable weapons. The medical scientists on the OSRD staff had performed miracles in developing such drugs as penicillin.

Meanwhile the energies of citizens without scientific training, who could not fight or work in war industries, were being harnessed by the Office of Civilian Defense—OCD—which had been organized in May, 1941. Some of the activities of OCD seem faintly foolish now, so swift is the pace of modern war. Now that Germany and Japan have fallen the black-outs and dim-outs, the air raid drills, the boxes of sand and the pails of water are the remnants of a gigantic false alarm. OCD was the home front agency. It stimulated rubber, tin, paper, and aluminum salvage drives. It encouraged first-aid training—to the peril of husbands who had to submit to practice bandages and splints. OCD served a double purpose. Through it millions of Americans, anxious to participate in the war, found useful outlets for their energies. OCD also organized the large centers of population against panic and needless casualties in the event of air raids.

No raids occurred. The defeat of the Luftwaffe, the destruction of German industry by the Army Air Forces, and the rapid advances across France and Germany blocked what plans Hitler may have had. We now know that raids by means of rocket bombs would almost certainly have taken place had the European war continued for another year. The Axis might have won the atomic race. The sirens, the sand, and the water buckets served their purpose. Their cost, together with fire-fighting apparatus, ran into hundreds of millions but they were among the minor expendables of war.

Americans—at least American women—learned to use a new form of currency: ration stamps and tokens. Americans accustomed themselves to little butter and almost no beef. They got along without bacon. As the war continued, shortages developed in cheaper clothes, leather goods of all kinds, kitchen utensils, paper, and other commodities. Nobody suffered, except possibly during the short-lived scarcity of whisky and cigarettes. But

America at war was curiously different from America at peace. Store clerks, cooks, and nursemaids flocked to the war plants. The old American custom of quick, efficient, courteous service was abandoned for the duration. Instead of being always right, the customer was always wrong.

"Don't ya know there's a war on!" was the snarling answer to any complaint.

In charge of rationing was the Office of Price Administration, the colossal agency which had once been part of the National Defense Advisory Commission. It had 60,000 paid employees and branches throughout the country. Hundreds of thousands of volunteer workers sat on War Price and Rationing Boards and tried to uncover black market operations. These flourished, nonetheless. There were black markets for gasoline, nylon stockings, meats and other foods. OPA, like all the other war agencies, made mistakes. During the optimistic summer of 1944 it looked as though Germany might collapse, so that autumn OPA lifted rationing from most foods. With the German break-through, it quickly clamped on the lid again.

The black markets flourished because Americans have always been inclined to disobey laws they do not like, as was proved during prohibition. Enforcement of price control laws was made additionally difficult by the huge purchasing power caused by high wages and full employment. Certain aspects of the prohibition era returned. The taxi driver who had known about a hidden speakeasy could now guide his fares to a filling station where gasoline coupons were sold. The bellboy could supply cigarettes. Many butchers sold steaks at illegal prices. Retailers and restaurant dealers conspired with wholesalers to get more than their share of rationed goods. Crack-downs were frequent, although OPA was handicapped by an inadequate enforcement staff and by a complacent public. Fines running into hundreds of thousands of dollars were collected. Counterfeiters who were printing millions of gasoline coupons were convicted.

OPA and other agencies working with it held the line against inflation fairly well, and thereby reduced the cost of the war by untold billions of dollars. In the last war the cost of living had increased 63 per cent by the time of the armistice. Prices, compared with 1914, had doubled by 1920. It would have been far better had the government acted more promptly this time. The price of food had risen 47 per cent over 1939 by the fall of 1943. Valuable months were lost before prices on essential commodities were fixed. Again, faulty administration was responsible. It was not until the Office of Economic Stabilization was created in October, 1942, that consistent policies were adopted and the friction among federal agencies cut down.

In the creation of OES and the establishment of the Office of War Mobilization and Reconversion in October, 1944, President Roosevelt conceded that the huge new Federal Government had been functioning badly. Former Supreme Court Justice James F. Byrnes was the head of each office, in turn, and was actually Assistant President of the United States until he became Secretary of State in the Truman Administration.

It may be stated categorically that the war agencies did an infinitely better job than in the last war, when not a single American airplane, and relatively few weapons, reached France before the armistice. Transportation broke down to the point where the government finally took over the railroads. Ably assisted by the Office of Defense Transportation, the railroads did a superb job in World War II. ODT created a system whereby it knew the precise location of every freight car in the country. It knew what goods waited at Atlantic coast ports and rerouted trains so that congestion of war material was rare. Civilian travel was too complicated to ration, however, except on the airlines, where priorities were instituted. Campaigns against unnecessary civilian travel were less than successful. Americans continued to take vacations, to visit the races, and to make other needless trips. But as millions of soldiers were shifted to the Pacific via already overburdened transcontinental lines, nearly all the Pullman sleepers in the country were requisitioned for military use. Sheer discomfort began to deter civilian travel where appeals to patriotism had failed.

The people of the United States did moderately well at paying the cost of the war. They could have done a great deal better. From time to time, before Pearl Harbor, there had been talk of "drafting capital . . . taking all the profit out of war production." Nothing like this occurred. Congress was never quite courageous enough in financing the war. Yet taxes were the highest in the history of the country. Under the 1941 Revenue Act, a married man with two dependents paid no tax unless his income was $2,400. Then he paid $6. If his income was $5,000 he paid only $271. Under the 1943 law a man earning $2,500 pays $179 as compared with $12. On a $5,000 income he pays $773 as against $271 under the 1941 Act.

Uncle Sam has collected about $123,000,000,000 in taxes since December 1, 1941. This represents about 40 per cent of the cost of the war. The difference was met by borrowing, of course, and the only sound way for a government to borrow is from the people themselves. Any sums needed could have been raised at the nation's banks, but this would have increased the currency in the country and would have raised prices. That was the basic reason for the War Bond drives. The sale of "E" Bonds, which are the smaller denominations, totaled almost $36,000,000,000 between May 1, 1941, and June, 1945. Although the holders could turn them in merely by presenting them at any bank, only $7,000,000,000 was redeemed during the same period. A very successful plan was payroll deductions for War Bonds. In just one month—April, 1945 —25,000,000 Americans bought $485,000,000 in War Bonds in that way. From the time when the plan was started, April, 1942, up to April, 1945, payroll deductions reached $16,000,000,000.

At frequent intervals, as the war progressed, gigantic bond drives were staged. These were marked by the usual ballyhoo. Motion-picture actresses paraded or auctioned off their more intimate garments to heavy purchasers. Nylon stockings, whisky during the shortage, seats to Broadway hit shows, and other valuable things were obtained by buying War Bonds which could, of course, be cashed in 60 days. Citizens were solemnly told that unless they bought bonds more Americans would be killed, which was absurdly untrue. The hand of the advertising promoter was apparent again. "He gives his life. You only lend your money," was the substance of the official slogan for one bond drive.

A safe assumption is that most Americans bought bonds because they were an excellent investment, a hedge against postwar depression, and because they felt a patriotic compulsion to do so. While a minority bought jewels, fur coats, and other luxuries, an overwhelming majority listened to the warnings about inflation and saved a percentage of their increased earnings. The total is almost unbelievable. Best government estimates are that between May 1, 1941, and March 31, 1945, the liquid savings of individuals reached $129,000,000,000. Of this some $39,000,000,000 went into life insurance and debt repayments—but $90,000,000,000 is new. Unless ceilings and other price controls are maintained for a period of years after the war, a disastrous wave of buying, sending prices to the sky, is probable.

One reason the war government grew so big and cost so much was that it had to solve postwar problems too. Surplus war goods have to be sold without disrupting business and wrecking prices. Government-owned plants must be sold or otherwise disposed of. Manufacturers formerly engaged in war work must be assisted in the complicated problems of conversion back to the goods of peace. These and innumerable other puzzles must be solved by the Office of War Mobilization and Reconversion and other subordinate government agencies. The responsibility of the officials in charge is heavy. Between $5,000,000,000 and $7,000,000,000 in contracts had to be terminated gradually when Japan surrendered. Unless this is done in an orderly manner, unless the plant owners are swiftly paid for the goods on hand and liberally financed for reconversion, a depression will certainly sweep the country. And then there will be few jobs for the 12,000,000 returning servicemen.

The proper deployment of the country's manpower continued to be a major problem even after V-E Day. President Roosevelt and spokesmen for the Army and Navy had pressed for a compulsory labor draft when, at times, production was lowered because of an inadequate number of workers. Congress refused, however, partly because some of its members regarded the Army itself as profligate in using manpower. Under the War Manpower Commission a hit-or-miss system of forbidding workers to leave their jobs was continued. The shipyards suffered most. Farmers, struggling to grow record crops, were also handicapped.

A revitalized Veterans Administration may be expected now that General Omar N. Bradley has been appointed head of it. With the United States Employment Service, functioning under the War Manpower Commission, it is the agency which must make certain that men and women returning from the service get all the benefits to which they are entitled. Under the G.I. Bill of Rights they will receive allowances for education, for vocational training, and for many other purposes. If disabled, they are, of course, taken care of until they can resume their places in normal civilian life. United States Employment Service offices are located in all principal cities. The veteran, in theory and on paper, will be treated as he deserves by a grateful nation. But this will be so only if the local branches of the Veterans Administration and the USES are manned by skilled and industrious experts. If the jobs are awarded as patronage, the G.I. Bill of Rights might better never have been passed.

Badly administered at times, the nation was about as close to total war as a democracy can attain. Never before in history had economic forces been used with such vigor and ingenuity. For war had grown infinitely complicated. Its tools required materials from all over the world or demanded the invention of substitutes when they could not be obtained. When the war started, a number of different agencies were fighting this economic warfare. Gradually they were largely consolidated into the Foreign Economic Administration.

The most powerful weapon used was Lend-Lease. This began on March 11, 1941. Between that date and March, 1945, a total of $39,000,000,000 in goods of every description had been shipped to our allies in all parts of the world. This was no one-way operation. The United States received about $5,500,000,000 in reverse Lend-Lease. Belgium, for instance, contributed almost twice as much as she received. By far the greater part of reverse Lend-Lease came from Great Britain. The AAF used bombs of British manufacture, auxiliary gas tanks, and other supplies. Great Britain, although it suffered terrible capital losses during the war, has supplied about $3,500,000,000 in reciprocal aid. England built 133 airfields for American fliers at a cost of $440,000,000. But the dollar is not a wholly reliable standard. A better test of Allied mutual assistance is found in the supply of materials desperately needed at home. Despite acute food shortages, Belgium furnished vegetables, including potatoes, which added to the United States Army's supply of fresh foods. France, wrecked by defeat, gave coal, steel, lumber, textiles, and food sorely needed for home consumption.

Americans have had little conception of the magnitude of reverse Lend-Lease. At first this was because German propagandists distorted the facts and portrayed the United States as a foolish, international Santa Claus. Later misunderstanding was caused, in part, by rumors spread by returning servicemen. They reported that Britain charged exorbitant sums for the use of airports and to bring American troops home. Actually these services, continuing long after V-E and V-J days, did not cost American taxpayers a penny. Credits were, of course, entered against the Lend-Lease totals provided by the United States.

Economic warfare was far more than Lend-Lease, however. It meant denying Axis countries vital necessities by buying them first in neutral markets. It meant, as the *Report to the Nation* issued by the government in 1942 described it, "fighting the Messerschmitt before it is a Messerschmitt, fighting the tank before it is a tank, smashing the submarine before it can go to sea."

War brings unity. People in deadly peril do not quarrel among themselves. Differences will rise again now that peace is restored, however, and this is the way it must be in a democracy. The problems of all government—village, city, state, and federal—are infinitely more complicated now than when the nation was young. Added to them are the problems brought by the war: preserving peace, maintaining a balanced economy, making real for the first time in recorded history the blessings of the Four Freedoms.

Americans are prone to extremes. When the last war ended they turned their backs on the Old World and sought to live behind the illusory barriers of isolation. Now, having had the biggest Federal Government in history, some of them may decide to cut it too drastically. The checks they impose may be so severe that nothing will get done. If this happens there will be real peril of still another extreme, the one most feared by thoughtful students of government. Power will again be concentrated almost wholly in the Federal Government, and the influence of Congress will fade.

This won't happen if the movement to modernize Congress is successful. It won't happen if the 12,000,000 men and women who have fought the war take an intelligent part in the government, in which they will hold the balance of power.

Part Three

Our Jobs and How We Did Them

I. WHAT LABOR DID

by R. J. THOMAS

R. J. Thomas *has been president of the United Automobile Workers, CIO, the largest labor union in the world, for the last six years. Many of his 45 years have been spent working as a welder in automobile factories in the Detroit area. He is a vice-president of the Congress of Industrial Organizations, and was a member of President Roosevelt's wartime Labor Advisory Committee and a labor member of the National War Labor Board from its inception. He has been an uncompromising supporter of labor's wartime no-strike pledge. During 1944 and 1945 he made three visits to Europe, once to the front lines under the auspices of the United States Army and twice later as head of the American delegation to the World Trade Union Congress in London.*

I LIKE the idea of having a chance to tell so many G.I.s, through the medium of this book, some of the things I was able to discuss with a lot of you in France and England, before V-E Day.

For various reasons it has fallen to me to tell you something of what the 14 million men and women of the Congress of Industrial Organizations, the American Federation of Labor, and the Railway Brotherhoods were doing during the months or years you were away. One of the reasons, I suppose, is that I am president of the world's biggest labor union—the United Automobile, Aircraft and Agricultural Workers of America (UAW-CIO). During the war this was a very big union indeed, reaching a maximum of 1,300,000 active members, with several hundred thousand more on leave in the armed forces. In terms of war production, we were first. We had a song, while you were gone—"It's that UAW-CIO, makes the Army roll and go." We were the men and women who built a great proportion of the tanks and practically all the jeeps, the trucks, the half-tracks, the ducks, much of the shells and bullets and rockets, and most of the aircraft. We're proud of our record.

I do not believe that the gap which some newspapers and people of ill will have tried to establish between the armed forces and organized labor really exists at all. It's more a matter of understanding each other's problems. Given that understanding, it's easy to have good will. Labor leaders in this country have tried hard to understand your problems, and when we've been able to meet you face to face (as I was lucky enough to do after D Day in France, on Omaha Beach and up to the front just outside of Paris before that city fell to us) it hasn't been hard to get you to understand labor's point of view. After all, the people in labor unions and the men in the armed forces are pretty much the same people, coming from the same towns, the same streets, often from the same houses. I can't believe there wasn't at least one trade union member in your platoon or group. And inasmuch as we are all the same kind of people, it shouldn't be too hard to appreciate each other's point of view.

For your part, I suppose you are interested in two principal matters. First, how come all those strikes we heard about? Second, how come those sky-high war wages? I'm going to answer both of these questions, I hope to your satisfaction. But before getting down on the mat with either of them, it might be to the point to try and tell you (in case you don't know) just what a labor union is and what it tries to do.

A labor union is a group of employees who have joined together so that they may bargain with management on something like an equal footing. Now, of course there is nothing like that in the Army or Navy or any of the armed services, and there shouldn't be, because the circumstances are entirely different from civilian life, and besides there are stringent and effective rules governing the conduct of every person in the armed services. For example, a private is just as much protected in his own particular rights by the carefully written regulations as is a colonel or a general (well, almost as much protected). This, of course, isn't so in civilian life, which is not on a regimented basis because it is intended for something entirely different from an army or a navy. The latter are intended to fight and win a war with; the civilian economy, obviously, is a way of life that continues in peace and in war.

Of course, in wartime we have to agree to certain modifications of our civilian rights and privileges in order to make sure the war is won, but it is always true, and especially so in a democracy, that these interferences with civil rights are looked on with suspicion by the people generally, and should be done away with just as soon as it may be safe for the nation to do so.

Now, most of you were really civilians in uniform. Very few of you were what might be called professional soldiers, because, thanks be, the U. S. A. is not a militaristic nation. We fight wars when we have to, but we don't like wars and we'd rather not have any. And as civilians again you know perfectly well that in a relatively free economy such as ours you have to protect yourself where the laws and the courts and the general customs do not protect you.

For many, many years the working people of this country had little or no protection from three things which you and I and all of us must be interested in: (1) the boss could lay workers off or fire them for bad reasons or no reasons at all; (2) the boss could and would reduce wages just as soon as somebody came along who would do the work for less, even if the wages didn't mean sufficient food and clothing and shelter for the worker and his family; (3) the working conditions were very often bad as regards health, safety, and the meanness and discriminations exercised by petty and incompetent men in foremen's and other supervisory positions.

Some one or all three of these wrong things applied in almost every place of employment. Working people came to feel that they were caught in the clutches of a vast machine which took them in, worked them hard for the least possible pay, then threw them out when they got older ór were sick or tired so they became paupers and dependent on charity. We felt that, unlike the old days of small companies and home ownership, it was impossible to talk to the boss and tell him our troubles; the only person you could see was an underling who could do nothing to help you because he was only an employee himself, without the authority to correct conditions, although usually with enough authority to make them worse.

So unions were organized, for the purpose of obtaining better pay for the union members and others; to establish contractual seniority rights so a worker could not be laid off and then never be called back although younger men still held their jobs; to negotiate on working conditions, classification of jobs, and indeed all the many things that are involved in the effort to get a better standard of living in the home and better conditions on the job; and to end the spying upon and blacklisting of workers who did not meekly accept whatever the boss chose to give them.

Most of the earlier unions were what are called "craft" unions; that is, the workers of a particular high skill would join together to improve the conditions of their own group. Later came the so-called "industrial" unions, in which were included all the employees of a particular factory below the level of foremen and confidential management people. An outstanding example of a craft union is the International Typographical Union, whose members are those who work in newspaper composing rooms and job printing shops. They do not take in, for example, the pressmen who work in the same plant; nor do they take in the stereotypers who often work in the same room with them; each of these groups has its own craft union, which separately negotiates for its members with management on wages and working conditions, generally speaking. Other examples of craft unions would be the Carpenters, the Boiler Makers, the Steamfitters (all affiliated with the AFL), many of whose members worked so competently and so courageously as Seabees during the war.

On the other hand, in a union such as the United Automobile Workers, CIO, we have as members, and bargain for, everyone in the Ford Motor Company's great River Rouge Plant near Detroit —tool and die makers, electricians and millwrights, production workers, sweepers, everyone below the level of a foreman. The same or a similar method of organization holds true in the steel mills (United Steelworkers of America, CIO), in the coal mines (John L. Lewis's United Mine Workers, not affiliated with either CIO or AFL), in the metal mines (Mine, Mill, and Smelter Workers, CIO), in electrical or electronics factories (United Electrical, Radio and Machine Workers, CIO), and in many other industries.*

In actual operation, collective bargaining means that the union,

* A number of veterans have asked me questions regarding the setup of unions, which, while not strictly relevant to this chapter, may be of some value as a rather lengthy footnote. The administrative setup usually is that in one particular plant there is a so-called "local" union or lodge or chapel (whatever that particular union may call its locals), which negotiates with the management for the members in the plant; and the local in turn is affiliated with a national or international union, which provides advice and guidance and financial resources in time of trouble; and the national or international union is usually affiliated either with the American Federation of Labor or with the Congress of Industrial Organizations, in each case a central body which establishes a unified policy on questions of national or international import. Now, most labor unions are really democratic; that is, those who pay dues have the right by secret ballot to decide who shall be their officers, and who shall speak for them in bargaining with management. Naturally, in a democratic union the members are very jealous of their rights and are usually willing to fight to protect those rights. They are properly suspicious of anything that tends to take away their democratic rights or limit them in any way.

If you have never belonged to a labor union it would probably be useful for you to know the structure of a union such as my own, which I quite naturally would nominate as perhaps the most democratic large organization in the United States.

The foundation of the Auto Workers is the local union. This consists of a majority or all of the workers in a single plant. The local union MUST hold elections of officers, committeemen, and shop stewards every year. These elections are by secret ballot and anyone is entitled to be a candidate who is a member in good standing of the local union. In the case of executive officers of the local and sometimes of committeemen, etc., a year's continuous membership prior to the date of nomination is required for eligibility to office.

through its properly chosen spokesmen, stands ready to bargain for any one of its members, or all of its members at times, on the contract between the union and the employer, on grievances, whether of working conditions, wages, hours, bad food in the cafeteria at the plant—almost anything you can think of that affects how people work and what they shall be paid for it. The union of course bargains with management, which nominates whoever it thinks can best do the bargaining for it, and they meet across a table, talk their troubles out, and eventually come to a meeting of minds and the grievance is disposed of. In some cases —and they should be very few in genuine collective bargaining— no agreement is reached and the issue is finally resolved by a strike, in which one side or the other loses and so settles the issue.

What I have said so far has to do with peacetime collective bargaining. In wartime, especially in World War II, which has been on a global basis and involved the entire economy of our

---

If any shop steward (who is the union spokesman in the plant for perhaps two hundred workers) or committeeman or chief steward (who will probably represent several groups of workers in the plant) fails to give satisfaction to his constituents, he may be recalled by a two-thirds vote of those attending a recall meeting, of which seven days' notice to the membership is required. If he is recalled, then a new election is held.

If any union member is accused of unbecoming conduct, a trial committee of at least seven members must be elected by secret ballot and the case heard. If he is convicted by the trial committee, the committee's report must be ratified by a two-thirds vote at a membership meeting for the verdict to be effective. On conviction, then, the accused member has the right of appeal to the International Executive Board, and if he loses there he has the right of appeal to the annual convention of the union, which consists of more than 2,000 individually elected convention delegates.

The local union has a very wide measure of local control of its own affairs. It has complete control of its finances, subject to audit by the International Union's traveling auditors, and subject to certain provisions requiring the setting aside of money in its own treasury for a strike fund, for educational purposes, etc. If, however, the local union officers are wasting or stealing the funds of the local, the International Union can take it over and suspend any or all of the officers on a vote of the International Executive Board, but it is provided that a new election of officers must take place within sixty days. So long as a local union is financially solvent, it cannot be taken over by the International Union except under special and unusual circumstances threatening the very life of the union. You can see from this explanation that a local union has a very wide measure of autonomy, the principal restricting

democracy, the situation was entirely different. Let me tell you now what has been going on while you were gone. First of all, let me say that most civilians have been honestly patriotic and anxious to do everything they could to win the war as quickly as possible. I think that is as true of the people in management as it is true of the working people who turned out the stuff you used to fight with, by their toil and sweat and long hours of hard, monotonous, and terribly dull work in the factory.

Of course, there have been profiteers and there have been companies that deliberately turned out shoddy and defective war material, just as there have been lazy and useless people who called themselves war workers, but on the whole the record is good. An honest and conscientious job was done by both management and labor, and the greatest flood of war materials of the highest quality in the history of warfare was there, ready for you to use when you needed it. In practically every instance since the

---

factor being that it must operate within the rules laid down by the International Constitution. The constitution was written by the conventions, which, as stated, are composed only of democratically elected delegates.

The International Executive Board is composed of a director for each geographical region of the union plus the president, vice-presidents, and secretary-treasurer. The officers are elected by the convention as a whole; the regional directors are separately elected during the convention by the delegates from each geographical region. Every officer and board member must face his electors annually at the convention.

The International Executive Board is the supreme power in the union between conventions; it is required to meet at least every ninety days. The International President is the supreme power between board meetings, and his actions are subject to review and approval by the Board, and the actions of either or both are subject to review and approval by the convention. The rate of dues (in the case of this union, $1.00 per month) is fixed by the convention, and under the constitution no more than one assessment of $1.00 can be levied on the membership by the International Executive Board in any one year. However, a local union, by going through an elaborate procedure and with the approval of the regional director, can levy special assessments in addition to the international assessment. This is frequently done, for example, to buy a building, or if the local's income is insufficient for its operating expenses. The $1.00 per month dues are divided, 60 cents to the local union, and 40 cents to the International Union, and the International Union in turn pays 5 cents per capita tax to the Congress of Industrial Organizations. I do not know how a more democratic organization than this could be set up.—R. J. T.

early days of the war if a shortage existed in any particular place it was because of difficulties of transportation and planning—not because of any production lack.

When Pearl Harbor came, the country was already producing a lot of war materials on Lend-Lease and for the equipment of our new Army and Navy. There was an increasing feeling among the leaders of labor and in the public generally that strikes which affected in any way the production of war goods for our own possible future use and for the immediate use of the anti-Axis nations were wrong and should not take place. With Pearl Harbor there was an immediate and practically unanimous decision by the leaders of organized labor that, through voluntary action of the unions, strikes should not be authorized until the war was won.

So, a few days after Pearl Harbor, labor's no-strike pledge was made to President Franklin D. Roosevelt. Under that pledge the responsible leaders of organized labor agreed that there would be no strikes authorized during the period of the war.

That pledge was not broken by any of the responsible leaders of the AFL, CIO, or Railway Brotherhoods who subscribed to it throughout the war. When wildcat or unauthorized strikes took place, and you know as well as I that there were many such strikes, the leaders of labor put forth every effort to get the people back to work. The result of that determined effort was that most work stoppages were ended in a few hours, or—with rare exceptions—in a day or two or three days.

Well, you may ask quite properly, why were there any strikes, unauthorized or authorized?

I personally did not and do not condone such strikes. I ended many of them myself by appealing to the workers involved and by use of the prestige of my office as president of the largest union of all—and the same stand was taken by every responsible leader in the CIO and in the AFL and most of the independent unions. But still some strikes did occur. I will try to explain why.

When labor gave its no-strike pledge to the Commander-in-

democracy, the situation was entirely different. Let me tell you now what has been going on while you were gone. First of all, let me say that most civilians have been honestly patriotic and anxious to do everything they could to win the war as quickly as possible. I think that is as true of the people in management as it is true of the working people who turned out the stuff you used to fight with, by their toil and sweat and long hours of hard, monotonous, and terribly dull work in the factory.

Of course, there have been profiteers and there have been companies that deliberately turned out shoddy and defective war material, just as there have been lazy and useless people who called themselves war workers, but on the whole the record is good. An honest and conscientious job was done by both management and labor, and the greatest flood of war materials of the highest quality in the history of warfare was there, ready for you to use when you needed it. In practically every instance since the

---

factor being that it must operate within the rules laid down by the International Constitution. The constitution was written by the conventions, which, as stated, are composed only of democratically elected delegates.

The International Executive Board is composed of a director for each geographical region of the union plus the president, vice-presidents, and secretary-treasurer. The officers are elected by the convention as a whole; the regional directors are separately elected during the convention by the delegates from each geographical region. Every officer and board member must face his electors annually at the convention.

The International Executive Board is the supreme power in the union between conventions; it is required to meet at least every ninety days. The International President is the supreme power between board meetings, and his actions are subject to review and approval by the Board, and the actions of either or both are subject to review and approval by the convention. The rate of dues (in the case of this union, $1.00 per month) is fixed by the convention, and under the constitution no more than one assessment of $1.00 can be levied on the membership by the International Executive Board in any one year. However, a local union, by going through an elaborate procedure and with the approval of the regional director, can levy special assessments in addition to the international assessment. This is frequently done, for example, to buy a building, or if the local's income is insufficient for its operating expenses. The $1.00 per month dues are divided, 60 cents to the local union, and 40 cents to the International Union, and the International Union in turn pays 5 cents per capita tax to the Congress of Industrial Organizations. I do not know how a more democratic organization than this could be set up.—R. J. T.

early days of the war if a shortage existed in any particular place it was because of difficulties of transportation and planning—not because of any production lack.

When Pearl Harbor came, the country was already producing a lot of war materials on Lend-Lease and for the equipment of our new Army and Navy. There was an increasing feeling among the leaders of labor and in the public generally that strikes which affected in any way the production of war goods for our own possible future use and for the immediate use of the anti-Axis nations were wrong and should not take place. With Pearl Harbor there was an immediate and practically unanimous decision by the leaders of organized labor that, through voluntary action of the unions, strikes should not be authorized until the war was won.

So, a few days after Pearl Harbor, labor's no-strike pledge was made to President Franklin D. Roosevelt. Under that pledge the responsible leaders of organized labor agreed that there would be no strikes authorized during the period of the war.

That pledge was not broken by any of the responsible leaders of the AFL, CIO, or Railway Brotherhoods who subscribed to it throughout the war. When wildcat or unauthorized strikes took place, and you know as well as I that there were many such strikes, the leaders of labor put forth every effort to get the people back to work. The result of that determined effort was that most work stoppages were ended in a few hours, or—with rare exceptions—in a day or two or three days.

Well, you may ask quite properly, why were there any strikes, unauthorized or authorized?

I personally did not and do not condone such strikes. I ended many of them myself by appealing to the workers involved and by use of the prestige of my office as president of the largest union of all—and the same stand was taken by every responsible leader in the CIO and in the AFL and most of the independent unions. But still some strikes did occur. I will try to explain why.

When labor gave its no-strike pledge to the Commander-in-

democracy, the situation was entirely different. Let me tell you now what has been going on while you were gone. First of all, let me say that most civilians have been honestly patriotic and anxious to do everything they could to win the war as quickly as possible. I think that is as true of the people in management as it is true of the working people who turned out the stuff you used to fight with, by their toil and sweat and long hours of hard, monotonous, and terribly dull work in the factory.

Of course, there have been profiteers and there have been companies that deliberately turned out shoddy and defective war material, just as there have been lazy and useless people who called themselves war workers, but on the whole the record is good. An honest and conscientious job was done by both management and labor, and the greatest flood of war materials of the highest quality in the history of warfare was there, ready for you to use when you needed it. In practically every instance since the

---

factor being that it must operate within the rules laid down by the International Constitution. The constitution was written by the conventions, which, as stated, are composed only of democratically elected delegates.

The International Executive Board is composed of a director for each geographical region of the union plus the president, vice-presidents, and secretary-treasurer. The officers are elected by the convention as a whole; the regional directors are separately elected during the convention by the delegates from each geographical region. Every officer and board member must face his electors annually at the convention.

The International Executive Board is the supreme power in the union between conventions; it is required to meet at least every ninety days. The International President is the supreme power between board meetings, and his actions are subject to review and approval by the Board, and the actions of either or both are subject to review and approval by the convention. The rate of dues (in the case of this union, $1.00 per month) is fixed by the convention, and under the constitution no more than one assessment of $1.00 can be levied on the membership by the International Executive Board in any one year. However, a local union, by going through an elaborate procedure and with the approval of the regional director, can levy special assessments in addition to the international assessment. This is frequently done, for example, to buy a building, or if the local's income is insufficient for its operating expenses. The $1.00 per month dues are divided, 60 cents to the local union, and 40 cents to the International Union, and the International Union in turn pays 5 cents per capita tax to the Congress of Industrial Organizations. I do not know how a more democratic organization than this could be set up.—R. J. T.

early days of the war if a shortage existed in any particular place it was because of difficulties of transportation and planning—not because of any production lack.

When Pearl Harbor came, the country was already producing a lot of war materials on Lend-Lease and for the equipment of our new Army and Navy. There was an increasing feeling among the leaders of labor and in the public generally that strikes which affected in any way the production of war goods for our own possible future use and for the immediate use of the anti-Axis nations were wrong and should not take place. With Pearl Harbor there was an immediate and practically unanimous decision by the leaders of organized labor that, through voluntary action of the unions, strikes should not be authorized until the war was won.

So, a few days after Pearl Harbor, labor's no-strike pledge was made to President Franklin D. Roosevelt. Under that pledge the responsible leaders of organized labor agreed that there would be no strikes authorized during the period of the war.

That pledge was not broken by any of the responsible leaders of the AFL, CIO, or Railway Brotherhoods who subscribed to it throughout the war. When wildcat or unauthorized strikes took place, and you know as well as I that there were many such strikes, the leaders of labor put forth every effort to get the people back to work. The result of that determined effort was that most work stoppages were ended in a few hours, or—with rare exceptions—in a day or two or three days.

Well, you may ask quite properly, why were there any strikes, unauthorized or authorized?

I personally did not and do not condone such strikes. I ended many of them myself by appealing to the workers involved and by use of the prestige of my office as president of the largest union of all—and the same stand was taken by every responsible leader in the CIO and in the AFL and most of the independent unions. But still some strikes did occur. I will try to explain why.

When labor gave its no-strike pledge to the Commander-in-

Chief, it was obviously necessary to provide some means of finally settling disputes other than by striking. Labor has only one finally effective weapon—the strike—which means the withholding of their labor from the employer by the workers. When you are bargaining and the employer knows that in the last analysis you have a real weapon, he will—unless he is silly—bargain genuinely and really try to get a meeting of minds and a mutually satisfactory settlement of grievances. But if labor gives up its only real weapon, the strike, it would be asking too much of human nature not to expect many, perhaps most, employers to take advantage of labor being disarmed, so to speak, and so collective bargaining would be largely destroyed. President Roosevelt was very well aware of this and therefore established the National War Labor Board to handle wage questions and many other grievances, giving the board certain powers to act, the whole being backed by the authority of the Congress. The board was a three-party board; one party was nominated by management, one party was nominated by labor, and one party represented the public. Most of the public members were people familiar with the relations between labor and management, and able to take a fair view of both sides of any given question. The public members, of course, were really the most important ones, because in any given dispute whichever way they voted would win. Decisions on matters brought before the board were decided by vote. Most decisions were unanimous.

Although the War Labor Board had no means in itself of enforcing its orders, it could, where either labor or management refused to comply with a directive, ask the Army or Navy to take over the establishment and operate it so there would be compliance. This is what occurred in the famous Montgomery Ward noncompliance case, in the Kearny Shipyards case, and in quite a few others. Pretty generally, however, its directives were obeyed because both management and labor recognized that to fight its verdicts could lead only to chaos in labor-management relations and would terribly injure the war effort.

Well, we got going with the War Labor Board, and really ran into headaches. In the first place, pretty soon thousands of plants were making war materials; the civilian economy in war production, transportation, and related activities expanded hugely; and all kinds of problems appeared that simply would not have occurred in peacetime with a relatively stable national economy. The consequence was that the War Labor Board fell far behind with its work; some cases were nearly two years in the works before being finally settled. Eventually, on the insistence of my own and other unions, regional War Labor Boards had to be set up (as they should have been from the first), so that quicker decisions could be made on cases which did not affect national policy; and an elaborate system of hearing panels, to hear the evidence so recommendations could be made to the board, was established. Yet it still took months to dispose of a case. Now, you know just as well as I do that there is nothing more aggravating than to have a grievance and be unable to get a decision on it. It is psychologically better to have an answer of no than to have the question left hanging in mid-air for months. And let me tell you how this whole setup tended to break down genuine collective bargaining—by which I mean the two parties sitting across a table and reaching a mutually agreeable settlement.

That had been the practice in most unionized industries prior to the war. But there were many managements which had never liked to bargain. They hankered for the good old days when the boss made all the decisions and told his men—and that was it. The good old days when the foreman could fire a man if he failed to polish the apple brightly enough. The good old days when a man past forty was too old to work in many plants. So here was a grand chance. When the union spokesmen tried to bargain out a grievance, the management would say, "Take it to the War Labor Board." They would say this even if they knew for sure the union would win before the board, because they could count on weeks or months of delay; they could probably expect lowered morale among the union men and women in the defense of their rights, and therefore a weakening of the union; and they hoped that eventually the union would fall into a "What's the use?" rut and become less and less effective for its members. It would be foolish to deny that these tactics, which were adopted by many corporations large and small, were effective. Collective bargaining did break down, and a feeling of blind exasperation developed that found expression in unplanned and sporadic work stoppages, some of which continued long enough or involved enough people to be properly designated as strikes.

However, although it cannot be denied that there were many work stoppages, no such strike, so far as I have been able to learn, was ever authorized by any responsible leader in the AFL, CIO, or the Railway Brotherhoods (certainly not in any war plant), and I do not know of a single instance where such responsible leaders did not do everything in their power to get the workers back on their jobs as quickly as possible. The result was that these "wildcat" strikes were of very short duration and the actual loss of production was so little as compared with the whole production that it could be considered infinitesimal. For example, in June, 1945, the time lost because of strikes and lockouts was only 0.23 per cent, and Secretary of Labor Lewis B. Schwellenbach commented: "It is estimated that workers in the munitions industry alone, by remaining on the job on New Year's Day, Washington's Birthday, Memorial Day, and the Fourth of July, put in more than five times as many man days of work as were lost through strikes and lockouts during the first six months of this year." The military authorities, however, are the best judges of whether strikes prevented needed war supplies from reaching the battle zones. During a hearing of the Senate's War Investigating Committee, Senator Mead asked General Brehon Somervell, army chief of supply, whether it was true that arms had to be "rationed" among soldiers because of shortages.

"Make no mistake about it," General Somervell replied, "no one has suffered from a lack of supplies. The boys at the front have had everything that could possibly be moved to the front."

An Associated Press correspondent, Wes Gallagher, during the Battle of the Bulge, cabled back: "There are undoubtedly multiple reasons for the American setback. It is not due, however, to any shortage of men and materials in the broad sense. The Allies have a superiority of men and materials along the Western Front, and no instance has come to light to date where the defeat of any particular unit was caused by running out of ammunition." If you have seen active service yourself, you will best be able to test the truth of irresponsible charges that strikes denied you the weapons you needed.

The unions themselves made great efforts to enforce the no-strike pledge. When wildcat strikes did occur the leaders of these stoppages were opposed and denounced, and we worked patiently and effectively among the rank and file who had been misled by a few irresponsible minor leaders. Where persuasive efforts to end wartime strikes failed, as very rarely happened, and the companies involved discharged the ringleaders, the unions refused to defend those who were guilty. Local unions have been suspended and their officers removed for defiance of the no-strike pledge.

According to the United States Department of Labor (March, 1945, issue of the *Monthly Labor Review*), the relative figures on strikes and lockouts are as follows:

> January, 1941, man-days lost 1.1 per cent of the total
> January, 1943, man-days lost 0.6 per cent of the total
> January, 1944, man-days lost 1.0 per cent of the total
> January, 1945, man-days lost 0.3 per cent of the total

Looked at another way, in January, 1945, 44,000 industrial workers were involved in these industrial interruptions, out of a total civilian labor force in the same month of 50,960,000, of whom 43,430,000 were industrial workers and the rest engaged in industrial labor. And not all of the 44,000 out of 43 million industrial workers who were listed as idle in January, 1945, went on strike. Some were locked out; many were involuntarily thrown into idleness because others in their plant or department went on strike. The government's figures include all who were "made idle . . . whether or not they were directly involved in the dispute." Nor should it be supposed that the 44,000 involved were out for the entire month of January. Workers out for one shift, or one day, are included in the government's total.

The insignificance of the loss of man-hours through dispute may further be judged by a comparison with man-hours lost through industrial accidents while you were away. From Pearl Harbor to January 1, 1945, according to the Secretary of Labor, accidents in wartime industry took a toll of 6,725,000 casualties. From Pearl Harbor to January 1, 1944, there were 4,500,000 industrial casualties; of these, 37,600 workers were killed on the job —7,500 more than the military dead for the same period. More than 200,000 workers were disabled for life through industrial accidents, while 4,500,000 workers were temporarily disabled.

It is pretty hard for you to understand, undergoing the hardships of war and the restrictions of military life, just how a war worker can strike, anyway. But it is necessary to remember that the war worker feels that he too is in the war, to preserve our democratic way of life. If in his judgment an attempt is being made to destroy part of that democratic way of life, he will be strongly tempted to take direct action—even against the advice of his responsible leaders, who are better acquainted with the overall picture than he is. However, the people who strike are the fellows who have their own folks in the armed services; they are just such people themselves, very often, as make up the armed services, except that they do not have quite the feeling of being part of a military team that you fellows have. As is human nature, the aggravation they have over something connected with their daily work is the nearest and most important thing to them, and sometimes—and quite wrongly—that overshadows everything else. And a strike starts. Mind, this has been true not only in unionized plants, but also in unorganized establishments during the war.

In all fairness to management, it must also be stated that they have faced some difficult problems because of the enormous increase in the nation's productive capacity. As a result a considerable number of men and women who would under past conditions have been considered unemployable have found jobs. This has caused many difficulties for supervision. Moreover, and also because of the great expansion, it has been almost impossible for management to obtain and train enough competent foremen and other supervisory employees. Obviously, incompetent foremen can cause an awful lot of trouble for the workers under them and for the company they work for. It is at the foreman level that most labor relations between workers and employer are conducted, and a few incompetent foremen can make things very tough indeed for all concerned.

Let me again emphasize: THERE WAS NOT ONE STRIKE IN THE UNITED STATES DURING THE WAR THAT CAUSED A SHORTAGE OF MATÉRIEL ON ANY WAR FRONT.

In the whole picture there were other features that were aggravating to the workers. They saw their employers making greater profits than ever before in history; they saw a great wastage of manpower during the earlier part of the war when employers rushed to hire all the people they could in the expectation of large war orders, knowing that Uncle Sam was paying the bills anyway; and so some of them became pretty cynical about it all, particularly when they saw insidious attacks being made on their unions. But the materials of war were produced and moved to the fighting fronts in quantity and on time. For that feat both management and labor will be given undying credit by the verdict of history, for in doing the job a nonmilitary nation became the arsenal of the United Nations and the greatest military force in all the world.

Now let me tell you what was wrong with the picture of labor as it was presented to you in the newspapers, on the radio, and in all the reports you received which were affected by newspapers and radio. In the first place, never forget that the newspapers make headlines of the unusual. They don't make a headline of the fact that 498,000 people are hard at work in Detroit factories turning out munitions when 2,000 men and women in some one plant have been on strike for a day or two. No, the headline is built on the strike; the other hundreds of thousands who are working are not mentioned. Nor does the paper mention that in the plant on strike for a short time the workers have been on seven days a week for many months; that they have had no furloughs with pay or even a 48-hour leave. That wouldn't be news, and I suppose the newspapers and radio commentators shouldn't be blamed too much for making a loud noise about the unusual.

Let me give you a pretty little example of how the newspapers handled strikes. Congressman Melvin Price, of Illinois, who is himself a veteran of this war, told me this one. He said that in his district, southern Illinois, there were in the early months of 1945 two strikes—temporary work stoppages affecting several thousand workers—in a big plant. He inquired into the cause of these strikes which he had not been able to find in the newspapers and discovered that the union local had ordered work stopped because the management had refused to give their jobs back to two discharged veterans. The management claimed the men were —for medical reasons—incapable of doing the required work. The union sent the men to the famous Mayo Clinic, where they were given a clean bill of health. But management balked. Simply refused to give the veterans back their jobs. P. S. Both these veterans have their jobs, today.

So there were these two brief strikes played up by the papers, but cause not mentioned.

Did you—while you were away—ever see in any of the newspapers or clippings that you read that the cause for the strike that made you mad was that the union was defending your buddy's right to his job? I don't think you did. That's not "news," for too many of our newspapers. Our newspapers were too often interested only in making you think the unions were sticking the knife in your back, while you were gone.

Let me give you a direct comparison with military affairs. The newspapers tell about victories, but they don't say anything about how many men went over the hill or were absent without leave. Yet when it came to labor, that's just the way they did report it —the number who went AWOL, but not the victories of production as the main news.

See what I mean?

I hope that the foregoing has at least helped to clarify your principal beef against labor—the question of those wildcat strikes. Now, how about the other point, those sky-high wages?

Well, generally speaking the sky-high wages were a myth. Lucius Beebe and one or two other pink-froth newspaper columnists filled their space in the newspapers while you were away with a lot of silly nonsense about how the bar of the Stork Club in New York was so crowded by shipyard workers buying all the champagne in sight that gentlemen couldn't find places to do their polite drinking. Too bad, too bad; it made a nice story but it simply wasn't true.

There were high wages in some plants, of course. These were chiefly those plants which were strictly war babies; which started during the war emergency and offered high wages in order to attract workers from other established factories and businesses. It was not the workers themselves, generally speaking, who established these high rates; it was the war contractors, spending Uncle Sam's money, who did it to lure people away from other jobs. In the established enterprises, like General Motors and Ford and Chrysler, on the railroads, in the food industry and so forth, these very high wages never were paid. The wages were "frozen" by the Wage Stabilization Act and were strictly in line with pre-war wages, with a slight increase allowed theoretically to take care of the higher cost of living. Actually, the increase in hourly rates never did catch up with the cost of living, which went up 50 per cent as against permitted increases during the war period of 15 per cent under the so-called "Little Steel formula" of the National War Labor Board. However, "take-home" earnings were usually quite a bit larger than during peacetime, because most industries had been on a five-day, 40-hour week during peacetime, and when we entered the war the wraps were taken off on hours and six or seven eight-hour days a week became usual, in some instances rising as high as seven nine-hour or ten-hour days. To facilitate this continuous operation (which was enormously important because it meant that vital machinery would be used continuously instead of remaining idle over week ends), organized labor agreed to relinquish, during the war emergency, premium time for Saturday, Sunday, and holidays as such. This meant that whereas in peacetime it was usual to pay at least time and a half for Saturday, and double time for Sunday and holidays, during the war, labor agreed that these days should not be considered as any different from other days. Immediately after hostilities ended, this provision was properly canceled by President Truman, as the necessity for continuous war production no longer existed.

However, the freeze on wages was a constant source of irritation, especially to the hundreds of thousands, yes, millions, of workers frozen into jobs paying around a dollar an hour and less. They saw the cost of living rising steadily, despite the efforts of OPA and an unwilling Congress to hold down consumer prices. The housewife knew beyond any argument that her husband's pay check of about $40 or $45 a week after deductions for income tax, social security, Red Cross, etc., represented a real decline in the family's standard of living. And in some industries, such as the vitally important textile industry, for example, pay checks were much less than that. So there was a lot of aggravation, made worse by the fact that American industry as a whole was making the largest profits in all history, *after* payment of taxes. These irritations were a background cause of many wildcat strikes, which, while ostensibly for some other grievance than wages (because the workers knew that under the law they could not get more money), really were an outburst of resentment against lowered living standards in the face of enormous industrial profits.

The wage freeze was instituted in 1942 by President Roosevelt as one point of a seven-point program designed to protect against inflation and keep the cost of the war within bounds. At the time the President declared that this economic program would work only if all of the seven points were followed. One point was that incomes be limited to $25,000 a year. Congress made short shrift of that one. Another was that retail prices must be rigidly held. That one didn't work either, because Congress never would let OPA do a complete job of holding the line on prices. Actually, only some of the seven points worked with real effectiveness: one of these was the point that froze wages.

Aside from the actual job of producing and transporting war materials, labor had some other interesting contributions to make to the war effort. In the early days of the war, when its global scope was perhaps not fully realized and it was not understood just how much of a job winning this war would be, there was a good deal of hesitation by business in actually converting and getting into war production with both feet.

The unions conducted a terrific pressure campaign, which was of great assistance to the armed services, to force conversion to war production with all possible speed. My own union insisted that the production of passenger automobiles be stopped; we insisted that the sights for airplane production, which had previously been manufactured principally in big tinsmith shops, must be raised and the principles of mass production be applied to the airplane industry.

As I indicated above, the unions took a leading part in insisting on the application of price controls to avert an inflation which would have destroyed the value of the dollar and wiped out our savings and your savings. Had there been no unions in this country, I doubt whether OPA could have done one-quarter of the limited job it was able to do in keeping prices somewhat in line with wages.

One of the outstanding achievements of the war was the integration of vast numbers of women, who had never before worked in production plants, in war work of a thousand different kinds. They learned new skills and they turned out vast quantities of the stuff you have been fighting with, especially in the aircraft industry. Another outstanding achievement in the interest of real economic democracy was the upgrading of Negroes and their acceptance for skilled and semiskilled work in many industries which had never before accepted them in any capacity, or in any but the most menial jobs. We cannot have a united democratic nation unless everyone has an equal chance to make a decent living. Out of this war at least came that opportunity for millions who never had the chance before. These Negro workers did a grand job and made an enormous contribution toward winning the war and toward a better understanding between all of us.

In the field of transportation, which certainly was just as important as production in this war of vast distances, a truly magnificent job was done by labor. The Railroad Brotherhoods and the railroad managements co-operated so that the greatest quantities of goods of every description in history were moved with a minimum of difficulty and with very little increase in plant and rolling stock. The traffic jams on the railroads which were a disgrace in World War I did not occur this time. If bottlenecks did appear, everybody worked to clear them and the goods kept rolling forward. On the highways the truckers (Brotherhood of Teamsters, AFL) worked long hours and made a great contribution to the transportation job. On the sea the maritime unions (notably the CIO's National Maritime Union), whose members suffered terrific casualties during the long period of submarine menace, set an example of devotion to duty and fearlessness that was an inspiration.

Space limits the mention of all the unions making real contributions to victory, but I should like to single out the Industrial Union of Marine and Shipbuilding Workers (CIO), who, together with the AFL's Boilermakers, built the thousands of ships—

Liberty ships, Victory ships, troopships, and all the myriad landing ships used on invasions—which combined to make a bridge
to victory.

Politically, organized labor—CIO, AFL, and the Brotherhoods
—was doing a job for you on the home front. There would be
little satisfaction for you in winning the war overseas and then
finding you had lost your rights as citizens when you got home
again and out of uniform. We have felt, and we feel, that what
is good for labor is good for you, because we are one. We fought
hard to make sure that income taxes were heaviest on those best
able to pay. We fought to do away with the poll tax, which was
originally established to keep the poor whites in certain states
from voting, and which has since been distorted into a racial
question although it still keeps the white workers from voting.
We led and are leading the fight for fair employment practices—
that is, to end economic discrimination based upon race, creed,
or color.

One of the great efforts of union labor during the war was to
establish labor-management committees which were intended by
labor at least to provide a means for a better understanding between labor and management, to develop methods and ideas for
faster and more economical production, and to channel war activities such as contributions to War Chests, the development of
blood banks, and so forth in a spirit of full co-operation. This
activity had the earnest support of President Roosevelt, and a
division to foster it was established by the Federal Government.
A large number of these labor-management committees were established, but most of them failed of their real purpose. There is
a fear on the part of management too often that any genuine
co-operation of this kind will mean a giving up to labor of some
part of the prerogatives and rights of management. As a result of
this, most labor-management committees degenerated into a
method of handling minor activities, but any attempt to promote
better production methods on a truly co-operative basis was discouraged by management. This was unfortunate, and I think

short-sighted, for committees such as this have been functioning in Great Britain for many years, and proved an immensely important factor in this war. However, some progress was made along these lines, and at least a few of the committees, out of the many hundreds that were established, worked well.

Because of the need to develop new methods and to work out new "know-how," a great many establishments were receptive to suggestions from the workers as to improvements in machines and methods. Many plants gave prizes for suggestions that were adopted, and union workers developed and turned over to management improvements that were undoubtedly worth untold millions and that did greatly accelerate production. It stands to reason, of course, that a man working on the job can often figure out for himself a better way of doing an operation. There is a strong urge to do so, even on the selfish basis of making his work easier. In prewar days it was often very difficult to get such ideas adopted, for various reasons—the foreman was apt to claim personal credit for the idea, thus robbing the worker of the credit and whatever reward there might be; some managements frowned on any advice from their workers as an infringement on the prerogatives of management; others simply didn't think the workers had any good ideas. However, in the process of changing over to the manufacture of war materials, management also had to learn, so everybody's ideas became acceptable. And the rate of productivity on the part of all workers soared unbelievably.

Labor also had to make a terrific fight to develop proper manpower controls. Some of the proposals that were made were either unworkable or would have hampered the war effort. But we were able to make our influence felt and to do a reasonably good job on manpower controls and job placement under government direction.

Early in the development of selective service, it became necessary for organized labor to take a firm stand for the protection of the seniority rights of the men in the armed services. In the face of considerable resistance, we forced the inclusion in our contracts with management of clauses which said in effect that anyone going into the armed services would accumulate seniority in his old job until his return. This was resisted by some employers, but eventually it became the pattern for industry. Later, when the G.I. Bill of Rights came along, we did everything possible to make the bill even more generous than it is, and played a great part in insuring its passage. At the time this was written organized labor had other bills in the hopper at Washington to extend and improve the benefits to ex-servicemen under the G.I. Bill.

As an example of the policy of labor unions toward veterans, I might cite the model clause which my own union is having incorporated in many contracts. Under this clause a veteran, upon being hired and passing through ɛ very brief probationary period, ranks on the seniority list with all of the time he has accumulated in the armed services since May 1, 1940. This, of course, is a great protection against layoffs in slack times and means that a great many veterans, coming in fresh to the factories, will hold their jobs when large numbers of war workers have been laid off.

Organized labor, generally speaking, is leading the political campaign for government policies that will insure full employment in peacetime—and that fight, of course, is your fight because you will no doubt be looking for a job when you are discharged. The hopes and ambitions of thousands of servicemen to become independent owners of businesses are certain to be disappointed; this statement is based upon the simple mathematical calculation by Dun and Bradstreet that 95 per cent of all businesses fail or discontinue. So most of you will have to get jobs. We are doing everything we can to make sure that there will be jobs for everyone in the postwar period.

There has been a lot of talk about the CIO's activities in political campaigns under the direction of the Political Action Committee. PAC had first the function of getting the people to vote. In so doing it was carrying out the most important principle of democracy: that as large a number of people shall participate in

political decisions as possible. PAC was highly effective in re-electing President Roosevelt in 1944. Its basic principle was and continues to be to endorse those candidates who will best support the cause of the common people, and then persuade the masses to vote for them. It is a basic political principle that in small elections reactionaries win; in large elections the people win. PAC has been naturally very disturbing to those who like to pull wires and keep control, because when the people speak at the polls the wire-pullers lose. It is only a secondary function of PAC to persuade the people to vote for liberal candidates, because in almost every instance if a large enough number of people vote, the liberal candidate will win anyway. The real problem, then, is to get people to vote. PAC mobilized thousands of workers to ring doorbells and ask people to get out and vote. It was in line with this principle that organized labor insisted so strongly, in Congress and in the states, upon a system of voting for the armed services that would enable as many servicemen as possible to cast their ballots in presidential and other elections. We were not completely successful, but we did at least make it reasonably possible for most of you to vote. You have been fighting for democracy, and we certainly need your help to make democracy real and effective through full use of your franchise.

While you were away organized labor and the people in it did a lot of other things. We bought billions of dollars' worth of War Bonds to back up the armed forces—although I don't feel that bouquets should be pinned on anyone for that. After all, Uncle Sam's 2.9 per cent is the best investment in the world, and anyone who can but doesn't make such an investment is just plain foolish. Labor gave unstinting support to the Red Cross, in donations of work, of money, of blood for the blood banks. President Philip Murray of the CIO and President William Green of the AFL are members of the National Board of the Red Cross, and their interest in its great work has been reflected all the way down through the rank and file of the unions.

In conclusion, let me say that I think the trade unions and the industrial unions can feel that they did a good job during the war. It was not perfect; there were many incidents that all of us must regret. However, human nature is not perfect either, and we must operate within the limitations imposed by human nature. But this we did—we provided the labor, skilled, semiskilled, and unskilled, to turn out the greatest flood of war supplies the world has ever known. Our people learned new skills to turn out goods of greater precision and more intricate design than they had ever seen before. And I think you know that both the quality and the quantity of the supplies you have been using and fighting with were good—very good. We supported all the related activities of the war effort outside of the actual work of production and transportation with effort and money and practical support, political and otherwise. We showed the world that a free enterprise democracy under the impact of war could be unified into a tightly knit, highly effective production machine that could overwhelm the best efforts of the totalitarian states. And we did all this while still maintaining most of our freedoms and a decent standard of living so that you might come home to a better country than the one you left. To do these things required hard work and unceasing vigilance for the protection of the rights of the people—and never forget that in so doing we were protecting you, because you are the people too.

II. WHAT INDUSTRY DID

by *DONALD M. NELSON*

In 1940 DONALD M. NELSON was borrowed by the Government from Sears Roebuck and Company, where he was Executive Vice-President and Chairman of the Executive Committee, to aid the national defense effort in a major post. After Pearl Harbor, President Roosevelt appointed him Chairman of the War Production Board. Under his leadership, American industry achieved the tremendous volume of production which insured victory. Later, as Personal Representative of President Roosevelt, Mr. Nelson aided Generalissimo Chiang Kai-shek in organizing the Chinese economy for war production. Special missions for the President also took him to England, Russia, Australia, and New Zealand. By early training a chemical engineer, Mr. Nelson holds honorary degrees from numerous universities, and is High Economic Adviser to the Republic of China.

THIS is the record: For nine years before Pearl Harbor, Germany, Italy, and Japan prepared intensively for war, while as late as 1940 the war production of peaceful America was virtually nothing. Yet two years later the output of our war factories equaled that of the three Axis nations combined. In 1943 our war production was one and one half times, and in 1944, more than double, Axis war production—a remarkable demonstration of power.

But the real triumph of wartime American industry lay in the fact that management and labor did their job voluntarily, cooperatively, in the great tradition of democracy. Dictatorial rule was not needed to make them become the world's most efficient producers of weapons, as they had been the most efficient producers of the goods of peace. Despite some strikes on the part of workers, and some cases of slipshod and greedy management, by and large both groups responded magnificently to the national need.

Industry surprised itself by the speed with which it turned from mass producing for peace to the mass production of weapons and equipment for war. Most of these wartime products were new to us, and many were highly complicated—big guns, antiaircraft guns, tanks, range finders, fire control units, radar, etc. Nevertheless, in an astonishingly short span of time American factories were making such high-precision mechanisms in quantity. Before we had been in the war a year, our war production was the wonder of the world.

It needed the high-voltage shock of Pearl Harbor to make this transformation possible. Prior to the rash Japanese attack, industry and government had been slow and uncertain in their approach to war production. Not unnaturally, businessmen were reluctant to stop peacetime production and convert their factories to war use, when it was not yet clear to them that we would enter the war. But the news of Pearl Harbor banished doubt. The nation stopped thinking in terms of defense and began to think in terms of all-out attack.

All over the country, once the word was given, manufacturers who had been making many kinds of civilian goods told their customers that they could no longer fill orders, because they were converting part or all of their plants to the making of weapons. These thousands of manufacturers immediately found themselves in a fantastic new world of production. Their customers were no longer wholesalers and retailers, no longer the familiar Mr. and Mrs. Consumer whose tastes and psychology they understood. Now they strove to please the American fighting man—in the air, on land, and on the sea. Failure to meet his requirements at any point meant not the loss of business, but very possibly the loss of

American lives. Very often, just when a manufacturer would think he had mastered the problem of producing his particular war item, an army or navy officer would appear in his plant to demand a change in design, necessitated by battle-front experience. Our soldiers were not getting the best results with the sight on this machine gun; the turret on this tank needed more head room; the nose armament of this airplane was not heavy enough. Production plans laboriously worked out over a period of weeks then had to be scrapped, and new plans made, while the government men cried, "Hurry, hurry!"

The manufacturers, with sons, brothers, and employees in the armed services, gritted their teeth and hurried. Workers eager to throw themselves into the war job, and held idle at their machines by model changes, fretted until the new designs came through. Often they had to learn to use new methods, new tools, new routines, new tempos of work, in order to meet the demands of the nation's new customers, the Army and Navy.

Businessmen and workers alike found themselves tackling jobs they had never dreamed of. A company which had canned citrus fruit began to make parts for merchant ships. A grower and shipper of ferns learned to manufacture bomb chutes. Manufacturers made guns who had a few months earlier made machinery for processing cotton. A maker of mechanical pencils turned out bomb parts and precision instruments. Mosquito netting became the chief product of a bedspread manufacturer. A soft drink company, which knew all about loading bottles with liquid, went into the business of loading shells with explosive. An automobile dealer took the technical know-how he had obtained by servicing cars and turned to the manufacture of airplane engine parts.

Naturally, the civilian economy had to be vigorously streamlined. Abruptly we stopped new production of automobiles, radios, washing machines, vacuum cleaners, and dozens of other products which used scarce metals. It is a startling revelation of the hidden power of America that we were able to produce for total war on a gigantic scale without disturbing civilian life more than we did. American industry turned out more goods for war than we ever produced for our peacetime needs—yet had enough power left over to keep civilian standards of living at an astonishingly high level. At the same time that our industry produced supplies for the most powerful army and navy in the world, and for the armies and peoples of our allies, it also enabled us to be the best fed and best clothed people, with the best equipped homes in the world. Nowhere else but in America were there enough resources, enough machinery, enough capital, enough skilled labor, enough able management, to perform such a feat of production.

I think I can safely say that the mobilization of all the productive resources of the nation was the biggest economic undertaking in history. Few people even now realize how staggering were the requirements which the war imposed on American industry. A 90-billion-dollar economy, measured in terms of 1940's gross national product, was stepped up in the years 1941 and 1942 to 150 billions; in 1943 to 180 billions, in 1944 to nearly 200 billions.

This record was made in the face of serious shortages of raw materials, notably steel and copper. Incredible amounts of these and other metals were needed to enable manufacturers to fulfill their war contracts. Often demands conflicted. Copper, for example, was needed by shipyards for ships, by arsenals for munitions, by railroads for train parts, by electric utilities for power transmission; and there was not enough to go around. The industries of the nation could not have all the materials they wanted, yet the "must" requirements of all of them had to be met.

It was in large part to solve this problem that the President, keenly aware of the gigantic production task confronting the country, created the War Production Board to work with industry. This was in January, 1942. The relation of the WPB to wartime industry was very much like that of the Chiefs of Staff to our Armed Forces. We had to take an over-all view of the productive side of the war effort and direct its grand strategy. For this purpose it was necessary to know intimately, and in the greatest detail, the capacity and essential requirements of each industry. The eternal questions were what to make first, when, where, how much, and sometimes how. Scores of thousands of separate parts had to be produced to go into modern tanks, planes, ships, guns, radar, radio. These parts were manufactured in tens of thousands of different plants. Each part had to be available in the right amount at the right time and at the right place. To ration materials and equipment and keep production of all these things in balance was a hazardous, as well as a new and immense, task for the government. We had to get all the facts, study them, make a decision—and be right. To be seriously wrong at any point might have meant disaster on the battlefield or on the home front.

The home economy was especially vulnerable, although not many people realized it. To an extent not approached in any other nation, this country depends for the necessities of life on an intricate network of mechanical things. Our farms and factories depend on machinery and electric power, our offices on switchboards, telephones, elevators, and typewriters, our homes on plumbing and furnaces. Virtually all of our transportation depends on engines, cars, signal equipment. Let even one standard element in the mechanical structure of American life break down, and the work and lives of millions would be sharply dislocated, with a consequent severe drop in production.

The only way to keep war production at top speed was to make sure that our population was adequately fed, clothed, housed, supplied with transportation and communications, and equipped for work. This meant that the countless mechanisms on which we depend had to be kept in good repair, with spare parts available at all times to prevent breakdowns.

The urgent need for war matériel threatened to close down not only nonessential civilian production, such as refrigerators and washing machines, but also production of essential parts and supplies. One of the jobs of WPB, and a vital one, was to make sure that the home front, on which our war industries depended, was kept going at high efficiency. The public heard little of the effort to preserve a healthy balance between production of munitions and production of essential civilian goods; but that balance enabled industry to operate at peak levels and made possible the tremendous war production record of the country.

In order to deal successfully with practical manufacturing problems, WPB drew heavily on industry for its personnel, and in addition tapped the experience and know-how of thousands of production men outside of its own organization. In the first World War, the War Industries Board, headed by Bernard Baruch, had been greatly helped by advisory committees made up of picked industrialists. WPB took a leaf from Mr. Baruch's book. Soon after Pearl Harbor, more than two hundred active Industry Advisory Committees were organized. One of their chief functions was to advise on the most efficient ways of dividing up the work of each industry among its component concerns. In normal times such an activity would have been pounced upon by the Department of Justice, as violating antitrust statutes. Because of the character of the emergency, however, and in view of legal safeguards taken to protect the public interest, the Attorney General granted the necessary permission. Every segment of industry was represented on these committees. The government's effort was to give equal representation to large, medium, and small concerns.

"Everything for the common cause" was the sentiment of these newly formed Industry Advisory Committees. The pooling of patents and the sharing of processes were immediate results. Competitors who had jealously guarded their manufacturing secrets, a few months before, now freely gave them up to each other in order to help win the war. The airplane industry particularly made rapid strides by patent pooling, but scores of other war industries were sharply benefited. Although a few concerns which held foreign patents under contract were for a short time hesitant to open them up to American competitors, and so violate their business agreements, they quickly recognized that in a world crisis the traditional ethics of international business had to give way to the greater ethic of patriotism. In the same spirit, manufacturers lent equipment and materials to former competitors who needed them to get production under way.

The Industry Advisory Committee made available to the government many of the best production men in the country, whose attitude was expressed in a remark frequently heard in meetings: "You tell us what you want, and we'll get it for you." The first and probably the most important advisory committee was drawn from the steel industry. In the early days of 1942 we were short not only of steel-making facilities but also of many of the metals which were needed for the alloy steels of modern warfare— tungsten, molybdenum, chromium, nickel, manganese, vanadium. Out of the Steel Industry Advisory Committee came a plan to put the research men of the industry to work to find substitute steels that would use less of these scarce alloys and yet do the job just as well. To the surprise not only of our army and navy but of the steel industry itself, many of these substitute steels turned out to be better than the original alloys. Armor plate for tanks and ships made with less alloy proved stronger and more resistant than the high-alloy steels produced before the war.

While thousands of industrial concerns were putting brains and know-how into the war effort through the War Production Board and the Industry Advisory Committees, the National Association of Manufacturers and the United States Chamber of Commerce were also throwing their weight into the war job. Right after Pearl Harbor, under the auspices of the National Association of Manufacturers, I met with 150 industrial leaders representing the most important companies in America, and I appealed to them "to get going." One sticking point was the length of time that it took to get a contract signed by the government. Our fighting men needed weapons and we could not wait for contracts to plow their way through government red tape. I took it upon myself to assure our industrialists that if they went ahead without waiting for contracts, they would not take a loss.

They did not hesitate. Contracts or no contracts, they agreed to put their plants to work without delay on the weapons and equipment we desperately needed. Moreover, they formed a strong committee which aroused businessmen all over the country to all-out speed and action, and their message was reiterated throughout the country by the NAM. The United States Chamber of Commerce rendered similar vigorous service. In this way, the inspiration and ideas required to stimulate the conversion from peace to war were brought to industry by industry.

It was clearly not enough to mobilize only the managers of industry. The other partner in industry, labor, had to have full understanding of the problem, and definite knowledge of what it could do to help. One of the first things we did at the War Production Board was to organize a sustained drive to form Labor-Management Committees in war plants throughout the country. The aim of the committees was to enable workers in war industries to get the facts about the war effort—to realize the importance of their jobs—to find ways to increase the speed and accuracy of their work—to learn to conserve tools and materials.

At first both management and labor were highly suspicious. Managers feared that the committees were a device to give power in management to labor. Labor leaders feared that the committees were a scheme for breaking the unions. Gradually, as the facts became clear, these fears dissipated and were replaced by hearty enthusiasm. Almost from the first, the committees did an outstanding job. They kept workers informed. They sponsored many thousands of practical suggestions from workers for the improvement of techniques, for saving time and materials, and in some cases for practical inventions which might otherwise not have come to light. In the upshot, over 5,000 Labor-Management Committees were formed in war plants. The result has been the saving of millions of man-hours and of untold amounts of scarce materials and tools, together with a definite strengthening of industrial morale. The workers threw themselves into the war job with intense zeal, working hard and long, often under difficult conditions. By and large, the contribution of labor to the war effort, as of management, has been splendid testimony to the fundamental patriotism and good sense of the American people.

The American Federation of Labor and the Congress of Industrial Organizations gave energetic co-operation to the War Production Board in getting a maximum effort from workers. Their enthusiastic response to the national need, like that of management, was largely due, I am convinced, to the democratic and voluntary methods which were used. Although WPB had virtually dictatorial powers of industry, powers unprecedented in American history, as a matter of basic policy it gave industry as much freedom of action as possible. Government put the nation's production problems up to industry, and for the most part industry solved them in its own way. American management and labor were not waiting to be driven; they were only asking to be led.

Naturally, industry was often troubled over wartime changes. The small businesses of the country were particularly alarmed by the impact of the war. The inevitable tendency of the government was to depend on the big mass-production factories for the vast output required; and concerns which could not afford to send representatives to Washington were obviously handicapped in getting war contracts. Under the National Defense Advisory Committee in 1940, a committee was formed to send information to small business on the needs of government and to invite their bids; but this merely scratched the surface of the problem.

After Pearl Harbor, with the cutting away of a vast amount of civilian production, the government had to take vigorous steps to maintain the position of small business in America during the war. To this end, the President and Congress set up the Smaller War Plants Corporation, which gave out and financed thousands of war contracts to small business, together with much-needed engineering assistance. At the same time SWPC urged big industries to farm out subcontracts to small concerns, and this campaign was also effective in keeping active many small businesses which might otherwise have been wartime casualties.

From my personal observation, I can say that the great majority of American industries did not try to make big profits out of war production. Aside from patriotic feeling, they recognized the danger to industry itself of profiteering, as a breeder of public resentment. Some large corporations, such as General Electric and Eastman Kodak, voluntarily turned back a part of their profits to the government.

At the outset of the war it was very difficult to figure costs accurately so as to set sound prices for war products. Most of these products were new. Designs had to be frequently changed. No one knew what a given product would cost next week. All that industry and government could do was guess at a price that would probably save the industry from loss. But after a product had been standardized and mass production had begun, costs dropped sharply. In 1943 a tank cost 27 per cent less than in 1942, a submachine gun 60 per cent less, a bomber 30 per cent less. Profits soared. It was obvious to industry, as to the government, that the only way to prevent excessive profits and public resentment was to renegotiate the original contract prices, as soon as experience had made it possible to estimate a fair price. I surmise that 98 per cent of industry felt that the "renegotiation" laws enacted by Congress were fair.

The attitude of most of industry toward high wartime taxes was similarly realistic. Businessmen recognized that the government needed immense sums to finance the war effort, and although they maintained the universal American custom of grousing about taxation, they paid readily enough. Even agitation over that old bugaboo, the excess profits tax, died down sometime in 1942. On the subject of postwar taxes, industrialists expressed grim determination to bring about reductions; but the wartime tax structure caused few hearts to break.

Many concerns, of course, put as much money as the government would permit back into large salaries to executives and into "good-will" advertising; and most of this money came out of taxes. On the whole, however, the government got its full tax revenue in one place or another. Tax money spent on advertising meant bigger taxes from the publication in which the advertising appeared; tax money spent on large salaries meant bigger personal income taxes; and the economy as a whole met the expectations of the Treasury. At the same time, of course, vast quantities of government bonds were purchased by the business community.

The chief concern of industry was not so much to make big profits out of the war as to prevent capital loss—always the great and natural fear of every industrial enterprise. The early days of the war required an enormous expansion of plants by private industry. Although these new facilities were financed in large part through government loans, it was necessary to give industry reasonable assurance against capital loss, so that it could confidently borrow capital, undertake new construction, and purchase machinery which in peacetime might be of little or no value. Congress therefore enacted the so-called five-year amortization plan. This plan enabled industry to write off, within a period of five years, new war plants and improvements in plants made for war purposes—subject, of course, to review and adjustment by the Treasury Department. In some cases this act may have enabled private concerns to pay for new plants out of war profits, but in the main it has proved a fair and reasonable arrangement for industry and for the public, and it helped enormously to speed up war construction at a time of great urgency.

Most serious of industry's headaches came from the need to adjust itself to the new restrictions and methods which the War Production Board had of necessity to impose. Even before we entered the war it was apparent that there would not be enough of some materials and equipment to go around among the manufacturers who wanted them. We could not allow scarce resources to be used in nonessential production. They had to be directed in an orderly way into the making of products for military use and for the essential civilian economy.

Industrial managers had to struggle with "priorities" and "allocations," to comply with a large number of restrictive orders issued by the War Production Board, to do a great deal of paper work and dull reading, and to learn many new and complicated rules. To the American industrialist, accustomed to a free market and famous for his independence of spirit and mind, the thousands of government regulations were an irksome nuisance. But in their hearts the managers of industry knew that these regulations were essential. On the whole, they gave WPB a remarkable demonstration of faithful compliance. Although there were a number of cases in which manufacturers violated complicated WPB orders without realizing it, they quickly fell into line as soon as the facts were brought to their attention. In a few other instances the heads of industrial concerns felt that the government had treated them unfairly in its orders, but here too explanation soon brought about voluntary compliance. Between 1942 and 1945 fewer than half a dozen attempts, all unsuccessful, were made by businessmen to obtain court injunctions preventing enforcement of WPB orders.

Adjusting itself, not without some groans, to wartime ways of doing business, industry teamed up with the government to drive production to ever new records. Between 1941 and the end of 1944 an almost magical transformation of American industry took place. Huge new plants dotted every section of the country. The agricultural South became heavily industrialized. Annual production of steel ingot rose nine million tons. Aluminum production rose from 807 million pounds to 2,179 million. An entirely new, huge, synthetic rubber industry was created. Plane production, in dollar value, was multiplied nearly by ten, tanks by five, naval shipping by more than five, cargo shipping by more than ten. In 1939 our total output of fabricated metal had been 13 billion dollars' worth, and in 1944 it was 70 billions; while in the same period the machine tool industry alone expanded production by more than seven times.

Thousands of individual manufacturers made remarkable records in speeding up production and improving quality in the face of all the obstacles created by wartime shortages and restrictions.

The few whom I mention by name here are only representative of many whose contributions were equally valuable. Everyone has heard of Henry Kaiser, the man who applied mass-production methods to the building of ships. Although without previous experience in this industry, his experience in constructing Boulder Dam had shown him what could be done to mass-produce large individual units. He knew the practical principles of mass production, and knew how to apply them to almost any industrial operation. He tackled the problem of building cargo ships of the Liberty type with such energy that he was able to reduce construction time from 280 days, as in the last war, to 80 days in early 1942, and to 22 days in 1944.

Another outstanding example of industrial ingenuity comes from Cleveland, where an aircraft parts manufacturer, the Jack and Heintz Company, evolved sensational new methods of increasing output through heightened worker morale. By paying exceptionally attractive wages, making sure that working conditions were congenial, developing a strong sense of team play, giving workers full credit for individual and group achievements, stressing the importance of the workers' jobs to the war effort, and appealing to patriotism by explaining the needs of the armed services, this company drove production and earnings to astonishing heights.

The names of General Motors and Chrysler figure prominently in the effort to get big production fast. The Oerlikon antiaircraft gun produced at great speed by General Motors is one of many war products of this company which have won wide acclaim for their quality; and Chrysler's 1942 achievement in swiftly building a fully equipped tank factory with specialized machinery greatly strengthened the Army's tank program. Packard's splendid performance in turning out the complicated Merlin aircraft engine was another powerful blow at the Axis.

One of the most remarkable instances of combined labor-management support of the government came in the second half of 1943, when a steel shortage threatened to handicap the entire armaments program. The war effort needed a million tons of steel beyond the estimated total productive capacity of the industry. A few of us went out to Pittsburgh and spoke to leaders of management and labor and frankly put the problem before them. They listened, talked quietly with each other—and pledged themselves to deliver the million additional tons which we were asking. How they would do it, no one quite knew, but they made good their promise in full—by the more efficient use of equipment, by the readiness of management to shorten the life of certain types of equipment in order to obtain greater immediate production, and above all by the willingness of labor to work harder for longer hours and with shorter rest periods.

Here and there, of course, black spots appear on industry's record—fortunately, very minor in comparison with the splendid over-all achievement. Some cases of gross mismanagement and even fraud in industry were revealed by the Senate Special Committee to Investigate the National Defense Program, first headed by the then Senator Truman, and later on by Senator Mead. This committee was an important innovation. Following the last war there had been a number of investigations which revealed cases of scandalous mismanagement and corruption, both in industry and government. This time the Senate determined to hold the investigations concurrently with the war effort. The decision proved wise, both in its moral effect of discouraging fraud and as a stimulus to production. All complaints of malfeasance and waste in industry were directed to the committee, which made thorough investigations with its own trained staff.

In one instance a copper-fabricating company was found to have circumvented inspection requirements, and to have sold a large quantity of defective material to the government. The management of a well-known aircraft corporation was cited by the Truman Committee for "faulty plans," resulting in "enforced idleness which led the workers to suspect sabotage, and which materially decreased their efficiency." But the bad taste left in the public mouth by these and other isolated episodes was soon washed away by mounting admiration for the fine and patriotic war job of industry as a whole.

When it appeared that the collapse of Germany could not be very far off, management and labor both began to be justifiably concerned over the situation which would confront them with victory in Europe. Presumably, the armed services would then cancel many contracts and reduce others. Advance estimates of these "cutbacks" ran from 10 per cent to 50 per cent of all war production. Everyone feared serious close-downs and unemployment after V-E Day.

Businessmen early in 1944 began to ask how soon they would be allowed to prepare for cutbacks and the resumption of civilian production. Bernard Baruch, with his long experience in war economics, prepared a report for the President on the reconversion problem, and followed it up with a statement in which he urged the government to hurry in its preparations, so as to avoid serious unemployment in the event of an early German surrender. In the late summer of 1944, when the end of the war in Europe by winter was freely predicted in high military quarters, WPB set up a mechanism by which the reconversion process could be speeded when the right time came—but not until then. The policy was to allow no civilian production that would draw needed resources away from the war effort, and to keep war production at whatever level was required to speed victory over Japan.

The problems involved in the eventual return of industry from wartime to peacetime production touched the very roots of American political life. Under the wartime system, competition in many industries had been virtually shut off as soon as those industries converted to war production. Such industries, operating through the Industry Advisory Committees, had more or less apportioned their production among themselves. Two questions were very much in the minds of many manufacturers when they contemplated the return to peacetime production: First, whether they would all get off to an equal start as they resumed competition; and, second, whether new companies would be allowed to enter into competition with them, perhaps before they themselves were able to resume production for the civilian market.

It was clear to me and most of my staff in WPB that the public interest did not allow the setting up of closed competitive systems in peacetime industry. The government above all else had to aim its policy at the maintenance of employment and the improvement of civilian living standards. In order to provide jobs and early production of goods needed by civilians, some manufacturers might have to be allowed to resume production before their former competitors who were still engaged on war contracts. Similarly, if a new concern chose to enter an industry, and by so doing could provide needed employment and satisfy consumer wants, then even if established concerns in that field were not yet in a position to resume civilian production the new competitor would be allowed to get started.

This was not an easy decision to make. It was bound to cause a certain amount of heartache here and there, and perhaps to work hardships on some manufacturers, through no fault of their own. Yet no other decision was compatible with the tradition of the American competitive system and with the public interest. On the whole, the business community of the country readily accepted the War Production Board point of view.

As Marshal Stalin said in his famous remarks at Teheran, when he proposed a toast to the war production of the United States, the war against the Axis could not have been won without American industry. In playing its great historic role in the war, our industry has opened up vast opportunities for itself and the nation. The profound wartime changes in America's industrial economy will have far-reaching effects on our future. We have developed many new products and better ways of making them. We have developed a deeper understanding of industrial psychology. We know more about the power of co-operation to produce great results.

At the same time, we face big new problems which must be solved before we or the rest of the world can feel secure. We know that to utilize all of our resources and new facilities effectively, an unprecedented number of jobs will have to be filled. If we are to find adequate markets for the products of our greatly expanded factories and so sustain employment at a high level, our foreign trade must greatly expand and our economic relations with other countries become far larger in scale than ever before.

All this we have learned, and more, and now it is up to us to put our hard-won, new-found knowledge to good practical use. Management and labor in voluntary co-operation have proved their wartime power, and we look to them to give equally triumphant proof of peacetime wisdom.

III. WHAT HAPPENED IN AGRICULTURE

by RUSSELL LORD

RUSSELL LORD (age 50) was a sergeant of artillery in the first World War. He wrote the first
draft of this chapter in England in June, 1945,
while doing a two months' turn as visiting con-
sultant to the British Ministry of Agriculture.
He is a founder of The Friends of the Land
and editor of its quarterly, The Land. He has
written a number of government publications
on agriculture and is a frequent contributor to
national magazines.

I

"YOU'RE a hero while it lasts, but war makes a bum out of
you afterwards." A professional soldier, Sergeant George Otten,
said that, instructing us fledgling noncoms in 1917; and of course
there is something to it. Soldiering as a business or occupation
falls between wars into relative disregard and low reward, but in
this respect soldiering is not unique. I find it depressing to recall,
even now, how many farmers said of their calling just about
what George Otten said of his, and had sound cause to say it,
after the first World War.

There have always been postwar depressions, and the farmer
as a rule has always been the one hit first and hardest; but that
war, which was Act I of this war, lifted agriculture higher and
then smashed it flatter in the interim years of peace than ever
before. There were a number of reasons, that time, why the economic slaughter of American agriculture was so widespread and
so merciless; and we had better have a look at them here, to begin

with, because the same special reasons, or accretion of circumstances, have not crept back into the womb of time.

This is not the country it was after the Civil War, or the Spanish-American skirmish, or World War I. The accelerating forces of change which made it so hard for farmers to hold their land and keep on their feet in the most recent postwar smash-up have kept right on accelerating, faster and faster.

The main hope for better luck this time lies in the fact that these disruptive forces have come, between wars, under a certain degree of governance, increasingly democratic. I believe that, whether we like it or not, we shall have to increase this sort and degree of governance. If we were now simply to whoop things up and let them ride, as we did from 1919 to 1929 or thereabouts, the same postwar forces that hammered us down then are likely to do us in for fair this time. They could, at the very least, wipe out all semblance of what we have come to call farm security for the ordinary man.

It is inaccurate to ticket off these forces one from another, separately, for they all operate together, all ends against the middle; but there are in general three propelling reasons why we can probably never return to ungoverned *laissez faire* in farming the United States:

1. We have a sharpening scarcity of land worth farming, in relation to the demand for it. We cannot sustain a democracy on the basis of having all the good land pass into "strong hands," financially, as they say on Wall Street.

2. Technological displacement, severe in the last war and postwar period, has been enormously accelerated by this war. Like it or not, we are a people in more and more rapid passage from the predominantly rural setup we started with. Originally, 90 per cent of our people were farmers. Farm census figures are much mixed up in terms of defining a farm, and existing figures lag well behind the actual present situation; but we are almost certainly down now to 15 per cent of the population farming, in the full-time commercial sense of the word, and plainly headed for a

complete reversal of our original structure of society, with 10 per cent or less doing all or most of the farming and 90 per cent or more who do not farm for a living.

3. We stand confronted with a climactic evidence that our former system of farming was ruinous. Soil damage, first dramatized by the dust storms of 1934, has since been thrust into our consciousness far more widely by unmistakable omens of soil wash and depletion. We have been forced to see plainly that our old ungoverned ways of land use cannot support a government or civilization that will be forever strong and secure.

The main device now used by our government to direct the use of land toward ends that are considered economically necessary or socially desirable is, in a word, *subsidy*. In consequence, our people pay for part of their food in the form of taxes. This has always been true in some part, but the tendency has advanced considerably in recent years; and I suppose this is almost inevitable in a land committed to cheap food policies, as ours has been and is likely, in changed ways, still to be.

Governmental subsidies paid to induce changed ways or patterns of land culture were no brand-new New Deal device. Before going to rack under the unstemmed tide of postwar crop "surpluses," President Hoover's Farm Board wrote it into a number of federal loan policies that the farmers receiving these loans or grants should limit or reduce their acreage and, in some instances, their applications of fertilizer thereto! And it was a Farm Board spokesman who first suggested plowing down cotton. Even the desperate agrarian New Dealers, grabbing hold of agricultural chaos in their turn, and plowing down cotton instead of talking about it, did not pay farmers to make the land less fertile. The performance was disgraceful enough without that, in a society imagined to be civilized and rational. Even more disgraceful were the years of lazy thinking that made the plow-down of one-fourth of the standing cotton the only thing the government could think of to do immediately in order to save the South from complete bankruptcy, which it did.

But some of the men who put on this show were really think-ing, beyond that, of using the same money to induce crop birth control, gearing production more nearly to the need and health of the people and to the need and health of the land. The early New Dealers made many blunders, but they did act boldly. They took the Farm Board idea of a loan or subsidy with a string to it, and pushed it out along the whole farm front on a constantly more defensible basis. For the land *is* vested with a public inter-est; and if the government puts money behind a man to help him farm better, the government, as a good banker, if nothing more, has a right to govern in some measure the ways in which that man farms, the crops he plants, and the care with which he tends them. This, at least, is the principle which seems now to have been firmly established in our governance of farming; and I think this principle will be far more widely invoked, with general con-sent, despite a lot of roaring and rumbling, in the years just ahead.

II

Fiercely, almost, as farming has been increasingly caught up in the warp and woof of an interdependent society, farmers have cherished an illusion of rugged independence. I do not blame them for that, exactly. The psychic income so derived has been, really, the main reward of farming, as such, and there was little or no money in land speculation, even between the two most re-cent wars. As an almost professional friend of the farmer, I do think, though, he ought to stop kidding himself occasionally and make an end to recoiling from subsidies with the air of a virgin who has just been propositioned for the first time. The only reli-able support of farming in this country, like the only real reliance of veterans of our wars out to make a new start, rests historically on repeated subsidies or handouts of mammoth proportions and real value. It could in fact be argued that the principal reason both farmers and veterans had to go through so long a period of apparent hopelessness after Act I of this war was simply that we as a nation had even then run out of our accustomed specie for subsidizing both farmers and veterans who wanted to be farmers: to wit, free, or cheap, rich, abundant *land.*

What a subsidy that was! Better, far, than cash handouts, which usually depreciate in value during war's aftermath, and do not usually breed more wealth or value, as land did in this country consistently for nearly the first two hundred years of our independence. From our Revolutionary War onward land grants to soldiers, civilians, educational institutions, and commercial entrepreneurs served a necessary public purpose in opening the country up and developing it for use. It provided jobs; for many it provided a fairly honored calling; and for many others who did not care for farming exclusively, it provided an increasing estate. Good farmer-businessmen like George Washington and the Byrds of Virginia, who really had a keen eye for land and loved to care for it, together with a horde of less admirable speculators, bought up veterans' land grants right and left, and so laid the foundations of large fortunes. The veterans got some money for their pension-grants and, often as not, more land, free or nearly free. That was a happy arrangement, for even when the money turned out to be worthless, or nearly so, the land kept going up in selling value.

Little local wars or fracases like the Whisky Rebellion in western Pennsylvania took the soldiers into virgin country and often led them to settle there as farm proprietors, building up to respected squiredom from a squatter or semisquatter basis. I read not many years ago in a history of Maine how the rich potato lands of Aroostook County provided, strangely belatedly, one of our last eastern farm frontiers worth taking. It came of a little war I had never heard of. In the late 1830's the British reasserted a claim to northern Maine. Ten thousand Maine militiamen in flaming red shirts and pea-green jackets marched north from Bangor in subzero weather to engage in the siege of the Little Madawaska. It was a good war, if ever there was one. The total recorded casualties were one; an American soldier engaging in horseplay fell on the ice and broke his hip. The troops sat around and swapped yarns while statesmen wrangled, until warm weather. The idle soldiers pawed at the soil that burst through the melting snow and were good soldiers no longer. They were Americans, and they smelled land. When the boundary dispute was settled in 1842 they trekked there to locate in some number. Certain of the most substantial potato kings of present-day Aroostook are grandsons of those militiamen who came in there around a hundred years ago and settled on some of the best land in America, almost free.

After the Civil War we still had the greater part of the West to spill over into, and we did. Original grants of 160 acres under the Homestead Act were raised, always too belatedly from the standpoint of providing an economic unit of dry-land farming or ranching operations, to as much as 640 acres—one square mile—as successive waves of migration spilled out beyond humid country onto the High Plains. Hundreds and thousands went broke or were starved out. The whole process of settlement and resettlement was enormously wasteful. Partly because the government had not then developed the device of making the recipient of the subsidy—a piece or stretch of our land—responsible for its proper care, tillage, or any form of development, the headlong damage that was done our soil and water sources had risen to all but catastrophic proportions almost unnoticed, by the outbreak of the first World War.

Even so, on paper, plundering American soil had paid. It had opened up and settled the country and paid the greater part of our debt to Europe. We had just made the historic turn from a debtor to a giant creditor nation when we entered the first World War. Land grabbing and exploitation had, moreover, served as a safety valve for high animal spirits and had served as an equalizer of social and economic opportunity, on the whole. It had paid in money to be a landowner, if not to farm. In Illinois, for example, from 1880 to 1920 the average farm acre rose in value from $29 to $364. That was extreme, but not unrepresentative of the better prairie blacklands in general; and the lesser consistent rise from year to year of midland soil less fertile and famous was definitely enough, on the average, so that if a man and his family holding title to a piece or block of land managed to hang on, farming however badly and losing money by any businesslike system of accounting almost every year, they could pretty well count upon selling out on the rise at somewhere along toward their twentieth to thirtieth year of it, and retiring to town or to the coast, on a competence. That was another reason why most of our farming has been so sinfully bad; but it provided a great argument for free enterprise and proved an invaluable shock absorber in times of business recession and unemployment, as long as free or cheap land lasted.

III

Insatiable markets abroad coinciding with a spurt of mechanization expanded our tilled land more than forty million acres during the first World War. We had beat the land by hand rather badly. Now we rolled out on wheels and gave it a terrific beating with machines. When the shooting halted, price supports for farm products were removed quite abruptly, and the Federal Reserve Board, by shifting discount rates, undertook more or less deliberately to get the water out of farm values. Land values hit the chute, and by 1921 the prices of some of our most important farm products had fallen to as little as one-fifth of what they had been in 1920.

That was only the beginning of what farmers have come to call "the twelve long years." Between 1920 and 1933 one farm in every four was sold for debts or taxes, and the net migration of young people alone from farm to city exceeded six million. Houses and fences sagged toward ruination; the land went thin and ragged. So did the people. It was a very doubtful refuge, our open country, after 1929, when the business smashup became general, and millions surged out from the cities trying to find a roof and enough to eat on farms. I remember a map, prepared by an economic aide of Henry A. Wallace, when he was Secretary of Agriculture in 1935. It showed an increase of 523,000 farms since 1930, with the new holdings dotted in, and the distribution of these dots at their thickest bore a startling resemblance to population maps of the United States in the eighteenth century. Refugee population was most marked along that thin and generally rather infertile spine of land, the Appalachian hill and mountain country from New England to Alabama. It was almost as if another great wave of Western migration were gathering, except that, this time, many of these new pioneers were squatting on inadequate little parcels of worn-out, punishing land.

With this map and figures before him Wallace went on the air. "Here have come home," he said, "unemployed and often penniless, the families of factory workers, miners, lumber workers, and others—unskilled, skilled, and highly trained workers, college graduates, teachers and others—to reoccupy the abandoned cabins, shacks, or old farmhouses of their fathers and grandfathers— or the abandoned premises of persons not known to them. This return to the land, this search of escape from unemployment, has a special tragic significance. Most of these people are on poor land, hilly, eroded, worn out, or grown up with weeds and brush-land stubborn to the touch of the men and their families, who usually have little in the way of equipment to carry on their unequal struggle with Nature."

Well, the tide has rushed the other way again now. During this war the open country is far more lightly populated and more prosperous than it was in 1939, when, despite all of the New Deal stays and measures, two million farm families were still on some sort of direct cash or food relief. Sharecropper families and families of migrants who never saw $200 cash a year are making as much as that or even more a week now, father, mother, and the youngsters between them, in factories and mills. These people could probably be spared, and well spared, from farming. The problem is to keep them productively employed. Farm production without them and without all the more spirited departing persons, including soldiers, was, in 1944, one-third more than it was in 1939. It was twice as great as in 1914 and three-fourths greater than in 1917–18, toward the peak of our expanded production for World War I.

The emigration from farms in the past four years has been the greatest in our history. The lowest estimate of it is four million persons, and some say seven million. Yet farm production has gone up one-third since the late thirties. God has had his arm around us, as the farmers like to say, on weather in these war years; but weather alone does not account for the achievement. The increase is mainly due to greatly advanced efficiency, to better farming, and to better, faster machines. The rubber-tired tractor has had much to do with it. The corn combine-harvester, the improved pickup baler, better-bred seeds and livestock, increased fertilization and modern contour farming, which soaks in the rain and restrains the soil from washing, all have helped. Cotton growing has made especially fast advances toward complete mechanization of seeding and tillage, with the long-expected mechanical picker about to become actually a practical proposition. In fields of truck crops, long a great and dreary provider for stoop-labor, mechanization marches fast. A new row-crop loader for harvesting potatoes, onions, carrots, lettuce, and sugar beets performs with fourteen hands to run it the work that required seventy hand laborers to perform. A new spinach harvester is displacing hands at a saving, its inventor says, of $300 an hour in the wages he used to have to pay. A new celery planter, operated by eight girls, waters and plants twelve thousand seedlings an hour.

Of such is progress. These extremes of mechanization do not, of course, affect all farmers all at once. It takes a great and increasing amount of money to lay in equipment of the larger order. It is obvious, however, that the availability of such equipment gives the big-money operator an increasing advantage. Farming—strictly commercial farming—is getting to be less of a poor man's business all the time; and the most enthusiastic advocates and practitioners of mechanization are saying that two million farmers, properly equipped, will be able to supply the postwar market, even if that market should hold up to present levels of demand. The number of farm operators listed in the census of 1940 was just above six million.

On June 22 of this year, 1945, the Census Bureau put out a sample count of the first 300 counties covered as to number and size of farms. Farms in these counties have increased on the average of one-tenth in size since 1940. The Bureau enjoins all concerned not to guess too closely for the country as a whole on this sampling, but warns that American farms are definitely getting bigger and fewer. My guess is that the completed count in 1945 will show around five and a half instead of six million farms, the bigger ones having swallowed the smaller ones, in general. But there are still an almost infinite number of potentially productive patches between.

IV

While marking time with other bored and restless returning soldiers at Cornell in 1920 I wrote a doleful little verse in dialect that seems to me rather on the babyish side now, but it did express our dominating mood at the moment. It was called "Back Home," with a soldier musing by the fire, thinking of dead comrades. "Sometimes I think they had it best," he says. For:

> *They died when they was going good.*
> *They're through; they played the biggest game,*
> *And maybe lost, and maybe won;*
> *And things back here; they ain't the same.*

That's right; and they never have been; certainly never in the surging, ever-changing field of American agriculture. As I have tried to indicate, things have been by no means rosy for farmers or even for agriculturists, year in and year out, since 1920; but then agriculture has never been the easiest way to make the most money anyway. Especially not if you depend on actual farming for your entire income. It is nevertheless true that the foundation satisfactions which always have attracted millions of our people to farming have not vanished, and have not diminished. It is further true that since 1920 agricultural work, including farming, has taken rapid turns which make it far more exciting, stimulating, and emotionally rewarding work than ever before.

We had settled this country at the shot of a gun. Only yesterday in historic terms of time the North American continent was an Indian paradise. Here was a vast and fruitful land, raised from the sea, ground into soil, and clad with a robe of plants that clasped and protected it for millions of years on end. Suddenly this body of land was thrown open to land-hungry men and women from Europe. With a rush and a roar we took it and beat upon it hungrily, wave by wave. By the beginning of the present century the hard fact of diminished basic resources had forced us to slow down on plunder and take stock. By 1910 natural-born prophets of a more reverent and provident husbandry—men like Gifford Pinchot and Liberty Hyde Bailey and Theodore Roosevelt—were crying ruin.

The late Seaman A. Knapp, a great agricultural teacher in our South, used to argue for learning to do by doing. He argued for the demonstration or action method as opposed to academic rote or preachment. "What a man hears he may doubt," he said. "What he sees he may possibly doubt. But what he does himself he cannot doubt." Dr. Knapp believed that a man must be led to take good care of land with his hands and mind before he will really care for his soil and his country at heart. Then, as the man feels the soil strengthening under his feet and sees it bringing forth strong new growth upon his fields, it is not only the crops that grow, Knapp said: "The man will grow faster than the crop."

Something much like this is happening to millions of farmers, gardeners, foresters, and water and wild-life technicians; yes, and to medical men, engineers, nutritionists, geographers, and geologists, who see this whole process of regeneration as a process inseparably at one with the conservation of human health and enduring human values all over the United States. As we have changed our ways we have changed our minds and our sense of values. The measurable physical results, while great, will, I think, prove in the end not as permanently important as this widespread and all but immeasurable change in personal and social attitude.

We have not yet conquered soil waste in the United States; we have barely half conquered it. But we have learned, we think, in the past ten years, how to halt our still accelerated soil runoff or blowoff; and now we are learning how to build up soil instead of diminishing or wrecking it.

Now we must seek some word more active and hopeful than "conservation" when we speak of regenerating soil, water sources, forests, livestock, wild life, people, and all the renewing sources of life. If all the fifty million acres of eroded American soil which our reconnaissance surveys of the early nineteen thirties reported as "destroyed" had been actually destroyed, that would have meant nearly eighty thousand square miles of land—an area almost equal to all of England plus all of Scotland—permanently out of production. This has not proven so. By developing processes of soil repair, soil building, and a restitution of the essential elements, we are raising fairly good crops on some of this "destroyed" soil now, and we are learning to do a better job of soil reconstruction year by year. If in the years to come more young research students and technicians can be led to regard the eternal interaction of soil, rain, sun, and air with the same constructive imagination which is now accorded that later and minor marvel, the workings of the internal-combustion engine, I would not be surprised if the human race would learn to build productive soil even on bedrock, and build it rather fast.

In addition to the fifty million acres initially reported destroyed, not less than another hundred and fifty million acres of the soil of our country was reported as more or less impaired. In total, then, some two hundred million acres of our entire area of 1,903,-000,000 acres was found upon survey—and I think rightly—to be seriously eroded, leached, or depleted by overcropping without proper replenishment or care. To put it in still another way, about half our present cropland of four hundred million acres showed plain signs of having been manhandled and abused by careless or faulty culture when we started this national campaign of repair and restitution in 1934.

The yield of all this land had run down, and in varying degrees, but discernibly, the quality of the yield had suffered. Not infrequently the diminished quality carried through visibly from stunted plants to scrawny livestock to sagging homes and fences and barns, and to sickly, spiritless people. The blight that had settled on such farming communities carried through, moreover, to the whole trading area around about them. When a soil runs down, as the saying goes, farmers are not the only sufferers. When the soil fails, everything fails.

Last spring when I was working as a writer for the Tennessee Valley Authority afield, I wrote something about the all but miraculous results of new farming methods on the foothill farms of the Great Smokies. I took the article for checkup to the wisest and most seasoned of TVA field men at the University of Georgia, where I also had my base. S. G. Chandler changed only one word of what I had written. He told me not to use the word "new" in speaking of modern conservation methods designed to rebuild fertility and control the destructive flow of water on the land. "It isn't what we didn't know," Sid Chandler told me. "It was what we had forgotten."

That is true. When you come to examine the essentials, we have invented nothing new in detail in our entire New Deal agricultural program. We have simply gone back to neglected or forgotten wisdom and applied it in a new working pattern or combination that suits our land and clime.

Agriculture has come out of the intellectual doghouse in this country. It is winning respect because it is facing and meeting its problems, at last, in a way that deserves respect. Why agriculture should for so many years have been accounted by the sophisticated a dull subject, why people should exclaim at the fact that writers like Bromfield and De Kruif actually make farming and farm research sound interesting, I hardly know. If farming or agricultural research is uninteresting, all life must be uninteresting; for here we touch on the intricate fabrication of the very stuff of life. I suppose it was because most of our farming and vital research was so ploddingly conventional, dumb, and complacent, turning up the wrong answers more often than not, and practicing outmoded methods with great damage. The same was demonstrably true of the let-be-as-is economic theories that were applied to agricultural matters, before the World War crackup forced a change. The smashup in dollar values and in actual land-productive values was painfully evident, but stimulating. We are not thinking or farming in just the same old way now.

What I am saying here is not intended primarily as explicit vocational guidance for you, the returning veteran. The government seems to have a pretty good setup, much better than it had last time, on that. But you will have to make up your own mind.

If you have come from a farm you will know without my hammering further the fact that bare earth is no cushion. Still, if you have a place to go to, you may well want to go back. When you get there you may find that your place has been filled, by iron hands. I suggest that there still may be a place for you in agriculture which may include farming; or you may serve farmers and the nation as a somewhat specialized outside agricultural attendant, honorably, on a salary not too toplofty, but regular.

In any event, farm-bred or not, if you feel that you *must* dig in the earth and live away from cities, it is the soundest of ideas to figure on a two-way income, partly in garden stuff and other sustaining edibles of your own rearing, partly from a pay envelope. The "rural amenities," as the British love to call them, have been principally sustained in our country as in theirs by country gentlemen who manage in one way or another to avoid an absolute dependence on farm income alone. And if that is a sound idea for the rich and mighty, it might work—it *will* work increasingly— for poor people and the middling well-to-do.

Despite all the jibes that have been directed at our Federal and Land Grant College bureaucracy, American agriculture will need and call for more and better technical assistance as the years go by. This assistance is and will be both commercial and scientific. Plows used to be made by the farmer himself or a local blacksmith; now they are designed or made in town. A man who makes plows or sells them is simply a highly specialized farm hand removed to town. The level of sense and competence as to basic design in this vital field of our culture has been until recently exceedingly low. Men trained in the engineering technique of killing other men out of doors may conceivably care to apply their knowledge on the upside of human progress now, working in commercial or in college laboratories and afield, on tools and engines to enrich the land and so feed hungry people. Men trained in the chemistry of destruction may want to shift their training to uses of a permanent and lasting reconstruction of humanity from the ground up. A whole new field of inquiry, as I have indicated, has recently opened, relating soil deficiencies to plant, animal, and human deficiencies; soil debility to human debility; sound agriculture to abounding human health and vigor. Or, if I were a younger man with a liking for geological or engineering research—especially if a grateful government stood willing to back me with college training—I would consider as a lifetime study and profession my country's failing underground water sources, the diminution of flow in great, secret subterranean rivers, the calamitous falling off in countless places of the standing water table. All this must be corrected, and the living waters of our land restored. We are such children when it really comes to knowing anything about the very sources of our being. We do not really know the facts of life. But we are learning.

To attain to what might be called an officer's grade and pay in all such work, you need special training. It is hard to go back to school after a war; I know that; but if you can possibly work it, or stand it, it pays. It pays you and it will pay the country. And agricultural or forestry studies are not, on the whole, as cramping and boring to the returning veteran as are most other studies. Not enough of the work, as yet, but some of it at least, is out of doors.

I think that as our attack on natural waste in the country continues and enlarges, more of the officers and high-grade field leaders should come up from the ranks by way of in-service training afield. The Forest Service has become a bit too West Pointed in its insistence on college degrees; so has the Soil Conservation Service. That can be altered. By reason of sheer competence and sound training gained with foot to earth, quite a few enrollees of our Civilian Conservation Corps and Veterans' Camps of the thirties have won their way up to technical and executive posts in these services. It would be well to have a great deal more of this. Most of the conservation measures being taught in our colleges now are, for one thing, anywhere from ten to twenty years behind the work afield. But that can change.

Meantime the American conservation movement has added at least a new and needed leaven to general education. It has tended to make us apprehend more clearly the eternal relationships of soil, rain, sun, man, and all the works of man. I have sometimes wondered at the blindness of working American farmers or agriculturists, who let our soil run down under our very feet, and saw attendant symbols of decadence arising at every hand without ever seeming to realize what was happening. I have wondered how old a man has to be, or how far he has to travel, before he can look at a living landscape and see what is going on. For my part, I did not begin to see landscapes, rural and urban, and seascapes, and cloudscapes, as parts of a unified, organic, living structure until I was thirty; and not until I was forty did I see the American scene in its entirety—forests, farms, wild life, gardens, mines, streams, factories, livestock, cities, and people—as a living structure "out of joint," going dead on us, running down.

Americans have definitely made the turn for the better now. But we have still a long way to go. Hugh H. Bennett, Chief of our Soil Conservation Service, tells me that simply to bring all our farmland and rangeland into such revised plowing plans and layouts as will make certain their permanent usefulness will require four million man-years of labor. He and his fellow Soil Rangers estimate that around half of this untechnical, relatively unskilled labor will be privately provided by farming operators and that the other half will probably be supplied from public sources. In addition to this S.C.S. tacticians see need of five hundred thousand man-years of skilled labor—an initial ratio of three skilled or trained men to each twenty workmen. "We believe," they report, "that we could employ, if need be, within two years after the war, as many as 200,000 to 250,000 workers."

In his book *Sixty Million Jobs,* "I am sure," Henry A. Wallace says, "that if we could only comprehend our potentialities we would never again have to resort to 'leaf-raking' as a way of making work for people whose hands are idle through no fault of their own." Wallace estimates that land conservation could offer four to five years' vital work for a million men; forest development, the same; rural electrification, a million men busy for three years; river valley development, a million men busy for ten years.

Hugh Bennett stated last spring before a Congressional committee that at the *then* prevailing rate of progress it would take fifty years to get done all essential and permanent land repair. Fifty years is too long. I do not believe it will take us as long as that. With the war ended, all of the skills and machines and ardor which we have had to throw into the business of destruction can be turned to works of peace and permanence, and we shall do better. No, I do not think it will take us another fifty years, or even twenty, to put all of our land into better order at the groundline. By the time we have done this, we shall have another generation in power; and I believe the young will have learned enough by that time to use the land more reverently, more permanently, and more productively than their fathers ever dreamed of when they were young.

Our Department of Agriculture, like the British Ministry of Agriculture, is conducting an open and emphatic propaganda urging returning soldiers not to return to Arcadia impulsively, only to find that Arcadia isn't there any more. Our leading farm organizations are joining in shouting this warning; and I think that is all right and perfectly natural, with things as they are. On the other side, an ardent back-to-nature-and-big-families arm of the Catholic Church, led by a good and able man, Monsignor Liguiti, is denouncing the strictly commercial attitude: "Private Property: Keep Out Except on Business." An increasing host of undenominational little-agrarian allies rise to support the view that people must be given access to the land as a way-of-life. They seem to be getting about as much attention as the cold-blooded commercial brotherhood (often absentees) who see our land more simply as an endlessly expansive food factory outdoors.

The romantics and moralists should be heard, emphatically. Our land is more than a cheap-food gestation factory, much more. The determination of a postwar land policy will arouse a thundering argument. It should. The strictly commercial brotherhood have been getting away with too much lately. They have crippled the Farm Security Administration, wiping out its subsistence homestead and co-operative farming experiments entire. As one who edited a critical report, quite critical, published by the Department of Agriculture, which administers such projects, I know how much waste and silliness there was in these enforced adventures. But it may well be that we shall have to cash in on that costly half-experience and do a lot more of the same thing, fairly immediately, right and economically, after this war.

When Harding was running for President, Bobby Clark, the comedian with the big eyeglasses, had a line in his act that was generally esteemed a knockout. "I'm thinking of running for President, myself. I play an awfully bad game of golf and I'm interested in agriculture," he said. We are beyond the baby-kissing stage of agricultural statesmanship now. We have action programs operating and bound to grow in many new and as yet uncharted directions. Farmers may or may not need more help in the field (machines may be too expensive again when hands are cheap) in the next reconstruction era. But farmers will need, I am certain, more of somewhat specialized help from without: scientific technicians, engineers, economists to help make working plans that work, organizers, further inventors of other such new social devices as Ever Normal Granary, Lend-Lease, and Food Stamps, architects of decentralization; yes, even talkers and writers, like me.

The days of our pioneering have not ended. But our first too simple and brutal concept of pioneering must and will be changed.

IV. WHAT HAPPENED IN
SCIENCE

by GERALD WENDT

DR. GERALD WENDT *(age 54) is technical adviser to Time, Inc.*

Formerly a newspaperman, he has been a captain in the Chemical Warfare Service during World War I, a chemist in the U. S. Bureau of Mines (where he helped develop a new way to extract radium), research director of both Standard Oil of Indiana and General Printing Ink Corporation, a professor at the University of Chicago, dean at Penn State, and Director of Science and Education for the New York World's Fair.

Dr. Wendt has also written and edited many books concerning science.

WAR demands power. Manpower by millions must be multiplied by machines. Man's weak muscles and weaker senses must be amplified by every available device. Moreover, modern war requires speed of observation and of action. To multiply that speed again requires power. And war is never static. Whatever the weapons of today, superior weapons in offense and defense must be available tomorrow. The only source for such steady increase in power is more knowledge, and the only source of more knowledge is scientific research. Thus wartime inevitably demands a complete mobilization of science which not only produces new devices and new principles, new industries, new strategy and tactics, but ultimately brings vast changes in civilian life as a result of the same researches.

The achievements of science in wartime are not a balanced whole. There are two reasons. One is that the deeper problems are not touched at all. Under the pressure of events we must postpone the study of remote galaxies, of the nature of life, and of the source of cosmic rays. Such fundamental problems await the leisure of peacetime, while present attention goes into utilizing what science we have. Progress is in applications, not in science itself. The second reason is that wartime research is secret. Military security demands that the new devices and processes be kept from the enemy. Even medical discoveries that might protect the enemy from disease or help him to rehabilitate his wounded have in this war been kept secret—one of the many incursions which distinguish total warfare from the milder, humane warfare of former years. Secrets are usually kept long after the enemy knows them—until every possible chance of his not knowing them is gone.

All of these attributes of wartime science crashed into the public mind with the explosion of the "atomic" bomb at Hiroshima on August 6, 1945. To a degree never before attained in man's history, here were incredible power, speed, creative research, organized production and secrecy. In ending the war it did all that was expected of it. But it will do far more. It may end warfare forever. It has already changed the international balance of power, with consequences beyond prediction. It has shown what can be done when a nation mobilizes its scientific and technical brains as it does its armies and industries. If the research is continued on the same scale, the power within the atom may become subject to control for constructive use, and also become much cheaper. In that case mankind will enter a new era in which few present institutions can survive unchanged.

The use of atomic energy in explosive form was a triumph of technology, but it would have been impossible without allies that are new to science. President Roosevelt himself had the vision and the courage to support appropriations that totaled some two billion dollars. The War Department had sufficient confidence to give the project priority over all others. Congress passed appropriations without question. Great corporations placed all their resources at the government's disposal, most of them on a cost basis. The Office of Scientific Research and Development and the National Defense Research Committee, with able leadership and superb organization, automatically had the complete loyalty of every scientist who was needed, including many from abroad, and engineered the colossal program as no research had ever been in all history.

But atomic energy was no new idea; the fundamental work had all been done. As long ago as 1905, the young Swiss, Albert Einstein, presented the revolutionary idea that matter can be converted into energy. Lord Rutherford in England and Professor Nagaoka in Tokyo some five years later proposed the idea that the chemical atom is not a "hard, massy particle," ultimate and indivisible, but has a nucleus at the center which contains concentrated matter and energy. Rutherford later showed that atoms of one element can be converted into atoms of other elements by bombardment with rays from radium. Dr. Enrico Fermi in Rome showed that small atomic fragments called neutrons are very effective in such conversion, and, finally, Dr. Otto Hahn and Miss Lise Meitner of Berlin, working at the Kaiser Wilhelm Institute, used neutrons to produce fission in uranium atoms and thereby released the tremendous energy that Einstein had predicted.

This was in 1939, the year which was later to see the German invasion of Poland. But all these experiments were done with single atoms, hence with quantities so minute that the actual energy evolved was infinitesimal and few outside the ranks of science were interested. Now it is already apparent that that experiment at the Kaiser Wilhelm Institute was even more important to mankind than the event for which 1939 is infamous—the beginning of World War II. The fragments of the uranium atoms flew apart with a velocity that indicated 200 million electron-volts, a far higher energy than had ever been attained by man. Above all, matter had been changed into energy. It was nuclear matter and nuclear energy, terms which should replace "atomic" because all energy from explosives and fuels and chemical reactions is atomic, though it comes from the outer, electronic regions of the atom.

The OSRD researches and the "Manhattan Project" began with these facts. Their task was to release this energy on a large scale, to produce the unstable form of uranium in quantity, to learn the conditions whereby one exploding uranium atom would explode all its neighbors so that in every bomb every atom of uranium would set off its colossal energy simultaneously with all others, to devise means of preventing such an explosion until the right moment, and then to devise means for setting off the explosive reaction. In all this they succeeded. The details are still secret but the result is history.

The horrible use of nuclear energy in military explosives is probably over, perhaps forever. Its civilian uses are not yet in sight. Its existence and availability are now certain. Equally certain is it that this energy can be harnessed if only a fraction of the money, time, and technical skill is devoted to further researches on it. Another two billion dollars or, more probably, another hundred million dollars a year is almost certain to produce means of slowing down the explosive reaction and of providing the materials in a form that can be used industrially. The internal-combustion engine fifty years ago accomplished just that for the uncontrollable hazard of gasoline explosions which were such a menace in the early days of the petroleum industry. It provided a means of exploding gasoline drop by drop in an engine which could utilize all its power at man's will. This is the next objective of research in nuclear energy.

The second must be the production of the uranium or other explosive atoms in inexpensive form. The over-all cost of the two bombs at Hiroshima and Nagasaki was a billion dollars each. The actual cost of the uranium has not been revealed, but its prewar cost was about one thousand dollars a pound. It is idle to speculate on what costs are attainable, and impossible to estimate when the time will come. Yet all the long history of science shows that no matter how revolutionary the concept is, once it has attained the reality of the nuclear bomb its further development, eventual usefulness, and ultimate social consequences are inevitable.

Assuming that the reaction can be controlled and that the cost can be gradually reduced, it is possible to forecast broadly the train of consequences. It is a concentrated, almost weightless source of energy and power. Its first use will probably be as aviation fuel because the actual cost of such fuel is a minor item in comparison to the cost of transporting many tons of it across the sky. A thousand gallons of gasoline weigh some three tons. If they are replaced by an ounce or less of uranium both the carrying capacity and the range of the plane can be enormously extended. Even at a thousand dollars a pound the new fuel would pay for itself. It cannot, of course, be used in the familiar internal-combustion engine, for there is no combustion. It could probably be used to provide a blast of expanding, superheated air in some type of jet engine which would thrust the plane forward by recoil as in present jet-propelled planes. If so, it could also operate a gas turbine and thus generate power for plane and ship propellers, for locomotive wheels—and all other industrial wheels.

All this is speculation, but it is safe to say that in the next phase of the use of nuclear power industrial power plants will substitute it for the energy from coal and petroleum—assuming that eventually its cost per unit of energy will be less than that of coal. Even this, however, does not mean that limitless energy will be available to all as freely as is the air we breathe. Probably the conversion of atoms into energy will for a long time require complicated machinery and such technical skill as only a great industrial powerhouse can have available. And power distributed from such plants for the individual use of consumers is costly because of the expense of distribution. A very cheap fuel would make little difference in the necessary price to the consumer.

Eventually—no one knows when—nuclear power will be available in "capsule form," to be conveniently used by anyone anywhere to generate heat or light and to do the world's work. Some future generation will live in a world where nearly all work is automatically done and is controlled by automatic electronic instruments. Then at last science will have freed the human race not only from disease, famine, and early death but also from poverty and work. Then at last science will enable humanity to live as well as to earn a living and will present it with what is far more valuable than things or dollars: time to live. Then materialism and mechanism will be merely the servants of the spiritual life. It is time now for educators, artists, clergymen, and governments to foresee this day, to speed its arrival by supporting atomic research, and to prepare the coming generations for a golden age—far better named in advance the nuclear age.

The uranium bomb was so colossal in its impact, both physically and mentally, that it threatens to overshadow the other achievements of wartime science. Its military effect was immediate but the new era that it promises is far distant. Yet the achievements of science in aviation, electronics, chemical industry, and medicine during the war were enormous and their civilian consequences will be immediate. Much of wartime science is still secret; it will be years before the full story can be told. But even the small fraction that has now been published indicates that a new era is upon us. Most spectacular have been the increases in speed and the extension of the human senses through time and space. To move a whole army fifty miles in a day, or two hundred miles in a week, requires chiefly multiplication of vehicles, plenty of radio-telephones, and a good military organization. But to move a single plane in combat faster than the enemy plane requires the concentrated research efforts of many specialists.

When the war began it was already commonplace for planes to fly at 200 miles an hour. Within a year the best planes were flying at 400. Today the published limit is 500 miles per hour, and aeronautical research is tugging at the sonic barrier—the stubborn behavior of air at the velocity of sound, 764 miles per hour.

Planes have not yet pierced that barrier though projectiles of all sorts have done so. The war's most concentrated research is probably devoted to this problem. At Aberdeen Proving Grounds in Maryland is a wind tunnel in which air moves at a velocity of 3,000 miles per hour, four times the velocity of sound. The flight of bombs and shells at such speed can there be studied to lay the basis for future plane design.

Sleek and streamlined as the ordinary 200-mile plane is, it creates too many eddies, too many restraining whirlpools to be capable of flight at twice that speed. Even the rivets and the dimples in the aluminum skin are a drag on the plane. They cut its speed and, worse, increase its fuel consumption, reduce its range, thus increase the fuel load and decrease its carrying capacity. The new planes are not only sleek but polished. At 500 miles an hour a thread, a splashed bug, a film of dust is far too costly a hindrance to drag through the sky. For this reason the planes now contemplated may well abandon aluminum in favor of plastic-coated glass fiber with smooth, very thin wings, much lighter than metal wings yet fully as strong. They can streak through the air with a minimum turbulence. Their drag is minute; their lift, enormous.

Prewar planes could lift eight or ten pounds for each square foot of wing surface; the first big bombers lifted twenty-five pounds. The B-29 lifts seventy. The new wings promise a hundred pounds for each square foot.

Even more important are the new engines. Niceties of design have increased the horsepower available from a single engine up to 3,000, more than half the power of the largest locomotive. The same engineering skill has reduced the weight of the engine to less than one pound for each horsepower. But the jet engine opens a new chapter in the story of power and speed. Here the explosion does not push a piston which turns the crank which spins the propeller, but instead the explosion roars almost unimpeded through the rear nozzle and sends the engine forward by recoil. With such engines the problem is not one of increasing the horsepower but of keeping it low enough. The 5,000-horsepower jet engine exists today. Planes with a total of 50,000 horsepower are possible.

Speed is only one consequence. Equally important is the fact that the jet engine has only one big moving part—no pistons, cams, crankshaft, valves, lubricating system, carburetor, and other accessories that contribute to weight. The jet engine needs only half a pound for each horsepower and has no problems of lubrication nor of special fuels. It burns kerosene or even crude oil. The result is decreased engine weight, less need of fuel load, increased carrying power, and a far greater range of flight.

The decisive advantage of the jet engine is that it is most efficient in the thinnest, highest air and at the highest speeds. It needs no propeller. It can skim through the air at a higher speed than sound, a thing that no propeller can do, for the propeller operates by biting into the air and thrusting itself forward. Long before the plane reaches the speed of sound the propeller tips have done so, and at the speed of sound the air becomes so thick, so immovable, that an almost solid film of air is formed between the propeller blades. In effect the propeller becomes a plastic circle, a mass of slush perhaps, which has no bite, no thrust, and impedes the plane rather than pulling it. The propellerless jet engine is the answer.

The latest pursuit planes of all nations are jet-powered. Their speed is 500 miles per hour—and up. The fastest, and most shocking, is the Japanese "Kamikaze," the suicide plane. It seems to appear "out of nowhere" because it flies a mile in a few seconds. It is designed only for high speed. Its wings are so small and so thin that it cannot fly slowly. It can neither lift itself from the airfield nor return to it. It is launched from a bomber and it never returns. Some such device will be needed if planes are ever to go faster than sound, for the wings that lift a plane at slow speeds would merely push a wall of air ahead of them at speeds higher than 750 miles per hour. Beyond that, flight must be by some type of wingless projectile like the V-2 bomb. Any future war will

be made dreadful by large numbers of such self-propelled projectiles flying at a thousand miles per hour or more. The airplane
was an infant in World War I and became a major weapon in
World War II. Just so will flight faster than sound be a major
weapon in World War III. This is a thought that should make
another war forever impossible.

The jet engine, however, has mundane uses too. It can be harnessed for the operation of slower planes and even of locomotives and ships when it is converted into a gas turbine. In that
form the roaring flame of the jet is directed at the blades of a
turbine wheel which absorb its power and spin under the impact.
The turbine wheel reaches a white-hot temperature of 1,500 degrees, may spin at 20,000 revolutions per minute (some thirty
miles a minute) with its axle geared to a propeller. Transport
planes will use this engine and with it comfortably attain speeds
of 400 miles an hour. The turbine engine, though heavier than the
jet engine, needs no more than half a pound of engine weight
per horsepower. Thus a 10,000-horsepower engine weighs 5,000
pounds as compared with some 10,000 for the reciprocating engine. The result is a saving of two and one-half tons, available
for passengers or for fuel. So confident are the aeronautical engineers in this field that one leading aeronautical engineer predicts
there will soon be no more reciprocating engines on any plane
anywhere. For railroads too the gas turbine will mean smaller
locomotives and lighter, with no boilers or condensers, no steam,
therefore no need to replenish the water tank. Finally, for ships it
means increased cargo space by a great reduction in the space
required for the engines.

These are the major technical consequences of wartime aviation. But the industrial consequences are equally important. Certainly the chief effect is our colossal production of planes. Even if
war planes are unfitted for civilian use the industry can produce
many more planes than are needed. Certainly air travel will be
commonplace. Hundreds of thousands of passengers will fly annually to Europe and to Asia, will fly to summer homes in Brazil

and the Argentine, Labrador and Alaska. Businessmen will think
no more of an overnight trip to Rome or Moscow than they now
do of a jaunt to Chicago. America enters an era of mobility which
exists in reality if not yet in the minds of the people. It is only the
veterans of global war who know what aviation is. They will lead
the way for civilians to life in the air.

Most civilians can look with sympathy on only one new plane,
the helicopter, which does not depend upon speed and is therefore congenial to earth-minded pedestrians. Although it demands
more skill of the operator, it seems simple and safe because it
frightens no one by too fast motion. It can hover, fly backwards
or sideways, can be parked as neatly as an automobile if the day
is not windy, can hop easily over mountains, streams, and cities,
yet can fly forward at 80 or 100 miles per hour—faster than an automobile and without hindrance from traffic or traffic lights. Here
too the important fact is that the helicopter is a reality, is being
made and used in large numbers, and can be produced for civilian use by tens of thousands.

If 100,000 helicopters are in use in the United States within five
years, as has been competently predicted, they will do to the
American city what every new form of transportation has done in
the past: they will remake the map. In the early days of America
it was the docks, the steamboat landing, and later the railroad
station which determined the location of the business district, the
industrial area, and the residences. With the advent of electricity
the trolley car changed the map by spreading retail business outward along the main streets. The automobile changed it again
with radial highways and shopping centers at the edge of town.
So, too, the helicopter will demand new centers. It will need
neighborhood airports, quite small and without runways, easily
accessible from home. These airports will become the new transportation centers and will be flanked by garages, grocery stores,
restaurants, and drugstores. They will become the new centers of
community development.

So aviation can transform America and American life with helicopters for the use of commuters and for short flights up to 50 or 100 miles, with "feeder planes" operating from every town to the nearest aviation center on the transcontinental lines, with planes carrying 50 to 75 passengers across the continent with only three or four stops on the way, and finally with great transoceanic planes carrying 200 or 300 passengers across the seas.

Probably more important than the dramatic advances in aviation is the blossoming of electronics in a multitude of military weapons and its growth into an industry which is now larger than prewar automobile manufacture. Only three major developments have been revealed in sufficient detail to produce public discussion. They are the radio telephone, radar, and electronic instruments for inspection and control.

Modern mobile warfare requires not only speed but precise timing in the action of many separate units. This was impossible in previous wars, for communication was by messenger and at best by telegraph and telephone signals. Today every mobile unit, be it plane, ship, tank, gun, or infantryman, can be equipped with a radio telephone. For the individual soldier a sending and receiving set, developed from the prewar walkie-talkie, need weigh but a few pounds and is compact because modern radio tubes are midgets—the size of an acorn or less. Even more vital is the fact that thousands of separate channels of communication are available so that almost any number of conversations may be carried on across the same area without interference. This is now possible because the radio waves which carry the impulse may vary in length from a half-mile to a small fraction of a millimeter. The study of short-wave, high-frequency radio has enormously increased the number of useful wave lengths and therefore the number of channels of communication.

To provide this radio equipment an enormous industry has grown up, and will provide the same facility of communication to civilian life. Already the police and army automobiles are equipped with two-way radio and are in constant touch with headquarters. In a few years taxicab fleets will be too, and busses, trucks, doctors' cars. Recently the Federal Communications Commission has allocated a large band of wave lengths to radio telephony, confident that such uses are inevitable, that railroad trains will increase the safety of operation by the universal use of the radio telephone.

Immediate as this application is, it does not compare in importance with radar. This device extends the range of human eyes far beyond any prewar dreams. It enables an antiaircraft battery to see the approach of planes through the blackest night and densest fog while those planes are still a hundred miles away. It operates, again, by radio waves. Each radar post is in effect a radio broadcasting station. It sends very short ether waves into the sky. Most of them are lost in empty space. But when they strike a metal object they are reflected, and a small percentage of those reflected return to the sending station, are received by special antennae, and are revealed on a screen so clearly that the type of plane or ship can be identified, its distance calculated.

Radar sets installed in planes can do more; they can observe the nature of the terrain beneath, in spite of night and cloud or fog. The operator can see the outlines of land and water masses, can even locate larger masses of metal such as an industrial plant. Radar has at one step accomplished what a million years of evolution would not have: it has extended the range of vision of human eyes to a hundred miles, given them night vision, and erased the mists.

Its consequences are beyond prediction. It will permit ships at sea to proceed at full steam ahead through fog and night with the certainty that any obstacle, be it ship or rock or iceberg, that protrudes above the waves will be visible. It may possibly increase the safety of automobile traffic by showing the approach of hidden cars at the crossroads. Certainly it will improve the safety of postwar flight.

But these are minor consequences. The major fact is that radar manufacture is so closely akin to television manufacture that television will be the first great industry to reach postwar maturity.

Within a year or two the eastern seaboard will be united under one or several television networks, and within five years nearly everyone in the continental United States will live within the high-pitched ether vibrations of the national networks. Screens are already large enough and bright enough to picture the events of the day, sports, and drama on the living-room wall without dimming the lights and in a size that will make human beings seem almost natural. Television in full color is ready in the laboratories. Here again the human eyes have been amplified so that the remote and neighborless farmer can yet see great events precisely as if he were sitting where the television camera is.

It is high time that statesmen, teachers, salesmen, and politicians thought well on what television will do to us—pondered on the qualities of charm and presence that will win the presidential election of 1948, the qualities of oral and visual persuasion that will sell goods to the assembled family in the parlor of 1947. It is time school teachers and correspondence schools foresaw the competition of trained experts who can thus enter the home via the ether. Above all, it is wise to realize that, unlike radio, television screens will not be in the homes of millions of people because they are expensive. People will congregate before screens that will be smartly provided by those who profit from crowds. Television will lure many a bored youngster and oldster from the home to the tavern or dance hall, to the school or church perhaps, will provide a needed audience to the advertisers by encouraging a neighborhood life, club life, community life. It may improve still further American sociability and perhaps social feeling.

The third great wartime development in electronics comprises those automatic instruments that are exemplified under the phrases "automatic pilot" and "invisible crew." They too improve on the human senses. The electric ear, the microphone, hears much more delicately than does the human ear. The electric eye exceeds the human eye in sensitiveness. It can see in the dark by infrared and ultraviolet light, it can see in a tenth of a thousandth of a second what it takes the human eye a tenth of a second to distinguish, and it can take instant action through amplifying tubes and a relay switch. Thus it can do with extreme discrimination and instant speed anything that can be done by throwing an electric switch off or on—and in this electric age that means it can do almost anything except smell and think. An enormous multiplication of labor-saving devices will certainly follow. Industry will replace the human senses by these superb electronic instruments. It could become another industrial revolution with such radical social changes as those of a century ago when the power of steam was substituted for that of human muscles.

Already the chemical industry has approached this status because of its need for enormous production during a shortage of labor. It is producing two billion pounds of aluminum a year, a million tons of synthetic rubber, and five hundred million gallons of 100-octane gasoline each day. The aluminum was needed for planes and will be used after the war for all articles that need to be constantly moved from place to place—at the cost of fuel or freight charges. The 100-octane gasoline was also needed for the modern planes with tremendous horsepower yet with small and light engines. If after the war the kerosene-burning gas turbine replaces the internal-combustion engine in the planes, the flow of 100-octane gasoline can go to the postwar automobiles to attain high speed and power by the use of small, high-compression engines which can be tucked under the rear seat.

The synthetic rubber industry is more than a mushroom growth: it is a new creation, quite unexpected because no one expected Pearl Harbor. It has succeeded not only in doubling the amount of rubber that had been available, but in producing it from petroleum at a cost less than that of natural rubber. It is doing so with extreme economy of labor. To collect our annual 600,000 tons of natural rubber from the scattered trees of the Orient required 9,000,000 Malayans, collecting an average of 150 pounds per year each. In American chemical plants that amount of synthetic rubber is made by 10,000 skilled workers producing 60 tons per year each. These figures are a measure of the productiveness of the new scientific industries.

This great new industry is important beyond the rubber market, for it is in fact making an endless variety of soft plastics. These new materials probably have as much future as did the hard plastics thirty years ago. Thin or thick, soft or stiff, tough, elastic, almost liquid or very hard, they can be made in such variety and can be embellished with such color and design that they will have as many uses as do hard plastics. In replacing articles like tablecloths and upholstery, wallpaper and drapes, floor coverings and articles of dress they will add to the competitive problems of the textile industry and to the luxuries of living.

Synthetic fibers—rayon, celanese, nylon—had, even before the war, replaced much cotton and even silk. It should surprise no one that synthetic fibers are superior to the natural. After all, the cotton plant covers its seed with a fibrous fuzz for its own biological purposes—not for man's sake. The fuzz was not designed for textile use. Nor do cattle have hides only because man needs leather for his shoes. It is just a lucky accident that many natural products fill our needs, and it is only natural when they are not quite perfect for us. But synthetic fibers are now made to prescription: long or short, thick or thin, hard or soft, straight or curled. Almost any desired quality, such as the elasticity of nylon, can be built into them by the ingenuity of the chemist. The natural textiles cannot be altered except by the long and fortuitous process of cross-breeding.

Each of the myriad new developments in plastics, except perhaps the most brittle, offers new possibilities for textile use, for rope and cord, for screens, nets, and tire fabrics, as well as for evening gowns, stockings, underwear, and fantastic accessories. But most materials that can thus be drawn into thin fibers can also be extruded in sheets to make substitutes for leather and rubber, for shoes, belts, and hats, and for outdoor furniture.

Textiles have felt the impact of the plastics industry in other ways. Wool can now be treated with melamine resins to render it shrink-proof in the laundry. Paper can be treated to make it as strong when wet as it is when dry. Supplies packed in paper bags and cartons can be thrown from the deck for a beachhead landing and can later be fished from the water with the paper still strong and intact. Wood, too, has been altered by the injection of plastics into its cellular structure so that soft woods become hard and all woods become proof against changes in length and shape from hot or cold, wet or dry weather. When wood does not expand, shrink, or warp with age and weather it can be machined as precisely as steel is. Better furniture and interior fittings result and wood becomes available in many uses for which it had been too soft and too unstable in size and shape.

Such are a few of the advances in chemistry and physics which have been developed by engineers and put into production by industry. Because these sciences are further advanced than the biological sciences, their by-products are too. And their chief by-products are the great industries producing power and things for war and later for peace. But the biological sciences and their by-products in medicine and health have also advanced. Here, too, progress has been in applications, not in fundamentals.

One chemical product has ended the age-old threat of typhus. To every army in all history typhus has been more dangerous than the human enemy and has cost more lives than have weapons. Now the threat of typhus is disappearing.

This was accomplished by a little known, yet long known, chemical. In 1874 a German chemistry student named Zeidler synthesized DDT, wrote a few dry words about his compound, and followed it into oblivion. But in 1939 Zeidler's formula got into the hands of Paul Muller, an employee of the Geigy Company, Inc. He found DDT so deadly to insects that the American branch of this dye firm called it to the attention of the U. S. Department of Agriculture. Soon the Surgeon General's Office and the Office of Scientific Research and Development undertook extensive research, and shortly the Cincinnati Chemical Works was producing it in quantity. During this time the formula was kept secret and referred to by the initials of its chemical name, dichloro-diphenyl-trichloroethane—hence, DDT.

The first large-scale medical test of DDT came in Africa in 1943 and again in Naples where the Allies were faced with a typhus epidemic. Millions of people were infested with lice, the lice infested with typhus. As a consequence of thorough dusting of our troops with DDT powder, the epidemic was checked.

Since malaria is transmitted by mosquitoes and since mosquitoes and their larvae are susceptible to DDT, this chemical has also been a primary weapon in the tropics by powdering the troops and all their supplies and by preliminary spraying of the Pacific beaches before landing.

Unique among insecticides, DDT is not a poison: insects do not need to eat it. It kills them on contact. When sprayed on the walls of a room, DDT is fatal to the fly or louse that touches it within three months. All sorts of domestic vermin can be eliminated.

With DDT available to civilians the farmer can give the barn a June spraying which will keep the cows at ease throughout the summer. And forests can be saved from the ravages of the gypsy moth caterpillar. The loss of food crops to insect pests in this country amounts to more than two billion dollars annually. It is within the expectation of experts that crop pests can be so controlled by means of DDT as to salvage the better part of this loss.

Another new chemical, forced into production by the needs of war, is penicillin, probably the most valuable drug ever discovered. It is not, however, manufactured by the chemical industry but must be extracted from the microscopic plants which somehow produce it. The culture of the mold *Penicillium* on a large scale, quite free from other microscopic organisms, and the extraction of its powerful germ-killing chemical is now conducted in twenty-two large plants in the United States and Canada. They have opened what is in effect a new profession: biological engineering. Already it promises to produce for the medical profession a large number of other antibacterial agents that can be harvested from a variety of new molds and bacteria. The production of chemicals from botanical plants is as old as agriculture itself, but the culture of micro-plants is new.

The story of penicillin begins with an accident—one that fortunately happened under the observation of a trained scientist. In 1928, Dr. Alexander Fleming of the University of London was trying to isolate pure cultures of various bacteria, seeking means to identify new infections. These cultures are allowed to grow for several days to permit the bacteria to multiply. Dr. Fleming chanced to notice that upon one plate a mold had started to grow—and that in a small circle around each spot of mold the bacteria had disappeared. It occurred to him that the mold was killing the bacteria. He made a pure culture of the mold and identified it as a variety of *Penicillium,* a relative of the common molds that grow on bread and cheese. Then he found that this mold was able to prevent the growth of a large number of different bacteria, and that the bactericidal action was exerted by a new chemical which could be extracted from the *Penicillium* mold. He named it penicillin. Yet his work seemed of little interest in medical practice and for ten years nothing more was done.

When war was imminent the need for antibacterial agents to counteract infected wounds became desperate. Dr. Howard Florey of Oxford University studied Fleming's work and confirmed the bactericidal effect. With the financial help of the Rockefeller Foundation and of the British Medical Research Council the value of penicillin was established by its use in British hospitals. Then the problem of its large-scale production was undertaken in the United States. The Northern Regional Research Laboratory of the U. S. Department of Agriculture at Peoria, Illinois, effected three great improvements. At a Peoria fruit stand a new strain of the mold was accidentally discovered growing on a cantaloupe, a strain which somehow produced twice the usual amount of penicillin. The Laboratory also discovered that "corn-steep liquor" is a unique nutrient for the mold and permits a very copious growth. Finally, the mold was grown in nodule form so that thousands of small pellets could be immersed in great 12,000-gallon tanks, there to grow under the surface, throughout the tank, instead of merely on the surface as is the usual habit of mold growth. As a result, a single one of the producing companies now makes enough penicillin for 100,000 treatments a month and the entire industry can provide for millions of patients.

The injection of penicillin into the blood stream has been used successfully to combat blood poisoning, pneumonia, and infections of the heart and brain. Its success in the treatment of gonorrhea has been spectacular. It may reduce gonorrhea to a disease of little consequence, and even syphilis responds to it. It is not effective against malaria and virus diseases like the common cold, influenza, and infantile paralysis.

Once in the blood stream, penicillin is short-lived, leaving by way of the kidneys within two or three hours. Repeated injections are needed. It would be much simpler to administer penicillin by mouth, but the drug loses its potency in the presence of acid, therefore is destroyed by the digestive acids in the stomach before it can reach the intestine for absorption. But special pills have now been devised which carry it through the stomach, and it promises to become a universal household remedy. Unlike the sulfa drugs, penicillin does no harm whatever to the human system.

Probably the best known of the medical advances of this war is the use of whole blood and of dried blood plasma in maintaining the life of wounded men in the front line until they could receive medical attention at the advanced hospitals. Fully 97 per cent of the battle-wounded were thus kept alive. Blood was collected from millions of willing civilian donors to supply the Army and Navy—more than 5,000,000 pints of blood in 1944 alone. By contrast, when disaster struck at Pearl Harbor 960 patients suddenly needed blood and only 750 pints were on hand.

The primary function of blood is to carry oxygen from the

lungs to the tissues. This is done by the red cells, or rather by a substance called hemoglobin in the red cells. When there has been severe loss of blood, when major operations are to be performed, and often during convalescence, whole blood which contains red cells and their hemoglobin is needed. But the blood performs many other functions also, and these do not require the aid of the red cells. For many purposes the plasma, which is the clear liquid left when the red cells are filtered out from blood, is equally effective and has the great advantage that it can be kept almost indefinitely, while the red cells do not remain active for more than a month. During this war the best means of preserving the plasma has been to evaporate it, to remove the water and leave a dry, white powder. When this is mixed with the right amount of distilled water the plasma is remade, as good as new.

The chief use of blood plasma is to counteract what is called combat shock. Shock results not from hemorrhage or actual loss of blood so much as from the seepage of plasma through the walls of the blood vessels into the tissues of the body under the severe strain of battle. The result is a loss of liquid in the arteries and veins, and a drop in blood pressure so that circulation is inadequate with a resulting daze and even unconsciousness. If blood plasma is injected, the volume of blood is restored, blood pressure becomes normal, circulation is renewed, and the shock is immediately checked.

Many a life has thus been saved, for in this war dried plasma has gone everywhere with the troops, vacuum-packed and accompanied by a bottle of distilled water, ready for use within five minutes. It has been dropped by plane and even shot in shells to isolated troops.

But blood plasma has done more: it has made possible an understanding of the function of the proteins which are contained in it and has made possible the extraction of specific life-giving chemicals that have opened a whole new chapter in medicine. In a careful study of blood plasma, Dr. Edwin J. Cohn of Harvard found that its chief constituent is a serum albumin. The molecules of this protein are the smallest of those present in the plasma and are the most effective in combating shock. A concentrated solution of serum albumin when injected into the blood is as effective as much larger quantities of plasma in drawing blood fluids back from the tissues into the blood stream and thus in restoring normal blood pressure and circulation.

After separating the serum albumin from the plasma Dr. Cohn was able to isolate other valuable proteins from the remaining plasma. For instance, about 1 per cent of the dried plasma is a protein called fibrinogen which stops the flow of blood from a cut or wound. A fibrin foam is now in use in military hospitals to speed the clotting of blood. But pure fibrinogen is a remarkable elastic material, similar to a synthetic plastic like nylon, so that films of fibrinogen have been used by surgeons to substitute for the membrane which lines the human brain.

But the most surprising and perhaps the most important of these discoveries in the chemistry of blood is still another class of proteins: the globulins. Among them are the heretofore mysterious substances which are the body's own protection against infectious diseases. In the case of measles a specific globulin has been concentrated from blood plasma and has been used with great success both to protect human beings from measles and to reduce the severity of the disease. The Red Cross is now supplying public health agencies with this antimeasles globulin. The globulin for jaundice is the next in line. Much research still needs to be done, yet the globulins from blood plasma may well be man's best protection against all infectious diseases, so that powerful chemical germicides will not in the future be needed.

These great scientific advances of medicine were called forth by military needs and have all played a part in the remarkable recovery of the battle-wounded. Only 3.3 per cent of the wounded have succumbed in this war, though in World War I 8.1 per cent died. This means that 60,000 men are now alive who would have died in the last war.

After the war civilian health will profit too. The balance sheet of the medical profession is kept by the insurance companies. Thus the net result of medical advances is expressed in terms of "life expectancy"—the average duration of life. These wartime discoveries, plus others that are yet secret, will appear on this balance sheet as an increase of some ten years in the life expectancy of American citizens. Since the average is already 65 years, it will jump to about 75 years. Babies born in 1950 can on the average expect to live until the year 2025. Rather soon American society and customs will change under the influence of a large number of elderly people. By 1970 we may have as many as twenty million people 65 years or older.

In the mental sciences, psychology and psychiatry, progress has been not so much in new discoveries as in the recognition by the public that the human mind is also a proper subject for scientific study. Some 500,000 men had been discharged from the Army by the middle of 1945 for mental disabilities which interfered with their military duties. Most of them were restored to normal civilian life and were there accepted with the full realization that mental disturbances are very common. Society will profit enormously from this realization that mental disease is not only real but that many "normal" people have peculiarities that can be understood and adjusted. Almost certainly the treatment of criminals, the divorce problem, and the care of underprivileged persons will benefit greatly by transfer from the field of morals and emotion to that of sound mental science.

In normal times the progress of science, though steady, is haphazard because it depends on the individual interests and inspiration of thousands of research workers in university laboratories scattered throughout the world and on the competing plans of industrial corporations and industries. Scientific research has always been an ideal example of private initiative and enterprise. But in wartime the threat from the enemy touches everyone, and co-ordinated action is needed in order to focus research on the vital military problems. The organization of scientists under government control is an outstanding and unique feature of this war.

It began in 1940, with an elaborate file of America's scientific manpower, set up in Washington as the National Roster of Scientific and Specialized Personnel. By means of this list, government agencies, industry, and education could promptly locate qualified personnel and specialists for co-ordinated attacks on war problems.

The largest war research organization is the Office of Scientific Research and Development (OSRD), started by executive order and intended to deal with research on military problems. It is headed by Dr. Vannevar Bush, president of the Carnegie Institution, and has two main branches. One of them is the National Defense Research Committee (NDRC), with President James B. Conant of Harvard as chairman, divided into agencies dealing with such specific weapons as radar, subsurface warfare, explosives. The other is the Committee on Medical Research (CMR), under Dr. A. Newton Richards of the University of Pennsylvania, devoted to the problems of military medicine. The whole structure of the OSRD worked in close liaison with military and naval authorities so that it was continually aware of war's newest demands and requirements.

Similarly, the War Production Board had its Office of Production Research and Development (OPRD), set up initially with Dr. Harvey N. Davis, president of Stevens Institute of Technology, as chairman to study industrial problems of the war industries: such vital matters as the production of aluminum and magnesium, synthetic rubber and motor fuels, substitutes for essential but unobtainable raw materials, and emergency problems of all sorts. Through the OPRD the government has made a superb record in providing facts and facilities that were beyond the reach of industry itself.

Through these and other research organizations more than $700,000,000 was spent in 1944. The results were spectacular and decisive for the history of the world. Organized co-operation had done for the crucial emergency what no amount of individual skill and initiative could have accomplished. Inevitably came the demand that the great scientific problems of peacetime be similarly attacked under government leadership. In every recent session of Congress, Senator Harley M. Kilgore of West Virginia has introduced a bill to that effect. He has encountered strong opposition, both because scientists are essentially individualists and because the most important single source of future profits for United States corporations lies in the exploration and exploitation of the frontiers of science.

Yet shortly before his death President Franklin D. Roosevelt asked Dr. Vannevar Bush of the OSRD for recommendations to continue government leadership in science and to apply the lessons of war research to the problems of peace. Dr. Bush's answer, a book entitled *Science, the Endless Frontier,* accepts the challenge and opens the door to a new scientific era. His committees recommend government expenditure of $90,000,000 a year at universities, medical schools, and research institutes for fundamental research on which the United States' future can be built. They recommend also no less than 6,000 federal scholarships a year for students in the sciences at American colleges and 300 fellowships for graduate students in the universities. This would make the advancement of science a primary project of the Federal Government. It is to be administered by a National Research Foundation whose first task is to formulate a national policy for science in order to keep permanently abreast of any possible enemy in military research, to achieve full employment in United States industry, and to promote international trade. Senator Warren Magnusson of Washington immediately introduced a bill into the U. S. Senate to carry out Dr. Bush's recommendations.

The social consequences of wartime research cannot be predicted in detail, but it is safe to say that, even without atomic or nuclear power, the few advances that have been briefly surveyed in this chapter will alter American life more than it was altered by the automobile and the radio, perhaps as much as it was altered by the thousand uses of electricity. Certainly science itself has been completely transformed. It is no longer a mere hobby for the specialist and a source of new gadgets. It is now recognized as a social force that is as strong as any and one under whose dictates we all live.

V. THE WOMEN IN THE WAR

by MARGARET MEAD

MARGARET MEAD *is an outstanding American anthropologist. Her expeditions to Samoa, the Admiralty Islands, New Guinea, and Bali have each resulted in a best-selling book embodying her findings. Since 1926, she has been Assistant Curator of Ethnology at the American Museum of Natural History.*

IN WARTIME men and women get out of step and begin to wonder about each other. "What will he be like after all those years in the Army?" "What will she be like after all those years alone at home?" "Will he be harder on the children and want them to toe the line too hard? After all, that's all he has seen for years." "Will she have learned to be so independent that she won't want to give up her job to make a home for me?" "Will he have got so used to having everything done for him, his clothes handed out, his meals set on the table, his allotment deducted, that he will hate having to sit down and plan how in the world we are going to pay the dentist's bill, or meet the payment on the house?" "What will he think about politics away off there where they say the men never get any papers and only want the baseball news?" "Wonder if she's got her head full of a lot of funny ideas while I was away." "What's happened to his morals?" "What's happened to her morals?" "I do hope he won't have changed too much." "I hope she will look the same."

All this is natural enough. Boys and girls grow up together in the same world, seeing a lot of each other, each knowing what the other is thinking. Husbands are used to coming home at night and telling their wives what they think of the news in the paper, and having their wives tell them they are exactly right—or exactly wrong. Either way, they know what's going on. In peacetime, for one young man who gets a bad jolt because he finds the girl of his special choice wants to keep her job instead of having a baby, or have a baby instead of keeping her job, there are several hundred young men who know just what their girls are going to think, whether they will want to go on working for quite a while to get enough money to buy the layette, whether they will elect to live in a very tiny house in order to have a baby right away, whether they have plans for combining a career and home. The boys not only know what is going on in the girls' heads, but have picked them out because they like the particular ideas. Once in a while somebody gets a rude surprise, but mostly they stay pretty well in step. If a man reads in the paper that women are working more and more out of the home and are less and less willing to stay in it, it doesn't make him look with knitted brow at his wife sitting placidly on the other side of the dining-room table to wonder whether she will be walking out, lunch box in hand, tomorrow. When the wife of an active trade union worker reads in the newspaper about opposition to some strike on which she has set her heart, she doesn't have to wonder if her husband feels like *that*, for she has just seen him off for the picket line or the union meeting. The things which the newspapers call "growing tendencies" or "rapidly developing trends" don't puzzle or frighten or anger people nearly so much, when their own particular girl, or man, is right there beside them.

Dramatic news, quintuplets and quads, double murders and triple suicides, bobby sox round-ups and bluebeard lovers, all fall into place in peacetime, as events which spice the even round of life, life in which most babies are born one at a time, husbands and wives may sometimes feel like murdering each other but hardly ever do, most high school girls are studying their lessons, and most men find it quite enough to have married one woman, without looking for extra wives. But in wartime, boys and girls, men and women, separated in time and in space, he living an entirely different kind of life which she often cannot even imagine, she living much the same old life, become flat and stale and tasteless because he has gone away, aren't in step any more, and both sexes begin to wonder what the other one will be like . . . after the war.

For during the war some twenty million people become anonymous overnight. John Smith, the son of the Bill Smiths, the one that was on the basketball team (you know, that boy who was always breaking his arm falling out of trees, the one who used to make those wacky posters for the games), becomes merely one of a group of young soldiers wandering about a strange town, where his good deeds and his bad will be laid to "the way those soldiers behaved." His sister, who in her own home town was singled out and protected by the memories and the watchfulness of her mother's friends (who would note how often she went out with that nice Brown boy or that wild Jones boy), is a thousand miles away working in a war plant, sleeping in a room with three strangers whose last names she may hardly know. When she appears in her war worker's getup—which she will make a little more like a war worker's getup every time somebody is rude to her—the comments of the unpleased townspeople will be very much like the comments on her brother, "How those girl war workers behave"—or don't behave. As for John's wife, she also, if she is one of the thousands of wives who have shifted about, baby on right arm, left hand grasping bundles, sitting on luggage, and stayed on in the last town, after her husband went overseas—she too isn't treated as a member of any community, but just as "one of those war wives."

All this is disturbing. So many people are doing things they haven't done before, seeing a part of life which their elders hoped they never would see at all. So much of life is being lived anonymously, far from home, away from the protection given by knowing that the girl in the office, or Uncle Jim, or your boy friend's brother is sitting at the next table in the juke box joint. The soldier or sailor, in a camp or port, far away overseas, has experienced this anonymity over and over again. Perhaps he has felt it most keenly when, after months of being treated as "an American" or "G.I." or "a good Joe," he suddenly meets a Red Cross girl who exclaims, "Why, Jack Smith, I haven't seen you since the senior dance" and becomes himself again, in a world of men and girls who know and, because they know, trust—or distrust ("He always was a wolf"—"She's a regular wolfess")—each other.

The man overseas reads his paper or his magazine filled with news that women are doing new and therefore, by definition, "unwomanly" jobs, for a womanly job is just a job that everybody is used to seeing women do. He reads about the mannish clothes women are wearing, the welding outfits they are wielding, and he worries. What's getting into women anyway? What will be the use of winning the war if when you go back home all the girls' heads are filled with a lot of unfamiliar and unwelcome nonsense? He knows his sister is a long way from home, and he has heard what the other men in the outfit say about other men's sisters. He knows his girl or his wife is far away from home, and he's heard plenty about fickle girls and wandering wives. The newspapers are full of wild tales, bobby soxers wandering about Times Square, or storming a performance by Frank Sinatra, the riotous living of war workers, the occasional but very conspicuous baby who is born after its father has been overseas for eleven months. If he were at home all this would fall into place. He would realize that the hundreds of thousands of babies who have been born discreetly, with due respect for the date on which their fathers left the country, aren't news to anybody but their close relations, and don't get their photographs into anything but V-mail. He'd have a chance to see that being a woman worker means long arduous hours at unfamiliar work, cramped and trying living conditions, hours of standing in line, waiting for busses, waiting for food, waiting once in a while to get into the town's one movie house. He'd know that every straying bobby soxer is balanced by a hundred youngsters who have added to their peacetime jobs of going to school and helping Mother with the dishes, many other tasks, sometimes a full eight hours of work in factory or store, sometimes the full burden of shopping and cooking because Mother is working; or doing their absent brothers' work on the farm. He would see the hundreds of little towns where there are no young men left at all, and the girls just carry on, as a counterpoint to the few bobby soxers of Times Square and the Loop. But he wasn't home, and he couldn't see things the way they were, and the newspapers only publish the sensational and the shocking—and so, he often wonders and worries.

As an anonymous soldier or sailor or marine, a thousand miles from home, he has also met more girls he wouldn't like his sister or his girl to be like, than otherwise. Even the "good girls" he's met have often been so foreign that he hasn't felt comfortable with them. Against all this background, separated from his own womenfolk, exposed in odd ways to other peoples', teased by newspapers and radio bits, it is small wonder that the hero of many missions answered the serious-minded reporter who asked him about his thoughts when he approached Berlin, "Well, mostly we've been wondering whether it's true that women are smoking pipes at home." The question he is asking is very simple: "Are the girls at home so changed that when we meet them we won't feel like ourselves either?" For after all, feeling comfortable in the world, as a man, depends a lot on the women, just as women can only be sure they are themselves when their men are there.

Besides the bobby soxers and the quads in the newspapers, there has been a continuous harping on the theme: "Will the women be willing to return to the home?" This worrying question is repeated over and over again, often inspired by those to whose interest it will be to discharge women workers, regardless of whether they are wives, widows, or spinsters, as soon as the war is over. To men far away from home, holding on to bits and pieces of memory of what the kitchen looked like on Sunday morning, or the feel of their baby's fingers curled around their own, it is almost more frightening than the old song, "I wonder who's kissing her now?" because it threatens the future. Perhaps women have all left the home, perhaps there won't be any homes! Across the pages of the mind march lines of women, in slacks, holding large fat pay envelopes which they brandish more effectively than the traditional rolling pin. Men who have counted on "supporting" their wives and receiving love in return, without ever having given much thought or much practice to making them happy in other ways, are naturally worried. Before they know it, bull sessions are developing, devoted to "putting the women back into the home and give the veteran back his job which the women have stolen."

Statistics on how many women are working and intend to work are paraded in headlines which add, "Eight out of every ten women queried say they will work after the war." The average man or woman doesn't go about with a headful of statistics to tell them that most of those women who say they will go on working are women who would have been working anyway, as the number of American women who work has been rising from two million and a half in 1880 to over five million in 1920 and to eleven million in 1940. In 1950—if you ask for official estimates—you'll find that about sixteen million women will be working in the United States. That's the kind of society we have, one in which many men aren't paid enough to support their wives, one in which women without husbands are expected to support themselves, one in which very few brothers are willing to support their unmarried sisters. Back of the headlines and the statistics and the ominous questions in the newspapers there lies the simple fact that more women have to work in the United States each year, and that more women will be working at some time in their lives than ever before.

This needn't worry the returning men very deeply. It was part of the America they left, and it's part of the America they are coming back to. The war has speeded the process up a little, that's all. After the war, just as it would have been if there had been no war, most girls will plan to work between school and marriage, many will plan to work until the first baby puts in an appearance, some will go back to work when their children are grown and they no longer have a full-time job running a home for two, and an increasing number will work because they have no husbands and no other means of support.

However, some striking things have happened during the war which are due to the war, and which the returning man will want to know about and understand—always against the background of the way men's work and women's work were developing anyway. During the war, over three million women have gone to work who would not have worked if there had not been a war. That means that over three million women will have done something they hadn't expected to do, and that their sons and brothers and husbands and boy friends wouldn't have expected them to do. If you allow two men to be surprised by what each of these women have done, have been able to do, you end up with over six million surprised men! A million girls between fourteen and eighteen who would ordinarily have been in school have been working part or full time. A million young married women, with and without children, have gone to work. Many of them are service wives, eking out an allotment or responding to urgent calls for more war workers in towns where there was no room to bring in any more workers because there was no place for them to sleep. Many of them are service wives who took jobs because it was easier to bear the waiting, the days and days of unrelieved anxiety, if their hands were fully occupied. Last, the remainder of the three million, women past the child-bearing years, who would not have been working otherwise, are now working. Many of these are women who have worked before, before they were married or before the children came, who have gone back to their old jobs, in factories, in offices, as teachers, nurses, telephone operators, social workers. Many of them are women who were thrown aside during the depression, who thought they would never work again, whose services have again become valuable. Some are mothers who cannot bear waiting for the mailman and some are mothers who already know their sons will never return.

These are the women, the little girls, the waiting wives, the tired older women, whom we can count because they have gone out to work for wages and salaries. In addition, there are the millions of women on farms, who for the first time in their lives have had to do men's work on the farms, run milking machines and tractors, dig potatoes and make hay. Seven hundred and fifty thousand women have voluntarily joined the women's Land Army and have been written up in magazines, but millions of women have not been written up at all, because they took on a second job, a man's job, in addition to their woman's job, just by stepping from the farm kitchen onto the farm.

There are several ways of looking at these things which have been happening to women. Some people find it more interesting that women have done jobs which no one thought they could do, become welders and machine setters, railroad conductors, taxi starters and taxi drivers. Most of these are strictly wartime shifts and will become men's jobs again after the war. In some kinds of work, women have proved themselves specially gifted, their smaller fingers deft and sure, their greater capacity to bear dull, repetitious work very useful. In some of these jobs, women will be kept after the war, and this will balance the increased number of men who in the Army have been practicing skills like stenography which used to be almost completely women's work.

To some, the fact that we had women's services in this war is the most striking thing that has happened. There are only a little over a quarter of a million women in the services. There always seem to be more, because at any point where there is one WAC or one Wave, there are likely to be more WACs and Waves. They have joined up in the face of a great deal of disapproval from brothers and boy friends and fathers; they have been given, for the most part, dull and inglorious jobs to do. The war for them has been about as exciting as being a clerk at an induction center or a hospital orderly in a hospital where there are no war casualties. They have listened to the whole railroad car sing, "The WACs and Waves will win the war, parley vous," and not taken much comfort from the concluding line, "So what the hell are we fighting for, parley vous." Men in the services who marry women in the services will have much in common to look back upon. The fact that the services existed and have acquitted themselves honorably is a solace to the women who desperately wanted to be allowed to do the same kind of things their husbands and brothers did, to be chosen, placed, trained, and used. Perhaps because a woman could—if she were fit—enlist and wear a uniform tailored for war, women's clothes have remained feminine for the rest of the women, the women whom war made feel less adventurous rather than more.

But what, concretely, do these figures mean? What will it mean to men that girls who wouldn't have worked will have worked, that their wives have been working while they were gone, that their mothers and their mothers-in-law—some of whom had never had a pay check in their lives—have worked? What will it mean that farm wives and farm daughters have done work that no one ever expected an American woman to do?

It means, for one thing, that women, as a group, are better informed than they were before. They understand what a time clock is and what a checkoff is; why you *have* to contribute to a charity or a drive which the plant or store is putting on; what it means when the foreman or the supervisor has an off day or a grudge against a given worker. The farm women have learned a great deal more about the drudgery and techniques of farm life. After the war they will go back into their kitchens and vegetable gardens, but with increased understanding of why their husbands need the new tractor, of what it means when the milking machine breaks or the shipment of feed or fertilizer doesn't arrive. Women in homes which used to employ servants will know a great deal more about housework and what they used to put their helpless maids through, and women who have left housework for the factory will come back with some new ideas of what it means to work definite hours. Millions of women will understand more of what their husbands are talking about, when their husbands talk sense, and will have a sounder idea of when they are talking non-sense. As traditionally American men have preferred women to have some sense—at least after they have married them—this should be counted as gain.

Women who have worked in large industries will know more about unions and be less puzzled and unsympathetic with their husbands' union activities. Women who have taken men's places in small businesses will know more about the agonies of filling out government forms. A great many more women will understand more about money, how hard it is to make, as well as how hard or how easy it is to spend. Here, perhaps, is one of the places where the experience of women in wartime America will be a useful supplement to the men's. While the men have had four or five years of less dealing with money, the women have had more. Arguments about the budget ought to be less acrimonious than they used to be, as men will now know how easy it is to relax when someone else—Uncle Sam—is doing the worrying, women how hard it is to be responsible for earning for a family.

Statistics show, too, that a smaller proportion of working women will come from the age group of women who marry and bring up their children, after the war, than hitherto. This means, concretely, that far from wanting to get out of the home, during the years when they are needed in it, more women want, if possible, to devote themselves to their homes and children. When the headlines scream, "Eight out of ten women wish to keep jobs after the war," remember those are the women without homes, or without homes which can afford them as full-time homemakers. There are a million and a half more women who have to support themselves. They are rivals of men only as all workers may become rivals of all other workers. Only by full employment will this rivalry disappear. Employed women are threats to employed men only if women's wages are lower; during the war we have done a pretty good job of insisting on "equal pay for equal work"—at least in war work.

So, while men have been away women have worked, and

learned more about working. They have seen close-ups of some of the ways in which the lot of working mothers could be made a great deal easier, and some of this experience they will carry back home. Many of them will realize that not only was the double job of being a working woman and a homemaker much too hard, but that full-time homemakers' lives could be made a great deal happier by the same kind of community planning, for nursery schools, cooked food centers, shopping pools. A good many wives will have new ideas about the way in which the community can supplement the home, and they won't be as frightened about going out and working in the community either.

For many women who didn't go out to work for money went out to work voluntarily, in the Red Cross, as nurses' aids in hospitals, as extra workers in schools, in canteens. They have learned to work in groups, to second a motion and to shut off discussion. Sometimes, a family has been elected to do a job, rather than a husband or a wife, because while one stayed home with the children, or nursed a cold, the other could go to a meeting. Men will find many women more interchangeable with men than they used to be, better able to fix a tire, or mend a faucet or fix an electric light connection, or preside at a meeting, or keep a treasurer's account, or organize a political campaign, than when they went away.

The second important experience women have had, while the men were away, is moving about. Small-town girls have gone to cities, city girls to the little country towns, factory and office girls to pick beets and milk cows, Northern girls have gone south, and Eastern girls have gone west. Girls who depended on cooking the way their mother—or His mother—cooked, have had to learn to cook new foods, in new ways. Young mothers who would have reared their children behind the shelter of house walls have had to travel around on trains and meet the approval, or disapproval, of many other kinds of women. Girls who would have lived and died in the same town, knowing the same people, and thinking they were eternally disgraced if the cake fell, the custard broke, or the curtains weren't laundered every six weeks, have seen in how many different ways life can be lived—when necessary. Some of this moving-about experience will match the men's; while the men have lived abroad, but mostly in camps, the women have not seen as strange ways of life, but they will have actually had to cope with them more, buy and prepare food, convert trailers, defense units, corners of shared kitchens and corners of rented parlors into homes.

And most of all women have waited. Many of them—those who have worked and traveled—have waited by doing something. Others have just waited. In their minds has been the echo of his "I want to find you just the same." Many women have sensibly interpreted this to mean that he wants her to be as good a 1945 model as she was a 1940 model, as smart a twenty-three-year-old as she was an eighteen-year-old.

But others, less realistic, have taken boy friends and husbands literally and tried not to change at all, to keep their minds, if not their hats, just as they were when their men left. Many of these girls, instead of moving out into the seething wartime world, have gone home to Mother, slipped back into dependent, little-girl positions, stayed eighteen years old or even slipped back a little. Getting reacquainted with a wife who has tried to stay as much the same as a flower in a still-life painting is really going to be more difficult than getting acquainted with a wife who has driven a truck or worn a uniform. These are the wives who will have to be wooed back to a point where they can start to grow again. Sometimes it will be very tiresome to find that a girl has kept her cute little ways until they are cute no longer. But she, and the man who asked her to stay just the same, have both been influenced by the advertisers who have exploited this longing for a remembered past as a way of keeping the American people longing for some well-known brand of soap or soup. For the reunited couples, or the boys and girls from the same age who will be falling in love after the war, for those who have kept moving, it will be like falling in step again after each has taken a different trail for a while, with all the excitement of a quick pace and lots to tell about the paths they traveled separately. For those men whose girls simply waited, like butterflies sitting on the edge of their chrysalises, there will be other satisfactions—for she will have to be tempted out into life all over again, the apron strings which have been reknotted, recut.

And women have learned new ways of love in these five years, new forms of fidelity and new forms of infidelity. They have learned to live for months on the memory of a few short days, to submit the whole of their hearts to the recollection of an acquaintance which is hardly more than a single string of memories, a shared ice-cream soda, the way he looked that night at the USO, the way they giggled over that M.P., his surprise that both her shoes would fit into his, the pattern of the wallpaper in the rented room, his last kiss at the station. Desperately treasured and poignant as such memories are, it's a new experience for American girls to have to live on them for years, and even write letters about them.

The American girl and the American man have always had to compete in the heart of the other with the Girl on the Magazine Cover and the Great Lover of the Screen. Now each has a new hurdle, each has to compete with a memory of the other, fostered in the heart, fed on an occasional snapshot and letters which could dwell on few shared experiences, through the years. But just as the surest way of guaranteeing that most people will fall in love at some time in their lives is to bring them up on songs and stories and pictures of romance, so because so many women have been able to believe in their fidelity to their three days with their husbands, most boy friends and husbands will find love waiting for them. This love will be a little like a suit which used to fit them, and which will need a little altering before it fits them now, grown plumper or gaunter through the years.

Women have come to value love and marriage through these years more and to be less exacting about the haircut or the income of their prospective husbands. When most girls can expect to marry because there are more men than girls, the girls become very choosy. When every unmarried girl is faced with the fear that she may not marry at all, and every childless woman who is unmarried or whose husband is overseas watches the years slip by without prospect of a child, marriage and motherhood are more eagerly sought. The war has seen a great crop of babies, some of them born to older parents who had had to wait all through the depression, but great numbers of them born to wives of servicemen, or men soon to enter the service. As the possibility of death came closer, giving life has seemed more important. This great group of wartime babies, whose experience has been so different from that of other children, will need special plans made for them, as they are ready to sally forth to school just about the time their fathers get home to help in the planning.

Young marriages have suffered because they have been deprived of the familiar courtship period, and of the steadying effect of a honeymoon among friends who always invited you to dinner together, of the steadying effect of a shared home. Even older marriages have been strained as husbands and wives who hadn't spent a night apart in ten years found it was very pleasant to read alone in bed. Women who knew how to deal with a husband who came home every night have found they didn't know what to do with a husband who has come home every week, or month, or three months. All of this will mean that there will be a lot of readjusting to be done after the war. It doesn't mean that women value marriage less, but only that they have been deprived of all the familiar ways of making marriages successful, and had to learn new ones.

People, especially young people, have come to grasp at the moment more, to marry now even though the day is inauspicious, to pour whatever they have into one hour or one evening, taking no thought for the morrow except that the morrow may not be there. This means that there has been more illicit love, technically speaking, as moments were grasped without benefit of clergy or divorce courts. But whether it means that women—and men—will be more or less interested in fidelity after the war isn't yet clear. As more people have been exposed to, and yielded or not yielded to, the temptation to cheat, they have become more aware of cheating and what it means. Some of this awareness will result in the point of view, "When I get married, I intend to mean it, and I mean *mean* it." Some of it will go into an inability to believe that the future of a human relationship may be more important than the present. American women with their men away (and American men, too) have had two related experiences: the experience of remaining romantically true over months and years to someone they hardly know at all, and the experience of giving everything at once, regardless of the future, to someone they hardly know at all. They will be out of practice in maintaining steady rewarding relationships with someone they do know. This is where the strain will come, in learning to live, day after day, in the Dream Home of the Future, about which both have been reading in the ads.

But one circumstance distinguishes American women and girls from all the other women and girls of the warring countries, that as a group they have suffered no important and catastrophic hardships of any sort. They have not been starved or bombed out, they have not been evacuated or had evacuees quartered upon them. Their parents and their children and they themselves have been safe. The war has come to many of them as individuals, through the absence or the loss of the men they loved. But physically, here at home, they have been safe and their children have been safe. They have been asked to go on living pretty much as they did before, in houses that were lit and reasonably warm, eating food that was harder to shop for but perfectly adequate, wearing clothes which wore out quicker but which were pretty and gay. There has been gas rationing which made it very difficult to keep house in the suburbs, shoe rationing which posed a problem for growing children, big cuts off small salaries for bonds and taxes, a thousand little irritations and no big ones. Nothing has happened on the home front to mobilize all of their strength and to put petty details in their places. Because there were no big difficulties, little ones have loomed large. When the men return from years of longing for the simple comforts of home, to find their women complaining about the hardships of a leaky faucet or a broken lamp or frayed car upholstery, they are likely to be impatient. When the returning man looks his wife or sweetheart in the eye, between them will loom his years of danger and hardship which she cannot share or even properly imagine, her flat empty years which she could not value because he was away, filled with comforts which he values highly because he missed them so keenly. Just as the man in the cartoon is pictured as looking at his rifle and saying, "I've given you the best years of my life," so the young women of the 1940's look at the pictures on their dressing tables, the service pins on their lapels, realizing the years which have been dedicated to absence, to breathless hope and to gnawing fear, and to a break in experience. In peacetime, men and women count upon living their lives side by side, watching children grow and gardens flower and houses go up and bank accounts accumulate and chins get double or beards get stubbier and life flow more quietly—together. All of our patterns for the relations between men and women were based on this simple expectation of their walking in step. This generation will have to make new patterns.

Last of all, the man who left the country in 1941–42 will come back to a new generation of girls, who were skinny little things without curves when they went away. These girls will be, inevitably, a new kind of girl, girls bred on the war years, on a different sort of romance, with a line which has a sharp staccato beat. They don't expect as much of boys as their older sisters did who grew up when dates were commoner. They will bear practically no marks from the depression years. War has stood at the beginning of their young girlhood, not crashed rudely into the middle, finding them unprepared. They will be standing on tiptoe for the postwar world.

VI. THE WORLD OF SPORTS

by *DAN PARKER*

> DAN PARKER *(age 52) has been Sports Editor of the New York* Daily Mirror *since 1926. He served overseas with the Hq. Co. 345th Infantry as a sergeant in the first World War and states that he is "one of the few guys who didn't win that war, never having fired a shot except at a practice target which I missed."*

WAR'S effect on sports was spottier than a prize fight manager's vest. Some branches throve on the war like munitions plants; others found that General Sherman had understated the situation. The over-all picture was a replica in miniature of how the world conflict affected the country as a whole. The sports world had its problems of inflation, manpower shortage, and transportation. Black markets sprang up and there was wartime profiteering in athletic commodities which often were inferior substitutes for the real article. Chauvinism of the peculiar brand which tried to palm off horse racing as a morale-booster and inflation preventive vied for top billing on the hypocritical side with the pat on the back that pugilism gave itself for keeping boxing alive during the crisis by charging grossly excessive prices for vastly inferior attractions. One fact that stood out above all the rest, however, was that America turned eagerly to sports as a means of escape from war's harsh realities. The result was the greatest boom in history for those sports which were least handicapped by wartime conditions. A by-product was an unprecedented wave of gambling on sports events which, when horse racing was suspended temporarily, found an unhealthy outlet in college basketball and caused a player-bribing scandal in that field which rocked the nation.

A betting man would have given odds during America's first year in the war that horse racing had the best chance of survival and baseball one of the poorest. Yet our country's fourth year in the conflict found the race tracks of America, victims of their own prosperity, padlocked by order of War Mobilizer James Byrnes, whereas baseball, having trimmed its sheets to ride the storm, was sailing serenely ahead. The tracks were closed for four months.

Baseball sent over 4,000 men into the service but managed to carry on with the 1,700 remaining players. Of the forty-one minor leagues in existence the season before Pearl Harbor, only nine remain. Travel restrictions and the power conservation measures sharply curtailed night baseball, without which many minor league clubs couldn't exist, and struck the hardest blow at the minors, although the shortage of players would have forced many teams to fold up even if the other two problems hadn't existed. Those leagues which were strong enough to survive the first impact of the war kept going as conditions grew worse for them by making adjustments they wouldn't have thought possible a few years previously.

From the outset, Commissioner Kenesaw Mountain Landis set a course for baseball that called for strict co-operation with the governmental agencies directing the war effort. Southern training trips were canceled in 1943, when the railroads of America began to creak under the strain suddenly imposed on them. Thereafter, the teams prepared for the campaign at Northern camps not far from home. To effect a further saving in transportation facilities, the major leagues made only three instead of four intersectional trips each season. A further reduction of 25 per cent in mileage was ordered by the ODT in 1945. Major league baseball gradually sank to the prewar level of Class A circuits, but there was no corresponding decline in admission prices. In fact, there was an upward adjustment which thoughtfully permitted the fan to pay the additional 10 per cent federal tax on baseball tickets voted by Congress.

Night baseball blinked on and off like a firefly. It was curtailed to some extent in 1942, was barred in all seaboard cities in 1943 when twilight games were substituted, but came back in 1944.

Grand-stand patriots (in mufti) who booed players such as Joe DiMaggio early in the war, because they weren't in the service, found it increasingly difficult to maintain their stand when Joe and most of the others who had been singled out for attention by the volunteer draft board agents went off to war, leaving their critics to battle it out with their consciences, if any.

At first, whenever the spotlight of publicity was focused on a ball player who had been rejected by his draft board for some such cause as flat feet or a punctured eardrum, there was grumbling of "Favoritism!" However, this feeling of suspicion that ball players were being favored died down as the game's Honor Roll grew longer. Although baseball made no claims for itself as a morale-builder, the importance of keeping the game going for the boys on the fighting front became increasingly evident as V-mail started to arrive from them. Soldiers who, back in the States, had resented the fact that able-bodied men were still playing ball found that distance had lent enchantment and mellowed their viewpoint when they were overseas. "Keep baseball going" was their plea.

The War Department gave the game its official endorsement when it arranged to have world series games broadcast to all fighting fronts. Since most of the star ball players in the service were assigned to teams which traveled from camp to camp entertaining the fighting men, it turned out that, whether soldier or civilian, a player was considered most useful in the role of morale-booster.

Two of New York City's boroughs, the Bronx and Brooklyn, were the rival capitals of baseball when America entered the war. A tree had grown in Brooklyn, and from its tip fluttered the National League pennant. The Yankees flew two standards at their Bronx ball yard—the World's and American League Championship flags. Manager Joe McCarthy's Yanks remained in the as-

cendancy in their league for two more years, but alas! Brooklyn's
hour of triumph was brief. In 1942 the Dodgers justified their new
sobriquet, "The Bums," by tossing off the 10½-game lead they
enjoyed in mid-August and losing out to the St. Louis Cardinals.
Brilliantly managed by Billy Southworth, the Cardinals went on
that year to wrest the world's championship from the Yanks. In
1943, however, the Yankees were back on top of the heap. Manager McCarthy, often accused of having pennants and world's
championships bought for him, proved himself a brilliant leader
by guiding one of the weakest teams he ever handled to a postseason triumph over Southworth's powerful Cards. The 1944
campaign was a runaway race for the Cardinals. It also produced
a miracle in the form of the first American League pennant winner St. Louis ever had. Luke Sewell piloted the Browns to their
first flag. With the world series all to itself, St. Louis thus solved
the transportation problem.

In a six-game series that was thrill-packed despite the deteri-
oration in the class of major league baseball, the Cardinals won
out.

During the off season between the 1944 and 1945 campaigns
two events occurred that will have a profound influence on the
postwar baseball picture. The first and more important was the
death of Commissioner Landis on November 25, 1944, of a heart
attack with which he had been stricken on the eve of the all-
St. Louis series. Landis was unique. Other sports, trying to copy
baseball, had installed commissioners. There was this difference,
however: Landis was boss; the others were bossed. The major
league club owners couldn't decide on his successor until a week
after the 1945 season got under way. Then they got together and,
steered gently by Colonel Leland Stanford (Larry) MacPhail,
the man who had pulled the Brooklyn Dodgers out of the mire,
they selected Albert B. Chandler, U. S. Senator from Kentucky,
for the office of commissioner. Chandler, the direct antithesis of
Landis, immediately antagonized his old friends, the horse-racing
interests, by committing the Kentucky sacrilege of warning ball

players to stay away from race tracks. It soon became obvious that the baseball magnates, tired of being dominated by Landis, had picked a man whom they could run.

The second important occurrence was the purchase of the vast Yankee Baseball Empire for $2,900,000 by a syndicate made up of Captain Dan Topping, owner of the Brooklyn Tigers' professional football club, Colonel MacPhail, Commissioner Chandler's chief sponsor, and Del Webb, a former professional ball player who had struck it rich in the contracting business in Arizona. Baseball men agreed that the Yankee property was a steal at that price and wondered whether Larry MacPhail, who was installed as president, replacing Ed Barrow, could tone down his fiery nature and circus ballyhoo tactics in his new role with the most conservative as well as most successful club in the game. MacPhail, a genius in his own peculiar way, had a difficult goal to aim at if he strove to top Ed Barrow's record over twenty-five years; but the capacity of the Stadium, the resources of the Yankees' rich farm system, and the expected war baseball boom made such an achievement possible, although Larry's first experiment with twilight baseball at the Stadium was a flop. MacPhail ran into trouble midway in the 1945 campaign by publicly criticizing his ball club. Thereupon Joe McCarthy, his manager, not used to such interference, "took sick" and left the club for three weeks. During his absence MacPhail sold Hank Borowy, one of his pitching aces, to the Chicago Cubs as pennant insurance, and Yankee fans, knowing their own club needed Borowy badly, showered MacPhail with futile protests.

Baseball didn't develop a single outstanding player during the war period for the obvious reason that all the promising youngsters were in the service. When things get back to normal, however, there's likely to be a Johnstown flood of pent-up talent. All in all, the game's future is bright: the development of airplane travel is bound to open up new major league territory, and modern illumination methods are making the possibilities of night baseball unlimited.

Horse racing, first major sports casualty of the war, gorged itself on war profits until it burst. There's something about war that makes even those on the home front reckless, and soon after we got into the conflict America was off on the damnedest gambling binge in its history. Almost everyone was playing the horses. With plenty of money in circulation, race tracks everywhere began to wallow in profits.

At first, racing moguls took bows along with their profits. The annual report of the New York Racing Commission in 1942 told of racing's brave resolve to help win the war by building up morale on the home front. The raucous roar that greeted this bit of buncombe influenced the Commission to try a new tack. The next benediction the turf bestowed on itself was motivated by the discovery that horse racing offered the most pleasant and painless form of taxation, since it took people outdoors and gave them entertainment in return for what it took from them. It remained for Herbert Bayard Swope, the turf's official spokesman, to discover that racing was also a powerful anti-inflationary measure. Nor did he neglect to point out that, by improving the breed, racing was helping the Cavalry. Then someone discovered that the Cavalry in this war rode in tanks, and the subject of conversation was changed to the Infantry.

The cause of improving the breed wasn't helped any by some race tracks showing only halfhearted co-operation with the war effort and a few being downright defiant. When gas rationing was started, the spectacle of race track parking lots crowded with cars, some of which doubtless were loaded with black-market gas, gave opponents of the sport plenty of ammunition. Narragansett Park refused to close its parking lot in defiance of an order from the ODT. The Kentucky Derby was run in 1943 after the ODT had expressed a desire that it be suspended. Early bond-selling efforts by race tracks were somewhat less than feeble. Twice, racing's powerful lobby at Washington killed a federal tax on bets. Finally, however, track owners and officials of the sport awoke to a realization of their wartime obligations, and from that point on, racing's record was good. Track parking lots were closed to discourage waste of gas and rubber. Bond sales were organized and pushed with all the resources available. Large contributions from excess profits were made to war funds. Racing's ballyhoo men saw that all these patriotic deeds were publicized, and the chances are that, if War Mobilizer Byrnes hadn't stepped in, the sport eventually would have broken its neck acknowledging its own applause.

One other mistake racing made was in accentuating the positive. As betting totals and attendance figures mounted, the tracks and racing commissions boasted about the new records in a mounting crescendo. The peak came in 1944. Although tracks everywhere in the country reported record-breaking attendance and receipts, it remained for New York to top them all. The attendance at the metropolitan courses was 4,497,127, and the wagering totaled $410,230,402. This represented an average daily "handle" of $2,170,531 for the season. Every person who went to the New York tracks bet an average of $12 per race and $91.22 for the day. There were seventeen racing days on which over $3,000,000 was bet, eighty-seven days when the handle was more than $2,000,000 and not one day when it dropped under a million. Even with a hurricane mowing down half of Long Island on September 13, and with transportation crippled, 10,909 persons went to the Aqueduct race track and bet $1,235,429. That's how crazy over horses America had become.

When the 1944 returns were in from all seventeen states where racing was conducted, it was found that America had bet $1,126,308,645 at race tracks and it was estimated that the amount wagered illicitly away from the tracks was at least twice as much more. In 1943 America had bet $705,142,257, and New York State, $284,635,711.

Intoxicated by these staggering totals, certain turf men—who, however, constituted a small minority—began to agitate for legalized off-the-course betting. Arguing that nothing could stop this type of betting anyway, and therefore that the state should legalize it and tax it the same as on-the-course wagering, proponents of unrestricted gambling had visions of betting bureaus on every corner which would yield the state and those who ran them an enormous profit. The Thoroughbred Racing Association and the National Association of State Racing Commissions, aware of the dynamite hidden in this project, opposed it vigorously.

Meantime, in Washington, War Mobilizer Byrnes was looking at racing with a baleful eye. With the front page headlines screaming of the manpower shortage and war-plant absenteeism, while the sports pages boasted of new attendance and betting records at race tracks, Mr. Byrnes decided the time for action had arrived; so, as a Christmas present to the Turf as 1944 waned, he announced that all race tracks must close until further notice, starting January 3, 1945. Thus burst the biggest bubble since the collapse of the Holland tulip speculation.

The suspension of a billion-dollar industry left a trail of hardships until relief finally came with the lifting of the ban on May 9. Many small horsemen had to dispose of their racing strings because they couldn't afford to feed them. Some took the easiest way out and destroyed the beautiful animals, which are practically useless except for racing. Many horsemen were stranded all winter in Miami and New Orleans, unable to get either the price or the shipping priority required before they could move their horses. Some owners shipped to Mexico City, where the most successful meeting in the history of the Hippodrome of the Americas was held. Don Meade was among the few American jockeys who rode south of the border, and he wound up in a jam, set down for insulting the stewards and all Mexicans.

The four-month suspension of racing had at least one salutary effect, besides the inestimable boon it proved to chronic players who found themselves with money to spare for the first time in years. That was the long rest it gave thousands of overworked race horses, many of them crippled. It also gave juveniles a chance to mature without having the strain of racing imposed on them prematurely. Race track men think that the records for attendance and wagering set in 1944 will seem picayune by comparison with those which will be hung up in the boom they predict for the postwar era. The amazing attendance and betting totals for 1945 gave ample support to this belief. There had been two $4,000,000 days at New York tracks by midseason, and all along the line old betting and attendance records were being smashed as people threw away easy money. The biggest race track in the world is planned for New York.

There was no interruption in the running of the big stake events during the war, even in 1945 when the ban threw the schedule out of kilter. The Greentree Stable's Shut Out missed racing's Triple Crown in 1942 when Alsab won the Preakness. Shut Out, which had won the Derby with Wayne Wright up, came back to take the Belmont Stakes also. Mrs. John D. Hertz's Count Fleet made a clean sweep of the three-year-old classics in 1943, with Johnny Longden in the saddle in all three events. Warren Wright's Pensive, ridden by Con McCreary, after winning both the Derby and the Preakness in 1944, bowed to Bounding Home in the Belmont Stakes and so was nosed out of the select little group which has won all three of these blue-ribbon events. F. W. Hooper's Hoop, Jr., ridden by Eddie Arcaro, won the 1945 Derby, run off on June 9; Mrs. P. A. B. Widener, 2d's, Polynesian, with Wayne Wright aboard, won the Preakness a week later, and the Belmont Stakes went to Pavot, Eddie Arcaro up.

Basketball is probably the major sport that suffered least as a result of wartime conditions. The radical change by which the center jump was eliminated had been put into effect before the war. This served to speed up play greatly, but there were other kinks that needed straightening. One of these concerned the "beanstalk goal tender." Suddenly a vogue for sky-scraping players who could reach up and push goals out of the hoop had sprung up, and teams that didn't boast a giant or two were at a great disadvantage. The practice of "freezing the ball" to protect a lead had also grown so common as to become a nuisance to the game from the spectators' viewpoint. Both of these problems were solved by new rules, but a more serious situation which couldn't be reached by revising the code was brewing. When college basketball was taken out of the small gyms and staged in large public arenas before tremendously increased crowds, it was thrown in direct contact with the gambling menace. Wagering on basketball games had been growing like tropical vegetation in recent years. When the race tracks were closed, the volume of basketball betting became enormous. There had been stories of key players on college quintets being approached by gamblers before important games. Phog Allen, coach of the University of Kansas team, frequently spoke up against the danger of college players' being contaminated by "fixers," but he was shouted down as a prophet of gloom. When the Brooklyn District Attorney's office announced early in 1945 that five members of the Brooklyn College quintet had confessed that they had accepted bribes from a couple of cheap neighborhood bookies, one of whom was a crook on the side, a scandal broke that threatened irreparable damage to college basketball. However, after a series of investigations which produced no further evidence of wrongdoing, basketball rode out the storm, undamaged. It is perhaps fortunate for the game that the boiling point of the public's indignation had been greatly raised by the war. What with the papers full of war atrocity stories, the public couldn't get too indignant over the venality of some college athletes.

The superiority of Western college basketball over the Eastern brand was demonstrated three years running, in Madison Square Garden, New York, when the unofficial national championship went to teams from west of the Mississippi. The 1942–43 season was capped by Wyoming's 52–47 overtime victory over St. John's of Brooklyn, in the play-off between these respective winners of the N.C.A.A. and the National Invitation tournaments. Utah came out on top in the 1943–44 campaign, beating St. John's of Brooklyn, 43–36, after winning the N.C.A.A. title. Oklahoma A. and M., with Big Bob Kurland, won the national laurels in the 1944–45 season by beating DePaul of Chicago, with Large Jarge

Mikan, by a score of 52–44 in the play-off between the tournament winners. The fact that the N.C.A.A. winners turned out to be the national champions in each of the three seasons since the play-off was inaugurated would seem to indicate that the N.C.A.A. tournament attracts the better teams.

If boxing had a voice, it would have walked up to the microphone after hostilities and chortled: "It was a tough fight, Mom, but I win the duke and didn't get hoited."

Pugilism was one of the sports that fattened grossly on the war. Though most of the champions and headliners were in the service, the promoters soon found that anyone who could lace on a boxing glove and climb into the ring under his own power would make an acceptable substitute. Later the promoters learned that not only could they palm off Gorgonzola on the public as ambrosia, but they could also charge fancy prices for it. This they did while reminding their customers what personal sacrifices they, the promoters, were making to keep the game alive. No one thought to ask, "What game?"

Although the number of boxers in the service ran into the thousands and many of them made the casualty lists, the spectacle of hundreds of able-bodied fighters who received medical discharges from the service, campaigning in the prize ring, brought the sport many bad notices. In 1944 alone about 300 boxers were discharged from the armed forces for such disabilities as flat feet, punctured eardrums, or "buzzing noises in the head." Some of them, including Willie Pep, the featherweight champion, who had been discharged from the Navy, were recalled. Willie was accepted by the Army at his second examination.

Sergeant Joe Louis's war record was something to which everyone in boxing could point with pride. Joe started out by donating his purses for two fights to the army and navy relief funds. Then he enlisted and settled down to the job of being a good soldier. That Joe wasn't sent into the front lines wasn't his fault. He went wherever he was sent, and wherever he went he did a good job of morale-building for his fellow soldiers.

Since most of the world's champions were in the service and, after the War Department tightened up its earlier liberal policy, couldn't participate in professional matches, boxing commissions everywhere "froze" their titles for the duration. As a cheap substitute, the promoters created "duration champions."

One striking effect of the war was to give colored boxers an unprecedented opportunity to make big money. Over 75 per cent of the boxers in action during the late stages of the war were Negroes. In normal times, the row of a colored fighter had been hard, unless he was outstanding. No promoter in peacetime would risk an all-colored main bout because it was a tradition of the business that such a match would be a box-office flop. But when no alternative was left to promoters but to risk flouting this time-honored matchmaking rule, they found to their delight that all-colored matches drew just as well as all-white ones.

Resolved to share in the boxing bonanza at any cost, unscrupulous managers trotted out defectives and cripples. The California Commission, examining Luther (Slugger) White for a bout in San Francisco, in 1945, discovered he had a glass eye. It developed that Luther had been passed, glass eye and all, by the commissions of several states, including California, before that.

At Madison Square Garden, in New York, Promoter Mike Jacobs was charging $12 and $15 tops for bouts he'd be afraid to use as semifinals on $5 cards before the war. The public paid uncomplainingly and asked for more, whereat Mike obligingly complied. Could he help it if people would pay Tunney-Dempsey prices to see two Quaker elders having a go at it with pillows?

Boxing made no progress toward unified national control during the war. The National Boxing Association was still working at cross-purposes with the New York State Athletic Commission, most powerful of the state bodies, which is prevented by state law from delegating any of its authority as it would have to if it joined other state commissions in the N.B.A. As a result of this division of authority, we still find two claimants to the championship in both the lightweight and featherweight divisions: Ike Williams and Bob Montgomery, in the 135-pound class, and Willie Pep and Sal Bartolo, in the 126-pound division. Under the administration of Colonel Eddie Eagan, former Yale and Olympic boxer who now is chairman of the New York State Athletic Commission, more co-operation among boxing administrative bodies may be expected.

Boxing's postwar prospects are bright. Among those returning from the fighting fronts will be a vast number of physically fit young men, many of whom have developed their natural boxing ability overseas. This group will produce the ring champions of the next decade. Of the new contenders for the heavyweight title developed in Joe Louis's absence, not one seems capable of dethroning him, which is as it should be. Joe, who owes the government a fortune because he donated to war funds his last two big purses out of which he had planned to pay his income tax, deserves a chance to get back on his feet financially.

Hockey felt the manpower shortage more acutely than boxing, but the results weren't evident at the gate. In fact, as the class of players deteriorated in the several professional leagues, the box office began to bulge. Since Canada produces practically all the hockey players, American magnates had visions of being forced to suspend operations when England and her Dominions entered the war. However, Canada's service laws were so flexible that there was no serious, immediate drain on the supply of top-line players. As the war continued and we became involved, players became increasingly scarce. Canada's strict labor laws also furnished a problem. But, as the magnates saw attendance increase while play deteriorated, they shed their misgivings and proceeded on the theory that as long as they could put six men on the ice, the public would pay without protest.

During the 1943–44 season the New York Rangers won only six of their 50 games but played to the biggest attendance in the club's history. An inferior brand of play and vastly increased gate receipts were the rule, wherever professional hockey was played.

Meantime, rule changes that made for easier scoring helped to distract attention from the lowered standard of play. The most radical of wartime revisions in the hockey code was the introduction of the red line across the center of the rink at the start of the 1944–45 season. This change in the zones speeded up the game, gave attacking teams more opportunities to work out combination plays, and reduced the amount of whistle blowing for offside play.

Montreal's Les Canadiens dominated the hockey world during the last two years of the European war, displacing Detroit's Red Wings, which had won both the National League championship and the Stanley Cup in the 1942–43 season. Detroit took the battered old silver mug in four straight games from the Boston Bruins that season. Les Canadiens made a sweep of things in the 1943–44 campaign, knocking off the Red Wings in four straight Cup final contests. But, after winning the league title in 1944–45, the Canucks were eliminated from the play-offs by the third-place Toronto Maple Leafs, who thereupon proceeded to take over Detroit in a seven-game Stanley Cup series.

The war was a lifesaver for hockey in both Montreal and Detroit, where it had been faring poorly up to then. Business was so good in the Eastern Amateur League that the salaries of many of the amateurs were increased to keep pace with mounting costs of living. Hockey, being one of the few sports which faces the amateurism problem without hypocrisy, sees no wrong in paying a salary to amateur players who have no other means of support. Perhaps that's basketball's "out," too.

The football world was affected like a large city by a mass bombing attack. Some teams weren't hit at all; others were obliterated. Those institutions which harbored servicemen's classes fared best on the gridiron. Scores of colleges dropped football for the duration the season after Pearl Harbor. The once proud Big Three resolved itself into the Small One as Harvard and

Princeton put the sport on an informal basis and Yale was left to carry on with a team greatly reinforced by Navy V-12 men.

It was only natural that the best athletes in the country should gravitate to West Point and Annapolis. This situation reached a peak in the fall of 1944 when the Army fielded one of its all-time great teams, a juggernaut that crushed all opposition, and chugged to the national championship at the rate of a point a minute.

During 1944 the football picture became so confused that it wasn't considered unusual to see a player in the Dartmouth backfield one Saturday against Yale and in the Yale backfield the following week against another team, as the Army or Navy switched him from one school to another. Most colleges waived the freshman rule. Otherwise they would have been unable to put a team on the field, what with upperclassmen being called into the service in droves. For the first time in history boys of high-school age played college football.

Postseason Bowl games, for the glorification of real-estate developments, etc., carried on during the most trying years of the war. True, the Rose Bowl game was transferred to Duke's stadium at Durham, North Carolina, in 1942, Oregon State traveling east to beat the Blue Devils, 20–16. The next year, however, the California fixture was back at the old stand in Pasadena with Georgia defeating U.C.L.A., 9–0. Because of travel regulations, the 1944 game was strictly a Pacific coast proposition, Southern California swamping Washington, 29–0. But the 1945 game reverted to type. Tennessee, chosen to represent the East, was turned back by Southern California, 25–0.

Professional football, which offers a more spectacular game than the college variety, took a bow when the Eastern Intercollegiate Football Association adopted a few of the pro rules in 1944. The most important of these was the rule making it legal to pass anywhere behind the line of scrimmage. In the next few years the trend in intercollegiate rules will doubtless be in the direction of the pro code. The professionals prospered throughout the war and at no time were seriously affected by a player shortage. It was possible for pro players to hold defense jobs and play week-end games, in which respect professional football had a distinct advantage over baseball. The war ended too late in the summer of 1945 to permit colleges which had suspended football for the duration to resume in the fall, since schedules must be drawn up a year in advance.

Although tennis and golf were all but eclipsed by wartime conditions, both sports look forward to a tremendous boom in the next few years because they have figured prominently in the rehabilitation program for servicemen. Many a recent recruit for the courts or links owes his new-found interest in the game to the fact that he was wounded or suffered battle fatigue overseas and helped fight his way back to health swinging a racket or a club in a rehabilitation center.

Most of the big tennis fixtures were canceled at the outbreak of the war. The Davis Cup, Wightman Cup, Wimbledon, French, and Australian championships, and the Newport Doubles tournament were among the casualties. The U. S. Nationals were held but, with so many top-ranking players gone to war, attracted vastly inferior entry lists. However, a touch of drama was lent to the otherwise drab 1944 season when Sergeant Frankie Parker, one-time boy wonder of the courts, finally fulfilled the predictions that had been made for him ever since he burst into prominence fifteen years ago. After twelve attempts Milwaukee's "golden boy," on furlough from Muroc Field, California, where he was serving with the Army Air Forces, finally won the national championship by beating Billy Talbert, 6–4, 3–6, 6–3, 6–3.

Pauline Betz, Los Angeles redhead, landed her pretty face in Tennis's Album of Notables by winning the women's championship for the third consecutive year. Alice Marble, Helen Jacobs, and Helen Wills Moody Roark had previously performed this "hat trick" of the courts. In the 1944 final, Pauline's speed and power vanquished Margaret Osborne of San Francisco, 6–3, 8–6.

Lieutenant W. Donald McNeill of Norfolk, Virginia, and Air

Cadet Bob Falkenburg, brother of beauteous Jinx, added to the military complexion of the 1944 tennis picture by winning the men's doubles title. For the third consecutive year the women's doubles crown went to Miss Osborne and Louise Brough.

Frederick R. Schroeder, Jr., of Glendale, California, beat Parker for the national singles title in 1942. Lieutenant Joseph R. Hunt defeated John A. Cramer for the title in 1943. Hunt became the first tennis star to give his life to his country when the navy fighter plane in which he was making a routine gunnery practice flight crashed at sea nineteen miles off Daytona Beach, Florida, February 2, 1945. Hal Surface, another top-flight player, was a minor casualty overseas. Besides those enumerated, among the other tennis players of importance who were in the armed forces were Lieutenant Seymour Greenberg, Army; J. Gilbert Hall, Army; Lieutenant Gardner Mulloy, Navy; Ensign John A. Cramer, Coast Guard; Lieutenant F. R. (Ted) Schroeder, Jr., Navy; Lieutenant Gilbert A. Hunt, Army; Jack McManus, Army; and Sergeant Gregory Mangin, who covered himself with glory and medals while serving as a tail gunner on a B-17 with the 15th Air Force in Italy. Greg completed his missions and returned safely to America, with minor wounds.

The tennis bum all but disappeared from the map. The Florida Association questioned the expense accounts of two civilian players, but that was the only flare-up of what used to be the principal peacetime problem of amateur tennis.

Byron Nelson, former Ft. Worth caddy who started out with a cross-hand grip, became the biggest thing in golf since Bobby Jones, if not indeed since the game was invented, during the 1944 and 1945 seasons. With a perfection of technique that won him the appellation of "the mechanical man" from the sports writers, Nelson swept the professional tournaments as no one ever had done before him. Up to the end of July, Nelson's winnings totaled $45,200, and he had won ten consecutive big-time tournaments before finally being stopped.

Many golf clubs had to suspend because gas rationing made it difficult if not impossible for members to get to the courses. Tournament play was cut to a minimum. Among the big fixtures that canceled out for the duration were the U. S. Open and Amateur, the British Open and Amateur, the U. S. Women's Open, and the British Women's Open. Such stars as Vic Ghezzi, Paul Runyan, Lawson Little, Horton Smith, Frank Strafaci, Bud Ward, Ben Hogan, Jimmy Demaret, Jimmy Thomson, and Sammy Snead were in the service. Ben Loving and Bill (Red) Francis gave their lives to their country. Wartime golf produced an amazing number of low scores. However, the catch was that most of the eyebrow-lifting cards were turned in under Winter Rules, which allow teeing up on the fairways.

Returning servicemen who seek recreation with rod or gun will find more game in the woods and more fish in the waters than ever were shot or caught in their time. Game had a chance to multiply and replenish, while the good shots were drawing beads on krauts and Japs. Many fishermen went to war. Many who didn't were prevented by travel restrictions from enjoying the sport. Thus Bountiful Nature took its course in streams that had been overfished in peacetime, and generous restocking helped restore the finny tribes where the job was too big for Nature.

One of the important discoveries in artificial fish propagation is that ponds and lakes need to be fertilized, just as gardens are, in order to produce bumper crops of fish. The fertilizer produces a growth of aquatic plants, which in turn provide food for minute organisms on which tiny fish thrive. The bigger fish fatten on the tiny ones, and everybody's happy. Formerly it was the practice to dump hundreds of fish into a pond which probably couldn't support those already in it. The result was that many fish starved to death and those which survived were stunted. Servicemen will recognize the situation as Poland on a small and aquatic scale.

Most of the big rowing fixtures were canceled at the start of the war. The Poughkeepsie Regatta hasn't been held since 1941. Yale and Harvard rowed on the Thames in 1942 but then called a halt for the duration. The Indianapolis Speedway Classic, a Memorial Day fixture since 1916, was another war casualty. The gas and rubber usually burned up in the 500-mile automobile race around the brick saucer was needed for war. Midget auto racing, a rapidly growing sport, also succumbed to the gas- and tire-rationing regulations.

Track and field sports prospered. America developed two out-standing performers during the war. Cornelius Warmerdam, a San Francisco boy who served as a naval lieutenant during the war, became the first and only human being to top 15 feet in the pole vault. To prove it wasn't an accident, Warmerdam did it forty-two more times after invading this virgin stratosphere. His forty-third 15-foot vault was made as Lt. (j.g.) Warmerdam, U.S.N.R., and gave him the 1944 A.A.U. championship. Gil Dodds, a divinity student who had specialized in the two-mile run, switched to the mile and in 1944 won seven consecutive races at this distance, two of which set new world's indoor records. Dodds' best mark was 4:06.4. Glen Cunningham ran a 4:04.4 indoor mile on Dartmouth's track when it was new, but it was a paced, not competitive, effort. Jimmy Rafferty, former Fordham runner representing the New York A. C., was the star miler of the 1945 indoor season.

Two visits to America by Gunder Haegg, great Swedish dis-tance runner, boomed track and field sports greatly. The swift Swede came here first in the summer of 1943 and beat all our run-ners with consummate ease over every distance at which they chose to meet him. Haegg returned early in 1945 and, two days off the boat after a 23-day voyage on a rolling tanker, finished last in a one-mile race that Rafferty won, in Madison Square Garden. This was Gunder's first indoor race. The lean Swede lost two more races, also, before finally winning one indoors in Cleveland. Rafferty, who won three races in which Haegg competed against him, didn't have a chance to meet him again during the tour as Jimmy couldn't get away from business to enter the Cleveland race that Gunder won and Gunder was put off a plane on his way from the Coast to Buffalo to compete in what was to have been his final test with the New York runner. They will probably meet again.

Two Hawaiians, Billy Smith and Keo Nakama, gave Ohio State pre-eminence in swimming until the Canal Zone sent a young man named Alan Ford to Yale. Ford has broken several world's records at Yale and appears to be just starting his career.

Hoping to revive interest in three-cushion billiards, the rules committee changed the playing code to enable players to select their own cue ball at the start of each inning. This was a crushing blow at safety playing, which made the game so dull for spectators. Welker Cochran beat the veteran Willie Hoppe in the first tournament under the new code. Willie was just back from a tour of military camps and weak from amoebic dysentery. Willie Mosconi was the champion pool player.

Wrestling sent many of its stalwarts into the service to act as instructors in judo and rough-and-tumble fighting. However, this didn't reduce the number of world's heavyweight wrestling champions still at large. At latest count there were 26 claimants to this title, each one insisting he was the only authentic champ. Despite the transparent theatricality of what now passes for wrestling, it still remains a favorite form of entertainment in certain centers where the sophistication quotient isn't high. Since Promoter Jack Curley died, the wrestling script hasn't been changed. What the business needs, besides someone to put it on the level, is a promoter with imagination enough to work up some new routines to replace the threadbare ones now in use.

All things considered, the sports world played a worthy part in wartime America. Besides sending thousands of well-conditioned athletes into the service of their country, this important segment of American life helped to raise money for war relief, sold billions of dollars' worth of War Bonds, and provided wholesome recreation for millions of war-weary people. To the boys in the front lines news about the world series or the Kentucky Derby had an effect almost as comforting as reports of another Allied victory. The spirit of fair play inculcated in young Americans on the field of sport made them braver soldiers, more resourceful leaders, better allies, and more humane conquerors. So, what if there was a little bragging and pointing-with-pride on the part of those who were left behind to see that Sportdom carried on?

VII. WHAT THE ANIMALS
WERE UP TO

by JAMES THURBER

JAMES THURBER *was fifty years old last December, still has a few ideas for writings and drawings, and lives behind an enormous oak tree in Connecticut. That is all the information this gentleman would give the editor, and it is about all that is necessary.*

ALTHOUGH this article may have some of the earmarks and paw prints of a survey, it is not a survey at all, it is merely a piece. A survey is the assembling and correlating of all discoverable data in a given field of research, and, just as its most honorable purpose is enlightenment, its highest virtue is comprehensiveness. A survey ought to prove or disprove something, honestly and thoroughly, so that men wrangling at three in the morning can turn to it in the confident hope of competent guidance.

If a controversy should arise at your house in the middle of the night over some phase of the Behavior of Animals on the American Home Front during World War II, do not assume that you can settle the dispute and pay off bets by referring to Thurber on Animals. The section herein on the famous dog Blaze is the completest or at least, the publishers of this book admit, the longest discussion of this subject that has appeared in print; but the rest, if not exactly hit-and-miss, is unquestionably a bit helter-skelter, leaping as it does more or less lightly from fiction to random fact. There are two chief reasons for this: first, no one man could keep track of, and set down, all the curious activities of all the birds and beasts, and second, no one would read it if he did. Let us, then, without further preface or apology, make our way among the scattered and fragmentary exhibits of this topsy-turvy zoo and museum.

We come first to two stories, not the kind you read, but the kind people tell. They seem to me the funniest two stories of the past few years, and both are concerned with animals: a frog and a turtle. Both were told on the air by Bob Burns, one of the drollest and most skillful storytellers in the country. These tales may be common knowledge now, they may even have been compiled somewhere else, but they belong in this particular record, and here they are.

It seems, then, that Grandpa and Grandma Snazzy gave a big family party down in Van Buren, Arkansas, attended by all the Burns aunts and uncles and cousins. A long table was set for supper, and when everybody was seated Grandma Snazzy went out to the springhouse and came back with a pail of milk. She began filling the guests' glasses. When she came to the host, Grandpa Snazzy, a small frog plopped into his glass with the milk and Grandpa just sat and stared at it without moving. Grandma proceeded along the table, and when she passed around to the other side she noticed her husband's trance. "Do you see something in your glass, Grandpa?" she asked. "Yes," said Grandpa, still staring transfixed, "and he sees me, too."

Bing Crosby, the sweet singer of Del Mar, has four sons, and it was on the youngest that Bob Burns hung, as the charming term has it, the turtle story.

Bing, the tale tells, had returned from a trip, bringing his smallest son one of those little round turtles whose shells the artists of California like to paint in gaudy colors. Little Lindsay—for that is our hero's name—became devoted to the garish pet and hovered over its swimming pool, a pan of water, whenever he was not in kindergarten or in bed.

One afternoon Lindsay came singing home to find Mike, the turtle, on its back, motionless, in the pan of water. There was a tremendous to-do in the household, but nobody could quiet

Lindsay's loud anguish. Finally Bing had to be sent for. He came home from the studio, put Lindsay on his knee, and told him that all turtles in their time must pass away to the great Heavenly Pan somewhere between the clouds and the stars, and so on and so forth. Lindsay was not consoled. Then his father took a large silver cigarette case from his pocket and said that he would line it with cotton, place Mike inside, and dig a fine grave for him on the sloping lawn under Lindsay's window. Bing would make a little granite headstone, and on it he would carve the name "Mike." There would be flowers on the grave and around it a lovely miniature fence. The little boy ceased crying and his eyes grew round in pleased wonder as his father went on with the details of this singular cemetery.

"Now," said Bing, "we will go out to the kitchen and get Mike and bury him."

Hand in hand, the two Crosbys walked to the kitchen and there in the pan was Mike, no longer motionless on his back, but swimming gaily around and around. Lindsay looked up at his father. "Let's kill him!" said Lindsay.

Your guide, in the manner of guides, will babble on about this and that pertinence or irrelevancy as we move from hall to hall. He has sometimes pondered writing a larger and graver monograph on a special aspect of our general subject, a monograph to be entitled *The Diminution of the Physical Stature of Menace through the Epochs of Life on Our Planet*. It would discuss the dwindling anatomy of peril, from the dinosaur to the microorganism—from the era of trample to the era of infection. It would trace the steady decline in the size of battle beasts, from the tank elephants of Hannibal to the soldier dogs of modern war. Even in the field of the imaginary creatures of dread and mischief there has been a great foreshortening: the big black furry bugbear and *bête noire* have given place to the little gremlin.

Your guide's theory and thesis come up against one considerable barrier, and unhappily it is an insuperable barrier. In the case of the greatest menace to Man there has been no change to speak of in stature. The greatest menace to Man is, of course, Man himself. Ah, here we are, ladies and gentlemen, in the section devoted to the miscellaneous activities of various individual animals that have had their brief moments in the public prints, from the New York *Times* to *Time* magazine, which always has its ear to the ground, listening for the thumping of five-legged rabbits or the hop flop, hop flop of two-legged dogs.

Over any given period of years the pattern of the lives of animals that live among human beings is much the same: devoted conduct, inexplicable behavior, singular accident, morphological phenomenon, and the distortion of values in the relation of human beings with their pets. To begin with the last category—after which we will just take my clippings as they come—at least two persons, in the past few years, left to their pets bequests the courts could not approve or relatives endure.

At Sparkill, New York, the late Elizabeth Miller left a $200,000 trust fund to an aged dachshund and a cheetah. One Betty Miller, a niece, promptly asked the courts to hold up the legacy. As far as I know, attorneys for Miss Smith and attorneys for the pets may still be arguing the case.

Three months later, in Dedham, Massachusetts, the late Woodbury Rand, a lawyer, bequeathed $100,000 to his eight-year-old cat, Buster, who, at last reports, was not going to be allowed to become the wealthiest cat in the country. Miss Margaret Thomson, Mr. Rand's housekeeper, inherited $40,000 of his fortune, and she agreed to support Buster in the style to which he was accustomed.

In New Jersey, a state inured to phenomena, a hound bitch gave birth, without much fuss on her part, to twenty-three pups, and at last report both the mother and her young were doing well. A hen named Bitsy in Mishawaka, Indiana, did not come out so well. She laid an egg nine and one-half inches long and seven and one-half inches around the middle and promptly died of a broken record. A Portland, Oregon, cow sauntered into the headquarters of the Humane Society and gave birth to a surprised calf, and in Saskatchewan, a steer rammed one of its horns through the side of a moving cattle car, caught up a switch lantern, and confounded railroaders with a series of new and incomprehensible signals all the way into Moose Jaw.

Trains up Saskatchewan way have a strange effect on animals: a horse there smacked into a moving freight train, flung his rider sprawling unhurt onto a flatcar, and fell dead. It is surely the only known case in which a horseman whose mount died under him landed in the next county. In Brockton, Massachusetts, a terrified and indignant woman phoned police to tell them that a puppy kept peeping at her, night after night, through a bedroom window. And in Milwaukee a female Irish setter adopted a brood of six motherless young rabbits. Farmers in Little Rock, Minnesota, found in a fox's burrow his vixen, seven fox puppies, twenty-five chickens, several pheasants, an owl, two toads, a muskrat, a pig, and no ration books. On the Hudson River, a stream that teems with legend and wild life, coastguardsmen in a cutter chased a stag from ice floe to ice floe, and finally pulled it aboard at the end of a lariat. Astonished sailors at the Little Creek, Virginia, training station caught a female seal in a fish net and roped her to a pier. She slipped her moorings in the night, and at dawn the bewildered sailors found on the beach a baby seal, weighing thirty-five pounds, which had come ashore hunting its mother. Once tied, twice shy, she did not return in spite of the young seal's constant yelping. The little seal refused condensed milk or anything else, and died. Nobody except a seal has ever successfully raised a seal, my zoologist informs me.

In the winter of 1943, Frank Rice, a Florida mechanic, and his wife arrived in New York with two black cats in separate carriers, and many pieces of baggage. They had come to New York to live. In the loud and confusing labyrinth of the Pennsylvania Station they continued an argument begun on the train, and suddenly Mr. Rice stalked away, carrying a suitcase and one of the cats. When after an hour he had not returned, Mrs. Rice became hysterical. She opened her handbag which contained $3,500 in bills and began handing fives and tens to passers-by, imploring them to help her find her husband.

Before station police intervened she had given away fifteen hundred dollars and Mr. Rice had not been found. Mrs. Rice was taken to Bellevue Hospital and later to the home of a relative on Long Island. Two months later, Mr. Rice's body was found in the East River. The police surgeon figured he had drowned about Christmastime.

Nothing was ever learned about the short, obscure life of Frank Rice in New York beyond the fact that he spent his first night in the great city at a small hotel near the Pennsylvania Station. He checked out the following morning, leaving behind him, for a floor maid to discover, the black cat he had taken with him. It was restored to Mrs. Rice, who returned to Florida after the finding of her husband in the river. Nobody seems to know what became of the second black cat.

"Thirty thousand people disappear in New York every year," said a member of the Missing Persons Bureau, "and a lot of them are married men. If a person is over twenty-one and there is no charge against him except getting the hell out, there is nothing the police can do. Frank Rice," he added, "just got the hell out."

In scrabbling through my disorderly notes at this point, I discover that my researchers have not, alas, supplied me with any reports on singing mice or delinquent carrier pigeons. In the years immediately preceding the war, mice stood up in the corners of rooms here and there around this unpredictable commonwealth and burst into song, according to usually reliable journals, and every now and then a banded homing pigeon on an official flight said the hell with it and dropped off in Wyoming or Indiana to live with people whose house it had taken a fancy to while passing over. Along with the house dog in the old, recurring story who held the lantern for the safe-cracker, I can only believe that the pigeons and the mice (except for one rascal over in Milford, New Jersey) have settled down to a more sober and disciplined way of life. Late one night in a paper factory, the Milford mouse distracted the attention of Albert Clauson, who turned from his finishing machine to watch the creature. Paper streaming through the machine tore and fouled several rollers so that they needed relathing. Clauson was laid off for four days, and two hundred fellow workers walked out in protest against this action.

There are among my clippings, I am glad to say, three instances of watchdogs barking their families out of sleep in the middle of the night to save them from death in burning houses; in New Jersey a dog stood by a baby mired in a bog and yelped for help till help came; and in Massachusetts, when bluejays were refused food, they attacked a baby in its carriage and were driven off by the family dog.

On the dark side of the recent record of canine pets there is a tragic happening to which I shall append a warning based on personal experience and some research on the subject of this particular peril. In Los Angeles, Mrs. Drusilla Derdenger rebuffed her bull terrier and a moment later caressed her two-year-old daughter. The jealous dog set upon the child and killed it. In this case, as in the vast majority of such cases, the owner had had the dog before the child was born. Many dogs, established in a household, will not accept graciously or understandingly the advent of what seems to them a rival and more popular pet. The incidence of attacks on infants in this situation, particularly infants old enough to crawl or toddle about, is too high to be ignored. Instances of the killing of children by dogs are extremely rare, but injuries and disfigurements of the face, especially the eyes, are far too frequent. Parents, even those who have heard warnings of this sort, are usually disarmed by the early tolerance and friendliness of the dog. His sudden lashing out is likely to come after months or even years of what has seemed a safe relationship.

There is an easy and dependable solution to the problem. Have the baby first and then buy the dog. To put it in words which I fondly hope may become a remembered slogan: Never bring the baby to the dog, always bring the dog to the baby. I realize that this editorial interpolation is likely to bring down upon me hundreds of letters indignantly defending certain breeds and individual animals. To these correspondents I reply, in advance: Never bring the baby to the dog, always bring the dog to the baby.

There is one other tragic item in my collection, and it proves that the signs reading "Do Not Tease the Animals," posted on many of the cages in all of the zoos in America, carry no idle warning. At a New York zoo late one night a group of roistering ladies and gentlemen decided it would be diverting to wake up the polar bear and tease him. The bear tore an arm off one of the ladies, putting a horrible end to the party's idiotic fun.

On our way to the Hall of Famous Dogs, with its Annex of Peculiar Dogs, let us step, for a moment, into the Bird House. I regret to say that it contains no wrackle-breasted tosscomb or crock-tufted gouse blown thousands of miles away from its home by a tropical hurricane. A great many of these exotic and unwilling visitors showed up along the Atlantic seaboard during the hurricane of 1938, but I find no record of more recent arrivals. We do have a stranger here, but unfortunately he is in too many pieces to be identified. I quote the United Press account of the violent end of this mysterious fowl:

Captain Fructuoso Perez Suarez of Compania Mexicana de Aviacion, a Pan American Airways affiliate, had a puzzling experience one night recently while flying a PAA clipper at 6000 feet between Punta Penasco and Hermosillo, Mexico. While the 21 passengers dozed and the crew kept watch, the cabin windshield was shattered and the remains of a bird splattered over the crew. Captain Suarez would like to know what kind of a bird flies 6000 feet above sea level in the dead of night.

We come next to a less mysterious bird, a parrot, who became involved not long ago in a curious international complication. The bird's owner lives in a house whimsically situated on a boundary line. When the parrot is in the kitchen he is in Canada, but when he is moved to the parlor he is in the United States. A 1930 statute obstructs the entry of parrots into this country, and the U. S. Public Health Service, somehow apprised of the situation, raised an alarmed and disapproving eyebrow whenever the parrot was moved into the parlor, where out of sheer cussedness he preferred to spend his afternoons. There was a great deal of squawking and fuss and feathers on the part of the parrot and the U. S. Public Health Service until somebody, possibly the bird's legal counsel, pointed out that the defendant was twenty-four years old and that the 1930 statute is not retroactive. Quiet settled down once more along the boundary line between the United States and the Dominion of Canada.

We need stop for only a moment before this small wild duck in the corner here. It was saved from drowning by a little boy in Astoria, Oregon, when it was going under for the third time—or perhaps with ducks it's the seventh time. Its wings had become fouled with oil. The duck now answers to its rescuer's whistle and, the boy's mother will tell you, is always underfoot; always underfoot.

Do not step too close to that handsome swan over there, for it has been through a lot with human beings. Along with four other swans, it was once the property of Mrs. Benjamin Halsey, of Irvington-on-Hudson. One day some months ago the five swans decided to move into a place of their own, and they flew to the Hudson River near Nyack. Everything went along swimmingly for quite a while. Then one winter's night the river froze over except for a thread of channel flow and the swans headed upstream, searching for open water. The next day four of them returned to their favorite haunt near Nyack, ice or no ice. Residents of both sides of the river worried and wondered about the missing member of the quintet. It showed up some hours later, limping and flopping and covered with blood, and managed to join its companions on an ice floe near the middle of the river. At this point, up rose Mrs. Frederick Branath, of South Nyack. She ran out across the thin ice and closed in on the swans, oblivious of a fact well known to ornithologists, if not to housewives, that it is safer to close in on an airplane propeller than to close in on a swan. On a firmer footing than ice, a professional wrestler would have his hands full grappling with even one swan, let alone (and good advice, too) five swans. But Mrs. Branath got her swan, braving the flopping wrath of its four partners and its own fierce and indignant infighting, and brought it safely ashore and took it into her house. The swan recovered from what turned out to be a gunshot wound, if not from its humiliation, and, for reasons unclear to me and possibly to its four companions and certainly to its owner, Mrs. Halsey, was given into the permanent custody of the New York Zoological Park.

So much for our bird exhibits.

In the Annex of Peculiar Dogs we stop for a look at Two Bits, a terrier of Medford, Oregon, who plunged over an eight-hundred-foot cliff into a snowbank and emerged unhurt. Some weeks later when the snow had disappeared, he made the same wild leap again, with the high disdain of a trapeze artist who works without a net. Once more he was not hurt, but his owners sent him away to a cliffless farm because they disagreed with him about the wisdom of his favorite exploit. I take no sides in the matter.

My next exhibit is the specter of a female chow, and when I describe her behavior in life as "peculiar," I realize the peculiarity of this facile word. It is the easy, offhand adjective for all goings on that are beyond the short comprehension of Man. Here was a grown dog which felt all of a sudden one day the sharp, insupportable cleavage between the way of life of the human being and the way of life of the four-legged beast. There must have been one final concession she could not make to the commands and restrictions of Man. So she decided to go it alone, making her own bed, finding her own food, living her own life. Who is there to prove that there was not a sudden clarity in her mind, rather than a sudden cloudiness?

That bewildering section of the world known as the Bronx has proved a good hide-out for more than one fugitive, and our chow also managed her secret life there successfully for many months. She selected the capacious precincts of the Botanical Park as her headquarters, but apparently foraged far afield. She was, unfortunately for her, still in the community, if not the company, of men, and the outlaw needs fingers, pocket money, and someone to call pal, if he is to survive among men.

As the problem of food grew larger with the deepening of winter, the chow turned not only away from men but against them. People began to report that a dog had leaped out of the darkness to snap at their heels, a dog variously described as a foot, two feet, and three feet high, an Airedale, a wolfhound, a Great Dane. Mrs. Smith told Mrs. Jones that Mrs. Brown had told her that Mrs. White's son was badly bitten by a hound that gave off a weird light in the night. Reports also came in to police that plants in the Botanical Gardens had been torn up by some mysterious and elusive vandal.

In the end the police, the Park attendants, and the S.P.C.A. banded together to hunt down the miscreant. But she evaded them all for many weeks. They traced her finally to a little known and well-concealed cave in the Botanical Park and built a fire to smoke her out. She didn't come out through the narrow entrance, but two undersized and undernourished puppies did. Their mother dug her way out through another wall with what remaining strength she had and fell at last into the hands of the law. No one came forward to claim the chow. It was too late, anyway. She and her pups were too far gone to save. No one, it came out later, had actually been bitten by the crazy outlaw. "Just imagine," said Mrs. Black to Mrs. Gray, "a dog not wanting to live with people." "The very idea," said Mrs. Gray.

This brooding collie on our left, leaning against the wall and staring into space, was called to the attention of the dog psychiatrists of the New York S.P.C.A. by persons who had observed it sitting motionless for hours on end, day after day, staring fixedly into the window of a house in which it had never lived. It growled at passers-by who tried to divert its attention and bit the official dog expert who finally dragged it off, protesting loudly, to its owner, a lady who lived, it turned out, a considerable way from the house of the strange fascination.

No use to snap your fingers at him, brother, he doesn't see you, he is looking right through you, remembering a wonderful window into which he was privileged to gaze for a while, beholding who shall say what garish dream, what bright illusion, what long atavistic memory. Yes, madam, it *could* have been a mere phosphene or a shred of opacity floating about in the vitreous humor of his eye, but here we are at the Hall of Famous Dogs.

The most celebrated animal in the world during the past few years was President Roosevelt's Scottish terrier, Fala. No dog has ever reached a higher eminence, and none could have taken his exalted position with greater strut and cockiness than the handsome black Scotty. He wore his exploits like a row of medals. When he sat beside the President at the launching of a battleship, he had the jaunty air of the late Admiral Beatty, who used to wear his braided hat rakishly over one eye.

Fala took the great men of the world in his stride. When he was patted on the head by General Doolittle or Winston Churchill, he flipped his admirer a casual salute, said, "How's it going, Mac?" and sauntered out into the kitchen of the White House to pass the time of day with the cook.

Fala's scrap book of clippings, if he kept one—and you felt that he did—must have been as thick as a dictionary. He was into everything, from a noisy affair with a female Scotty who pinned his arrogant ears back, to a scandalous legend which held that his distinguished master had absent-mindedly left him on an island somewhere and had sent a gunboat to pick him up at great expense to the American taxpayers. President Roosevelt dragged Fala and the mythical gunboat into one of his campaign speeches, to the merriment of millions of radio listeners and the discomfiture of the idiots who had publicized the apocryphal adventure.

In America's most sorrowful April since the time of Lincoln's death, Fala stood beside the grave of his great master and added his sharp agonized barks to the solemn thunder of the cannon. It became known a few days later that under an arrangement with the President, Fala was to be returned to his former owner, Miss Ruth Suckley, if anything happened. So the first dog of the land has had his gaudy day and now lives in a quiet and dignified retirement which I am sure is not to his restless taste. At last reports he was teaching two puppies he had sired the fine art of thrust and parry. I have no doubt that he occasionally slips out of the house to brag to the other dogs of the neighborhood about his high participation in world affairs from 1941 to 1945.*

As for animals in the arts, an enormous rabbit named Harvey padded softly and invisibly through a Broadway hit of the same name, and in the movies a beautiful male collie perversely called Lassie put on a performance in a technicolor picture that I believe should have won both the male and female Oscars. Since the heyday of Rin Tin Tin movie producers had been, for the shadowy reasons that turn the turgid wheels of their minds, wary of animal stars, in spite of the great popularity of the fox terrier Asta in the *Thin Man* pictures and others. Lassie's subtle and moving performance touched the stony hearts of such eminent dog haters as Stanley Walker and Gene Fowler, and the movie men threw the gates wide open to the animal actors in Hollywood. In *My Friend Flicka* and its recent sequel, *The Return of My Friend Flicka* or something of the sort, a horse star and a large supporting cast of horses were hits at the box office. Horses who hadn't worked since the great days of William S. Hart combed out their tails, slicked their manes down with water, and showed up at the casting offices. There they found hundreds of dogs who had heard rumors that the brilliant French director, René Clair, was preparing the script of a full-length movie that would star five different dogs of five different breeds. I will con-

* The present White House dog is an Irish terrier named Mike, a gift to President Truman's daughter from Robert Hannegan.

clude the artistic, or temperamental, phase of this motley chronicle by quoting a paragraph from the New York *Times*.

This is to note a slight confusion among the canine actors on the Metro-Goldwyn-Mayer lot during the filming of "Son of Lassie." Lassie, the beautiful Scotch collie who played the title role in "Lassie Come Home" portrayed Laddie in "Son of Lassie," while Major, who served as the stand-in for Lassie in "Lassie Come Home," appeared as Lassie in "Son of Lassie." And, to round out the record, and perhaps add to the confusion, Lassie, despite the name, is a male and the reported sire of a litter of five collies —all male.

It would be unfair to the hard-working and put-upon dogs which take part in the Westminster Dog Show every February if I did not list the proud winners of the Best of Show title for the past few years in this most important of all canine competitions: Wolvey Pattern of Edgerstoune, a West Highland white terrier, 1942; Pitter Patter of Piperscroft, a miniature poodle, 1943; Flornell Rare-bit of Twin Ponds, a Welsh terrier, 1944; Shieling's Signature, a Scottish terrier, 1945.

And now, ladies and gentlemen, we come at last to Blaze. Don't stick out your tongue or point your accusing finger at this gigantic and puzzled mastiff. He never knew what the sound and the fury were all about, and neither did most irate citizens who got the story of Blaze in bits and pieces. Let us see if we can fit together into a sensible pattern the scattered news stories, editorials, letters to the editor, resolutions, and demonstrations that were called forth during this four weeks' American wonder.

On January 17, 1945, an eighteen-year-old sailor, Seaman 1st Class Leon LeRoy, walked into the headquarters of the Red Cross in the little town of Antioch, California, with two problems and a grievance. He was well known in Antioch, because his father, the late Al LeRoy, had once been Chief of Police there. The young sailor's problems were routine problems, familiar to Red Cross ears anywhere: he had lost his leave papers, and he was a long way from his ship with his furlough time running out. He wanted the Red Cross to trace his papers and to expedite his return to his post. The grievance of Leon LeRoy, however, was not so easy to classify and file. It was, indeed, a unique grievance and it smelled of news. Later in the day, Seaman LeRoy found himself repeating his story, from the beginning, to reporters.

On January 4, LeRoy said, he had come into New York Harbor aboard a navy tanker on which he served as gunner. When he went ashore he learned for the first time of the death of his father in Antioch a month before, and he applied for and received an emergency leave to visit his mother. He was put aboard a west-bound cargo plane of the Army Transport Command, at Newark. When the plane landed at Dayton, Ohio, a large wooden crate containing a bull mastiff, weighing between a hundred and ten and a hundred and thirty pounds, was put aboard. The crate took up the space of three seats. The dog's papers, which were handed to the flight engineer, included an A travel priority, and instructions on the care, exercise, and feeding of the animal. The crate was marked for delivery in Los Angeles to Faye Emerson, movie actress and wife of Lieutenant Colonel Elliott Roosevelt.

When the plane took off for Memphis from Patterson Field, it carried not only Leon LeRoy, but two other servicemen, the time and place of whose advent my dossier of newspaper clippings does not make clear. They were Sergeant David Aks, back after thirty-one months in the Orient, and a Navy Seabee whose name and destination the newspapers did not reveal. Sergeant Aks was on his way to Riverdale, California, on emergency leave, to visit his wife, who was ill. All three men were traveling on C priorities, two notches below the A priority rating of our innocent villain, Blaze, who was soaring through the air with flight credentials usually reserved for men of the highest eminence or cargo of vital and urgent importance to the war effort.

It was at Memphis that the trouble began. A lieutenant of the ATC there examined Blaze's priority and then the priorities of the servicemen. He said the men would have to get off the plane to make room for three hundred pounds of B priority freight that had piled up at the Memphis field. Blaze outranked the cargo, but the cargo outranked the servicemen. They got off the plane or, as ATC parlance has it, they were bumped off. The Seabee at this point disappears from our story forever, and we lose sight of Sergeant Aks for a time while we follow the misadventures of Leon LeRoy.

The young sailor went out into the highway and began thumbing rides. He hitch-hiked his way slowly to Dallas, bemoaning the dwindling hours of his leave, and cursing, no doubt, all mastiffs and all colonels. Somewhere along the tedious route he lost his leave papers, and when he got to Dallas the M.P.'s picked him up and held him for two days. As soon as he was released he went to the ATC in Dallas and managed at last to get on another plane headed for California.

When LeRoy had finished his story to the reporters, the press services went into action. Here was a news editor's dream story. It involved a dog, servicemen, a movie actress, and the Roosevelts. It smacked of arrogant goings on in high places. There was a great shouting and scurrying and telephoning and telegraphing. Someone got hold of Sergeant Aks in Riverdale, and he corroborated the sailor's story. Mrs. Al LeRoy, Leon's mother, was worried. She told reporters she was afraid the Navy might discipline her son because of the publicity he had started.

In Granite City, Illinois, Mrs. Ola Vee Nix added to the complicated situation a new figure, Maurice Nix, Carpenter's Mate second class, U.S.N. His wife said that Nix, who had been home on emergency leave because his whole family was sick, could not get on a plane in Dallas, Texas, to return to his station because a huge mastiff had a higher travel priority. Nix had to borrow ninety-eight dollars from the Dallas Red Cross, with which he bought transportation to San Francisco on a commercial plane.

Reporters now began to knock on high official doors in Washington, demanding to know who had requested the high priority for Blaze and what official had assigned it to the dog. Secretary of War Stimson said that there had been a mistake somewhere down the line. General Harold L. George, commander of the ATC, admitted that somebody had committed an error of judgment. Presidential Secretary Stephen T. Early declared that there had been a regrettable combination of mistakes. One reporter, probing for the name of the ATC officer who had granted the A priority, asked if anybody would be punished. "If you mean Sailor LeRoy," Early said, "certainly not." "No, that boy's safe all right," bawled another newsman. In Antioch a navy representative told LeRoy that he would be given a five days' extension of leave and promised him a ride back to his tanker in a plane of the Navy Transport Command. Mrs. Al LeRoy breathed easier.

Mrs. Eleanor Roosevelt, cornered in Washington, said she did not believe any plane dispatcher would be stupid enough to put a serviceman off a plane in favor of a dog. Reporters closed in on Faye Emerson at Albuquerque when a train carrying her to Chicago stopped there. The Colonel's wife said she did not believe the dog had a travel priority, and suggested that the story be carefully checked. The first she knew of Blaze's transcontinental trip, she said, was when he was delivered to her in Los Angeles by an army major in a truck. For the first time a waiting world learned something about the bull mastiff's background. Colonel Roosevelt's wife explained that her husband wanted to breed mastiffs and that he had bought four of them in England. One had been delivered to her some months before, without any tumult or shouting, two others were still in London, and Blaze—well, the whole planet knew the whereabouts of Blaze.

In London, reporters could not find Colonel Roosevelt, but one of his aides said Elliott had left the dog with his family in Washington some time before and had asked that it be sent to his wife in Los Angeles in case any empty bomber or something was making a flight to the Coast. A War Department official, who didn't want his name used, mumbled something about comparative priorities, freight displacement schedules, and the precedence of cargo over passengers on cargo planes. All this the New York *Herald Tribune* branded as "hilariously unsatisfactory" in an editorial which began, "We would not go so far as to say that the story of Elliott Roosevelt's dog has blanketed the news of the great Russian offensive, but we venture to guess that as a subject of discussion from coast to coast it is a strong rival," and which ended: "But let us halt before breaking into tears—unless we shed them for a family some of whose members have never learned the first rule of royalty, which is noblesse oblige." The *Tribune's* stand was supported by dozens of indignant letters in its correspondence columns.

At this juncture there was a sputtering from Congressmen here and there. Representative George P. Miller, of California, wrote a letter to Secretary Stimson demanding a full report on what he called a deplorable incident, and Representative Clare E. Hoffman of Michigan brought the matter formally to the attention of the Lower House in an impassioned speech. He asked his colleagues what the boys in the Pacific would think if they found out that three of their buddies had been bumped off a plane to make room for a dog. At this same moment reporters were presenting a list of typed questions to Major General Alexander D. Surles, head of the War Department's Bureau of Public Relations. The newspapermen wanted the name of the culprit who had established the A priority, and they demanded to know what action was going to be taken to punish the fellow. Stephen Early said he would not put the finger on anybody, but the affair had gone too far to be dropped so easily. The American public and the American press had found something pretty special to kick around, and they kicked it around in that peculiar American way, which encompasses everything from elaborate gags to solemn Senatorial investigation. Everybody picked up his phone, or got out his typewriter, or stood up and had his say.

In Detroit, a lawyer named Herbert Denis announced that he, too, had intended to breed mastiffs but that the U. S. Bureau of Animal Husbandry had refused to let him bring a male mastiff into the country three years before. The Bureau of Animal Husbandry retorted that it had no record of such a case and did not believe Mr. Denis' dog had been refused admittance to the United States. In Granite City, Illinois, the local carpenters' union held a meeting and voted to refund to the Dallas Red Cross the ninety-eight dollars it had lent to Carpenter's Mate Maurice Nix. In Dallas thirty members of that city's famous Bonehead Club tried in vain to get one of the local air lines to send to President Roosevelt, by plane, a large sad-eyed Saint Bernard wearing an opera hat. The club members then voted to send the two hundred and sixty dogs in the Dallas pound about the country in airplanes, and passed a resolution changing Groundhog Day to Ground Dog Day. On this day, February 2, all dogs would be grounded so that people would get a chance to fly.

Senator Styles Bridges, Republican, of New Hampshire, hearkening to the clamor of the papers and the people, recommended a Senatorial investigation of the high courtesies extended to a foreign-born mastiff. Senator Elbert D. Thomas, chairman of the Senate Military Affairs Committee, agreed with Senator Bridges and appointed a subcommittee to probe into the origin of the high priority. At this crucial and impressive moment a perfectly lovely thing, to use a city room expression, happened. While journalists clucked and gloated and rubbed their hands together in fine excitement, it was revealed that the War Department had recommended seventy-seven colonels for promotion to the rank of brigadier general, and that President Roosevelt, coolly oblivious of the horrible mastiff scandal, had sent the list of names to the Senate for its approval in spite of the fact that Elliott Roosevelt was one of the seventy-seven. "Why do they have to pick *this* time for it?" wailed Senator Albert B. ("Happy") Chandler, of Kentucky. Eyebrows lifted and tongues wagged in corridors and living rooms all over the country. A little man in a Washington restaurant observed to a tableful of total strangers that he had never heard of a colonel in all his life that he had any use for. A woman in Ohio wrote to her favorite afternoon daily crying, "Do you mean to say, for God sakes, that any Roosevelt can't just make himself a general if he wants to?"

The *Herald Tribune* added another man to the imposing battery of editorial writers it had assigned exclusively to the Blaze story. This new man had volunteered to tie up the Blaze episode with all the other tactless and arrogant mistakes of the Roosevelt regime. He wrote in part, "It will seem to a great many besides these Senators that the President might have omitted his son's name from the list until he had been cleared, if that is in the cards, of responsibility for his dog's privileges. But Mr. Roosevelt's tact appears to have suffered an eclipse since his fourth inauguration. His letter to Secretary Jones asking him to make way for Mr. Wallace is a conspicuous case in point. His appointment of Aubrey Williams to head the Rural Electrification Administration is another. And now, on their heels, comes this climacteric challenge to Congressional and public indignation. On top of all this can anyone be sure that he hasn't a commission in store for Blaze?"

Other newspapers followed the *Herald Tribune*'s lead, and a nasty rumble arose throughout the land. Many mothers, churchmen, and other right-thinking citizens began to fear that there would be rioting in the streets and that mastiffs and colonels would be strung up on lamp posts from Tallahassee to Tacoma and from Dallas to Danbury.

It was, of all people, the United States Senators, including the Republicans, who got off the first wisecracks, thus lessening the dangerous and rapidly mounting tension. "How in blazes," said Senator Bridges, "was Blaze to know he had a preferred claim? Blaze likely is an innocent victim of a poorly regulated priority system. He probably wasn't conscious of his position, except that it was comfortable and he did not care to leave the plane." Another Senator who would not, understandably enough, allow his name to be used, said, "Way I look at it, the Army Transport Command is putting on a lot of dog." And he went from room to room of the Senate Office Building, repeating the gag and guf-

Now that the warm light of humor had begun to play about the celebrated case, things began to fall into a proper perspective. The Senators perceived that Colonel Roosevelt's connection with the notorious flight, whatever that connection may have been, had precisely nothing whatever to do with his merits as a soldier and his right to promotion. The anti-administration press continued to squawk loudly, but nobody any longer paid much attention. The affair had dragged along for almost a month, and the volatile American mind was turning to other interests.

The whole business was cleared up, once and forever, on February 10, when General George submitted a 900-word report to the subcommittee of the Senate Military Affairs Committee, in which the general placed all blame for the "inexcusable incident" on the Army's Air Transport Command. While the nation held its breath, General George pointed a shame-on-you finger at the true culprit, the official for whose blood some of the press and a part of the populace had panted since January 17. The man who had established the high priority for Blaze was Colonel Ray W. Ireland, assistant chief of staff for priorities and traffic, headquarters Air Transport Command. Colonel Ireland said that he had established the priority just as a favor. The Roosevelt family was completely absolved of any responsibility in the matter. Mrs. John Boettiger had called up the ATC from the White House about shipping Blaze to the Coast, but she had not asked for a priority of any kind. Blaze, it turned out, had been flown from London to Washington in three different army planes, but in making the long journey he had displaced no servicemen and had broken no War Department regulation. The ATC was instructed, however, not to transport dogs, cats, mice, penguins, goldfish, or any other kind of animal life in army planes ever again.

General George's report was all right as far as it went, but it left the regulation of priorities and the freight-passenger differential still pretty cloudy in the American lay mind. One of my friends, brooding over the confusing case of the bull mastiff, has suggested a card game to be called "Bumpo." If in the rapid give-

and-take of cards in this game you are the first to fill your hand with seven A priority dogs, you jump to your feet, cry "Bumpo!" and are permitted to throw your opponent or opponents out of the house.

Colonel Roosevelt and the other colonels whose promotions had been held up for nearly two weeks were made brigadier generals. In Antioch it was announced that Seaman LeRoy was going to marry a lovely girl named Barbara Warren. Thus the remarkable case of Blaze ended in a flurry of hand-shaking and congratulations all around.

A slight, gray, but alert gentleman to whom I assigned the task of observing the behavior of birds and beasts during the summer of 1945, while I was busy with other matters, has just made his report. He finds only three items worthy of perpetuation in this monumental archive. A small dog named Bosco, shipped, against his will, to Glendale, California, for a visit last winter, escaped from his crate at the express office in that town, and set out for home. Since Bosco's home was in Knoxville, Tennessee, twenty-three hundred miles away, his journey was a considerable undertaking. The trip took Bosco seven months, but he made it, setting a new world's record for homing dogs.

In June, two peregrine falcons came out of the Middle Ages to take up their residence on the roof of a high New York apartment building. Members of the City Department of Falconry who finally trapped the swift, savage birds found the remains of two hundred pigeons on the roof. A dozen of the dead pigeons wore official bands on their legs.

My agent's report ends with a notation about a Wisconsin dog named Fido who died leaving in his will $30,000 "to sick and needy dogs." That does it, friends. This thing has definitely gone far enough.

Part Four

What We Saw, Read, and Heard

I. THE NEWSPAPERS

by LESTER MARKEL

LESTER MARKEL (*age 51*) *is the Sunday Editor of* The New York Times. *His has been solely a newspaper career since his graduation from the Columbia School of Journalism thirty-one years ago. For nine years he was a staff member of the old* New York Tribune *and served successively as reporter, rewrite man, copy reader, telegraph editor, cable editor, city editor, night editor, assistant managing editor. He has been Sunday Editor of the* Times *since 1923, with jurisdiction over all sections with the exception of straight news. Under his supervision, the* Magazine *has been developed, the* Review of the Week *established, the* Book Review *expanded, and* Drama *and* Travel Sections *enlarged.*

IN THE course of World War II the newspapers of the country printed the news of Okinawa—and the news of Main Street; the story of the atomic bomb—and the story of the Chaplin trial; the accounts of the havoc in Europe—and the blueprints for the new post office; the news of tremendous things—and the news of trivial things, too.

There were newspapers that devoted themselves primarily to the news—and there were other newspapers that were more concerned with circuses and trick circulations; there were newspapers that made a genuine effort to be unbiased—and there were others that carried the torch (or the bludgeon) in their news columns; there were newspapers that printed the news without fear or favor—and there were those that headlined fears and italicized favoritism.

In other words, during these war days, the newspapers of the country performed as their consciences and their interests dictated. They printed what they wanted to print; they attacked those they saw fit to attack; they gave the news accurately or they distorted the news, as they chose. In short, they acted as a free press acts.

Now, a lot of eye-wash has been spilled and a good many excellent adjectives have been maltreated in talk about the "freedom of the press." The phrase has been used so often as camouflage and as cant that it is in a somewhat shop-worn state.

Yet the words still have a large meaning. It is no mere coincidence that, in totalitarian lands, the first institution to vanish is the free press. "Where the press is free and every man able to read," Jefferson wrote, "all is safe." Where the press is shackled, the dictators can black out the truth and spread their poison unchecked.

It did not happen here. That is the outstanding, the tremendous fact about American journalism during the war years.

IF THIS BE BIAS, SO BE IT

This chapter is a report on how the newspapers of the country used their freedom in the period since Pearl Harbor and what that means for the future. The theme is full of controversy; that is as it should be, because the question merits complete and even overheated debate.

Right at the start, I confess a prejudice in favor of the newspaper. Out of a long acquaintance with them, I have developed a deep respect for American newspapermen. They are in the business, in most instances, not for money and very little for glory, but mainly for the love of it.

As for newspaper publishers, there are those, to be sure, who keep their eyes on the counting rooms rather than on the editorial sanctums. And, what is much more cause for concern, there are those who distort the news to suit their economic purposes or to further their political or social ideologies. I deeply deplore both groups and I hope that eventually they will move into the commercial enterprises or the pamphleteering businesses to which they properly belong.

Yet their existence is almost inevitable under our system of a free press, for that freedom encompasses freedom to misuse as well as freedom to use. And their number is not nearly as great as their stridence might indicate. I am convinced that most publishers are aware of the large degree of public responsibility that attaches to their properties and recognize that freedom of the press is a trust as well as a privilege.

I believe, then, that even though there are bad newspapers— bad because they are biased or because they are inadequate —they are outnumbered by the good.

I believe that the newspaper has an important future, just as it has had an important past and just as it has an important present.

I believe that the newspaper business is, by and large, a good business and I am proud to be part of it.

If this be bias, make the most of it.

A WORD ON BIAS AND THE BIASED

At this point a critic will doubtless make something of it. It has become fashionable in certain circles, intellectual and political, to take pot-shots at the newspapers. So I shall be accused of espousing the "conservative" side, of harboring "bias" in an unholy degree.

Now, in my time, I have heard a multitude of complaints about "bias." But I have yet to find a single complainant who was really plugging for objective presentation. Almost invariably the complaint is, not that the newspaper is slanted, but that it is slanted in the wrong direction, that is, not in the direction of the critic.

I do not deny that the critics have something, a good deal, to their case. But let them examine carefully the "liberal" journals which they applaud and they will find the slant as compared with the "conservative" press far greater—ten adjectives, I should say, to one.

(I regret that I am not using more precise words than the much-misused "liberal" and "conservative," but no adequate substitutes seem to be available. At any rate, I assure the reader that the quotation marks have no ideological significance and that the terms are not intended to express condemnation or admiration one way or the other.)

Let me try to make myself entirely clear. I condemn the "conservative" press when it reports "conservatively" and I condemn the "liberal" press when it reports "liberally." I insist that the report be neither right nor left, but factual, right down the middle. I do not ask that opinion be outlawed from the newspaper or that the editorial pages be abolished; I ask only that it be confined to the editorial pages.

I urge the critics to put their criticisms on the right basis; by all means let them condemn bias, but let that condemnation be uniform. Because only through the fair presentation of facts on all sides can true public opinion be guided.

But I did not mean to plunge into the debate this early in the chapter. Before passing judgment, let us look at the record.

BACKGROUND VERSUS OPINION

In appraising that record there are these three tests: First, how good and how complete was the coverage? Second, was the news free of slant? Third, how was the news displayed?

For the first test the Pulitzer formula—"accuracy, terseness, accuracy"—still applies. But a vital ingredient must be added: "background." Increasing attention must be paid to the task of interpretation; it is as important as the task of news-gathering itself. More and more the reporter is required to be the expert; he must write as much between the lines as on them.

This matter of "background" deserves special attention. Let us make sure that the word is understood. "Background" is the deeper meaning of the news; it places a particular event in the flow of current history; it provides the setting and the sequence and thus the significance.

But "background" *does not* mean opinion. Background is factual —it explains; opinion is editorial—it argues.

What you *see* is news; what you *know* is background; what you *feel* is opinion. To say that Stalin does not like Franco is news; to explain why he does not is background; to remark that you do not blame Stalin for disliking Franco is opinion. To report that President Truman has canceled Lend-Lease is news; to set out the reasons for the cancellation is background; to state that the cancellation was a mistake is opinion.

Explanation, interpretation, belong in the news columns; opinion, editorial slant, must be kept out.

On the question of slant the reader has acquired some wisdom. He has learned to spot the falsehoods of a Goebbels or a Haw Haw and even the more subtle. insinuations of our home-bred purveyors of propaganda. Where, as in the case of the isolationist press, he recognizes slant, he will often accept it because he approves of it or he will disregard it because he is more addicted to features than to news.

But on the question of display the reader has little sophistication. He does not generally realize that, from the propaganda viewpoint, the way a story is written is no more important than the way it is "played"—by which is meant the way it is placed in the newspaper, on page 1 or on page 3 or on page 19. The judgment as to what stories shall go on the first page of a newspaper is as editorial a decision as there is.

If these three tests are applied to the war record, the balance sheet might look like this:

On the credit side: 1) The war coverage was admirable; 2) There was a substantial increase in "solid" news; 3) There was a growing concern about slant; 4) The task of news interpretation had greater attention.

On the debit side: 1) Certain segments of the press showed a reckless irresponsibility; 2) Some categories of news were handled with a good deal of bias; 3) The news perspective was at times askew; 4) The newspapers did not exert, as fully as they might have, the influence at their command.

The debits are heavy, yet, on balance, the record gives encouragement for the future of the newspaper. Even though there is still a long road to travel, distinct headway has been made.

I — THE WAR COVERAGE

The big headline news during the war was, of course, the reports dispatched from the fronts. Journalistic enterprise and integrity were tested there as never before. The flow of the news was tremendous; here are some random statistics:

In the year 1944 approximately 200,000,000 words were transmitted from the fighting fronts to the newspapers of the U. S.

The correspondents covering World War II for American newspapers numbered between 500 and 700 as compared with not more than 100 assigned to World War I.

The three main press associations alone are estimated to have spent some thirty million dollars on war coverage since Pearl Harbor.

In a single day a newspaper such as the New York *Times* receives 500,000 words of news, out of which 125,000 must be selected for publication.

But more important than the number of words is their quality. Of the war correspondence, it can be said immediately that it was, on the whole, vivid and accurate, and that the correspondents have been, with few exceptions, courageous and painstaking. The reporter has shared, so far as he could, the emotions of the fighter, from the brooding silences before battle to the exultant releases of victory. The correspondents have covered the whole range of our citizen soldiery, from a portrait of a Patton to a profile of a private; they have been at headquarters with the commanders and at the fronts with the troops; they, too, are found in the casualty lists. Never before had a war been reported like this one; for example, the June 6th invasion was covered by 450 correspondents—"the best coverage of any military operation in all history," Elmer Davis called it.

Of most of the reporters, it can be said, as it was said of Ernie Pyle, that they made this war "truly a people's war." That was done not by preaching or by exhortation or by the piling on of color and of adjectives, but by the simple, swift, true narration of events.

TWO PICTURES OF MEN AT WAR

Because of the high standard of the war reporting, it is difficult, almost unfair, to select any one or three or even thirty passages out of the dispatches as those deserving of laurels. But there are certain ones that remain vividly in memory.

There was, for example, Ernie Pyle's description of the Normandy beachhead as he saw it only a few hours after the first wave of the invasion had broken over it:

There was another and more human litter. It extended in a thin little line, just like a high-water mark, for miles along the beach. This was the strewn personal gear, gear that would never be needed again by those who fought and died to give us our entrance into Europe.

There in a jumbled row for mile on mile were soldiers' packs. There were socks and shoe polish, kits, diaries, Bibles, hand grenades. There were the latest letters from home, with the address on each one neatly razored out—one of the security precautions enforced before the boys embarked. There were toothbrushes and razors, and snapshots of families back home staring up at you from the sand. There were pocket-books, metal mirrors, extra trousers, and bloody, abandoned shoes.

There were torn pistol belts and canvas water buckets, first-aid kits, and jumbled heaps of life belts. I picked up a pocket Bible with a soldier's name in it, and put it in my jacket. I carried it half a mile or so and then put it back down on the beach. I don't know why I picked it up, or why I put it down again.

Two of the most dominant items in the beach refuse were cigarettes and writing paper. Each soldier was issued a carton of cigarettes just before he started. That day those cartons by the thousands, water-soaked and spilled out, marked the line of our first savage blow.

Writing paper and air-mail envelopes came second. The boys had intended to do a lot of writing in France. The letters—now forever incapable of being written—that might have filled those blank abandoned pages!

And this dispatch by Kenneth L. Dixon, of the Associated Press, written as our men moved into Germany:

As seen from a ditch, the two tall trees made a perfect picture frame through which the column slowly advanced.

Ten paces apart, company A was moving into the combat line.

The men walked upward along a gradually rising ridge, entering the picture one by one. Each drab, muddy outline held the scene a moment as it topped the crest. It seemed suspended there against the gray, smoky sky just before it stumbled on.

All along the rainswept slope, the wet earth seemed to boil with muddy mortar bubbles bursting and splashing around the men.

Through it all the doughboys walked slowly, grim, strained—ten paces apart.

Sometimes when a shell landed too close they hit the dirt, but mostly they just kept moving. Twice men were hit. The column paused briefly. Then it flowed forward again, with sticky reluctance, like heavy motor oil on a cold morning.

The dead of the company up ahead still lay where they had fallen. The pathway was narrow and mines were thick on both sides. Heavy-footed doughboys stepped carefully over the bodies of men they'd swapped cigarettes with just a few hours before.

Some turned their eyes aside. Some stared, fearful and with magnetized fascination, at the torn bodies. Strangely there seemed to be no wounded on the slope. Only the walking and the dead.

With faces pale and tight under the beards and dirt, the soldiers neither hurried nor lagged as shells fell about them. Still there was no straggling.

There was a complete absence of human sound. No one shouted orders, cried out or talked. They just pushed on toward an invisible enemy. Their job was to concentrate powerfully on putting one foot ahead of the other regardless of what happened.

Watching them you began to tremble and you weren't sure why. These men displayed no heroics, no hate, no enthusiasms, no crusading zeal.

There seemed to be nothing whatsoever to help spur them on. But they marched. Their steps seemed to drum into your brain. These men didn't want to go forward. That was heartbreakingly clear in every line of their flinching forms.

It was even more clear that they would not stop short of that inferno beyond them. And you knew that if they fell others would follow and they too would keep on going.

Reluctant heroes—ten paces apart.

This kind of reporting, warm and non-Olympian and full of human detail, kept the nation fully informed about the course and the nature of the war. And, as a consequence, it helped greatly in establishing links between the men at the front and the people at home.

The grimness of the war and the achievements of the troops were realized too, with dramatic impact, through the photographs from the fronts. Never before has there been such pictorial coverage of the news and never before have the men with the cameras ventured so much in the way of their own comfort and safety to bring back the record. On all fronts the news photographers were present, landing with the first waves on the assault beaches, reaching the summits of battle-scarred peaks even as the flags were going up, living with the troops and partaking of their thoughts and their dangers. Their work supplemented the work of the reporters in an extraordinarily vivid way.

EVERY MAN HIS OWN REPORTER

Some of the troops have reported, in their private communiqués to the folks back home, or more publicly in letters to the editors, that the correspondents have not been too accurate.

Take, as an example, the reports of the Battle of the Bulge, that final German fling in December, 1944. For the men who took part in that struggle the going was very, very tough, and among many of them there was the feeling that the correspondents did not tell the whole story and what they did tell was colored with a large pigment of optimism.

The facts are that, for a period of days, there was confusion at headquarters as well as at the front. In some sectors correspondents were told that a crisis was at hand; in others, that everything was under control (and no report to the contrary could get past the censors). As for the charge of "optimism" made against some reporters, there is this bit of evidence in their behalf: when General Eisenhower was asked in June 1945 whether he had been worried about the outcome of the battle he answered, "You bet! Three months later, when I got the American papers."

Yet those "pessimistic" dispatches were based on what the briefing officers had told the correspondents; and they had been passed by the censors.

Every man is his own reporter and arrives at his own version. The soldiers were there and they saw and they know. But what they had was a view of one small sector of the front, whereas the job of the correspondent was to present the picture as a whole, with the help of such briefing as he had at headquarters—briefing which was at times, to hear the correspondents tell it, neither too complete nor too unslanted. Moreover, it should be realized how large an assignment it is to get agreement as to detail between any two spectators of any event. Take fifty witnesses of a single occurrence and you will get fifty accounts of it; each observer has his own set of sights, psychological as well as physical.

THE MAZE OF THE CENSORSHIP

The censorship, of course, presented its special problems. For the question of censorship is one of many facets and much argument, and it is easy, in considering it, to go to extremes. The military authorities are generally on the side of repression; their job, as they see it, is to fight the war and to win it and the less said about it the better, because words lead to debates and debates hold up action. The newspapers are naturally on the side of publication; their job, as *they* see it, is to record events and to provide the information for a sound public opinion.

There are extremists in both camps. For example: on the military side, it is related that one high-ranking leader in Washington has always believed that the coverage of the war should be limited to two communiqués: *Number 1—*"We have been attacked." *Number 2—*"The enemy has surrendered." As an offset, on the journalistic side, there is the reporter or the editor who seems to think that the war is being fought so that he can attain scoops; to him military security is an intrusion on life, liberty, and the pursuit of circulation.

The true position can be stated simply: that the newspaper shall respect to the utmost the limits laid down for military security, but that it shall be ever vigilant that, behind the veil, the prosecution of the war shall proceed without blunders and without favoritism. But, having stated the theory, one is confronted with its execution, and that is a task for a Solomon, a Diogenes, and an Atlas all rolled into one. For it is very difficult to decide where military security ends and a smoke screen for mistakes begins; or where public interest ceases and selfish newspaper enterprise takes over.

A noteworthy example of this kind of dilemma was presented to the New York *Times* in 1942. Hanson Baldwin, military expert of the *Times*, made a swing through the Pacific, encountered brass-hat inefficiency and duplication of command, and found that censorship was throwing a smoke screen over all of it. The question was: Would the publication of these facts help or hurt the war effort; would such publication lead to correction and thereby more than offset the possible blow to morale?

The decision was made to publish; the articles (which were written without any pulling of punches) were submitted in uncompromising form to the censors at Washington; they were passed for publication and the result was an improvement in the censorship so that it became one designed more for military security and less for concealment.

The famous Patton incident provided another such test. Soon after it happened that story was known to many newspaper correspondents in Sicily; for months it was an open secret that Patton had slapped a soldier in a hospital and that Eisenhower had reprimanded him for it. It became such general knowledge that Eisenhower called the correspondents together, told them of the incident, said that he thought publication would be harmful to morale, conceded that inasmuch as there was no question of military secrecy involved, he could not impose a censorship, and urged that the story be withheld. No correspondent sent it.

A month later Drew Pearson broke the story in a broadcast. This was a case of every man for himself, with the chance that the devil would take the foremost. It was an individual decision and a decision with which many, including this observer, would disagree.

A notable debate over newspaper ethics arose in the case of Edward Kennedy, of the Associated Press, who was one of a group of reporters brought by the Army from Paris to Amiens to witness the signing of the German surrender. The group was pledged not to transmit any stories until the official release was given. Kennedy beat the gun by telephoning his story from Paris to London, thus eluding the censor. He justified his action on the ground that no military security was involved, inasmuch as the war was over.

But it seemed to many of us that the question ran much deeper than that. The sanctity of the release—the observance by the newspaperman of an agreement made with those from whom the news is obtained—is one of the foundation stones of newspaper work. Unless there is this mutual trust, journalism becomes a game of typographical cops and robbers.

Most secrets were kept with extraordinary vigilance. Plans for D-Day in Normandy had obviously to be laid well in advance and many correspondents were in on the preparations; but there was no leak whatsoever. And the mystery of the atomic bomb began when the newspapers were requested not to speculate on experiments with uranium, among other elements; that was in June, 1943, and for more than two years no word about the tests was printed, with the result that the physical explosion over Hiroshima was no more epochal than the psychological.

"The plain and sober truth is," said Byron Price, then Director of Censorship, "that in no war in history and in no country in the world has the common man been given access to such detailed and comprehensive reports of warfare as those that are placed hourly before readers of American newspapers and listeners beside American radios. The correspondents on the fighting line and the newspapers and broadcasters at home have done a fabulously successful job of protecting the national security."

THE TEST OF PERSPECTIVE

But how about the "playing" of the news? That, too, is a test, and an acid one. It has been charged that the papers were overoptimistic in their appraisals of the war news and, especially, that minor advances were played up as considerable victories. Many newspapers, especially afternoon journals, whose sales depend to an important degree on the size and the shock of the headlines, are prone in wartime, as in peacetime, to apply major captions to minor items. Here are four typical, if not actual, samples:

HALF GERMANY'S INDUSTRIES IN RUINS

(This according to a rumor of a compilation made by an obscure and unnamed official at the British Air Ministry.)

GERMAN HOME FRONT COLLAPSING

(This according to a Swedish traveler just returned from a two-day stay at the Adlon Hotel in Berlin, mostly at the bar.)

JAPAN *ROCKED* BY OUR AIRMEN

(This a dispatch that fifty bombers had attacked a coast town and inflicted a modicum of damage—and the verb, mind you, was *"rocked."*)

REMNANTS OF JAP FLEET SUNK

(This every other week—and in the weeks between it was usually the merchant fleet that was finally sunk.)

Now a good part of German industry was destroyed and the German home front did collapse and the very samurai was blasted out of Japan and the Japanese fleet was knocked to bits. But this all came later; at the time the headlines appeared they might well have engendered a false optimism and so brought about a letdown in the war effort.

But the newspapers were not the sole offenders. A good deal of glowing prediction emanated from high military quarters. Some of our generals have not been exactly fanatics for under-statement, and their communiqués have sometimes had a gorgeous hue. Often the newspapers have been accused of originating these purple reports when in fact they were only publishing, as they should have, pronouncements handed down from on high.

In many instances the stories from the front gave a picture that was truer and less optimistic than that contained in the communiqués. But the communiqués were released before the corre-spondents' reports, in nine cases out of ten—due to the delays of censorship and other causes—and thus the correction, as usually happens, failed to catch up with the primary exaggeration. This was the case in the reports of the Battle of the Bulge, which told of the rough days after the first German smash-through but which were stopped by the censor or held until the turn of the tide was at hand.

Just as important, and just as vexing, was the censorship at the source. At times the Public Relations Officers kept certain facts from the correspondents or, through the release of some facts and not others, gave a distorted picture.

In many instances, then, the criticism on the grounds of inaccuracy or of overoptimism should be leveled, not at the newspapers, but at the Army.

The Navy was more direct in its public relations. But its communiqués and information were scantier, its censorship was sterner, because, presumably, the Navy brass hats are older, shinier, and more proof against the winds of opinion. Thus the heavy losses in the Pacific fighting and particularly those of the desperate Kamikaze days were shrouded by censorship.

These decisions, made for security reasons, could not be questioned at the time. But the argument can be made that this kind of news was needed to offset our early complacencies. Certainly without Pearl Harbor this nation would never have been aroused as it was; we are a nation that gets fighting mad when the odds are against it and takes it mighty easy when it believes there is no need to expend energy. We are spurred not by denial but by disaster. As the war went on, Washington came to recognize this —and the tone of the communiqués changed and the truth was released in greater quantity.

II — THE INTERNATIONAL COVERAGE

In the longer view, the reporting of international news is of more importance than the reporting of the fronts. The battle stories are as simple as they are dramatic; they do not involve the deep issues and the complicated problems inherent in the coverage of world affairs. Moreover, if we are to master the atom rather than to allow the atom to master us, the task of establishing good relations among nations is one that must have a prime priority. And a large part of that task must be assigned to the newspapers.

In the coverage of the diplomatic and other global fronts, the newspapers did a more comprehensive job than ever before. For example, American correspondents at the San Francisco Conference sent to their press associations and individual newspapers some 200,000 words a day. Likewise vital discussions in the economic and social areas, even though they do not have the drama of political events—issues such as Bretton Woods, UNRRA, minority rights and the like—have had increased attention.

But again it is the kind of words, not the number of them, that counts. Immediately, when that is said, questions are raised about the isolationist press. This is the way the indictment runs: that before Pearl Harbor, it condoned the Hitler crimes; that, after Pearl Harbor, it urged concentration on the Pacific war, at a time when the President and our ranking military men believed we had to mass everything we had to beat Hitler; that, even during the war and certainly in the post-European-war period, it has revealed anti-Russian and anti-British attitudes; and that now, having failed to achieve political isolation through the defeat of the Dumbarton Oaks plan, it is seeking to attain economic isolationism.

To one who, like myself, believes that our fate is bound up utterly with the fate of other nations and that when the bell tolls for one it tolls for all of us, these attitudes are wrong and this reasoning is false. And so I believe these newspapers did and do the nation and the world a grave disservice.

There is another accusation that is likely to escape notice— and it should not. It is a much simpler and a much more fundamental charge: that these same newspapers allow—and, more than that, implant—these slants in their news columns. Thus they fail, I say, in a primary duty.

THE TANGLED RUSSIAN ISSUE

Against other parts of the press, there have also been charges that the news was angled. Especially has there been debate about the handling of news about Russia. The Russian issue is the most incendiary of all; it would take the Gestapo, the Ogpu, and the F.B.I. combined to find any observer who is neutral on the subject. The argument rages in and outside the press. There is the extremist on one side who, unless you have a picture of Stalin in your home, will blast you as a fascist; and the extremist on the other who, if you remark pleasantly that the Kremlin is an imposing building in Moscow, will brand you a communist.

The basic difficulty is that the discussion proceeds over political issues or over questions of geography, whereas it belongs properly in the realm of psychology, of the psychology of fear. When that is recognized and the fears are analyzed and understood, our relations with Russia will improve and some of the energy now expended in superheated adjectives will be devoted to more constructive ends.

Against the newspapers it is said: that they picture Russia as an imperialist nation, intent on the eventual destruction of this citadel of free enterprise; that stories such as the Polish and the Finnish episodes are played up, out of all proportion, to Russia's detriment; that the press, being capitalist, is fearful of communism and fights it openly in its news columns.

On the other side of the ledger there are these items: that the Russian bear, even though it is now a Red Bear instead of a White One, still deals gruffly with us; that Stalin *et cie.* make almost a fetish of secrecy and suspicion; and that our American Communists are not very fetching representatives (if they are representatives at all) of Mother-in-law Russia.

Because the real issues are rarely joined, it is difficult to appraise properly the charges and the counter-charges. Certainly on the editorial pages much opposition has been expressed to the tenets of communism; that is to be expected of a "capitalist" press. And in too many instances the slant has been carried over into the news columns. Yet the story of Russia's part in the war was well and fully told.

Russian censorship and Russian secretiveness have made the newspaper task much more difficult. There may be good reasons for both—a suspicion of the outside world based on the long record of history; a desire to conceal weaknesses arising out of a kind of inferiority feeling; a general uncertainty about the future. But the fact remains that even a newspaper intent on giving the Soviets a square deal has found almost insuperable handicaps in the way of getting the facts.

Time and again I have tried to get from our men in Moscow background articles dealing with fundamental and simple questions—Russia's postwar policy, her feeling toward the United States, her attitude toward the Comintern in general and the American Communists in particular, and so on—and too often the pieces arrive by cable accompanied with this apology: "Sorry but this is all that fellow left," that fellow being the censor and what was left being very little.

The reporting about Russia will be more objective when it is less frustrated—that is, when the Russians give the American press more of a chance to do its proper job.

CONFERENCES OR CIRCUSES?

The coverage of the San Francisco Conference is another excellent case history in the study of newspaper handling of international affairs. There the press was revealed at its best and at its worst. Its best was the work done by correspondents who tried honestly to interpret the great fact of the meeting: that the delegates were intent on making a start toward a new world order. Its worst was the work done by the men who found a new crisis every day; who were intent on having their headlines, as though this were one of the more sensational murder trials. And there is no doubt that there were too many of these last.

At times, too, the meeting was treated as a circus or a community sing or a national convention. The gossip writers and the keyhole commentators, the sob sisters and the blab brothers descended on it in force. And freedom of the press really reached its zenith at a conference held by Molotoff, when the saloon editor of a New York newspaper, after hearing questions of large international concern discussed for a half hour or so, put this atomic query: "How, Mr. Molotoff, do you pronounce vodka?" It is to be hoped fervently that this kind of coverage is not the pattern for the future; if it is, international amity is in serious danger.

Moreover, some newspapers seem to believe that these meetings are being held not to achieve the solution of world problems but to enhance circulation. At San Francisco, and later at the Potsdam meeting of the Big Three, a number of correspondents complained bitterly and publicly in their dispatches that they were not in on the secrets, that freedom of the press was being jeopardized—in other words that they were not getting enough "good copy."

It is greatly to be desired, of course, that all these international gatherings shall be subject to the scrutiny of public opinion through the eyes of the press and of the radio. But in delicate negotiations, a considerable amount of secrecy is needed, for once a delegation is publicly committed to a position, it cannot retreat from it without losing too much face; the chances of working out a solution are much greater if it is done tête à tête rather than on the rostrum under the limelights. "Open covenants openly arrived at" is an excellent ideal, but the difficulties must be taken into account. And the truth is that the complaints against such secrecy often are made not because the reporter is hugely concerned about the world's future but because he is wholly intent upon his own by-lines.

There are times, to be sure, when pitiless publicity is vital. At the meetings of the Council of Foreign Ministers in London an effort was made in the first days to keep all the negotiations under cover. Yet the world of the future was being mapped out. Obviously the limelight was needed and the full benefit of debate. As Secretary Byrnes said on another occasion, when the question of observation of the Balkan elections was brought up: "I would rather have unrestricted and uncensored reporters on the watch than any number of official observers." But that, in turn, requires a full responsibility on the part of the press—a responsibility, as has been indicated, which is not always recognized.

ALSO A SLANT TO THE LEFT

But if the "conservative" press is guilty at times of permitting slant in its news columns—and I repeat that is a primary, even *the* primary, test of a newspaper—consider the "liberal" press. Take, for example, what has been one of its favorite themes, the "derelictions" of the State Department: "its Fascist background"; "its opposition to Russia"; "the Darlan Deal"; "the failure to recognize de Gaulle for too long a time"; "its benevolence toward Spain"; "its traffic with the Argentine Government" and the like.

Now I am not defending the State Department. I have no doubt that it contains too many Dollar Diplomats and too much of the Palm Beach Peerage, that it has had too great an attachment to the Old Order and too great a fear of the New. But I deplore the nature and the place of the attack. It was made not only on the editorial page but even more violently in the "news correspondence," from Washington and other observation posts. There was no pretense at objective reporting.

Why should there be, my "liberal" friends ask? You can't be a sexless, emotionless creature; you write what you feel, you crusade. Yet once you concede that principle, then the bottom drops out of the complaints about the other side.

The strangest part of this whole controversy is that these are the same newspapers that were such ardent supporters of Roosevelt. Our foreign policy during the war was Franklin Roosevelt's foreign policy; he ran the show, in Washington and at diplomatic points, West and East. The syllogism might then run like this: 1) The State Department was fascist; 2) Franklin Roosevelt ran the State Department; 3) ergo, Franklin Roosevelt was a fascist. Somehow that does not sound right.

III—THE NEWS OF THE HOME FRONT

Now, how about the home front? How was the domestic news played?

Certain general credits can be set down immediately: the newspapers cut their newsprint quota 30 per cent; they sacrificed millions of lines of advertising in order to give the news; they played an important part in the war drives—for bonds, for scrap, for fats, for paper, for what-not—allotting millions of dollars' worth of space for these purposes without cost to the government.

All these are achievements deserving of praise; yet they are, after all, what might have been expected of the newspapers in wartime. Just as it was to be expected that they would cover, as they did, fully and competently, the stories of home-front activities—such as volunteer defense and Red Cross and recruitment and war work in general—and home-front concerns—such as wartime production and rationing and victory gardens.

But how about "trivialities," and how about controversial matters, and how about perspective? Let us start with the simpler items and proceed to the more complicated.

TRIVIA FOR THE GENERAL

If the reader were to run through the files of the war years he would find on the first pages many stories which he would assign to the category of "trivial" if they were stacked up against the war news. And from the global viewpoint they were undeniably inconsequential.

Notably there was the Lonergan case in the second year of the war—the case of that strange, perverted young man who was accused of the murder of his wife. Here was the story of one man and one woman—neither of them, weighed by standards of real importance, of any significance whatsoever—spotlighted at a time when millions were embattled in the four corners of the earth. No fewer than eighty-five accredited reporters attended the trial; all the wire services were represented and requests for press seats came from papers as distant as Australia.

Well, how about that one? the critic asks. And, to take them at random, how about the large news displays given to stories such as these:

In 1942: a fire in a Boston night club; the debate over gasoline rationing; the burning of the *Normandie*—these in 1942, a year which saw the American landing in Africa, the Battle of Stalingrad, and the fall of the Philippines.

Or in 1943: the Sir Harry Oakes murder case; a to-do over shoe rationing; the controversy over pay-as-you-go taxation—these in 1943, a year which saw the turn of the tide in Russia, the German withdrawal from North Africa, and the fall of Mussolini.

Or in 1944, the ban on horse racing; a circus fire in Hartford; the Montgomery Ward feud with the government—these in 1944, a year which saw the invasion of Normandy, the advent of the V-1 bomb, and the liberation of Paris.

How are all these to be explained?

The answer is that the folks at home, like the men at the front, wanted now and then to get away from the war. This does not mean that they were insensitive to the struggle and the sacrifice. It means that the home front is prone to its own brand of psychoneurosis and is likely now and then to indulge in an orgy of escapism. The Lonergan case was one such; the psychological thrillers in the movies another. It is true that some newspapers, taking undue advantage of the opportunity, played this kind of story to the last lurid adjective and the final breathless headline, but such excesses were always soon corrected by the war news.

With the end of the war and of the period of breath-taking

news, there is bound to be an overplay of this type of news. In England the trend has been very marked; murder stories and sex crimes have been played with all the type fonts and the headline fervor once reserved for the Drama of Dunkirk, the Battle of Britain, and the Invasion of Germany. We can expect something of the same here. But it is no serious matter; all it means is that the reader is getting what he wants or what the editor thinks he wants.

DICK TRACY, FLATTOP, ET AL.

Speaking still of "trivialities," there are the so-called "comics," an extremely important item in the newspaper inventory. (Note that in speaking of the comics the adjective is "so-called." The fact is that the "comics" are for the most part not funny; they are adventure yarns.) As an example of their selling power, it is reported that 60 per cent of the income of the Hearst newspaper organizations is derived from the sale of the comics. As proof of their influence, there is the case of a Dick Tracy character named Flattop who, killed by his artist creator, was the subject of obituary notice all over the country. Yes, the "comics" are taken seriously; they are surely a social phenomenon. They are covered fully in Mr. Caniff's chapter, so I shall have only a few things to say about them.

In the beginning they were really comic. When the first of the tribe made their appearance in the gay Nineties—the Yellow Kid and the Katzenjammers and Foxy Grandpa and later Alphonse and Gaston and Mutt and Jeff—they were designed strictly for laughs, direct from the midriff. But somewhere in the period between the wars and especially after the Great Depression of 1929 the new trend set in—adventure became the dominant theme. Maybe it was a reaction from unemployment and monotony and the drabness of life, but at any rate this was the time when Tracy and Terry and the Pirates and especially Superman were born.

With the war there was a swing away from the extravaganzas

of Superman—apparently on the proper theory that fiction could not compete with wartime fact—and the strips based at least partly on humor took on a new lease of life; in fact, such outstanding favorites as Li'l Abner and Blondie never did get really involved in the war. The syndicate editors report that "on the whole they found that readers preferred to keep the war on the front page and off the comic pages to which they turned apparently for escape."

But the thriller has lost none of its popularity and most of the rest of the strips depict the adventures of daily life in the same tug-at-the-heart, lump-in-the-throat manner as the soap operas played out on the radio for the sewing and sighing housewife.

Likewise, the war, except for such curtailments as were brought about by the newsprint shortage, had no revolutionary effects on other features. The gnu and wak continued to graze in the crossword pasture; advice was still offered to—and presumably acted upon by—the lovelorn; folks were still kept Emily Posted on their table manners and sidewalk salutes; the problems of problem children were set out for the puzzlement of problem parents; health hints, tasty tidbits, and kiddies' kracks could still be found in their accustomed places.

The only two innovations of note were an increased interest in astrological writing—doubtless a result of the war, with its suspense and its preoccupations with destiny; and a surprising nascence of features devoted to teen-agers—to be attributed presumably to the fact that this group assumed a much more important role in the social scheme, what with the male twenties away at the fronts and the female twenties occupied with homefront activities.

But otherwise life among the comics and the features went on as usual. Thus, for those who fear the coming of communism or the imminence of the Revolution, there must surely be comfort in the knowledge that the Gumps, Moon Mullins, Dorothy Dix, and Elsie Robinson are still doing duty at the old stands and, as it were, manning the ramparts of the Old Order.

In other words, "triviality" in the wartime newspaper meant for the most part "escape" or diversion and the trend is of no great importance. The more serious issue is again the question of slant; certain accusations on that score deserve special examination.

ROOSEVELT: PRO AND CON

The most widespread and the most heated of these charges is to this effect: that the press was unfair to Franklin Roosevelt and the New Deal, even though the people, as shown conclusively by their votes, were overwhelmingly for him. The critics charge that in matters of legislation and especially at election time, the news columns were distinctly angled against him. They cite instances such as these:

There was a persistent effort to identify the New Deal as a share-the-wealth movement and the New Dealers as economic crackpots.

There was in the 1944 campaign a series of articles written for a large newspaper chain and printed in the news columns which made a highly editorial effort to link New Dealism and Communism.

There was the tremendous whispering campaign about the President's health—a campaign which forced him to take unnecessary risks to prove that he was not critically ill.

There was the unusual play given to unfavorable news about any member of the Roosevelt family and especially the attacks on Mrs. Roosevelt as a radical.

Many of these accusations are true. Newspapers which for three years and eleven months preserve their objectivity and their perspective will every fourth November turn completely partisan and electioneer even on their first pages.

These tactics, the critics continue, get the newspapers no place and leave them with a considerable loss of face. They summon the statistics:

PERCENTAGES	1932	1936	1940	1944
Newspapers supporting Republican candidate	52.0%	57.1%	63.9%	60.1%
Newspapers supporting FDR	40.5	36.1	22.7	22.0
Popular vote for FDR	57.3	60.2	54.7	53.4

These are tough mathematics for most of the editors and their most constant readers. Many among us would have liked to have seen much more extensive newspaper support of the President and felt that personal, economic reasons dictated the editorial policies of too many publishers.

Yet the facts need careful analysis so that no false conclusions will be drawn from them. It must be kept in mind that "support" of a candidate means only that the newspaper has declared editorially—that is, on its editorial page—for that candidate. In some newspapers this preference colors the news columns, but in more cases it does not.

What is more important is this: that almost all newspapers, whether they were for Mr. Roosevelt or against him, printed his speeches and recorded his doings and goings in their news columns. And so Mr. Roosevelt was able to make his case despite the editorial pages.

In that connection there is a pertinent story—one that reveals, incidentally, Mr. Roosevelt's journalistic astuteness. The President was preparing an important economic address and ten days before its delivery he invited to the White House the editor of a leading newspaper which had editorially opposed his economic program. He told this editor that he wanted to explain fully to him the purposes of the speech, "not to influence editorial policy but to prevent misstatements."

But, on a previous visit, Mr. Roosevelt had remarked to this same editor that he was not bothered about the editorial page because he had it on good authority that not more than 10 per cent of the readers paid any attention to it. So when Mr. Roosevelt set out the reason for this second visit the editor recalled the remarks made during the first one and asked the President why, if the editorial page was so unimportant, Mr. Roosevelt was going to all this trouble to set it right.

"You see," replied Mr. Roosevelt, in effect, "even though your editorials are not read very widely on your editorial page, papers throughout the country reprint them in their news columns—and I don't want to miss those readers."

As to anti-Roosevelt slants in the news columns and on the editorial page, it must also be remembered that these same newspapers that opposed Mr. Roosevelt on their editorial pages printed syndicated columns by such writers as Walter Lippmann and Dorothy Thompson expressing vigorous support of the President.

HAS LABOR HAD A FAIR DEAL?

Another charge that has had a good deal of currency is this: that labor has not had a fair deal in the press and, in particular, that the strike situation has been overplayed. This accusation attracted a great deal of attention because the stories of strikes were communicated to the troops and aroused resentment and resolutions of protest among them. It is alleged that such stories spread the view here and abroad that labor had neglected its duty and that production had been seriously curtailed.

It is true that there has been a tendency on the part of anti-New Deal newspapers to play up labor difficulties and to create the impression that labor got all the possible breaks under Roosevelt. The Wagner Act, and its progeny, the War Labor Board, became in the war years almost symbolic of the struggle between New Dealers and Old. Some of this crept into the news displays: difficulties in administering the act were played up; the news of strikes was surely not underemphasized. When a coal walkout was threatened by John L. Lewis the news stories were almost editorial in tone.

There is only a partial answer to these accusations. The critic, in pointing out that the newspapers played up the fact that there were strikes and failed to report that these strikes affected only one-half of 1 per cent of the labor force, does not recognize that news, of necessity, is not the normal thing but the departure from the norm; that in everyday matters news is likely to be "bad" news. And in the case of the coal crisis, there was general indignation throughout the country. But the record in these instances is not easily defended.

Another case of this kind is the reporting of the Full Employment Bill. Concededly there is no issue more important for the country. Yet in two ways the over-all picture of newspaper coverage has been bad: first, the opponents of the measure have had, on the average, the break in news display—their statements have had fuller treatment and better position than those of the proponents; second, some newspapers have carried in their news columns signed articles attacking the bill—and even though the newspaper may say that the signers assume the responsibility, nevertheless the publication and surely the play are in the nature of endorsement.

The labor difficulties in Detroit that came to a head in September 1945 provide another enlightening case history in the same field. In announcing the demand for a 30 per cent increase, Walter Reuther, Vice-President of the United Automobile Workers, issued a statement justifying the demand on two main grounds: that it would help prevent depression; and that the companies could afford to pay it. Only the New York *Times,* of 28 papers surveyed, printed the statement in full. The Associated Press report did not include the second argument at all—and 16 of the 28 papers printed the A.P. story. It may be argued, of course, that space limitations made it impossible to carry the complete statement. But in the case of so important a story, more space might well have been given to the Reuther argument, primarily, for sound news reasons, and, secondarily, as refutation of any charge of anti-labor bias.

The newspapers, I feel, should scrupulously present both sides in labor disputes and give them equal emphasis. Any other course surely does not win friends and certainly does not influence people. But here again the critics take the wrong tack. They indict, and with justice, the slant against the bill—and at the same time make it abundantly clear that what they want is not an impartial presentation but a crusade for the measure in the news columns. And that, again, is no solution.

"FREE" PRESS OR "CONTROLLED" PRESS

One other accusation on the score of slant—and a most vehement one—is made in peacetime as well as in wartime. It was said earlier that American journalism enjoyed "freedom of the press." The critics retort that it is not really free—that it is controlled by capitalists leagued against collectivists, or by industrialists united against laborites, or, especially, by advertisers.

Immediately it should be said that if such controls exist, they are private usurpations that can be set down just as they were set up, not governmental seizures from which there is no appeal.

As to the charge that the publisher is likely to be a "capitalist" believing in the "free enterprise" system, the answer is: Why not? We are a capitalist democracy and the press is, on the whole, big business. So why should the critic expect that, on the editorial page, where the viewpoint of the publisher is revealed, any other than the capitalist philosophy should be expressed? If it were not, the accusation of dishonesty could certainly be made.

The charge that the advertiser is likely to dominate the newspaper is really old hat. The more advertising there is, the more likely it is that the newspaper is free of pressures. For if a newspaper has a large quantity and a great variety of advertising, then its advertisers are five hundred or a thousand persons, each with his own economic and political convictions and his own slants on the news, and thus one will cancel out another.

On the other hand, the newspaper without advertising, unless it is that extraordinary production that can make a living out of circulation, is likely to require a subsidy—and that subsidy is often the largess of one man. The dangers of this kind of situation were revealed strikingly in prewar France where the press was corrupt and poisonous.

IV—THE INFLUENCE OF THE NEWSPAPER

The war brought a great increase in instruments of communication, in number of publications, and in circulations. Radio came of age and took full advantage of its opportunity, both in news coverage and in feature treatment. Magazines of all types—and news magazines in particular—flourished. The newsreel and the documentary picture won new audiences. It was a period of intense interest in every field of the news, written, spoken, or photographed.

How did the newspaper fare amid all this competition? Did it lose or did it gain in influence?

By certain critics, the newspaper has been described as a dying institution, hanging on only with the aid of Dick Tracy, Orphan Annie, and others of the thriller tribe, until such time as facsimile or television or some other electronic device shall relegate it into some dusty corner of the Smithsonian Institution.

The mathematics do not bear out these prognosticators. In the war years, in spite of newsprint shortages and increases in price, daily newspaper circulations have risen steadily. Total daily circulation in 1941 was some 42 millions; in 1944 it was close to 46 millions. Sunday circulation in 1941 totaled about 33½ millions; in 1944 it was close to 38 millions. So there is still equity in the Fourth Estate.

There was in that period, however, a shrinkage in number of newspapers—a drop in daily newspapers from 1,857 to 1,744 and in Sunday newspapers from 510 to 481. That, too, is a Trend and, likewise, Viewed with Alarm by these same surveyors of the newspaper scene. What we are having, these critics say, is more and more canned stuff and less and less genuine local journalism reflecting the spirit and the needs of the community. They point with pride—and pride that is fully justified—to William Allen White and Henry Watterson and other Thunderers of the Hinterlands. There, they say, is what the country needs. And there is no denying it.

But what made the Emporia *Gazette* and the Louisville *Courier-Journal* was not the news, but the White and the Watterson touches. And for every White or Watterson there were fifty other editors without the White talent or the Watterson genius; so their papers had nothing in the way of editorial distinction and little in the way of news. Now these papers at least have access to the news of the world through the press associations, and to that extent they are better newspapers.

It is, on the whole, less biased news. The Associated Press serves approximately 1,250 newspapers (and as a result of the government's verdict over the AP, the number may be increased) and the United Press about 950. The press association, having a responsibility not toward one but toward some thousand newspapers, each with its own editorial view and each with its favorite aversions and diversions, is more likely to rule out slant.

It is possible, too, that a careful survey might reveal that the decline in the number of newspapers is due not so much to the expansion of the newspaper chains as to the fact that, with the intensification of the automobile age and the consequently greater radius of interest and operation, the area of newspaper circulation has been proportionately widened and so one newspaper is covering territory previously covered by two or even more.

Finally, one wonders whether local coverage was ever as sparkling as we think it was. The Good Old Days were once the Bad New Days—and so with the Good Old Institutions. With the broadening of reader interest and the widening of news coverage, a certain amount of general news, either national or international, has supplanted some of the local intelligence. All this is in the direction of One World, and so to be applauded.

ITEM NO. 1: THE NEWS

But the critic has another string to his bow. Even if all the above is true, he says, and the newspapers still have circulation, that is due to the comics, the cross-word puzzles, the bill-and-coo columns, and the features. The emphasis in the American newspaper, he asserts, has shifted from information to entertainment.

It is true that many newspapers depend for a good part of their circulation on features. But they do not neglect the news. Measure the news content of the most feature-minded of the newspapers with a similar journal of the prewar days and you will find that the news content of the former is considerably greater and considerably better. In other words, the feature—the comics, the columns, the etiquette and epigram departments—is still a plus element (even though a big one) and not the basic factor even in the most tabloid of the tabloids.

Evidence to that effect is supplied by a recent Roper survey. During the deliverers' strike in New York in July, 1945, this question was put to a cross-section of New Yorkers: "What two or three things in your newspapers have you missed the most?" The answers given most frequently were these:

	PER CENT		PER CENT
News (kind not specified)	31.5	Business and finance	6.2
War news, foreign news	26.5	Entertainment features—	
Comics	15.2	theatre, movies, radio,	
Editorials	14.2	etc.	5.7
Sports	12.0	Magazine section, feature	
Advertisements, sales	11.3	stories, etc.	3.7
Columns	8.7	Front page, headlines	3.4
Domestic news—local, political, government, etc.	7.4		

The appeal of the news, it seems, is twice as great as the appeal of the comics. We have not capitulated utterly to the bobby-soxers.

Additional proof of the importance of the news appeal to all newspapers is found in the fantastic bidding for the memoirs of the insiders in the European war—whether they be the oddments of a Mussolini or the remainders of a Goering. In this bidding the tabloids take part more energetically even than their full-size competitors. No, the Number One Item in the newspaper stock-room is not the comics—it is still the news.

THE MOLDERS OF OPINION

The editorial page is also the subject of much debate. Its power, it is said, is gone; the "leader" no longer leads and does not even follow, but is only a voice crying in a wilderness of words. The figures on the Roosevelt elections are always Exhibit A in any such argument.

Yet that influence is surely not as meager as the critics picture it to be. In the shaping of national thought about the urgency of our entrance into the war and the need of victory in the peace, the editorial pages have had considerable effect. There is un-doubtedly less thunder in the editorials of today than in those of Greeley's time, but there is likely to be more light. If their impact is not as great, it is largely because there are competing voices—namely, the editorial writers of the columns and of the air waves.

The columnist deserves special inspection. It has been said that he plays an important role in the education of the reader and in helping to bring about a balance in newspaper opinion. But do not get the idea that this is proof that the nation has gone pretty intellectual; fears of that kind are still premature. You get the true view if you look at the line-up of columnists:

Walter Winchell—800 papers, with a circulation in the twenty or thirty millions.

Drew Pearson—600 papers with a circulation of some ten millions.

Westbrook Pegler—between 175 and 200 papers, with a circu-lation of some ten millions.

Walter Lippmann—some 140 papers, with a circulation of approximately ten millions.

Dorothy Thompson—125 papers, with a circulation of about eight millions.

Two names are missing from the list. Ernie Pyle, at the time of his death, ranked second only to Winchell. At the start of the war he had 44 papers with a circulation of three millions, but when his last column was written he was serving almost 700 papers with a circulation of some fourteen millions. Raymond Clapper is the other. He had an audience of ten million readers in some 200 newspapers.

If, out of the list, you try to determine what makes a successful column, you will find yourself stumped. One columnist, you discover, combines gossip, news, and editorial comment in a mélange of 72-point excitement. Another has attained his reputation through awesome predictions and resounding scoops. Another is the intellectual, devoting himself solely to the interpretation of the news. And so on right down the line, through the 52nd Street Contingent and the Droll Fellows, to the Hollywood troupe, which has a credo and a grammar all its own.

Essentially, though, there are two types of columnist: the Gossip Gatherers and the Editorialists. At the moment the Gossip Gatherers seem to have the edge so far as circulation is concerned. But the Editorialists have no mean audiences of their own and are becoming more numerous and more influential in the shaping of public opinion, especially at election time. In a way their function is not greatly different from that of the editor of the old days, although their approach, even though it may be just as personal, is generally more thoughtful and less vitriolic.

YES, WE ARE STILL NEWS-WORTHY!

I had not thought of the news weekly as another one of these Mortal Threats to the newspaper until I read the chapter by Mr. Hodgins in this same volume. Mr. Hodgins seems to believe that the news weeklies, not the newspapers, did the real news job during the war; that they are, in peacetime as well as wartime, the only true expositors of the news because they excel (a) in coverage, due to their "huge" staffs, and (b) in perspective, because they do not have breathlessly to meet deadlines.

I shall not attempt, speaking of coverage, to compare the comprehensiveness and the authority of the news report in the newspaper with the condensation and the casualness of the news weekly. Nor to contrast the news weekly correspondent, hunting for dashes of color here and dots of information there, with the newspaper reporter seeking only the facts and unconcerned with "news-worthy items" or "time-worthy adjectives."

I shall not attempt, speaking of perspective, to compare the delectable details and the frothy footnotes that the news weeklies call "background" with the solid interpretive article of the newspaper. Nor to contrast the orderless presentation of the news weekly with the orderly arrangement of the newspaper—especially the play of the news on the first page, which is, in its way, an index to current history.

I shall not point out that the breathlessness of the newspaper is as nothing compared with the frenzy of the news weekly trying to guess on Monday what Thursday's news will be. Nor shall I, even though it is of vital concern, call attention to the slant which leaks, or is hosed, into the news columns of certain of the weeklies.

I shall not be so immodest as to call Mr. Hodgins' attention to such productions as the New York *Times Review of the Week* or the weekly summaries in other newspapers where the "background" job is done with balance and without bias.

No, I shall content myself with putting this question: Why, if the newspaper has so little value in Mr. Hodgins' eyes, why does Mr. Hodgins' *Time* buy from its news dealer every day 135 copies of the New York *Times*—every day, weekdays and Sundays? *

* I really don't know, Mr. Markel; I should think two copies would be plenty. But two copies of the *Times*, weekday and Sunday, are certainly invaluable, as are the copies of one hundred and sixty-three other U. S. news-

AND, OF COURSE, THE RADIO

Finally there is the radio, which, to hear these aforementioned critics tell it, is also doing the newspaper out of business. And the mathematicians among them cite the polls, disregarding the unscientific imponderables in "scientific sampling" (but that is another chapter, and a long one). They quote Dr. Gallup's figures to the effect that where a newspaper report does not agree with a radio broadcast 39 out of 100 quizzees are more likely to believe the radio and only 38 out of 100 the newspaper; and they quote Mr. Roper, who reports that, to the question "which do you think gives the more accurate news about the war," 41 per cent said radio and only 22 per cent said newspaper.

But the figures do not reveal how many pollees meant really to

---

papers to which the diligent editors of *Time* subscribe, and which they read, clip and file every day to supplement their own world-wide staff of news-gatherers and the full news and picture services of the AP. I am no more a traducer of newspapers than any of my colleagues; with them, I venerate the *Times* as I do my grandmother. As a matter of fact, your figure of one hundred thirty-five copies, daily and Sunday, is incorrect; it's actually one hundred fifty-one copies—plus ninety-one others for *Life* and *Fortune*. Accuracy, terseness, accuracy, Mr. Markel.

Your other points, I suppose, will have to go unanswered, since you say you are not making them. You certainly would have had me at a disadvantage about the *orderless presentation of the newsweekly* compared to the *orderly arrangement of the newspaper* if you had mentioned it out loud. *Time,* just to pick it at random as an example of a newsmagazine, doesn't put the story of the little girl who has lost her bunny on Page 1, where every newspaper man over fifty knows it belongs, alongside of MacArthur's latest orders to the Mikado, and the bit about the newest two-headed calf to be born in Winsted, Conn.—all of which have in common that they can be set on the linotype if the operator punches the right keys. And if you *had* been so immodest as to speak of the New York *Times Review of the Week,* I guess I would have had to be so immodest as to mention that *Time* began publication in 1923, whereas your invaluable summary, The News of the Week in Review, in 1935; in fact that many newspapers now publish weekly news reviews on Saturdays or Sundays, and that somehow the newspaper publishers began getting the idea from seven years to fourteen years after *Time* began.

Thank you for yielding the space on this page, which the publishers kindly lent me, because you saw the galley proofs of my article before I saw the galley proofs of yours. I hope I haven't distracted anybody's attention from your excellent piece; it's a little rough on the newspapers, but it's all worth saying.
                                                    —Eric Hodgins

say only that the radio news is later and therefore more likely to be correct. And the whole computation seems to mean little when you realize that most of the news broadcasts are based on the same news sources as those on which the newspapers rely—namely, the big press associations.

On the other hand, there is a statistic also contributed by Dr. Gallup. He asked: "When you hear news broadcast over the radio do you usually try to get more of the details from the newspaper?" To this query there were 77 per cent yes answers and only 23 per cent noes. And asked whether they read a daily newspaper regularly 79 per cent of those queried answered yes.

The radio has turned its attention diligently to its news assignment. For example, of the total broadcasting time on the National Broadcasting Company Network, only 3.6 per cent was devoted to news in 1939; in 1941 it was 10.5 per cent; in 1942, 15.4 per cent; in 1943, 19.6 per cent; and in 1944, 20.4 per cent.

Yet this is not enough for those seeking all the news. In the course of a survey made during the strike of deliverers in July, 1945, this question was put: "You are probably getting most of your news now from the radio. Is radio completely fulfilling your need for news?" The answers averaged 82.3 per cent in the negative and only 17.2 per cent in the affirmative.

On a single day during the strike more than 165,000 copies of the New York *Times* were sold over temporary counters set up at the *Times* Building; would-be purchasers formed queues five blocks long. Thus, in an amazing way, the importance and the meaning of the newspaper were demonstrated.

The radio has, of course, its great and its good uses. It reports with a speed no newspaper obviously can ever hope to achieve. Its spot broadcasts, as demonstrated during the war, have a vividness and a sense of immediate drama that few written reports can equal. But it cannot supply the full report, to be read when the reader wants to read it, and the perspective, without which news bulletins and headlines have little meaning. These are supplied only by the newspaper.

V — *THE FUTURE OF THE NEWSPAPER*

Yes, I believe that the newspaper has a future—a large future.

I do not believe that any mechanical device will put it out of business. Even in the Atomic Age, I am sure, people will still be reading, as well as talking and listening. Reading habits are strange and stubborn things and no political ukase or scientific contraption can change them perceptibly. People want their reading spread out before them for selection; and they want to set their own paces for perusal. So no televisionary ticker is likely to take the place of the newspaper.

Not that we have achieved the Perfect Gazette any more than we have attained the Perfect State. Many newspapers should carry more news; they should remember that they are primarily *news*papers and not magazines or cartoon anthologies. Bias is still found in considerable quantity; if we had a Pure Fact Law, there might well be a goodly number of indictments. Too many editors do not realize that a change has come in the world and that the old dogmas and the old formulas and the old headlines are gone with the Wind of Yesterday.

Yet the picture of the press during the war, despite the blurrings and the occasional distortions, reveals progress. More news, more news background, less bias—these are the measures of advance and these are the direction posts for the future.

The crusade against slanted news must be carried on, inside the newspaper profession and out. The remedy does not lie in suppression, for the pattern of censorship is too easily set and even more easily misapplied. No, the remedy lies with the reader; let him withdraw his support and the journalistic weeds will vanish.

The facts and the background, yes; but slant, never—even though it is the kind of slant we happen to like. That is a cardinal principle and now is the time for all good men, liberal as well as conservative, to come to its aid.

In various ways more background must be supplied through fuller and more expert reporting, through more articles of interpretation in the daily newspaper, through the presentation of both sides of an issue in the form of debates or editorial symposiums, through weekly reviews of the news.

The assignment of the newspaper in these days is greater than ever before; never has the news been so complex and the need of understanding it more urgent. Likewise the responsibility is great: to give the news, without fear and without favor; and to interpret the news, without distortion and without bias.

There are vast blanks in our national knowledge. It is reported, for example, that of the 138,100,000 estimated Americans, 138,000,000 have never read the Dumbarton Oaks plan and 100,000,000 have never read the Atlantic Charter.

The newspaper can help greatly to fill these gaps. It can supply the information to convince us that we cannot afford again to slip back into isolation and disaster; and that we must not revert to the dog-eat-dog days of economics.

The full report and the true perspective—these are the contributions of the real newspaper. Only if it provides these can the press do its part toward building an informed and effective public opinion—the kind of public opinion without which democracy cannot function. Therein lie the great challenge and the great opportunity.

II. THE RADIO

by *NORMAN CORWIN*

NORMAN CORWIN *had an antifascist grudge
long before things got to the shooting stage,
and his personal war via radio was the kind
which made Robert E. Sherwood say of him,
"The finest writer developed in radio in the
United States—which probably means the entire world . . . one of the most eloquent,
vigorous, and tireless exponents of the cause of
liberation."*

*Born in Boston 35 years ago, Corwin spent
twelve years as a newspaperman before breaking into network radio in 1938. From before
Pearl Harbor to V-J Day he devoted himself
almost exclusively to war radio, and his works
include such outstanding broadcasts as "We
Hold These Truths" (on the Bill of Rights),
the "This Is War!" series, and "On a Note of
Triumph." In 1942 he went to England for
CBS to write and produce "An American in
England" and returned to this country to continue pioneering in international-minded radio.*

THERE is a story in radio about a commercial producer who,
finding the Lord's Prayer in a script, wanted to rewrite it. He
felt it was slow. I happen to think the Lord's Prayer is pretty
good as it stands. But then, in American radio everybody is entitled to his own opinion. It's a free country.

You should bear in mind when you read this report that I am
prejudiced. I believe radio has a higher destiny than merely to
sell soup and soap. I think it's an art apart; a social force which

can figure vitally in the keeping of the peace and the making of a clean and orderly world. This point of view may have colored my opinion about what was transmitted while you were gone, so if you disagree with my basic approach you are entitled to discount any and all gripes and mutterings hereinafter contained.

First of all, let's face the fact that radio is no jerkwater business. There are still a few newspaper publishers and sterile intellectuals who, as we will see later, wishfully think broadcasting is a fad, like yo-yo or pogo, and that it will go away. It won't go away.

Radio is a great, sprawling industry which, unlike any other, reaches into the home day after day, hour after hour. It lives intimately with the listener, is at his bedside, in his kitchen, under his automobile dashboard, and as often as not is blaring from his neighbor's window. It is no exaggeration to say that a man could walk around any suburban block during an important Presidential address and hardly miss a word of the speech.

Naturally, any phenomenon so vast, so penetrating, so immediate, cannot mean the same thing to all people. Like the elephant described by blind men, this behemoth presents many faces, tails, tusks, and contradictory aspects: one to the housewife, another to the FCC Commissioner, a third to the salesman of radio time, still others to writers, actors, critics, management, labor, commercial agencies, and sustaining artists. It may be that the part of radio's anatomy which I describe as its big fat backside might to others seem its cherubic face. Don't think I haven't tried to be objective in these pages. But if I've failed, your only recourse is to sue me, and the courts are slow these days.

All right, so you've returned. It will be a while before you're really back in the swing, and feel like a veteran civilian, but you should have little trouble getting oriented to your radio. Whereas the movies have come up with new queens (including The Face and The Look and The Body) and baseball has developed new pitchers during your absence, the top programs and voices that were your radio favorites before you went to war are still around.

Comics who were getting laughs before Pearl Harbor are at the same old stand and so are some of their routines; quiz shows radiate fairly useless data to all I.Q. levels; detective dramas have mushroomed like mushrooms, and variety shows pursue the uneven ways of their tenors.

The top programs are mostly the sponsored ones and will be found, as usual, in the best commercial time, from seven to eleven in the evening. And, as usual, the sustaining shows * will be found scattered around in the less popular hours. There may be fewer sustainers now, but otherwise the picture is about the same as far as the programs and performers are concerned. In short, the radio industry's conversion to wartime operation caused only minor dislocations, and there was a revision upward in audience ratings.

Now hold on. This is not to say that radio did not make notable contributions to the prosecution of the war. It did. But on the other hand—as the cautious news analyst says—on the other hand, it may have overlooked certain obligations in the public interest. You can judge for yourself.

At the outset, radio's biggest organisms, the networks, were quick to respond to the government's call for "voluntary mobilization of the brains, the heart, courage, and experience of the radio industry toward winning the war." They soon packaged programs to give listeners a better idea of whom, where, why, and how you were fighting. News coverage was broadened to step up transmission of full information on war developments on all fronts, at all times. Sponsors bent their programs, in whole or in part, to the task. Some produced special shows on war topics; others integrated war themes into the plots of their regular programs, or provided time for government messages on rationing, food, gasoline, paper- and fat-conservation, price control, recruiting, bond and blood drives, V-mail. This was a free and voluntary service which, as it happens, did not greatly interfere

---

* Let's clear this up right now: By "sustaining" is meant unsponsored—selling nothing and bearing only the name of the radio organization which foots the bill for the production. The commercial, or sponsored program, advertises and promotes the sale of a product.

with the sponsor's schedule of commercial announcements. Wartime prosperity brought to radio a record income from advertisers, some of whom preferred to spend their money for air shows rather than have it go for taxes. Newsprint shortage and the subsequent reduction in advertising space contributed to the rush. Time was at a premium. Even symphony orchestras, never considered a top attraction in radio, had no trouble in finding sponsorship. There were not enough hours—good evening hours—to go around, and seekers of air time just had to wait their turn in line. Business, as any amateur economist could see, was good.

This was radio's golden period. It will interest your slide rule to know that in 1944, 836 stations reported a total broadcast income of $68,888,110, representing an increase of 125 per cent over 1942. The income for the average station rose from $36,488 in 1942 to $82,402 in 1944.

It is perhaps pertinent to ask what kinds of program the advertisers put their money into during the most critical period in the nation's history. Chiefly they chose detective-mystery dramas for escapist entertainment, comedy-variety shows for laughs, and news programs. These, at any rate, were the programs that grew most in popularity from Pearl Harbor to V-J Day.

In the detection department, radio's sleuths certainly knew there was a war on, although of course no situation was critical enough to shake their imperturbability. They put their techniques to work smashing wartime misdemeanors and crime. Enemy undercover agents were covered by "The Man from G-2"; black market racketeers trembled at the trilling of "The Whistler"; enemy bigwigs got theirs from "The Man Called X"; ration-coupon counterfeiters were foiled by "David Harding—Counterspy." True-story sleuthing turned out to be as gripping as the fictional kind in Jerry Devine's "FBI in Peace and War," a series based on actual FBI records of public enemies, and broadcast to show "just how these agents in the preservation of democracy really work."

In spite of their preoccupation with wartime problems, radio's detectives did not shirk a jewel robbery or a murder now and then. There were specialists to handle all types of crime, foreign and domestic, and this they did in their suave, unhurried, slightly bored manner.* In some programs laymen guests were given the privilege of solving a mystery; in others, the radio audience was invited to send in solutions. It was all very elementary, my dear Crossley.

In war as in peace, the biggest money was put into the comedy-variety program. Sheerly as a war measure, comedy was a good thing for the public morale and continued to draw the highest ratings via Crossley and Hooper analyses. Advertisers paid as much as $22,500 a week for comedy talent on a half-hour show to plug a brand of cigarettes you couldn't get at your drugstore for love or money, especially love.

Many comedy programs originated from army and navy bases, with the result that joke routines often touched on life in the service. This in itself was a fine thing for morale, considering it helped reduce tired gags on Bing Crosby's horses, Lamour's sarong, Bob Hope's yo-yo, Eddie Cantor's wife Ida, and the delicate state of Frank Sinatra's health.

Incidentally, it was Sinatra ("The Voice"), the frail crooner from New Jersey,† and not any news from the war fronts, who created the nearest thing to mass hysteria in the country—a phenomenon which I leave to psychiatrists and Sinatra's press agents to explain. Frankie was the particular idol of teen-agers, the bobby-soxers. They mobbed him in the streets. They sighed,

---

* Characters who made good escapist listening on the networks included Father Brown, The Saint, Bulldog Drummond, Private Detective Michael Shayne, Ellery Queen, Sherlock Holmes, Charlie Chan, Dick Tracy, Bill Lance, Hercule Poirot, Perry Mason, Philo Vance, and Casey, Crime Photographer. Funniest was the Thin Man (Nick Charles), who satirized the profession.

† There is a tendency among men who think themselves red-blooded to despise any idol—especially a crooner—who makes women's hearts beat wildly. But even the most rugged Sinatra-despiser had to admire the forthrightness with which he electioneered in the 1944 campaign. Except for Orson Welles, no radio performer was so effective a speaker for either candidate.

screamed, swooned wherever and whenever he sang. It seemed for a while that no comedy show in radio could be complete without a Sinatra gag. Example.

MAN: A voice like Sinatra's comes once in a lifetime.

CROSBY: Why does it have to come in my lifetime?

There was friendly scorn as well as corn in the repertoire of radio comedians, and the routine of ridiculing the star was always good for a laugh. Stooges kidded Bob Hope's chin, Jimmy Durante's nose, Jack Benny's pinch-penny habits, the bags under Fred Allen's eyes, Milton Berle's stolen jokes, Cantor's daughters, Crosby's twins, Edgar Bergen's shiny pate, and so on down the ratings.

The comedians could take it; and dish it out, too. When they toured military camps, they had no inhibitions about kidding G.I. regulations, officers, and brass hats. Many stories were told at the expense of young second lieutenants, and the G.I.'s roared. Crosby told this one:

2ND LIEUT: (Anxiously): Did General Eisenhower arrive yet?
SENTRY: No, sir.
2ND LIEUT: Well, let me know the instant he does.
SENTRY: Yessir.
2ND LIEUT: (10 minutes later): General Eisenhower here yet?
SENTRY: No, sir.
2ND LIEUT: (For the fifth time): General Eisenhower here yet? Let me know immediately.
SENTRY: (As jeep with five-star general approaches): Are you General Eisenhower, sir?
GENERAL EISENHOWER: I am.
SENTRY: Boy, are you going to catch hell. There's a second lieutenant here been looking for you for hours.

According to NBC, Edgar Bergen, with his precocious dummy Charlie McCarthy, was the first radio star to take his program from the studio to a military base. In March, 1942, four months after Pearl Harbor, Bergen and McCarthy broadcast their regular show from March Field, California. Seems that Charlie, who was already a master sergeant in the Air Corps, committed the indiscretion of accepting a commission in the Marines. At a later broadcast from Stockton Field, the blockhead was court-martialed, with no less than Jimmy Stewart acting as prosecutor.

Comedy shows were not all buffoonery and high jinks during the darkest days of war. Comedians gave curtain talks on their programs that were often eloquent and sincere. They discussed war subjects allocated by the Office of War Information, and spoke in their own or someone else's words, and what they said made good sense. Coming from a comedian, the serious approach was doubly impressive. Eddie Cantor explained:

... a serious note from a comedian today isn't as screwball as the sponsors or agencies or broadcasters at first thought. Today, every name comic has a serious note, whether it's for bonds or blood or conservation or tolerance or what. Perhaps the punch is heightened because of its very contrast.

Imagination and resourcefulness went into the integration of war "messages" on the better comedy programs. Perhaps the outstanding example was that of "Fibber McGee and Molly." Its writer, Don Quinn, successfully avoided the clichés which tempted so many other commercial programs. Instead of just tacking an OWI ukase on the end of his program, to be read by an announcer at record speed as though a government agent were holding a gun at his temple, Quinn managed to write *entire* programs on subjects ranging from the black market to the recruiting of Nurses' Aides. This combination of service and entertainment did not damage the popularity of the show, as may be gathered from the record of Fibber's consistently high ratings.

War indeed penetrated the comedy program. Top comedians were not content merely to entertain the home-front radio audience. With other stage, screen, and radio people, they toured the hospitals to entertain convalescent G.I.'s, and they crossed the oceans (some of them several times) to give laughs to you men in the Pacific, in Alaska, in Europe. Bob Hope, an indefatigable traveler, became practically an institution. Not only did his program set an all-time high in ratings for a continuing series,* but Hope's book, *I Never Left Home*, based on his camp tours, was a national best seller, and the comedian enjoyed the publicity, rare for a radio personality, of having his face on the cover of *Life*.

These were the times, too, when comedians began to reflect soberly on their medium, to evaluate it critically. Fred Allen, in a lower-case letter to the editor of *Variety*, wrote:

... a comedian who has had only radio knows only the reactions of transient mobs, who float from program to program posing as audiences, and tends to gear his antics and material down to the mental level of this moronic element, forgetting the millions of intelligent listeners in homes. Having had no contact with theater audiences in various parts of the country he has no knowledge of the type of matter that might appeal to a nation-wide group.

But there were problems in radio that were more serious, and they were beyond the control of the radio comedian. The comedy program had its place in wartime radio. There was need for it. But there was no less need that the public be kept fully informed on war issues. Comedy shows could not be expected to do the job. "Public service" programs—forums, round tables, discussions, dramatic documentaries—helped to clarify and crystallize issues in the minds of the people. But first people had to know what the issues were. And while the sponsored comedy shows invariably got the best evening time and were carried on full networks of one hundred and fifty or more stations, some of the unsponsored "think" programs were either dropped or relegated to unpopular listening hours. On the other hand, at least one big out-and-out "think" show ("Town Meeting of the Air") was sponsored, and as

---

* He never got much competition from Corwin, who was fated to be opposite Hope on three distinct series. At one time *Billboard* carried a headline to the effect that Corwin had cut into (or perhaps scratched would be a better term) Hope's ratings, but the ratio was constantly about forty to eight, and your writer seemed forever in the position of hoping against Hope.

a result gained many more stations and listeners than it had previously enjoyed.*

In 1944, a survey by Hadley Cantrell, director of Public Opinion Research of Princeton University, revealed that the majority of Americans never heard of or read the Atlantic Charter, or knew what a price subsidy was or how a peace treaty is approved. It was inevitable that accusing fingers be pointed at radio as well as the press, and the fingers were pointed by men as varied in political complexion as Senator Wheeler, FCC Chairman Paul Porter, and Niles Trammell, NBC president. In an address before a district meeting of the National Association of Broadcasters (NAB) in March, 1945, Porter said:

> Many influential broadcasters have expressed to me deep concern over what they themselves describe as an alarming trend toward excessive commercialism. Somehow there must be a determination as to whether broadcasting is simply going to operate as an advertising and entertainment media, or whether it will continue to perform in increasing measure public service functions in addition. I want broadcasters themselves to provide the answer to that question.

The answers varied with the opinions of individual broadcasters. FCC Commissioner Clifford J. Durr, in a speech (June 23, 1945) before the Conference of the Independent Citizens Committee of Arts, Sciences, and Professions, pointed out the "two basic philosophies" of radio; the first laid down by Herbert

---

* That is often the way with sponsorship. A company, out of an initial interest in selling cheese or jello, pays not only for its act, but rents, in a manner of speaking, the theater. In this way, the sponsoring angel guarantees a definite network to his show week after week. But sustaining programs must seek their fortunes on all save the few network stations which are *owned* outright (others are "affiliates") by the network. Most local outlets carry sustaining programs at their *option*—a situation which makes the local station operator almost an absolute censor over most of the unsponsored cultural importations via the network's telephone lines. In such a case a live symphony concert might be running into the local station's control board and expiring there, while the station itself was transmitting a local wrestling match. (If this footnote confuses you, write a letter of exactly fifty words explaining why. You will receive free our special gift offer of a miniature atomic bomb for the kiddies.)

Hoover (never known as a radical) when he was Secretary of Commerce:

The ether is a public medium, and its use must be for public benefit. . . . The dominant element for consideration in the radio field is, and always will be, the great body of the listening public, millions in number, country-wide in distribution.

The second philosophy, said Durr, was exemplified by a statement of the President of the NAB * at the end of 1944:

One must consider balance sheets to measure the progress of radio. For balance sheets represent an index to the medium's effectiveness. . . .
American radio today is the product of American business. It is just as much that kind of product as the vacuum [cleaner], the washing machine, the automobile, and the airplane. . . .
After twenty-five years, if the legend still persists that a radio station is some kind of an art center, a technical museum or a little piece of Hollywood transplanted strangely to your home town, then the first official act of the second quarter century should be to list it along with the local dairies, laundries, banks, restaurants, and filling stations as a member of the town's business family.

It was, and is, this stuffy kind of Babbitt who stands responsible for the dreadful mediocrity of so much of American radio. He invests in radio as he would in a laundry, dairy, or restaurant, and his product bears every mark of it. At least in the theater, a financial backer will take a chance. He will support a daring or unconventional play *because* it is fresh and different. A film studio will gamble millions on a picture. But there is little courage in radio, as practiced by the advertising agencies. The average sponsor and agency want to play it safe, very safe; so they borrow, imitate, plagiarize, and perpetuate formulas which have been tested and proven by others (sustainers, probably), and become fast slaves to the ratings. In such an atmosphere, originality and

---

* An association which represents about two-thirds of the broadcasting stations in the United States.

experimentation are not only unwelcome, they are firmly rejected.

Fortunately, washing-machine salesmen are not altogether running your radio system. There are men of open and vigorous mind who, while considerate of the virtue and desirability of healthy balance sheets, look to wider horizons. It was their courage and initiative which was responsible for the great things broadcast to America's rooftops during your absence . . . and there *were* some great things.

A far cry from the philosophy of the NAB president was that of another executive, William S. Paley, president of the Columbia Broadcasting System. In an address before the very same NAB on April 29, 1943, Paley said:

Elevating standards and striving for new fields to conquer must be the spirit of radio, if we are to take advantage of our great opportunities and discharge our great obligation to the American people. . . .

The lifeblood of American radio is an awareness on the part of the radio broadcaster that his first duty is to serve the best interests of the people and the nation. That awareness is a springboard for action and the action consists of programs designed to inform, to entertain, and to educate the people of this country. . . .

It is up to us now to concentrate on and to develop to its fullest possibilities the art of broadcasting. Our future freedom, our future rewards, our future satisfaction will depend on how well we do this. . . .

The eternal struggle between editorial content and the box office abated none during the war years; and radio, like newspapers, films, and other media, suffered before the influence of leaders like Paley and Trammell could be felt throughout the industry.

Just after Pearl Harbor there were instances of bad taste on the part of sponsors who tied up their copy with the war. One commercial went: "Here is a late important news bulletin: Use Smith Brothers Cough Drops." Another: "Use Gillette Blades which last longer, and thereby conserve steel for national defense." After news announcements of heavy fighting and casualties, one New York station permitted commercials advertising a funeral parlor and cemetery. "You never know when to expect bad news," said the announcer, "so be prepared. Buy a family lot."

These violations of good taste were eventually corrected. One network cut down on long commercials on news programs and insisted that the advertising be clearly distinguished from news content. Restrictions were placed on commercials attempting to capitalize on the war. Some stations took steps to reduce or eliminate the singing commercial * and the middle commercial. Spot announcements using gunfire, airplane motors, and the hooting of a destroyer to advertise Pall Mall cigarettes were banned by one network because the effects too closely approximated the real thing. These are instances of radio's efforts at self-regulation, at putting its own house in order.

Not even the most hostile critic will deny that radio performed an important war service in bringing to the listening public war

---

* These got to be radio's biggest pain in the ear. They were probably inspired by Western Union's singing telegrams, but however they originated, suffering listeners were impatient to hear the last of them. A superior example was the commercial for the Prince George Hotel in New York, sung daily over Station WJZ in the early morning hours. Playwright-producer Russel Crouse, a connoisseur of the singing commercial, entertained his friends with a rendition of this one. The words went:

The Prince George Hotel
Is a friendly hotel
Won't you stay there when you are around?
The Prince George Hotel
Where the service is swell
When you slumber, there's hardly a sound.
And should you want to play, forget your cares,
The Prince George Hotel is just a couple of minutes from everywheres.
Convenient, it's great,
Fourteen East 28,
New York City.
It's a pity
If you pass us by.
With a thousand rooms to choose from,
Won't you try?
You can never get the blues from
The friendly Prince George Hotel.

This commercial mentioned the Prince George Hotel only four times, thus was somewhat on the conservative side.

news promptly, effectively, and conscientiously. From the pre-
Munich days through the third V-J Day there was the greatest
concentration of highly dramatic news in all history, and radio
lost little of that drama and less time in transmitting the news to
the public. In periods of crisis, commercials were interrupted for
bulletins or canceled entirely to make way for special pickups
here and abroad. Key stations remained on the air all night to
accommodate possible sensational developments, and they presented news summaries on the hour, filling the interims with
music for every taste.

The rise of the news program as a popular feature was distinctly a wartime phenomenon. On NBC, 1944 news programs
accounted for more than five times as many network hours as
were used in 1939. CBS estimates that war news programs made
up 38.7 per cent of the network's total war program hours from
Pearl Harbor to V-E Day. The news program became so popular
that it was broadcast in many instances under the joint sponsorship of several advertisers.

Unquestionably the most spectacular news coverage of the war
was furnished by radio's reporters on the fighting fronts. They
experienced the same hardships and faced the same risks as the
flier and the foot soldier. The radio reporter's news coverage was
brilliant, and often as dramatic as the news itself. Examples:

George Hicks, broadcasting from an American warship under
heavy fire, gave an eye-witness account of the invasion of Western Europe. The farmer in Iowa, the housewife in California, the
schoolboy in New York, could feel the impact of battle thousands
of miles from home as Hicks began, "The platform on which I
am standing is vibrating to the concussion of the guns and the
exploding shells. . . ." His was the first on-the-spot account of
the Allied landings.

Edward R. Murrow made the first broadcast by an American
correspondent direct from a bomber on a mission over the Continent and gave listeners a vivid description of the bombing of
Berlin. In England, Murrow, with Robert Trout and others,

brought to American listeners what the British felicitously call "actuality" broadcasts from London's pubs, factories, and bomb shelters.

Larry Tighe, flying in a B-29, was the first radio reporter to cover an actual Pacific invasion from the air.* He described the first landings on Okinawa against a background of machine-gun fire as his plane beat off an attack by a Jap Zero. The broadcast was picked up and amplified at the navy radio station on Guam for instantaneous relay to America, more than eight thousand miles away.

Cecil Brown, who survived the sinking of the British battleship *Repulse* and was bombed on the Burma Road, told of his experiences in a series of remarkable broadcasts.

Richard Hottelet parachuted from a burning Flying Fortress over Germany, flew back a few hours later to a transmitter, and told his story while it was still hot.

Eric Sevareid bailed out from a transport plane over the Burmese jungle and later, after reaching what we loosely call civilization, related his experience to millions of American listeners.

William L. Shirer, who made some memorable broadcasts from Prague and Berlin before our entry into the war, was on the scene at Compiègne, France, when Hitler handed his armistice terms to France.

You get the idea. Radio covered the waterfront, and then some. And while its correspondents were risking their necks in the field, analysts and commentators were editorializing back home. The complexities of international life had grown so vast from Munich onward, that listeners looked more and more to analysts to make sense out of it all. Few analysts did, but most rated an E for Effort. Their number increased tenfold, and they ranged in political outlook from extreme reactionary to independent liberal.

By and large, American commentators enjoyed a freedom of

* Earlier, Murrow had covered the air-borne invasion of Holland, speaking into a wire recorder which was then flown back to London and reproduced for American transmission.

expression to be found in no other country in the world. Commentators so minded attacked our commander in chief, our British and Russian allies, the big conferences, the Administration, our conduct of the war. Some consistently followed a disruptionist line which could hardly be distinguished from the Berlin radio— or from the Chicago *Tribune*. When they got *too* bad, of course, public opinion forced them off the air. One of the worst reactionaries, Upton Close, was invited to scram by the American Network. The patriotic and outspoken *Variety* delivered a swift kick in the pants to solemnize his exit. In a trenchant piece headlined "A Healthy Departure," *Variety* paralleled Close and Father Coughlin, a prewar fascist commentator who was likewise shown the door. "Both men," said the editorial, "were sources of dissension, embarrassment and potential trouble to radio, and their departure is a healthy development for the industry. Indeed, it seems fair to suggest that Close's loss (like Father Coughlin's), is America's gain."

The Presidential campaign of 1944 gave radio its hottest months. In the fury of battle some commentators, making no pretense of objective reporting, aired biased and even irresponsible judgments. People tuning in to programs listed as "news" in their radio logs, heard instead partisan and prejudiced commentaries on candidates and campaign issues. H. V. Kaltenborn, Fulton Lewis, Upton Close, Boake Carter, Lowell Thomas, Earl Godwin, and others who shared their political slant were generally bitterly hostile to the Administration, to labor, to New Deal legislation, to Russia, sometimes to Britain, and almost always to the acts and accomplishments of the Big Three parleys. Offsetting the influence of these commentators were such voices as Walter Winchell, Johannes Steel, William S. Gailmor, Shirer, Murrow, Brown, Ned Calmer, John B. Hughes, Drew Pearson, Chet Huntley, Raymond Swing, Sam Balter. They took almost diametrically opposite points of view, and neither side hesitated to larrup the other.

Even before the candidates for the 1944 race were nominated, radio analysts covering the conventions were taking sides. Commentators who gave circulation to unsubstantiated reports that Sidney Hillman was dictating to the Democratic National Committee, that the Democrats were under the spell of communists, etc., turned out to be the same commentators who later were to root for the failure of the San Francisco Conference.

It was natural that radio should be the greatest arena of political battle in the Presidential campaign. The Gallup, *Fortune,* and other polls of candidates swayed after each broadcast, and once again the press took a back seat as the campaign was slugged out.

I think it only fair to notify you voters that I was wholeheartedly pro-Administration and personally involved in the campaign, before here declaring my conviction that the kind of radio strategy conducted by the Republican National Committee, under Herbert Brownell, was mean and dangerous. The Republicans used as their campaign slogan the phrase, "Clear everything with Sidney," putting it in spot announcements broadcast throughout the country to give the electorate the impression that President Roosevelt, running for re-election, was clearing, and would continue to clear, matters of state with Sidney Hillman, chairman of the Political Action Committee (PAC). Arthur Krock, of the New York *Times,* who reported that the President used this expression when the choice of a running mate for the fourth term was under consideration, publicly denied it had any significance beyond that. In spite of this, the Republicans continued to plug the canard, with anti-Semitic overtones, adding that *their* candidate, if elected, would clear everything with Congress, with the people.

I became so alarmed at the striking resemblance of this and other cynical techniques to Axis propaganda methods that when the Democratic National Committee approached me to write and produce the culminating broadcast of the campaign, I accepted with little hesitation. The form, substance, and merit of that program I leave to the estimation of others, but it is safe to say that Democrats generally loved it and Brownell-type Republicans loathed it.

An old campaigner who worked for the radio division of the Republican National Committee estimated that the broadcast set radio back ten years, but at Democratic headquarters it was considered a revolutionary departure in concept which could not fail to liberalize radio's policy toward campaign broadcasting in the future.*

A subject of keen controversy in the election was the activity of the PAC. It invaded radio with a vigorous campaign, including a Radio Handbook designed "to explain to the people their rights to radio time and how to secure and make effective use of that time." It put a staff of monitors to work for a seven week period just before the election "to see what the commentators and analysts were saying about labor and to determine whether radio was living up to its obligation to present a fair balance of viewpoints on important issues." The survey claimed that for every favorable item broadcast on labor, there were six unfavorable ones. It may be that PAC's activities influenced radio to give more time to labor. At any rate, following the elections three of the four major chains gave labor coast-to-coast programs where only one network had carried a labor program before.

The shortcomings of radio during war, such as an unbalance in points of view, overcommercialization, a neglectful attitude toward public service programs and so on, began at last to be adjusted through radio's own conscience and experience and the

* Democratic National Committeemen in Washington credited the broadcast with affecting upwards of two million votes.

The program, an hour in length, consisted of statements by plain people from all walks of life, each telling why he was voting for Roosevelt. Picture stars and celebrities of the arts and sciences were also on the program but only as background to the unknowns. The use of satirical songs, like "Gotta Get Out and Vote," "Don't Look Now, Mr. Dewey, but Your Record Is Showing," and "The Dear Old Days" (of Republican misrule), and the integration of music in a roll call of celebrities were innovations in radio campaigning, though they remained well within the continuing network strictures against "dramatizing" any political issue. The President himself was introduced by an eighteen-year-old Georgia girl who was casting her first vote for him.—EDITOR'S NOTE.

impact of public opinion. What must not be overlooked in any reckoning is the fact that World War II was radio's first war. Broadcasting was born in 1920 and reached its voting age in 1941, the year President Roosevelt asked for a declaration of war against Japan. Radio had no wartime precedents or experiences to guide it. In World War I, radio meant wireless telegraphy. By 1939 the infant industry found itself with the muscles of a giant, a powerful weapon of war confronted with its most important challenge. All of the important crises leading up to the situation which sent you to war were the first radio had encountered. The death of Franklin Delano Roosevelt was the first loss of a transcendentally great American in radio's life. D-Day, V-E Day, V-J Day, were other such momentous occasions, and all firsts. As a young industry untested by war, American radio came through in the pinch, and had many accomplishments to which it could point with pride. Such as these:

Many stations early in the war operated on a 24-hour schedule to serve as monitors for the Army Fighter Command, as part of the air radio defense system.

The four major networks donated time and costs for the broadcast of a wartime morale series, "This Is War," carried simultaneously by about 550 stations.

Short-wave listening posts were established to monitor enemy propaganda.

Superpowered short-wave transmitters beamed broadcasts to enemy countries.

Special programs were transmitted south and east to create good will and understanding among the Americas and between us and our European allies.

Home-front programs gave Americans an insight into the problems of rehabilitation and readjustment of the returning G.I.

Microphones were taken into submarines and fighting planes, war plants and aircraft carriers, to give the people word- and sound-pictures of the weapons their War Bonds made possible.

Aired over the networks were many hard-hitting social-minded programs, including William N. Robson's "Open Letter" on CBS, after the Detroit race riots; Jerry Devine's "Mr. District Attorney," promoting unity; NBC's "Words at War"; Mutual's "This Is the Enemy"; Ranald MacDougall's "The Man Behind the Gun," and the tough-minded, and often macabre plays of Arch Oboler.

Documentary radio made great strides in spite of the fact that sustaining programs were produced less frequently than before the war. Columbia's famed "Workshop," first and best of the experimental series, expired early in 1942, largely because of insufficient material from new writers. No out-and-out experimental series took its place in this country, although late in the war Canada enjoyed programs of Workshop caliber by the Canadian Broadcasting Corporation's Fletcher Markle and Andrew Allen.

But a new kind of documentary developed with the rise of world-consciousness, of global concepts, of the fact and spirit of the United Nations. CBS led the way in the international field, with programs called "An American in Russia" (Larry LeSueur on his war years in Moscow and Kuibyshev), "Hello, America" (Pan-Americana), "Transatlantic Call" (an exchange series alternating between originations in Britain and the United States); "An American in England" (produced by myself in London for short-wave transmission, and broadcast simultaneously by CBS); "Passport for Adams" (a quasi documentary using fictional characters but real-life situations and authentic foreign detail); William K. Clarke's "Promise Us the Dead," which ran into censorship trouble and folded.

Radio units of the armed forces themselves did great work with programs such as the "Army Hour" and "Assignment Home." Many army and navy installations maintained radio production units corresponding to camp and ship newspapers, and their product was given free time on local and network stations. The biggest of the Army's wartime radio agencies was the Armed Forces Radio Service, which had almost 500 outlets all over the world. Its studios in Hollywood poured out 50,000 transcriptions monthly, and these were distributed from the Aleutians to India.

The disks helped to keep men who were overseas in touch with home by bringing them their favorite programs as well as an additional diet of strictly service shows. Domestic radio made a singularly unselfish contribution by permitting a wealth of program material to be exported by AFRS without commercial advertising or royalties of any kind.

Of course broadcast material going to troops overseas came under various types of censorship, including political. On this latter score there seemed to be no consistent policy pursued by the War Department. On the one hand, the Army's School for Special Services, in Lexington, Virginia, encouraged material like the tough-minded radio play, *Untitled* (CBS, April, 1944; printed in *Coronet,* November, 1944), and staged it at a number of national conferences of Special Service officers; but the AFRS did not clear it for overseas reproduction. Nor did they clear *On a Note of Triumph,* or a synthesis of the works of Carl Sandburg—among examples of censorship that I know about. The personal opinions of key officers, with respect to labor and some of our allies, were apparently exercised in the censoring of outgoing material, and it was felt by a number of critics that insufficient emphasis was being placed by the AFRS upon antifascist orientation of troops. This sort of orientation was the special province of documentary radio, and by an unfortunate paradox the best of such material (including the more powerful of the "Words at War" shows) was never made available to you men overseas.

There were civilian and domestic censorship troubles, too. Walter Winchell, who fought an immense war against fascism at home and in our State Department, was always running into somebody's blue pencil. Usually that of some clerk in the Blue network, when it was still the Blue. There would be some objection to his calling a rat a rat, and Winchell would turn the deleted portions of his text over to the newspaper *PM* and/or the New York *Post,* or would run it in his own column.

For a while the OWI, under Elmer Davis and a hybrid group of dollar-a-year-men, former time salesmen, copy-writers, and account executives, had a puzzling radio policy. Seems there was some division of opinion as to whether one should use the term "fascist" loudly and publicly. One of the more celebrated rumpuses was set off when an overseas broadcast, beamed by the OWI's short-wave division to Italy, quoted Samuel Grafton's allusion to King Victor Emmanuel as an idiot (which he is). Followed a great uproar. Men were bounced from their jobs. There was a split between the Davis camp in Washington and the Joseph Barnes (OWI short-wave) wing which operated in New York. Davis won.

And then, around the time of the 1944 elections, Cecil B. DeMille, an old union-hater, screamed bloody murder because the radio actor's union (AFRA), to which he belonged, assessed each member one dollar in order to fight a vicious referendum in the state of California. This (the notorious Referendum No. 12) would in effect have wiped out most unions. DeMille wouldn't pay his buck. The union, which for years had had a closed-shop agreement with the networks, enjoined him from appearing on the air. And, as DeMille was emcee of the popular Lux Radio Theater, this turned out to be quite a dislocation. He took to the air (on the March of Time program) to state his case, and was answered a week later by Edward Arnold, speaking for the union. At this writing, DeMille and AFRA had not yet made it up, the referendum was dead, and Lux Theater's rating was undamaged.

Yet all in all, there was little censorship. These examples were conspicuous, of course, and controverted. What didn't make the news were the many uncensored and hard-punching documentaries produced by both commercial and sustaining radio.

Three of the most ambitious one-time documentaries ever undertaken were Columbia's round-the-country *Bond Show* in 1944, its round-the-world *Word from the People,* on the eve of the opening of the San Francisco Conference, and, a few weeks later, *On a Note of Triumph,* celebrating V-E Day. All this, together with the forenamed international series, represented only part of the documentary output of only one network. The other systems, though somewhat less active in this sphere, were nevertheless busy with documentary pursuits, and all came at length to regard the one-time superbroadcast on social themes or war issues as their highest home-built offering. The American (née Blue) Network, in its first such enterprise (June, 1945), broadcast an hour's program on the theme of freedom of expression.

The greatest broadcasts of the entire war came, of course, out of real life, current history, death. Its most tragic news was that of the loss of America's commander in chief on the threshold of victory in Europe. The death of President Franklin D. Roosevelt * was broadcast to the nation one minute after it was announced at the White House on April 12, 1945. The networks, unlike newspapers, canceled commercial advertising for three whole days. Radio brought to the nation the sorrowful progress of the funeral train from Warm Springs to Washington, D. C., and a description of the rites in the Capitol and at Hyde Park. Radio's necessarily impromptu performance during this period was little short of phenomenal, and even the usually grudging press was outspoken in editorial commendation of radio's dignified and sincere treatment of the tragedy. As it happened, one of radio's own creations took on special meaning in this hour, and was widely broadcast during the period of mourning. It was "The Lonesome Train," a musical legend of the progress of Lincoln's funeral train, written by Millard Lampell with music by Earl Robinson. It had been produced less than a year earlier, and recorded commercially—a fact which enabled it to be replayed by independent stations during the sad days of the funeral procession.

Together with the rise of the documentary form, radio during

* Roosevelt had recognized the importance of radio in keeping people informed, and he was the first President to insist that radio correspondents be permitted to attend White House press conferences. "We pay tribute," said Chester J. LaRoche, former v. p. of the American Broadcasting Company, "to the enormous contribution President Roosevelt made to radio as a means of communication. More, perhaps, than any other American, he demonstrated how it could be used to draw government and the people closer together, and to create an aware and informed public opinion."

the war years developed as an art form and a medium of entertainment worthy of criticism. The best prose in the field came from John K. Hutchens while he was radio editor of the New York *Times*. Hutchens gave the industry its first mature criticism outside of the trade publications. His brilliance was especially conspicuous in that he succeeded two editors who had science fixations. They were forever writing long Sunday columns about a television that nobody could yet see, and which was still years away. Hutchens in 1943 was removed to another department of the *Times*, and it was a great loss to a medium whose competent critics could be counted on one-and-three-fifths hands. He was replaced by Jack Gould, a younger and less sensitive writer, but a man with honest judgment and a growing perspicacity.

Time and *Newsweek*, among the big-circulation magazines, developed radio departments, and these were well written, spicy, resourceful and slanted. Both criticized boldly and generally soundly, although their straight reporting suffered intermittently from a tendency to be inaccurate—a common enough failing among us mortals, but in *Time's* case the inaccuracy was often at somebody's expense. The policy of anonymity common to the criticism of both magazines encouraged a kind of bumptiousness which radio had not encountered up to then, and a turnover in editors would occasionally produce startling changes in attitude. John T. McManus, later movie editor for *PM*, and Williston Rich, still at *Time* in another capacity, were Luce's best radio critics.

Variety's criticism was the most consistent, comprehensive and penetrating of all, the tradition established by Robert J. Landry (later of CBS) being carried forward by George Rosen and his staff. Others of first rank were Lou Frankel, who passionately fought for progressive and better radio in his columns in *Billboard*; Leonard Carleton, while radio editor of the New York *Post*; Ben Gross and his desk-mates of the New York *Daily News*; Betty Burns of the Chicago *Sun*, Harriet Van Horne, a bright and provocative voice in the New York *World-Telegram*; Arnold

Blom, Jerry Franken and Edwin Levin of *PM;* Paul K. Damai of the Hammond (Ind.) *Times.*

Cities other than New York developed a certain amount of responsible radio criticism during the war, but there remained many deserts like Los Angeles, where the only daily column of radio comment was an advertisement, and so labeled. In southern California one needed powers of divination to find out when a program was on the air, and it was impossible to learn in advance anything of the nature of that program. Though most of this attitude was dictated by the old-fashioned notion on the part of publishers that radio was an upstart and a temporary advertising competitor which could be discouraged or injured by being ignored, there was also the element of contempt. It is true that radio's lesser product is, if anything, below contempt; but so is that of the stage, screen, press, and the world beyond the compounds of "entertainment." There has never been any justification for the static snobbishness of periodicals which undertake to criticize all the media save radio. A good example was the *New Yorker,* which during the war maintained departments on the film, stage, horse racing, shopping, ballet, art, music, and books, but none on radio.

As radio began to sense its artistic potential, its efforts attracted serious criticism from other, recognized fields. Thus, NBC's Toscanini concerts, which were produced not in a concert hall, but in a radio studio, drew the same respectful criticism from Olin Downes and the New York *Times* as did Carnegie Hall symphonic performances. Published radio writings were reviewed by the leading critics, and the *Saturday Review of Literature* more than once gave its front cover to works from this allegedly primitive literary medium. The *Theatre Arts Monthly* was quick to accept radio drama as a sister among the arts, with full voting rights and page space for good scripts.

Now and then an intellectual who confined his radio listening almost exclusively to news bulletins honored some big broadcast by lending it his ear. The more successful the broadcast, the more infuriated these people became. Archibald MacLeish's pioneering verse dramas drew sniggers from fancy critics who felt he had betrayed his literary class by condescending to this gauche new medium. They bragged about never listening to the radio, one of the best ways of guaranteeing ignorance on the subject. Automatically they sprang into grotesque postures every time they attempted to criticize it.

Such critics were described by Christopher Morley as "imitation sensitives who can't see a whole new art in birth under their eyes." *

Magazines like *Harper's* and the *Atlantic Monthly* now and then opened their columns to solemn accounts of the decay of the American people as induced by radio. The writers in most cases behaved as though they were discovering something. All this was dreadfully easy, for radio is a fat sitting target, no harder to hit than a hangar door at twenty paces. This sort of criticism was as helpful as it would be if a professor of drama at Yale suddenly announced with alarm that Broadway turns out more flops than hits, that burlesque is on the vulgar side, and that a great deal of money has been made from enterprises like *Abie's Irish Rose.*

Criticism can be astringent and salutary, and radio is in dire need of more and tougher and sounder comment. But radio's severest critics may turn out to be the men who are returning from the battlefronts. War has certainly sharpened their sense of values. They speak up and talk back. The magnificent outspokenness of such G.I. publications as *Stars and Stripes* and *Yank*, the trenchant and penetrating criticism of a Bill Mauldin, have had no small effect on the soldier. The news stories trickling in from the European theater indicated that American boys could say sharp and incisive things to a Gertrude Stein or a Leni Riefenstahl, or to a delegation of congressmen touring the front lines.

America faces serious postwar problems, and the G.I. will want

* Letter to the author, October, 1945.

to be in on them. He has heard some of our programs broadcast overseas without benefit of overbearing or singing commercials, and he may have liked the sound. He may want radio at home to bring him sober consideration of social, economic, and political issues at hours when it is convenient to listen, and not always through the courtesy of a soap concern, a magazine publisher, or an automotive magnate. He will grant commentators and others the right to speak their mind, but not the right to abuse the privilege by inciting masses of listeners to prejudice and intolerance through innuendo and misrepresentation of facts.

When men return home after long absence, they see things they never noticed before. They may discover certain shortcomings about the state of radio in their home towns. They may not like the idea that local stations devote most of their time to transcriptions, leaving little room for creative programs in the community interest. Many local radio stations no more serve in the community interest than a newspaper which prints almost exclusively the canned copy received from syndicates in New York and Cleveland.

The level of local programs can be raised with small effort or expense. Writers are the most important single ingredient in radio programs. Yet in 1944, 747 full-time stations in the country employed fewer than 600 writers, or eight-tenths of a writer apiece, and their average wage was about $40 a week—about half of the salary paid to salesmen of spot announcements.

But increasingly, during the latter part of the war, enterprising station managers demonstrated that the local program can be more than a stereotype; that it can bring to light new talent, fresh and original ideas, and a new concept in public service programming. A program such as that developed by WHAS in Louisville, entitled "Wake Up, Kentucky," suggested what could be done at the local level. *Variety*, reviewing the program, said, "It makes a potent case for bringing wrongs and inequalities to the surface, thus throwing the strong light of frankness and truth into dark places, which have retarded the state's progress in

many ways." Station WTAG in Worcester, Mass., blazed a path
with a program called "Worcester and the World," in which it organized and led the entire city through weekly activities honor-
ing our allies and contributing to the understanding and awareness of the meaning of the United Nations. Station WMCA in
New York won a national award for "New World A-Comin'," a
series treating frankly of the Negro (or white?) problem.

In motion pictures during the war, a group of high-strung
Nervous Nellies known as the Motion Picture Alliance for the
Preservation of American Ideals organized to combat the tendency of the medium to grow up and think like a big boy. Its creed
was Entertainment, and to hell with the big, bad world. Though
radio suffered no such formal disgrace, it was nevertheless the
chronic victim of a correspondingly jittery neutrality—a sort of
sexlessness. Before Pearl Harbor only the brave among radio
broadcasters suggested that fascism was an ugly business. The
late Alexander Woollcott broke with a sponsor over the issue of
whether Hitler and Mussolini could be spoken of with disparage-
ment. Always there was the fear of "offending." On this score
Commissioner Durr made some sharp comment:

Never to offend anyone may be good salesmanship. But is it
good radio? Is it good sense in times such as these in which we
are living? The best in literature and drama, and even art and
music has offended. Milton offended in his time. So did Shakespeare and Victor Hugo . . . and even Galileo, in theirs—but their
works have survived long after even the names of those whom
they offended were forgotten. Tom Paine and Sam Adams and
Jefferson and Hamilton and Madison and many others whose
names we honor today did a lot of offending prejudices and vani-
ties and fixed habits of thought. Out of their courage to offend came
a Declaration of Independence and a Constitution and a Bill of
Rights. . .

They say we must have a competitive radio. I agree. Let us
have a radio that is competitive for listeners as well as for advertising accounts; that competes for the quality and sincerity of
programs as well as for listener ratings; that competes for the
privilege of using the people's frequencies in the best interests of

the people and on the basis of public service promised and rendered. . . .

Radio, most radiomen agree, is a vast and growing industry which cannot but play an increasingly important role in the social and political life of the nation. There are sufficient forces for good within its ranks to guarantee that it will not get much worse before it gets better, and when it gets better it may well climb to a position of highest eminence among the cultural media of the world.

Steps were taken in 1944, by a group representing many walks of radio, to inaugurate an Academy of Arts, Sciences, and Professions. One of the principal aims is "the facilitation of closer collaboration among all branches of the broadcasting industry for cultural, educational, and technological progress." The blueprints called for a permanent archive of recordings of the best work done here and abroad, an expanding library of technical, historical, and critical literature, a bureau of international liaison, a yearbook of radio's public services, a research division, a system of awards, and such publications as a talent directory, a news-letter for its membership, and a periodical for public circulation. At the time of this writing, stations, networks, agencies, guilds, and unions were pretty much for it, but the washing-machine wing of the NAB, which apparently is the majority, voted to reject participation. Instead of injuring the Academy idea, the NAB's action will probably end up by killing the NAB.

An academy, while still far off and faced by complex and difficult obstacles, will eventually be realized; and when it is, it will be one of the signs by which we shall recognize the full maturity of the medium. Meanwhile, the ether of this land will continue to crackle with programs which are at once the best and worst, the most restricted and the freest, the most venal and altruistic, in the world. That's America, boys. Melting pot.

III. THE MAGAZINES

by *ERIC HODGINS*

ERIC HODGINS *(age 46) is a Vice-President of* Time, Inc. *He has been successively, and successfully, within eighteen years, Managing Editor of* The Youth's Companion, *Promotion Manager of the McCall Company publications, Associate Editor of* Redbook, *and Publisher of* Fortune.

EVEN before the war began there was nothing else in the world that resembled the family, the system, the network, the aggregation of U. S. publications roughly grouped as "the magazines." There were, there are, six and a half thousand of them—more than twice as many as the counties in the nation, and more than three times as many as all the daily newspapers from coast to coast. The war brought to most of them the mightiest boom in their history.

Most of these magazines have always been unknown to that great body, the General Public; the great majority existed to serve their readers not as seekers after the true and the beautiful but as interested parties: they served alumni, soft drink bottlers, undertakers, ophthalmologists, and cement manufacturers. Yet the editors of *The Bottler's Gazette* had something in common throughout 1939–45 with the editors of *The Reader's Digest,* and the war similarly bound the editors of *The Nation* and of *Life* together in a way equally distasteful to both. For these, and all the other editors in the country were forced, or thought they were, first in 1939 and then all over again in 1941, to produce a wartime "angle" for almost everything that went into print.

For every magazine in America had, and has, a Policy. Magazine publishers and editors cling more tenaciously to policy than their fellows of books or newspapers. A book publisher can, and happily does, publish one volume today extolling the art of the dry-fly fisherman and another tomorrow rending the political fabric of the republic into fluttering rags, and it occurs to nobody (and certainly not to him) that he has done anything contradictory, random, or irreversible. A newspaper confesses, of course, to being (*Rep.*) or (*Dem.*) or even (*Ind.*), but unless it is the Chicago *Tribune* or New York's *Daily News* this has singularly little effect on its over-all content.

A magazine editor is bowed down by deeper cares. His policy is with him through the day and through the night. It faced him in the war, and now it haunts his peace. He is grappling with a continuum: his year is not over until 12 or 52 issues have—sprung isn't the word—been yielded forth by his printer's presses; linked, consistent, organic, homologous. Yet he is in a worse fix than this: although he knows he has a policy, and knows what it is, he cannot put it into words; when he tries, it spills down his shirt-front like a home-rolled cigarette. By usage, his masthead may no longer carry anything similar to "Dedicated to a furtherance and wider diffusion of ——." Even as unexceptional a sentiment as the Scripps-Howard newspapers' "Give Light and the People will find the Way" is somehow out of place as a magazine editor's announcement; accordingly, "Founded by Benjamin Franklin A°. D¹. 1728" is by convention about as far as he can go with a formal statement of his aims. Yet he feels policy all the time, and his moments of inarticulate frustration are never greater than when he is declining a manuscript he really likes, but which somehow or other won't do. Then all he can say is, with a sincerity that sounds hollower to him than to the rejected author, "It's a swell piece, Jim, and I liked it from beginning to end, but it just won't do for us. I think maybe the *Post* would snap it right up. Oh, the *Post* has seen it? Hibbs said he thought it might be just our dish? Hibbs ought to—well in that case why don't you send it right over to Freddie Allen at *Harper's* . . ."

This sounds like evasion but it is not. Each editor is engaged in a formal, ritualistic dance with *his* contributors and *his* ideas. He knows when a step is awry in his own set but he can no more truly explain what is wrong than Pavlova could have gotten Beardsley Ruml satisfactorily geared into *Les Sylphides*. This asperses neither Pavlova's genius for the ballet nor Mr. Ruml's almost infinite capacity for adaptation. It just wouldn't work, and an editor instinctively knows when he is up against the same sort of brick wall. Mr. Harold Ross of *The New Yorker,* expressing criticism of a manuscript, becomes in this regard not merely an editor but a veritable arch-editor. "It gets sort of foggy in *here,*" he will say, indicating the last sixteen pages of an eighteen-page manuscript. He is then likely to add, "And it's slow in getting started." Inadequate as this may seem to instructors in English A, it serves the occasion; Mr. Ross has the knack of feeling the way his readers would feel if he didn't feel that way first. Neither magic nor brains is involved.

Into this vast process of empathy between editor and audience, the war thrust a thousand new entanglements. We can dismiss here the problems of the trade-paper editor anxious to get a war-time slant into his columns on point-of-sale display or soda-fountain merchandising. We can also, because we must, let slide the dilemmas of the editors of those 100% fiction carriers, the pulps. They have their own world, their own ethos. Nobody even knows exactly how many of them there are, for as one title wanes in popularity its entire contents, staff, and policy are next found appearing under another; *Romantic Strangle Stories* gives place to *Popular Perversions* without much awareness among either "the trade" or the "reading" public. If we agree not to discuss this sort of thing our magazine statistics become much easier to handle; the sixty-five hundred magazines now reduce themselves to not much more than fifty. Yet fifty magazines with fifty editors studiously pursuing fifty policies is still a lot to generalize about.

Among these fifty there were many wartime changes in psychology, some in physiology, and few in anatomy: the leading magazines of 1939, '40, and '41 remained the leading magazines in 1945. But the newsstands changed. As the paper shortage deepened and the War Production Board slowly reduced consumption tonnage to 75 per cent of prewar, the piles of the larger magazines diminished fast; the more popular the magazine the more acute its shortage until, for a while, the process of getting some of them became a matter of whisper and preferment, like getting a package of recognizable cigarettes. First they went under the counter as "stoopies," then they disappeared altogether. As with cigarettes, this produced a burgeoning of the unfamiliar; a magazine that had been growing fast before the WPB restrictions was at a heavy disadvantage compared to a magazine that had been growing slowly or not at all.

As the efflux of males to the war theatres increased the country's percentage of women in circulation a minor revolution took place in "the woman's field." Street & Smith, hitherto mostly dedicated to the pulps, struck it rich with *Mademoiselle*, a sort of junior *Vogue;* this threat spurred the firm of Condé Nast to the production of *Glamour* and Walter Annenberg to *Seventeen—*all this evidencing a restored nubility in an area that until then had seemed many years beyond the menopause.

Elsewhere, things were quieter. The deep longing in a dozen publishing bosoms to make a million dollars *quick* in the service of society continued to produce new imitator-competitors for *The Reader's Digest,* all of whom equally continued to be out-Dewitted by Mr. Wallace. The newsstands have sometimes thronged with fifty-odd active *Digest* imitators, but this population has been more of floaters than of citizens. Meanwhile *The Reader's Digest* continued to pursue its imperturbable, incomparable way; its circulation in the continental United States is now some 8,000,000 copies a month, excluding those editions sold elsewhere in English or in Spanish, Portuguese, and Arabic. But if Mr. Wallace could not be successfully imitated in catering to the vast American yen for self-improvement or in his magazine's capacities for condensing all human knowledge into 750 words, he was at least successfully challenged on trim-size. *Coronet*, *The American Mercury*, *Current History*, and *Encore*, to name a diverse four magazines having little in common with the *Digest* except linear dimensions, are successful in their own way; along with the pure-and-simple *Digest* imitator and a vast increase in pocket-size, paper-covered books, they have wrought a further change in the appearance of the American newsstand. The news magazines *Time* and *Newsweek*, the pictorials *Life* and *Look*, while circulating widely overseas were in heavy demand at home and the visible piles of them correspondingly shrank. The older line magazines of fiction and nonfiction combined were able to keep a more even balance between demand and supply—although all large circulation magazines were up from prewar days; up, on a rough average, about a quarter of a million copies each.

Behind these figures all sorts of diversities were concealed. The war's paper stringencies were a boon to some magazines of overextended circulation which were able to reduce their more expensive forms of distribution in the name of patriotism and save money in the process. Circulation and advertising managers both tended to suffer from King Midas trouble; whatever they touched was likely to turn into a subscription or an advertising space order, when certainly both could not be accommodated and possibly neither. For several years things could not have been stranger: magazines urged readers not to buy copies but to borrow them; advertisers and their agencies bought cocktails and lunches for advertising salesmen in the hope of shoehorning a favorite client into a precious and expensive page of space. The waters ran uphill.

There are no figures to tell the quantitative extent of a brand-new magazine reading public brought about by the war. To what level magazine circulations would have soared with a sufficient supply of paper can only be conjecture; the enormous increase of readers per copy of all magazines can be estimated, but the figures can take no account of the U. S. magazines that were read by servicemen overseas until each copy was ready to vanish into dust. The public had money to spend; the public was ready to devour anything about the war that could be made to transpire through censorship; the public, reaping the slow fruits of education, could read as it couldn't read twenty-five years ago. If advertising and circulation managers were living in a dream, so was the magazine editor. Whoever he was, he was *good;* the public wanted more of what he had to offer.

With an audience clamoring for more and more, the war encouraged a new politicalization of U. S. magazines, which went beyond inarticulate policy and had its say on what the political U. S. should and shouldn't do in a way that magazines had not found the boldness or the method to say before. The editorial pages of *The Saturday Evening Post,* in the days of Mr. George Horace Lorimer, could always have provided the safest imaginable haven in which an editor could espouse *anything* with safety: it was never discovered that anybody ever read them and there was some doubt as to whether it was intended that anybody should. The *Post's* editorial pages today are another matter; it is obvious that an editor is addressing an audience in the expectation of being read, believed, and followed. *Collier's* has made it a practice to say what it thinks. *Life's* editorial page is conspicuous and aggressive. Among other major magazines *Time, The Reader's Digest,* and *The New Yorker* make no direct pronouncements of opinion, but don't need to: their editors are all, in their several ways, crusading editors. None of them, however, are professional controversialists, and it is curious indeed that it is these non-controversialists around whom most of the political controversies of the magazine world today revolve. The "magazines of opinion" —*The Nation, The New Republic,* and some others—have scarcely produced a stir.

This politicalization of the magazines revolved, in general, around their regard for U. S. foreign policy: implicitly or explicitly they stated their own editorial positions as to the stand the U. S. should take *vis-à-vis* its own world leadership, Russia, the politics of democracy, "free enterprise," collectivist economics, and the "police state." *The Reader's Digest* lived out a policy strongly nationalist and with a touch of xenophobia in its make-up; *Life,* and to a lesser degree *Time,* espoused "The American Century"—a viewpoint that could be described as internationalism-with-U. S.-interests-first; *The New Yorker* in a nebulous way was the champion of international brotherhood. The argumentation was pitched on an intellectual plane that probably no editor of a mass magazine would have thought his readers remotely capable of understanding ten years ago.

Perhaps the one thing all editors most truly possessed in common during the war years was an immensely hypertrophied conscience. This took the form of assuming that no reader would know anything about anything—the war, jet propulsion, the challenge to our civilization, the meat scandal, full employment, or the German entry into Poland—unless he read about it in the editor's own magazine. This was quite proper; the desire to share surprise (or shock) and delight (or alarm) at something he has never known before is the mark of the successful editor of anything. But in 1939–45 it led to a good deal of shouting and jostling in the corridors of journalism, magazine and otherwise. And since bad news was often more salable than good news, and usually, in the war's early days, was much more plausible, the magazines from 1939 onward for a while fairly drooled of doom. This was better, certainly, than drooling a fatuous optimism. Indeed, it was not until the autumn of 1944 that editors generally let it become apparent that they had known the final score all along but had felt the necessity to withhold from their readers the possibly contaminated fruits of overoptimism. This attitude of avuncular omniscience, coupled with a certain nervous yammering about chaos, bungling, crisis, incompetence, stupidity, blundering, fraud, misfeasance, imminent dissolution, and the immediacy of the Apocalypse made the magazine editor seem occasionally like a refugee Prime Minister clogging his own warriors' egress with the limousine he was using to transport his mistress's rescued canary.

But this attitude was not new. Sometime between the Great

Muckraking Era (*circa* 1905) and the Dawn of John Siddall
(*circa* 1915) * the late John Reed put magazine psychology into
verse in the course of writing the libretto for the first Dutch Treat
Club show ever given. This was a Reed who had not yet undergone the tremendous change in temperament and outlook that
later produced *Ten Days That Shook the World;* who had not
yet been outside the Continental U. S. and whose job was as an
assistant editor of *The American Magazine* (1911–13). His hymn,
"The Freedom of the Press" from an offering titled "*Every-
magazine:* An Immorality Play," went like this:

> When God the earth created
> And saw that it was good
> He was naturally elated;
> He did the best He could.
> But not to knock Jehovah
> (He wisely used His means)
> It had to be done over
> By all us magazines.
> We do not mean to be unkind—
> How could He know the public mind?
> We do not mean to give offense;
> He hadn't our experience.
>
> * * *
>
> God made the earth and heaven
> And things that creep and crawl
> It took but mornings seven;
> It wasn't bad at all.
> But not to criticize Him
> The world was raising hob
> Till the magazines came forward
> And finished up the job.†

---

* The Muckraking Era is commonly dated as beginning in 1903 with the
publication of Lincoln Steffens' *The Shame of the Cities* and Ida M. Tar-
bell's *History of the Standard Oil Company*, both in *McClure's Magazine*,
but 1905 saw its lushest flowering. It subsided rapidly after 1912. John
Siddall, perhaps the greatest editorial accentuator of the positive and *vice
versa* in U. S. magazine history, served *The American Magazine* from 1906
until 1923, but 1915 was his first year as editor-in-chief.

† Lyrics by Jack Reed; music by Bill Daly. Produced before the Dutch
Treat Club, February 19, 1913. The above version is metrically altered from
the original to compensate for the absence of Mr. Daly's music.

This same attitude, translated into terms of World War **II, re**-
sulted in the overworking of a few of the hardier formulae. **It is**
possible to go through the tables of contents of only a few magazines for the earlier years of the war, and discover an innumerable variation on the following themes. (In the spaces left blank,
insert your own phobia; you have as much right to yours as the
editor had to his.)

THE MYTH OF ———   AFTER ———, WHAT?
            HOW GOOD IS OUR ———?
WHY ——— FAILED   CRISIS IN ———
            ———: MASTERPIECE OR MENACE?

But if these are blemishes they deserve to be discounted in the
larger view. After all, a world in which everything is just as it
should be calls for no next issue of anything. "We have here," as
Charles Merz once said on a weightier occasion, "not a plot but
a quotient." The larger view, the view that really takes in all aspects of magazine contribution and participation during the last
five years of our existence, is of huge importance: the magazines
espoused, adapted, and made great *the reporter*. They supplied
him with a set of working tools more powerful by far than his
typewriter alone. With expense accounts, subsidies and allowances—but above all with a set of assignments, objectives, and,
yes, policies, they instituted a journalistic system of travel and
reportage unheard of until five years ago. James Gordon Bennett
made history in 1870 by sending Stanley to find Livingstone; the
magazines since 1939 have sent a hundred Stanleys to find a thousand Livingstones. Almost all of them turned up with their quar-
ries. They have been in process of acquiring from the newspapers
the principal asset that once, and in a simpler day, made the Ben-
netts and Greeleys and Danas and Pulitzers great. *The Reader's
Digest* lists nineteen names, most of them illustrious, under the
single heading of "Roving Editors"; *Collier's* lists twenty-seven
working Associate Editors, most of them in the field, and *The*

Saturday Evening Post acknowledges thirteen. The number of editor-reporters deployed over the globe for *Time, Life,* and *Fortune* at one time or another totaled over thirty. During the last war a magazine with an editorial staff of six would have been ripe for what the business office used to call retrenchment. In today's world, at home or abroad, working in reportorial fields that range from medicine to the Levant, to Guam, to political science, these men and women represent as formidable an army of fact-gatherers as journalism has ever known. Magazines of smaller resources but disproportionate influence, like the *Atlantic* and *Harper's,* took a leaf from this book; they no longer found it sufficient to depend upon wandering essayists or amateur volunteers to bring in the news from the far or difficult places.

Now a cry of protest is likely to go up here that this belittles the contribution of those newspaper war correspondents who were, after all, some hundreds strong, whose devotion is recorded by some twenty of gold stars in the journalism service flag, and whose roster had in it such names as Ernie Pyle and Raymond Clapper. But it is not the newspaper correspondent himself who is to be criticized; the trouble lies in his editor's perverse throwing away of the correspondent's very best material; an act of sabotage the editor has indulged in as part of his service to a set of journalistic conventions as out of date as a Washington toggle hand-press.

It is important to pause on this, for it is the pivot on which the war contribution of the magazines almost wholly revolves. The magazines have picked up what the newspapers have for years been discarding and have discovered in it treasures beyond any comparison with the conventional news story beginning, "More than 6000 tons of bombs were dropped today on the vital . . ."

The magazines are wide awake to the fact that the newspapers are twenty years out of date in serving a fetish that, in reality, was taken from them in 1925. The fetish is *speed.* The power-driven rotary press and the telegraph line started the fierce competition of one newspaper to be on the street four minutes ahead of its rival with the news of a Boss Tweed's indictment, or of one wire service to get the news of McKinley's election into a distant telegraph sounder thirteen seconds before the other. This frenzy still continues, long after it has become senseless. Mr. Edward Kennedy of the Associated Press was the victim of this hypnosis of tradition when he broke his word of honor and several other things in "scooping" his rivals at SHAEF in Reims, May, 1945, on Germany's final capitulation. In actuality there was no imaginable felony that Mr. Kennedy could have committed that would have made it possible for one of his association's member newspapers to be on the street with the news sooner than a million loud-speakers could have brought it into a million living rooms, had radio's correspondents also decided to do the dirty. The radio has destroyed the newspapers' primacy in speed, but the newspapers have not given in. And in striving for speed where speed no longer counts they are forgoing many of the virtues of insight, penetration, scope, grasp, understanding, perspective, and reflection which are possible to a correspondent when he is not yelling into a telephone to a rewrite man at the other end of the line, or trying to compose a cable in the toilet of a C-47, but instead can sit down at his own typewriter, take a long drink of something, and think before he writes.

Into the breach left by the newspaper's yearning for the split second, the magazine editor walked with astounding results. So eager was the public for some flesh with which to clothe the bare bones of "Yesterday at 1:18 A.M. marked the . . ." that it is now the magazines that have the money to spend, the top talent to hire, the adequate space to provide. The journalistic scoop, in so far as it still existed, moved from the domain of the newspaper to the domain of the magazine—which once was not even considered a part of journalism at all.

The rise of the reporter in the policy of magazine making had to be accompanied by another, and compensating, movement. This was the decline of the soothsayer. Magazines in the U. S. have made, in recent years, many more valuable contributions to

contemporary letters and to mass understanding via their non-fiction than their fiction. Their percentage of nonfiction has also been steadily rising; for one thing, facts since 1939 have been outrunning fantasy. Moreover, the nature of that nonfiction has been changing swiftly and emphatically, as the men and women chosen to write it have changed. The word reporter, for example, does not mean the lovable hack with the pint of whisky in his overcoat pocket who used to be the hero of most of the drama's enactments of journalism. It means today a man who may be either a writer, artist, photographer, or public opinion investigator—but, whoever he is, carries with him some apparatus for shedding light on facts and is more interested in that than in confusing them with his own beliefs. The word soothsayer can mean anything from the most dishonest and cynical propagandist to the most genteel essayist who weaves together a pleasant but indistinguishable fabric of fact and opinion. Twenty years ago, this latter contributed almost the whole content of magazine nonfiction; it was the sort of business against which Sir Leslie Stephen inveighed years ago when he said (the London *Times* happened to be in his mind's eye when he spoke), "Journalism consists in writing for pay on matters of which you are ignorant."

Two things happened in the years before World War II which enormously altered the approach of magazines toward their responsibility in reporting. The first was the application of thorough-going research methods to the journalistic process, with results going far beyond the effect on any one article. The second was the adding of the modern camera to the equipment of journalism, with results outrunning the mere taking and printing of new profusions of pictures.

It cannot be said *when* the reporter supplanted the essayist, since the process is still going on. The Muckraking Era certainly resulted from a good deal of deep, exact reporting, yet the magazines of that era were edited in a literary, not a journalistic, tradition. During, and perhaps because of, the first World War, the literary tradition in magazine editing all but expired, and left no recognizable heir. The essayist had lost touch with the great body of consequential facts that needed to be generalized and organized to make their meaning clear; he was snowed under by the sheer weight of meaningful news. For a good many years it occurred to no editor that *he* had a responsibility for what his essayist was saying in his magazine or, more than that, that the essayist needed the help of *organization* to marshal and present his facts. Not until magazines began to assemble their own reference libraries and services to augment the dictionary and the almanac in the proofroom, and trained research investigators to provide sources and checks for the writer (instead of merely correcting his spelling, in the proofroom tradition) did magazine journalism really begin to take on weight, knowledge, and responsibility.

By this time the essayist was up to his chin in the rising waters of fact. In the middle 1930s a new danger assailed him: the survey of public opinion came into being. He had previously been his own authority on such matters; there now came a rational method of inquiry to supplant his dicta.

The public opinion survey antedates the outbreak of the war by only four years. The *Fortune* Survey, first to appear, saw its first public print in July, 1935; George Gallup brought his American Institute of Public Opinion into the light in October of the same year. Both of these models have since been widely copied, and adapted to ends both worthy and unworthy. But the significance that resides in them beyond themselves is that they are supplanting an older journalistic method. The comparison is extravagant, yet the temptation is to say that they are doing the same sort of thing for journalism that the experimental method did for natural philosophy: putting matters to the test of the laboratory instead of expecting truth to spin itself out of a cocoon of speculation. It will be a long time before the journalistic soothsayers wholly cease the practice of spending 48 hours in a town, city, nation, or hemisphere, and then pronouncing upon its total problems—but these wise men have now been so heavily challenged that their own consciences may begin to tell them that something must be wrong with their methods. When a writer no longer feels easy in saying, out of his own unsupported hunch or prejudice, "It is obvious that the people of Detroit . . ." or "Regardless of his station in life every Catholic is as one in the belief that . . ." or "Of whatever race or creed, it is clear that the privileged classes are conspiring to . . ." we are bound to see a new approach to the question, What, indeed, *is* reporting?

So the swami, the soothsayer, the dictumist is seeing one profound modification come over his practices in the knowledge that opinion, which he was at once supposed to affect *and* to disclose, can actually be felt and measured and weighed. There can now be verified one of the great intangibles in what he writes: is what he *says* important, really important? There remains the verification: is what he *says* true, really true? Another piece of new apparatus enters the magazine field here. It is the camera.

There will someday be explained a great mystery: Why did the journalism of pictorial representation wither and decay in the U. S. for over half a century after the Civil War? The answer is perhaps—again!—that daily journalism became so bemused with speed that it forgot its other values. It forgot Mathew Brady and the now priceless photographs of the Civil War and its high participants that Brady took with an apparatus of *camerae obscurae* and messy chemicals that no present-day photographer would demean himself to touch. It forgot the documentary conscience and journalistic acumen of the editors of *Harper's Weekly* —that wonderful and precocious magazine that flowered from 1857 until into the eighties. It is sad indeed that the halftone-engraving process, which could have wedded Brady and the editors of *Harper's Weekly* into such a significant editorial union, came along too late by some thirty years. It was ready, or almost, by the outbreak of the Spanish-American War, by which time Brady was gone and there was not much left of *Harper's Weekly*. And it was more than ready by 1914. But by that time American picture journalism was embedded so deeply in the stupid trivialities of the Sunday rotogravure section that a whole epoch of history took place without engaging our visual notice. The ingenuity of editors was directed toward devising the various irrelevant cookie-shapes into which a picture could be cropped by the "art editor"; this left no time for consideration of what pictures could *reveal*. Thousands of photographs were taken of World War I; taken without direction, published without relevance. The day-by-day and week-by-week record now left behind is almost non-existent; the editors abandoned to the anthologists and the curators of the future the job of sorting and winnowing and collating that is today the heart of their journalistic process.

The strange fact thus remains that photographs played no substantial part in creative periodical journalism until less than three years before the outbreak of World War II. It remained for magazine journalism to bring them into sensible focus. The occasion was the establishment of the modern *Life,* whose first issue appeared in November, 1936. Pictorial journalism was not new to England, which had its *London Illustrated News,* its *Sketch,* and its *Sphere;* it was not new to Europe, which had its *Vu* and its *Illustrierte Zeitung;* it was not, indeed, "new" to the U. S. if you include in its lineage such varied efforts as *The Police Gazette* and the New York *Times Midweek Pictorial.* But it was wholly new in asking of pictures, as the new *Life* did, that they should tell a connected, continuous, and logical story, with the same sort of beginning, middle, and end that is exacted of other reporting.

Pictorial journalism was ready for the war; it did not have to improvise its techniques. It had to, and it did, however, enormously refine and increase them. Its methods serve to highlight one important change that has come about in many a magazine as the war progressed. It was no longer enough that a correspondent (whether with his typewriter or his camera) merely leave the office for a theatre of war to pick up what random scraps he could. The matter of assignment and control must now be worked out in magazine journalism in precisely the same way as the editor of a newspaper deploys his city room staff—although on a different scale. The lucky break, the chance shot, will always turn up, let us hope, but reinforcing such fortunate accidents is now a policy of calculation and arrangement. (This policy of "arrangement" has been criticized by those who forget that you cannot take a photograph of a third-rate diplomat on the steps of the State Department without stopping him, straightening his tie, dusting him off, and setting him in the best light available.) It is only by the most painstaking arrangement that such photographic essays can be assembled as those that have shown precisely, and almost moment-by-moment, the existence of an infantryman from the instant he was wounded through his procession of dressing stations, field and base hospitals, evacuation, convalescence, and discharge. Random snappings of the shutter and random jottings in the notebook do not serve any longer to provide the magazine reader with what the magazines have now led him to expect: the treatment of contemporaneous history as a stream of related and continuous events, and not as bright, sporadic, disconnected flashes.

As the war progressed it became evident that the possibilities of pictorial journalism were not limited to the camera. In one sense, the "best" picture could never be taken: despite all the planning and contriving the lens was always pointed a few degrees off course or the shutter clicked a couple of seconds too late. The addition of the artist to the roll of magazine contributors became, accordingly, another development of major importance.

To the everlasting discredit of all concerned, the painters of America recorded substantially nothing at all of the epoch in history which was World War I. Newspapers could have no use for them; magazines once again forgot the elder genius of *Harper's Weekly*, which commissioned Winslow Homer to go into the field and sketch scenes from the Civil War. Seven months after our first troops reached Europe in 1917 the U. S. Government commissioned eight—count them!—eight artists to proceed more or less to the front lines and sketch what they could observe. But in choosing illustrators rather than painters the Army tackled its problem in precisely its most difficult and unrewarding perspective; consequently nothing exists today in the way of first-hand artistic observation and record of what went on among U. S. troops.

The record of 1939–45 is quite different. Starting in 1941, the magazine *Life* commissioned, and the U. S. armed services accredited, some thirty painters whose work already forms the impressive body of some seven hundred canvases. The U. S. Army later undertook a similar program of its own—but when, in 1943, the Congress disapproved an appropriation to continue it, the War Department turned to the magazines as the only aggregation which could keep the program going.

If this discussion has treated magazines primarily as conveyors of *information,* that is because, in greater and greater measure, the war presented that role to them as their challenge and their opportunity. They spent impressive sums of money to meet and face it. Happily, they had it to spend. The American advertiser invested in magazines $100,000,000 *more* in 1944 than in 1942. This just about footed the new bills that faced the magazine editor. His rising ambitions to do the best possible job he could in competition with his fellows swallowed one large chunk of his new revenues; generally rising costs swallowed the rest. On balance, he was left with just about as much net income in 1944 as he was left with in 1939. But he had a lot more fun. "It is much easier to forget about money and edit for glory than it used to be," said Frederick Allen of *Harper's.* But then he added: "What kind of a fool's paradise we are getting into, what kind of bad habits we may be forming, I don't know."

Certainly the war has added to U. S. magazine publishing one dimension which it will be difficult and undesirable to eliminate if the day comes when shrinking revenues call for another new set of economics. The war made *exporters* out of the magazine publishers. Where before the war U. S. magazines had a few thousand subscribers in the British Isles and in Canada they now measure their subscribers overseas and in Latin America by the hundreds of thousands. The vast deployment of U. S. troops over the face of the earth was the primary, but not the only, cause of this new publishing interest in Wendell Willkie's One World. The not inconsiderable result has been the growth of an export trade in American ideas; Hollywood is no longer alone in displaying the U. S. for better or for worse to its cousins abroad. The return of the troops may noticeably diminish this new trade, but it is hard to imagine that it will suppress it altogether.

But in one respect the magazines did little to enhance their own, or America's, reputation either abroad or at home. That respect was the magazines' fiction. The heroes and heroines changed from civilian clothes to the appropriate uniforms, and the locales changed from the corner of Main and Centre to the more exotic crossroads of Europe, Africa, and Asia—but the plots went on and on. *McCall's* magazine, which, in the women's field, often presents its readers with the unexpected, serialized Mr. Glenway Wescott's notable novel, *Apartment in Athens;* elsewhere, in other large circulation magazines, there was not much to report. Magazine fiction isn't as good as it used to be and, like *Punch,* it never was. If World War II has as yet brought forth any notable literature that fact will be happily recorded elsewhere in this volume (see Lewis Gannett's piece on books), but it will probably also there be demonstrated that it did not appear *because of* any magazine, even though some of it may have had the magazine as a vehicle. The magazine editor, of all save the smallest and most gem-like, no longer looks on his fiction as rewarding the same sort of creative and co-operative effort that he puts in with his reporters: he buys it with the shrewd conscientiousness of a tip-top grocer, up early in the morning to find the best in the dockside markets. It used to be a generality in publishing that "no magazine can succeed on fiction alone, but no magazine can succeed except with fiction in it." The war left that generality, rusty and weed-grown, in the ditch of the 1930s. That the fiction record of the magazines from 1939–45 is in general so blank (except for the extraordinarily consistent high record of *The New Yorker*) is a sad matter. What the war did for the magazines, by and large, was to reconvert them into *journals*—perforce they have been practicing journalism as they never did before. This is not inconsistent with the discovery of a new Kipling or Conrad or Stephen Crane or Jack London: men with a strong narrative to tell. It *is* inconsistent with the discovery of more subtle and perhaps more precious talents—but so, it is said, is the American public. Journalism is the conveyance of information from here to there; with accuracy, insight and dispatch; in such a manner that the truth is served and the rightness of things becomes slowly, if not immediately, more evident. That was the not inconsiderable order that the magazines, 1939–45, undertook to serve. It was enough.

IV. ADVERTISING

by *RAYMOND RUBICAM*

RAYMOND RUBICAM (*age 53*) *recently retired as head of Young & Rubicam, Inc., which under his leadership grew to be one of the world's largest advertising organizations.*

Although he does not mention it in this article, he is the author of "Johnny Russell, In Memoriam," one of the outstanding war advertisements, which received a voluntary circulation of more than thirty million.

With Dr. George H. Gallup he pioneered in the application of public opinion research to advertising, radio, and motion pictures. In 1942 he was special assistant to the Chairman of the War Manpower Commission. He is a member of the Research Committee of the Committee for Economic Development.

Time: December, 1941

Place: Any American home

AUTOMOBILE MANUFACTURER (*speaking to Pop and Mom through full-page advertisement in newspaper*): "Never have you settled back into such deep-cushioned comfort, nor sleeked along the highway to the country club with such compelling power. You owe it to yourself to see, to drive, this new——"

COSMETIC MANUFACTURER (*whispering to Betty Lou from color page in magazine*): "Tonight . . . tonight . . . he may speak . . . in reality . . . those words you have heard him say so often in your dreams. . . . Will you be glamorous? Will your make-up be an invitation to come closer . . . closer . . . closer?"

BREAKFAST CEREAL MANUFACTURER (*speaking to Junior on radio*): "Know the secret every athlete knows—the secret that wins games, builds champions! Send for our booklet——"

NETWORK ANNOUNCER (*breaking in on above*): "This broadcast is interrupted for an important news announcement. . . . The Japanese fleet has attacked Pearl Harbor . . . all commercial broadcasts on this network are suspended until further notice to bring you continuous news of the war. . . ."

The network announcer's sweeping words, "all commercial broadcasts on this network are suspended until further notice," led many a listener to muse on more than a temporary interruption of advertising. Would there be a place for it at all in the war? And, if so, how much of a place, and what kind?

So far as radio was concerned, a hint of an answer came almost immediately. Not all networks suspended all commercial programs the day of Pearl Harbor; some continued them but interrupted them when news was received. Those who suspended them soon found there was too little real news to fill the time, and too much repetition and padding to hold the public. The commercial programs actually gathered and held bigger audiences for the moments when real news came in.

But this quickly proved point seemed trifling in the face of many other questions about advertising. What had happened to it in the first World War? Had it decreased or increased? Had it been a real war help in spreading important information to civilians? What had been happening to it in England, *this* war? Will Roosevelt clamp down on business advertising? Will the government itself advertise? These and other questions sent business, advertising, and government people hurrying to the records and to conferences.

Briefly, the record showed that during the last war there was about as much advertising by business as there had been just before it. Little of this advertising carried a message directly devoted to helping win the war. Large numbers of advertising writers, artists, and executives volunteered to help George Creel, head of government information, and their talents were used in many ways on special campaigns; but no organized effort was made to put the main body of business advertising to work for the war. Individual manufacturers and publishers donated, according to Creel, about $2,500,000 worth of national advertising space to the government in 1918, but not all of it was used, and even the full amount was only a trickle from the main stream—about 1½ per cent of the total. Generally speaking, advertising stuck to business in the first World War, although some companies made a fatal mistake in stopping advertising while other companies hurried into the opening to help the public forget the old favorite.

The record showed that in England, *this* war, with the enemy less than twenty minutes away, things were different. Carrying blitz and submarine losses on its back, industry strained to supply the war and the barest elements of civilian life. Shortage of paper reduced newspapers to four-page bulletins, and advertising space was cut to the bone. The government paid for its own advertising campaigns on war themes and became the largest single advertiser, although business collectively continued to do about five times as much advertising as the government, to protect trademarks and future markets.

While this searching of the record was going on in the United States after Pearl Harbor, advertising groped its way and the government groped with it. Some customary advertisers, like the food and drug companies, knew they would still have goods to sell the public but did not know how much; others, completely converted to the war, like the automobile and household appliance companies, knew they would have nothing to sell. Both groups feared the greatest catastrophe that could happen to them—that the public would forget them if they stopped advertising; but both groups were at a loss to know what kind of advertising to use.

Some businesses quickly canceled or reduced their advertising. Many put their worst foot forward with quick and easy solutions, like the bread manufacturer who told the nation to slice its way to victory with his enriched bread, the cigarette maker who put the Army and Navy to work measuring the length of cigarettes, and the cast-iron pipe advertiser who had the soldier telling his girl not to worry about him, that he was as tough as cast-iron pipe.

Meanwhile, scores of "information" officials in scores of government war offices were, unknown to each other, telephoning and ·telegraphing to friends and acquaintances connected with advertising and asking immediate production of campaigns to aid the particular war activity which the individual official represented. From the advertising end a stream of other individuals telephoned and telegraphed friends and acquaintances in the government with assorted suggestions, or demands to know what they could do to help. Nobody knew what anybody else was doing. Half a dozen groups would be working independently on one project and nobody on another that was perhaps more important. Advertisers and radio networks were getting five and six government requests for the same radio time on the same day and program. There were no priorities. Nobody had authority to settle anything. While some government people welcomed advertising's help, others sneered: "No soap salesmen wanted."

But there were wiser heads in both government and in the ranks of advertising. A group of patriotic advertising men who first called themselves the Advertising Council, and, later, the War Advertising Council, set out on the hard multiple task of (1) finding useful work for advertising in the war, (2) planning and organizing that work, (3) persuading thousands of firms and individuals to donate advertising space, time, and talent without charge, and (4) getting solid government backing for the job.

It has been said that advertising was unpopular in some circles in Washington before the war because it was associated with making money. But this does not seem a sufficient reason, because advertising is also associated with spending money, and this has been an activity of which Washington thinks highly. Perhaps that depends on who spends the money; but whatever the reason for advertising's ill-favor, it was real and it was earnest, and it was not improved by the slice-your-way-to-victory approach, or by picturing the General Staff measuring cigarettes in the War Map Room, or by comparing our sons and heroes to cast-iron pipe, especially as there might be a faint suggestion that army food required that kind of constitution.

Fortunately, the Advertising Council lost little time in organizing for direct and practical usefulness in the war effort. In advertising parlance, the "advertiser" is the company which pays for the advertising and signs it; an "advertising agency" is a separate and independent organization which prepares advertising for certain firms who are its "clients"; and advertising "media" are the newspapers, magazines, radio networks and stations, outdoor posters, etc., which circulate the advertising. All of these had to be represented in the Council, and their co-operation won, if the organization was to be successful.

Under the chairmanship of Chester J. La Roche, who represented the advertising agencies, a strong board of directors, drawn from all the major divisions of advertising, was formed, and the aims of the organization were communicated to Donald Nelson, chairman of the War Production Board. He was told that only a few men in the government and a few men in business and advertising were aware of advertising's full possibilities for usefulness in the war; and it was suggested to him that a call from him for a meeting of government, business, and advertising people to discuss the subject would be an important first step.

Nelson, faced at that moment with a serious shortage of scrap iron and steel, and looking for ways and means to stir the nation to action in collecting it, promptly wrote a letter to the Council group and said, "One of the pressing requirements of the government is to have the help of the established organizations representing the creative ability of advertising and the channels of communication for reaching the public. . . . We must have the means of quickly and effectively disseminating the facts to the American people. . . . It is, therefore, our patriotic duty to establish a working relationship. . . . I suggest a meeting."

But preliminary organization for the national scrap drive was an enormous task, and Henry Morgenthau, Secretary of the Treasury, who was then pointing toward a payroll savings plan of bond purchase, became the Council's first government "client" by inviting its services to help form and "sell" the Treasury plan.

To equip itself to carry these and future war messages to the country, the Council's board now had to knit thousands of advertisers, thousands of media, and hundreds of advertising agencies into a voluntary organization to hammer home to the people by all available means the points which the government selected as being most important to the war. In some cases this meant that companies or industries would finance special campaigns, as in the case of the scrap and fat salvage campaigns; in more cases it meant that companies would devote part of their regular advertising to approved government themes. In all cases it meant that volunteers from advertising agencies and industrial companies would work with the government and prepare basic campaign guidebooks and sample advertising for the use or adaptation of advertisers and media across the country.

This recruiting of men and money was not undertaken in a limpid atmosphere of universal agreement that it ought to be done. Some public officials believed that the government ought to pay for its own advertising as a matter of principle; some mistrusted the partnership with business. Some thought that literary men and journalists could deal more fittingly with war themes than commercial writers could—the "soap salesmen" epithet did not die easily.

The Council found business and advertising men beset with comparable doubts. With some, sentiment had not changed much since the *New Yorker* ran its cartoon of the little girl in front of the prosperous home saying to her mother, "Mama, Johnny wrote a bad word on the sidewalk!" When mother looked, the bad word was "Roosevelt."

Many businessmen hesitated to advertise either war themes or their own businesses, fearing that the administration would later oppose allowance for advertising as a wartime business expense. Some shared the view of some public officials that the government ought to do its own advertising. Many had limited vision as to the part in the war which war advertising could play.

The Council's view of all this was that the argument as to whether the government should or should not pay for its own advertising might drag out in Congress for the greater part of the war, and that in the meantime there was immediate work for advertising to do. It urged that the practical course was for business to pay for the needed jobs, and that if these were well and unselfishly done doubts would begin to disappear regarding both the war usefulness of advertising and the motives of business. Last, and extremely important, the Council contended that no amount of money which the government would, or should, appropriate, could provide the power that a voluntary effort could be made to yield.

The air was cleared when the Treasury Department announced that advertising, in "reasonable" amounts, would continue to be regarded as a legitimate business expense. The Council's first campaigns were launched and it began a steady acquisition of support in both government and business circles. In its first year, 1942, it planned and executed 14 separate government information campaigns for 8 different government agencies. In 1943 the number of campaigns grew to 34, and 17 government agencies made use of the volunteered service. In 1944 the number of campaigns almost doubled again, to reach a total of 62, and 27 government agencies employed the service.

It is estimated that $150,000,000 in space and radio time was turned over to these government projects by business in 1942. The amount grew to $284,000,000 given in 1943, and to $302,000,-000 in 1944. It is probable that in final total over a billion dollars' worth of space and time was given to these campaigns.

Among the home front jobs which advertising tackled for the government were the scrap metal and fat salvage drives, the curbing of absenteeism, the recruitment of aviation cadets, cadet nurses, army nurses, WACs and WAVEs, and the recruitment of victory gardeners and farm crop harvesters. Several campaigns on food, including one on conservation and another on price control, drives for fuel and rubber conservation, Red Cross and National War Fund drives, campaigns for the early mailing of overseas Christmas packages, for the greater use of V-mail, tin can conservation, recruitment of man and womanpower for war industry, and, biggest of all, for war financing, won strong support.

Many of these campaigns came up on a moment's notice to meet a sudden turn in the war situation. They required teams of research men to gather background material, teams of artists, writers, and radio men to produce the material. More than 400 advertising agencies volunteered to do without compensation whatever work was called for. Advertising managers in major industries volunteered as "campaign managers" to work with the advertising agency "task forces" in executing the campaigns.

Executives and salesmen of leading publishing houses, radio stations and networks, and outdoor posting companies made personal calls on thousands of advertisers to win their co-operation. Handbooks of information and sample advertisements were mailed to all advertisers and advertising agencies explaining the campaigns and offering material for use.

Even with all this volunteer effort, the Council had to have a full-time paid staff. The money for this was donated each year by the same business groups who did the work and provided the space and radio time.

Not all the campaigns were of such nature that results could be measured in numerical terms, but some could. By the end of 1944, 85,000,000 Americans owned War Bonds. When the U. S. Cadet Nurse Corps was created by Congress in 1943, many people thought it unrealistic to expect to recruit a quota of 60,000 girls by 1944. Actually, by that time, 65,291 cadet nurses were at work in American hospitals. One series of magazine advertisements accounted for 40 per cent of all the inquiries received.

Nine months after the campaign had finished, coupons from it were still being received, accounting for about 10 per cent of the inquiries.

In 1944 shortage of shipping space slowed up soldier mail and hurt morale. Only one letter in five was a V-mail letter, yet an increase in V-mail would save space and speed delivery. The armed services asked the Council for help in appealing to the public for a greater use of V-mail. Within a few months the proportion of V-mail was jumped to one out of three, in spite of the fact that the total amount of mail had increased 50 per cent.

In 1944, 18,000,000 victory gardens were planted in the United States and furnished 40 per cent of all the fresh vegetables consumed by civilians. Nearly 25,000,000 households put by an estimated 3,500,000,000 quarts of preserved foods, over and above commercial production. Four million workers were recruited to supplement the regular food-processing labor force on a full-time or part-time basis.

Advertising alone did not bring about these results, but it played an important part in all of them.

In 1944 the need for merchant seamen was desperate; shipping schedules were disrupted. There was an urgent need for 43,000 additional experienced seamen within twelve months. A Council campaign played a major part in achieving satisfactory enlistments and restoring shipping schedules.

Although the Council tested the method of soliciting business interests to make special appropriations for war theme advertising apart from their regular advertising appropriations, this method proved far slower and productive of less total space than a drive on all advertisers to incorporate government war information themes in their regular space, combining it in appropriate instances with their own institutional or product advertising. Also, the country was faced with a paper shortage, and it was felt that if this grew more severe the extra war information campaigns would suffer.

One of the major problems which the government and the

Council faced in the war's early days was the working out of a system for a fair and orderly use of commercial radio programs. Both the government and the Council recognized that radio was a quick and flexible means of transmitting messages to the public. So much so, in fact, that before the official Radio Allocation Plan was adopted, government officials sometimes sent advertisers lengthy messages an hour before a show went on the air, with a request that they be read in full and exactly as written. More often than not, the style in which they were prepared would not fit the show, and often several government agencies would request the same time.

At the request of the Office of War Information, the Council worked out the Radio Allocation Plan. Under this plan radio stations, networks, and advertisers all agreed to give a certain amount of time each week for war messages. The OWI then decided what government programs were important enough to put on the air, ranked them in importance, and created a priority system. Then advertisers and stations were supplied with fact sheets from which the radio producers could develop their own messages.

In addition, plans were worked out to have the entertainment portions of many leading radio shows built around a war message. For example, a popular dramatic show might build the plot for an entire quarter-hour or half-hour period around the problem of food growing, food conservation, and keeping down the cost of living. Children's shows dramatized tin and paper salvage and subjects similarly appealing to youngsters.

In all these war information campaigns, just as the Council co-ordinated and represented the diverse interests in the field of advertising, the OWI was the co-ordinating agency and clearing-house representing the government. Requests for the Council's assistance were transmitted by each government department through the OWI, which then worked shoulder to shoulder with the Council and the government department in charge of the particular activity.

The Council defined war advertising as advertising "which induces people, through information, understanding, and persuasion, to take certain actions necessary to the winning of the war." This excluded "brag" advertising, in which a company or industry boasted of its own achievements, "political" advertising glorifying private enterprise, and advertising which painted rosy pictures of the postwar world.

The Council's attitude, spirit, and efforts were, indeed, a needed offset to brag advertising. They did not shut off the flow, which continued throughout the European war, but they cut its volume and brought to advertising a positive usefulness and a definite place in the struggle for victory.

Some people felt that in the early and dark days of the war, when America's confidence rested on her future arms production, even the brag advertising contributed to national morale by bringing us progress reports as our industrial resources were trained on the war objective. Granting some merit in this point of view, the fact remains that the brag advertising continued long after the asserted need was gone, and the charge is justified that most of it claimed mountainous importance for molehills of accomplishment.

As the war continued such advertisements were pilloried not only by servicemen, civilians, and government officials, but increasingly by advertising men as well.

"As soon as a pea canner runs short of peas he shouts 'Canned peas have gone to war!'" wrote one serviceman; "and as soon as an umbrella maker starts building parachutes he has us in Berlin."

A few advertisers even went so far as to kid the brag ads in print. One manufacturer of lipstick said of his product, "It won't build morale, it won't preserve our way of life, all [this] lipstick will do is make you look prettier. If it's victory you want, better buy bonds."

A furniture store ran a cartoon of two paratroopers floating to earth. On the way down one was pictured as shouting to the other, "What are your postwar aims?" Then the advertisement chortled, "If you can believe the majority of institutional advertisements appearing in the magazines today, most of our ten million men in uniform spend a large part of their waking hours talking in well-turned phrases of their personal postwar aims."

But the problem of the advertiser was not easy, particularly in the early days before the Council showed him the way to greatest usefulness. He had to explain to his customers either a total absence or a severe shortage of goods; he had to convey somehow the fact that the war was the reason. He had the additional problem of holding workers in a tight market, and he tried to present his plant, his product, and his work as importantly as he could. Even in the comfortable atmosphere of peace, advertising is a common inspirer of the "Oh yeah?" reaction in the popular breast. It suffers from the disadvantage of having to speak well of everything, and it compounds this handicap by all too often extolling the zipper in the same cathedral tones used to persuade you that you cannot be easy in your final resting place without a headstone of Vermont marble.

What was offensive in peace was ten times more so in war.

One serviceman put it this way: "When I read the ads I don't see why I'm here in camp. We don't need men in this war—our machines are so perfect they'll do the job themselves." Even more to the point was the protest which greeted an advertisement headed "Who's Afraid of the Big Focke-Wulf?" A flier in a bomber station clipped the ad from a magazine, wrote across it, "*I* am," signed his name, and then got every other flier in the station, including the commanding officer, to sign his name also. The advertisement was then mailed to the company which sponsored it.

Another advertisement heralded, in classical type, "The Great Gift to the Mothers of Men!" In the first two paragraphs we learned that the great gift was sulfa. In the next five paragraphs we learned that the advertiser had nothing to do with the development of this "gift," but merely produced the air conditioners employed in its production and keeping.

Another air conditioner advertiser, describing a torpedo hit on a Jap ship, asserted that "air conditioning helped make possible the hit itself," because part of the periscope used by the Navy was ground and polished in an air-conditioned workshop.

Not to be outdone by the air conditioner firm, a water conditioner firm boasted that water conditioning drives our shot all the way through the armor of enemy tanks.

There was also "the gun that comes out of an oil well," because the barrels were bored in a bath of oil.

A ball bearing manufacturer informed us that "the subject of ball bearings is on everyone's lips nowadays." A second ball bearing firm promised the soldier "a safe highway home," because the advertiser's bearings "still ride with him."

A metal fastener company, picturing a soldier in a hammock, boasted that "*His* cradle won't drop, because it's furnished with clamps 30% stronger than specified."

We were comforted with the news that "back of every attack is wire rope"; that "cotton cloth can help win an air fight"; that grinding wheels made bombers tougher; that alarm clocks kept America on time in the war; that sugar was an Axis-killer; and that castor beans had left the medicine cabinet for the battlefield.

And we were warned that we must have the right eyeglass lenses to recognize our soldier sons when they come home.

Wire rope promised its invaluable services in peace as well as war by "playing its part in the clearing away of the rubble of destruction and in the rebuilding of a better world."

Rising to supreme heights of ineptness was an advertisement called "Angel in Muddy Boots" picturing a nurse leaning over a wounded soldier. It quoted the boy's reverie: "I remember you ... you are the girl with flying feet who led the way to laughter ... you are all the girls I ever liked who brightened a fellow's life. ...

"You didn't always wear muddy boots.

"Once you raced over summer lawns in bright, skylarking shoes. ..."

Then the advertiser's reverie: "Yes, she grew up. . . . Her muddy boots are an example of that. The men and women—skilled craftsmen, all . . . that first gave her the delight of casual shoes in color, turned their hand to meeting the need for a sturdy boot that would carry a nurse through mud and rain. . . . When the war came, these same bootmakers . . . created the Nurses' Arctic, the Soldiers' Arctic, the Jungle Boot, the war Pilots' Boot, the deck-gripping Sea Boot, the Arctic Mukluk. . . .

"Someday peacetime living will come again. Someday there will be girls again who . . . fly over sun-flecked lawns with the lilt of summer in their hearts and rainbows on their feet."

Then, says the advertiser, his play shoes "will be back." Presumably that is in case the girl with the lilting heart gets tired of rainbows on her feet.

If "fertilizer can win the war" as still another advertiser claimed, the brag ads were surely spreading it around.

Although this type of advertising continued throughout the war, it reached its peak in quantity in late 1942. Thereafter, largely through Council efforts, a steadily mounting volume of advertising really went to work on specific and useful war tasks. A check of several leading national magazines illustrates this.

In issues checked in 1942, from 50 to 75 per cent of the advertisements made no reference to the war, and a high percentage of those which did were brag ads. In 1943-44, however, the over-all figures were reversed, and from 50 to 75 per cent of the ads dealt in some degree and in some way with the war. The treatment ranged from short notices on war themes to complete advertisements on them, with markedly fewer brag ads.

In one respect advertising was turned upside down in these campaigns, because so many of them, instead of urging people to buy products, urged them to conserve products—dealt with ways to use less of a company's commodity, ways to make possessions last longer. People were entreated to make fewer phone calls, to stay off trains, to avoid telegraphing, to share their automobile, and to lend their vacuum cleaner to neighbors. The appeal of ad-

vertising was literally hurled at the idea of thrift in everything—
save food, clothing, tires, gas, paper, tin, grease and oil, typewriters, and almost all the things that go to make up daily life.

The slogan "Use it up, wear it out, make it do or do without"
was officially adopted by the government and given widespread
circulation, not only by numerous industries, but by the publishers of some 400 magazines and periodicals who supplied a page a
month with a total of 90,000,000 circulation to drive home the
basic thrift theme and the danger of inflationary spending.

Many advertisements aimed telling arguments at women who
hung back from taking war jobs. One quoted the woman who
says, "But I've never worked before!—what kind of war job could
I do?" and then proceeded to answer her question. Another pictured a woman war worker, with the headline, "My husband's in
the Army. I'm in a shipyard. . . . We're in the war together."

Such was the shortage of manpower and womanpower throughout the two-front war that the lowly "Help Wanted" ad borrowed
some of the colorful and persuasive character of "display" advertising. Women were a particular target for this kind of effort because they were being urged to take types of jobs women had
never held before or which were not considered as "socially desirable" as the more familiar feminine occupations.

"Will it take a bomb to break up that afternoon bridge game?"
asked one advertisement, which urged women to "Get out and
drive a truck, load a freight car, work in a day nursery, operate
an elevator." Even cosmetic firms, whose prewar advertising had
aimed to create an atmosphere of luxury and beautiful leisure,
occasionally sang the virtues of riveting and welding.

While most such appeals made sense, there was also the case
of the valve manufacturer who hired a society editor to write and
sign a full-page "Help Wanted Female" advertisement. She
urged women to take a war job and fight for "the caviar of life."

Almost every war theme had its share of advertisements of
high effectiveness. "Keep it under your Stetson" was the catch-
line in an effective series which warned people against loose talk.

"Idle words make busy subs" was one headline in the series. "The less said, the less dead" was another.

"Can you pass a mail box with a clear conscience?" was one of many advertisements in which industry urged more letters to service men. The campaign to increase the use of V-mail told the public "how to make a letter hustle overseas." To illustrate shipping space saved, it pictured the fact that a cigarette package would hold 1,700 V-mail letters. It showed that V-mail letters go 300 miles per hour by air, as against 10 miles per hour for heavier mail by ship.

"Quiz on junk" told people in definite and forceful terms what to save for the scrap collection campaign, how to save it, where it goes, and the importance of what it makes.

At a time when arguments were raging as to whether there was or was not a real gasoline shortage, one advertisement showed a group of men disputing the point in a barbershop. The headline of the advertisement said, "These men don't know the true facts. Do you?"

"Who gets hurt if you buy gas in the black market?" asked another advertisement in this series.

An advertisement for cadet nurses had two parents saying to a friend, "We feel awfully good about Mary's joining the Cadet Nurse Corps."

Another, for the grease salvage campaign, pictured a woman who said, "I'm straining bullets—not grease."

An appeal for blood donors asked, "Will you give a pint of life insurance?" Another pictured a woman who had just given her donation saying, "To think I had to be coaxed!"

"I haven't any kick coming about food" was the title of one advertisement which explained how lucky the American civilian was in his food supply, while "The food you save can help win the war" was the blunt statement of another.

"I have freed a Marine to fight. You can do it too!" said a recruiting advertisement for women Marines.

"Want to give a soldier something to be thankful for? You can do it just by spending the holiday at home" advised an advertisement urging less travel.

Appealing for less use of the telephone so that men in the service might use it more, one advertisement said, "Help him get that long-distance call through tonight." Another in the same series was headed: "Joe needs the long-distance lines tonight."

An effective page pointing out that loose spending led to higher prices and inflation was headed: "How to prevent inflation in one easy lesson. *Put that money back in your pocket.*"

Another on the same theme showed a young war worker displaying his wages to his family while his father cautioned him, "Careful, son—don't let that money bite you."

At the opening of War Bond drives, as many as a thousand magazines would run War Bond pictures or feature material on their covers; often, in entire editions of newspapers every advertisement in the issue would be devoted to War Bonds; and radio coverage would be on a comparable scale. Supplementary media of every type supported the effort. Even wrappers on diapers were pressed into service to advertise War Bonds. Messages on the importance of bond buying were published from the President, Stalin, Churchill, and all the leading generals and admirals of the American armed services. Radio and motion-picture stars originated or were furnished with ingenious and colorful ways of bringing their talents to bear.

Slogans like "Back the attack with War Bonds" and "You've done your bit, now do your best!" were rallying forces for the drives.

Altogether, advertising space and time estimated to be worth $400,000,000 was donated to War Bond campaigns alone, and the number of individual ads ran into the millions.

There were many brilliant advertisements which made telling emotional appeals for war support all along the line. One powerful example of this type showed three young girls lined up along the wall in a Nazi headquarters with a bullet-headed Nazi official leering at them. The headline of the advertisement was: "A high honor for your daughter," and the text then said that if the Nazis win the war "You they may cast aside and put to some ignominious task, such as scrubbing the sidewalks or sweeping the streets. But your daughter . . . well, if she's young and healthy and strong, a Gauleiter with an eye for beauty may decide she is a perfect specimen for one of their experimental camps. A high honor for your daughter."

Another dramatic page in the same series pictured a hangman's noose with a smaller picture in the background of five people hanging. The headline was: "Try this for size." "This type of collar," said the text, "is designed for conquered people. . . . It's not a minute too soon to get the picture straight . . . not a minute too soon to pitch in and help turn the tide . . . not a minute too soon to do everything humanly possible, now, to save our necks."

Another advertisement showed a civilian in his shirt sleeves asleep on his living-room couch. "Are you comfortable, brother?" asked the headline. And then the text went on to say, "That's good, brother. Just sleep right through this war. Let some other guy do your share! What's it to you that a kid just got bumped off in the Solomons . . . because *you* couldn't be bothered with scrap collection? Sure, you out-smarted the ration board on gas all right . . . and kept a certain Army plane in Africa out of the air. You're exhausted thinking up reasons why *not* to buy War Bonds . . . while thousands of American boys are going without food and sleep to protect your hide. Come on, get up off that fat can of yours . . . stop riding and start pushing! If this doesn't apply to you, tear it out and send it to someone it does!"

Perhaps the most widely quoted single advertisement of the war was one entitled "The Kid in Upper 4." While the specific job of this advertisement was to explain the problem of the railroads in handling both military and civilian travel, the advertisement had an appeal far beyond this. It told of a youthful soldier traveling away from home and shipping overseas. "Wide awake . . . listening . . . staring into the blackness," the kid reminisced about "the taste of hamburgers and pop . . . the feel of driving a roadster over a six-lane highway . . . a dog named Shucks, or Spot, or Barnacle Bill," and of the family left behind him. "There's a lump in his throat," the advertisement said, "and maybe a tear fills his eye. It doesn't matter, Kid. Nobody will see . . . it's too dark. . . ." Then to the public came this closing message: "Next time you are on the train, remember the kid in Upper 4. If you have to stand en route . . . If there is no berth for you . . . If you have to wait for a seat in the diner . . ." it is so that he may do his job. "To treat him as our most honored guest is the least we can do to pay a mighty debt of gratitude."

The brag ads quoted earlier and the war messages just cited are samples from the two main streams that flowed side by side throughout the war. Not all brag ads were as bad as those quoted. A few told of really important industrial achievements, and did so with a sense of fitness and with modesty. And not all of the war theme advertisements were as ably or as unselfishly done as the ones cited. But there is no escaping the fact that advertising would have done a better war job if next to nobody had told us that the war was in the bag because snap fasteners and spot welding had put it there, and if more had reminded us that the job was up to us, as people, wherever we might be and whatever we might be doing.

Servicemen in the United States saw and heard much more advertising than servicemen abroad. Commercial radio programs, when broadcast to the services, were sent minus the advertising. Publications were rarely seen by many troops abroad, and in some cases publishers, to facilitate delivery, published special editions containing no advertising.

While vociferous condemnation of many of the brag campaigns emerged even from the jungles of the Pacific theater or the desert of Africa, the absence of advertising was also often lamented by fighting men far from home. One magazine wrote a letter to armed forces subscribers abroad offering them a choice between its regular edition containing advertising and a special light-paper edition without advertising. Although the latter was offered at a lower price and would speed up delivery, a large percentage of the servicemen wrote back that they still wanted the issues with the ads.

One soldier wrote, "You people back there are not in a position to realize how much those advertisements mean to us over here; how they bring back memories of home and evoke pleasant thoughts of what used to be."

Another said: "I have your letter in which you beguile me with the advantages of a lighter edition. I say, no dice. I will not be deprived of the advertisements. All the women look like my wife. . . ."

Another: "Most of our diet over here is so dehydrated that I like to keep the reading robust and natural."

Another: "Out here on New Britain, part of the breath of civilization that comes between the covers of your magazine comes through the medium of your advertisements. . . ."

And another: "Without the advertisements your little publication would be sadly emasculated. I might even forget what a perfume bottle looks like. By perfume, I refer, of course, to Vat 69."

And speaking of perfume, its advertising, like that of cosmetics and toilet soaps, lived in a world by itself—a superheated atmosphere of sensuality which shut out the war except for the fervent moments of heart-thump when the boys and girls got together. In this respect, war copy made prewar copy seem pallid. "This is It," said one advertisement, commenting on the rapturous embrace in its illustration. "The starry eyes . . . the fireworks in the bloodstream . . . this is what the songs sing about . . . this is what little girls are made for."

Another advertisement, labeled "Contact," rhapsodied: "So one and one *really* make one. A moment bright with rapture, and suddenly you know . . . you are whirling through space, *lost* . . . you've just found yourself for the first time! This is the beginning of your life. This is love, love, love. . . ."

Perfume slogans specialized in the "irresistible" theme. Examples:

"A perfume to leave alone unless you can meet its challenge."

"Easy to wear, but not always simple to manage."

"There's no escape from it."

"He will if you wear it; she will if you give it."

When American troops and publications began to filter through France after D-day, the news carried reports that the French population craved our magazines, particularly the advertisements. And of the British, a soldier wrote: "When I give them my old copies of magazines, they read nothing but the advertisements. They get a faraway, misty look in their eyes as they look at the luxuries denied them for five years (I do myself, come to think of it)."

A survey in the South Pacific in the spring of '45 reported that advertising was among the most popular off-duty reading wherever it was obtainable.

The *Harvard Business School Alumni Bulletin* published part of a letter from an army lieutenant in a German prison camp, who said that one of the "best sellers" in the prison camp was a book called *Economic Effects of Advertising*, by Neil Borden, a Harvard professor. The lieutenant said there were three copies of the book in camp, that rental of the copies was paid for in chocolate, but that he feared he had little chance of getting to the top of the waiting list.

The pin-up picture craze drew most of its inspiration from press agents' pictures of movie stars, but toward the end of the war one advertising series became a major contender for popularity honors. Entitled "Back home for keeps," the pictures in this series abjured bold sex and featured romantically sentimental pictures of handsome servicemen and beautiful girls in soulful home-coming embraces. Requests for reproductions of the illustration have passed the hundred-thousand mark as this is written, helped along perhaps by an Irving Berlin song, "Back Home for Keeps," which the series inspired.

In spite of a paper shortage which resulted in cuts totaling 25 per cent in paper available for newspapers and periodicals, advertising volume in dollars rose from approximately $2,000,000,-000 in 1940 to about $2,800,000,000 in 1944. Some of the increase came from higher advertising rates, but more came from greater volume.

When paper cuts were first announced American ingenuity went to work and produced the seeming sleight-of-hand trick of making more paper out of less. Paper allotments were figured in tons of paper; by using lighter-weight papers, by reducing page sizes through trimming margins, by using smaller type, and by many other devices publishers "stretched" their paper so as to accommodate both more editorial matter and more advertising—and often more circulation.

New businesses born in the war, and which hoped to continue afterwards, contributed many new advertisers; general prosperity and the excess-profits tax contributed the rest. To the extent that a business firm was in the excess-profits bracket it could advertise at a cost of fifteen cents on the dollar, since the other eighty-five cents would have gone to the government in taxes if it had not been spent for advertising. In the end the government was likely to collect anyway, because what it did not get from the advertiser it probably got later from the firms to which the money was passed on. Undoubtedly the excess-profits tax was a major factor in swelling the volume of advertising, both that which was effectively devoted to the war and that which stirred resentment for its self-centered and foolish boasting.

But there were over-all advantages which were clear to the government. It needed the power of advertising to appeal to the civilian through popular media. No advertising which it would buy for itself could approach, in amount, distribution, or variety of skill, the total which business could put at the service of the war. And, at the same time, business could keep its products—and the American standard of living—fresh in the public mind for the day when demand would be needed quickly to sell the goods that make the jobs for peace.

Although the great bulk of the advertising in support of the war was done by business, the government paid for several extensive recruitment campaigns for the armed services, beginning as early as 1940. Because there was peacetime precedent for such campaigns, they did not bring to a head the issue which arose early in the war as to whether the government itself should engage in government-paid war advertising. But the issue did have its big test in Congress in 1943, when Senator Bankhead of Alabama introduced a bill authorizing the United States Treasury to spend from $25,000,000 to $30,000,000 "in connection with the sale of U. S. bonds and other purposes."

The reason for the bill was not "ideological"; it saw no special virtue in government advertising as against nongovernment advertising; its principal purpose was to provide financial support for newspapers in small towns and rural areas. At the time of the bill's introduction such publications were still suffering financially from the decline in advertising volume which came immediately after the war's beginning; they had been the hardest hit and the slowest to recover. Under the provisions of the bill one-half of the money appropriated was to be spent in weekly, semiweekly, triweekly, and monthly newspapers and the balance in dailies.

While some members of the country press inspired the bill and many fought for it, others in their field who would benefit financially opposed it just as actively. The latter were backed up by the American Newspaper Publishers Association and the American Society of Newspaper Editors on the ground that government advertising of such magnitude was a serious danger to the freedom of the press. The bill was also vigorously opposed by the War Advertising Council and by the Treasury Department on the ground that, through the Council, business was furnishing without cost all the War Bond advertising needed.

Seven months after the bill's introduction it was passed by the Senate, but with the appropriation reduced to $15,000,000 and with additional restrictions on the type of publication to be used.

The opposition then carried their fight to the members of the House, where the bill died in committee.

While a similar proposal arose again, the chance for success was gone. Increased advertising volume had improved the situation of the country publisher, and war advertising by business was covering more and more sectors of the information job which the government wanted done. Recruitment advertising, mentioned a few paragraphs before, furnishes an illustration of the latter point. As the war progressed the government-paid recruitment campaigns were augmented by growing amounts of industry-donated space and radio time; and as such free advertising proved its effectiveness and mounted in volume it tended more and more to displace the government effort.

As the war with Germany moved toward its end, the pattern of advertising moved with it. Brag advertising almost disappeared, which was good in itself, but a rash of utopian word-pictures of the postwar product-world broke over the nation so fast that the faithful Advertising Council, remembering Japan, sent warnings that the war job was not finished. There were still bond drives, food shortages, conservation needs, the inflation specter, and other continuing assignments to be met—with new tasks looming as we entered the state of part-peace, part-war.

In many an earlier letter, servicemen had said they would feel better in their foxhole homes if their old firms would assure them through advertising of having their old jobs back when they returned. They knew their rights under the law, but they wanted friendly reassurance. Now was the time for it, and many firms took up the theme, some well, some badly. A good example of a good approach was the advertiser who said: "We will have jobs for our service people when they return. They will get a warm welcome and a generous restoration of employee benefits as well. Furthermore, through growth and development of our present products, and by launching new products immediately after the war, we expect to make many new jobs . . . jobs that don't exist today."

Contrasting were advertisers who printed pious generalities, like the one who said: "Now is the time for good business to plan good jobs for good fighters," and let it go at that.

Rehabilitation of wounded veterans received growing advertising attention. One forceful example pictured a soldier who had lost a leg: "I don't want a handout. I just want to stand on my own feet!" was his message. The advertiser then told readers: "This advertisement is . . . to remind you that rehabilitation is your responsibility as well as that of the medical profession . . . that it is a social as well as a medical problem."

Another company, quoting its own example of what individual employers can do to help, announced: "We are working now to analyze every job which men with physical disabilities could perform, so that these jobs can be made available first to returning wounded servicemen."

After V-E Day it was inevitable that advertising would veer as the economy veered, toward peace. This meant more emphasis on civilian merchandise, more getting ready for the selling job ahead. The Council acted to prevent the swing from coming too early and going too far—but the biggest job in advertising's history would soon be faced, and business knew it.

Advertising's role in the war was a minor one, no matter how you stretch it, but advertising's role in peace would be major. Even if the needed 7 to 10 million added peacetime jobs were created, goods produced must move into consumption at an even greater rate of increase or the structure would be a house of cards. Accumulated need for civilian products, due to wartime denial, might lead to the required rate of buying for a time, but after that a plentiful supply of jobs would depend on a permanent level of current demand far higher than prewar levels. Everybody knew that we had more than ample production facilities; not everybody knew that we must have two other things:

ample wages to buy, and the active desire to use. Inside of business there was not enough appreciation of the first of these two; outside of business there was not enough appreciation of the second. People forgot that mass demand does not exist unaided—forgot that it took more than a quarter of a century to bring the automobile into universal use in America, and that it still had not reached that point anywhere else in the world. They forgot that in all things and in all countries the greatest resistances to change are mental and emotional—that higher standards of living call for imagination and enterprise in the consumer no less than in the producer.

The devotion of advertising to the war had been as inconsistent as the devotion of civilians. Some had given much, some nothing. By comparison with the countries which were battlegrounds, we still had not experienced total war. But no nation ever gave so much to a war in which the fighting was so far away—and gave so largely by voluntary action of its people. This does not count for nothing in judging human capacity to grow into the responsibilities of civilization.

In the war the men and women of advertising had their first major chance to devote the content of advertising to themes of noncommercial public service. One result was a strong sentiment in the Advertising Council for the continuance of such work not only through the reconversion period, but into peace. During the San Francisco Conference a special Council task force prepared a series of advertisements on the need for international co-operation and found funds among business firms and others for their use. Another Council group studied the possibilities of a similar co-operative effort to encourage businessmen to bolder postwar job-making.

All this is good. But in the final test the great contribution of advertising has been and must be the selling of goods and services—new and old—into use and consumption. It carries its real Sunday punch in its everyday job. And now it must be getting down to business.

V. BOOKS

by LEWIS GANNETT

LEWIS GANNETT (*age 54*) *has been the daily book critic of the* New York Herald Tribune *since 1930. In* World War I *he was a war correspondent, and during 1944 he reverted to form, becoming a combat correspondent with the 1st and 9th U.S. Armies in France, Belgium, Holland, and Germany before and during the Battle of the Bulge.*

THE books of World War I were at first heavily loaded with a traditional American pacifism, then argumentatively "pro-Ally" or "pro-German," and finally dreamily and utopianly internationalist. It was different this time.

America had done her home work before Pearl Harbor, and much of it before the Germans invaded Poland. Dozens of correspondents had been warning us of trouble ahead; we had read at least parts of *Mein Kampf;* no one in America except hirelings and utter crackpots defended Adolf Hitler. We weren't quite sure whether or when we would enter this war, but we knew which side we wanted to win. We hated war; we were reluctant to take an active part in it; but not a single isolationist book made the best-seller lists. Long before Pearl Harbor the Gallup poll of readers' tastes indicated an overwhelmingly war-minded America.

William L. Shirer's *Berlin Diary* stood at the top of the non-fiction best-seller lists from Portland, Maine, through Chicago to San Diego as recorded in the book supplements on the quiet Sunday when Japanese planes over Pearl Harbor bombed the United States into the World War. That was typical; as a reading public we were in the war long before the armies crossed the seas. From

447

the perspective of a foxhole the civilian public may seem always to have been dismally calm and remote. But it read all the war it could.

You can trace the stages of civilian interest in war in the procession of best-seller lists. William L. Shirer, a son of Iowa not widely known before he began broadcasting from Berlin, was a calm, patient, conscientious man who made up his mind slowly, but firmly; he was, perhaps, a typical Middle Westerner. He didn't shout, over the air or in his book; but he was powerfully convincing. America was in the business of being convinced in December, 1941.

The book which succeeded *Berlin Diary* as the nation's Number 1 nonfiction best seller—and all through the war nonfiction has played a bigger role in the bookstores than ever before in their history—was, appropriately, former Ambassador Joseph Davies's *Mission to Moscow*. Mr. Davies, a Wisconsin businessman, had been in Russia in those shadow-years when Moscow was nominally the ally of Berlin and when America was full of propaganda to the effect that Russia wouldn't fight and couldn't fight, and would fight on Germany's side if she did. Mr. Davies didn't agree. He said that Russia's much-discussed and still debatable purges hadn't weakened the country; that they had, on the contrary, eliminated pro-German elements. His book was long, and ponderously written, but Americans diligently plowed through it. They were ready to be convinced, particularly by a businessman. *Mission to Moscow* played an historic part in preparing America for the difficult business of being a capitalist ally of a socialist state.

In the spring of 1942, when the Army was still in training and most of the Navy was in the repair yards, when the Japanese were busily chasing the British and Americans out of Southwest Asia, the uneasy public read a succession of books indicative of its perplexity.

Actually the best-selling book of that period—though, since it was classified as a pamphlet, it never appeared on the published best-seller lists—was the Red Cross First Aid Manual. In 1942 eight million copies of it went into the homes of civilian Americans eager to "do something," and uncertain what to do. All sorts of technical books also had huge sales in 1942.

The war books of the period were, inevitably, epics of heroism in retreat; there wasn't much else to write about or read about. One of the best of them was Robert St. John's *From the Land of Silent People,* the story of his long trek, along with other cursing newspapermen, from Yugoslavia to Cairo. They watched the German planes drop their loads on Belgrade unopposed, and go home for more, and then they rushed to cable the story. But there were no cable terminals. So they dashed over the mountains to the coast, passing on the way pitiful long lines of little Yugoslav ox-carts lumbering toward the front to meet the German tanks. There were no working telegraph offices on the coast, either. So the correspondents bought a leaky little boat and tacked down the Dalmatian coast to Greece, still seeking an open wire. They found the Germans in Greece ahead of them. They fled on to Crete, were evacuated thence with the British, and when at last they found a functioning cable in Cairo, the censor stopped their too grim stories. *From the Land of Silent People* was a dramatic book, symbolic of a stage of the war, and helped, like others of its kind, prepare the American public for a long wait.

There was Captain Antoine de Saint-Exupéry's *Flight to Arras,* the beautiful but too philosophical meditations of a French flier who did his duty in the air with a sense that his country was doomed. There was the quite different book by young Richard Hillary, an English boy who grew up in the air over the English Channel with a sense that he, but not his country, was doomed— as indeed he was. *Falling Through Space* told how he fell into the Channel from a burning parachute, and it is one of the most rereadable of British war books; after writing it, Hillary returned to the air, and was lost.

There were also a host of books upon the fall of France, as later there were stories, sometimes springing rather from the soil of

Hollywood than from that of France, of the French Underground. Among the best of the books on the fall of France were *Scum of the Earth,* by Arthur Koestler, a brilliant Austrian refugee who later joined the British Army, and *A Thousand Shall Die,* by Hans Habe, a German refugee who later joined the United States Army and became editor of the first newspaper issued in German on German soil under American Army auspices.

Civilian America, remote from the war, needed grim realism, but it also needed reassurance. War books provided that, too. Colonel W. F. Kernan's *Defense Will Not Win the War* cheerfully asserted that it would be possible to land on the soft underbelly of Europe in that spring of 1942, and Major Alexander de Seversky glowingly prophesied other alluring patterns of victory in *Victory Through Air Power.* It is obvious today that both the American colonel and the Russian major grievously underrated the United States Navy; infantrymen grumble today at Seversky's dithyrambs about precision bombing, just as they mutter at Air Corps publicity, and the men of the carrier planes today can laugh at his contempt for sea-based aviation; but in 1942 the major's book was rousing reading, and it and the movie made from it helped nerve the country to give up pleasure driving and turn out planes by the hundred thousand. It is worth recalling that soon after his book appeared a man who was to be a Presidential candidate still could sneer at President Roosevelt's "impossible" talk of building a hundred thousand planes a year.

These, of course, were not the only books that civilians read, and read avidly. Now and then pure "escape" literature topped the best-seller lists. There was Marjorie Kinnan Rawlings's amiable story of her back-country life in cracker Florida, *Cross Creek;* there were also Ilka Chase's glittering and entertaining recollections of stage life, *Past Imperfect.* In a sense Elliot Paul's nostalgic book, *The Last Time I Saw Paris,* was escape literature too, though its fade-out was war. His Paris was the shabby rue de la Huchette, of the Left Bank; respectable Right Bank lovers deplored his disreputable cast of characters, but most Americans had what would later be known as a healthy G.I. taste; they loved the book and its rowdy cast.

In July, 1942, a meteor burst across the publishing skies, and a shy, gangling North Carolina boy found himself famous. Pvt. Marion Hargrove, who, like most privates, needed cash, had sent a few sketches of life at Fort Bragg to his home-town newspaper, the Charlotte, North Carolina, *News*. Maxwell Anderson, visiting Fort Bragg, saw them and sent a batch to a New York publisher, Henry Holt and Company. They sold pretty well—12,500 copies in the first two months. Then *Reader's Digest* and *Life* reprinted excerpts from the book—and civilian America, tired of reading what other people's sons were doing on other continents, took to its heart Private Hargrove's unassuming stories of what American boys were doing in American training camps. *See Here, Private Hargrove* has sold two and a half million copies at this writing, which puts it well up among the top best sellers of all American publishing history. Its phenomenal success was obviously a reflection of the American's parochial interest in American boys, wherever they might be. At that time our boys were in the camps, and so Americans preferred to read of the training camps rather than of the war in Europe.

As our boys went into action, however, we were avid to read about them in action. The first of the best-seller American-boys-in-action books was William L. White's *They Were Expendable,* a thriller of the PT boats in Philippine waters. Like the European war books of the period, it was, necessarily, a story of heroism in retreat, but it was American heroism and we gobbled it up. The first American success story, and a tough-bitten one it was, was Richard Tregaskis's *Guadalcanal Diary.* Three Guadalcanal books appeared almost simultaneously, two of them by men whose names were soon to be rising stars in American letters. The second was Ira Wolfert's *Battle for the Solomons;* the third was *Into the Valley*, by John Hersey, whose *A Bell for Adano* was to win the Pulitzer Prize in fiction in 1945. None of them pictured life on "the Canal" as we heard of it when the survivors came home, but for that censorship, rather than the authors, was to blame. One can argue about censorship until doomsday. Perhaps the Japs didn't know the facts of life in the Solomons at the time, as the censors argued, but to a good many civilians as well as soldiers the record seems to show that army and navy authorities overprotected the home public from grim news. Yet the public always reacted well to grim news; it never behaved better than after Pearl Harbor when it suspected the worst. Most of the faults of civilian life can be traced to inadequate knowledge of the facts of war, and for that censorship directives are largely responsible.

Another little book which had one of the most fantastic histories in American publishing appeared on April 8, 1943. Wendell L. Willkie, Republican candidate for President of the United States in 1940, had flown around the world in the summer of 1942 and returned with a passionate sense that America's view of the war and the world was parochial. He wrote *One World*—and he wrote it himself, despite malicious legends to the contrary.

One World had no book-club sponsorship to help launch it. Its author's name was sufficient to guarantee a good sale, but the highest prepublication estimate of its sales made in the office of its publishers, Simon and Schuster, who are not noted for conservatism, was 250,000. The American public gobbled it up. No book in publishing history—not *See Here, Private Hargrove*, and not even *Gone With the Wind*—had ever sold faster. Within two months after its publication date sales topped a million. Within two years sales topped two million. A paper edition was issued simultaneously with the cloth-bound edition, but both editions sold. The original publishers sold 970,000 in paper, 350,000 in cloth. The Book-of-the-Month Club, which had passed it by prior to publication, put *One World* into an omnibus volume, *Prefaces to Peace*, and sold 350,000 copies of that. Pocketbooks sold half a million copies of a pocket edition. England, Switzerland, Sweden, and other foreign countries issued *One World* in translation. The Danish Underground brought out what was probably the handsomest edition in the history of underground political publishing.

The book was a bullet. It helped kill the lingering moods of complacency at home. It was a crippling blow to the powerful isolationist wing in Mr. Willkie's own party. Isolationists were still powerful enough to stop his campaign for renomination in 1944, but they had to camouflage their tracks. *One World* was probably the most influential book published in America during the war. For sixteen consecutive weeks it stood at the top of the New York *Herald Tribune's* best-seller list, a composite of records from bookstores all over the United States. It was still selling a year after publication; like *Uncle Tom's Cabin,* its history is a part of the history of the country.

Walter Lippmann's sober study of *U. S. Foreign Policy* for a time competed with it for top place. Sumner Welles's *The Time for Decision* rivaled it in popularity, but it is a striking fact that blueprints for peace and charters for the future had no such vogue in World War II as in World War I. The American public was healthily skeptical; it seemed to realize that blueprints and charters could never be enough, and that the day-to-day working realities of international partnership are more important than the paper patterns of charters.

Under Cover, an exposure of the phony "shirt" movements which masqueraded under a guise of patriotic "nationalism," also had a significant run as top best seller. Its author, an Armenian immigrant, had worked as an undercover agent with some of the organizations which opposed American participation in the war; he hated them all. His book's sales reached 700,000, which, in view of its loose construction and turgid rhetoric, was significant of an extraordinary change in the national temper. A very different book that had a phenomenal sale was Bob Hope's *I Never Left Home,* full of Hollywood G.I. guffaws and groans.

And then came Ernie Pyle. He had been wandering about the U.S.A. for years writing small-town stuff for the Scripps-Howard newspapers, but thousands of newspapermen were better known.

He covered London in its blitz, but scores of reporters did so more memorably. Then Ernie Pyle followed his American G.I. to North Africa and, instead of writing strategy, continued writing home-town Americana. His *Here Is Your War,* published toward the end of 1943, a year after the American invasion of North Africa, made his a household name throughout the U.S.A. In his modest, matter-of-fact, G.I. reporting, the civilian public had its most effective contact with its neighbors at the front. Pyle brought the monotony as well as the drama and drudgery of war into the American home. That book sold 240,000 copies in the original edition, 150,000 through the People's Book Club, a million copies in a twenty-five-cent Pocketbook reprint, 100,000 in a dollar reprint edition—and then it went overseas in an Armed Services Edition, and Ernie Pyle began appearing in the *Stars and Stripes.* Pyle's second book, *Brave Men,* sold a million copies before a Japanese sniper killed its author, close to the front as usual, on the Japanese-held island of Ie in April, 1945, and the reprints had not yet begun. It was still topping all best-seller lists in the summer of 1945, though by that time Sergeant Bill Mauldin's *Up Front* was beginning to challenge it.

Mauldin's book was a real G.I. product, and naturally a bit different from the somewhat slicker and more sentimental versions of front life produced by visiting correspondents, even by Ernie Pyle. Mauldin's book began as a collection of drawings which had first appeared in *Stars and Stripes* and, despite a few frowns from some of the loftier brass, had won general army approval. His characters didn't shave and button up in accordance with rear-echelon prescriptions, and their language had at least a whiff of the unpoliced jargon of the front. And when Mauldin was persuaded to write a text to accompany his drawings, it turned out that he could write, perhaps, even better than he could draw—and he wrote with the same hard-bitten, angry honesty with which he drew. He gave civilian readers almost their first unscreened sense of the combat infantryman's bitter and independent attitude toward his officers, his orders, his isolation, toward the high and low brass, all the rear echelons, and all the civilians at home.

Those were the most-read war books, and in the succession from Shirer through St. John and Seversky, Hargrove and Willkie, to Pyle, you can trace a kind of history of the shifting patterns of civilian America's war interest.

Novels usually outsell what the book trade, for want of a better word, calls nonfiction; in this war that has never been true. Even Lloyd C. Douglas's *The Robe,* probably the fastest-selling wartime novel, did not match the records of *See Here, Private Hargrove,* of *One World,* or of Ernie Pyle's books.

Nor is it easy to discern in the public's wartime choice of novels any indication of public taste and public interest, or any hint of any literary "trend." Dr. A. J. Cronin's *Keys of the Kingdom,* Lloyd Douglas's *The Robe,* Franz Werfel's *The Song of Bernadette,* and Sholem Asch's *The Apostle,* all very popular in wartime, exploited what are called "religious" themes, but religious themes have always appeared high on best-seller lists, and none of these books seemed to have any significant impact on American thought or feeling.

War novels, it is true, never held the spotlight as the war narratives and war arguments did. Many reasons may be assigned for that. Primarily, they weren't good enough. But for that in its turn many reasons may be assigned—first of all, that the novelists did not know enough.

The great war novels, of course, are written by veterans, after a war is well past. Fighting soldiers have lots of time to stand in line and wait, but little time to write. Newspaper correspondents are always in a hurry, and their experience of war, however close they may come to the shells, is different from that of the man who lives with the enemy night and day; moreover, few correspondents are natural novelists. The well-established novelists, of course, are over-age.

Ernest Hemingway, to be sure, emerged from his hide-out in Cuba, covered the advance on Paris, and, dissatisfied with the role of spectator, joined the French Army. John Dos Passos, after covering the home front in a series of magazine articles, went to the Pacific as a correspondent. But neither wrote war novels. William Saroyan, after writing *The Human Comedy,* Saroyan's own ode on intimations of immortality, joined the Army as a private but was assigned to action in London, which left him free to live at the Hotel Savoy, hardly a foxhole despite the buzz bombs. Sinclair Lewis watched the war from his native Minnesota. Louis Bromfield wrote about his Ohio farm. Theodore Dreiser, even before the war, had lapsed into silence in Hollywood. Pearl Buck wrote a parable of war in China, *Dragon Seed,* but for the most part her wartime role was the useful one of an oracle of interracial understanding. John Steinbeck was the only one of America's major novelists who essayed a war novel, and for that he was roundly abused by an army of frustrated civilian critics.

Steinbeck's greatest success, *Grapes of Wrath,* his odyssey of the penniless Okies trekking to California in depression-time, had appeared in 1939. He followed it with an escapist record of a biological expedition to the Gulf of California, *Sea of Cortez.* Then, early in 1942, he dashed off at white heat a little parable of invasion in an unnamed country, obviously Norway, *The Moon Is Down.* It was a story of a pacific people overwhelmed by sudden invasion, confused at first but never conquered in spirit. Its hero, the mayor, was killed, but not before he had told the German major that while herd men win battles, free men win wars. Its motto was the shriek of a crazed German officer, "the flies conquer the flypaper." But it also pictured a philosophic old German officer, who remembered Belgium in the last war, and recognized in his heart that the mayor was right, though in fact the major ritually performed his ruthless German "duty." For that inclusion Steinbeck was fiercely attacked as a defeatist.

The silly affair was a revelation of one of the weaknesses of civilians, including many writers, in wartime. They feel guilty for their ease and passivity, and express their sense of guilt in pathological excesses. The attack on *The Moon Is Down* was an echo, in a new form, of the foolishness of 1917, when good American housewives suspected German-born bakers of selling bread made with powdered glass. The critics of Steinbeck's novel lived in a world of propaganda warfare, in which every German soldier had to be regarded as a super-SS fanatic; they adopted a kind of race philosophy in reverse which made the discovery of dazed, docile Germans in 1945 a bewilderment and a puzzle. Such critics were in fact denying the writer's essential right to picture diverse types, even among the enemy.

Steinbeck, actually, saw more of the war than most novelists. He too felt under obligation. He trained with the Air Force and wrote a handbook for Air Force families, *Bombs Away*. He went overseas for six months as a correspondent for the New York *Herald Tribune*, writing daily articles. But he refused to permit his articles to be reprinted as a book, and so far he has written no novel based on his war experience. Apparently he knows that it takes time to ripen apples.

The best of the correspondents' novels were simple, unpretentious affairs, written by men who had lived close to the Army. Richard Tregaskis, author of the first of the Guadalcanal reports, contracted malaria in the Pacific, and was wounded in Italy, but could live nowhere except at the front. On sick leave after the fall of Aachen he wrote *Stronger Than Fear*, the story of a combat soldier who conquered his own fear during a street fight, not so much out of any sense that he was making history as because he had to fight to retain his sense of personal dignity. Tregaskis's book was an episode as much as a novel, but far closer to front psychology than most of the hero-stories rewritten by civilian writers aglow with patriotism.

John Hersey's first book, *Men on Bataan*, was a rewrite job of *Time* and *Life* correspondents' reports from the Philippines. Instead of attempting, as so many other correspondents did, to sum up "the decisive battle of the war," Hersey, in his second book, *Into the Valley*, told simply and sensitively of a minor and in itself unsuccessful skirmish by a company of green Marines. That book brought home to a headline-weary public the forgotten fact that if nine-tenths of war is waiting, most of the rest is skirmishing for position. It also revealed a young writer of power, and in the spring of 1944 his *A Bell for Adano* for a time topped all the best-seller lists.

Partly it was a *succès de scandale.* Hersey's book was the story of a little "Wop" major from the Bronx, who tried to do the right thing in a Sicilian town and ran into difficulties with a hot-tempered general. Appearing about the time stories of General Patton's impatience with shell-shocked American soldiers were making headlines, it was read in that light. But at root it was an honest story of the difficulties of democracy, and its more durable merits eventually won it a Pulitzer Prize. John Hersey was not yet thirty when it appeared.

In the same period Lillian Smith's *Strange Fruit* had a success which astonished no one more than its own author. Florida-born, Lillian Smith had grown up in Georgia, where she still lives. Hers is an honest story of a white man's love for a colored girl, a hopeless affair in a Georgia town.

Aided, possibly, by the fact that Boston banned the book (because it contained, in an incidental and a natural context, a four-letter word commoner in G.I. conversation than in print), it leaped to the top of the best-seller lists. But Boston has banned many books which never sold, and for the popularity of Lillian Smith's book one must seek other causes.

Race prejudice in an America fighting race-mad Nazi Germany would not appear to be a naturally popular topic. Yet it is a topic which always lurks uneasily in the American subconsciousness. And the amazing success of Lillian Smith's novel, together with the almost equally striking record of Richard Wright's *Black Boy,* the bleak story of its author's childhood in Tennessee and Mississippi, suggests that more may be happening in the South than the Bilbos and Talmadges suspect. The United States Army, in this war, was still a Jim Crow Army, but no Jim Crow law or convention applied to civilian reading.

It is hard to find any meaning in the success of John Marquand's story of an overaged intellectual in wartime, *So Little Time*, except that in detail it is very good reading; or of Betty Smith's story of slum childhood, *A Tree Grows in Brooklyn*, except that the mud out of which water lilies grow always seems romantic. As for the flash best sellers of the winter of 1944–45, the meaning is clear. Kathleen Winsor's *Forever Amber* was a lush, loose, romantic "historical novel" of the roistering days of King Charles II; Adria Locke Langley's *A Lion Is in the Streets* was a lusty parable of Huey Long's Louisiana, with democratic overtones and sex-in-the-bayous underpinning. The moral, of course, is what every bookseller knows: Sex sells.

Many writers deliberately abandoned "creative" writing to fill some niche in the war effort, none of them more effectively than the frail poet Stephen Vincent Benét, who turned from his unfinished American epic, *Western Star*, to write war scripts for radio and war poems for any occasion, and died of overwork, a true civilian war casualty. Unquestionably the most immediately effective and popular war poem was Alice Duer Miller's *White Cliffs of Dover;* written before the United States entered the war, it passionately voiced her crisis-sense of common heritage: "In a world where England is finished and dead, I do not wish to live."

A mystery-story writer organized as a part-time bit what became a full-time job, the incredibly active Writers' War Board. Two days after Pearl Harbor, Rex Stout, author of the Nero Wolfe stories, called the board into being, to help the Treasury enlist writers in selling War Bonds. Within a few months it grew into a ramifying liaison office between writers and government departments, a kind of unpaid extension of the Office of War Information.

The Writers' War Board enlisted name writers from the Rev. Harry Emerson Fosdick to Gypsy Rose Lee, from Alexander Woollcott to John P. Marquand. Before Germany surrendered, more than two thousand writers with established markets had written scripts or articles at its request; an accountant-author reckoned its total output at more than three tons of manuscript. Among these tons of material were Treasury slogans, radio scripts, editorials, and articles for virtually every magazine in America. The board suggested topics to authors, and authors to magazines; it publicized the tragedy of Lidice internationally; it served as a voluntary American board of editors for the magazine *Transatlantic,* which told England what Americans were doing in the war.

The Writers' War Board worked primarily on the East Coast; in the West, the Hollywood Writers' Mobilization served a similar purpose, enlisting writers for documentary films, a "Free World Theatre" series, radio scripts, and army camp plays.

Meanwhile, the book publishing industry, which, like most civilian groups, had floundered about in an effort to be of some use just after Pearl Harbor, had stumbled into the extraordinary publishing adventure known as Armed Services Editions, with which most soldiers are more familiar than civilians.

The publishers had early organized a Council on Books in Wartime which sought to promote not only the idea that books may be bullets, but the kind of books which are good bullets. It set up a committee consisting of three critics, a colonel, and an admiral who designated certain books as "Imperatives," and the Council actively promoted the sale of these. W. L. White's *They Were Expendable* was the first Imperative; John Hersey's *Into the Valley,* Wendell Willkie's *One World,* Walter Lippmann's *U. S. Foreign Policy,* John Hersey's *A Bell for Adano,* and Edgar Snow's *People on Our Side* followed. These were the Council's Silver-Star war books.

The Armed Services Editions developed into the greatest mass publishing enterprise of all history. The Army's and Navy's first appeals for books for soldiers and sailors, made through the American Library Association, had dug more than ten million books out of civilian homes, but not all of them were of much interest to the G.I.'s, and as the services expanded it became obvious that civilian donations would never meet the servicemen's demand for current best sellers, funny books, technical books, sexy books, or even classics. Accordingly, early in 1943 Editions for the Armed Services, Inc., was organized, with Philip Van Doren Stern, an experienced publisher, as its director. Before the end of the year it delivered six and a half million books to the Army and Navy, in 1944 the figure was twenty-eight million books, and in 1945 it will be about sixty million—mountains and mountains of books!

The plan, drawn up in co-operation with representatives of the Army and Navy, was to supply small paper-bound books on an essentially nonprofit basis to American armed forces stationed overseas, on a schedule calling for the delivery every month of thirty titles, 40,000 copies of each to the Army and 10,000 to the Navy. This schedule expanded until it called for forty titles a month, 130,000 copies of each for Army use, and 25,000 for the Navy, and no serviceman paid a cent for them. The titles were selected by a group of critics, librarians, and booksellers, subject to army and navy veto, and eventually constituted a library of nearly a thousand titles. Authors were paid a royalty of one-half cent per copy, as contrasted with the usual royalty of 25 to 50 cents.

The first list ranged from Ambassador Joseph Grew's *Report from Tokyo* through Dickens's *Oliver Twist*, Conrad's *Lord Jim*, and Steinbeck's *Tortilla Flat* to Thurber's *My World and Welcome to It* and Jack Goodman's *Fireside Book of Dog Stories*. Later, as the evidence of G.I. taste made itself felt, the selections became more low-brow. Mystery stories and "Westerns" were most popular; the editors could never locate enough humor, and there was a constant demand for any story whose title suggested sex. The most printed author was Ernest Haycox, a "Western" writer with eight titles; Max Brand's "Westerns," the ever-popular Thorne Smith books, and C. S. Forester's sea stories ranked next.

All these titles were subject to veto by army and navy boards, and some of the vetoes seemed odd to the board of critics. The Army, for instance, had no objection to Hersey's *A Bell for Adano;*

the Navy, speaking through its lady librarian, did! At an early stage army authorities, interpreting literally a congressional prescription, held that they could not buy books having political angles, and they scrupulously counted as such, even Catherine Drinker Bowen's *Yankee from Olympus* (a biography of the late Supreme Court Justice Oliver Wendell Holmes) and Professor Charles Beard's symposium on the Constitution, *The Republic*. The consequent storm was terrific, and Congress changed the law.

Textbooks, scientific books, and "educational" books were not included in these editions; but the Army and the Navy bought some millions of copies of such specialized books direct from the publishers. Out of the venture grew the phenomenon that the armed services in the remotest outposts, in New Guinea, Iceland, Ascension Island, and Alaska, read the top best sellers almost as soon as the civilians did at home, and long before they went into cheap reprint editions at home. The servicemen also had an ample supply of selected "pulp" fiction; hopefully a few classics were sent them, and even some poetry. Inevitably the books were read more intensively at sea, in hospitals, and at base camps than in foxholes and cellars, but they reached the front. They were combat books. No army in history had ever had so ample a supply of reading matter.

Every publisher co-operated. In fact, the book publishers' record in the war, of quiet co-operative contribution to the war effort, compares very favorably with that of other industries. The home-market situation was such that books—all kinds of books— sold phenomenally well; but the publishers, while counting their profits, did a bit less flamboyant flag-waving than most of their business confreres. Their advertising, generally speaking, would bear a tolerant G.I. scrutiny. None of the successful war novels matched in bathos the conventional Hollywood war story; and, as should be the case with the book world's more leisurely product, the books were soberer than newspaper headlines or radio thrills. If the wartime book output includes little which seems likely to rank as enduring world literature, a shelf of World War II books is likely to look more sensible, as well as more readable, in 1975, than a shelf of World War I books does today. It reflects a maturer civilian world, less hysterical but as soberly and as realistically at war as it had been permitted to know how to be.

For any realistic picture of the world in which the servicemen lived, on the well-advertised as on the forgotten fronts of this excessively world-wide World War, of course, the civilians, like the servicemen, will have to wait until the men who lived the war have had time to digest their experiences, to adjust their perspectives to the civilian world to which they are returning, and to learn the art of writing. No war in history was ever as fully reported, or as avidly read, as this; but no war has ever been understood in its own time. If great novels, great poetry, or any kind of great writing comes out of this war, it will come, as out of previous wars, long after the event. Such books will be written in a mood determined not only by a grimmer picture of war experience than morale permits in wartime, but also by the as yet unpredictable convolutions of what we still vaguely call "the postwar mind." No one has yet written anything about that postwar mind which makes any sense at all. Presumably, sometime someone—and presumably a veteran of this war—will.

VI. THE THEATRE

by *WOLCOTT GIBBS*

WOLCOTT GIBBS *is the drama critic, the movie
critic, and a general editor for* The New Yorker
magazine. He has been with The New Yorker
*since its inception and prepared for this career
by taking the precaution of being born in New
York City forty-three years ago.*

TOWARD the end of November, 1941, the producing firm of José
Ferrer and Ruth Wilk hopefully announced the opening of a play
by Lowell Barrington called *The Admiral Had a Wife*. The date
set was Wednesday, December 10, the theatre was the Playhouse,
and the stars were Uta Hagen, Mr. Ferrer's wife, and Alfred
Drake, a young actor soon to ride to glory in *Oklahoma!* According to reports from out of town, the piece was a comedy, dealing
with an ambitious navy wife in Hawaii and her efforts to obtain
promotion for her husband through the influence of an uncle,
agreeably potent in Washington; it was further described as "a
good-natured spoof on the Navy," which, it seemed, was humor-
ously honeycombed with nepotism. On Sunday, the seventh, the
Japanese bombers, swarming in over Diamond Head to blast
Pearl Harbor and Hickham Field, scored an unplanned but nevertheless disastrous hit on the Playhouse, some five thousand miles
away. The nautical spoof was hastily abandoned by her crew on
Monday, the eighth, going down in theatrical history as the first
local casualty of the war. In addition to winning this unhappy
distinction, it also marked the beginning of a period of unprecedented confusion, anxiety, makeshift, bad taste, and just plain
nonsense on the American stage.

Running at the time were such substantial successes as *Lady in
the Dark*, Moss Hart's handsome wedding of psychiatry and the

464

magazine business; *Best Foot Forward,* a very engaging musical about the high-school set; *Let's Face It,* another musical, this one based on a lively old farce called *The Cradle Snatchers; Blithe Spirit,* Noel Coward's cheerful essay on haunts; *Junior Miss,* a neat, touching comedy adapted from a series in the *New Yorker; Sons o' Fun,* Olsen and Johnson's maniacal successor to *Hellzapoppin; Angel Street,* a fine, chilly melodrama imported from London; and, of course, those great permanent exhibits, *Life with Father* and *Arsenic and Old Lace.* However, these nine, none of which had even the remotest bearing on the war, were just about all the really rewarding original material New York had to look at during the remainder of that troubled season.* Two excellent revivals turned up during the spring—a return engagement of the musical version of *Porgy and Bess,* which was, on the whole, superior to its first showing in 1935, and a magnificent production of *Candida,* with Katharine Cornell, Raymond Massey, and Burgess Meredith—but the rest ranged from mediocre to ghastly.

Of the nonmilitary exhibits, *Jason,* based on the extremely dubious premise that drama critics lead interesting lives; *Guest in the House* and *Uncle Harry,* two psychological studies of a somewhat languid nature; and a musical called *By Jupiter,* which was largely devoted to the hypothetical humor of effeminacy, were probably the most satisfactory, though there was nothing about any of them to warrant elaborate critical scrutiny. The other entries in this class, which bore such forbidding titles as *The Lady Comes Across* (3 performances), *They Should Have Stood in Bed* (11 performances), *What Big Ears* (8 performances), and *Comes the Revelation* (2 performances) caused on the whole nothing but suffering on both sides of the footlights, and most of them, in the words of Richard Maney, the most articulate press agent since St. Paul, flew shut like so many doors. This was especially discouraging since among the authors of these melancholy works

---

* *The Corn Is Green* and *The Watch on the Rhine* ended their long runs too soon after Pearl Harbor to warrant inclusion here, but it might be noted that the latter, immeasurably the best play to be written about this war, was produced some eight months before the United States was actually involved.

were men like Clifford Odets, Charles MacArthur, Ben Hecht, John van Druten, Marc Connelly, and Paul Vincent Carroll, all of whom had performed with distinction in the past. It might be noted, incidentally, that George S. Kaufman, Maxwell Anderson, and Somerset Maugham escaped this list only because their contributions to the season's misery happened to be made a little before Pearl Harbor.

The war plays were even worse. Some notion of what we were in for might have been gathered from a drama by Frederick Hazlitt Brennan called *The Wookey*, which had opened the previous September. This was the saga of a Cockney tugboat captain who was transformed from a sardonic critic of British war policy into one of the heroes of Dunkirk when a bomb demolished his humble dockside home. It was one of the noisiest productions in memory, featuring a special sound track made on the scene during the blitz and costing fifteen thousand dollars to import, but somehow this expensive racket failed to fetch the reviewers. George Jean Nathan, who considered *The Wookey* as mechanical and doughy as an Automat pie, wrote further: "The mental and psychical changes in the heroes of fine drama are not wrought by bombs. . . . Thinking quickly back over the war plays of all history, I cannot recall one of any authentic quality that was not practically soundless." In addition to this external application of high explosives as opposed to any inward growth of the spirit as a means of bringing about its hero's regeneration, Mr. Brennan's drama suffered from a painful overdose of that quietly whimsical fortitude which has rendered almost every play about Englishmen at war, not excepting the vastly overrated *Journey's End*, somewhat absurd and even a little embarrassing to the actual warriors thus canonized.

From December 8 to the close of the season, there were five plays dealing exclusively with the war, and three of these— *Golden Wings*, a piece of appalling nonsense about the RAF; *Heart of a City*, a well-meaning but hopelessly inept tribute to a vaudeville troupe that carried on through the blitz; and *Plan M*, an ephillipsoppenheim of really majestic imbecility—had a great deal in common with *The Wookey,* being compounded largely of loud noises and modestly bogus heroics.

The other two, both of native origin, were somewhat different. *Letters to Lucerne,* laid in a girls' school in Switzerland immediately before and after the outbreak of war, dealt with the agony suffered by a German girl faced with the gathering hatred of her schoolmates. Basically an interesting idea, it was handicapped by its Noah's Ark construction, each of the warring nations being conscientiously represented; the strictly utilitarian quality of its prose; and a slickness of plot (the Russian girl was in love with the German's brother, and he gallantly crashed his plane rather than bomb her family in Warsaw) that seemed to mirror Hollywood rather more accurately than life. It may even have been that the sympathetic treatment given the heroine operated against it with a public in no mood for compromises with the devil. In any case, it closed after two weeks, though it won a sort of consolation prize when Burns Mantle named it in his annual selection of the season's ten best plays.

The Moon Is Down, by John Steinbeck, was a far more ambitious project, a good deal harder to evaluate. In it Mr. Steinbeck, who had previously written such bitterly effective novels attacking native fascism as *In Dubious Battle* and *The Grapes of Wrath,* showed a curious tenderness toward the Germans. Essentially, *The Moon Is Down* presented the tragedy of the Occupied Countries in microcosm. A small village, presumably in Norway, was taken by the invaders, largely as a result of fifth column activities; the conquest was easy, almost bloodless, but the spirit of resistance was never crushed. Nazi soldiers and native collaborationists were the victims of mysterious attacks; railroads and mines were sabotaged; in the face of the silent, implacable hatred of the townspeople, panic began to creep into the German garrison. "The flies have conquered the flypaper!" one lieutenant cried hysterically, and his words became the mocking refrain of a song that spread over the countryside. In the end, the Nazi commandant ordered the execution of the mayor, a gentle, courageous old man, unless he instructed his people to co-operate with the invaders. Naturally, he refused, and as the curtain fell, there was the sound of an off-stage explosion that was presumably his death warrant but also the sound of doom for the men who dreamed that murder could stamp out freedom.

No exception, of course, could be taken to Mr. Steinbeck's thesis. His treatment, however, aroused a lively storm of protest and derision in critical teapots. One of his German officers was the cold, fanatical product, not so much of National Socialism—for Mr. Steinbeck had no apparent concern with racial or economic theories—as of a professional military caste. The others, however, were generally felt to be very odd specimens for an army that had overrun most of Europe. They were sentimental, homesick, almost humbly anxious for the friendship of the vanquished and unable to understand the hostility they found instead; they had even come to doubt Hitler's magnificent crusade; one of them said he had dreamt the Fuehrer was crazy. Even the commandant, a veteran of the last war and a realist, was a man of basically humane impulses, ordering his victims shot with genuine reluctance, making it clear that he was only carrying out the policies, personally distasteful to him, that were formulated in Berlin. The general critical reaction to all this was summed up by Richard Lockridge, who wrote in the *Sun:* "By making his invaders more sinned against than sinning Mr. Steinbeck has dissipated his drama. The drama needs two hostile forces face to face. Here are pleasant, reasonable people on one side and on the other only disembodied orders from 'the capital.' Mr. Steinbeck proves himself tolerant to a fault and his play suffers. So, I suspect, does his argument." A more acid critic was pleased to credit *The Moon Is Down* to another hand, well known for its skill in reducing the forces of good and evil to a general level of sunny charm. "I think it's the best thing that Robert Nathan ever wrote," he said.

From the vantage point of the present, it must be admitted that Mr. Steinbeck was an accurate prophet of German psychol-

ogy in defeat—the anxiety, that is, of the individual soldier to dis-
claim any moral responsibility for his behavior—but that, and the
not unpoetic quality of the prose, were about all that could be
said for the play. In short, if *The Moon Is Down* presented a true
picture of the enemy, the average German's belief in the doctrine
of the superman was so feebly and even apologetically held that
it was almost impossible to regard him as a serious threat to civilization. Taken in conjunction with the desperate news then arriv-
ing from Europe and the Pacific, Mr. Steinbeck's message inevitably seemed rather vacant and literary. It was, however, just
about all that American playwrights had to offer during our first
half year at war.

Customarily, the metropolitan stage takes a rest from the middle of June until Labor Day. A few plays may come into town,
but they are seldom anything to summon the critics away from
the mountains and beaches where for a little while they try to
live like other men. In 1942, however, their rest was violently
disturbed by the arrival of Irving Berlin's *This Is the Army,* which
opened at the Broadway Theatre on the Fourth of July. Because
of its wide distribution, practically unaltered, as a film, and the
even wider distribution of its songs via the phonograph and radio, it isn't necessary to describe *This Is the Army* in any detail.
It had approximately the same function in this war as Mr. Berlin's
Yip, Yip, Yaphank had in the last. It was a service show entirely
executed by servicemen, and it told more, through the medium of
vaudeville, about the qualities that made it possible for a nonmilitary nation to raise an effective fighting force than any ten
plays celebrating desperate and rhetorical gallantries on the battlefield. Mr. Nathan, whose attitude toward the current war plays
up to then had been what Booth Tarkington once described as
that of a duchess looking at bugs, said of this one: "There are
two points of view from which to report on the show. One is the
patriotic, which would warmly assert that it was great stuff. The
other is the critical, which would coolly assert that it certainly
was. For in the experience of the present recorder, there hasn't

been a frankly designated patriotic spectacle that was in quieter and better taste, that had so much merit in it of its independent own, and that so strainlessly and modestly persuaded its audience into emotional response." He was not excessive.

To appreciate the singular virtues of *This Is the Army,* it is necessary to go forward almost a year and a half to the night when Moss Hart's *Winged Victory,* another all-service show of imposing dimensions, opened at the Forty-Fourth Street Theatre. Mr. Hart's offering, however, was not vaudeville; it was a conventionally plotted drama, taking a group of boys from their diverse homes, through a long and often disheartening period of training as flight cadets, and delivering them finally on an island in the Pacific, subject to Japanese bombing. Beyond any question, *Winged Victory* was a valuable recruiting poster, as stirring and gaily colored as any ever drawn by James Montgomery Flagg, and it also had a good deal of documentary interest, since the technical details were clearly authentic and brilliantly staged. But as a serious play (and Mr. Hart certainly intended to be taken seriously) it was as vacant and obvious as a moving picture. Each hero (there were no villains, except the Japanese, nor even any who harbored impure or destructive thoughts) was, allowing for regional variations, the typical American boy; each had his separate emotional involvement with a chaste young woman, also typical; each contributed his separate cliché to the plot—the nerveless student who failed his flight test, the illiterate who delivered what Mr. Hart must hopefully have regarded as the profound, intuitive philosophy of the common man, and even at the end, that handiest of all stencils, the pilot who learned about the birth of his son while he himself was confronted with death.

On the stage the presence of some two hundred and fifty actors engaged in impressive military rituals before acres of high-class scenery occasionally had a tendency to disguise the essential banality of these proceedings. Even the most casual reading of the script, however, revealed with dismaying clarity not only the

Klieg-lit nature of Mr. Hart's plot but also his extremely peculiar conception of the behavior of twenty-year-olds. One of the earliest stage directions, for instance, reads: *They . . . stop and turn as they hear a voice singing: 'Off we go into the wild blue yonder' and watch Pinky Scariano come in the gate. He doesn't just come in, however. He has his arms outstretched on either side for wings, his body twists and spins, and he makes a fine series of airplane noises in his throat before he stops.* A little later the wife of one of them observes with emotions not clearly indicated in the text, "They're such kids, Mom—such babies! . . . It's all they think about. They talk about it like kids, as though it were some wonderful party they were going to." It can be presumed that Mr. Hart was trying to indicate the poignant survival of the boy in the man. What he seemed to get, however, was just an oversized, spiritual image of Penrod busily whittling a good ol' ottomatick out of a piece of wood in the Schofield barn.

To revert to the comparison with *This Is the Army*, both plays were alike in that they peopled their stages with actual soldiers. The difference was that Mr. Berlin was wise enough to say simply, this is what they are like, these are their jokes and their songs; he was wise enough, that is, to allow his audiences to discover any deeper emotional content for themselves. Mr. Hart used all the big words—pride, love, sacrifice, patriotism—and achieved only an enormous vacuum, since the American theatregoer is no longer in that state of happy innocence when he can be readily seduced by the waving of a flag or *morituri te salutamus* addresses on the battlefield. There can be no question which was a more moving tribute to the armed forces.

The summer of 1942 passed without further notable incident. There were revivals of *The Merry Widow* and *The New Moon*, and William Saroyan, the Armenian cornucopia, came up with two one-act plays that seemed more or less in the nature of finger exercises, but otherwise the hot months were quiet. The new season, opening in September, was to produce war plays, both comic and serious; musicals, some touching dutifully on the war; and completely disassociated exhibits, including revivals, in about equal proportions.

The comedies had, in general, an air of rapid contrivance, suggesting that their authors had fallen passionately on their typewriters with the first explosions in the Pacific. *Janie*, something about suburban schoolgirls and adolescent soldiers; *Kiss and Tell*, more of the same, with special emphasis on the humor of teenage pregnancy; *Three's a Family*, a further obstetrical note; and *Vickie*, a glum hash about women in war service, explored the more obvious aspects of the situation and were all practically innocent of merit. *The Doughgirls*, a rowdy farce having to do with three predatory young women and the housing shortage in Washington, was apparently another quickie, but it was directed by George S. Kaufman at such a dizzy pace and with such a superb instinct for chaos that it seemed a good deal better than it was. Its virtues, however, were certainly more physical than mental. Philip Barry's *Without Love*, a comic valentine of the marriage-in-name-only school, was also based on the congestion in the national capital, though not perhaps as firmly as it was on the well-known box-office appeal of Miss Katharine Hepburn. Mr. Barry, in his latter-day role of political medicine man, attempted to draw some vague analogy between the tangled romance of his principals and the state of affairs between England and Ireland, but nothing much came of it.

The comparative poverty of all these offerings could conceivably be laid to the fact that it requires some daring, as well as talent, to write lightly about a war when one is going on—except, of course, on the musical stage, where homosexual comics in uniform are always greeted with rapture; the continuing failure of the serious wartime drama, however, still remained a formidable mystery.

Of the twelve that were produced, eight were the customary rubbish, demonstrating in general that there is nothing like high explosive to reveal a man in his true colors. Three—*The Morning Star*, *Lifeline*, and *Flare Path*—were standard British contraptions.

One, *This Rock*, was also a hymn to our ally, though the work of the adoring vice-president of an American oil company. The rest were such assorted odds and ends as *Yankee Point*, a rather frantic attempt to wring some excitement out of the saboteurs' landing on Long Island; *The Russian People*, a horrific melodrama that performed no especial service either to the Soviet Union or the Theatre Guild; and three samples of what might be called the drama of arbitrary confinement—*Proof through the Night*, a desperate ingenuity in which an all-girl cast was trapped in a cave on Bataan; *Men in Shadow*, approximately the same thing, except that the players were men and they were caught in a Dutch windmill; and *Counterattack*, again the same, this time dealing with a Russo-German scuffle in the basement of a ruined factory. In all these pieces, to borrow a phrase from a prominent thinker of the period, it just seemed that somebody had gone out of his way to write a play.

The other four, though very far from being completely satisfactory, had at least the merit of some sincerity and originality. *Winter Soldiers*, produced in a small theatre off Broadway, was perhaps the season's greatest military surprise. An unabashed melodrama about the Russian guerrillas who slowed down the Nazi drive on Moscow, it suffered from rigid economies of production, some crudities of style and form, and the fact that the Nazi officers sometimes betrayed a philosophic acceptance of final defeat that recalled Mr. Steinbeck's similar optimisms in *The Moon Is Down*. For all that, it was a graphic and vigorous instance of theatrical journalism, and deserved much better than the comparative obscurity it got. *Sons and Soldiers*, by Irwin Shaw, who has yet to prove that an admirable talent for short prose can be successfully stretched and adjusted to the theatre, was at least a valiant effort to get away from established patterns. Mr. Shaw asked himself if a mother would face a ten-to-one chance of dying in childbirth if she could see in advance the troubled course her son's life would take. The play was an interminable series of her visions of the future, always literary and mainly doleful, that somehow convinced her that any life is worth living, but left Mr. Shaw's status as a playwright just about where it was before. *Tomorrow the World* turned up on the screen not very long after the end of its Broadway run, and possibly that was where it belonged in the first place. The re-education of a young Nazi in an American household was, and still is, a provocative theme, but the authors stated it in terms of such precocious savagery—among other pleasantries, the little visitor stopped only slightly short of braining his hosts' daughter with a book end—that the portrait was partially dissolved in caricature. It seemed a pity.

In spite of his well-known and exasperating tendency to set only partially digested ideas to derivative music, to borrow the form of Shakespeare to convey the philosophy of an editorial writer on *PM*, Maxwell Anderson still commands respectful attention in the theatre. A great many people, of course, have been so bewitched by the miracle of scansion, together with the grandiose productions usually accorded Mr. Anderson, that they have been more or less indifferent to content, and even the professional critics, remembering such very satisfactory exhibits as *What Price Glory?*, *Winterset*, and *High Tor*, and overlooking more recent indiscretions like *Star Wagon*, *Key Largo*, and *Journey to Jerusalem*, have continued to regard him with hope. So far, he has made four contributions to this war, at the nearly incredible rate of one a year, all of which were gratifyingly selected by Burns Mantle as among the ten best plays of the season. *Key Largo*, which dealt with the preliminary phase in Spain, and *Candle in the Wind*, laid in France during the first days of the occupation, both preceded our own appearance as a belligerent, and both were more valuable as mirroring the prevailing confusion in the American mind, as evidenced by the author's tendency to retreat into metaphysical underbrush, than they were as theatre or even propaganda. The other two, considered here simultaneously for the sake of convenience, were *The Eve of St. Mark*, which appeared in the season now under consideration, and *Storm Operation,* which opened in January, 1944.

Of the two, *The Eve of St. Mark* was certainly the more rewarding. Basically, it was just the story of a boy from a farm in upstate New York and the course of events that led to his heroic death in a delaying action on a little island in the Philippines. Avoiding, except in one regrettable instance, the rhythms of Avon, Mr. Anderson caught the gentle, timeless simplicities of life on the farm, the raucous humors of the training camp, and finally the brave, hopeless ordeal on the rock. In all the scenes that dealt with groups of people, he wrote directly and with some eloquence, putting down living men and women rather than those rich literary abstractions that have so often enchanted him (and the Pulitzer Prize Committee) in the past. The only real trouble with his play, in fact, was that its hero was almost as stupefying a prig as the delayed adolescents in *Winged Victory.* He was a young man, not only of blood-curdling nobility, but also relentlessly determined to talk about it.

Once, with another soldier, he encountered two amiable young women in a juke joint. The ladies retired momentarily for repairs, and his lecherous colleague was planning the final phase of their campaign.

"Now what do we do?" he asked.

"We take the bus back to camp and crawl into our own truckle beds," replied the young Galahad sternly.

"I don't know as I like a man with so much character," the sinner said, possibly expressing the private emotions of most of the audience.

Again, there was the following passage in what purported to be a duet *con amore:*

JANET: Quizz, have you ever——?
QUIZZ: No, darling. You see, somebody told me—the way to be happy—was to wait till you were in love—and I waited.

JANET: Who told you?
QUIZZ: My mother.

And, finally, there was a scene in which his spirit materialized in his fiancée's bedroom to explain why it was necessary for his body to remain on the rock although his commanding officer had said he could withdraw with honor. It was here that Mr. Anderson seemed to have found his thought too luminous for prose:

JANET: Who asks this of you?
　　　　They shouldn't ask it!
QUIZZ: Nobody asks it, dear.
　　　　It's something in myself I don't understand
　　　　that seems to require it of me. It seems to be
　　　　the best of me—the inner self that turned
　　　　to love you and love no one else, that says
　　　　give more than is asked of you, be such a man
　　　　as she you love could honor at a secret altar
　　　　knowing all you've thought and done. But as for orders
　　　　we have none now. We're free to go back or stay
　　　　save for what's in our minds.

John Mason Brown, writing in the *Post*, said, "Whether *The Eve of St. Mark* is a good play or not seems almost beside the point. It is deeply affecting. It speaks to the heart irresistibly even when the head says No." The idea that the strict theatrical merit of a play can ever be regarded as being beside the point by a critic is, of course, open to a good deal of argument. Mr. Nathan, in this connection, noted, "The present criticism of drama in ratio to the acceptability of its themes is just a small step removed from the older criticism of drama in proportion to its morality, chiefly sexual, and must lead to the same artistically dubious end. . . . Let us be patriots all, surely, but let those of us whose job is dramatic criticism not confuse it with the job of flying a bomber over Berlin." In the case of *The Eve of St. Mark*, there was even some doubt about how irresistibly Mr. Anderson had addressed himself to the heart, since some were disagreeable enough to say that a hero so acutely aware of his own perfections aroused in them only a dim sensation of having been belted over the head with a Gideon Bible.

Hardly anything needs to be said about *Storm Operation*. Feeling that the times called for a first-hand report of American activities at the front, Mr. Anderson had himself duly accredited as a correspondent and journeyed to North Africa, where he turned out his composition under the personal supervision of General Eisenhower. The mice emerging from these twin mountains were, first, a carefully documented account of the landings in Algiers, rather inferior to the newsreels on the subject, and, second, a love story, intended to demonstrate, according to the author, that "the best soldier is the one with a picture of his girl in his pocket." This proposition proving too much for critical composure, *Storm Operation* withdrew in embarrassment after twenty-three performances.

The musicals and the plays that swung free in space are not primarily within the province of this essay, but three of them—Sidney Kingsley's *The Patriots,* Thornton Wilder's *The Skin of Our Teeth,* and, of course, the already legendary *Oklahoma!*—require some passing reference, if only because they attracted far more critical and popular attention than anything written about the war. (*Harriet,* a thorough but rather attenuated biography of the author of *Uncle Tom's Cabin,* captivated that special audience which would pay handsomely to hear Miss Helen Hayes read a cookbook, but it was without dramatic significance and can be ignored.)

In a sense, *The Patriots* was a war play in that it dealt with the basically antagonistic conceptions of government held by Thomas Jefferson and Alexander Hamilton and could be regarded as a neat, ready-made parallel to the crisis of today. To achieve this analogy, Mr. Kingsley was obliged to overemphasize Hamilton's distaste for his Great Beast, the people, and to create in Jefferson a figure of such overwhelming moral splendor that it seemed impertinent to suspect that he was also a rather tiresome man. Either because they were dazzled and abashed in the presence of so much nobility or else conceivably because they had practically nothing else to vote for, the drama critics chose *The Patriots* for their annual award. It was cautiously described as a worthy selection, but nobody's heart was really in it.

The Skin of Our Teeth, which won the Pulitzer Prize, was also a prominent contender for the critics' accolade until an educated member of the group discovered in it some evidence that Mr. Wilder had been unduly influenced, subconsciously or otherwise, by James Joyce's *Finnegan's Wake*. The majority of the critics had read no more of Joyce than the anatomical section of *Ulysses*, but they bowed to superior culture and the play was eliminated. However the author came by his inspiration, *The Skin of Our Teeth* seemed to many a gay and exciting evening in the theatre, while to others it was rather more like a visit to Bedlam. To intrude a single personal note in this dispatch, the present writer was one of those who were persuaded to abandon Mr. Wilder's play in favor of *The Patriots*. Rereading them both now, he is compelled to say that he ought to have been shot.

On March 31, toward the end of a musical comedy season that had been largely devoted to an attempt to resuscitate vaudeville, *Oklahoma!* opened at the St. James. The epic of *Oklahoma!* began in 1931, when the Theatre Guild produced an American folk-play by Lynn Riggs called *Green Grow the Lilacs*. It was original and literate, but probably the times were against it. Mr. Hoover was in the last disastrous year of his presidency, and audiences may have found it difficult to focus on a drama about the love-life of a cowhand, even though it was punctuated by regional ballads. Anyway, it had a run of sixty-four performances, after which the script was bought by a moving-picture company which, apparently seeing nothing in it worthy of its current supply of grandiose bosoms and chemical hair, just put it away in a safe. It might have stayed there forever, if the directors of the Guild hadn't had the happy idea of employing Richard Rodgers and

Oscar Hammerstein II to turn it into a musical. Their work, plus the incorporation of two superb and perfectly integrated ballets, made *Oklahoma!* not only a historic money-maker but also a powerful force in giving new impetus and direction to a form then painfully set in its ways.

In addition to *Winged Victory* and *Storm Operation*, both previously covered in these notes, the season of 1943–44 came up with three plays, dealing exclusively with the war, that deserved at least some critical attention, and another, a war play only in the sense that its hero wore a uniform, that proved to be the year's happiest contribution. The other military operations belonged to what might be described as the Arms and the Ham division, and the civilian offerings were also spotty, with at the most five shows worth the considerable scuffle by then involved in getting into a theatre to look at them.

Although it lasted no more than five performances, *South Pacific*, featuring that excellent actor Canada Lee, was based on an original idea and possessed a certain measure of crude power. The Negro survivor of a torpedoed merchant ship is marooned, along with his white captain, on a little island held by the Japanese, and here for the first time in his life he finds himself, by virtue of his color, the member of a dominant group. The play is the story of his gradual and angry decision to fight for the men who have always treated him with contempt and against a race apparently willing to accept him as an equal. The motivation behind this change of heart is a little obscure; whether, that is, it is an abstract moral choice between the white civilization that has degraded him personally and the totalitarian principle that would degrade all men impartially, or whether it is his immediate reaction to isolated acts of Japanese violence. The authors' cloudy statement of their case, plus some unfortunate casting and direction, doomed *South Pacific* at the box office, but it was at least an adult and dignified effort, which was considerably more than could be said for either *Winged Victory* or *Storm Operation*.

The second pure war play was *Jacobowsky and the Colonel*, a

comedy adapted for the Theatre Guild by S. N. Behrman. Werfel's original story of the ceremonious but helplessly impractical
Polish officer and the humorous, endlessly resourceful Jew, fleeing
together before the Nazi advance, is said to have been a good
deal more sentimental, more insistent on the proud, sorrowful
heritage of Jewry than the version Behrman finally contrived. It
is also said that Mr. Werfel felt that his script had been somewhat
vitiated by Mr. Behrman's amiable anxiety to entertain his audience rather than to instruct it in the special virtues of a race.
There may have been some truth in this, but the play as produced
was graceful and witty, which, after all, was probably all that the
Guild hoped for from it.

The trouble, obviously, with being Lillian Hellman is that people are inclined to expect a constantly ascending scale in her
work, and when it seems apparent that she has momentarily lost
her way the critics come down on her with a happy ferocity accorded no other current playwright. In the case of *The Searching
Wind*, their disapproval was justified to some extent. Wishing to
damn appeasement to the end of time, Miss Hellman, whose
sense of form had previously been impeccable, threw all the rules
out the window and, writing in a voice choked with indignation,
produced a drama that wandered irresolutely back and forth in
time, that seemed rather unfairly to judge the political behavior
of its principal characters in 1922 in terms of the fuller information available in 1944, that masqueraded a conventional and
somewhat preposterous emotional triangle as a symbol of the
larger ethical struggle going on in her protagonist's mind, and
that finally employed the very dubious device of placing the
truth as she sees it, the enormous, complex truth, in the mouth of
an immature character, a young soldier who had been wounded
in Italy and whose opinions, distilled out of his own bitter and
immediate suffering, were offered as the cool, inarguable judgment of history. Miss Hellman, in other words, seemed to be trying to speak simultaneously from her own adult and intellectual
point of view and from the passionate but politically unsophisti-

cated mind of an adolescent. Her play was a failure in that its valid message was more or less lost in the unhappy contrivances of its form, but her position as the most nearly articulate social conscience in the theatre remained beyond dispute.

John van Druten's comedy called *The Voice of the Turtle* was a triumph of literate charm. With a cast of only three characters and no more plot than the immemorial one of a sudden, happy love so limited by time (the warrior has to go back to his war) that it is consummated without the assistance of the church, Mr. van Druten persuaded his audiences that promiscuity can be a merry and even virtuous business when engaged in by attractive people and, far more difficult than that, that a play with only three people in it isn't necessarily to be classified as a stunt. He was immeasurably assisted by the fine performance of Margaret Sullavan, Elliott Nugent, and Audrey Christie, by an extremely cheerful and original set by Stewart Chaney, and by his own nicely restrained direction. The whole thing was a delight and presumably still is.

Of the civilian offerings, *A New Life,* by Elmer Rice, was noted for the most explicit delivery-room sequence in the history of the theatre and the embarrassing absence of anything that could be identified as thought; *Outrageous Fortune,* by Rose Franken, was a wayward conglomeration of many themes, including perversion, anti-Semitism, psychiatry, and a touch of voodoo, that failed to develop any of them to a satisfactory degree; *The Innocent Voyage* was adapted from Richard Hughes' novel by Paul Osborne, who apparently confused it somewhat with *Peter Pan* and so lost all the fine diabolical quality of the original; and *Decision,* by Edward Chodorov, was another essay on native fascism, done this time with such florid strokes that it seemed almost a parody on its predecessors. Of them all, in fact, only *Carmen Jones,* a ghostly collaboration between Bizet and Oscar Hammerstein II, could really be defined as wholly satisfactory entertainment. Two troupes of colored actors, of course, had already dealt hilariously with *The Mikado* so that the extension of the same treatment to the opera wasn't precisely a new idea. It was accomplished, however, with enormous spirit and charm and established its producer, Billy Rose, more firmly than ever in the hearts of his countrymen.

According to the New York *Times,* which has a childlike faith in statistics, the season of 1944–45 was a fruitful one. There were ninety-five openings, two more than the previous year and eighteen more than the year before that. Twenty-four plays and musicals were successful, measured by the somewhat arbitrary yardstick of one hundred performances. It was all wonderful, but the unfortunate fact remained that the best plays had to do with such strictly nonmilitary personnel as an enchanted rabbit, a Norse matriarch, a pillar of Boston society, a neurotic cripple, and a colored daughter of joy. "The final play about the weariness, the hatred, the savagery, and the pathos of the second World War has yet to reach Broadway," wrote Lewis Nichols, the *Times* critic. It was rather worse than that. One drama of respectable stature appeared in *A Bell for Adano,* and a couple of others made earnest attempts to say something or other, but on the whole it was the most vacant season since Pearl Harbor. The greatest disappointment, incidentally, was an exercise in sophomore metaphysics called *The Streets Are Guarded* and written by Laurence Stallings, who, of course, had been partly responsible for the most exciting of all American war plays when he collaborated with Maxwell Anderson on *What Price Glory?* It closed after twenty-four performances, demonstrating among other things the unwisdom of attempting to clear up earthly problems by the introduction of a hero apparently of divine origin.

A Bell for Adano was the work of John Hersey, a young writer employed at the time by the Luce publications. To a certain extent the influence of that brisk, informed, and calmly superior organization was reflected in Mr. Hersey's work. The play dealt with the United States Military Government in a small Italian town; the hero was one Major Joppolo, an Italian-American from the Bronx, who succeeded in winning the confidence and affection of the villagers largely because he was intuitive enough to know that the restoration of the bell that had rung out for centuries in Adano meant more to them than any large abstractions about freedom, being, in fact, almost on a par with food and drink. In the end, he was broken for countermanding a brutal and senseless order given by a general, whose derivation at the time Mr. Hersey's play was produced seemed rather more apparent than it might now, but he got his bell and the public got its moral; in effect, that it is just as necessary to understand and respect the immemorial traditions of a conquered people as it is to tidy up their country. It might perhaps be said that Mr. Hersey's treatment of his theme was oversentimental and a little too pat for comfort—the bell, for instance, rang out with split-second irony just as the Major was preparing to leave in disgrace—and it could certainly be said that the natives were presented as picturesque children with something of the same amiable condescension with which *Life* attends and photographs the quaint gambols of our own peasantry. Nevertheless, in Joppolo's weary integrity Mr. Hersey created the most appealing character to come out of this war, and what he had to say was wiser than most of the messages that have been delivered to us so far.

The Hasty Heart was described by Miss Wilella Waldorf of the *Post* as the best play of the war, "profoundly touching, deeply moving . . . one of the merriest pieces on Broadway," while Walter Winchell of the Stork Club remarked that it struck him as "all white meat." Other criticism, however, was slightly more vegetarian, the consensus apparently being that while the author, John Patrick, was dealing essentially in hokum, he had handled it with some discretion and also that he displayed in the main a cheerful wit. On rereading, the play hardly seems to bear out even this temperate estimate. The story is about a Scotch soldier in a base hospital in Burma who is unaware that he has only six weeks to live. His companions, five men of assorted nationalities —the standard microcosm, of course—and a beautiful nurse, know that he is doomed and do their best to treat him kindly in spite of his fiercely proud and conspicuously thorny disposition. Just when they have finally broken down his reserve, he accidentally learns the truth and passionately rejects the friendship he believes has been given simply out of pity. He is convinced of their sincerity only when a black man, who speaks no English, coyly offers him a string of beads, after which he is able to face death secure in the knowledge that for the first time in his life he is not alone. Not only would all this appear to be the material of sure and easy pathos, but also, in his attempt to indicate the bitter struggle between pride and loneliness in his hero's heart, Mr. Patrick produced a figure so malignantly lacking in charm that when one of his comrades wished to be assured that the Scot was really going to die so that he would be spared the bother of killing him, it seemed in many ways the soundest observation of the evening. The quality of the humor can be judged by the following random samples:

"Well, I'm a sort of waiter by profession. Me father owns a pub and I'm waiting for 'im to kick off."

"Snoring? Sounds more like the mating call of the hippopotamus."

"This tea tastes like a baby's been boiled in it."

The prosecution rests.

Foxhole in the Parlor, also passionately admired here and there, considered the case history of a soldier, discharged from the service as a psychoneurotic, who was desperately obsessed with the idea of getting a message to the San Francisco Conference, giving his private formula for a permanent peace. There are certainly a great many things that ought to be said on this subject, but Elsa Shelley's drama, being generally as confused and overwrought as its protagonist's mind, failed to deliver any coherent message and must be put down as a loss. It might be complained, incidentally, that the consideration of any problem from a disordered point of view is to some extent just an evasion of the issue. The other military offerings, among them *Soldier's Wife, Dear Ruth, Kiss Them for Me,* and *Common Ground,* had occasional meritorious scenes, but none was much more memorable than yesterday's newspaper and certainly none could be described as a really useful contribution to the theatre. This was the total output of American thought about the war for that season.

So much has been written about *The Late George Apley, Anna Lucasta, I Remember Mama, Harvey,* and *The Glass Menagerie* that it is quite unnecessary to discuss them here. Each was superlative in its special field and each would have been a credit to any season. The musical stage also did very nicely, with *On the Town, Carousel, Bloomer Girl,* and a couple of others succeeding handsomely in spite of the problem of casting male choristers who would resemble neither the inmates of a veterans' home nor the bearers of a daisy chain. Enchanting as all these exhibits were, however, they were also profoundly disturbing in the evidence they gave of how resolutely many of the best and most original talents in the theatre had turned their backs on the primary and almost exclusive concern of the nation.

While this was sufficiently apparent in a single season, the total roll-call of the four and a half years between Pearl Harbor and Hiroshima was very nearly appalling. If a list patterned on Mr. Mantle's were drawn up for the whole period, including all plays dealing with the war with the exception of those, like *The Voice of the Turtle,* whose connection with it was purely arbitrary, the Ten Best, roughly in the order of their merit, might easily read:

This Is the Army	*Tomorrow the World*
A Bell for Adano	*The Moon Is Down*
The Searching Wind	*The Eve of St. Mark*
Winter Soldiers	*South Pacific*
Jacobowsky and the Colonel	*Letters to Lucerne*

With the exception of the first title, it is a melancholy catalogue and one about which the theatre has every reason to be deeply concerned.

Dismissing the contention that people just don't want to be reminded of the war, which too often has the air of an excuse rather than an explanation, there are still a good many reasons advanced for the astonishing poverty of the militant stage. The playwright, it is said, is confronted with two equally disastrous choices. He can write in the strict terms of black and white demanded by an aggressive public temper, but such an extension of the comic strip technique of "Terry and the Pirates" is hardly likely to attract a man of any perceptible attainments, and it is very doubtful if such a man, even if he wanted to, *could* write in this vein, it being more difficult to turn out any composition in a spirit of pure cynicism than is generally supposed. Or he can approach his material with the idea that it is the duty of the mature and reputable playwright to deal with it in somewhat more complex terms, even though this may mean conceding that fascism has no precise geographical frontiers but is latent in any political organism, including our own. But this is a very dubious box-office recipe, both because it offends the sensibilities of a great many people who honestly believe that these are no times for detached investigation and also because it is very likely to baffle or just bore those who emphatically don't go to the theatre for political instruction, especially of a nature hostile to practically everything they've been taught by the radio and screen. This, of course, is a cynical opinion, but unfortunately it is held by many whose judgments dictate what shall appear upon our stage.

Another reason, and a good one, put forward for the nonappearance of plays of any particular stature is the vastly increased effectiveness of the moving pictures in their factual reports from the front. Magnificent films, covering every theatre of action, have shown the true nature of the conflict with such terrible urgency and such unmistakable authenticity that tin-sheet and red-flare imitations on the stage are reduced to absurdity and even the works of adult writers, who are actually trying to say something, inevitably seem a little pale and disassociated in comparison with pictures that can and do say almost everything, except perhaps what makes men fight. This is not, of course, to argue that a really great war play couldn't succeed on Broadway today. It is only to suggest that bad writers are helpless against any such competition, and good ones on the whole have either declined the challenge or else, too conscious of it, have written away from life in the direction of cloudy symbolism and eccentric construction.

There is undoubtedly something in all these explanations, but the most valid one may easily be that the young men who have known the dull, dirty, murderous business of war at first hand are still to be heard from. Many of them are still in Europe or the Pacific, and it is still too soon to expect very much from those who have come back. The atom bomb, too, is bound to call for certain readjustments in any serious playwright's thought. The appalling explosions that mushroomed over Hiroshima and Nagasaki shook the foundations of every idea in the world, and men need a little while to look around and think. The ethic, after all, may also split. Sooner or later, however, the plays will come. They will come because there will be a compulsion in the writers much stronger and deeper and more important than the usual considerations that move people to write plays, and they will be good, too. The information the young men have now, both sardonic and appalling, and the conclusions they draw from it, the personal, immediate conclusions of men in a very fine position to know what price in agony was asked for peace, to judge how close to the limit of their endurance men and nations came in the war just over and how good anybody's chances of survival would be in the next one—this information and these conclusions are the materials from which enduring plays will certainly be made. At the moment, in the writing of such personal histories, before anything is blurred or forgotten, lies the brightest hope of any theatre prepared to face its full artistic responsibility.

VII. THE COMICS

by *MILTON CANIFF*

MILTON CANIFF *(age 38) is the creator of "Terry and the Pirates," one of the most successful of all comic strips. Servicemen will also recall Caniff's strip, "Male Call," which ran in more than 2,000 camp newspapers and in Stars and Stripes, featuring the delectable war activities of "Miss Lace."*

THE cartoonist makes love to his reader a meager minute or two each day; for the remainder of the twenty-four hours that elfin darling who paid for the copy of the newspaper is gamboling about among the other strips in the same and similar sections. Because of the brevity of assignation, the comic artist tries to fashion a thin, taut wire of continuity upon which he hangs baubles of incident, hoping to hold the customer's affection even while his worship cavorts below the fold with the blowzy product of a rival syndicate.

It has been estimated that 60 per cent of the newspaper readers who follow any strips at all will follow *all* strips, good or bad. Part of this loyalty is habit, part is the hope (often justified) that a once-loved cartoon is merely in a slump and may one day brighten up. Too, there is the matter of constant but ubiquitous devotion in which a comics fan will switch intense interest from one feature to another while never completely forgetting the pleasures of the old stimulation.

Recapitulation of a comic strip story is a sad thing; the cartoonist appears to be getting away with more murder than that of which the Mothers' Clubs complain. In some features there is no continuity in the chronological sense. A review of the most popular narrative and gag cartoons covering the time you were gone reveals that characterization is what remains in the reader's mind. Those of us who have done chalk talk shows for Allied troops returning from enemy prison camps have learned to expect the standard questions: "Is Orphan Annie still wearing that red dress?" "Did Captain Easy get his majority?" "Did Daisy Mae catch Li'l Abner last Sadie Hawkins day?" We learned that incoming kriegies (as our people in German camps called themselves) were met at the gates by delegated representatives of different sections of the prisoner body who hammered the newcomers for the latest fill-in on news of anything American, rating the funnies high for inquiry priority. There are always gaps in such recitals, so the released men unfold their pent-up curiosity when they are back home and have a journeyman paper doll maker at hand and willing.

It is difficult for anyone who himself produces a newspaper cartoon strip feature (notice that there is still no adequate substitute word for "comics") to view other strips dispassionately for a review of this kind. One conclusion inevitably reached by looking over old releases is that our American-type comics come closer than any medium of public entertainment to being all things to all men. In a time when every sort of ideology was banging the eyes and ears of the nation, four comic features boiled to the top of the ten most popular strips in the *Esquire* magazine poll. The trend of public affairs sentiment in each was: "Joe Palooka," left of center; "Blondie," straight down the middle; "Li'l Abner," hard to classify in that Al Capp, its creator, although as opinionated as anyone I know, does not speak his mind through his strip as obviously as do Ham Fisher in "Palooka" and Harold Gray in "Little Orphan Annie." This last, the fourth in the poll, is the outspoken champion of the right in the political sense. Author Gray defends his stand against all comers, including in some cases paying clients who buy his work on a syndicated basis.

The importance of all this is that these are the first four comic strips in the affections of millions of people. This is not a single-choice affair in which the readers consulted voted for just one favorite and let it go at that; enough people named them in that order to establish the fact that they liked the liberality of Palooka and the reaction of Warbucks in O. Annie. Of course they liked Blondie because everybody likes Blondie. The syndicate for which Chic Young produces the strip is happy about many aspects of the Bumpstead family, not the least being that this feature is the only one which never draws a reader criticism (in the negative sense, that is. People complain bitterly if the refrigerator from which Dagwood produces the ingredients for those towering sandwiches is moved from its regular position in Blondie's kitchen).

Al Capp is the true caricaturist in his Li'l Abner. To the delight of his devotees he has pulled the leg of such worthies as: Margaret Mitchell (whose attorneys said she didn't like it, but who is, in my opinion, too sharp a Georgia gal to have resented such priceless publicity in the waning days of the sale of GWTW); Orson Welles (who devoured it); and Chester Gould (Gould *is* Dick Tracy), who thoroughly relished the unique role of having the first comic strip to be lampooned by another right out in front of God and the customers. Capp had his fun with Iron Richard by introducing "Fearless Fosdick," a strip within a strip, in "Li'l Abner." Except for necessary alterations to keep the lawyers off his inky trail, Capp drew Fosdick in the Gould-Tracy tradition; it was a keen but friendly caricature of the popular detective, and was quickly recognized by fans of both funnies.

Capp is indeed the sly fellow of the four-color sections. He has one simple ambition: he wishes to be the highest paid cartoonist in the world. As of his most recent contract he seems to have a leg-up on his laudable (if surtaxable) object of desire.

To expand the lack of accountability for the presence of Palooka, Blondie, Abner, and Annie together in the highest bracket of reader esteem: Fisher and Capp devoted many hours of their spare time during the war to the preparation (at no cost to the government) of training manuals, pocket guides to foreign countries, language guides for invasion troops, bond-selling campaigns, etc., as well as including ardent boosts for such activities in the regular continuities of their respective strips (this last was especially true of Fisher). Gray and Young on the other hand participated but modestly in extra-curricular drawing for the war effort, although each did most effective work within the confines of their strips. Gray's Junior Commando campaign for scrap salvage was taken up by individual newspapers carrying Orphan Annie and doubtless resulted in the collection of many tons of material that might never have been brought to light without the day-to-day goading of the tireless and ageless urchin in the red dimity.

Chic Young's very off-handedness about the war earned him a unique place in the hearts of the G.I.s in that Blondie represented home and the days when the only uniforms in a man's life were those of the postman, filling station attendant, policeman, fireman, etc. When the commercial syndicates offered their material free to the editors of *Stars and Stripes,* Blondie was one of the three selected to fill the limited space available in the G.I. daily. (Li'l Abner and Terry were the other two. When *Stars and Stripes* subsequently introduced a color section, Dick Tracy was added to the list. As presses became available after the surrender of Germany, the line-up of *Stars and Stripes* comics looked like those in any solvent newspaper back home. There were other daily papers published by G.I.s, but the many-editioned *Stars and Stripes* was the largest operation under one head. It and *Yank* will probably be used as yardsticks by historians in large-scale conclusions on G.I. opinion.)

Most syndicates prefer their comic strip creators to avoid all controversial issues and especially subjects that deal with specific individuals, living or dead. Fisher and Gray have turned this policy into a most profitable reversal of custom. In Palooka the late President Roosevelt was not only supported but appeared as a character (by permission). There is no question that Joe's early entry into the Army via the peacetime draft did much to shine a positive spotlight on the unpleasant prospect of 21 bucks per month. Roosevelt was happy about it and said so, publicly. Fisher has reiterated his pro-New Deal stand through Palooka and his secondary people whenever the opportunity occurred.

In taking the opposite view, Harold Gray has had rougher going. An entertainer speaking out against a war measure is juggling volatile stuff. At one time during the war years Orphan Annie was a sort of side-line vehicle for an extended discussion by Gray of the shortcomings of the rationing system. He had spoken earlier against organized labor, so the readers and editors who disagreed were quick to point a finger his way, condemning him for raising an editorial voice in a space dedicated to divertisement.

Just before the death of Roosevelt, Daddy Warbucks could stand the pace no longer and threw himself to certain death in a situation which left little room for even the most far-fetched comic strip reincarnation. Gray revived Warbucks on the note that, "since the climate is different around here recently," it would be possible for a man of sense and substance to breathe again.

Both Gray and Fisher have collected many new followers during the emergency years; their strips have often appeared side by side in the same newspaper; the theses they uphold have been as clear to their readers as those of any two opposed debaters on an open forum. Gray had the more difficult tune to play in that, like a vaudeville theatre to which people come to relax and escape from their humdrum lives, the comic section of a newspaper offers a program of turns which the publisher hopes will please as many different types of customers as possible. As in the variety house, it is not considered good showmanship to introduce a controversial note. Popular and mass butts such as Congress and the local public utilities may be kidded a bit by a single comic like Will Rogers who has enough reputation to get away with it, but the proper tone is provided by an act in the tradition of the Four Cohans, which would break out an American flag and go into a snappy Chauvin Nocturne at no advance in prices.

That Gray has managed to buck tradition in the midst of a

conflict and get away with it in the largest sense is a tribute to his avowed position of businessman rather than artist. He saw that there would be a market for the negative approach, provided it could be properly ballyhooed (as witness the amount of space it is occupying here) and that a contentious objector would find a ready and vast audience among people disaffected by the war if not by the hostilities; these in addition to the millions of readers who find pleasure in Annie's doings with no thought of their relation to national affairs.

It is extremely healthy and American that such opposites should occur in apposition in newspapers of all political faiths.

What astonishes me about the comic strips is that we lowly dispensers of picture prose should have been picked by a quirk of fate to guess the real function of art in wartime so much more accurately than the bigger men in the higher brackets of the story-telling craft.

Pass over the apparent bumptiousness of that remark. Or let it go for what is so generally expected of us—that we comic strip artists have come to expect some degree of bumptiousness of ourselves; not in vain, some will agree. Bumptious or not, the idea that we, the latest newcomers to the story-telling field, kept faith with fiction while its hereditary practitioners were in default is worth exploring if true.

Well, what happened, for instance, to Theodore Dreiser, to pick one from the top drawer? I recall that he was asked about work in progress back in the early days of the war and that the great man answered sharply: "Only a slacker would set about writing a novel when there were so many cartridges to be milled and ditches to be dug." The answer had a lot of impact at the time, I can testify personally, remembering the week when it had me looking pretty helplessly at blank white paper while it got between me and my drawing board. Now that many cartridges are spent and ditches in the Ardennes are filling up with weeds, a second guess occurs to a lot of us who would have been heartened when heartening was scarce if there had been another

American Tragedy to keep Americans reminded of what we are.

Then there is Edna St. Vincent Millay, who wrote one excruciating poem of exhortation, the winter England was sticking it out all alone, and has said nothing, nothing at all, ever since.

There was Thomas Mann. He shelved his calling to turn propagandist. So doing, and being Thomas Mann, he greased a slide for others of his general rank and grade to follow pell-mell down to the bottom of the copy-writing heap. He's a "distinguished contributor" now.

Dmitri Shostakovitch put up a better fight, over in the musical wing. He dissented, at least, from the popular proposition that the whole wartime duty of the man of art is to lure his muse up a dark alley and cut her throat. However, he did empty the emptiness of his personal battle fatigue into his score describing the siege of Leningrad, surely the least of his symphonies if indeed it rates among the previous six; so that, if the war did not stop Shostakovitch, neither did the war add to Shostakovitch nor Shostakovitch to the war.

I believe the list could be extended, conclusively, to sum up to a Big Blackout among the aristocrats of the tale-spinning craft.

And all through the twilight of these gods the cartoonists were working out ways to right themselves after the sickening skid of the first shock of war and now are fairly certain to come away from V-J Day surer of themselves, of what it is they are doing, of what they want and what is wanted from them and of the continuity of things in general and of their products in particular than they ever were before.

I hope at this point not to be tempted to shriek, nor suspected of shrieking, the comic strips' success. It is true we are doing well. As to that, the arts take turns living high, and it seems to be our turn to move uptown. The money success of the strips has inspired a false explanation of the phenomenon I am attempting to describe, which is an entirely different kind of success. This false explanation would have it that, if the comics flourish while better stuff wilts on the stalk, that is because we are planted in

pay dirt. There is perverse public taste for our fruit. We are the weed that gets a rose's care. Specifically, we enjoyed a special privilege, probably wangled by sinister means, in the matter of allotments during the paper shortage, so that where the publisher of that unwritten Dreiser wartime novel would have been up against a blighting necessity to keep his editions down to a fraction of the demand, the newspaper publishers who purvey our output were mysteriously permitted to raze irreplaceable forests in order to tease, appease, and ultimately sicken the appetite of America, civilization's juvenile delinquent, for its daily Strasbourg goose stuffing on the liverish doings of Wonderbum, the squiggle that talks like a man.

Arithmetically, all this is true enough. The figures show we profited during, and maybe by, the war. As of 1944–45 turn of the year, the previously mentioned survey of the readerships of the top ten comic strips brought out awesome figures, to the accuracy of which I will not attest. Nevertheless, they will probably be accepted as gospel for the period.

1. Ham Fisher's "Joe Palooka"   40,000,000 readers
2. Chic Young's "Blondie"   35,000,000   "
3. Al Capp's "Li'l Abner"   32,000,000   "
4. Harold Gray's "Orphan Annie"   32,000,000   "
5. My own "Terry"   31,000,000   "
6. Chet Gould's "Dick Tracy"   30,000,000   "
7. Frank Willard's "Moon Mullins"   28,000,000   "
8. Frank King's "Gasoline Alley"   27,000,000   "
9. George McManus' "Bringing Up Father" 26,000,000   "
10. Gus Edson's "Gumps"   26,000,000   "

Thinning out these war debt figures to account for the overlap of addicts of more than one strip, the statisticians wind up with an estimate that at least 70,000,000 Americans patronize the players of the paper playhouse day in, day out, while wars come and go and markets and empires rise and fall. More significantly, they show the comics taking a steep upward climb during the war, which means to me that they probably benefited (though "benefit," in the circumstances, is a nasty fratricidal word) by the flat failure of most of the other departments of the narrative craft to claim and do their share of the job.

For that matter, the figures can prove anything, except the one point I think worth making before I am through. Because, while they prove almost embarrassingly that the comics kept going during the war, they hint nothing about how and why. And the comics kept going, I argue, not because of some depraved and improbable tendency, inborn or induced, on the part of the American public to deflate its IQ at the drop of Moon Mullins' iron hat, but because at a crucial wartime juncture they kept going in the right groove, whereas other arts and artists untracked themselves and went wrong.

At a time when almost anybody who could spell or picture a word was pulling every sort of wire to get himself and his paraphernalia shipped in khaki overseas and Hollywood couldn't keep a first-grade actress on a movie lot, the comics decided on the whole NOT to master-mind the war.

In view of the fact that the comics live closer to the crowd— even closer, I take it, than the movies; almost as close as radio— and might be expected to follow any band up any street any time, anywhere, this abstention of a majority of the comics from direct on-the-scene participation in the shooting seems to me to be the key story of my craft in the last four years. Parenthetically, if I who undertake to tell it happen to conduct a strip which was drawn into military events in the East by the logic of its scheme, that is something I hope to fit into the argument that the comics guessed right when they decided to let the generals win it on their own.

The story tells itself perfectly in terms of the personal war-year adventure of one of the comic strip teams, Jerry Siegel and Joe Shuster, continuity writer and artist respectively of the strip "Superman." I tell it as I saw it.

The pair's collaborator career got its start in a Cleveland high school where Jerry and Joe got a chance to fiddle around with the strip technique in the columns of the campus publication—a start so typical that it might serve with blanks for filling in names to start off the grubby workshop story of any of us. I spotted it as my own. I know that high school. They were operating it over in Dayton, Ohio, when I happened on that news story about the late Sid Smith, when he signed the comic strips' first million-dollar contract to draw Andy Gump, with an imported right-drive Rolls thrown in. That news release populated the present-day comic strip field. I know I quit sleeping for a week after it appeared, while I tried to see if I too could draw a human face, full and profile, and have them turn out two views of the same man.

The Siegel-Shuster combination seem to have had slightly worse than average bad luck peddling their "Superman" idea, which, exceptional to their case, came full-fledged out of their first experiments. They got the royal turndown from all listed newspaper feature syndicates, plus quite a few which had not yet built up to the dignity of owning a whole telephone. The given reason for the turndowns was a formula: Superman was too fantastic. He would never get by with the strips' audience, which is a few million hero-worshiping but liberal-minded American kids.

Hindsight has spotted the reversible errors in that verdict. One of them is obvious. Everybody knows by now that the national shriek of agony which rises every week on the Sunday morning air emanates from Junior, who is getting his teeth kicked down his throat for violating the rule that Daddy gets the colored section first. The other misconception is challenged less often, in fact never so far as I know, although it is one which is disproved by the very existence of the comics. It is the notion that Superman is a fantastic character: or, let me put it, that he is a more fantastic fictional character than most.

All fictional characters have one fantastic characteristic in common. They are imperishable. They cannot die. Even when an author elects to kill them off, none need be fooled by the funeral. Dickens has us see Sidney Carton's head roll into the basket, but that is simply the dodge of the book-writing craft. Novelists must end their tales. The book format will have it so. Comic strip authors must not end theirs. The newspapers' endless chain format will have it so. The difference between the two workers at the same trade, quality of product apart, is purely departmental. The characters in the terminable book and the interminable strip are of the same nonperishable stuff. They cannot die as you and I shall die, out of our skins and out of all but one or two carefully tended memories. This is a point which Conan Doyle settled once for all when he resuscitated Sherlock Holmes after having squashed him like a bug in an Alpine crevasse. The point is vital here. Being nonexpendable, the fiction character cannot go to war on a fair and square footing of equality with the expendables, the flesh-and-blood G.I.s. Follow that out and you will see how difficult it is, even unseemly sometimes, to send a fiction character to war at all.

Siegel and Shuster followed it out. Having reached the daily newspaper comic strip field by way of the comic book periodicals (a branch of the publishing industry which they set on its paying feet), their Superman one day came face to face with the problem of what to do about the war. It was posed in terms more categorical than was the luckier case with most of us. Superman, of course, could win the war singlehanded. So could Little Orphan Annie, for that matter, or any other fiction character ever drawn, from Alice in Wonderland to Paul Bunyan, indestructibility being as much the attainable reality of fiction as it is the unattainable dream of generals.

Superman was tempted. I understand that his fans took him to the top of that mountain; that Siegel and Shuster were answering their mail when, one fine Lend-Lease Sunday, back before we got in, their irresistible Mr. Force met up with the immovable Maginot Line and ripped it from Belgium to Belfort. It was a grand piece of pictorial bulldozing, right up the alley of a pair who have a superior flair for the terrific.

Right here, I see, I ought to polish off the argument left suspended a page or so back that the terrificness of Superman is not fantastic—certainly not in the fiction-craft sense of being implausible. Superman has superior means of locomotion, yes. At best, they are about as superior, say, as the generally accepted ability of leading characters in the English fiction tradition to live splendidly untrammeled lives on no income. So Superman levitates instead of riding streetcars, the net result being an author's convention whereby the reader is spared those recurrent stretches of utility filler, so exasperating in most tales, wherein the hero must be observed riding the 5:36 accommodation local to Schenectady, complete with list of stations. Otherwise, Superman remains nicely within the Robin Hood mold, and his creators have taken admirable care to give him anchorage in an alter ego, that of an obscure newspaper reporter with an average man's worries about the rent and the risks of being fired. Superman's plagiarizers, by the way, have missed the point of the original's mealtime normality, and anyone may properly call *their* creations fantastic—or worse.

Superman's devastating attack on the Maginot Line, by the way, was delivered after the fall of France and was meant to confound Hitler and the Junkers. To the amazement of Joe and Jerry, I imagine, it did exactly that. It seems that copies of the strip were circulated among German troops, producing an effect which is certified in the historic record by countermeasures, taken forthwith by the late Herr Goebbels, who ordered publication in *Das Schwarze Korps,* organ of the Sturmtruppen, of a virulent attack on Superman as a Jewish-American plutocrat whose infamous record was well known to the Ausland Dienst.

Oddly enough, foreign observers of the American scene, particularly foreign enemies, are much more impressed by the phenomenon of the American comic strip than are Americans themselves, not excepting the comic strip artists. The Japanese war lords were even more impressed than his compatriot readers when Frank Miller happened to pick the historic Sunday of Doolittle's Shangri-La bombing of Tokyo for release of a full-page colored comic episode in the adventures of his freebooter aviator, Barney Baxter, exactly duplicating the Doolittle exploit. The Japs are convinced (as are some native comic strip fans) that some of the comic strip artists have pipe-lines into anteroom No. 1 of General Marshall's Washington quarters. An episode involving myself gave me early insight, around the period of Pearl Harbor, into this curious conviction on the part of the Japs, who are pretty literal and level-headed in sizing up the Western world except when the West in question is fabulous America, about which they will swallow any fairy tale. My strip, "Terry," had been running for some time prior to 1941 in a Tokyo newspaper—naturally with all the dialogue in the "balloons" carefully edited to eliminate any inference that the villains of my perpetual China coast plot were Japanese. The strip was run daily up to and including December 7, 1941, which means that a file of unpublished "Terry" strips may still be lying around whatever the B-29s may have left standing of that Tokyo newspaper plant. What was the idea? Did they hope to pick up some indication in the "Terry" continuity that the stupid Yankees were not as stupid as they seemed —that the Jap Air Force would dive into something hot when it delivered its carefully elaborated sneak attack on Pearl Harbor? I don't know. I do know that a long overdue check for the last six months of publication in my Tokyo outlet never came through. I was counting on framing it. Total war is sure hell.

But I digress from Superman, who, following the Maginot Line episode, found himself heading into an impossible dilemma, the one I have been trying to blueprint all along. It is a dilemma of allegiances. A parallel comes to mind. Key war workers—coal miners, for instance—are told to stick to their civilian posts, and the finest minds and the most silvery tongues are recruited for the special purpose of convincing them that there is virtue, even heroism, in resisting that wartime impulse to enlist. But the problem in conduct for the coal miner is relatively simple. It involves only the matter of his disposition of himself. It gets really tricky in the dual identity case of the fictionist and his protagonist. Obviously, the fictionist can do any one of four things: (1) go to war and leave his hero behind; (2) send his hero to war and stay at home; or (3 and 4) accompany his hero into battle (that was Mauldin's case) or stay with his hero at home. Moreover, nobody in authority tells the fictionist what to do, nor what a swell fellow he could be, doing it. On the other hand, quite a few volunteer editors, without official status, are eager to help. My information is incomplete, but I gather that all of us, not excepting Harold Gray of the Orphan Annie strip, have been offered, free gratis, a thousand times apiece, a startling idea which I copy herewith from the first piece of fan mail that comes to hand:

"How come your bimbo didn't parachute down on the Imperial Palace and tell that heel where he headed in long before the atom bomb?"

At one time, everyone was for sending the comic strip people off to war: the fans, the newspaper syndicate editors, a good many of the Washington master minds, and, last and least, the comic strip artists themselves. It looked like the easiest, most obvious move, timely, popular, and offering for good measure limitless possibilities for action plot. Imagine Dick Tracy assigned to counterespionage! Imagine Superman on the Berlin bomber run! All right, go ahead and imagine it! Or rather, let Superman's creators imagine it, and let's see what they saw.

What they saw was ruin. Here they had built up a character who is known to millions of strip and radio fans to be superior to all opposition in the realm of physical combat—which is a way of saying, of course, that like all fiction characters he is immune to all the vicissitudes of life save one, the whim of the fellow behind the pen. Plainly, Superman had to be kept out of uniform. Either the war would ruin Superman or Superman would ruin the war. Superman's creators solved the problem neatly. Among his other supernormal attributes, Superman has X-ray eyes. On the day he reported to his draft board in his workaday character of newspaper reporter he passed all tests with a grade of perfect or better, until he flopped in the eye-test booth. He had read off the wrong chart—the one hung in the last booth down the line.

Superman had other brushes with the war. He played god-out-of-the-machine to bring about a battlefield reunion of a kid G.I. and his dog. The incident served as pretext for a rounding out of the philosophy back of his authors' staggering decision to put Superman through the draft-board wringer and let him come out 4-F. He bows off the scene. Certainly Superman could have taken over the war, reflected his authors, but had he the moral right as a nonexpendable to deprive these others of their opportunity to expend themselves in acts of heroism?

I suppose that, were I to undertake to get down to the roots of this matter of keeping war and fiction from mixing and spoiling each other, I would soon be out of my depth in questions of free will and other intangibles of pure philosophy.

The comic strip fans in the armed forces have handled the moot question straightforwardly and without hunting out the fine points of reasoning. They have pleaded with the authors of certain comic strips *not* to militarize their characters. In the case of Al Capp and his Ozarkian folkways strip, the phenomenally popular Li'l Abner, the mail from the foxholes, I am told, added up to a spontaneous Gallup poll of the inducted ten million. In one voice homesick American youth begged Al Capp to keep Dogpatch and the Yokum clan intact, beyond the reach of the draft board.

The same G.I. electorate tolerated, or actively approved, induction of some other comic strip characters into their ranks. Ham Fisher's pug, Joe Palooka, was every doughfoot's buddy. In the case of my character, Terry, I reason that it was more a matter of the war coming to Terry than one of Terry going to the war. Long before Pearl Harbor and before anyone could have guessed that farm-bred lads from Kansas would be crossing Terry's back trail in half tracks fresh from Detroit assembly lines, I had planted my juvenile adventurer on the China coast—probably in a lazy man's hope that history would not come nosing into my scenery with her taskmistress demands for accuracy of detail. I was caught in a trap of my own making. A million American eyes, every pair a critical editor's, looked into the details of the things I used to draw so glibly and safely, a few years back, from an imagination fettered only by the descriptive matter in a ten-dollar atlas. During the war I dared not gloss over the chevrons on the sleeve of a New Zealand corporal, seen in one panel of a weekday strip, lest I be deluged with mail in scornful vein pointing out that they slant them different down under.

This is all by way of saying that the militarization of my Terry, along with Fisher's Joe Palooka and Frank King's Skeezix, seems to have been accepted as smoothly as the failure to go military of the majority, probably for what amounts to the same reason. It would have been as violent a wrenching of the fictional probabilities for free-wheeling able-bodied Palooka, the itinerant pug, or draft-age Skeezix, or my instinctive guerrillist Terry, to side-step the war as for Blondie's Dagwood or mob-buster Tracy or wisecracker Mullins to step out of civilian character to get into it.

No one has ever established for certain whether superior distribution, public relations and publicity, or just plain quality is responsible for some comics being household favorites while others languish. I know from my own experience there is nothing more deflating for a cartoonist than to travel from a city in which his strip appears to one in which it does not. In the first he has only to sign a hotel register (most hotel employees are comics addicts) to be recognized as the creator of So-and-so. When the local newspaper carrying his feature learns he is in town there are interviews and other pleasantries the visitor modestly accepts as his due. In the second he is plain Joe Drummer and, "Sorry we can't cash your check!"

Media other than the client papers of a strip will sometimes contribute to the general whoopla surrounding a well-known comic. The fascinating string of villains in Dick Tracy has so captivated Bob Hope that he seldom fails to build at least one gag on each program around the incumbent louse in Tracy's professional hair. Lesser comedians follow the big boys, and Gould's monsters have become as good for laughs as Crosby's horses, Cantor's daughters, Hope's nose, and Benny's assumed parsimony when the lower-shelf wits unburden themselves on the aerial backwash.

The result of this focusing of attention on a few features is that in pieces like this as well as in casual conversation, the same strips are discussed over and over, when your own favorite may be a cartoon nobody else seems to have heard of. Some newspaper syndicates specialize in selling strips to the smaller city dailies; hence, a feature that has millions of readers may not even be known to people in Chicago, New York, or Los Angeles. A high-light cross section of what happened while you were away might read like an observation post report in the field. *Abbie and Slats:* Bathless Groggins emerges as the number one attraction, with Slats in uniform and Abbie running out of the money. *Alley Oop:* The Beaver Boy ignores the time element and flits hither and beyond, to the distress of Bogies of all periods. *Barnaby:* May be new to you, but worth hunting for if you're after a fresh slant in funnies. *Barney Google and Snuffy Smith:* You know by now that the terms "Yard Bird" and "Feather Merchant" and many others resulted from Snuffy joining the Army and Barney the Navy. *Believe It or Not:* Ripley hasn't run out of material; in fact, his contest for service people's most outstanding BIONs brought him reams of copy and heavy sugar to the G.I. winners. *Blondie:* Even mimeographed service newspapers which could carry but one weekday-size strip a week would often use a continuityless Blondie to give the gang a breath of home. *Bringing Up Father:* The war has changed your old friends very little, although Jiggs and Maggie had shortage troubles along with other civilians. *Buck Rogers:* Working like mad to keep ahead of those A Bomb people. *The Captain and the Kids* and *The Katzenjammer Kids:* SOP (standing operating procedure). *Captain Easy:* Trade-mark registration triumphs over derring-do, and Easy keeps the railroad tracks on his collar. *E. Simms Campbell's Cuties:* You probably have some of them pinned up. *Dick Tracy:* Old Dick took a commission in Naval Intelligence; his work to be done in plain clothes . . . so don't go asking why he wasn't in uniform.

Dixie Dugan: The whee! that grew in Brooklyn is still in there rounding things out for the guys who come back to Flatbush. *Flash Gordon:* Continued to encounter atom and evil by means of stand-by artists while his pappy answered the U. S. Marine muster as Captain Alex Raymond. *Gasoline Alley:* The comic which handled the war theme best of all in my opinion. Skeezix' life in the Army, his marriage, and his relationship with the home-front crowd was written and drawn with great skill by Frank King. *The Gumps:* Old Andy tried to enlist but the man said no. Gus Edson, Andy's boss, has been to every hospital he could reach to draw for the maroon pajama gang. *Harold Teen:* While the name boy was in navy blue, Shadow and company kept the rivets hot and handy. *Jane Arden:* Still poking her pretty profile into peril. *Joe Palooka:* Pfc. right through V-J Day. The Table of Organization in the comics is fouled up again. Imagine a guy like Palooka with one lousy stripe while a punk kid like Terry Lee makes First Lieutenant just because he's a throttle bender in the Air Corps? *Li'l Abner:* The Yokum family and friends got painted on more aircraft than the slickest chicks in other strips. The fly-boys found the Dogpatch crowd just far enough out in that wild blue to suit an airman's taste. *Little Orphan Annie:* Like most everyone else, she went out and blew herself to a change of clothes after the Japs quit. *Micky Finn:* Via the FBI and Coast Guard, the Big M is back in mufti, while Uncle Phil continues to make his brag in the Bars and Grills. *Mickey Mouse:* For this you need sound. *Miss Fury:* Many G.I.s never let the plot of this baby interfere with their enjoyment of the firmly packed white meat displayed in each installment. *Moon Mullins:* One of the few really funny strips. Moon-struck followers of this top drawer humor will tear out M. M. and throw you the residue of the paper.

Mutt and Jeff: Those of us who were weaned on this comic have not been out of the country. *Napoleon and Uncle Elby:*

Things haven't changed much around here. Owners of large dogs particularly appreciate those expressions on Napoleon's face which the untutored claim to be exaggerations. *Nancy:* Real relief from taut nerves. You may have known the bouncy kid as a secondary character to Fritzie Ritz. The shrimp has now edged the cutie out of the number one spot. Sex is just not enough, even in the tragics (suggested word to replace "comics"). *The Neighbors:* This is a single panel cartoon with no established characters in the strip tradition; however, I think George Clark has done in this home-front feature what Sgt. Bill Mauldin did so admirably under fire. If you would like to know what the trend of thought was in the Zone of the Interior at any given time while you were away just look up the Public Library's file of "The Neighbors." *Out Our Way:* Continues to be the most incisive of the panel cartoons not labeled "editorial." *Polly and Her Pals:* This strip felt the war early when Neewaw the Jap valet got the literary ax. *Popeye:* Still the spinach growers' delight. In spite of continued threats, old Chomp-Chin hasn't yet lost his pants. *Prince Valiant:* Val and his Singing Sword continue to beat their way over the ETO in an earlier version of this latest misunderstanding. That 1927 shingle bob Val wears is strictly practical. You probably wished you had hair like that when *your* helmet was good and cold. The strip is as beautifully drawn as always.

Right Around Home: Has balanced the small trials of home-front difficulties in one hand while extending the other in invitation to you to return and spice up the local scene. *Scorchy Smith:* Brought fictional glory to the insigne of the Fifth Air Force all through the war, then got caught by the surrender just as we all did. There were enough Japs killed in the comic strips after capitulation to form the basis for a Domei "incident." *Secret Agent X-9:* Kept the faith on the home front for the FBI. I was sorry we never had a chance to see what Mel Graff, devoted to realism as he is, would have done with a combat sequence. *Smilin' Jack:* Two major mysteries in this strip remain a puzzle to readers: 1. What does Downwind Jaxon's face look like? 2. Where could a fella find a li'l de-icer of his own built to the specifications of those in Jack's life? *Smitty:* Was ruled too young for the Army, although his pop, Walter Berndt, admits the kid is at least twenty-four years old. *Superman:* The Man of Tomorrow has had as much trouble as any other comic strip hero keeping up with quickly outmoded Today. *Tarzan:* Still speaking the unknown tongue to the stars of Ringling Brothers' player farm in the Loin Cloth League. *They'll Do It Every Time:* Hatlo's Foible Foundry has come closest to holding up the mirror to our manners since the death of the great Tad Dorgan. *Winnie Winkle* and *Tillie the Toiler:* These two hard-working gals had their brushes with the war and the wolves: Winnie married into the Army and Tillie joined it. Both are now back at breadwinning.

Of the comics more or less in the war-baby classification, Bill Mauldin's panel called successively *Up Front, Sweating It Out, Back Home,* and finally *Willie and Joe* is easily the best known. It is rare enough for a cartoonist to receive a Pulitzer Prize during his first year of syndication, rarer still for the prize to be given for a drawing that was meant to be entertaining and not to express an editorial policy. *Johnny Hazard:* A comic strip hero who smoked and made eyes at girls right off the bat; very daring stuff. Johnny was another pilot-hero who had no idea there was a peace on and was caught with combat on his hands after V-J Day. *Kerry Drake:* The opposition paper's answer on what to do about the Dick Tracy problem, and *Bruce Gentry:* Honorably discharged from the USAAF and lately a pilot on a South American air line. Two strips I follow with much interest. *Penny:* Darling of the N. Y. *Herald Tribune* and sundry other papers over the country. This chick is the sharpest young blood to show herself around the corner soda fountain in a long time.

Sorry if I skipped your pet. Think what will happen when I see the by-passed authors; some of them outweigh me.

If it is true that the comics have negotiated the war crisis more wisely—certainly more productively, in any event—than the poets and musicians and novelists, maybe the editing we got from the 'fans was what saved and steered us. Reader-editing of the comic strips is an unprecedented phenomenon of publication history. It is not the fan mail phenomenon, as the movies know it. A movie, or a play or a novel, is a completed product before the fan mail starts coming. But the course of events in a comic strip can be influenced, practically, sometimes even advantageously, by fan letters. I have mentioned the technical fan mail I receive in quantity from soldier and sailor readers who spotted errors of service detail in a strip which depicted fighting men of a dozen nationalities and countless ranks and ratings. That helped.

However, I am not sure that anything much was accomplished by a controversy with the gentlemen of the cloth into which I was plunged a few months after I undertook to supply the Armed Forces publication services with a strip, "Male Call," designed to appeal specially to the forlorn fellow in the foxhole. It was a girl strip, as racy as is permissible under the Supreme Court ruling reversing former Postmaster Walker in the Varga girl case. There would have been no particular point in providing girl-hungry G.I.s, isolated in remote defeminized badlands, with a special strip of any other description.

"Male Call" had been running along, smoothly enough, producing no reported outbreaks of animal violence in the ranks when it suddenly became the target of a series of furious editorial attacks in the Brooklyn *Tablet*, a superpurist sectarian publication, from which I quote a typical passage:

"This week we received a copy of 'The Camp Wallace Trainer.' . . . Marked were columns written by the chaplains and an editorial on Easter—messages intended to lift the morale of the boys —and a comic strip by Milton Caniff, cartoonist who draws the series, 'Terry and the Pirates.' The Caniff contribution was a beckoning to the soldier readers away from the appeal to decency and respect for womanhood made by the chaplains. While it was too disgusting to describe, it may be noted that the cartoonist seemed to have one object: to arouse the base, animal instincts in our service men. Since it is obvious that no soldier can be anything but a poorer soldier after he is fed a dish of such filth, it seems strange that the morale officers of the camp permit such men as Caniff access to the boys in our armed forces. This type of stuff certainly is waging a strong fight against the Army chaplains."

The blast had its echoes in the form of some correspondence with army chaplains in different parts of the globe. Reactions were varied. From Camp Wallace, Texas, Father Alfred Barrett, Catholic Chaplain, wrote in part:

"You are aware of the Church's position towards immodesty in women as being provocative of lewd thoughts and desires to normally constituted men. The Church reflects the teaching of Our Lord. He who looks upon a woman to lust after her has already committed adultery with her in his heart.

"The point then is, does 'Male Call' provoke in the minds of readers such lewd thoughts and desires? I am far from being a prude, but I should say it does. What is Miss Lace doing in an Army Camp? She is not a WAAC nor a nurse nor a civilian worker. If she were any of these and pranced around in low-cut gowns which emphasize sexual characteristics, she would be run in by the M.P.'s. To give one specific example of immodesty, you will recall the strip which showed a girl taking a sun bath in the nude, as she was spied on by soldiers repairing telephone lines.

"I cannot therefore agree with the attitude of Chaplain James M. Butler, USNR, whom you quote as saying: 'We Chaplains especially appreciate the clever and tasteful way in which you treat the fighting man's frank and animal interest in the opposite sex.'"

The last of the series came through later. It was signed by Father C. A. Sullivan, Seabees Chaplain on the island-hopping circuit in the remote South Seas, and I can only wonder whether liberalism is not developed in ratio to the distance of the liberalized from home base:

"To say that your 'Queen Bee' illustration was jubilantly received would be an understatement. Distribution of the paper yesterday brought numerous congratulations and everyone here was delighted with the drawing. Enclosed is a copy of 'THE SEABEECON.' We sincerely hope we did justice to 'Burma.' Copies of the paper were sent yesterday to the outlying islands. I know how much these isolated men will enjoy your drawing."

See what I mean? Advice is such a help. Looking back over what I have written, I conclude I ought to take some. I have certainly dished it out.

VIII. THE MOVIES

by BOSLEY CROWTHER

BOSLEY CROWTHER *(age 40) is film critic of*
The New York Times, *a job he has had for the*
last five years. During the war he has visited
several invasion areas, and he spent some time
on a navy carrier in the winter of 1944.

NOW let's go to the movies and see where they came in. . . .

To get this picture in focus, you have got to keep in mind that
"movies," the way we use it, is a catch-all or baggage-car word.
It embraces not only the products turned out by Hollywood—the
star-spangled entertainments which are the standard of the American screen; the wishful-thinking fables so beloved by us romantic
souls—but it includes other types of motion pictures that have
become more conspicuous during the war: the newsreels, the
"fact" films, the "teach" films, and, especially, the ones that help
you think.

Also, that satchel word "movies" contains, in the visions it calls
up, all of the glamorous people who are part of the mythos of
our screen—the actors and actresses, directors, and those vaguely
anonymous folks who make and convey the movies from the studios to you. They are the Movies Incarnate, the shadows reduced
to flesh and blood. What were they doing in the war years?
Where did they figure in? Take the Gables and Stewarts and
Rooneys—the ones who got into uniform, along with some 12,-
000,000 other American guys and girls—or the Hopes and the
Browns and the Crosbys who went out on entertainment tours
and bucked up the kids with home-grown cornstarch in bivouacs
all over the world. And then "the industry" in general: how did
it give of itself with bond sales and war drives and whoop-la and

free movies sent overseas? . . . This all makes a big, broad picture, and you've got to see it from the beginning and as a whole.

First things come first, however, and Hollywood's films are that. They have the top priority as the test of American movies during the war. They were seen by millions of people, both here and in foreign lands; they probably reached a vaster audience than any other form of visual stimuli. The masses swarmed to see them for refreshment, replenishment, release; next to mail, they were readily acknowledged as the serviceman's closest touch with "home." And so they had a responsibility—much greater than they had ever had before—to nourish the spirits of their patrons with the most bracing and satisfying food. How well they fulfilled it is the question. How successfully did they entertain? How nearly did they realize their potential for expanding men's hearts and minds?

This is an estimation in which most everyone is qualified to join—everyone, that is, who went to movies between 1941 and now. And that, of course, includes the fighting forces, which saw almost as many as folks back home. From the Main Street theatre in your own town to the "beachhead Bijou" wherever you were, the same films were shown, with some exceptions; the same images flickered on the screen. The only thing is that all of us didn't see them through precisely the same eyes. Some, such as fighters in the rest camps or weary war workers, say, looked to movies for utter diversion and judged them on how much they gave. Others, desiring more from them than music, wisecracks, and shapely girls, gauged them according to how much dramatic validity they had. And still others who felt that movies should have strived to clarify the real drama of this momentous era took a much different slant on what they saw.

It depends upon where you were sitting. But this you must understand: the making of movies is a business with the big boys in Hollywood—a business which the war, for all the obstacles that it placed in the way, did a great deal to boom. More people had more money during the war years than they had ever had before; more people were willing to spend it for entertainment, no matter what. Theatre box-office grosses reached unprecedented heights. It took a pretty crummy picture not to show a return. So the Hollywood nabobs, in the manner of good business people, inclined—with a few rather notable exceptions—to play their tickets safe. They didn't go in for bold experiments. They stuck generally to familiar routines. Remember, too, that Hollywood was never particularly famed for an accurate scan of life. Remember, because these facts have bearing upon the quality of Hollywood's wartime films.

You probably recall the general nature of our movies during 1941—the year before Pearl Harbor; the year that we sat on the fence. A none too profound comprehension of what was cooking showed in Hollywood's films. (A few previous anti-Nazi pictures had been more or less candidly made and had provoked senatorial isolationists to raise a ruction which soon came to naught.) The big and most popular pictures that year were *Kitty Foyle*, *Sergeant York*, *The Philadelphia Story*, *Citizen Kane*, and such as those. *Gone With the Wind* was still stirring considerable box-office dust. *How Green Was My Valley* had its premiere just six weeks before the Japs let fly.

Oh, sure—the war was distantly suggested in such fictions as *A Yank in the R.A.F.*, *I Wanted Wings*, and *Dive Bomber* and a spate of so-called "service comedies." These latter were pictures which kidded the experiences of "selectees," and most memorable among them were Bud Abbott's and Lou Costello's *Buck Privates* and *In the Navy*. Out of England did come a few pictures such as *Target for Tonight* and that brilliant little fact film, *London Can Take It*, which told bravely of that city's trial by blitz. But, in general, the screens of our theatres were as peaceful as a bright summer day. Our movies were giving us pleasure in the familiar escapist groove.

Wham! Pearl Harbor! (Or BOOM! "December 7th"—as they flash it on the screen.) Hollywood rubbed its eyes one morning and heard we were in a war. The men who produce motion pictures were confronted with a fact which now put it up to them squarely: What is to be the function of the screen? Skipping, for the moment, the many forthright and direct things that Hollywood people did—their organizations for war activities, the enlistments, all of that—let's have a look at the consequences of the productive decisions the big boys made.

The best way to take them is in order. During the first year that we were in the war—and the first year, as a consequence, that some of you were away—a pretty strong smell of high explosives got into Hollywood's films. Indeed, the war figured somehow in about one out of every four. The fact that most of these pictures were begun at least a year in advance was evidence that the producers had been following the news headlines.

Mrs. Miniver was the first one that you would call a top-notch job. It came along in early summer, about the time that we were catching our breath. Although it was questioned in England as a silly representation of their case, it gave to secure Americans a sudden heart-shocking sense of total war. That wonderful English lady and her darling family! So *that's* how it was! (Of course, it really wasn't—but the effect, in movie idioms, was intense.)

Wake Island, which opened in September, when the papers were full of Guadalcanal, was likewise a sock in the kisser for such folks as were still rubbing their eyes. Sure, the fellows who had seen the real McCoy said it looked awfully phony to them. But to us back here in the theatres, reading daily about the Marines and their fight on that other fuming island, it carried a credible punch. Also, *Joe Smith, American* brought the peril pretty close on the home front, and *Casablanca* and *Journey for Margaret* looked sharply behind some transatlantic scenes. At the year's end there also came from England Noel Coward's *In Which We Serve,* a moving saga of the British Navy, which was "limey" as all hell but solid stuff. (As it happened, the American public was strangely lukewarm towards it.)

On the other hand, there were such "war" films as *Eagle Squadron, Captains of the Clouds, To the Shores of Tripoli,* and *Des-*

perate Journey—sheer glamour-boy-in-uniform hoke, as far from realities as dreamland, as heroic as a Superman cartoon.

For straight entertainment, however, that first year of the war did bring some pretty sweet movies—*The Man Who Came to Dinner, Woman of the Year, Sullivan's Travels, Road to Morocco, The Pride of the Yankees,* and—the best of the lot—*Yankee Doodle Dandy,* in which Jim Cagney played George M. Cohan. It waved the flag like the mischief, but that kind of waving was good.

Now, let's see what sort of pictures Hollywood gave us in 1943 —the year of the clean-up in North Africa, the beginning of the Italian show, and the big Pacific island hopping. You would think the producers, by now, would have been pretty well on the war beam. And, in their way, they were. The Warners' *Air Force—* and we mention especially that studio's name because it had a good record of honest, hard-hitting war films—began the year well with a tribute to the spirit of a B-17 crew. The same studio's *Action in the North Atlantic* was a tough film about the Merchant Marine (which, indeed, was shown to trainees as a picture of how things generally were), and its *Watch on the Rhine* won prizes as the best picture of that year. It was a drama of the peril of complacency towards fascist operators at large in the world.

As a matter of fact, Hollywood gave us a big bunch of war films that year—some of them good and some of them elaborately overdone. *Sahara* showed desert warfare in a mixture of realism and Hollywood. *Corvette K-225* was tough sea-fighting, laced rather tenderly with love. *Bataan* and *Guadalcanal Diary* were dubious dramatizations of those dirty shows. And *So Proudly We Hail* was strictly grease-paint, but people liked its story of nurses on Bataan. (Did you see it? Claudette Colbert, Paulette Goddard, and Veronica Lake were spectacularly brave.) *The Moon Is Down, This Land Is Mine, The North Star,* and *Commandoes Strike at Dawn* were various fictitious notions of resistance to the Nazis in occupied lands, shot through with platitudinous mouthings, but well-intentioned, at least.

But with strictly un-war-clouded movies, the boys did much in 1943. *The More the Merrier, Madame Curie, Best Foot Forward,* and *Coney Island* were their speed. Warners filmed *This Is the Army,* the famous Irving Berlin army show, and donated all the profits, plus a quarter million for screen rights, to Army Relief. And Sol Lesser made *Stage Door Canteen* with a large cast of free-talent stars and turned over most of the proceeds to the American Theatre Wing.

This is notable, however: two films of that year caused considerable argument and stir. (When a movie arouses indignation, that's a new twist on man biting dog.) Paramount's prettified version of Hemingway's novel *For Whom the Bell Tolls* got loud boos for reducing the issues in the Spanish Civil War (the thematic crux of the novel) to the vague perplexities of a mountaineers' feud. (Sam Wood, who produced and directed, claimed the "politics" didn't matter, anyhow.) And the Warners' uncommonly daring exegesis on current affairs—their idealized dramatization of *Mission to Moscow,* former Ambassador Joseph E. Davies' diary—got lots of people hot and bothered because it made Russia look like Paradise. It also skipped very politely over the details of the famous Moscow trials. *For Whom the Bell Tolls,* with Gary Cooper and Ingrid Bergman in the cast, was generally successful. *Mission to Moscow,* without star players, laid an egg.

(Incidentally, it might here be noted that the box-office headliner of that critical year, as picked in a poll of theatre operators, was Betty Grable. Does that prove anything?)

Came 1944 and Hollywood's product began to show a pronounced trend towards lighter and mellower diversion, away from the serious thoughts of war. The fact that the year's most popular picture was Bing Crosby's *Going My Way,* the story of two priests in a New York parish, was just one manifestation of the trend. It touched a human note of spiritual triumph which was plainly gratifying in these times. *The Song of Bernadette,* also popular, was as much in the current of this trend as were Preston Sturges' howling satires, *Hail the Conquering Hero* and *The*

Miracle of Morgan's Creek. National Velvet and *Meet Me in St. Louis, Home in Indiana* and *Cover Girl, See Here, Private Hargrove* and *Laura*—they were all significantly "escape."

It is interesting to note, psychologically, that there came along towards the year's end a run of elegant "shockers," of which *Laura* was a type. Among them were *Double Indemnity, The Woman in the Window,* and *Murder, My Sweet*—films of vicarious violence. And the public loved them. Now, figure that one out.

There were some notable war films, for all that—especially *Destination Tokyo, The Purple Heart, Gung Ho!, Thirty Seconds Over Tokyo,* and *A Wing and a Prayer.* All of them had their faults, obviously—glaring errors at which the serviceman could scoff. But they did show a steady development towards a more honest treatment of war. And Darryl Zanuck's production, *Wilson,* which told a story of our first World War President, was a courageous and timely dramatization of a personalized ideal of world accord. It was a rare contribution to public thinking—the sort that Hollywood usually avoids.

On the other hand, the picture *Lifeboat* was occasion for a bitter critical row. Based on a story by John Steinbeck and directed by Alfred Hitchcock, it told of a group of torpedoed Americans and Britishers adrift in a small boat with a Nazi submarine captain. It was widely accepted as a compelling drama of the sea, with the Allied men and women stacked up against the Nazi properly. But several critics and Dorothy Thompson, not to mention a lot of just plain folks, felt it made the Nazi out to be a champion and the democrats a bunch of bungling dopes. This writer concurred with that opinion. It seemed a strangely antidemocratic film, excusable on no basis, even in our enlightened society.

But, to get on with it—the trend towards lightness continued into 1945. Outside of *Objective Burma,* which had Errol Flynn doing a fine job on the Japs, there wasn't a fictional war film of any moment from Hollywood in the year's first half. *Counter-*

Attack was a minor episode in which Paul Muni as a Russian guerrilla foxed the Huns, and *God Is My Co-Pilot* was a flamboyant and distasteful flying-hero film. Just after the Japanese capitulation, however, there did come along two very good Hollywood war films, *Pride of the Marines* and *The Story of G. I. Joe*. The former was an understanding study of a blinded veteran's readjustment, frankly based on the real-life experience of a marine who fought on Guadalcanal, Sergeant Al Schmid. And *The Story of G. I. Joe* was documented from the articles of Ernie Pyle. It was fully endorsed by veterans of the Italian campaign, who saw it in preview.

Otherwise, the top Hollywood pictures up to mid-1945 were such as *A Song to Remember,* a wistful musical about the composer Chopin; *A Tree Grows in Brooklyn, Without Love, The Valley of Decision,* and *Wonder Man.*

Looking back on the over-all record of Hollywood's films in the war, one might reach the dispassionate conclusion that it was neither as good nor as bad as it might have been. There is not the slightest question that it shows evidences of bad taste and occasionally horrible obtuseness. Such films as *Four Jills in a Jeep,* which showed four Hollywood actresses having the jolliest, romantic time touring war fronts; or *Hollywood Canteen,* a quite offensive display of self-esteem; or *Ladies Courageous,* in which the female ferry-pilots were saved by one brave dame; or *Keep Your Powder Dry,* a wretched fiction about three glamour girls in the WAC, were terrible. That's the only word for them.

Furthermore, it cannot be denied that the familiar "hero" pattern was unhappily overused. As he was from the beginning of movies, the individual two-fisted guy was too frequently winning for our side beyond a possible shadow of doubt. And he wasn't always a very pleasant fellow. He was either an elegant sort of snob who finally heard the stern call of duty, or he was a suddenly regenerated punk. The plainly fictitious warfare in which such characters engaged gave the public a dangerous conception of the real kind our men were up against.

And that is the sternest indictment to be drawn against Hollywood's films: they did not give a consistent or reliable impression of the wartime world. Many producers, underrating the public's intelligence as they often do, felt that their films were sufficient if they stated such platitudes as the Nazis are cruel, the Japs are fiendish, the Russians are nice and the Chinese are, too. They did not perceive that the chief thing was to give to audiences a sense of the immense and impersonal conflict into which all peoples have been collectively drawn.

Of course, there is always the question whether Hollywood could have been expected to make any broad and profound clarification of the drama that has baffled expert minds. To expect that it could is assuming an undemonstrated competence. If its films caught a surface indication of the physical nature of war, of the suffering and courage of peoples, then they did about as much as they could. The dramatic comprehension of deep conflicts and of the impersonal tragedy of war was a big bite for fellows in Hollywood who were trained in the mills of make-believe.

Furthermore, added to the confusions and limitations of the makers of Hollywood films there was always the pressure of exhibitors against serious and realistic films. Their periodic yammer was that "the public wants to be entertained," "the public is fed up with war films," and "the theatre is not the place for woe." This thesis, of course, was a bogey. The public did go for *good* war films, such as *Mrs. Miniver, Air Force,* and *Destination Tokyo.* But it was either indifferent or resentful towards the phony and mock-heroic ones. So the exhibitors, rather than take chances on the ratio of good war films to bad, and naturally anxious for fat pickings, said (generally), "Let's stick to 'escape.'"

Also exhibitor pressure on the makers of Hollywood films was supported by the argument that servicemen overseas weren't interested in realistic dramas about the war or anything else. "Just give 'em lots of girls and comedies"—that's what these standpatters said. Hollywood, meshed in its anxiety to please everybody, took the cue.

But, for all that, our screens did get some "war" films of a réal and persuasive sort—pictures that showed what actually happened in straight, photographic detail. These were the documentary pictures of the nation and its forces in action. They were movies, of course—emphatically *movies*—but very different from Hollywood's fiction films.

Again, to get the continuity, we must go back a bit and understand what was doing with "factual" films before the war. Pictures which showed realities had been familiar on the commercial screen ever since movies started flickering, in the shape of newsreels, travelogues, and filmed reports. But in the early 1930's there began to emerge a new school of actuality film-makers who took their cameras out and photographed real life, then composed this material into pictures aimed to catch the true drama of daily events.

These films, known as "documentaries," advanced more rapidly in England at first, gained some momentum on the Continent, and spread to the United States. The March of Time represented the first considerable effort in this line, with its monthly releases of short pictures which dramatized and discussed current happenings. Pare Lorentz made two pictures for government agencies, *The Plow That Broke the Plains* and *The River,* classics in this medium, which further developed the style. Numerous independent producers had made a variety of these fact films before the war, and even the Hollywood shorts departments had made a few interesting tries. But the documentary was still a stepchild on the commercial screen in 1941.

With the outbreak of war, however, it was immediately manifest to public-relations experts that films were a powerful medium for conveying to the people information and inspiration. They were labeled a "weapon of war." The old saw about a picture being worth 10,000 words could be multiplied by twenty when the picture moved, they said. So steps were forthwith taken to bring the movie medium into use. Most appropriate to the purpose was the documentary film.

It so happened that, long before Pearl Harbor—a year and a half before, in fact—the motion-picture industry (meaning the producers, distributors, and exhibitors of Hollywood films) had organized a committee—the Motion Picture Committee Co-operating for National Defense—designated to co-ordinate the industry with outside groups in the national emergency. Even before Pearl Harbor, this committee had helpfully arranged to give distribution in regular theatres to government-made information films—short pictures such as the National Defense Commission's *Power for Defense* and the Office of Emergency Management's *Bomber, Food for Freedom,* and *Women in Defense.*

Immediately after Pearl Harbor this group was renamed the War Activities Committee of the Motion Picture Industry, and a request was sent to President Roosevelt asking that he appoint a co-ordinator of government films. Six days later the President appointed Lowell Mellett, then serving as director of the Office of Government Reports, to fill this additional job. When the Office of War Information was established a few weeks later, Mr. Mellett was named chief of its Bureau of Films, through which were passed to the industry all government- and service-made films.

The relations of the War Activities Committee (or the WAC) with the OWI—and with the armed services for which it acted—could fill a whole chapter in this book. But it is enough to say that the industry, despite some painful groans, did give release to more than one hundred information and war-combat films. These ranged from films made specifically by the OWI's own producing unit—such films as *The World at War, Troop Train,* and *Manpower*—to such splendid combat pictures as *The Memphis Belle* and *With the Marines at Tarawa.* It included fact films made in England and sponsored by the OWI over here, films made by the Army for "orientation," and special films made in Hollywood. Among the latter was the excellent little cartoon which Walt Disney made for the Treasury, encouraging people to enjoy paying their income tax in 1942.

All of these films—most of which were made at the government's expense—were distributed free of charge by the industry to some 16,000 theatres. This was the number of houses that pledged themselves to show the films, and it is fair to assume that most of them abided by their pledges, more or less. The fact that some theatres took exception to the quality of some of these films—if, indeed, they weren't outright resistant to "war" pictures—occasions the doubt.

It is true that many of the items turned out by the OWI were not particularly impressive. They were hurriedly and sometimes haphazardly made. And they fitted no long-range pattern of information. They were made for "spot" jobs. But then the domestic film unit of the OWI was dropped by a congressional economy in the budget in July, 1943, and the making of information films thereafter was left to volunteers in Hollywood. The fact that they didn't do much better bespeaks an incompetence in this line.

However, the factual combat pictures which were made by the services, with their own combat photographers, were something else, when they came along. It was in these that the documentary method was put to excellent use. First of the lot was *The Battle of Midway,* made by Commander John Ford, former Hollywood director (*The Informer, The Grapes of Wrath*), which gave (with only a touch of "Hollywood" faking) a grim picture of the attack on that island. It was released in August, 1942, was in color, and was widely shown.

Less successful but still effective was the Signal Corps's *At the Front,* which described the initial phases of the North African campaign. It was made under the supervision of Darryl Zanuck (then a lieutenant colonel), it was in color, too, and it went out through the WAC to theatres early in 1943. Later that year *Report from the Aleutians* was sent through by the Signal Corps, and it gave a bang-up picture of the rugged conditions in that frozen combat zone. Captain (later Major) John Huston, another former Hollywood director, was in charge of its production. It was a significant finger-post.

For the real combat *documentaries* began coming in 1944, and they clearly manifested the new, realistic "shock" approach. *With the Marines at Tarawa,* made by that service's combat cameramen under the direction of Captain Louis Hayward, was a vivid and sobering illustration of the terrible cost of that little isle. *The Memphis Belle,* filmed by an Air Force Photo unit under Major William Wyler (also of Hollywood), gave a spectacular conception of a bombing mission over Germany. *Attack!—The Battle of New Britain* showed the Arawe Beach assault and the subsequent drive on Cape Gloucester in all its grueling jungle-fighting detail, while *Target Japan* and *The Battle for the Marianas* were brief but tough glimpses of the Pacific naval war.

This flow of vivid combat pictures continued—and, indeed, increased—in 1945. It included the Navy's *Brought to Action,* the Army's *The Enemy Strikes* (Battle of the Bulge), and the joint services' *Fury in the Pacific,* recounting the capture of Peleliu. It also included *The Fighting Lady,* a tremendous feature-length film put together by Louis de Rochemont of Twentieth Century-Fox from footage shot by navy cameras. It told the story of life on an aircraft carrier and was climaxed by spectacular combat scenes. Commercially released to theatres, it was one of the brilliant pictures of the war. (And, we might add, it was eminently successful.)

List, too, among the year's good combat films *To the Shores of Iwo Jima,* made by navy, marine, and coast guard cameramen; *Target Tokyo,* an Air Force picture recounting a B-29 raid; and the Navy's film of kamikaze resistance off Okinawa, *The Fleet That Came to Stay.* A little late but solemnly impressive was the Signal Corps's *San Pietro,* showing the action for that small town in Italy during the winter (1943) campaign. And the full-length review of the invasion of Europe, from the inception to the fall of Berlin—*The True Glory*—was a fine comprehension of that great effort, when it was shown in the early fall.

Widely exhibited in regular theatres, these films had a marked effect in bringing home to audiences the grim realities of war.

Maybe the average movie-goer didn't see all of them; maybe he missed, for various reasons, all but five or six. But whichever and however many of them he happened to see, his knowledge and comprehension of the real thing was sharpened thereby. And, re-member, the showing of these pictures was a public service of the industry.

This calls to mind a story recounted by a service cameraman who was going ashore in an assault boat during one of the Pacific island attacks. A rifleman, crouched next to him, tossed him a nasty crack about how he could be more helpful with a rifle than with that camera. "Look here, pal," said the cameraman, "do you ever write letters home?" "Sure," said the guy with the rifle. "And does the stuff that you write get through—I mean, the stuff about the fighting and the dying that you've already seen?" The rifleman looked at him coldly. "The censors cut it," he growled. "The folks back home have no idea what it's like." With that the cameraman smiled and tapped his camera: "That's what I've got this thing for—to show the people back home exactly what you're going through." From then on, he said, the rifleman was his most con-siderate friend. . . .

In addition to our own combat pictures, there were also shown on our screens similar films from other countries—the British-made *Desert Victory,* recounting the Eighth Army's fateful de-feat of Rommel at El Alamein; *Moscow Strikes Back,* a splendid fact film of the Russian repulse of the Nazis at Moscow's gate; *The Siege of Leningrad,* a grim, cold document of that city's long and painful stand; and *The City That Stopped Hitler—Heroic Stalingrad,* another Russian film.

Mention should also be made here of the Army's famous "orien-tation" films which were put out for public showing through the OWI and the WAC. These were the "Why We Fight" pictures, which were officially required to be shown to every man in the Army before he went overseas. There were seven films in the se-ries, all made under the supervision of Lieutenant Colonel Frank Capra, another famous director from Hollywood and, incidentally, one of the foremost innovators with films during the war. Of the seven, only three—*Prelude to War, The Battle of Russia,* and *War Comes to America*—were publicly released. But, despite rather limited showing, they helped clarify the war's background. And the whole series marked a rare advancement in the use of films to reach men's minds.

As for the role of the newsreels during the war, it was adequate. No one, least of all the newsreel people, were entirely satisfied with it. In the first place, the newsreel companies were put under strict security; their cameramen were generally restricted overseas and all of their footage was "pooled." That is to say, whatever pictures one of them got were distributed to all—after passing the usual censorship. But the fact is that most of their stuff on the war and everything pertaining thereto was furnished to them by the services, share and share alike. As a consequence, the newsreels were dependent almost entirely upon the services for really important war coverage—a condition which plainly limited them. The length of the reels was also limited (by the War Production Board) to 750 feet for each release, but this limitation was politely winked at when the boys had something hot.

And they did get a few sensational stories. The navy footage from Tarawa, and the joint material from Peleliu and Anguar made up into fine, timely newsreels. The films of the liberation of Paris, most of them made by a regular newsreel man working with the resistance forces before the city's "release," were historic, as were the pictures of Manila's capture. Most impressive of all newsreel issues during the war, however, were the films showing the Nazi prison-camp atrocities, released after the fall of Germany. These films were so stark and unstinting that a few theatres declined to show them. But they did reach the public very widely, and were classics in news-film reportage.

The commercially made "think" pictures which were released periodically by the March of Time, the World in Action (Canadian National Film Board), and Pathé's This Is America series contributed, too, to the public's understanding of issues and problems during the war years. A great deal of attention was given in these factual films to the international scene—a healthy indication of broadening horizons on our screens.

And the *movies* still served other purposes—significant purposes —during the war, many of them in areas removed from the general public's eye. There were, of course, the elaborate programs of service training films—a vast new function of motion pictures developed during a few fateful years. (It is proper to note that the Hollywood studios assisted these programs in their initial stages by making many training films on order, before the services completed their own production units.)

There were the special-purpose films produced by Hollywood and other commercial studios—especially by Walt Disney's outfit —for release in Latin America by the Office of the Co-Ordinator of Inter-American Affairs; the films made by the Overseas Motion Picture Bureau of the OWI for exhibition to foreign audiences to acquaint them with our country and our ways. There were the fact films produced by the services and released nontheatrically by them for showing in schools and factories as part of large "industrial incentive" programs. And there were films put out for such occasions as bond and war-charity drives. No one can ever say that movies didn't win their service stripes in World War II.

Now, let's make a hasty survey of the participation of movie people in straight war work. First, of course, there were those who entered the services—some voluntarily, some by request— among them Clark Gable, James Stewart, Robert Montgomery, Douglas Fairbanks, Jr., Henry Fonda, Louis Hayward, Tyrone Power, Mickey Rooney, Victor Mature, David Niven, Wayne Morris, Gene Autry, and Lew Ayres. William Wyler, Frank Capra, John Ford, Anatole Litvak, Anthony Veillier, John Huston, and Gene Markey were among the writers and directors. These are just some of the "star" names. At least one-fourth of the male employees of Hollywood—and from other branches of the industry —went into uniform.

And those who stayed in "civvies" did much work, too. Three days after Pearl Harbor the Hollywood Victory Committee, a wartime outfit, was enthusiastically formed. This organization, embracing virtually all of the people of Hollywood, mobilized the colony's talents and energies for the many activities to which they were called—for bond rallies, camp entertainments, and USO tours overseas. Between the day of its formation and June 1, 1945, the Hollywood Victory Committee enlisted a total of 3,865 players for 47,330 free appearances in 6,810 events contributing to the purposes named above.

Or, to break those figures down into categories:

One hundred and thirty-eight artists played 9,187 days on entertainment tours overseas.

Three hundred and eighty-six personalities played 5,560 days in camps and hospitals in this country.

Two hundred and thirty-nine personalities played 2,919 days on 26 national tours, largely for the Treasury Department bond rallies.

Fifty-two personalities played 221 days on Canadian bond tours.

One thousand seven hundred and seventy-four performances were staged at West Coast embarkation points and staging areas to entertain men headed for the Pacific.

This is not to mention players provided for radio programs, transcriptions, and personal appearances at numerous other rallies.

These figures, of course, do not capture the personal drama and sometimes sacrifice involved. They do not reveal, for instance, that Carole Lombard lost her life in an airplane wreck during a bond tour; that Joe E. Brown made four lengthy trips into practically every war area in which American forces fought, from the Aleutians to North Africa; that Bob Hope and his company were out on the "foxhole circuit" for as many months, almost, as they were at home, or that hundreds of familiar—and unfamiliar—troupers gladly took discomfort in their stride to bring to our fighting forces (and to our wounded veterans) a measure of cheer and hope. If there were a few unfortunate incidents connected with their overseas tours, as occasionally reported, they were exceptions and may now be dismissed.

And the industry itself gave to our forces the most salubrious gift of all when it contributed *all* of its product for free showing at bases overseas. In February, 1942, the WAC presented on behalf of the industry to the Special Services Division of the War Department an initial gift of 1,200 prints on 16-mm. film of feature films released up to that time and assured the Army that any pictures made thereafter might be taken for free showing overseas. In short, the Army was invited to take whatever pictures it desired.

The organization of the overseas facilities for distributing and showing films was, of course, the Army's responsibility, and it was a little slow in shaping at first. Reports came back that the pictures were old and were not widely shown. But the kinks had been pretty well ironed out by the summer of 1943, small projectors were abroad in large numbers, and four new features were going out every week.

Eventually the Army established twenty-one film exchanges overseas, supplying pictures for an average of 5,850 showings a night. A total of 982 different feature films had been sent abroad by mid-1945—or exactly 34,232 prints. It might be mentioned that the raw stock on which these films were printed was contributed free by manufacturers and that the industry, through its subsidiaries, was helpful in bringing it about that the Army had approximately 7,500 16-mm. projection machines available at all times for the showing of entertainment films throughout the world. Many of Hollywood's top pictures were exhibited to troops overseas long before they were released to theatres here at home.

And finally, through exhibitor organizations, rallied by the

WAC, our movie theatres and their screens were made available for bond sales and war charity drives. In addition to showing shorts and trailers encouraging the sale of bonds, many of the nation's 16,000 houses (the total reached 4,280 in the Seventh War Loan drive) had booths placed in their lobbies for the direct vending of bonds. It was roughly estimated that 11 per cent of the total E Bond sales during the war were made in movie theatres or as the result of stimulation by films. And through straight pass-the-hat collections among the nation's audiences, more than $30,000,000 was realized for the Red Cross, Army-Navy Relief, and March of Dimes.

Such were the war-inspired activities of the motion picture industry. Such were the ways in which film folks did their considerable "bits." And yet this would not be an accurate observation of movies during the war if it did not report that that strange cosmos known as Hollywood continued very much as of old. On the surface, of course, there were the obvious indications of a people "geared for war." The stars—especially the females—rushed to volunteer auxiliary work and jauntily showed up at functions in their trim tailor-made uniforms. Food and gasoline rationing put a sharp crimp in social life, as well as in normal transportation, and the studios adjusted to war needs. But the broad exhibitionistic nature of the whole bizarre place remained unchanged. By virtue of inveterate publicity, Hollywood was still the nation's goldfish bowl.

During the war's first few months, a certain caution in conduct was observed, it is true. The annual Academy dinner, in February, 1942, was somewhat subdued and informal, in contrast to the pomp of previous years, and military uniforms and titles were solemnly put on display. The popular Hollywood practice of gaudy premières was dropped—at least, until the danger of a Japanese attack was past. And nobody slugged anybody or got a divorce while the first heat was on.

But pretty soon the film folks were back in their old accustomed stride, being divorced and married and doing other odd and ostentatious things. And, of course, the fan and gossip columnists sped the news to a waiting world. Greer Garson startled everybody by marrying youthful Ensign Richard Ney, who had played her son in *Mrs. Miniver* before he joined the fleet. Mickey Rooney, the fun-loving Andy Hardy, stepped out of character somewhat and was married, divorced, and remarried before his draft board finally found him physically fit. Rita Hayworth shed one husband and then married Orson Welles; and that oft advertised "perfect couple," Dick Powell and Joan Blondell, were split. Lana Turner, Betty Grable, and Carole Landis were also domestically involved.

Outstanding Hollywood romance of the war years, however, was that of middle-aged Humphrey Bogart and his youthful leading lady, Lauren Bacall. Miss Bacall, a sultry charmer who was aptly tagged "The Look," appeared opposite Mr. Bogart in the film *To Have and Have Not*, and the pair were subsequently married (after Mr. Bogart shed a previous wife) in a press agent's dream ceremony on Louis Bromfield's Ohio farm. (The rustic affair was fully covered by a national picture magazine.)

However, domestic tranquillity also had great virtue during the war, especially in the cases of certain male stars who were of notable fighting age. Such romantic lads as might, in peacetime, have kept their families discreetly in the shade were suddenly publicized as happy husbands and fathers of beautiful tots. By an odd twist, the closing of the race tracks brought Bing Crosby's brood into the public eye; when the gag writers couldn't use Bing's horses for "copy" they used his kids.

New stars were born in great abundance, especially new male stars who were rushed in to take the places of the glamour boys who went away to war. Van Johnson, Robert Walker, Dana Andrews, Sonny Tufts, Danny Kaye, and Gregory Peck were tops among the several who emerged, as it were, overnight. And the ranks of the glamour ladies welcomed some new ones in four years.

Much less agreeable to mention—but a part of the picture,

withal—were several unpleasant scandals, notably the cases of
Charlie Chaplin and Errol Flynn. Mr. Flynn, whose social behavior was never especially subdued, was brought to trial in Los
Angeles in January, 1943, on charges of criminally attacking, on
unrelated occasions, two teen-age girls. The twenty-day trial
made a Roman holiday for the curious and the war-heavy press;
the most lurid descriptions of intimacies were boldly and frankly
publicized. Even in Washington, curious people rushed to the
Capitol to attend a Senate committee hearing on the appointment of Edward J. Flynn as Minister to Australia, thinking it
the trial of the movie star. Women swooned in the corridors
when the actor passed to and fro the court. Mr. Flynn was eventually acquitted by a jury of nine women and three men. Said
he: "My confidence has now been justified in essential American
justice. I didn't become an American citizen for nothing." It was
notable that attendance at his pictures boomed during the period
of the trial.

Mr. Chaplin's involvement was equally unsavory. Furthermore,
there was the factor of the public affection in which he was held.
After a great deal of preliminary rumor and developments of a
sordid cast, he was brought to trial in Los Angeles in March,
1944, on charges of transporting Joan Barry, a former "drama
pupil" of his, to New York for the purpose of immoral relations.
The trial was similar to that of Mr. Flynn in that it was occasion
for scandal-mongering by the press all over the land. Although
Mr. Chaplin was acquitted of the federal charge, he was later
declared the father of Miss Barry's child in a second trial. Mr.
Chaplin alleged that he was victimized by persons who resented
the fact that he had made a speech advocating a "second front"
in October, 1942.

These two cases and the public interest in them were miserable
reflections, it is true, of the worst aspects of Hollywood "glamour" and its cultivation by the press. It was ironic that the
movie colony should have suffered such exposure during the
war. Yet, as one West Coast reporter observed in the New York

Times, the morbid public interest displayed by the people on the Coast was more an indication of an "escapism desire" than a callous and conscious indifference to the serious events of the day.

You may question now, in conclusion, what has been the total effect of the war upon American movies. Where do they stand now—and where do they go from here? Those are questions which even the film folks have not fully weighed and appraised. Time alone—and the public's own reactions in the postwar scheme —will answer them.

But this much is fairly obvious: the makers of entertainment films see a greater responsibility to society than they saw before the war. They know that the public—and particularly the fighters who return to civil life—have a broader concept of peoples and of the organization of this world. They know that the mind of the masses, awakened to sharp realities, will not henceforth be susceptible to unmitigated "escape." They know that our films of the future will have to come to a closer grip with life.

The fact that many film-makers have gained combat experience in this war and have seen a new function for movies beyond entertainment is good. These creative men will be anxious to make a richer type of film when they return. They will want to project their experience and their maturity in new dramatic terms. Add to this the fact that the techniques of the documentary have been so well advanced that the public is now accustomed to them and you have a whole new horizon. Films of the future should stimulate, not lull and delude, men's minds.

But that is the "coming attraction"—"next week at this theatre." Our job was to scan the current epic. And this is where we came in.

Part Five

How We Prepared for Tomorrow

I. HOW WE PLANNED FOR THE VETERANS' RETURN

by *CHARLES HURD and CHARLES G. BOLTÉ*

CHARLES HURD (*age 42*) *was, for a year after Pearl Harbor, Washington military reporter for* The New York Times. *In September, 1944, he became Veterans' Editor and started producing the column, "The Veteran," which appears in the Sunday* Times *and the weekly overseas* Times *for servicemen.*

CHARLES BOLTÉ (*age 25*) *is chairman of* The American Veterans' Committee. *He lost a leg in the battle of El Alamein. His book,* The New Veteran, *was recently published by Reynal & Hitchcock.*

SO YOU are confused by a lot that you have read about veterans' benefits? You undoubtedly think they involve too much of the same paper work that you hoped to leave behind when you get or got your discharge papers and your mileage home. A lot of people who were not in uniform agree with you on that.

It may help if we just talk for a few minutes about the *idea* behind the programs planned for you, the benefits and the limitations that enter into them. And remember that no one in his right mind will consider them complete until you veterans have had your say about them. (Amendments to the G.I. Bill of Rights have been introduced in Congress already, and some of the provisions described in this article will probaby have been changed by the time you get this book.)

535

If there is anything at all on which everyone in the United States agrees it is that veterans have got something special coming to them. Only a few people believe that the veterans want a lot of special babying; most people realize that there is no complete pay-off possible. But running through the country there is a widespread conviction that the veteran *should be helped to return to the status he would have held if he hadn't gone to war.* That, we think, is the test that should be applied to all veterans' programs.

By that test, the existing programs of legislation and community action vary widely in their effectiveness. There has been no over-all *strategic* plan devised for returning you to normal civilian status. There are, instead, dozens of unco-ordinated *tactical* plans, each aimed at reaching a specific objective on the road to your full and final readjustment. It's a little as if General Patton and General Keyes and Colonel Snooks and Lieutenant Brown and Bill Mauldin's Willie and Joe had set off to capture Berlin without having General Eisenhower to co-ordinate their actions—and without any radio intercommunication among their separate commands. The result is that much good work and good planning are being done, but that many veterans have become confused and discouraged by the run-around from agency to agency which has inevitably grown out of this situation.

Several reporters—including your present correspondents—have been beating their brains out trying to tell this to the folks at home, and there are encouraging signs that the run-around is being ended. President Truman has helped a lot by appointing that master strategist, General Omar Bradley, as head of the Veterans Administration, the federal agency with which most of you will have to deal at one time or another. We're sure that General Bradley, a soldier's soldier if ever there was one, will bring the VA up to date, streamline its operations, cut most of the red tape which has lowered its efficiency, and improve the quality of medical care in the veterans' hospitals.

Another encouraging sign is the increase in the number of veterans' community service centers. Most of you won't have terribly complicated problems, but almost all of you will have one or two or several comparatively small problems, and you'll certainly have questions that will need answering. These problems can best be dealt with in your own community, in a single center where trained workers can give you quick answers and help you with your job-rights, disability allowances, conversion of your National Service Life Insurance (a good thing to hold on to, by the way), education, vocational rehabilitation, any family problems you find, and so on.

Centers like this are already functioning in many communities, with New York City, Los Angeles, and Bridgeport, Connecticut, having outstanding examples. If you get home early and there isn't one in your home town, you'll be doing your buddies a favor if you suggest to the town fathers that they put their heads together and set one up.

That, in brief, is the background of national legislation and community organization which proceeded on the basis of trial and error as large numbers of veterans were released, from month to month while the fighting still went on, and in much greater totals since V-J Day.

Now for some specific information on what's coming to you:

JOBS

THE OLD ONE:

Away back in 1940 Congress passed the Selective Service Act, which eventually put most of the men into the armed forces. You will remember that then the National Guard was called up for a year. It was planned to draft men for what looked like only a year of training. Into the draft law was written Section 8, which guaranteed that any man pulled out of a job into military service would have the legal right to his old job or to a similar one, without loss of seniority, status, or pay. That provision seemed to answer most of the questions of five years ago.

This law says that if you had a permanent job before you entered military service you have the right to reclaim it at any time within ninety days after your discharge. You must be physically and mentally able to take up the old work, and it must not be "impossible or unreasonable" for your employer to take you back. If these conditions are met, the job is yours for at least one year, and you are secure against lay-off or arbitrary dismissal. Of course, if the plant closes within that year, you're out along with everybody else.

The law is still in effect today, but there are wide differences of opinion as to what it means and as to just how effective it really is. Selective Service itself estimates that only 20 per cent of all servicemen and veterans have the right to a job under the act. There are several reasons for this:

In all the shuffling of war production, many of the old jobs have disappeared.

Some jobs have had five or six men drafted out of them.

And the director of Selective Service has ruled in his famous Local Board Memorandum 190-A that a veteran must be restored to a specific "position," and that only the first man drafted out of a job has the right to get it back, because all subsequent employees in that job are classed as "temporary."

In this same memorandum General Hershey set forth the principle of "superseniority," which means that a veteran who held a "permanent" job must be restored to it even if it means discharging a worker with greater seniority; for instance, a welder with twelve years' seniority who had been transferred to your job on a punch press when the welding department was cut back would be discharged when you returned, although you had had only a year in the plant and six months in service.

The labor unions and many experts in industrial relations hold a completely opposing view of what the act means. They say the definition of "temporary" should be narrowed so that more veterans would have job-rights, and that Section 8 is intended to give you not the right to a specific "position" but to "the totality of job rights," which would include seniority figured on the basis of your time in the plant plus your time in the armed forces. Under this interpretation you would be rehired on the basis of a seniority list, if necessary replacing a worker employed *after* you were, but not a worker employed *before* you were.

A federal court has upheld the Selective Service reading of the act in one case; the War Labor Board and an arbitrator's decision have upheld the union interpretation in two other cases. It's not likely that there will be a Supreme Court ruling for some time. The result is that many a veteran will find himself in a law court instead of in a job, unless the law is amended so that Congress makes its intention clear. It seems self-evident that the law should make more than 20 per cent of you eligible for jobs.

Aside from the legal aspect, there is this important angle when it comes to considering the old job: hundreds of thousands of veterans have grown older, have learned more, and have got new ideas. There is no particular benefit to the combat major in guaranteeing him the right to go back to the shipping clerk's job he held as a kid. This is a problem that can hardly be met by legislation; it can best be met by community and group understanding, *and by your own understanding and patience.* The unpleasant fact is that you're probably worth more to Uncle Sam piloting a B-29 than you are to some private employer when you walk in on him and want to start work. Your progress back up to pilot's pay will then depend on your skill in your new job—which is the way it's always been in America.

A NEW ONE:

There is no *guarantee* of a job for a veteran who didn't have one when he was drafted, who held one defined as "temporary" by Selective Service, or who decides he doesn't want to go back to his old one. But most employers are giving special consideration to job applications from veterans; you may have learned new skills in the armed forces which will help you get a new job; and there are provisions in the G.I. Bill of Rights and elsewhere which will give you educational or vocational training to fit you for almost any line of work you care to go into.

You'll get some dope on this from the separation center when you leave the service. Then when you report back to your local draft board, you will have a chance to talk to the employment counselor there. These men are not specialists, but they usually know the opportunities and problems in the local community, and they should have the practical experience you'll want to draw on. Then, either at the veterans' service center or at one of the eight thousand field offices of the United States Employment Service that are scattered over the country, you'll find someone who specializes in counseling veterans on jobs and getting them into the jobs that are available.

The USES has been working for years to help supply the job requirements of some of the biggest as well as the smallest industries in the country. It helps highly paid specialists to get the right jobs, as well as skilled and unskilled labor. It knows where the jobs are, what they are worth, and how peacetime jobs can be developed out of the skills you may have learned in service. It can tell you also what supplemental training may lead to in the field you want to develop for yourself. Every USES office has got or soon will have a specially trained man known as a "Veterans' Counselor." He is supposed to have the information you are looking for, and if he doesn't have it he knows where to get it fast.

After you have talked with the counselors at USES and Selective Service, you will be in a position to have a really honest count on the job outlook. You should get a pretty good idea of the apprentice training and in-plant training programs and many other details of plans designed to help you land solidly on your feet in the place where you want to be. If you're not sure what job you want, or if the available jobs don't suit you, you can take your time, look around, and investigate the possibilities of further education or training. There are a lot of benefits available here, and you might as well make the best of them.

FOR THE DISABLED:

Some of you are going to have this job problem badly complicated by disabilities suffered in service or resulting from it. We won't tell you that these don't matter, because a man with a disability is the only one who knows whether it matters to himself or not. But it's a fact that a great deal is being done to help the man disabled in service to establish himself both economically and socially so as to make his disability unimportant, at least so far as earning a living is concerned.

While you were away, as one example, twenty thousand different industries combed all of the things that are done in their offices and plants to find out which jobs actually need only one hand, to segregate the stand-up jobs from the sit-down ones—in other words, to list the jobs so that disabled men need not actually be disabled in their work at all.

As an additional help, there is a specific service, carried out in co-operation between the Veterans Administration and many of the leading universities and colleges, which any veterans' service agency can tell you about. It is a service primarily designed to guide disabled men to the best possible jobs, but it is equally available to any able-bodied man who wants to use it. These aptitude tests and the job-counseling that goes with them are the practical application of principles that have been fully proved by experience.

EDUCATION AND VOCATIONAL TRAINING

The educational part of the veterans' program is about the simplest section of it, and it is working well.

The education program breaks down into two sections. There is one section, written in the G.I. Bill of Rights, that covers everyone, able-bodied or disabled, which we will discuss first. Then there is a special one, aimed at disabled veterans, which we shall take up later.

The G.I. Bill authorizes every veteran with a discharge other than dishonorable to education comparable with his period of service, the only condition being that he shall have served more than 90 days on active duty, not including attendance at school while in uniform. This provision stipulates that every veteran, from General Eisenhower down, shall have available at least a year of this educational training or its equivalent at part-time studying of his choice.

The law states that provision should be made for completion of the education of all veterans whose schooling or training was "interrupted" by the war. The veterans whose education was "interrupted" can get additional education equivalent to the time spent in service, up to three years, provided they apply for this within two years after the war or two years after discharge, whichever is later.

The Veterans Administration has ruled that any veteran who was under 25 years of age when he entered service can consider his education "interrupted," and can get at least one year of education no matter how old he is. It has also ruled that the extended education benefits based on actual service can be given to anyone, regardless of age, who can prove that his education actually has been interrupted. In other words, if a man was 32 years old when he was inducted and was studying for a Ph.D., his education was interrupted.

The veterans who go in for this education are being paid a subsistence allowance of $50 a month if single or $75 a month if they have dependents. The schools they attend are being paid up to $500 for a school year in tuition and fees.

The simplest application of this benefit is to the man or woman who wants to go to college, but the program only begins with that special class. A veteran can collect the living allowance if he is attending full time any recognized trade school or business college or institution. What he studies is conditioned only by the question as to whether he can qualify for the school he wants to attend. One hitch is that the VA will pay the full tuition only if you attend an institution which runs on a normal-length school year; but there are indications that this ruling may be amended.

Many men will want to do part-time studies leading to professions or skills while they are holding down full-time jobs. If you have a full-time job, the government will pay your tuition but no subsistence allowance. These subsistence allowances may be supplemented by part-time earnings, but not by regular full-time jobs.

Here is what is offered to the men who have disabilities certified by the Veterans Administration, whether the disability is 10 per cent or 70 per cent:

If the veteran will take the advice given by vocational guidance people designated by the Veterans Administration, the sky is the limit on the type of training he may receive, in a school or on the job. The government will supply all books, equipment, and tuition, regardless of their cost, for as long as necessary to complete the recommended course of training, up to three years. The training will be recommended by the VA's vocational guidance people on the basis of a man's prior educational background and experience.

Thus the disabled veteran who had finished his premedical work in college may be certified, if he is physically able, to go ahead and take his medical degree. Or a man may want to be a toolmaker or a bookkeeper. If the vocational guidance people consider him able to do this sort of thing, he will be trained as nearly in accordance with his desires as possible.

The living allowances for disabled veterans taking this special training are considerably more liberal than those provided by the G.I. Bill. Every disabled veteran in this program, if single, gets a minimum of $92 a month. If his pension is greater than $92, he gets the pension instead. The disabled veteran who is married gets a living allowance of $103.50, plus $5.75 for each child. There is a special allowance of $11.50 a month for each dependent parent. Again, if a veteran's pension is greater than this total, he gets the pension.

If you are one of the hundreds of thousands of men with minor disabilities that do not actually affect your life or work one way or another, you will doubtless check these two programs over against each other, forgetting the immediate size of the subsistence allowance and determining which one seems to offer the best long-range benefit. And, if you follow the experience of many veterans, you will take these two educational and vocational-training programs and check them over against the job outlook which you can get from USES and the draft board counselors.

LOANS

A number of the states have set up loan and assistance programs varying so much in detail that there is no room to go into them here. We will limit our discussion to the grand-daddy of the loan programs: the one written into the G.I. Bill by the government, which has undertaken to guarantee half of the money a veteran is able to borrow, up to $4,000, to establish or buy a business, to go into farming, or to buy a house.

There has got to be a lot of simplification in the administering of this loan provision to make it mean all that you may wish it to mean. It's a very businesslike proposition, and you can't simply walk into a bank and say, "Where's my $2,000?" Safeguards that had to be devised to protect a few veterans may seem crippling to a great many others. For instance, one thing that the Congress and the Veterans Administration had to worry about was the possibility that racketeers and shysters would devise a lot of schemes to get the money away from you before it did you any good.

The safeguard against this is to get the best advice available in your community before you put your name on the dotted line for anything. Your local banker is there to talk to you; so is the veteran's counselor at your draft board. And the local representatives of federal agencies like the Reconstruction Finance Corporation are at your disposal. If you want to go into farming there is a Department of Agriculture agent in every county in the United States whom you'll want to see, and he usually has working with him a committee composed of the most solid farmers in his region.

As for the loan program itself, the Veterans Administration is prepared to guarantee 50 per cent of loans up to $4,000, so long as the money is to be repaid within 20 years and the interest is not greater than 4 per cent. You may be able to arrange a much larger loan, in which case the VA will guarantee no more than $2,000.

The Veterans Administration will pay the interest on the guaranteed part for the first year but otherwise it puts out no money at all. It only guarantees its fraction. If you go in default of the loan, the government will pay off the guaranteed part—*but you are still liable for anything you may have to make good the government's claim against you.*

Now, you may use this guarantee for any one of the three purposes outlined, or for any combination of them, as long as you can get the money from the lender and can pass muster with other investigating agencies of the government, designated by the Veterans Administration to approve applications for guarantees.

You may wish to go into partnership with some other veteran in business or farming. In that case you may pool your borrowing capacity and get the advantage of one special little ruling that can be very important. Under most laws, all partners are equally liable for all debts. But on these guaranteed government loans, each veteran is liable only for his own share. Incidentally, if you happen to be a veteran married to another veteran you each have your own individual borrowing capacity.

HOME LOANS:

Up to now the biggest business done in loans has concerned homes. Some veterans in small communities have found that $4,000 is enough to buy a home, and they have been able to set up housekeeping simply on the basis of making a long-term semi-guaranteed loan. Others have used their savings but needed a little more money and have borrowed possibly $1,000 or $2,000, leaving the rest of the borrowing capacity—the remainder of that $2,000 guarantee—in reserve for some future purpose.

Unfortunately, very few home deals have been possible in many communities because the war boom has pushed all property values beyond the "reasonable normal value" specified in the act. Here again, efforts are being made to have the act amended so that you can float a loan to get yourself a home even if the price is above the prewar level.

In addition to the G.I. Bill, there is one standard procedure by which a veteran without any cash, but whose income prospects are in line with his desires, can get a house. Long before the war the Federal Government set up a home mortgage insurance system to underwrite mortgages up to 80, and in some cases 90, per cent of the value of homes of small and medium size. The Veterans Administration has specified in a regulation that wherever a veteran can buy a house covered by federal mortgage insurance, the 80 per cent insured part can be considered a first mortgage and the VA will insure all of a second mortgage up to 20 per cent of the value of the property, as long as that 20 per cent does not exceed $2,000. That is the one means of getting a house costing no more than $10,000 without making any down payment out of your own pocket.

When you look into this project you will find that there is a lot of investigation to be gone through, but all of it simply heads up into the requirement that you have a reasonable chance of being able to repay the loan on the home you want to buy.

The way to find out about this whole home-buying opportunity is to go to a bank or a building and loan association. If your ideas and your outlook, and the house you have in mind, fit the bill, the paper work will turn into work that the lender will be glad to handle for you, because he is looking for customers.

FARMS:

The farm loan program falls into the general pattern of the home loan program. Again, it's a question of getting good counsel from the county agent, and then of showing the lending agency that you are a good risk. The Department of Agriculture warns amateurs to stay out of farming on their own hook until they have the experience and the training that will give them a reasonable chance of success—which any farmer can tell you is good advice.

The technicalities for getting the money are about the same as for getting home loans. There are various means, too, of getting additional credit from various farm loan agencies, which your county agent will explain to you in detail.

In all of this loan program, we'd like to emphasize again, nothing is being given away. Whether you borrow from an old-line federal agency or use the guarantee covering half of a smaller loan endorsed by the Veterans Administration, you still are borrowing—you're not getting some left-handed kind of bonus.

BUSINESS LOANS:

The business loans are the most complicated of the lot. The chief reason for this is the high percentage of failures in new small-business enterprises every year. Going into business on your own is a risky proposition; so the government, for your protection, for the protection of the lending agencies, and for its own protection, has hedged the business loan provisions with restrictions. The result is plenty of red tape and a very long application blank.

For instance, you can't use any VA-guaranteed loan for working capital, which would cover running expenses and inventory. The guaranteed loan can be used only for setting the business up or for buying a partnership interest in a going concern. And right there you find one of the reasons for all the red tape: some businessmen might see in the veteran a chance to get a new infusion of capital and paint a glowing picture of big profits if you would only buy a partnership with them. The cumbersome regulations are here designed so as to reduce the possibility of your being played for a sucker.

On the other hand, government agencies such as the Department of Commerce and private organizations such as the Committee for Economic Development are planning for an increase in the number of small businesses, in order to counteract the concentration of capital and enterprise in the hands of a comparatively few great corporations. You can get a line on the likely prospects for a new business enterprise or small industrial establishment from these agencies; and if you're thinking of going into a retail enterprise, the retail trades associations are developing a program designed to help veterans set up shop which should prove useful to you. Your local chamber of commerce should also have information about what enterprises are needed, which ones have the best prospects of success, what some of the pitfalls in each line amount to, and how to avoid them.

This brief account of complications should help explain why the business loan is the most businesslike of the G.I. Bill loan provisions. There has been a lot of malarkey circulated about the G.I. Bill, and many veterans have been disillusioned at finding that it wasn't so easy as it had been made to sound. The fact is that it can be of considerable benefit to you, but only if you do some pretty sharp investigating first.

YOUR STAKE IN THE FUTURE

One of the problems in working out this program has been to do it in such a way that the whole thing won't kick back on *you* in a few years. This is because veterans are also citizens, and citizens pay taxes. After the war the veterans will comprise at least a fourth and possibly a third of the taxpayers. So you have a personal interest in seeing that the program is run efficiently, without waste or duplication or overlapping.

President Truman said awhile ago that the veterans will be running the country for years to come, and that therefore they had to accept responsibility as well as benefits. The reason for this is obvious: with 12,000,000 or more veterans, making up the most vigorous and powerful single element in the nation, there can't be any lasting benefits for veterans unless the nation as a whole is healthy, prosperous, and peaceful. There can be no island of security for veterans in the middle of a sea of unemployment and depression, because unless all our people have decent jobs they can't buy the goods and services produced by the veterans, and then the veterans will be out of luck themselves. That's why, in the long run, the only solution to the veterans' problems depends on the solution to the national problems.

Because the veterans of this war will have tremendous political power, they can do much to help solve these national problems, thereby providing the best solution to their own problems.

But—let's be blunt—there are people in this country who would like to harness your collective power to their own selfish plans for domination. Some of them are already using the familiar techniques of the fascist demagogues you've defeated on the battlefield, the old techniques of setting class against class, of weakening the people by dividing them against one another so that they themselves can vault into the saddle. You as a veteran are the most desirable asset anybody with an ax to grind can hope for. So, for your own protection and for the protection of the things you fought for, you'll want to be pretty careful about whom you link yourself up with.

Alone, you can't do a great deal to bring about the kind of America you want to live in; acting together with your comrades, you can do a lot. You'll therefore want to be sure that you join a veterans' organization which is going the way you want to be going, and in which you know your own voice can be heard. That way you can help guarantee both your country and your own future, in peace as you did in war.

HOW TO GET YOUR QUESTIONS ANSWERED

Sometime a question is going to arise that probably will make you ask, "Why didn't they tell me about this?"

Well, that is one of the problems that has run all through this program. Most of the people who have worked on answers to your questions became convinced a long time ago that any man who has been in service is pretty tired of being "told." The idea behind the whole program has been to lay the answers on the line, where they could be obtained with the least possible difficulty, but without saying to any veteran, "You must do this or that."

There are a lot of other details in the program that lack of space has made impossible to describe here, but you can find out generally about them from the little booklet, *Your Rights and Benefits,* which was given to you when you were discharged. (If it wasn't, you can obtain it from any Veterans Administration office or veterans' service center.)

Finally, here is a brief guide to the places where your most important inquiries can be answered:

FOR GENERAL INFORMATION: Your local Selective Service Board, the Red Cross, veterans' information or service center, or veterans' organizations.

GOVERNMENT INSURANCE: Director of Insurance, Veterans Administration, Washington 25, D. C.

RE-EMPLOYMENT: Your former employer or Re-employment Committeeman of your local Selective Service Board.

NEW EMPLOYMENT: U. S. Employment Service; U. S. Civil Service Commission; veterans' service center.

EDUCATION: Veterans Administration; college or school of your choice.

VOCATIONAL TRAINING: Veterans Administration; also (if disability is not due to service) your State Department of Education.

LOANS FOR HOMES, FARMS, BUSINESS: Veterans Administration, bank, lending agency, veterans' service center.

DISABILITY: Veterans Administration (disability pensions, hospital care, insurance, national soldiers' homes, burial allowance). Veterans' organizations or the Red Cross will help file a claim for disability allowance.

LEGAL AID: Red Cross, County Welfare Office, local bar association.

INCOME TAX: Federal—nearest Internal Revenue Office; State—State Tax Commission, at state capital.

SOCIAL SECURITY BENEFITS: Nearest Social Security Board field office.

UNEMPLOYMENT BENEFITS: Nearest U. S. Employment Office.

II. HOW WE PLANNED FOR THE POSTWAR WORLD

by *JOSEPH H. BALL,*
U. S. Senator from Minnesota

SENATOR JOSEPH H. BALL *(age 40) was appointed to the U. S. Senate by Governor Stassen of Minnesota in 1940 and in 1942 was elected for a six-year term. In March 1943 he introduced the so-called B2H2 Resolution, for U. S. participation in an international peace organization, which is described in this chapter. His major Senate activities have been as a member of the Special Committee to Investigate the Defense Program, the so-called Truman Committee; of the Education and Labor, Appropriations, and Immigration Committees. In 1944 he was one of the leading young Republicans to vote for Franklin Delano Roosevelt.*

PLENTY of plans for that postwar world were concocted in the U.S.A. while you were gone. Only a few of them have jelled so far, and those few are mostly concerned with the part America will play in various international agencies aimed at preventing another war.

So if you've been concerned about just how you would fit into a changed and utopian world, forget it. There have been changes, but nothing to marvel at, and you'll have plenty of opportunities to do your share of postwar planning.

The greatest changes have been in our foreign policy, and that's where most of our concrete postwar plans have been made.

In case you've forgotten it, foreign policy was rather a sizzling subject back in 1940 and 1941, and even up through 1944 there was considerable difference of opinion in the country as to how far the United States should commit itself to various international enterprises. Those differences seem to be evaporating rapidly today, and the United States is stepping out in the world in a way that would have seemed incredible in the 1920's or 1930's or even 1940.

After our fight over the League of Nations in 1919 following the first World War, winding up with its defeat in the Senate, we went isolationist with a vengeance. It was a rare politician who got elected to Congress without declaring flatly against "foreign entanglements." Big Bill Thompson was elected mayor of Chicago time after time by campaigning against the King of England, and the late Senator William Borah was the authentic spokesman of our overwhelming desire to stay clear of other nations' wars.

We had a boom and a depression. We got the New Deal, the Blue Eagle, CWA, WPA, NYA, CCC, and a host of other agencies. We didn't like some of the things that slightly comic dictator in Germany was doing, and noticed the headlines about the fighting between the Japanese and Chinese. But most of us were too busy with our own problems to worry very much about what the United States should do about it. Congress passed a Neutrality Act, which forbade our mixing up in any way in any war that might happen, regardless of who was involved or on which side our sympathies might lie. We were determined to remain aloof.

We continued that determination while Italy grabbed Ethiopia, the Nazis and Fascists helped Franco establish his dictatorship in Spain, the Japs seized more chunks of China, and Hitler first marched into the Rhineland and then occupied Austria.

In the spring of 1939, President Roosevelt and Secretary of State Hull both pleaded with Congress to amend the Neutrality Act so that we could at least send a few arms to our friends in the war that appeared all set to explode in Europe. They got nowhere. We were still determined to remain aloof. President Roosevelt tried again after Germany attacked Poland in September of 1939, and again was turned down by Congress. Republicans were almost solidly opposed to any change in the Neutrality Act, and, despite overwhelming Democratic majorities in both houses, there were enough members of the President's own party likewise opposed to block any action. We remained stubbornly isolationist.

President Roosevelt and Secretary Hull, as well as some other leaders and many newspapers (our reporters all through the thirties had been reporting accurately the gathering storm in Europe), argued and pleaded, pointing to our own danger if the democracies in Europe were beaten, but it was an uphill battle.

The William Allen White Committee to Defend America by Aiding the Allies was organized, and the America First Committee took up the cudgels against any involvement. Then two things happened.

The invasion, on April 9, of Norway and Denmark and their quick conquest, followed by the blitz through the Low Countries and France, jolted our complacency as reasoned arguments had failed to do. All through this change in America's foreign policy, events have been more effective in changing opinion than words, and the might of the German war machine revealed in that incredibly quick conquest of France gave us a real scare.

The second thing that happened was Wendell L. Willkie. A businessman and Wall Street lawyer, almost completely unknown politically in January of 1940, Willkie stumped the country in an evangelical campaign that won him the Republican nomination for president in June. A shaggy bear of a man with a hoarse, vibrant voice, Willkie stood squarely for American support of England, and won the Republican nomination on that platform. Many Republicans who had long been suspicious of the party's isolationist position were encouraged by Willkie's leadership to fight actively within the G.O.P., and for the first time there appeared to be a chance of substantial bipartisan support for our intervention in the war.

Willkie's position encouraged President Roosevelt to send arms to England during those black weeks after France fell and in September to trade fifty U. S. destroyers for American air and naval bases in the West Indies, Newfoundland, and Bermuda.

President Roosevelt was re-elected for a third term in November, but Willkie's contribution to building unified public support for a strong American foreign policy cannot be overestimated. During the next four years, while he was titular head of the Republican party, his support, both of the war effort and of all moves toward postwar international co-operation, never wavered. America lost a great fighter when Willkie died suddenly shortly before the 1944 election.

The German blitz played no small part in the passage by Congress in September of 1940 of the Selective Service Act, with which you no doubt are familiar. At the same time President Roosevelt inaugurated a national defense program, and the first of many subsequent appropriations of the billions of dollars which built our army, navy, and air force went through.

The controversy over whether the United States should take an active hand in the war reached its peak in January of 1941, when President Roosevelt proposed to Congress the Lend-Lease Act. Under the Neutrality Act, Britain and China could buy munitions in America, but they had to take title at the water's edge and transport the munitions in their own ships. Both countries had used up virtually all of their dollar balances in the United States, and both were extremely short of ships to transport the supplies they were getting.

The President proposed briefly that he be authorized to buy and transfer munitions to countries whose defense he considered vital to the defense of the United States, which of course meant those countries still fighting the Axis. The debate was pretty vitriolic. Both the America First Committee and the Committee to Defend America by Aiding the Allies sponsored mass meetings and radio broadcasts throughout the country. Opponents of the bill contended it was a first step toward war and inevitably would mean our involvement. Proponents argued that if the Axis won in both Europe and Asia we would eventually be attacked anyhow, and in that case we would fight alone. Some pretty harsh terms were tossed around, such as "warmongers," "Anglophiles," "Nazi sympathizers," and others. One Senator accused President Roosevelt of planning to "plow under every fourth American boy."

The opponents had all the emotional arguments on their side: our hatred of war and our deep distrust of European power politics. On the other side were the frightening power and ruthlessness of the German war machine and the plain evidence that democracy and freedom were blotted out wherever the Nazis conquered.

The Lend-Lease Act passed both the House and Senate and became law on March 11, 1941. In the House the vote was 260 for and 160 against. Democrats voted 236 for and 25 against, while House Republicans were 24 for and 135 against. In the Senate, the vote was 59 for and 30 against Lend-Lease, with Democrats splitting 49 for and 13 against, while Republicans voted 10 for and 17 against.

Under Lend-Lease, around 35 billion dollars of munitions, food, shipping services, and other supplies have been transferred to our allies, chiefly to Britain and Russia. Passage of the act threw the power and strength of the United States into the war on the side of the Allies and against the Axis, although we still maintained a pretense of neutrality and were not actually in the war.

That there was still a deep division of opinion in the country over our actual participation showed clearly when an amendment was proposed to the Selective Service Act to extend the training period limited to one year by the original law to the duration of the national emergency which the President had declared. The bill passed the Senate with nearly a two-thirds majority but barely squeaked through the House with a single-vote margin.

Failure of the bill would have meant tearing to pieces the army we were just beginning to build and starting all over again less than six months before Pearl Harbor.

It was also in the summer of 1941 that President Roosevelt and Prime Minister Churchill met on a cruiser off the Atlantic coast and announced the now-famous Atlantic Charter, which was in effect a statement of our joint war and peace aims, similar to Wilson's Fourteen Points, even though we were not yet officially in the war. The Atlantic Charter, proclaimed in August, was also our first official step in international postwar planning.

The Charter's eight points, among other things, called for no territorial aggrandizement, self-determination of peoples, freer world trade, international co-operation on social and economic problems, and a wider and permanent system of security against war.

The reception in America of this statement of postwar aims was mixed. A few isolationists derided it. More were silent, and most interventionists hailed it as the first step toward effective psychological countering of Nazi propaganda.

One more controversial foreign policy measure was passed by Congress before Pearl Harbor. It was a bill repealing the Neutrality Act embargo on arms shipments to belligerents and also authorizing the arming of our merchant ships, some of which had already been sunk by submarines. It passed the House, 259 to 134, and the Senate, 49 to 36.

These pre-Pearl Harbor foreign policy measures were extremely important, not only because they strengthened our allies sufficiently so that they were able to hold off the Axis until our full power could be mobilized and brought to bear, but because they in effect reversed completely the isolationist, strict neutrality policies which had dominated our international actions for two decades. By these legislative acts we recognized and admitted that we had a stake in any major war, wherever it occurred, and that under modern circumstances we could not by ourselves alone assure our own security and peace. The logical conclusion was that once the war was won we would not again do what we did in 1919 and withdraw from joint international efforts to prevent future wars. It was against that background and with that implied commitment that we began a year or so later to plan our postwar foreign policy.

The sneak attack on Pearl Harbor on December 7 ended our public debate and united the nation. Congress declared war the next day with only one dissenting vote. Pearl Harbor—because it proved, as only events can, that the United States was vulnerable to destructive attacks across huge oceans—cut the ground from under the strongest argument the isolationists had had, namely, that our oceans made us secure from any attack. Later the B-29's, the development of paratroops, and, above all, the V1 and V2 bombs strengthened the argument. The atomic bomb was the final clincher, shattering the last vestiges of isolationism along with Japanese resistance.

Outside of a few crackpots and the remnants of the old America First group led by rabble-rousing Gerald L. K. Smith, virtually all Americans are convinced that we must co-operate with other nations after the war in maintaining the peace. There will be plenty of arguments over the methods and extent of our co-operation, but no serious clash over the basic principle.

After Pearl Harbor, 1942 was a year when all our efforts were devoted to mobilizing for war, with little time left over for postwar planning. The executive branches were busy building camps, factories, and shipyards and getting them into production, and Congress was kept busy passing appropriation bills that ran into astronomical figures, granting various war powers to the President, establishing price, rent, and wage control, and wrestling with priorities, rationing, conversion, and production problems, with the 1942 elections thrown in for good measure.

Churchill came to Washington to discuss war plans, and the combined chiefs of staff and combined war resources boards were organized to integrate the war efforts of all the Allies. In January of 1943 Roosevelt and Churchill met again at Casablanca, primarily to plan war strategy, but with the "unconditional surrender" formula as a by-product of their meeting.

With the pressure relaxed somewhat, federal officials in the spring of 1943 began to think and talk about what we would do about the peace once we had won the war. Because it was the United States Senate that had blocked our participation in the League of Nations after World War I, public attention focused on the Senate, where a two-thirds majority would have to ratify any treaty committing us to international co-operation after the war. Under the Constitution, only the President or his representatives can negotiate treaties, but they are not binding until ratified by two-thirds of the Senate, and this requirement had killed the League, which obtained a majority but not two-thirds.

A number of resolutions seeking to place Congress, particularly the Senate, on record in favor of United States participation in a postwar international security organization were offered in both houses, the most notable being the Fulbright resolution in the House and the so-called B2H2 resolution in the Senate.

The Fulbright resolution, offered by Democratic Representative J. William Fulbright of Arkansas (elected to the Senate in 1944), was very brief, simply calling for the creation of and our participation in international machinery with power adequate to maintain peace.

The B2H2 resolution was more elaborate and was offered by two Democrats, Senators Carl A. Hatch of New Mexico and Lister Hill of Alabama, and two Republicans, Senator Harold H. Burton of Ohio and yours truly. It proposed that the United States take the initiative in the immediate establishment of a United Nations organization, to help prosecute the war and to plan the peace and to have at its command joint military forces to maintain the peace in the future.

Congress at first received these proposals rather coldly, and there were strong arguments made against Congress' committing itself too hurriedly. However, a number of national organizations got behind the resolutions, and bipartisan stumping tours, with one Democratic and one Republican member of Congress as speakers, were arranged. In all, eighteen such bipartisan speaking trips during the summer covered some thirty of the forty-eight states.

These bipartisan tours and the enthusiastic reception accorded them, particularly in the supposedly isolationist Midwest, built up public interest to the point where members of Congress were being asked to go on record both in conferences at home and in thousands of letters pouring into Washington. On September 7, 1943, a conference of Republican governors and congressmen at Mackinac Island, Michigan, adopted a cautiously worded declaration in favor of United States participation in joint international efforts to preserve the peace.

Two weeks later, on September 21, the House beat the Senate to the punch and adopted the Fulbright resolution, which had been unanimously recommended by its Foreign Relations Committee, by the overwhelming vote of 360 to 29.

These developments stirred the Senate Foreign Relations Committee to action, and a bipartisan subcommittee of eight members, to which had been referred the B2H2 and other resolutions, finally agreed on the draft of a resolution to place the Senate on record in favor of international co-operation. It was introduced by Senator Tom Connally, committee chairman, and became known as the Connally resolution. After two weeks' debate and adoption of an amendment adding a paragraph of the Moscow declaration calling for the establishment at the "earliest practicable date" of a general international organization to keep the peace, the Connally resolution was adopted by the Senate, 85 to 5.

The tremendous significance of the Senate's action becomes apparent when it is recalled that it was a similar resolution, the famous "round robin" offered by Senator Lodge of Massachusetts in the spring of 1919 while President Wilson was attending the Versailles Conference, which foreshadowed the subsequent defeat of the Versailles Treaty and the League of Nations by the Senate. Lodge's resolution was never acted upon, but it was signed by more than one-third of the Senators and it pledged the signers to oppose the whole Versailles Treaty unless the League Covenant was stricken from it.

The overwhelming vote for the Connally resolution in the Senate enabled President Roosevelt and Secretary Hull to go forward with their preliminary negotiations for the establishment of a United Nations security organization with confidence that the Senate would support their efforts and not reject them as in 1919. Secretary Hull greatly strengthened this senatorial support by working through the ensuing months with the same bipartisan subcommittee of Senators and keeping them informed of every move made in this field by the executive branch of our government.

Meanwhile, the executive branch had been moving ahead with plans for postwar co-operation by the United States in other fields. Secretary Hull attended the conference of foreign ministers of Russia, China, Britain, and the United States at Moscow in October, which resulted in the Moscow Declarations, pledging the four powers to postwar unity and co-operation in keeping the peace and seeking peaceful means for adjustment and change. In December, President Roosevelt and Prime Minister Churchill had their first joint meeting with Marshal Stalin at Teheran. While their meeting was devoted primarily to military problems, they did agree to call conferences on postwar problems the next year.

The United Nations Conference on Food and Agriculture, seeking means of solving the paradox of famines and food surpluses existing at the same time in the world, met at Hot Springs in June and recommended establishment of a permanent international commission on basic food supplies to make recommendations to the member nations for more reasonable controls than now exist. Its recommendations were approved by Congress in the summer of 1945.

A United Nations Relief and Rehabilitation conference also was held and agreed on the establishment of the United Nations Relief and Rehabilitation Administration to provide immediate relief to war-stricken nations which are unable to pay for their own. UNRRA, as it is known, was approved by Congress November 9. The Senate vote was 47 to 14; that in the House, 285 to 58. Herbert Lehman, former Governor of New York, was chosen as its director. The nations have pledged $2,225,000,000 to UNRRA, with the United States to contribute $1,350,000,000. So far it is supplying relief to Poland, Greece, Yugoslavia, Italy, and Albania. France, Belgium, Holland, and Norway are all so-called "paying" nations in which UNRRA does not function.

All in all, 1943 saw considerable progress made by the United States and the other United Nations in their postwar plans in the international field, and the planning went forward at an accelerated pace in 1944.

The economic phases of international co-operation had been moving along, although with less public discussion and considerably more controversy, at the same time political co-operation advanced. In 1943 our government had begun discussions with Britain on proposals for exchange stabilization and promotion of international investment in the postwar period.

Two main reasons were behind the planning. It was obvious that there would be a tremendous postwar need for credits to finance reconstruction of war-devastated countries and also to develop resources of backward nations. Because of the unfortunate experience of private investors, particularly in the United States, with defaulted foreign loans after the first war, as well as the tremendous need, it did not appear that private capital could or would carry the whole load—certainly not without some governmental guarantees.

Likewise, if we were to achieve the free flow of international trade and commerce essential to postwar prosperity, it was necessary somehow to achieve stability in currency exchange rates and protection against sudden and arbitrary changes and restrictions on exchange by any single nation. If business is to buy and sell freely across international boundaries, it must have some assurance that the various currencies in which it deals will remain stable, that the currency devaluation race of the 1930's will not be repeated.

Both England and the United States developed plans, the former known as the Keynes and the latter as the White plan, to meet these problems. Finally, in the summer of 1944 after preliminary discussions with the other United Nations, a Monetary and Financial Conference was held at Bretton Woods, New Hampshire, and plans were agreed upon for the establishment of an International Monetary Fund and an International Bank for Reconstruction and Development.

The Fund would have a capital of $8,800,000,000, with the United States subscribing $2,750,000,000 as its quota; Russia, $1,200,000,000; Britain, $1,300,000,000; and the other members in proportion. Members of the Fund would pledge themselves not to change the value of their currencies in excess of 10 per cent without approval of the Fund and also not to impose any restrictions on exchange of their currencies. In order to balance its foreign exchange, each member would be entitled to exchange its own currency for any other currency it required up to the amount of 25 per cent of its quota annually, with a limit of 100 per cent of its quota, in our case 2¾ billions. In other words, the Fund would function like a local bank clearinghouse, where checks drawn on the various banks are canceled out in a bookkeeping transaction. Its principal value would be in encouraging multilateral trade, where one nation buys from a second but sells to a third and the balances are canceled out.

The Bank would have a total capital of $9,100,000,000, the United States' quota being $3,175,000,000. Its function would be to either make loans or guarantee (up to 90 per cent) loans made by private capital for reconstruction and development purposes in member nations. Any nation whose currency was to be loaned would have a veto on any particular loan.

Virtually all groups in and out of Congress approved of the Bank setup, but there was at first considerable controversy over the Fund, the American Bankers Association particularly feeling that its credit facilities would be open to abuse at the expense of America. However, after some safeguarding amendments limiting the Fund to short-term loans were adopted, the legislation approving the agreements passed the House, 345 to 18, on June 7, 1945, and a month later was approved overwhelmingly by the Senate.

Closely linked to the issues involved in the Bretton Woods agreements is our own tariff policy. You will recall that one of the early policies of the New Deal approved by Congress was embodied in the Reciprocal Trade Agreements Act, which authorized the President to negotiate agreements with other countries reducing our tariff rates up to 50 per cent in return for similar reductions for our exports on their part. This act has been renewed every three years and would have expired in June, 1945. President Roosevelt and later President Truman asked for another three-year extension, with the additional authority to lower tariff duties 50 per cent below rates prevailing on January 1, 1945. Inasmuch as most rates had already been lowered 50 per cent under existing agreements, this in effect authorized for most of them an additional 25 per cent reduction, or 75 per cent below the 1932 Smoot-Hawley Act rates.

There was strong Republican opposition in both houses to this additional 50 per cent reduction power, but despite that the bill passed both houses by substantial majorities and is now law, virtually committing the United States in the postwar period to a policy of gradually lowering tariffs and encouraging both exports and imports. The basic fallacy of the high protective tariff policy —namely, that we could sell without buying—has long been exploded by economic facts and now seems to be on the way out as a political theory.

An International Civil Aviation conference was held in November and December of 1944 at Chicago in an effort to develop general multilateral agreements on postwar civil international aviation. The United States took the lead in efforts to obtain general acceptance of these five freedoms for international air transport:

Each contracting state grants to the other contracting states the following freedoms of the air in respect of scheduled international air services:
1—The privilege to fly across its territory without landing;
2—The privilege to land for non-traffic purposes;
3—The privilege to put down passengers, mail and cargo taken on in the territory of the state whose nationality the aircraft possesses;
4—The privilege to take on passengers, mail and cargo destined for the territory of the state whose nationality the aircraft possesses;
5—The privilege to take on passengers, mail and cargo destined for the territory of any other contracting state and the privilege to put down passengers, mail and cargo coming from any such territory.

Forty-six of 54 nations at the conference signed the first freedom, 41 signed the first two, and 26 nations accepted all five freedoms, subject to ratification by their governments. Some of our allies seem fearful, perhaps with cause, that America will dominate international air transport in the future.

Meanwhile, quite a scrap developed in Congress, particularly the Senate, over the question of whether the United States should turn all postwar international air routes over to one company, on the theory that that would be the best way to compete with other nations having monopolies in this field, or whether we should have several American companies competing in international aviation just as we do in domestic aviation. Pan American Airways, which had a virtual monopoly on international routes prior to the war, was the chief proponent of the one-company proposal, while it was fought vigorously by all but one of the major domestic airlines, several of which have flown transocean routes on contract for ATC during the war and have their applications filed for postwar international routes.

Sponsors of the one-company bill have failed after many months to muster enough votes in the Senate Commerce Committee even to get their bill reported, and finally the Civil Aeronautics Board has gone ahead and licensed two of the domestic airlines for transatlantic routes, so that controversy appears to be settled.

Plans for a postwar world security organization made equally good progress in 1944. The so-called Big Four—the United States, Russia, China, and Britain—met at Dumbarton Oaks, in Washington, in August of 1944 and after seven weeks of discussions finally agreed on a set of proposals for a United Nations security organization, made public on October 7. Under those proposals the policing job on future aggressors would be turned over to a Security Council of eleven members, with the United States, Russia, England, China, and France holding permanent seats and the other six members to be elected biennially by a General Assembly of all the member nations. Each member nation would make available to the Security Council on call an agreed-upon quota of military force.

Coming in the midst of the presidential campaign, the Dumbarton Oaks proposals naturally were widely discussed. President Roosevelt was committed to the program, and Governor Dewey, Republican nominee, accepted it. And the people generally approved, although there was considerable criticism of the great power given to the so-called Big Five.

As you know, Roosevelt and Truman won the election, by a popular majority of 3,500,000. It is this writer's opinion that the fear of an interruption and delay in the war effort, plus greater public confidence in the Roosevelt and Democratic pledges for postwar international co-operation to maintain peace, were the determining factors in the election results. Significantly, a substantial number of the most irreconcilable isolationists in Congress, including Congressman Ham Fish and Senators Bennett Clark, Rufus Holman, and Gerald Nye, were defeated and succeeded by men pledged to participation of the United States in a world security organization.

At the conference of Roosevelt, Stalin, and Churchill at Yalta in the Crimea in February, 1945, the San Fransisco conference to draft the charter for a world security organization was called for April 25, and a formula on voting procedure in the Security Council, which had deadlocked the Dumbarton Oaks conference, was agreed upon. The formula, subsequently written into the charter, requires a majority of seven of the eleven votes on all procedural matters and a similar majority on all other questions, with the additional requirement that the votes of all five permanent members must be included in the majority. In effect it simply means that the Big Five must agree on any joint measures taken by the council to prevent war or to punish future aggressions.

President Roosevelt before his death named both Senator Connally and Senator Arthur Vandenberg of Michigan, a Republican, along with Representatives Sol Bloom and Charles Eaton, to the United States delegation at San Francisco, thus continuing the close co-operation with Congress which Secretary Hull had inaugurated.

The Charter agreed upon by fifty nations at San Francisco follows closely the Dumbarton Oaks proposals, but with some liberal additions. The power of the General Assembly to debate and make recommendations has been broadened and strengthened, the statute of a new world court added, and a Trusteeship Council set up under the assembly, which also will have jurisdiction over the important Social and Economic Council, designed to co-ordinate the work of existing international agencies in that field and tackle any new problems that arise.

There isn't space here to discuss the Charter in detail, and anyhow you who have the greatest stake in preventing future wars will want to read its text, which you can obtain simply by writing the State Department or your congressman or senator. Despite obvious weaknesses and compromises, the Charter has been received with overwhelming approval. The general opinion is that while the organization is not perfect, it offers our best and only hope of preventing another great war and therefore we should join it and support its efforts to the limit.

This was reflected in the overwhelming Senate vote for ratification of the San Francisco Charter, 89 to 2, on July 28, 1945. Since then failure of the London Conference of foreign ministers to agree on peace terms for Europe has caused a resurgence of nationalism just as we are setting up the United Nations organization. Support for collective security as opposed to individual national security appears to be weakening.

That gives you a brief but fairly complete picture of the postwar plans the United States has made in the international field. Now let's take a look at the domestic field.

There is not anywhere near the volume of concrete planning set to go in this field as there is in the international field, partly because there has not been time for it, partly because the issues are more controversial, and partly because the Army and Navy frowned on too much talk of postwar planning at home as tending to make many people forget the war in the Pacific.

Generally, both major political parties and most public leaders, political and otherwise, are agreed that we must aim at full employment of a postwar labor force of from 55 to 60 millions with a national standard of living and prosperity substantially above prewar levels. The general consensus is that we must keep the national income at 120 to 150 billions annually after the war, as compared to between 50 and 90 billions in prewar years. That of course would require full employment at high wage levels. With the tremendous productive capacity we have demonstrated during the war and all the new plants and machine tools available, it probably also means within a few years a further shortening of the standard work week, from 40 hours down to 35 and perhaps less.

Also there is general agreement, though as yet no specific program on the federal level, that any slack in the economy should be taken up by a flexible public works program of federal, state, and local projects. Many states and communities have set aside postwar construction funds and have the blueprints all set to go whenever materials and manpower become available.

Congress has authorized $1,700,000,000 of postwar Rivers and Harbors and Flood Control projects estimated to take eight or ten years to complete as well as some 750 millions for highway construction, spread over a three-year period. In addition bills are pending for a 500-million-dollar airport construction program, with the states matching on a 50-50 basis, and a billion-dollar hospital construction program, again on a federal-state matching basis.

The Committee for Economic Development, a businessmen's research and promotion group, consulting with labor and agriculture, has organized throughout the country to encourage and stimulate businessmen to plan their postwar employment early so that government can get some kind of estimate of how much employment slack there will be. A number of communities have made complete surveys and plans to provide postwar jobs for all their employables.

Early in the war the National Resources Planning Board, created by President Roosevelt, published some very ambitious postwar plans along the lines of the English "cradle to the grave" security program, but its proposals got a cold reception from Congress and the committee died when its funds were cut off.

The most concrete job of planning is embodied in the G.I. Bill of Rights, passed by Congress in 1943, which provides for business and farm loans of up to $2,000 for returning veterans, federal help in continuing education, and a variety of other employment aids, in addition to enlarging the Veterans Administration and its facilities. This planning is covered more fully elsewhere in this volume. Various bills also have been introduced for veterans' bonuses, but so far Congress seems inclined to wait until more veterans are back before taking any action along those lines.

There are various estimates as to how great the postwar opportunities will be in such fields as plastics, radar and electronics, civil aviation and light metals, where tremendous advances have been made in research under the spur of war needs. Generally, however, we are optimistic, and most observers believe jobs and business will boom for sure for at least the first few postwar years.

Except for the construction program and the G.I. Bill of Rights, however, most major domestic postwar plans remain plans, as reported at the beginning of this chapter, with congressional approval still to come. Here is a brief summary of the major proposals in the various fields:

TAXES:

Bill passed to pay 10 per cent holdback on excess profits tax to corporations now and also increase excess profits tax exemption from $10,000 to $25,000 so as to provide small business with reconversion capital. A postwar tax bill repealing excess profits tax on corporations and reducing individual rates passed late in 1945. No overall fiscal program yet proposed.

LABOR RELATIONS:

Hatch-Burton-Ball bill pending to require unions and managements to exhaust federal peaceful settlement procedures, including collective bargaining, conciliation, mediation, voluntary arbitration, and recommendation of special fact-finding commission, before either strike or lockout, with compulsory arbitration of grievances under contracts and disputes involving essential public utilities or services. Bill also would make unfair labor practices of Wagner Act applicable to employees as well as employers, prohibit wildcat strikes and slowdowns, and require unions having closed shop contracts to admit anyone seeking employment without discrimination.

Monroney bill pending to make labor unions subject to antitrust and antiracketeering statutes.

SOCIAL SECURITY:

Wagner-Murray-Dingle bill pending to expand social security

coverage to nearly all employees, increase employer and employee contributions, provide increased benefits including medical services, and federalize unemployment compensation, now administered by states.

FULL EMPLOYMENT:

S 380, proposed by Senators Murray, O'Mahoney, Thomas, and Wagner, was passed by the Senate and is pending in the House. It would require the President, through a special commission, to estimate each year the probable total national income for the following year and the amount by which it might fall short of providing full employment and report such estimate to Congress together with a recommendation for a public works program to fill the gap.

NATIONAL DEFENSE:

Special House committee has recommended universal military training after the war and the House Military Affairs Committee is to begin hearings on a specific bill. Measure is extremely controversial, and there seems little prospect of early action despite pressure from the War and Navy departments. The atomic bomb probably has killed this bill.

No bill has been introduced but many proposals for consolidation of the War and Navy Departments after the war have been made, both in and out of Congress, and some action along this line is likely to be considered fairly soon.

RIVER DEVELOPMENT:

Bills for establishing authorities similar to the Tennessee Valley Authority on the Missouri, Columbia, and other rivers have been proposed, but Congress has turned thumbs down and gone ahead instead with the usual program under Rivers and Harbors and Flood Control projects.

This brief outline is far from complete, but it gives you some idea of the issues which are likely to be hot politically in the next few years. And it likewise becomes apparent that you and your organizations will have considerable to say, if not the determining voice, in the postwar plans that finally emerge from these various proposals.

The unexpectedly early end of the Japanese war has speeded up domestic postwar planning considerably, but not enough to deprive you of a voice in it. We also face many new domestic and international problems created by the release of atomic power, which may prove to be the most revolutionary discovery since man first found that fire could be useful.

ATOMIC ENERGY:

Discovery and use of the atomic bomb not only has created new international problems but also has raised the immediate issue of the kind of domestic government control we should set up for this two-billion-dollar project and its future development. Several bills already are pending and a hot controversy developing over the degree of secrecy which can or should be imposed.

Appendix

How Your Congressman Voted

How Your Congressman Voted
While You Were Gone

THIS IS *an analysis of the key votes in Congress and the voting records of your Senators and Representatives in the Congress which was elected on November 7, 1944. It has been prepared by Press Research, Inc., Washington, D. C. The issues are those discussed by Thomas L. Stokes in his chapter on Congress— p. 133. They date from January, 1941, when the 77th Congress met and most of you began to go into the armed services, to the summer of 1945 when V-E Day began to turn you back into civilians and the 79th Congress ended its wartime legislation.*

I — FOREIGN POLICY

1. LEND-LEASE — 1941

Senate *March 8, 1941 passed* 60-31
House *February 6, 1941 passed* 260-165

The first Lend-Lease Bill was devised to extend credit to the nations fighting the Axis in Europe and make the United States, in fact, "the arsenal of Democracy." It placed the resources of the United States behind the enemies of fascism. The vote against Lend-Lease is regarded as a list of the pre-Pearl Harbor isolationists in Congress. Many of these, both Republicans and Democrats, were defeated in the 1942 and 1944 elections. Their successors, for the most part, have been internationalists and include seven veterans of World War II in the House.

575

2. *RECIPROCAL TRADE AGREEMENTS* — 1945

Senate June 20, 1945 *passed* 54-21
House May 26, 1945 *passed* 239-153

The vote on the extension of the Reciprocal Trade Agreements Act continued the liberal international trade policy established by Cordell Hull and confirmed our postwar foreign economic policy. Thirty-four Republicans in the House and fifteen in the Senate bolted the party "high tariff" line to vote for the bill. Twelve Democrats in the House and five in the Senate voted against the Administration.

3. *BRETTON WOODS* — 1945

Senate July 18, 1945 *passed* 61-16
House June 7, 1945 *defeated* 29-326

This bill committed the United States to join with the other United Nations in establishing an International Bank and an International Monetary Fund. A pressure campaign against the Monetary Fund was conducted by the American Bankers Association and allied interests. The general public, according to polls and mail, seemed to be for the bill and most Congressmen followed the will of the people. The most revealing vote in the House was on an amendment, introduced by Rep. Jessie Sumners (R., Ill.), which would have eliminated the Fund from the bill and would have affected the whole international stabilization policy. That vote is given in the following table, rather than the vote on the final passage, because it shows the Congressmen who may be expected to fight against other aspects of world economic co-operation in the future. The amendment was defeated 326-29. Voting against it were 202 Democrats and 122 Republicans. The House vote which finally passed the Bretton Woods agreements was 345-18 with 205 Democrats and 138 Republicans recorded for the bill. The vote shown for the Senate is on the final passage.

4. *UNITED NATIONS CHARTER* — 1945

Senate July 28, 1945 *passed* 89-2
House does not vote on charters

Ratification of the Charter written at San Francisco required a two-thirds vote of the Senate. The House does not vote on treaties. There were only two votes recorded against the Charter —Senator Langer (R., N. Dak.) and Senator Shipstead (R., Minn.). Senator Hiram Johnson (R., Cal.), who fought Woodrow Wilson and the League of Nations in 1919, reported from his deathbed that if he had been present he would have voted against the Charter. The almost unanimous vote, however, does not mean that all the Senators were wholeheartedly for the bill. Remembering the situation after the last war, and besieged by mail from their constituents in favor of the Charter, many of them did not want to go on record against a United Nations Organization. Several of them, notably such isolationists as Sen. Burton K. Wheeler (D., Mont.) and Sen. Robert A. Taft (R., Ohio), served notice that although they were voting for the Charter, they intended, in the future, to fight some of the more specific measures to implement the Charter.

II — CIVIL LIBERTIES

5. *SOLDIER VOTE* — 1944

Senate February 4, 1944 *tied* 42-42
House March 15, 1944 *passed* 328-69

Aware of the inadequacies of the Soldier Voting Act of 1942, under which only 28,000 ballots had been cast, Congress spent months debating the question of State vs. Federal ballots for the armed forces, before the 1944 elections. President Roosevelt denounced the bill proposed in Congress as "a fraud on the soldiers, sailors and marines" and moreover warned the Congress against attempting to pass a bill without a roll call vote. He said: "I

think most Americans will agree with me that every member of
the two houses of Congress ought in justice to be willing to
'stand up and be counted.'" The Administration federal ballot
bill was defeated in the House 224-169 and the so-called "States
Rights" bill was passed 328-69, with 65 Democrats and 3 Republicans voting against it. The Senate defeated this bill with a tie
vote of 42-42, with 35 Democrats and 6 Republicans against the
"States Rights" measure. A compromise bill was finally passed
by the House 273-111 and the Senate 46-40, which the President
allowed to become law without his signature, labeling it wholly
inadequate. The bill provided that if a state ballot had not been
received by October 1, a serviceman could use the federal ballot,
provided that the Governor of his State had certified that the
federal ballot could be accepted under the laws of that State.
Under this bill, 84,835 federal service ballots were counted in
the 1944 election, out of 2,691,000 soldier votes.

6. ANTI-POLL TAX — 1944–45

Senate May 15, 1944 *passed* 41-35
House June 12, 1945 *passed* 251-105

Bills to eliminate the poll tax as a voting qualification have
been passed by the House in the 77th, 78th, and 79th Congresses.
Sponsors of the bills claim that if the matter were allowed to
come to a vote in the Senate, it would pass with a large majority.
But in each Congress, Southern Senators have conducted a
filibuster to prevent a vote. The chief argument is the States
Rights issue, which changes its political complexion with the
subject. It is used by the Democrats on such issues as the poll
tax and the FEPC and by the Republicans on federal service
ballots and federal unemployment compensation. In 1945 the
vote in the House on the elimination of the poll tax was 251-105
with 118 Democrats and 131 Republicans voting for the bill and
86 Democrats and 19 Republicans voting against it. The strength
of the forces arraigned against the poll tax in the House can be

measured by the fact that 218 members signed a petition circulated in 1945 by Rep. Mary Norton (D., N. J.) to bring the anti-poll tax bill to a vote on the floor of the House. Of the signers of the petition, 109 were Democrats and 107 Republicans. The Senate in 1942 passed a bill to eliminate the poll tax for soldiers (afterward incorporated in the soldier vote bill) by a count of 33-20 with only Democrats opposed, but there was no roll call on the subject in the House and the names of the Representatives in favor of a poll tax for soldiers were not recorded.

In 1944, the Senate voted on a bill to lay aside consideration of the poll tax question. This is the vote shown below and one of the few records of the division in the upper chamber on this question. Voting 41-35 to lay aside the anti-poll tax bill, the record shows 29 Democrats and 12 Republicans in favor while 18 Democrats and 16 Republicans voted for consideration of the problem.

7. *FAIR EMPLOYMENT PRACTICES* — 1944

Senate June 20, 1944 defeated 21-39
House did not vote on this issue

In direct contrast to the line-up on the poll tax in the House and Senate is the attitude of the two houses on the Fair Employment Practice Committee. The House has consistently attempted to abolish this Committee, which was established by Executive Order as a wartime agency to guard against discrimination because of race, creed, or color, and the House has just as consistently refused to "stand up and be counted" on the issue. The Senate, however, in 1944, defeated 39-21 an attempt by Senator Russell (D., Ga.) to eliminate the FEPC appropriation, and again in 1945 when the House abolished the FEPC by cutting out its entire budget, the Senate restored part of it. In the 1944 vote, 23 Democrats and 16 Republicans voted to keep the FEPC; 14 Democrats and 7 Republicans voted to abolish it by eliminating its appropriation.

III—STABILIZATION

8. PRICE CONTROL—1942

Senate September 29, 1942 *passed* 48-43
House September 23, 1942 *passed* 205-172

In passing the original Price Control Act, Congress included a provision that farm prices could rise to 110 per cent of parity—that is, 10 per cent higher, in proportion, than the standard set for other prices and wages. In April, 1942, the President set forth an anti-inflation program and asked Congress to revise the provision favoring the farmers. Congress retaliated by fixing farm prices at 100 per cent of parity, but adopted an amendment to include farm labor costs in figuring parity. Known as the "farm bloc" amendment, it was introduced by Rep. Brown (D., Ga.) and passed the House 205-172 and the Senate, 48-43. Voting for the dividend to farmers were 105 Democrats and 99 Republicans in the House; 31 Democrats and 15 Republicans in the Senate. In the fight on this issue between President Roosevelt and the farm bloc, the President threatened to stabilize prices himself unless the Congress acted by October first, and repeated his objections to the bills showing undue favoritism to the farmers. A compromise bill was passed in the last days of September, 1942, which modified the farmers' bonus but was still acceptable to such powerful sponsors of what Roosevelt labeled "farm relief" as Senator Bankhead (D., Ala.) and Senator O'Mahoney (D., Wyo.). The vote which follows shows the members of the House and Senate who voted for the farm bloc bill to include labor costs in parity.

9. ANTI-SUBSIDY BILL—1944

Senate March 11, 1944 *passed* 43-28
House February 18, 1944 *defeated* 226-151

The wartime price control program to keep food costs to the consumer at prewar levels was based not only on a ceiling on food prices, but a floor on prices the farmer could obtain for his produce. A subsidy plan, administered by the Commodity Credit Corporation, provided for the payment of subsidies in order to maintain the balance of farm profits and consumer costs. At the end of 1943, C.C.C. was due to expire and further legislation was necessary to prolong its life. The bill extending C.C.C. to June 30, 1945, became known as the anti-subsidy bill, because it contained a provision forbidding payment of consumer subsidies on dairy products, meats, and bread. It was passed by the House 278-117 and by the Senate 43-28. The President vetoed the bill, calling it "an inflation measure, a high-cost-of-living measure, a food-shortage measure." The House voted to override the veto 226-151, which was 26 votes short of the required two-thirds majority. After the failure of the attempt to defeat the Administration program, a joint resolution was passed by both Houses eliminating the subsidy clause. The votes recorded here are the Senate vote for the anti-subsidy bill, in which 25 Democrats and 17 Republicans voted against the Administration, and the House vote attempting to override the veto, in which 58 Democrats and 166 Republicans went on record against the President's program.

IV — NATIONAL DEFENSE

10. EIGHTEEN MONTH DRAFT EXTENSION—1941

Senate August 7, 1941 passed 45-30
House August 12, 1941 passed 203-202

On May 27, 1941, the President declared that the country was in a state of national emergency. This was done, in part, because the first Selective Service Act of 1940 provided for drafting men for 12 months only, unless the "national interest is imperiled," in which case the President was authorized to extend the length of service. Congress, anxious to retain its prerogatives, debated the length of the draft extension for months. On August 7, 1941, four months before Pearl Harbor, the Senate, by a vote of 45-30, passed the 18 month extension bill. Opposing were 16 Democrats and 13 Republicans. A few days later, the House passed a slightly amended version of the bill by the historically important vote of 203-202. The one vote majority opinion was cast by 182 Democrats and 21 Republicans. Against the draft extension were 65 Democrats and 133 Republicans. Of these, 82 members of the 1941 Congress—41 Democrats and 41 Republicans—are no longer in the House. Some of them have died, but most of them were defeated or did not run in 1942 or 1944.

11. *$50 BASE PAY FOR SERVICEMEN* — 1942

Senate June 8, 1942 passed 58-20
House May 13, 1942 passed 332-28

The first bill to increase the pay of servicemen from $21 a month would have given the lowest ratings $42 a month and increased the pay for the higher grades. This was passed by the House and Senate with only one dissenting vote (Rep. Disney, D., Okla.). The House, however, then revised the bill to raise the base pay to $50 a month, on an amendment by Rep. John Rankin (D., Miss.), by a vote of 332-28 with 17 Democrats and 11 Republicans voting against it. The Senate accepted the $50 minimum by a vote of 58-20, with 13 Democrats and 6 Republicans in opposition. This is the roll call vote shown in the table.

V — *POSTWAR PLANNING*

12. *RECONVERSION ACT* — 1944 *(State vs. Federal Jobless Benefits)*

Senate August 11, 1944 passed 49-25
House September 18, 1944 passed 174-156

Two competing bills for industrial reconversion were debated in the Senate in 1944, one submitted by conservative Senator George (D., Ga.), the other by liberal Senators Murray (D.,

Mont.) and Kilgore (D., W. Va.). The important difference between them was that the George bill wanted to maintain state control of unemployment compensation, while the Murray-Kilgore bill proposed a uniform national unemployment compensation rate. Both bills provided for the coverage of federal workers in government shipyards, munitions plants, and arsenals, and the final version of the George bill adopted the Murray-Kilgore proposal of a $200 transportation grant for migratory war workers to return home. The Senate voted for the George bill 49-25 with 23 Democrats and 26 Republicans supporting "States Rights," as recorded in the table.

The House avoided a roll call vote on the several versions of the reconversion bill and voted to refuse transportation to war workers by 238-90, with 69 Democrats and 19 Republicans favoring helping war workers to get home. The House vote, shown in the table, refused unemployment compensation to some 3,000,000 federal war workers by 174-156, with 100 Democrats and 54 Republicans in the minority. In conference with the Senate over the differences in the bills, the House was obdurate on these two provisions and the Senate finally eliminated them from the Reconversion Act of 1944. The final vote in both Houses was not recorded.

13. *NATIONAL RESOURCES PLANNING BOARD* — 1943

Senate May 27, 1943 *defeated* 31-43
House   did not vote on this issue

The new Congress, elected in November, 1942, began immediately, in its first session, to defy the President. Two early New Deal agencies were the first to feel the ax: the National Youth Administration, which had little to do after the 18 year old draft was passed, and the National Resources Planning Board, which was engaged in working out programs for the postwar period. The House first withheld appropriations and then, fearing that the President might use money from his war emergency fund to continue the board, voted to forbid the President to use this fund to continue NRPB and other agencies cut off by Congress. Moreover, in ordering the liquidation of the NRPB by August 31, 1943, the Congress instructed the President that none of the functions of the Board were to be transferred to any other agency or continued after that date. The Board had submitted to Congress a plan for full production and full employment in peacetime, which was killed off by the House without a roll call, so that the stand of its members is not recorded. The Senate defeated an amendment offered by Senator MacKellar (D., Tenn.) which would have given NRPB $500,000 (about a third of its budget) by a vote of 43-31. Recorded in favor of the Board were 26 Democrats and 4 Republicans. Against the Board were 17 Democrats and 26 Republicans,

VI—SPECIAL INTERESTS

14. SMITH-CONNALLY ANTISTRIKE BILL—1943

Senate June 25, 1943 *passed* 56-25
House June 25, 1943 *passed* 244-108

This bill presented by Senator Connally (D., Tex.) and Rep. Smith (D., Va.) was passed by Congress in a wave of indignation over John L. Lewis's call for a strike in the coal mines. It gave the President power to take over striking war plants, it provided penalties for anyone instigating a strike in a government-operated plant in defiance of the no-strike pledge, it provided for a 30-day cooling off period, after which a strike vote could be taken, and it prohibited labor contributions to political campaigns. The President vetoed the bill, saying, "Far from discouraging strikes, these provisions would stimulate labor unrest and give government sanction to strike agitations."

Two minutes after the veto was received, the Senate voted 56-25 to override it, with 29 Democrats and 27 Republicans in favor of the bill, and 19 Democrats and 5 Republicans supporting the President's veto. Three hours later the House voted to override the veto 244-108, with 67 Democrats and 37 Republicans siding with Roosevelt.

The effect of the Congress' hot-tempered war against John L. Lewis was as the President had predicted. Philip Murray of C.I.O. and William Green of A. F. of L. found difficulty in holding some of their unions to the antistrike pledge, once Congress had allowed them to take a strike vote. The activities of the C.I.O.'s Political Action Committee during the 1944 campaign were ruled by Attorney General Biddle not to be covered by the Smith-Connally bill. Much to the dismay of the antilabor faction on Capitol Hill, the firm of Montgomery Ward was seized by the government under one of the clauses of the bill, and John L. Lewis continued to call coal strikes.

15. *OVERRIDE THE TAX BILL VETO* — 1944

Senate February 25, 1944 *passed* 72-14
House February 24, 1944 *passed* 299-95

On Washington's birthday in 1944, the first veto of a tax bill in the history of the United States was sent to the Congress. The President called it "not a tax bill, but a tax-relief bill providing relief not for the needy, but for the greedy." The bill as originally passed by Congress cut down the Treasury's request for an additional ten and a half billion dollars to what the President described as an increase of a little over a billion dollars. Wendell Willkie had attacked the Treasury for not asking for enough money from Congress. The President's message criticized the bill on five points: 1. insufficient revenue, 2. granting relief from social security and other existing taxes, 3. terminating the authority to renegotiate war contracts, 4. special privilege to favored groups, 5. not simplifying tax laws and tax returns.

The veto precipitated a dramatic revolt in Congress climaxed by the resignation of the majority leader, Sen. Alben Barkley

(D., Ky.), and a joint statement by Rep. Doughton (D., N. C.) and Rep. Knutson (R., Minn.) of the House Ways and Means Committee, severely censuring the President. The House voted to override the veto 299-95 with only 89 Democrats and 3 Republicans supporting the President and the Senate followed by a vote of 72-14, with 13 Democrats and 1 Republican upholding the veto. The Congress acted quickly and in a burst of temper at what it interpreted as an insult to its members, without attempting in any way to answer the President's criticisms of the bill or to prove its adequacy.

16. *INSURANCE BILL* — 1945

Senate February 27, 1945 *passed* 68-8
House February 14, 1945 *passed* 315-58

In June, 1944, the United States Supreme Court rendered a decision declaring that the insurance companies were engaged in interstate commerce and therefore were subject to the provisions of the federal antitrust laws. Before the Court decision, the House passed a bill exempting insurance companies from federal regulation and putting them under state control. The bill was held up in the Senate to await the Court decision. Then, to relieve the pressure on the insurance companies, Congress passed a moratorium giving the companies until March, 1946, to adjust themselves to federal regulation. Nevertheless, in February, 1945, the House again passed a bill allowing the states to regulate insurance and providing that the insurance companies should not come under the Sherman and Clayton antitrust laws until 1948. Chief sponsors of the bill in the House were Representatives Francis E. Walter (D., Pa.) and Clarence Hancock (R., N. Y.). Advocates of the bill called for quick action to correct the "confusion" created by the Supreme Court decision. Opponents of the bill said that for 75 years the insurance companies had avoided regulation by the various states on the ground that their business was in several states. They claimed that now that the Supreme Court had reached a decision agreeing with them, the insurance companies, with the specter of the antitrust laws before them, had reversed their position and were throwing themselves on the mercy of the states. The insurance bill passed the House 315-58 with 56 Democrats and no Republicans voting against it. The Senate vote was 68-8, all eight opponents being Democrats.

How Your President Voted

President Harry S. Truman was United States Senator from Missouri from January 1935 to January 1945 when he took office as Vice-President. Here is the record of how the President voted on the key issues discussed by Thomas L. Stokes.

HOW SENATOR TRUMAN VOTED

1. Lend Lease Bill—Passage 3-8-41   Y
2. "States Rights Soldier Vote Bill" 2-4-44   N
3. Anti-Poll Tax Bill—Motion to lay aside 5-15-44   A
4. Eliminate funds for F.E.P.C. 6-20-44   PN
5. Include Farm Labor in Parity Formula 9-29-42   AN*
6. Anti-Subsidy Bill—Passage 2-11-44   N
7. Draft Extension—Passage 8-7-41   Y
8. $50 Pay for Servicemen—Passage 6-8-42   N
9. State vs. Federal Job Benefits 8-11-44   N
10. Continue National Resources Planning Board 5-27-43 Y
11. Override Veto Smith Connally Anti-Strike Bill 6-25-43 N
12. Override Veto Tax Bill 2-25-44   Y*

* Position in opposition to President Roosevelt's.

U. S. SENATE—*79TH CONGRESS*

Key on Voting: N—Nay; Y—Yea; GP—General Pair; PY—Paired for; PN—Paired Against; A—Absent, not voting; AY—Absent, declared for; AN—Absent, declared against.

	LEND LEASE	RECIPROCAL TRADE	BRETTON WOODS	UNITED NATIONS CHARTER	SOLDIER VOTE	ANTI-POLL TAX	F.E.P.C.	PRICE CONTROL	ANTI-SUBSIDY	18 MONTH DRAFT	$50 BASE PAY FOR SERVICEMAN	STATE VS. FEDERAL JOBLESS BENEFITS	N.R.P.B.	SMITH-CONNALLY ACT	1944 TAX	INSURANCE CO. REGULATION
	1	2	3	4	5	6	7	8	9	10	11	12	13	14	15	16
ALABAMA																
Bankhead (D)	Y	PY	PY	Y	Y	Y	Y	Y	Y	PY	Y	Y	Y	Y	Y	Y
Hill (D)	Y	Y	Y	Y	Y	Y	Y	Y	Y	Y	Y	N	Y	Y	N	N
ARIZONA																
Hayden (D)	Y	Y	AY	Y	N	Y	A	Y	N	Y	Y	N	Y	Y	Y	Y
McFarland (D)	Y	Y	Y	Y	N	N	N	Y	N	Y	Y	N	Y	N	Y	Y
ARKANSAS																
Fulbright (D)		Y	Y	Y												Y
McClellan (D)		Y	Y	Y	Y	Y	Y		Y			Y	N	Y	Y	A
CALIFORNIA																
Downey (D)	Y	Y	Y	Y	N	N	AN	Y	N	N	AY	N	A	N	A	N
Johnson (R)*	N	A	PN	AN	A	A	A	Y	AY	N	Y	Y	A	A	PY	Y
COLORADO																
Millikin (R)		N	N	Y	Y	Y	Y	Y	A		Y	Y	N	Y	Y	Y
Johnson (D)	N	N	Y	Y	N	N	Y	N	N	N	A	N	N	N	Y	Y

* Hiram W. Johnson died Aug. 6th, 1945 (replaced by Wm. F. Knowland Sept. 9th).

	1	2	3	4	5	6	7	8	9	10	11	12	13	14	15	16
CONNECTICUT																
McMahon (D)		Y	Y	Y												Y
Hart (R)*		A	N	Y												Y
DELAWARE																
Buck (R)		A	Y	Y	Y	N	PN		AY			Y	N	Y	Y	AY
Tunnell (D)	Y	Y	Y	Y	N	N	N	N	N	Y	N	N	Y	N	N	Y
FLORIDA																
Andrews (D)	Y	PY	Y	Y	N	A	PY	Y	Y	Y	Y	Y	AY	Y	Y	A
Pepper (D)	Y	Y	AY	Y	N	N	N	N	N	Y	Y	N	Y	Y	N	N
GEORGIA																
George (D)	Y	Y	Y	Y	Y	Y	Y	Y	Y	Y	N	Y	Y	Y	Y	Y
Russell (D)	Y	PY	Y	Y	Y	Y	Y	Y	Y	PY	Y	Y	Y	Y	Y	Y
IDAHO																
Taylor (D)		Y	Y	Y												A
Thomas (R)†	N	PN	PN	AY	A	Y	A	Y	Y	N	Y	A	A	Y	Y	AY
ILLINOIS																
Brooks (R)	N	Y	N	Y	Y	N	AN	Y	A	N	Y	Y	AY	Y	Y	AY
Lucas (D)	Y	Y	Y	Y	N	N	N	N	N	Y	Y	A	AY	A	Y	A
INDIANA																
Capehart (R)		Y	Y	Y												Y
Willis (R)	N	PN	Y	Y	Y	A	N	Y	PY	PN	AY	Y	N	Y	Y	Y
IOWA																
Hicken-looper (R)		PN	Y	Y												Y
Wilson (R)		Y	A	Y	Y	N	A					Y	N	Y	Y	Y
KANSAS																
Capper (R)	N	N	N	Y	Y	N	N	Y	Y	N	Y	Y	Y	Y	Y	Y
Reed (R)	PN	Y	AY	AY	A	Y	N	N	Y	AY	N	AY	N	Y	AY	AY
KENTUCKY																
Barkley (D)	Y	Y	Y	Y	N	Y	N	N	N	Y	N	N	AY	A	Y	Y
Chandler (D)‡	Y	Y	Y	Y	N	Y	A	N	AN	Y	Y	Y	N	AY	Y	Y
LOUISIANA																
Ellender (D)	Y	Y	Y	Y	Y	Y	PY	Y	N	Y	Y	Y	Y	A	PY	Y
Overton (D)	Y	Y	A	Y	Y	Y	Y	Y	Y	Y	N	Y	N	Y	Y	N

* Thomas C. Hart sworn in Feb. 15th, 1945.
† John Thomas died November 10th, 1945.
‡ Albert B. Chandler resigned November 1st, 1945, replaced by Wm. A. Stanfield. November 23rd, 1945.

	1	2	3	4	5	6	7	8	9	10	11	12	13	14	15	16
MAINE																
Brewster (R)	Y	N	A	Y	Y	Y	Y	Y	A	Y	Y	Y	Y	Y	Y	Y
White (R)	Y	N	Y	Y	Y	Y	Y	N	Y	Y	Y	Y	N	Y	Y	Y
MARYLAND																
Radcliffe (D)	Y	Y	Y	Y	N	Y	N	N	PN	Y	AN	Y	Y	Y	Y	Y
Tydings (D)	Y	PY	PY	Y	N	Y	PN	N	Y	N	N	Y	N	Y	Y	Y
MASSACHUSETTS																
Saltonstall (R)		Y	Y	Y												Y
Walsh (D)	N	N	Y	Y	N	N	N	N	N	N	Y	N	A	N	Y	Y
MICHIGAN																
Ferguson (R)		Y	Y	Y	Y	N	N		N			Y	N	Y	Y	Y
Vanden-berg (R)	N	GP	Y	Y	N	N	N	N	N	N	N	Y	Y	Y	Y	Y
MINNESOTA																
Ball (R)	Y	Y	Y	Y	Y	Y	N	N	AY	PY	A	A	Y	N	Y	Y
Shipstead (R)	N	N	PN	N	Y	A	N	Y	Y	N	Y	N	AN	N	Y	Y
MISSISSIPPI																
Bilbo (D)	Y	Y	Y	Y	A	Y	Y	Y	Y	A	AY	A	Y	Y	Y	A
Eastland (D)		Y	Y	Y	Y	Y	Y		Y	Y		Y	Y	Y	Y	Y
MISSOURI																
Briggs (D)		Y	Y	Y												A
Donnell (R)		Y	Y	Y												Y
MONTANA																
Murray (D)	Y	A	Y	Y	N	A	N	N	N	A	Y	N	AY	N	N	N
Wheeler (D)	N	PN	N	Y	Y	N	AN	Y	Y	N	Y	AN	A	N	Y	Y
NEBRASKA																
Butler (R)	N	N	N	Y	Y	A	N	Y	Y	PN	AY	Y	N	Y	Y	Y
Wherry (R)		N	N	Y	Y	N	N		Y			Y	A	Y	Y	Y
NEVADA																
McCarran (D)	N	PN	Y	Y	AN	N	PN	Y	PN	N	Y	AN	N	N	Y	Y
Scrugham (D)*		A		Y	N	A	A		A			AN	A	N	Y	A
NEW HAMPSHIRE																
Bridges (R)	Y	Y	AY	Y	A	A	A	AN	AY	Y	A	AY	N	Y	Y	AY
Tobey (R)	N	Y	Y	Y	Y	A	AN	N	AY	N	Y	Y	N	Y	Y	AY
NEW JERSEY																
Hawkes (R)		N	N	Y	AY	Y	A		PY			Y	N	Y	Y	Y
Smith (R)		Y	Y	Y								Y				Y

* James G. Scrugham died June 23rd, 1945 (replaced by E. P. Carville, July 26th).

	1	2	3	4	5	6	7	8	9	10	11	12	13	14	15	16
NEW MEXICO																
Chavez (D)	N	Y	Y	Y	N	N	N	N	Y	PN	Y	N	Y	Y	Y	Y
Hatch (D)	Y	Y	Y	Y	N	Y	N	Y	N	Y	N	N	Y	Y	Y	Y
NEW YORK																
Mead (D)	Y	Y	Y	Y	N	N	N	N	N	Y	Y	N	Y	N	N	Y
Wagner (D)	PY	Y	Y	Y	N	N	N	N	N	AY	Y	N	Y	N	N	GP
NORTH CAROLINA																
Bailey (D)	Y	Y	PY	AY	Y	Y	PY	Y	Y	Y	AN	PY	Y	A	Y	Y
Hoey (D)	Y	Y	Y													Y
NORTH DAKOTA																
Langer (R)	N	N	N	N	N	N	AN	Y	PN	N	Y	N	Y	N	N	Y
Young (R)*		N	Y	Y												
OHIO																
Burton (R)	Y	Y	Y	Y	N	N	N	N	Y	Y	N	Y	Y	PY	Y	Y
Taft (R)	N	N	N	Y	Y	N	N	N	PY	N	AN	Y	N	Y	Y	Y
OKLAHOMA																
Moore (R)		N	N	Y	Y	Y	A		Y			Y	N	Y	Y	Y
Thomas (D)	AY	Y	Y	Y	A	A	N	Y	Y	Y	Y	AN	Y	Y	AY	Y
OREGON																
Cordon (R)		PN	Y	Y		N	N					Y				Y
Morse (R)		Y	Y	Y												Y
PENNSYLVANIA																
Guffey (D)	Y	Y	Y	Y	N	N	N	N	N	Y	N	N	Y	N	N	N
Meyers (D)		Y	Y	Y												Y
RHODE ISLAND																
Gerry (D)	N	N	A	Y	Y	Y	N	N	Y	Y	A	Y	N	Y	Y	Y
Green (D)	Y	Y	AY	Y	N	N	AN	N	N	Y	AY	N	Y	N	N	N
SOUTH CAROLINA																
Johnston (D)		Y	Y	Y												Y
Maybank (D)		PY	Y	Y	N	Y	Y	N	Y			Y	Y	AY	Y	Y
SOUTH DAKOTA																
Bushfield (R)		PN	N	Y	Y	Y	Y		Y			PY	N	AY	Y	Y
Gurney (R)	Y	N	N	Y	Y	A	Y	N	Y	Y	N	Y	N	Y	Y	Y
TENNESSEE																
McKellar (D)	Y	Y	Y	Y	Y	Y	Y	Y	Y	Y	Y	Y	Y	Y	Y	Y
Stewart (D)	Y	Y	Y	Y	N	Y	Y	N	Y	Y	Y	Y	Y	Y	A	Y

* Milton R. Young sworn in March 19th, 1945.

	1	2	3	4	5	6	7	8	9	10	11	12	13	14	15	16
TEXAS																
Connally (D)	Y	GP	A	Y	Y	Y	Y	Y	Y	Y	Y	Y	A	Y	Y	A
O'Daniel (D)		N	N	Y	Y	Y	PY	Y	Y	N	Y	Y	N	Y	Y	Y
UTAH																
Murdock (D)	Y	Y	Y	Y	N	N	N	Y	N	AY	Y	A	AY	N	N	Y
Thomas (D)	Y	Y	AY	Y	N	A	N	N	N	A	Y	N	Y	N	N	Y
VERMONT																
Aiken (R)	N	Y	Y	Y	N	N	N	Y	Y	AN	Y	N	Y	Y	Y	Y
Austin (R)	Y	Y	Y	Y	N	A	A	N	Y	Y	N	Y	N	AY	Y	AY
VIRGINIA																
Byrd (D)	Y	Y	Y	Y	Y	Y	Y	N	Y	Y	N	Y	N	Y	Y	Y
Glass (D)	Y	AY	A	AY	A	A	A	AN	A	Y	N	A	A	PY	PN	A
WASHINGTON																
Magnuson (D)		PY	Y	Y												A
Mitchell (D)		Y	Y	Y												A
WEST VIRGINIA																
Kilgore (D)	Y	Y	Y	Y	N	N	N	N	N	Y	Y	N	AY	N	N	N
Revercomb (R)		N	N	Y	Y	Y	N		A		Y	N		Y	Y	Y
WISCONSIN																
LaFollette (P)	N	Y	Y	Y	N	N	AN	Y	Y	N	Y	PN	Y	N	Y	Y
Wiley (R)	N	N	Y	Y	A	N	AN	Y	Y	N	Y	Y	Y	Y	Y	Y
WYOMING																
O'Mahoney (D)	Y	N	Y	Y	N	Y	N	N	PN	Y	N	Y	A	Y	AY	Y
Robertson (R)		N	N	Y	Y	Y	Y		PY			Y	N	Y	AY	Y

SENATE VOTE TOTALS

	1	2	3	4	5	6	7	8	9	10	11	12	13	14	15	16
YEAS	60	54	61	89	42	41	21	48	43	45	58	49	31	56	72	68
NAYS	31	21	16	2	42	35	39	43	28	30	20	25	43	25	14	8

DEMOCRATS

	1	2	3	4	5	6	7	8	9	10	11	12	13	14	15	16
FOR	49	38	41	53	19	29	14	31	25	38	41	23	26	29	39	35
AGAINST	13	5	2	0	35	18	23	30	25	16	13	22	17	19	13	8

REPUBLICANS

	1	2	3	4	5	6	7	8	9	10	11	12	13	14	15	16
FOR	10	15	19	35	23	12	7	15	17	7	16	26	4	27	32	32
AGAINST	17	16	14	2	6	16	16	13	3	13	6	3	26	5	1	0

HOUSE OF REPRESENTATIVES

DISTRICT	LEND LEASE	RECIPROCAL TRADE	BRETTON WOODS	UNITED NATIONS CHARTER	SOLDIER VOTE	ANTI-POLL TAX	F.E.P.C.	PRICE CONTROL	ANTI-SUBSIDY	18 MONTH DRAFT	$50 BASE PAY FOR SERVICEMAN	STATE VS. FEDERAL JOBLESS BENEFITS	N.R.P.B.	SMITH-CONNALLY ACT	1944 TAX	INSURANCE CO. REGULATION
	1	2	3	4	5	6	7	8	9	10	11	12	13	14	15	16
ALABAMA																
3 Andrews (D)		Y	N			PN						Y				Y
1 Boykin (D)	Y	A	N	Y		N		Y	A	Y	A	A		Y	PY	GP
2 Grant (D)	Y	GP	GP	Y		PN		Y	Y	Y	A	Y		Y	Y	Y
4 Hobbs (D)	Y	Y	GP	Y		PN		Y	PY	Y	Y	Y			PY	Y
6 Jarman (D)	Y	Y	GP	A		PN		Y	Y	Y	A	Y		PY	Y	Y
7 Manasco (D)		Y	N	A		N		Y	PY	Y	Y	Y		Y	A	Y
9 Patrick (D)	Y	Y	N			Y		A		Y	A					Y
5 Rains (D)		Y	N			N										Y
8 Sparkman (D)	Y	Y	N	Y		N		Y	Y	Y	A	Y		Y	Y	Y
ARIZONA																
(AL) Harless (D)		Y	N			Y			N				N	Y	N	A
(AL) Murdock (D)	Y	Y	N	N		GP		N	N	Y	Y	N		Y	N	Y
ARKANSAS																
4 Cravens (D)	Y	Y	N	Y		PN		Y	Y	N	Y	Y		Y	Y	Y
1 Gathings (D)	Y	Y	N	Y		PN		Y	Y	Y	Y	Y		Y	Y	Y
7 Harris (D)	Y	Y	N	Y		N		Y	Y	Y	Y	Y		Y	Y	Y
5 Hays (D)		Y	N	Y		N			N				A	Y	Y	A
2 Mills (D)	Y	Y	N	Y		N		Y	Y	Y	Y	Y		Y	Y	Y
6 Norrell (D)	Y	Y	N	Y		N		A	Y	Y	Y	PY		Y	Y	Y
3 Trimble (D)		Y	N			N										Y

593

DISTRICT	1	2	3	4	5	6	7	8	9	10	11	12	13	14	15	16
CALIFORNIA																
8 Anderson (R)	N	N	N		N	Y		Y	Y	Y	Y	N		Y	Y	GP
14 Douglas (D)		Y	N			Y										N
18 Doyle (D)		Y	N			Y										N
10 Elliott (D)	Y	N	N		Y	Y		Y	Y	Y	Y	A		Y	Y	GP
2 Engle (D)		Y	N		Y	Y			Y			A			N	Y
9 Gearhart (R)	N	N	N		Y	Y		Y	Y	Y	A	Y		Y	Y	Y
4 Havenner (D)		Y	N			Y										PN
13 Healy (D)		PY	N			Y										N
20 Hinshaw (R)	N	N	N		Y	Y		N	N	Y	Y	N		Y	Y	Y
19 Holifield (D)		Y	GP		N	PY			N			PN		N	PN	N
23 Izac (D)	Y	Y	N		N	Y		N	N	Y	Y	PN		A	N	GP
3 Johnson (R)	Y	N	GP		Y	A		A	A	N	Y	Y		Y	Y	Y
17 King (D)		Y	N		N	Y			N			N		A	N	N
1 Lea (D)	Y	N	N		Y	Y		Y	Y	Y	Y	N		Y	Y	N
15 McDonough (R)		Y	N			Y										Y
6 Miller (D)		Y	N			Y										N
11 Outland (D)		Y	N		N	Y			N			N		N	N	N
16 Patterson (D)		Y	N			Y										N
22 Phillips (R)		N	N		A	Y			Y			A		PY	Y	Y
21 Sheppard (D)	Y	Y	GP		N	GP		A	N	PY	Y	A		A	Y	N
7 Tolan (D)	N	Y	N		N	Y		N	N	N	Y	PN		A	N	Y
12 Voorhis (D)	Y	Y	N		N	Y		N	N	N	Y	N		N	N	N
5 Welch (R)	N	Y	A		N	Y		N	N	N	Y	A		N	N	Y
COLORADO																
3 Chenoweth (R)	N	N	N		A	Y		Y	Y	N	Y	Y		Y	Y	Y
1 Gillespie (R)		N	N			Y						N				Y
2 Hill (R)	N	N	N		Y	Y		Y	Y	N	Y	Y		Y	Y	Y
4 Rockwell (R)		N	N		Y	Y		Y	Y		N	Y		Y	Y	Y
CONNECTICUT																
3 Geelan (D)		Y	A			Y										Y
1 Kopplemann (D)	Y	Y	N			Y		N		Y	Y	Y			Y	Y
4 Luce (R)		Y	N		A	Y			A			N		PN	Y	Y
(AL) Ryter (D)		Y	N			Y										Y
5 Talbot (R)		N	N		Y	GP		N	PY		Y	N		Y	Y	Y
2 Woodhouse (D)		Y	N			Y										Y
DELAWARE																
(AL) Traynor (D)	Y	A	N			Y		A		Y	Y					Y
FLORIDA																
4 Cannon (D)	Y	N	GP		Y	PN		Y	N	N	Y	Y		A	A	GP
5 Hendricks (D)	Y	Y	N		A	N		A	N	Y	Y	A		Y	Y	Y
1 Peterson (D)	Y	N	GP		Y	N		Y	N	Y	Y	N		Y	Y	Y

DISTRICT	1	2	3	4	5	6	7	8	9	10	11	12	13	14	15	16
2 Price (D)		Y	N		Y	N			PN			Y		Y	Y	Y
6 Rogers (D)		N	N			N										Y
3 Sikes (D)	Y	Y	GP		Y	PN		Y	N	Y	Y	A		Y	Y	A
GEORGIA																
10 Brown (D)	Y	Y	N		Y	N		Y	Y	Y	Y	Y		Y	Y	Y
4 Camp (D)	Y	Y	N		Y	N		Y	Y	Y	Y	Y		Y	Y	Y
2 Cox (D)	Y	Y	N	PY		N		A	Y	Y	Y	Y		Y	Y	Y
8 Gibson (D)	Y	Y	N	A		N		Y	Y	Y	Y	A		Y	Y	Y
3 Pace (D)	Y	Y	N		Y	PN		Y	Y	Y	Y	Y		Y	Y	Y
1 Peterson (D)	N	Y	N		Y	N		Y	Y	Y	Y	Y		Y	PY	Y
5 Ramspeck (D)*	Y	Y	N		Y	N		N	N	Y	Y	N		Y	A	Y
7 Tarver (D)	Y	Y	N		Y	N		Y	Y	Y	Y	Y		Y	N	Y
6 Vinson (D)	Y	Y	N		Y	N		Y	Y	Y	Y	A		PY	Y	Y
9 Wood (D)		Y	N			N										Y
IDAHO																
2 Dworshak (R)	N	N	N		Y	Y		Y	Y	N	Y	Y		Y	Y	Y
1 White (D)	N	Y	A		Y	GP		A	N	PN	Y	N		N	Y	A
ILLINOIS†																
13 Allen (R)	N	N	N		Y	Y		Y	Y	N	Y	Y		PY	Y	Y
17 Arends (R)	N	N	N		Y	Y		Y	Y	N	Y	Y		Y	Y	Y
25 Bishop (R)	N	N	Y		Y	Y		Y	Y	N	Y	Y		N	Y	Y
15 Chiperfield (R)	N	N	N		Y	Y		Y	Y	N	Y	Y		Y	Y	Y
10 Church (R)		N	N		Y	Y			Y			Y		Y	Y	Y
1 Dawson (D)		Y	A		N	Y			N			N		N	N	N
16 Dirksen (R)	N	Y	PN		Y	PY		N	PY	N	Y	Y		Y	PY	Y
8 Gordon (D)		Y	N		N	Y			N			N		N	N	N
4 Gorski (D)		Y	N		N	GP			N			N		N	N	Y
21 Howell (R)	N	N	N		Y	Y		Y	Y	N	Y	Y		Y	Y	Y
14 Johnson (R)	N	N	N		Y	N		Y	Y	N	Y	Y		Y	Y	Y
3 Kelly (D)	Y	Y	N			Y		N		N	Y					N
7 Link (D)		Y	N			Y										N
19 McMillen (R)		N	N			Y						Y				Y
12 Mason (R)	N	N	Y		Y	N		Y	Y	N	Y	Y		Y	PY	Y
6 O'Brien (D)		Y	N		N	Y			N			N		N	N	N
22 Price (D)		Y	GP			PY										N
11 Reed (R)	N	N	N		Y	GP		Y	PY	N	Y	Y		N	Y	Y
9 Resa (D)		Y	N			Y										Y
2 Rowan (D)		Y	N	PN		Y			N			N		N	N	PN
5 Sabath (D)	Y	Y	GP		N	Y		N	N	Y	A	PN		N	N	N
20 Simpson (R)		N	N		Y	Y			Y			Y		Y	Y	Y

* Robert Ramspeck resigned November 27th, 1945.
† Seat vacant 24th District of Illinois.

DISTRICT	1	2	3	4	5	6	7	8	9	10	11	12	13	14	15	16
18 Sumner (R)	N	N	Y		Y	N		Y	Y	N	Y	Y		Y	Y	Y
23 Vursell (R)		N	Y		Y	Y			Y			Y		Y	Y	Y
(AL) Douglas (D)		Y	N			Y										Y
INDIANA																
3 Grant (R)	N	N	GP		Y	PY		Y	Y	N	Y	Y		Y	Y	Y
4 Gillie (R)	N	N	N		Y	Y		Y	Y	N	A	Y		Y	Y	Y
2 Halleck (R)	N	N	N		Y	GP		Y	Y	N	Y	PY		Y	Y	Y
5 Harness (R)	N	N	N		Y	Y		Y	Y	N	Y	Y		Y	Y	GP
6 Johnson (R)	N	N	GP		Y	A		Y	Y	N	Y	N		A	Y	Y
8 LaFollette (R)		Y	GP		Y	PY			N			N		N	Y	GP
7 Landis (R)	N	N	N		Y	A		Y	PY	N	Y	Y		PY	Y	GP
11 Ludlow (D)	N	Y	N		N	Y		A	N	N	Y	N		N	Y	Y
1 Madden (D)		Y	N		N	Y			N			N		N	N	A
10 Springer (R)	N	N	N		Y	Y		Y	Y	N	Y	Y		Y	Y	Y
9 Wilson (R)	N	GP	N		Y	Y		Y	Y	N	Y	Y		Y	Y	GP
IOWA																
5 Cunningham (R)	Y	N	N		Y	Y		Y	Y	N	Y	N		Y	Y	Y
6 Dolliver (R)		N	N			Y										Y
3 Gwynne (R)	N	N	Y		Y	A		Y	Y	N	Y	Y		Y	Y	Y
8 Hoeven (R)		N	N		Y	Y			Y			PY		Y	Y	Y
7 Jensen (R)	N	N	GP		Y	N		Y	Y	N	Y	Y		Y	Y	Y
4 LeCompte (R)	N	N	N		Y	Y		Y	Y	N	Y	A		Y	Y	Y
1 Martin (R)	N	N	GP		Y	GP		Y	Y	N	Y	Y		Y	Y	GP
2 Talle (R)	N	N	N		Y	Y		Y	Y	N	Y	Y		Y	Y	Y
KANSAS																
6 Carlson (R)	N	N	GP		Y	GP		Y	Y	N	Y	Y		Y	Y	Y
1 Cole (R)		Y	N			Y										Y
5 Hope (R)	N	Y	N		Y	Y		Y	Y	N	Y	Y		Y	Y	Y
4 Rees (R)	N	N	Y		Y	Y		Y	Y	N	Y	Y		Y	Y	GP
2 Scrivner (R)		N	Y		Y	Y			Y			Y			Y	Y
3 Winter (R)	N	N	A		A	A		Y	A	N	Y	Y		Y	PY	GP
KENTUCKY																
8 Bates (D)	Y	Y	N		N	Y		N	N	Y	A	A		N	N	Y
6 Chapman (D)	Y	Y	N		N	GP		Y	N	Y	Y	Y		Y	Y	Y
4 Chelf (D)		Y	N			Y										Y
2 Clements (D)		Y	N			PY										A
1 Gregory (D)	Y	Y	N		Y	N		N	Y	Y	Y	Y		Y	Y	Y
7 May (D)	Y	Y	N		Y	N		N	Y	Y	N	Y		Y	Y	GP
3 O'Neal (D)	Y	Y	N		N	Y		N	N	Y	N	A		N	Y	Y
9 Robsion (R)	N	N	Y		Y	Y		Y	A	N	Y	A		N	Y	Y
5 Spence (D)	Y	Y	N		N	Y		N	N	Y	A	N		N	N	N

DISTRICT	1	2	3	4	5	6	7	8	9	10	11	12	13	14	15	16
LOUISIANA																
8 Allen (D)	Y	Y	N		Y	N		Y	Y	Y	Y	N		Y	Y	Y
4 Brooks (D)	Y	Y	N		Y	N		Y	N	Y	Y	A		Y	Y	Y
3 Domengeaux (D)	Y	N	GP		Y	N		Y	A	Y	Y			Y	A	Y
1 Hebert (D)	Y	GP	GP		Y	GP		Y	N	PY	Y	Y		A	Y	GP
7 Larcade (D)		Y	N		Y	GP			N			N		PN	Y	Y
5 McKenzie (D)		Y	N		Y	N			Y			A		PY	Y	Y
2 Maloney (D)		Y	N		Y	N			N			N		Y	Y	Y
6 Morrison (D)		Y	GP		Y	N			PY			PN		PY	PN	GP
MAINE																
3 Fellows (R)	N	N	N		Y	PN		N	Y	Y	Y	Y		Y	Y	Y
1 Hale (R)		N	N		Y	N			Y			N		Y	Y	Y
2 Smith (R)	Y	Y	N		Y	Y		N	Y	Y	Y	N		N	Y	Y
MARYLAND																
2 Baldwin (D)		Y	N	PY	N				Y			Y		Y	A	Y
6 Beall (R)		N	N		Y	Y			PY			N		A	Y	Y
3 D'Alesandro (D)	Y	Y	N		Y	Y		N	N	Y	Y	N		N	Y	PY
4 Fallon (D)		Y	N		Y											Y
1 Roe (D)		Y	N		N											Y
5 Sasscer (D)	Y	Y	N		Y	Y		N	N	Y	Y	N		N	Y	Y
MASSACHUSETTS																
6 Bates (R)	Y	N	N		Y	Y		N	Y	Y	Y	Y		A	Y	Y
2 Clason (R)	N	N	GP		Y	GP		N	Y	N	A	A		Y	Y	Y
11 Curley (D)		Y	N		Y	GP			PY			N		N	A	Y
9 Gifford (R)	Y	N	N		A	Y		N	PY	N	N	A		Y	A	Y
8 Goodwin (R)		N	N		Y	Y			Y			Y		Y	Y	Y
10 Herter (R)		N	N		Y	GP			N			N		Y	Y	Y
1 Heselton (R)		Y	N		Y											Y
4 Holmes (R)	Y	N	N		Y	Y		N	Y	N	Y	Y		Y	A	Y
7 Lane (D)		N	N		N	Y		PN	N		Y	N		N	N	Y
12 McCormack (D)	Y	Y	N		N	Y		N	N	Y	A	N		N	N	Y
14 Martin (R)	N	N	N		Y	Y		N	Y	N	Y	N		Y	Y	Y
3 Philbin (D)		N	N		Y	Y			PN			N		A	AY	Y
5 Rogers (R)	N	N	N		Y	Y		N	Y	Y	Y	A		Y	Y	Y
13 Wigglesworth (R)	N	N	N		Y	Y		N	Y	Y	Y	Y		Y	Y	Y
MICHIGAN																
6 Blackney (R)	N	Y	N		Y	Y		A	Y	N	A	A		N	Y	Y
11 Bradley (R)	N	PN	GP		Y	Y		A	Y	N	A	PY		PY	Y	Y
8 Crawford (R)	N	N	N		Y	Y		Y	Y	N	Y	Y		Y	Y	Y
15 Dingell (D)	Y	Y	N		N	Y		N	N	Y	Y	N		N	N	Y
17 Dondero (R)	N	N	N		Y	PY		Y	Y	N	A	Y		Y	Y	PY
9 Engel (R)	N	N	N		Y	Y		Y	Y	N	Y	N		N	Y	Y

DISTRICT	1	2	3	4	5	6	7	8	9	10	11	12	13	14	15	16
4 Hoffman (R)	N	PN	Y		Y	N		Y	Y	N	Y	Y		Y	Y	Y
12 Hook (D)	Y	PY	N			Y		N		N	Y					N
5 Jonkman (R)	N	N	N		A	Y		Y	Y	N	Y	Y		Y	Y	Y
16 Lesinski (D)	Y	Y	N		N	Y		N	PN	Y	Y	N		N	N	N
2 Michener (R)	N	Y	N		Y	Y		Y	Y	N	A	Y		Y	Y	Y
13 O'Brien (D)	N	Y	N		N	Y		N	N	N	Y	N		N	N	N
14 Rabaut (D)	N	PY	GP		N	PY		N	N	PN	A	N		N	N	Y
1 Sadowski (D)		Y	A		N	Y			N			N		N	N	N
3 Shafer (R)	N	N	GP		Y	Y		Y	Y	N	Y	N		Y	Y	PY
7 Wolcott (R)	N	N	N		Y	Y		N	Y	N	Y	Y		Y	Y	Y
10 Woodruff (R)	N	N	GP		Y	Y		Y	Y	N	Y	Y		Y	Y	Y
MINNESOTA																
7 Andersen (R)	N	N	PN		A	Y		Y	Y	N	Y	Y		Y	N	Y
1 Andresen (R)	N	N	GP		Y	GP		Y	Y	N	Y	A		Y	Y	Y
3 Gallagher (D)		Y	N			Y			Y							Y
9 Hagen (R)		N	N		Y	GP			Y			A		N	Y	Y
5 Judd (R)		Y	N		Y	Y			N			A		Y	Y	Y
6 Knutson (R)	N	N	Y		Y	GP		Y	PY	N	N	Y		Y	Y	Y
2 O'Hara (R)	N	N	Y		PY	N		Y	Y	PN	Y	N		Y	Y	PY
8 Pittenger (R)	Y	N	N		Y	Y		Y	Y	Y	Y	N		N	Y	Y
4 Starkey (D)		Y	N			Y										Y
MISSISSIPPI																
4 Abernethy (D)		Y	N		Y	N			Y			Y		Y	Y	Y
6 Colmer (D)	Y	Y	N		Y	N		Y	Y	Y	Y	N		Y	Y	GP
7 McGehee (D)	Y	Y	N		A	N		Y	Y	Y	Y	Y		Y	Y	Y
1 Rankin (D)	Y	Y	N		Y	N		Y	Y	Y	Y	Y		Y	Y	Y
2 Whitten (D)	Y	Y	GP		Y	PN		Y	Y		Y	Y		Y	Y	Y
3 Whittington (D)	Y	Y	N		Y	N		Y	Y	Y	N	Y		Y	Y	Y
5 Winstead (D)		Y	N		Y	N			Y			Y		Y	Y	Y
MISSOURI																
1 Arnold (R)		Y	N		Y	N			Y			Y		Y	Y	Y
4 Bell (D)	Y	Y	N		Y	N		Y	A	Y	N	A		Y	Y	Y
6 Bennett (R)	N	N	Y		Y	Y		Y	Y	N	Y	PY		Y	Y	Y
9 Cannon (D)	Y	Y	N		N	Y		Y	Y	N	Y	N		Y	N	N
8 Carnahan (D)		Y	N			Y										N
13 Cochran (D)	Y	Y	N		N	Y		A	N	N	Y	N		A	N	N
3 Cole (R)		N	Y		Y	N			Y			Y		N	Y	Y
12 Ploeser (R)	N	N	GP		PY	PY		N	Y	N	Y	PY		Y	Y	Y
2 Schwabe (R)		N	Y		Y	N			Y			PY		Y	Y	Y
7 Short (R)	N	N	PY		PY	GP		Y	Y	N	A	Y		Y	Y	PY
5 Slaughter (D)		PY	GP		Y	N			Y			A		Y	PY	Y

DISTRICT	1	2	3	4	5	6	7	8	9	10	11	12	13	14	15	16
11 Sullivan (D)	Y	Y	N			Y		N		Y	Y					N
10 Zimmerman (D)	Y	Y	N		N	Y		Y	N	Y	A	Y		Y	Y	Y
MONTANA																
1 Mansfield (D)		Y	A		N	Y			N			N		N	N	Y
2 D'Ewart (R)°																
NEBRASKA																
2 Buffett (R)		N	Y	Y	Y	Y		Y				Y		Y	Y	Y
1 Curtis (R)	N	N	Y	Y	N	Y		Y	Y	N	Y	PY		Y	Y	Y
4 Miller (R)		PN	PY	Y	Y	Y		Y				Y		Y	Y	Y
3 Stefan (R)	N	PN	GP	Y	PY	Y		Y	N	Y		A		Y	Y	Y
NEVADA																
(AL) Bunker (D)		A	N			Y										Y
NEW HAMPSHIRE																
2 Adams (R)		Y	N			Y										Y
1 Merrow (R)		Y	GP	Y		A		Y				Y		Y	Y	Y
NEW JERSEY																
3 Auchincloss (R)		Y	N	A		Y		Y				Y		Y	Y	Y
8 Canfield (R)	N	N	GP	N		Y		N	N	N	Y	N		N	Y	Y
6 Case (R)		Y	N			Y										Y
5 Eaton (R)	N	GP	GP	Y		A		N	Y	N		N		Y	Y	GP
2 Hand (R)		N	GP			Y										Y
14 Hart (D)	Y	Y	GP	N		Y		N	N	N	Y	N		N	N	N
10 Hartley (R)	N	Y	N	N		Y		A	PN	N	Y	A		PY	Y	Y
12 Kean (R)	N	Y	N	N		Y		N	Y	N	Y	Y		Y	Y	Y
13 Norton (D)	Y	Y	N	N		Y		N	N	Y	Y	N		N	N	N
4 Powers (R)†	Y	N	N	Y	Y	A		N	N	Y		N		N	Y	GP
11 Sundstrom (R)		Y	N	Y	PY			Y				Y		PY	Y	Y
7 Thomas (R)	Y	Y	N	Y	Y			N	Y	A	Y	Y		PY	Y	GP
9 Towe (R)		Y	N	Y	Y			N				N		PY	Y	Y
1 Wolverton (R)	Y	Y	N	N		Y		Y	N	N	Y	N		PN	Y	Y
NEW MEXICO																
(AL) Anderson (D)‡	Y	PY	N		N	GP		Y	N	Y	Y	N		Y	Y	Y
(AL) Fernandez (D)		Y	N		N	Y		N				N		Y	Y	A
NEW YORK																
42 Andrews (R)	Y	Y	N	N		Y		N	Y	Y	N	Y		Y	Y	Y
17 Baldwin (R)	•	Y	GP	A		Y		N	N	Y	A	N		PN	Y	Y
4 Barry (D)	N	Y	N	N		Y		N	N	N	Y	A		N	Y	Y

° Wesley A. D'Ewart sworn in June 25th, 1945.

† D. Lane Powers resigned August 31st, 1945 (seat vacant).

‡ Clinton P. Anderson resigned June 30th, 1945 (seat vacant).

DISTRICT	1	2	3	4	5	6	7	8	9	10	11	12	13	14	15	16
29 Bennet (R)		Y	N			Y										Y
20 Bloom (D)	Y	PY	GP		N	GP		N	N	Y	Y	N		N	N	N
16 Buck (R)		N	A			Y						Y				Y
25 Buckley (D)	Y	Y	N		N	Y		N	N	Y	A	N		A	N	Y
44 Butler (R)		N	N		Y	Y		N	Y	N	Y	Y		N	Y	Y
32 Byrne (D)	Y	Y	N		N	Y		N	N	Y	A	N		A	N	Y
15 Celler (D)	A	Y	N		N	Y		N	N	A	Y	N		N	PY	N
39 Cole (R)	Y	PY	GP		Y	A		Y	Y	N	N	Y		Y	Y	Y
6 Delaney, James (D)		Y	N			Y										Y
7 Delaney, John (D)	Y	Y	N		N	Y		N	N	Y	A	N		A	N	N
19 Dickstein (D)	Y	Y	N		N	Y		N	N	Y	Y	PN		N	N	N
43 Elsaesser (R)		N	N			Y										Y
35 Fuller (R)		N	N		Y	N			Y			Y			Y	Y
28 Gamble (R)	Y	N	N		A	Y		N	A	Y	Y	Y		PY	PY	Y
27 Gwinn (R)		N	N			Y										PY
37 Hall, E. A. (R)	N	N	N		Y	Y		Y	Y	N	Y	N		Y	Y	Y
2 Hall, L. W. (R)	Y	PY	N		Y	Y		N	Y	Y	Y	Y		Y	Y	Y
36 Hancock (R)	Y	N	N		Y	Y		Y	Y	Y	N	Y		Y	Y	Y
11 Heffernan (D)	Y	Y	N		N	Y		N	N	Y	Y	N		A	N	PN
31 Kearney (R)		N	N		Y	Y			N			N		A	Y	Y
9 Keogh (D)	Y	Y	N		N	Y		N	N	Y	Y	N		PN	N	GP
34 Kilburn (R)	Y	N	N		Y	PN		Y	Y	Y	A	Y		PY	Y	Y
3 Latham (R)		Y	A			Y										Y
30 LeFevre (R)		N	N		A	Y			Y			Y		Y	Y	Y
23 Lynch (D)	Y	Y	N		N	Y		N	PN	Y	Y	N		N	N	PN
18 Marcantonio (ALP)	N	Y	N		N	Y		N	N	N	Y	N		N	N	N
13 O'Toole (D)	Y	Y	N		N	PY		N	N	N	Y	N		N	N	PN
8 Pfeifer (D)	Y	Y	N		N	Y		N	N	N	Y	N		A	N	PN
22 Powell (D)		GP	N			Y										N
26 Quinn (D)		Y	N			Y										Y
24 Rabin (D)		Y	N			Y										N
14 Rayfiel (D)		Y	N			Y										N
45 Reed (D)		PY	Y		Y	N		Y	Y	N	Y	Y		Y	Y	Y
5 Roe (D)		Y	GP			GP										Y
40 Rogers (D)		Y	N			Y										Y
12 Rooney (D)		Y	N			Y						N				N
1 Sharp (R)		GP	A			A										Y
10 Somers (D)	Y	Y	GP		N	Y		N	N	N	Y	N		N	N	N
38 Taber (R)	N	N	N		Y	N		Y	Y	Y	N	Y		Y	Y	Y
33 Taylor (R)		N	GP		Y	Y			A			N		PY	Y	Y

DISTRICT	1	2	3	4	5	6	7	8	9	10	11	12	13	14	15	16
21 Torrens (D)		Y	N		N	Y						N				N
41 Wadsworth (R)	Y	GP	N		A	N		Y	Y	Y	N	PY		A	Y	Y

NORTH CAROLINA

DISTRICT	1	2	3	4	5	6	7	8	9	10	11	12	13	14	15	16
3 Barden (D)	Y	Y	N		Y	N		Y	Y	Y	Y	Y		PY	Y	Y
1 Bonner (D)	Y	Y	GP		Y	N		Y	N	Y	A	Y		Y	Y	Y
11 Bulwinkle (D)	Y	Y	N		N	N		N	N	Y	N	Y		Y	Y	Y
8 Burgin (D)	Y	Y	N		Y	N		Y	N	Y	Y	A		Y	Y	Y
7 Clark (D)	Y	Y	N		N	N		Y	N	Y	N	A		Y	Y	Y
4 Cooley (D)	Y	PY	GP		N	PN		Y	N	Y	Y	Y		Y	Y	Y
9 Doughton (D)	Y	Y	N		Y	N		Y	A	Y	Y	Y		Y	Y	Y
6 Durham (D)		Y	GP		Y	PN		Y	N	Y	A	Y		Y	Y	Y
10 Ervin (D)		Y	N			N										Y
5 Folger (D)	Y	Y	N		N	N		N	N	Y	Y	N		N	Y	N
2 Kerr (D)	Y	Y	N		Y	N		Y	N	Y	Y	Y		Y	PY	GP
12 Weaver (D)	Y	Y	N		Y	N		N	N	Y	Y	A		Y	Y	Y

NORTH DAKOTA

DISTRICT	1	2	3	4	5	6	7	8	9	10	11	12	13	14	15	16
(AL) Lemke (R)		N	Y	Y	Y			Y				PN		N	Y	Y
(AL) Robertson (R)	N	N	N			Y		Y		N	Y					Y

OHIO

DISTRICT	1	2	3	4	5	6	7	8	9	10	11	12	13	14	15	16
22 Bolton (R)	N	Y	N		N	Y		N	Y	N	Y	A		N	N	GP
11 Brehm (R)		N	Y		Y	Y			PY			A		Y	Y	Y
7 Brown (R)	N	PN	N		Y	PY		Y	N	Y	Y	Y		Y	Y	Y
5 Clevenger (R)	N	N	Y		Y	N		Y	Y	N	A	Y		Y	Y	Y
21 Crosser (D)	Y	Y	N		N	Y		A	N	N	A	N		N	N	N
1 Elston (R)	N	N	N		Y	Y		N	PY	N	Y	Y		Y	Y	GP
20 Feighan (D)		Y	N	PN		Y			N			N		N	N	N
3 Gardner (D)		Y	N			Y										A
15 Griffiths (R)		N	N		Y	Y			Y			Y		Y	Y	Y
2 Hess (R)	N	PN	GP		Y	Y		N	Y	N	N	Y		Y	Y	Y
14 Huber (D)		Y	N			Y										N
10 Jenkins (R)	N	N	Y		Y	Y		Y	Y	N	Y	Y		Y	Y	Y
4 Jones (R)	N	N	Y		Y	GP		Y	Y	N	Y	Y		Y	Y	Y
19 Kirwan (D)	Y	Y	N		N	Y			N	Y	Y	N		A	N	N
18 Lewis (R)		N	N		Y	Y			Y			N		N	Y	Y
6 McCowen (R)		N	N		Y	Y			PY			Y		Y	Y	Y
17 McGregor (R)	N	N	N		Y	Y		Y	Y	N	Y	Y		Y	Y	GP
9 Ramey (R)		Y	N		Y	Y			Y			N		N	Y	Y
8 Smith (R)	N	N	Y		Y	A		Y	Y	N	Y	Y		Y	Y	Y
16 Thom (D)	Y	Y	N			Y		N		N	Y					Y
12 Vorys (R)	N	N	N		A	Y		N	Y	N	Y	Y		Y	Y	PY
13 Weichel (R)		N	GP		Y	Y			Y			Y		Y	Y	Y
(AL) Bender (R)	N	GP	N		N	Y		N	Y	N	Y	N		N	Y	Y

DISTRICT	1	2	3	4	5	6	7	8	9	10	11	12	13	14	15	16
OKLAHOMA																
4 Boren (D)	Y	A	A		Y	GP		Y	Y	Y	Y	Y		Y	Y	Y
6 Johnson (D)	Y	GP	N		N	Y		Y	Y	Y	Y	Y		Y	N	Y
5 Monroney (D)	Y	Y	N		A	Y		N	N	Y	Y	N		Y	N	Y
8 Rizley (R)	N	N	Y		Y	N		Y	Y	N	Y	A		Y	Y	Y
1 Schwabe (R)		N	Y			N										PY
3 Stewart (D)		PY	A		Y	GP			Y			Y		Y	Y	Y
2 Stigler (D)		PY	N			Y						Y				Y
7 Wickersham (D)		Y	N		Y	N		Y	N	Y	Y	N		Y	N	Y
OREGON																
3 Angell (R)	N	Y	N		Y	Y		N	N	N	Y	N		N	Y	Y
4 Ellsworth (R)		N	N		Y	Y			Y			A		Y	Y	Y
1 Mott (R)*	N	N	N		Y	Y		Y	Y	N	Y	N		Y	Y	A
2 Stockman (R)		N	GP		A	Y			Y			A		Y	Y	Y
PENNSYLVANIA																
1 Barrett (D)		Y	N			Y										Y
3 Bradley (D)	Y	A	GP		N	A		N	N	N	Y	N		N	N	N
22 Brumbaugh (R)		N	GP		Y	Y			Y			Y				Y
29 Campbell (R)		N	N			Y										Y
30 Corbett (R)		Y	N			Y				Y						Y
32 Eberharter (D)	Y	Y	N		N	Y		N	N	Y	Y	N		A	N	Y
12 Fenton (R)	N	N	N		Y	Y		N	PY	N				N	Y	Y
11 Flood (D)		Y	N			Y										Y
31 Fulton (R)		Y	N			Y										Y
19 Gavin (R)		N	N		Y	Y			Y			Y		PY	Y	Y
8 Gerlach (R)	N	N	N		Y	Y		N	PY	N	Y	N		Y	Y	Y
14 Gillette (R)		N	N		Y	Y		Y	Y		Y	Y		Y	Y	Y
25 Graham (R)	N	PN	N		Y	Y		Y	Y	N	Y	Y		Y	Y	Y
2 Granahan (D)		Y	N			Y										Y
5 Green (D)		Y	N			Y										N
21 Gross (R)		N	N		Y	Y			Y			Y		Y	Y	Y
13 Hoch (D)		Y	N		N	Y			N			N		N	N	Y
27 Kelley (D)	Y	Y	N		PN	Y		N	N	Y	Y	N		N	N	N
9 Kinzer (R)	N	N	N		Y	Y		Y	Y	N	Y	Y		Y	Y	Y
18 Kunkel (R)	Y	N	N		Y	Y		N	Y	N	Y	A		N	Y	Y
16 McConnell (R)		N	N		Y	Y			Y			Y			Y	Y
6 McGlinchey (D)		Y	N			Y										Y
24 Morgan (D)		Y	N			Y										N
10 Murphy (D)		Y	N		N	Y			N			N		A	N	Y
28 Rodgers (R)	N	N	N		A	GP		Y	Y	N	Y	Y		Y	Y	Y
15 Rich (R)	N	N	Y			N		N		N	N					Y
4 Sheridan (D)	Y	Y	N		N	Y		N	N	N	Y	M		A	N	PN

° James W. Mott died November 12, 1945.

DISTRICT	1	2	3	4	5	6	7	8	9	10	11	12	13	14	15	16
17 Simpson (R)	N	N	GP		Y	A		N	Y	N	Y	Y		PY	Y	Y
23 Snyder (D)	Y	Y	N		N	Y		N	N	Y	Y	N		N	N	Y
26 Tibbott (R)	N	N	N		Y	Y		N	Y	N	Y	Y		Y	Y	Y
20 Walter (D)	Y	Y	GP		N	Y		N	N	N	A	N		A	Y	Y
33 Weiss (D)	Y	Y	N		N	Y		N	N	N	Y	PN		N	N	N
7 Wolfenden (R)	N	N	N		Y	Y		A	Y	N	Y	N		N	Y	Y
RHODE ISLAND																
2 Fogarty (D)	Y	N	N	PN	Y			N	N	N	Y	N		N	N	Y
1 Forand (D)	Y	Y	N		N	Y		N	N	Y	Y	N		A	N	Y
SOUTH CAROLINA																
4 Bryson (D)	Y	Y	N		Y	N		Y	N	Y	Y	Y		Y	Y	Y
3 Hare (D)	Y	Y	N		Y	N		Y	A	Y	Y	Y		Y	PY	GP
6 McMillan (D)	Y	Y	A		Y	PN		Y	A	N	Y	Y		Y	Y	GP
5 Richards (D)	Y	Y	N		Y	PN		Y	PN	Y	Y	A		Y	Y	Y
2 Riley (D)		Y	N			N										Y
1 Rivers (D)	Y	Y	GP		A	N		Y	N	Y	Y	Y		A	Y	A
SOUTH DAKOTA																
2 Case (R)	N	N	N		Y	Y		Y	Y	N	Y	A		Y	Y	Y
1 Mundt (R)	Y	N	N		Y	Y		Y	Y	N	Y	A		A	Y	Y
TENNESSEE																
9 Cooper (D)	Y	Y	N		Y	N		N	N	Y	Y	Y		Y	N	Y
7 Courtney (D)	Y	Y	N		Y	N		N	Y	Y	Y	PY		Y	N	GP
10 Davis (D)	Y	Y	N		N	N		N	N	Y	Y	N		Y	N	Y
5 Earthman (D)		A	A			GP					A					Y
4 Gore (D)	Y	Y	N		N	Y		N	N	Y	Y	Y		Y	N	
2 Jennings (R)	N	N	N		A	PY		Y	Y	N	A	Y		Y	Y	Y
3 Kefauver (D)	Y	Y	N		Y	PY		N	N	Y	Y	N		Y	N	Y
8 Murray (D)		Y	N		Y	N					A	Y		Y	Y	Y
6 Priest (D)	Y	Y	N		N	Y		N	N	Y	Y	N		Y	N	Y
1 Reece (R)	N	PN	GP		Y	GP		Y	Y	N	A	A		Y	Y	GP
TEXAS																
3 Beckworth (D)	Y	Y	N		Y	N		Y	N	Y	Y	N		Y	Y	Y
2 Combs (D)		Y	N			N										Y
21 Fisher (D)		PN	N		Y	N			Y			A		Y	Y	Y
13 Gossett (D)	Y	Y	N		Y	N		Y	Y	Y	Y	Y		Y	Y	Y
6 Johnson,L.A.(D)	Y	Y	N		Y	N		Y	N	Y	Y	Y		Y	Y	Y
10 Johnson,L.B.(D)	Y	A	A		N	N		Y	N	Y	A	N		Y	PN	GP
20 Kilday (D)	Y	Y	N		Y	N		N	PY	Y	N	N		Y	PY	Y
12 Lanham (D)	Y	Y	N		Y	N		Y	Y	Y	Y	Y		Y	Y	Y
14 Lyle (D)		Y	N			N										Y
19 Mahon (D)	Y	Y	N		Y	N		Y	Y	Y	Y	N		Y	Y	Y

DISTRICT	1	2	3	4	5	6	7	8	9	10	11	12	13	14	15	16
9 Mansfield (D)	A	Y	N		Y	N		Y	Y	Y	Y	Y		Y	Y	Y
1 Patman (D)	Y	Y	N		N	N		Y	PN	Y	Y	A		Y	PN	Y
7 Pickett (D)		Y	N			N										Y
11 Poage (D)	Y	Y	N		Y	N		Y	Y	Y	Y	A		Y	A	Y
4 Rayburn (D)*																
17 Russell (D)	Y	Y	N		Y	N		Y	Y	Y	Y	A		Y	Y	N
5 Sumners (D)	Y	Y	N		Y	N		Y	PY	Y	Y	Y		Y	PY	Y
8 Thomas (D)	Y	Y	N		N	Y		A	N	Y	Y	N		Y	Y	Y
16 Thomason (D)	Y	Y	N		Y	Y		N	Y	Y	Y	N		PY	Y	Y
15 West (D)	Y	N	N		Y	N		A	Y	Y	N	Y		Y	Y	Y
18 Worley (D)	Y	A	N		Y	N		Y	Y	Y	A	N		N	Y	Y
UTAH																
1 Granger (D)	Y	N	N		N	Y		Y	N	Y	A	PN		N	N	Y
2 Robinson (D)	Y	Y	N		N	Y		N	N	A	Y	N		N	N	Y
VERMONT																
(AL) Plumley (R)	Y	N	GP		Y	GP		Y	Y	Y	A	Y		A	Y	Y
VIRGINIA																
1 Bland (D)	Y	Y	N		Y	N		Y	N	Y	Y	Y		Y	Y	Y
5 Burch (D)	Y	Y	GP		Y	N		Y	A	Y	Y	N		Y	Y	Y
2 Daughton (D)		Y	N			N										Y
4 Drewry (D)	Y	Y	GP		Y	N		N	N	N	A	Y		Y	Y	Y
9 Flannagan (D)	Y	Y	N		N	N		Y	N	Y	Y	N		N	N	Y
7 Robertson (D)	Y	Y	N		Y	N		N	Y	Y	N	N		Y	Y	Y
3 Gary (D)†		Y	N			N										
8 Smith (D)	Y	Y	N		Y	N		N	A	Y	A	N		Y	Y	Y
6 Woodrum (D)	Y	Y	N		Y	N		N	Y	Y	Y	N		Y	Y	Y
WASHINGTON																
6 Coffee (D)	N	Y	N		N	PY		N	PN	Y	Y	N		N	N	N
1 DeLacy (D)		Y	N			Y										PN
4 Holmes (R)		N	N		Y	PY			Y			A		Y	Y	Y
5 Horan (R)		N	N		Y	Y			Y			A		Y	Y	Y
2 Jackson (D)	N	Y	N		N	Y		N	N	PY	Y	A		N	N	N
3 Savage (D)		GP	N			Y										N
WEST VIRGINIA																
3 Bailey (D)		Y	A			GP										N
4 Ellis (R)		N	Y		Y	Y			Y			Y		Y	Y	Y
6 Hedrick (D)		Y	N			Y										Y
5 Kee (D)	Y	Y	N		N	Y		N	N	Y	Y	N		N	N	N

* Sam Rayburn as Speaker of the House does not vote.
† J. Vaughn Gary sworn in March 13th, 1945.

DISTRICT	1	2	3	4	5	6	7	8	9	10	11	12	13	14	15	16
1 Neely (D)		Y	N		Y											N
2 Randolph (D)	Y	N	N		N	Y		N	N	Y	Y	N		Y	Y	Y
WISCONSIN																
5 Biemiller (D)		Y	N			Y										A
8 Byrnes (R)		N	N			PN										Y
2 Henry (R)		N	N			Y										A
9 Hull (Prog)	N	N	N		N	Y		Y	N	N	Y	N		N	N	N
6 Keefe (R)	N	N	N		Y	Y		Y	Y	N	Y	N		Y	Y	Y
7 Murray (R)	N	N	N		Y	Y		Y	Y	N	Y	N		A	Y	Y
10 O'Konski (R)		PN	Y		Y	Y			N			Y		Y	Y	Y
1 Smith (R)		N	N		Y	Y		Y	Y		Y	N		Y	Y	Y
3 Stevenson (R)	N	Y	N		Y	Y		Y	Y	N	Y	AN		N	Y	Y
4 Wasielewski (D)	Y	Y	N		PN	Y		N	N	N	Y	PN		Y	Y	GP
WYOMING																
(AL) Barrett (R)		N	N		Y	Y			Y			Y		Y	Y	Y

HOUSE VOTE TOTALS

	1	2	3	5	6	8	9	10	11	12	14	15	16
YEAS	260	239	29	328	251	205	226	203	332	174	244	299	315
NAYS	165	153	326	69	105	172	151	202	28	156	108	95	58

DEMOCRATS

	1	2	3	5	6	8	9	10	11	12	14	15	16
FOR	236	205	0	134	118	105	58	182	195	67	114	99	150
AGAINST	25	12	202	65	86	118	130	65	17	100	67	89	56

REPUBLICANS

	1	2	3	5	6	8	9	10	11	12	14	15	16
FOR	24	33	29	191	131	99	166	21	133	107	130	199	165
AGAINST	135	140	122	3	19	53	19	133	11	54	37	3	9

Index

INDEX

an, J.
While you were gone